Linguistic Variation: Structure and Interpretation

Studies in Generative Grammar

Editors
Norbert Corver
Harry van der Hulst

Founding Editors
Jan Koster
Henk van Riemsdijk

Volume 132

Linguistic Variation: Structure and Interpretation

Edited by
Ludovico Franco and Paolo Lorusso

DE GRUYTER
MOUTON

ISBN 978-1-5015-2670-1
e-ISBN (PDF) 978-1-5015-0520-1
e-ISBN (EPUB) 978-1-5015-0510-2
ISSN 0167-4331

Library of Congress Control Number: 2019940604

Bibliographic information published by the Deutsche Nationalbibliothek
The Deutsche Nationalbibliothek lists this publication in the Deutsche Nationalbibliografie;
detailed bibliographic data are available on the Internet at http://dnb.dnb.de.

© 2021 Walter de Gruyter Inc., Boston/Berlin
This volume is text- and page-identical with the hardback published in 2020.
Typesetting: Integra Software Services Pvt. Ltd.
Printing and binding: CPI books GmbH, Leck

www.degruyter.com

Contributions in Honor of M. Rita Manzini

Contents

Leonardo M. Savoia
Introduction —— 1

David Adger
A labelling solution to a curious EPP effect —— 7

Laura Bafile
The question of overgeneration in Element Theory —— 19

Benedetta Baldi
Linguistic and pragmatic procedures in the political discourse —— 29

Josef Bayer
Why doubling discourse particles? —— 47

Adriana Belletti
(Reflexive) *Si* as a route to passive in Italian —— 73

Andrea Calabrese
Irregular verbal morphology and locality: The irregular Latin perfect forms, their Proto-Indo-European ancestors and their Romance outcomes —— 87

Anna Cardinaletti and Giuliana Giusti
Multiple agreement in Southern Italian dialects —— 125

Carlo Cecchetto and Caterina Donati
Relabeling participial constructions —— 149

Noam Chomsky
Puzzles about phases —— 163

Guglielmo Cinque
On the double-headed analysis of "Headless" relative clauses —— 169

Gloria Cocchi
Bantu class prefixes: Towards a cross-categorial account —— 197

Marcel den Dikken
Differential object marking and the structure of transitive clauses —— 217

Elisa Di Domenico
Countability and the /s/ morpheme in English —— 231

Ludovico Franco
(Im)proper prepositions in (Old and Modern) Italian —— 249

Jacopo Garzonio
Not even a crumb of negation: on *mica* in Old Italian —— 273

Mirko Grimaldi
From brain noise to syntactic structures: A formal proposal within the oscillatory rhythms perspective —— 293

Kleanthes K. Grohmann
When *seem* wants to control —— 317

Richard S. Kayne
Some thoughts on *one* and *two* and other numerals —— 335

Rosangela Lai
Stress shift under cliticization in the Sardinian transitional area —— 357

Adam Ledgeway
The causative construction in the dialects of southern Italy and the phonology-syntax interface —— 371

Paolo Lorusso
Lexical parametrization and early subjects in L1 Italian —— 401

Ana Madeira and Alexandra Fiéis
Inflected infinitives in Portuguese —— 423

Guido Mensching
Some notes on the Sardinian complementizer systems —— 439

Léa Nash
Structural source of person split —— 453

Ad Neeleman and Hans van de Koot
The non-existence of sub-lexical scope —— 501

Diego Pescarini
An emergentist view on functional classes —— 531

Francesca Ramaglia and Mara Frascarelli
The (information) structure of existentials —— 561

Luigi Rizzi
***Che* and weak islands** —— 599

Anna Roussou
Complement clauses: Case and argumenthood —— 609

Tarald Taraldsen
The internal structure of Nguni nominal class prefixes —— 633

Jeroen van Craenenbroeck
Expletives, locatives, and subject doubling —— 661

Kenneth Wexler
Arbitrary control instead of obligatory control in temporal adjuncts in Child Grammar: An ATTRACT analysis —— 691

Language Index —— 717

Subject Index —— 719

Leonardo M. Savoia
Introduction

Maria Rita Manzini has been my colleague sharing the teaching of General Linguistics in the University of Florence since 1992. Previously I had heard our common supervisor at the Scuola Normale Superiore, Prof. Alfredo Stussi, and other then young researchers – now well-known linguists like Luigi Rizzi and Giorgio Graffi – speaking about her during the time she was at MIT. They depicted Rita as a truly promising scholar, a very capable and original linguist. She was awarded her Ph.D. at the Department of Linguistics and Philosophy, MIT, discussing a Dissertation entitled *Restructuring and Reanalysis*, under the supervision of Prof. Noam Chomsky, in 1983. Her studies in Italy, preceding her stay in USA, showed clear signs of excellence, including a Diploma from the Scuola Normale Superiore (Pisa), and her Arts (lettere) degree at the University of Pisa, with a thesis on *Il Controllo e la Sintassi Generativa dell'Italiano* (supervisor Prof. Alfredo Stussi), in 1979. After her Ph.D. in the USA, Maria Rita Manzini became Postdoctoral Fellow at the Centre for Cognitive Science, in the University of California at Irvine (1983–1984) and was Visiting Assistant Professor in the Romance Languages and Linguistics Program, UCLA, Los Angeles, in 1984. Her career continued in London, at University College London as a Lecturer in the Italian Department (1984–1990) and as Reader and then Visiting Professor in the Department of Phonetics and Linguistics 1990–1999. In the 1990s she was appointed to a professorship at the University of Florence where she has been full professor of General Linguistics for many years. The above is an outline of her academic life, starting from studies at the Scuola Normale till she came back to Italy after crucial and decisive years which surely shaped her deep knowledge of our field of studies by virtue of many important varied experiences in linguistic research and teaching, and collaboration and interaction with a number of excellent scholars. More to the point, to the extent that she was a genuine student of Chomsky, I think, she is a direct and authentic connoisseur of generative theory and its inspiring conceptualization, as, however, shown by her well-known ability in facing its crucial theoretical points with in-depth competence, critical and clear vision of descriptive and theoretical problems and innovative ideas.

The first time I met Maria Rita Manzini, as far as I remember at a conference of the Società di Linguistica Italiana in Rome, the idea of coming back in Italy did not seem to attract her. Italian universities are, all things considered, nothing but a typical academic world, naturally with the positive and negative characteristics of Italian culture and style of life! However, the professorial position in Florence persuaded her to remain in our university system. When she began to work at Florence University she was already world-famous in the field of linguistic studies, and her reputation as a sharp, deep, expert linguist characterized her as one of the most highly considered and influential scholars in theoretical linguistics, specifically in generative syntax and related domains of research, as her excellent list of publications shows. M Rita Manzini has provided a very important contribution to the linguistic studies in the Florentine University and we owe relevant results both in the field of research and teaching to her. In fact, several young researchers, some of which are now excellent scholars, were formed under her teaching.

Turning now to her scientific activity, we remind that crucial stages in her research activities are represented by some publications always quoted because of their very important role in the theoretical debate, i.e. the articles with Kenneth Wexler on Binding Theory and learnability, the book *Locality. A theory and some of its empirical consequences* (Cambridge, Mass.: The MIT Press, 1992), the collaborations with Michael Brody, and her several articles on issues concerning the structure of the sentence, locality, parameters, and acquisition. In Florence, Rita Manzini started working on the morpho-syntactic variation on the basis of a broad empirical complex of data concerning Italian and Albanian varieties, generally in collaboration with Leonardo Savoia. Her deep mastery of syntactic theory and original sensistivity for linguistic facts gave rise to important results. Specifically, she used the possibility of testing theoretical hypothesis against the real organization of languages in order to theorize allowed her deep mastery of syntactic theory and original sensitivity for linguistic phenomena to be applied to field data concerning Italian and Albanian varieties. A complex of morphosyntactic phenomena provided the study of linguistic variation with a broad empirical basis that made testing theoretical hypotheses possible and inspired new theoretical elaborations in the Chomskyan minimalist model. Books such as *I dialetti italiani e romanci. Morfosintassi generativa* (3 volumes, Alessandria, Edizioni dell'Orso, 2005), *A Unification of Morphology and Syntax. Investigations into Romance and Albanian dialects* (London, Routledge, 2007), *Grammatical Categories: Variation in Romance Languages* (Cambridge, Cambridge University Press, 2011) belong to this period. Finally, The Morphosyntax of Albanian and Aromanian Varieties, Berlin/ Boston: De Gruyter Mouton, 2018, brings together recent articles inspired by a thorough rethinking of the minimalist conceptualization. Many articles aim at developing new theoretical lines anticipating and promoting many of the theoretical points characterizing the most recent perspedtives in the design of grammar, Specifically, they address, the critical revision of the cartographic approach, the notion of agreement, the traditional categories of case and prepositions, the DOM and voice phenomena, the treatment of inflection, the identification of complementizers with nominal elements, all in the light of an application of the authentic minimalist conceptualization of the relation between lexical elements and syntax. The spectrum of her scientific interests is very wide, embracing now also the analysis of morphological phenomena, such as noun class inflection and inner word processes, treated on the basis of the same computational mechanisms underlying syntax. However, her main interests remain in the domain of sentence syntax phenomena, such as sentence complementation, case and agreement, clitics, pronouns, linkers, DOM and OCP, with a clear theoretical turning point in the direction of a true minimalist treatment of syntactic phenomena.

Her wide and articulated scholarly production, encompassing different phenomena and languages, is reflected by the rich contribution that longstanding and more recent friends and colleagues, starting with Noam Chomsky, her Ph.D. supervisor and true master, offered to Rita for her 60th birthday. If we examine the contributions gathered in this book, we see that they embrace the topics that have influenced and guided the theoretical reflection on language and the syntactic debate. Indeed, the purpose of this book is twofold, celebrating the honouree and providing a survey of the recent research in linguistics capable of representing the various interests that have inspired her theoretical work. Classic syntactic phenomena such as the syntax of the complex sentences, dependent clauses and the status of complementizers are the object of several articles: Adam Ledgeway in *The Causative Construction in the Dialects of Southern Italy and the Phonology-Syntax Interface,* addresses a subtle distinction between different types of causatives depending on the position of object clitics; Anna Cardinaletti and Giuliana Giusti in *Multiple Agreement in Southern Italian Dialects* analyse constructions with double verb agreement; Ana Madeira and Alexiandra Fiéis in *Inflected infinitives in Portuguese* address the problem concerning controlled sentences with an inflected T; Guido Mensching in *Some notes on the Sardinian complementizer systems* aims to reconsider the complex complementizer system of Sardinian, also taking the proposals of Maria Rita Manzini into account. In Anna Roussou *Complement clauses: case and argumenthood*, an important idea, upheld also by Maria Rita Manzini is discussed, i.e. the fact that "complementizers are nominal elements and as such they can be associated with the range of features (projections) of the nominal system". An alternative treatment to the classical control theory inspires Kleanthes K. Grohmann that in *When seem wants to control* resumes and elaborates the analysis of the control constructions proposed by Maria Rita Manzini and Anna Roussou. Caterina Donati and Carlo Cecchetto, in *Relabeling participial constructions*, propose an analysis of the participial relatives in terms of (re)labeling, that allow them to explain the unaccusative/ passive nature of the participial constructions and the structural differences with the absolute participial clauses.

Another line of research to which Maria Rita Manzini devoted herself in the last years is the interpretation and distribution of the pronominal elements, specifically the person split phenomena, here represented by the works of Léa Nash on *Structural source of person split*, that identifies the source of the split between 1st / 2nd persons and 3rd person in the structural representation of the (pro)nominal arguments themselves, and of Marcel den Dikken on *Differential object marking and the structure of transitive clauses*. This work assumes an object position outside VP, lower than the lowest structural position for the external argument, and mapped outside the nuclear scope of the object and connected with differential object marking. The morpho-syntax of the words is touched by Andrea Calabrese, in *The Irregular Latin Perfect Forms, their Proto-Indo-European Ancestors and their Romance Outcomes*, where he explains the development of perfective forms from Proto-Indo-European (PIE) to modern Italo-Romance by assigning a crucial role to locality principles, applying to athematic forms. Elisa Di Domenico, in *Countability and the /s /morpheme in English* proposes a unified interpretation of the sigmatic occurrences of the morpheme s in English; Tarald Taraldsen, in *The internal structure of Nguni nominal class prefixes*, proposes to separate gender and classifiers in Bantu languages, identifying the classifiers with silent nouns. This solution has interesting effects on the notion of agreement, understood as a semantic mechanism and on other aspects of the treatment of morphosyntax of nouns. Gloria Cocchi in *Bantu class prefixes: Towards a cross-categorial account* illustrates the strict parallelism between the structure of Bantu nouns and verbs, arguing that the same set of inflectional projections are to be assumed at both syntactic and morphological levels;

All in all, the effective, suggestive and in-depth picture of the different aspects in the syntactic analysis emerging from the whole of the works, confirms our conviction and highlights the fact that natural language, though somehow tied up with the general human capacity to communicate meanings, has a recognizable and self-evident specialized status. So, its fundamental combinatory mechanism, recursion, Saussurean arbitrariness and other intrinsic properties characterize language as the optimal solution to interface conditions, connecting S-M and C-I systems. This accounts for why explaining linguistic phenomena needs a sophisticated and specialized theory of the organization of linguistic units in wider strings. The articulation and the richness of the issues discussed tells us just this, the unicity and the specialized nature of human language both as regards its internal organization and its link with communication. And, in fact, the path towards the C-I and S-M interfaces assumes a crucial interpretive role that involves the properties of the lexical items. Richard Kayne in *Some Thoughts on One and Two and Other Numerals* enters into the subtlest mechanisms of the interpretation by highlighting the concealed grammaticalized content of numerals. The recurse to the lexical properties is crucial also in the two contributions that Guglielmo Cinque (*On the double-headed analysis of "Headless" relative clauses*) and Luigi Rizzi (*Che and weak islands*) devote to the behaviour of the relatives; Cinque appeals to functional silent nouns that specify the content of elements such as *what*, *who*. Rizzi accounts for the different distribution of *che* and *che cosa* on the base of their internal structure. In *Not even a crumb of negation: on mica in Old Italian*, Jacopo Garzonio analyses the distribution of the postverbal negation *mica* in Old and Modern Italian, excluding that the change from quantifier to negation involves the interpretability of the Negative feature and proposing an interpretation in terms of attraction properties of Focus and Ludovico Franco, in *(Im)proper prepositions in (Old and Modern) Italian*, addresses the question concerning the status of the Italian prepositions *su* and *tra/fra*, proposing to characterize them as Axial Parts, so patterning with complex adpositions. Ad Neeleman and Hans van de Koot, in *The Non-Existence of Sub-Lexical Scope*, argue for the conclusion that simplex causatives cannot be treated as syntactically complex verbs, insofar there is evidence that modifiers never take scope over part of their lexical semantics. Jeroen van Craenenbroeck, in *Expletives, locatives, and subject doubling*, analyses *there*-expletives in a dialect of Dutch and, taking their distribution and syntactic behaviour into account, proposes an explanation whereby their behaviour is parasitic on the regular locative use.

The other externalization implies non-strictly linguistic factors interacting with different aspects of the computation. So, the way the discourse interpretation of constituents is connected with formal features is the conceptual space in which Francesca Ramaglia and Mara Frascarelli place *The (information) structure of existentials*, Josef Bayer *Why Doubling Discourse Particles?* Other contributions concentrate on the acquisition, throwing light, in turn, on the involvement of computational limitations and other factors, not necessarily specific of the faculty of language, as Paolo Lorusso in *Lexical Parameterization and early subjects in L1 Italian* and Kenneth Wexler, which in *Arbitrary Control Instead of Obligatory Control in Temporal Adjuncts in Child Grammar: an ATTRACT* takes important cues from the proposals of Maria Rita Manzini and Anna Roussou introducing a reinterpretation of the notions of movement and control; Adriana Belletti, in *(Reflexive) Si as a route to passive in Italian*, concludes that Italian-speaking children adopt the reflexive passive as favoured by its simplicity in comparison of the more complex syntax of the true passive, connected to a *smuggling* operation. Finally, in an authentic neurolinguistics approach, Mirko Grimaldi, in *From brain noise to syntactic structures: A formal proposal within the oscillatory rhythms perspective* proposes a connection between linguistic and neural structures and operations. If morphology and phonology implement the path from computation to externalization, the reflection on the organization of phonological theory, Laura Bafile *The Question of Overgeneration in Element Theory* and the morpho-syntactic accommodation of clitics in Sardinian dialects that select specialized clitics in modal contexts discussed by Rosangela Lai in *Stress shift under cliticization in the Sardinian transitional area*, represent the more external linguistic phenomena. The ultimate step, namely the transmission of meaning by the discourse processes is discussed by Benedetta Baldi in *Linguistic and pragmatic procedures in the political discourse*, where the rhetoric of the political speaking translates language into the experience of the linguistic interaction.

However, all of us know that the interaction between S-M and C-I is very difficult to draw. The interaction involving the three factors in the language design suggests a mutual contribution in the defining even the most specialized devices of the language. Save Merge and other computational properties, language is sensitive to the requirement of the S-M and C-I systems, more specifically, language theory needs to satisfy two crucial requirements, learnability and evolvability, refusing too complex and over-elaborated structures, unpredictable on the base of the evidence available to the child, redundant unvalued features, up to usually accepted notions like Agree. Noam Chomsky in *Puzzles about Phases* remind us this point, by discussing two theoretical problems concerning the traditionally assumed raising of the subject. Raising of the subject poses a problem connected with the fact that nothing seems to forces it and a more crucial counter-cyclicity problem. The solution involves a conceptually different approach to the syntax, whereby 'common assumption on triggering of operations', based on the probe-goal relation, should be abandoned in favor of the principle of 'minimal computation'; in other words, we can expect that Merge freely applies and that also deviant expressions are generated. Naturally only interpretable results will be relevant for language.

David Adger
A labelling solution to a curious EPP effect

1 Introduction

McCloskey (1996) examines a curious phenomenon in Modern Irish, where there is an alternation between what he calls `salient' versus `putative' unaccusatives. These are predicates which take their single argument either as a PP, or as a DP:

(1) Neartaigh   ar a   ghlór
    strengthened on his voice
    'His voice strengthened'   Salient Unaccusative

(2) Neartaigh   a   ghlór
    strengthened his voice
    'His voice strengthened'   Putative Unaccusative

McCloskey shows that the DP argument of a putative unaccusative is in the same position as the subject argument of a transitive: that is, it is in the standard subject position. The PP argument of the salient unaccusative, however, is in a lower position (the complement of the verb). This is most clearly seen when the verb types appear in progressive constructions:

(3) Bhí ag neartú   ar an nglór
    was PROG strengthen on the noise
    'The noise was getting louder'   Salient Unaccusative

(4) Tá mo shaibhreas ag   méadú
    is my wealth   PROG increase
    'My wealth is increasing'   Putative Unaccusative

(3) shows that the PP argument occurs after the non-finite form of the verb (in the usual complement position) while in (4), the DP argument occurs before the non-finite verb (in the usual subject position). McCloskey argues that there is

---
Note: Many thanks to an anonymous reviewer, and to Coppe van Urk for comments.

David Adger, Queen Mary University of London

https://doi.org/10.1515/9781501505201-002

no null expletive in (3), (as is evident from the absence of definiteness effects) so that there is, in these examples, no subject at all. He concludes that the Extended Projection Principle does not hold in Irish.

The following characterization of the phenomenon seems appropriate: when there is at least one nominal argument present in a finite sentence, the highest obligatorily raises to the structural subject position, but in the absence of nominal arguments, that position remains unfilled.

McCloskey's analysis of this pattern takes there to be an optional functional projection in Irish clause structure that bears nominative case features and to which a subject raises (so the verb itself raises to a higher functional position):

(5)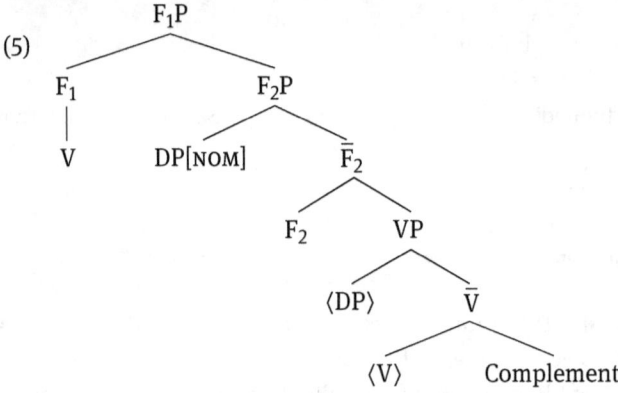

In a putative unaccusative, F_2 is present, and requires movement of a DP to its specifier to check nominative case. If the derivation does not contain F_2, the single argument DP will not have its case checked, and the derivation will crash. In a salient unaccusative, a derivation that contains F_2 will crash, as the DP inside the PP argument of the verb will already have its case checked, while in the absence of F_2, the derivation will converge. It follows that the single argument DP of a putative unaccusative will always raise, and that the PP argument of a salient unaccusative never will, even though the projection of F_2 is optional.

While this proposal is sufficient to capture the generalisation, inserting an optional head to make movement happen in a putative unaccusative but not in a salient one is uncomfortably close to simply stating that movement must happen in the former and can't in the latter. Adger (2000), noting this, suggests an alternative analysis that relies on a (morphological) surface filter, requiring DPs to be adjacent to a case assigning governor, but that is equally unappealing.

2 A labelling alternative

The system developed in Chomsky (2013) and Chomsky (2015) suggests a more satisfying solution to this problem. In contrast to systems where features of some head H attract lower elements of structure into H's specifier, in Chomsky's approach, some XPs are effectively ejected from their Merge position, while others are not. The capacity for an XP to remain in situ is dependent on whether the constituent containing it can be labelled. A labelling algorithm (LA), initiated on Merge of a phase head, searches each constituent in its domain for a label. In the simplest case, a constituent will be labelled by the lexical item that heads it (6-a). However, when two phrases are Merged, LA searches into each for lexical items to act as the label. In the typical case, the heads will not match and no unambiguous result can be returned by LA, so the search fails. However, if the two heads bear a (relevant) feature in common (say a ϕ feature), then that feature is returned as the label for the whole constituent (so in (6-b), the whole constituent is labelled by the ϕ features on the heads X and Y). Alternatively if one of XP or YP raise, leaving a trace, LA treats the trace as invisible to search, and so returns the label of the non-moved phrase (in (6-c), where angled brackets notate a lower occurrence of a moved element, LA will therefore return Y as the label of the whole constituent). Chomsky connects the inability of LA to see traces to the idea that it needs access to all copies of the relevant element, and this is only possible in the topmost position[1]:

(6) a. { H, XP }
 b. {{ X[ϕ], ZP}, {Y[ϕ], WP}}
 c. {⟨XP⟩, {Y, WP}}

Schematically, we have a derivation that looks as follows for the external argument (see Chomsky 2013 for details). Categories such as DP, v*P etc are used for expository convenience. Such nodes actually have no category in this system:

(7) a. { DP, v*P } no head and no agreeing features, so not labellable
 b. { DP[ϕ] {$_\alpha$ T[ϕ] {⟨DP⟩ v*P } } } DP bears ϕ-features, as does T, so the constituent immediately containing both can be labelled by these ϕ

---

[1] Labelling takes place at Phase level, allowing limited counter-cyclicity, so that the label of vP and TP are determined only once the phase is complete.

features (cf (6-b)). The smaller constituent with the trace of DP in its specifier can be labelled by the v* head of v*P, as the DP trace is invisible (cf. (6-c)).

What of the constituent α containing just T and its sister? Chomsky's proposal is that, in English, T cannot serve as a label unless there is a DP bearing ϕ features merged to its mother, in which case it is 'strengthened' and can thereby label its mother.

What about an object? In this situation we have the following structure:

(8) [$_\alpha$ root DP]

Chomsky proposes that roots, adapting Borer 2005 et seq., cannot serve as labels, so α cannot be labelled by the verbal root. He proposes that a root selected by v* inherits the ϕ features of v*, and eventually raises to conjoin with v*. Since the root bears ϕ features, and the object DP bears ϕ features, the following would be a well formed structure:

(9) root+v* [$_\beta$ DP [$_\alpha$ ⟨root⟩ ⟨DP⟩]]

Here the ϕ-features on root and on DP allow the labelling of β. I'll assume that α, being empty, does not require a label.[2]

(9) is well formed, but is it required? Standardly, DP objects are taken to be case checked in situ. Chomsky discusses ECM subjects, which he shows can raise to adjoin to the constituent headed by the root, but he does not discuss simple objects. It turns out that these too are forced to move in this system.

Under the extension of the system developed in Chomsky 2015, when the root raises to v*, it effectively deletes v*, and the various properties of v*, which have been inherited by the root, become active on the root (and hence on its copy). Crucially, for Chomsky's analysis of ECM, the root inherits v*'s phasehood, and therefore the root's complement is Transferred. This is problematic if the object remains in situ for two reasons: first, it incorrectly predicts that the object will no longer be subject to later syntactic computation; secondly, if the object bears a structural case feature, this will be transferred unchecked. Assuming that DPs do

---

[2] A reviewer points out that this configuration violates anti-locality. Chomsky's system does not encode anti-locality intrinsically, so its effects, such as they are, would have to come from some interface constraint. I leave this aside here.

indeed bear a structural case feature, an object DP will have to move from its in situ position, or the derivation will crash. It follows, then, in Chomsky's system, that objects, whether they are direct objects or ECM subjects, are forced to raise.[3]

This system predicts the Irish pattern with two further well-motivated assumptions. The first is that, in Irish, as in *pro*-drop languages like Italian, T is able to serve as a label, parametrically distinguishing these languages from English (see Chomsky 2015).The second assumption is that unaccusative v acts as a phase head for Transfer, but bears no ϕ features. The idea that unaccusative v behaves in the same way as transitive v* in terms of its phase properties is expected if phasehood is linked to propositionality, and receives empirical support from work that shows that the edge of unaccusative v provides the same reconstruction sites as v* (Fox 2002, Legate 2003).

The idea that unaccusative v nevertheless lacks ϕ features is supported by various facts that show unaccusatives have a distinct capacity to agree, compared to transitives. As is well known, unaccusatives usually allow participial agreement with their objects, even in cases where the object has not moved. However, this is likely to be related to a relationship between T and the functional head (Asp) supporting the participle. In cases where T directly Agrees with a post-verbal unaccusative subject, we find variation in agreement. This is well known for expletive constructions in English, but is also found in Romance. For example, Costa (2001) shows that postverbal subjects of unaccusatives can fail to trigger number agreement in European Portuguese. Other phenomena support this general view. Anagnostopoulou (2003) argues on the basis of the behaviour of unaccusatives in Person Case Constraint contexts that unaccusative v does not check case and lacks ϕ features. The correlation between unaccusative verbs and reflexive clitics with reduced ϕ specification is well documented (Embick 2004). There are also more general theoretical reasons that motivate this assumption: if structural case assignment is connected to agreement, then unaccusative v must have a different set of ϕ features from transitive v.

To see how a system incorporating these assumptions works, consider a salient unaccusative in Irish with a single PP argument:

---

[3] Chomsky discusses the possibility of the movement being optional for CP complements of verbs like *think*, but since these do not carry a case feature, the argument sketched here does not apply. Indeed, if the movement of CP complements to a higher spec is possible, this should allow successive cyclic movement from their specifiers, possibly providing an account of why some languages do not allow successive cyclic wh-movement (they do not raise CP complements).

(10)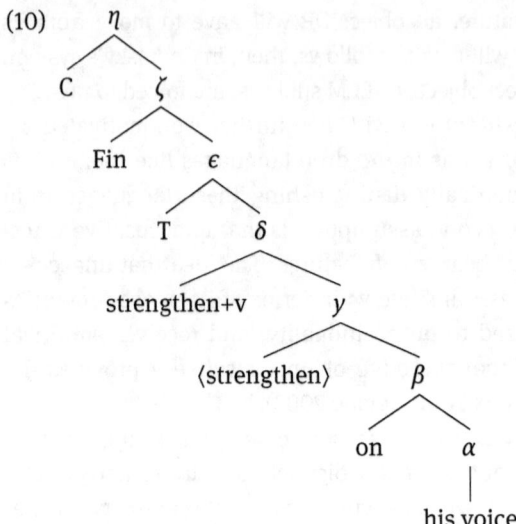

The lowest phase head here is v, which searches in its domain to ensure a label can be found for each constituent. Since v is a phase head, and its properties are transfered to the ⟨copy of⟩ the root, the PP *on his voice* is Transferred. The DP inside that PP already has its structural case feature checked (I leave aside how this happens) and α and β are labelled by their heads. The root in γ is invisible to labelling, so γ simply has the same label as β. The next phase head is C and here the labels are straightforward: η is labelled by C, ζ by Finiteness, ε, δ by T and v respectively. Nothing moves, and all constituents have a label. The PP has the independent phonetic and semantic coherence expected of Transferred units. Like Chomsky's treatment of Italian, which follows Manzini 2009 in taking there to be no syntactically active EPP position, Irish does not require movement to satisfy any property of T. I'll assume that the verb-initial order is derived by post-syntactic raising of v to Fin (perhaps by a direct linearization procedure that simply pronounces the chain of head positions at Fin, as in Adger 2013).

Now consider a structure for the putative unaccusative, which is close to identical aside from the P:

(11)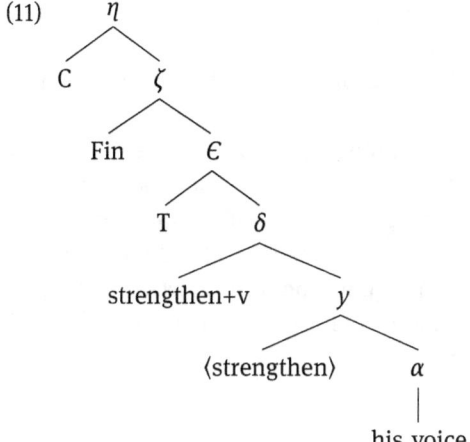

Since v is unaccusative, it bears no ϕ-features and so the root does not inherit ϕ-features from it. However, the root inherits v's phasehood after root to v raising, and therefore the DP *his voice* should Transfer. However, Transfer of this DP will lead to a crash, as the DP bears an unchecked case feature. However, in this case, the DP cannot internally Merge with y, since the root bears no phi-features and the result would not be labelled. The same holds for Internal Merge of the DP to any of the intermediate categories until it reaches T. At this point, the DP Internally Merges with the constituent headed by T, both share ϕ-features, and the resulting constituent can be labelled as usual. The following structure shows this:

(12)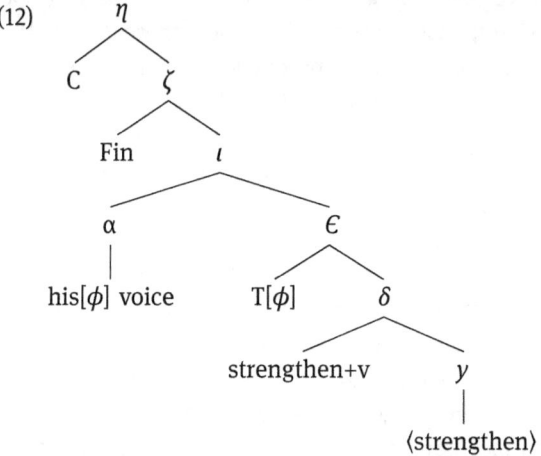

Since everything in γ is invisible to LA, γ does not require labelling and the various other syntactic objects are labelled just as before, with the addition that ι will receive a label, as the heads of its subconstituents (D and T) agree in ϕ features.

There are two core intuitions underpinning this analysis. The first is that, in Irish, T does not require a subject (that is, like in McCloskey's analysis, Irish does not have the EPP property). The second is that the object of an unaccusative is forced to leave its base position because there is no head that can serve to label the constituent containing it, and there is no head to whose specifier it can move (resulting in a label via ϕ-feature sharing). The first such head is T, giving rise to the pattern.

3 Is this an improvement?

McCloskey's analysis sought to capture the somewhat anomalous nature of subject positions in Irish via an optional functional head bearing case features. This analysis captured the anomalous nature of EPP-type effects in Irish. However, the technology proposed there basically restates the problem. Adger's (2000) solution tried to capture the pattern by a filter requiring nominative case to be checked in a surface head-XP configuration, but that is equally unsatisfying, as it makes nominal licensing in Irish quite distinct from what happens in other languages, and quite distinct from accusative case.

The new proposal takes from Adger (2000) the relevance of the lack of a head inside the VP in an unaccusative base configuration, and from McCloskey (1996) the notion that T can, but need not, host a specifier, but places these ideas within a theoretical context which makes them natural consequences of a larger system.

The system proposed here adds to Chomsky (2015) nothing beyond the idea that unaccusative v is a phase head but bears no ϕ features. Salient unaccusatives leave their single argument in situ, as the case licensing of the DP is met by it being a complement of P. The single argument of a putative unaccusative, in contrast, cannot stay in situ, it would be transferred with an unchecked case feature. Since unaccusative roots are selected by v, they do not inherit ϕ-features, so the DP object cannot internally Merge with the constituent containing the root. It is therefore forced to Internally Merge with the constituent headed by T, which has inherited ϕ-features from C. The net result is to capture the same pattern as McCloskey's and Adger's systems do, but without an optional functional head or a surface government requirement. In fact, the virtue of the proposal developed here is that it does not require any special stipulation to capture the pattern, the differences between English, and Irish reducing to easily detectable properties of the input (whether unaccusative V selects a PP (Irish) or a DP (English); whether T can serve as a label allowing *pro*-drop (Irish/Italian) or not (English)).

A final comment on in situ unaccusatives without a P (as in Italian, for example Belletti 2001): salient unaccusatives in Irish show no sensitivity to definiteness (McCloskey 1996, page 261), while in situ unaccusatives in Standard Italian do, suggesting a somewhat different syntax for the verb classes in the two languages. Moro (1997) has proposed that certain unaccusative subjects are actually the subjects of a small clause complement of the unaccusative verb, where the predicate of the small clause is a locative, so that (13) could be assigned a rough structure as in (14):

(13) É arrivato uno studente al giornale
 is arrived a student to-the newspaper
 'A student arrived at the newspaper'

(14) v arrive [$_\alpha$ a student [at the newspaper]]

Here *a student* Externally Merges with the PP *at the newspaper*. However, this is an {XP, YP} construction and hence α has no label. Following Koopman (2000) and much subsequent work, we can take there to be a functional directional P that takes the locative small clause as its complement.

(15) v arrive [$_\beta$ P [$_\alpha$ a student [at the newspaper]]]

Assuming either that P's ϕ features are inherited by *at*, leading to labelling by agreement, or that *a student* internally Merges to P which bears ϕ, we derive a post-verbal subject which is internal to the vP (in fact, to the PP in this analysis). The former analysis looks as follows:

(16) v arrive [$_\beta$ P [$_\alpha$ [a[ϕ] student] [at[ϕ] the newspaper]]]

Here P transfers its ϕ-features to the preposition *at*, and α is labelled because LA sees the relevant ϕ-features. The alternative analysis is:

(17) v arrive [$_\beta$ [a student] P [$_\alpha$ ⟨a student⟩ [at the newspaper]]]

Here β is labelled by the agreeing ϕ features of DP and P, and α is labelled by the locative P, since the trace of DP is invisible to labelling. If P is a phase head here, it may be that it is associated with existential closure, giving rise to definiteness effects. The difference between Italian unaccusatives and Irish ones (which are in quite different semantic classes), is that the former involve a small clause predication structure, with the subject licensed by an abstract P head, while the latter are simple DPs, case licenced by an overt P head. In both languages the P head is optional, allowing the lower argument to escape to a higher position.

4 Conclusion

The partcular approach to labelling proposed in Chomsky's (2013)/(2015) system derives one half of the solution that is proposed here to the Irish EPP pattern: rather than elements being attracted to positions, Chomsky's proposals about labelling effectively eject them from positions where they would lead to unlabelled structures. Crucially, the single argument of an unaccusative is moved from its base position, because little v is too weak to license it in that position, a weakness in little v's capacity to label. Although this is elegantly statable in Chomsky's system, the core ideas, that unaccusatives cannot license their objects in situ, and that there is a distinction in the capacity of DP vs PP to relate to the specifier of TP can of course be stated or derived in other approaches. I have used Chomsky's system here primarily as an example of an explicit system that encodes the 'ejection' view of movement, as opposed to the 'attraction' view.

The second half of the solution to the EPP problem is the development of a theory that allows subjects in pro-drop languages to raise to the specifier of TP, without requiring them to do so. This is effectively Manzini's (2009) proposal that there is no syntactically represented EPP position in *pro*-drop languages. Chomsky's theory relies here on the notion that some languages have sufficiently strong ϕ features on T that no subject is required; however, moving some ϕ-bearing element to the specifier of T will do no harm. Other languages, like English, require some specifier for T, to strengthen T's features so that the containing phrases can be labelled. This is the core novelty here: in *pro*-drop languages, the subject does not move to the specifier of TP because it has to, but because that position is available and of the right sort.

Notice, however, that if there were other positions of the relevant sort, the DP could come to rest in these instead, giving rise to further parametric variation between languages where moved objects of unaccusatives have topical readings, and those which do not. In fact, Adger (1996) provides evidence that, in Standard Italian, the moved arguments of unaccusatives are interpreted as topical, in contrast to what McCloskey reports for Irish. It may be the case then, extending

Chomsky's parametric account somewhat, that, while in Irish the single argument of an unaccusative indeed finally stops in the specifier of TP, in Italian the relevant functional category is one encoding topicality (Manzini and Savoia 1997).

References

Adger, David. 1996. Economy and optionality: the interpretation of subjects in Italian. *Probus* 8:117–135.
Adger, David. 2000. VSO clause structure and morphological feature checking. In Robert Borsley, ed., *Syntactic Categories*, 79–100, New York: Academic Press.
Adger, David. 2013. *A Syntax of Substance*. Cambridge, MA: MIT Press.
Anagnostopoulou, Elena. 2003. *The Syntax of Ditransitives: Evidence from Clitics*. Berlin: Mouton de Gruyter.
Belletti, Adriana. 2001. Inversion as focalization. In Aafke Hulk and Jean-Yves Pollock, eds., *Inversion in Romance and the Theory of Universal Grammar*, 60–90, Oxford: Oxford University Press.
Borer, Hagit. 2005. *In Name Only: Structuring Sense*. Oxford: Oxford University Press.
Chomsky, Noam. 2013. Problems of projection. *Lingua* 130:33–49.
Chomsky, Noam. 2015. Problems of projection: Extensions. In Elisa Di Domenico, Cornelia Hamann and Simona Matteini, eds., *Structures, Strategies and Beyond: Studies in honour of Adriana Belletti* 1–16, Amsterdam: John Benjamins.
Costa, João. 2001. Postverbal subjects and agreement in unaccusative contexts in European Portuguese. *The Linguistic Review* 18:1–17.
Embick, David. 2004. Unaccusative syntax and verbal alternations. In Artemis Alexiadou, Elena Anagnostopoulou, and Martin Everaert, eds., *The Unaccusativity Puzzle: Explorations of the Syntax-Lexicon Interface*, 137–158, Oxford: Oxford University Press.
Fox, Danny. 2002. Antecedent-contained deletion and the copy theory of movement. *Linguistic Inquiry* 33:63–96.
Koopman, Hilda. 2000. Prepositions, postpositions, circumpositions and particles. In *The Syntax of Specifiers and Heads*, 204–260, London: Routledge.
Legate, Julie. 2003. Some interface properties of the phase. *Linguistic Inquiry* 34:506–516.
Manzini, M. Rita. 2009. PRO, pro and NP-trace (raising) are interpretations. In Kleanthes K. Grohmann, ed., *Explorations of Phase Theory: Features and Arguments*, 131–180, Berlin, New York: Mouton de Gruyter.
Manzini, Rita and Savoia, Leonardo M. 1997. Null subjects without *pro*. *UCL Working Papers in Linguistics* 9:1–12.
McCloskey, James. 1996. Subjects and subject positions in irish. In Robert D. Borsley and Ian Roberts, eds., *The Syntax of the Celtic Languages: A Comparative Perspective*, 241–283, Cambridge: Cambridge University Press.
Moro, Andrea. 1997. *The Raising of Predicates*. Cambridge: Cambridge University Press.

Laura Bafile
The question of overgeneration in Element Theory

1 Introduction: The nature of primitives in classic Element Theory

Element Theory (henceforth ET) assumes that primitives of segmental systems are privative units, autonomously interpreted by phonetics. Both characteristics differentiate elements from binary units of generative standard feature theory. By privativity, each element may only form part of a segment or be absent from it. Given autonomous phonetic interpretability, each element is directly pronounceable, and therefore can be the only content of a consonant or a vowel. Moreover, ET maintains the Dependency Phonology (Andersen and Jones 1974) view that elements have asymmetric relations within segments. The minimal hypothesis about dependency is the one assumed in classic ET models (e.g. Harris and Lindsey 1995), whereby only one element may be the head in the compound, and thus determine the dominant properties of the segment. As a result of headedness, given two elements, e.g. **A** and **I**, three different compounds are possible (the head element is underlined): |A I|, |A̲ I| and |A I̲|.

Elements can be individually translated into sounds, but they do not serve the same role as binary features in most approaches within Feature Theory, which is, in Bromberger and Halle's words, encoding "the information that enables a speaker to produce the sound sequence [and specifying] the vocal tract gymnastic necessary for uttering the word" (1989: 54). Given that acoustic signal is what speakers and hearers share, in ET, grammar mainly elaborates auditory symbols (cf. Kaye, Lowenstamm, and Vergnaud 1985, Lindsey and Harris 1990, Harris and Lindsey 1995, Backley 2011). It has been remarked, however, that linguistic content is only a part of the information carried through speech sounds, since acoustic signal also contains stable or variable non-linguistic information, consisting of human group-recognition signals, expression of emotions and other individual features (Kaye 1989, 2005, Traunmüller 1994). Elements are associated with auditory patterns, or "acoustic signatures" (Kaye 2005: 285), which are contained in the signal and are to be found in it.

The correspondence between phonological categories (elements and segments) and phonetic forms may be slack to some degree. For example, the

Laura Bafile, Università di Ferrara

https://doi.org/10.1515/9781501505201-003

corner vowels consisting in the elements **A, I, U**, are not necessarily phonetic [a], [i], [u].[1] Instead, they may be realised in different languages as slightly different phones belonging to corner vowel space, although still interpreting the categorical information of **A, I, U**. For example, in a language with only one low central vowel, a given phonetic object, that could be [a], [ɑ] or [ɐ], is the realisation of the linguistic information corresponding to the element **A**, and will be identified as such by learners and then by adult users.

One of the consequences of the ET conception of subsegmental units, whereby segments are made up of one or more elements (in most cases from two to four), is that the inventory of primitives in ET is smaller than in binary Feature Theories. For example, Harris and Lindsey (1995) assume ten elements, but from the beginning of ET up to present day, revised models have been provided, that almost without exceptions eliminate elements in order to make the inventory smaller.

2 Shrinking the set of elements

The set of elements identified by Harris and Lindsey (1995) consists of five place units, **A, I, U, R** (coronality) and **@** ("neuter" i.e. placeless element, corresponding to *schwa*, and in consonants to velarity); two manner units, **ʔ** (stop) and **h** (noise); two units concerning laryngeal activity, **L** (low frequency energy, low tone in vowels, voicing in consonants) and **H** (high frequency energy, high tone in vowels, aspiration in consonants); **N** (nasality). As already mentioned, revised formulations of the model propose smaller inventories.

Aiming at a reduction of the inventory, revised ET addresses three aspects of the element systems. The first is the subset of place elements and the distinction between consonantal and vocalic elements. Harris and Lindsey (1995) are the first to acknowledge that both **@** and **R** are too vague categories. In socalled Standard ET (Backley 2011), the weakness of the neuter element, due to its quality of inactive category, results in the elimination of **@** as an element for vowels and its merger with labiality as the element for velar place; therefore, labiality and velarity are expressed by **U**. As for coronality, **R** is problematic both for the acoustic elusiveness of the element, and for the special status of coronals, which are known to behave passively in many languages, in processes like assimilation and vowel harmony (cf. Harris and Lindsey 1995: 68–69; Backley 1993). Coronality disappears as an autonomous category in Standard ET, by merging either with palatals into **I**, or with pharyngeals into **A**,

---

[1] We may ignore here that IPA symbols also imply a certain degree of approximation.

depending on the language or on the kind of coronal (cf. Backley 2011). A more general aim of the elimination of **R** is a totally unified representation of consonants and vowels as far as melodic content is concerned, since in Government Phonology and ET view, no melodic category is inherently vocalic or consonantal. What makes a segment belong to one or to the other class is its syllabic constituency, i.e. the association to a Nucleus or to an Onset (or a Coda).

The latter consideration also extends to manner elements, which are the second target of criticism in revised versions of ET. In Standard ET, the element **h** ('noise') contained in stops and fricatives, is merged with **H** ('high tone' in vowel and 'aspiration' in consonants). The 'stop' element **ʔ** is maintained, e.g. in Backley (2011), given the existence of glottalised vowels. However, the proposal of removing **ʔ** dates back to Jensen (1994), and has been developed in the more recent approach (called "Progressive ET" by Backley 2012) which considers the segmental properties corresponding to **ʔ** and **H** to depend on the structure of segments rather than on their melodic content (cf. Pöchtrager 2006; Pöchtrager and Kaye 2013).

The third change concerns nasality. For reasons of acoustics and phonological behaviour, in Standard ET nasality and voicing are represented by the same element **L**: both nasal murmur and glottal signal consist in low frequency energy; besides, many languages show distributional constraints or processes suggesting a tight link between voiced and nasal stops, as opposed to voiceless stops (cf. Nasukawa 2005; Backley and Nasukawa 2010).

To sum up, the Standard ET inventory (e.g. Kaye 2000; Backley 2011) contains **A, I, U, H, L, ʔ**. Jensen (1994) proposal for five elements (**A, I, U, H, L**) has been further developed recently in work we will not survey here, so that we are ultimately left with a total of three elements: **I, U** and **L** (cf. Pöchtrager and Kaye 2013).

3 No fear of overgeneration

The reduction of the number of elements, described in the previous section, pursues an adequate representation of relevant phonological categories, independently from detailed phonetic forms. To give an example, nasality and voicing are different phonetic features, but, as mentioned above, convincing reasons are provided for considering them as corresponding to the same property at a more abstract linguistic level.

A further argument of different kind is generally adduced in support of inventory reduction, i.e. prevention of overgeneration. Overgeneration refers in this case to the capacity of the model to generate, by means of element combination, a set of segments much larger than the segmental inventories that can be observed in natural languages. Notably, this concern attracts considerable attention in ET work, and it is not by chance that almost all the proponents of a reduction of the classic set of elements also mention overgeneration. The issue is raised, for example by Backley (1993: 301): "the ten elements inventory [...] still has the capacity for generating a significant number of expressions which are either unobserved or non-contrastive in the world's languages"; Jensen (1994: 72–73): "Most of the segments generated by the fusion operation [...] seem to have no interpretation. Even the [...] Revised Theory with only {A, I, U, H, L, ?} and no dependency nodes generates a total of 256 representations. But languages typically seem to support between 50 and 100 linguistically significant contrasts in their phonologies"; Charette and Göksel (1996: 2): "The main idea [of Revised Theory of Elements] is to overcome the overgeneration of phonological expressions by reducing the number of elements"; Pöchtrager (2006: 14): "P[honological] E[xpression]s only encode what is *phonologically relevant*, and current estimates are that the number of expressions needed will be well below 100. Any theory generating more than that is certainly wrong"; Backley (2011: 142): "There is no doubt that [employing a 'noise' element |h| in addition to |H|] increases the richness and expressive power of representations; however, a larger set of elements always brings with it the risk of overgeneration".

However, authors that express concern for overgeneration do not usually go in much depth about why exactly it should be an issue in a theory of grammar. Preventing overgeneration may be deemed a general matter of parsimony and elegance of the model. From this point of view, ET proves a competing theory, since even its richer set, e.g. the one consisting of ten elements, allows 6,144 combinations, as against 1,048,576 produced by binary feature theory with a relatively small set of twenty features. On the contrary, for a segmental model whose goal is to exclude unattested languages from the set of possible grammars, ten elements are still too many, since 6,144 largely exceeds not only the size of a single segmental inventory, but also the set of all possible segments in the world's languages.

Although, in current ET approach, preventing overgeneration is considered a sufficient and overriding reason for curtailing the set of primitives, this is inevitably a costly move. An obvious consequence of it is the risk of undergeneration, i.e. that the total of possible combinations of elements is not sufficient to express the segmental contrasts attested in the world's languages. This problem can find at least a partial solution if we conceive elements as having quite low phonetic resolution, so that languages may exist that have identical sets of abstract segmental representations, while showing fine-grained variation at the phonetic level (Breit 2013: 42–43). This being the case, a single segmental compound, e.g. |**A** I| may be [ɛ] in some languages, but [æ] in others (Backley 2011: 20).

Interestingly, the elimination of elements may have a further, somewhat paradoxical drawback of preventing significant generalisations. In his argumentation against overgenerating models, Backley (2012: 82) observes: "Once again, using two elements instead of one has the obvious advantage of greater expressive power. [...] In such a situation, theorists must consider the question of cost". A good example of this situation is the above-mentioned unification of velarity and labiality, both expressed by **U** in Standard ET. According to Backley, this move is motivated by the fact that the two classes of segments share acoustic properties (in Jakobson's theory, expressed by the feature [grave]) and that they pattern together as a natural class in some languages (cf. Backley 2011: 79 81.). It should be noted, however, that languages do not provide consistent evidence that labiality and velarity are one and the same category. As Scheer (1999) remarks, while vowels *u,w* interact with both classes of consonants, therefore revealing a labial and velar elemental content, velar consonants, being definitely unrounded, cannot contain a labiality element. Therefore, Scheer (1999: 210) claims that "consonantal representations should reflect the affinity of [u, w] with both labials and velars" and proposes two different primitives for velarity and roundness: thus, vowels *u, w* contain both **B** and **U**, velar consonants contain **U** and labial consonants contain **B**. This example illustrates the situation, that we can expect to be not isolated, where the unification of different properties under the same abstract category may allow generalisation in some cases, or for some languages, but may impede it in other cases, or for other languages.

Given the significant consequences of prevention strategy against overgeneration, it should be established in the first place whether overgeneration is a truly relevant issue for segmental theory.

Typological studies indicate that most languages have segmental inventories containing from 20 to 40 units. For example, in the *UCLA Phonological Segment Inventory Database* (UPSID), languages with 20–40 segments amount to the 78% of the 451 languages that compose the sample. The minimal cardinality in UPSID is 11 (in two languages) and the maximal is 141 (in one language); only eight languages have 15 segments or fewer, and nine languages have 60 or more. Besides, in UPSID there are 919 different segments, but the 80% of them only appear in ten or fewer languages, which means that almost all the languages of the sample make up their inventory by taking segments from a subset of 184 units.[2]

---

[2] If scrutinised through the lens of Kaye's (2005: 283) *Phonological epistemological principle,* whereby "The only source of phonological knowledge is phonological behaviour" as opposed to phonetic details, many of the 919 segments of UPSID would probably prove to be just phonetic variants of the same phonological categories.

To sum up, on the one hand, regarding segmental inventories, languages show strong preference for a subset of all attested cardinalities and for a subset of all attested segments. On the other hand, within the range of preferred subsets, languages vary to a large degree. In other words, there are extreme limits – represented in UPSID by minimal-maximal cardinality (11/141) and possible segments (919) – and preferred ranges, within which languages display variation. From the viewpoint of phonological theory, a fundamental question should be addressed, whether this state of affairs relies on specific phonological constraints, or rather on more general factors, not specifically belonging to language.

As for the number of segments that each language uses, we can reasonably conjecture that the lower limit to inventory dimensions may be owing to the fact that a smaller number of segments would be not sufficient to the externalisation task of expressing lexical contrasts. The upper limit may be due to some non-linguistic factor concerning computational capacity, as well as to properties of sound perception, wich allow language users to manage a limited number of phonological contrasts. Properties of perception and articulation obviously limit also the number of sounds that can be pronounced and discriminated by human sensory-motor system, i.e. the set of all possible segments. Non-specifically linguistic considerations of the same kind can also explain the above-mentioned "preferred ranges" observable in most languages, concerning both the dimension of inventories and the quality of segments. We can plausibly conceive that an inventory of 30 segments is a better, and therefore preferred compromise between the needs of expressive power on the one hand, and of efficient computation on the other, compared to inventories of 11 or of 141 segments, which are rare, although attested.[3] Regarding the frequency of different segments, the reason why, for instance, the voiced bilabial nasal occurs in the 94.2% of the UPSID languages, while the palatalized voiceless dental/alveolar lateral fricative occurs in only one language, is to be found in principles of perception and of articulation.[4] Notice that we are not referring here to the traditional – and rather simplistic – notions of 'easy of articulation' and 'avoidance of ambiguity'. To clear this point, let us consider a well-known typological universal concerning vowel systems: languages with at least three vowels generally have (a vowel of the kind of) *a, i, u,* and hence mid vowels

---

[3] The upper limit of the range concerning segmental inventories can also be attributed to a general linguistic principle of "*feature economy,* according to which languages maximize the combinatory possibilities of a few phonological features to generate large numbers of speech sounds" (Clements 2003).

[4] See also footnote 2.

imply corner vowels (cf. Crothers 1978). No argument of easy of articulation applies to this implication, since the articulatory gesture to utter [a], [i] or [u] is not, in any reasonable sense, easier than the gesture for [e] or [o]. From the point of view of perception, an intuitive consideration is that, being at the corner of the vocalic space, *a, i, u* are more distant and therefore more different from each other. However, a deeper analysis (Stevens 1989) reveals a less trivial property of corner vowels, consisting in their quantal nature, whereby their acoustic-auditory quality is very stable, despite the considerable variation that characterises their articulation. In other words, one of the causes of the priority of *a, i, u* over the other vowels is a specific, non-trivial interaction between phonetic parameters.

To sum up, preferences and limits observable in languages, concerning the size and the content of segmental inventories, can be attributed to properties of perception and articulation on the one hand, and to constraints of human cognition on the other. These factors are not specific to language and therefore fall outside of a theory of grammar. Within the space created by segmental primitives (i.e. elements) and delimited by non-linguistic factors, languages display random variation, exhibiting inventories that differ widely as for dimension and quality of segments.

If this premise is correct, and a part of the logically possible combinations of elements is excluded by non-linguistic factors, it follows that grammar is not what determines how many and which segments languages may have, and thus, that overgeneration is not an issue in a theory of grammar. It must be underlined that this claim does not entail opening the door to proliferation of elements. Rather, the assumption in it is that a cognitively adequate model of grammar should identify all and only the categories that prove to be relevant to phonology and related fields, including, for example, language acquisition and speech disorders.

A very valuable contribution to our understanding of generative power of segmental systems comes from Reiss (2012). Reiss criticises the tendency within linguistics to worry that our models of grammar are too rich in the naive sense of "defining a too-large space of possibilities" (Reiss 2012: 189).[5] As he observes, the combinatoric explosion of feature systems is not problematic if we characterise sets of features intensionally, i.e. from the perspective of

---

5 According to Reiss (2012), great combinatorial power is a desirable outcome of segmental models, since it allows to reduce the feature set attributed to Universal Grammar, and therefore to converge to Chomsky's (2007) approach "from bottom up", condensed into the following question: "How little can be attributed to UG while still accounting for the variety of I-languages attained, relying on third factor principles?" (Chomsky 2007: 4).

language acquisition and of explanatory adequacy, instead of extensionally, i.e. from the perspective of typology and of descriptive adequacy. From the viewpoint of language acquisition, this means that there is no reason to hypothesise that language learners start from the assumption that each one of the elements must combine with each other; and even less, that learners pursue the goal of evaluating the thousands of logically possible segmental inventories in order to single out the one that matches the target inventory. A more plausible picture is that, starting from a given knowledge of the set of primitives with specified properties (privativity, autonomous pronounceability, compositionality) as a genetic endowment, and making use of highly developed auditory perception, infants parse input signal in search of the acoustic signatures corresponding to the elements, and thus to the segments that make up words in their target language.

4 Conclusions

A position generally assumed in Element Theory is that a segmental model should be "data-fitting [i.e. able to] exclude unattested languages from the set of possible grammars generated by the model" (Blaho and Reiss 2014: 101). This concern involves in particular the generative capacity of the set of primes.

The goal of this paper is to reaffirm the essential nature of ET as a theory of grammar with the primary objective of a cognitively adequate model of linguistic competence. With this in mind, we have tried to draw attention to the negative consequences of reduction of element set on the one hand, and to highlight the weakness and inconsistency of overgeneration as an issue of phonological theory, on the other hand.

Both quantitative and qualitative variation concerning segmental systems can largely be explained as a result of third factor principles, such as properties of sensory-motor system and constraints of human cognition. Furthermore, the residual variation (e.g. between a language with 20 segments and one with 40 segments, or a language with nasal vowels and a language without nasal vowels) needs not to be explained in terms of principles of Universal Grammar, being simply a matter of lexical acquisition.

In this perspective, overgeneration has no relevance to a theory of internal/intensional language. Our claim is therefore that the primes of phonological representation, their properties and number should only reflect categories of linguistic competence and not account for data belonging to the external/extensional dimension of language.

References

Anderson, John, & Charles Jones. 1974. "Three theses concerning phonological representations". *Journal of linguistics* 10, 1: 1–26.
Backley, Phillip. 1993. "Coronal: the undesirable element". *Working Papers in Linguistics* 5: 301–323.
Backley, Phillip. 2011. *An Introduction to Element Theory.* Edinburgh: Edinburgh University Press.
Backley, Philip. 2012 "Variation in element theory". *Linguistic Variation* 12.1: 57–102.
Backley, Phillip, & Kuniya Nasukawa. 2010. "Consonant-vowel unity in Element Theory" *Phonological Studies* 13: 21–28.
Blaho, Sylvia & Curt Rice. 2014. "Overgeneration and falsifiability in phonological theory". In Jacques Durand, Gjert Kristoffersen, Bernard Laks, Julie Peuvergne (eds.) *La phonologie du français: normes, périphéries, modélisation: Mélanges pour Chantal Lyche.* Paris: Presses Universitaires de Paris Ouest: 101–120.
Breit, Florian. 2013. *Formal aspects of Element Theory.* MRes dissertation, University College London.
Bromberger, Sylvain & Morris Halle. 1989. "Why phonology is different". *Linguistic Inquiry* 20.1: 51–70.
Charette, Monik & Asli Göksel. 1996. "Licensing constraints and vowel harmony in Turkic languages". *SOAS Working Papers in Linguistics and Phonetics* 6: 1–25.
Chomsky, Noam. 2007. "Approaching UG from below". In Uli Sauerland & Hans-Martin Gärtner (eds.) *Interfaces+ recursion= language?: Chomsky's minimalism and the view from syntax-semantics.* Berlin: Walter de Gruyter: 1–30.
Clements Georges N. (2003) "Feature economy as a phonological universal". In Maria Josep Solé, Daniel Recasens & Joaquin Romero (eds.) *Proceedings of the 15th International Congress of Phonetic Sciences.* Barcelona: Futurgraphic: 371–374.
Crothers, John. 1978. *Typology and Universals of vowel systems.* In Joseph Harold Greenberg, Charles Albert Ferguson & Edith A. Moravcsik (eds.) *Universals of human language: phonology.* Vol. 2. Stanford: Stanford University Press: 93–152
Harris, John & Geoff Lindsey. 1995. "The elements of phonological representation". In Jacques Durand & Francis Katamba (eds.) *Frontiers of Phonology: Atoms, Structures and Derivations.* Harlow: Essex: Longman: 34–79.
Harris, John & Geoff Lindsey. 2000. "Vowel pattern in mind and sounds". In Noel Burton-Roberts, Philip Carr & Gerard Docherty (eds.) *Phonological knowledge: conceptual and empirical issues.* Oxford: OUP: 185–205.
Jensen, Sean. 1994. "Is ? an Element? Towards a Non-segmental Phonology". *SOAS Working Papers in Linguistics & Phonetics* 4: 71–8.
Kaye, Jonathan. 1989. *Phonology: a cognitive view.* New York/London: Routledge, 2013.
Kaye, Jonathan. 2000. *A User's Guide to Government Phonology (GP).* Unpublished ms.
Kaye, Jonathan. 2005. "GP, I'll have to put your flat feet on the ground". In Hans Broekhuis, Norbert Corver, Riny Huybregts, Ursula Kleinhenz & Jan Koster (eds.) *Organizing Grammar. Studies in Honor of Henk van Riemsdijk.* Berlin: Mouton de Gruyter: 283–288.
Kaye, Jonathan, Jean Lowenstamm & Jean-Roger Vergnaud. 1985. "The internal structure of phonological elements: a theory of charm and government". *Phonology Yearbook* 2: 305–328.

Lindsey, Geoff & John Harris. 1990. "Phonetic interpretation in generative grammar". *UCL Working Papers in Linguistics* 2: 355–369.
Nasukawa, Kuniya. 2005. *A unified approach to nasality and voicing*. Berlin: Walter de Gruyter.
Pöchtrager, Markus A. 2006. *The Structure of Length*. Dissertation zur Erlangung des Doktorgrades der Philosophie aus dem Fachgebiet Sprachwissenschaft, Universität Wien.
Pöchtrager, Markus A. & Jonathan Kaye. 2013. "GP2.0". *SOAS Working Paper in Linguistics* 16: 51–64.
Reiss, Charles. 2012. "Towards a bottom-up approach to phonological typology". In Anna Maria Di Sciullo (ed.), *Towards a Biolinguistic Understanding of Grammar: Essays on Interfaces*, Amsterdam: John Benjamins: 169–191.
Scheer, Tobias. 1999. "A theory of consonantal interaction". *Folia linguistica* 32.3–4: 201–237.
Stevens, Kenneth N. 1989. "On the quantal nature of speech". *Journal of phonetics* 17: 3–45.
Traunmüller, Hartmut. 1994. "Conventional, biological and environmental factors in speech communication: a modulation theory". *Phonetica* 51.1–3: 170–183.
UPSID (*UCLA Phonological Segment Inventory Database*). Compiled by Ian Maddieson & Kristin Precoda. Accessed on 15.07.2016 through Henning Reetz's Interface: http://web.phonetik.uni-frankfurt.de/upsid_info.html#seg_freq.

Benedetta Baldi
Linguistic and pragmatic procedures in the political discourse

1 Introduction

According to Edelman (1987), the policy differs from other value assignment methods because language is used to legitimize the action and achieve immediate results, but it also gains the consent of the people. Social interaction takes place within a cultural context: the culture of a group is the way of life of the group – language, ways of perceiving, classifying and thinking, non-verbal forms of communication and social interaction, rules and conventions concerning behaviour, values and moral ideals, the technological level and standards of life, art, science, literature and history. The relations within a society are influenced by the different aspects of culture and conventions that regulate social behaviour, moral conventions on interpersonal behaviour, verbal and non-verbal means of communication, social, technical, etc. (cf. Argyle 1974 [1972], Noelle-Neumann 1984).

An interesting aspect of the large linguistic communities with strong internal socio-cultural differentiation, as societies with high population density and socio-economic organization of the industrial and post-industrial system, is that integration in reference networks is mainly symbolic (cf. Fishman 1972). This integration mechanism through linguistic devices, and more generally communicative strategies, is also involved in the case of political discourse: the symbolic integration into a reference network and to a political and cultural belonging, is conveyed by particular linguistic expressions, that regardless of their content, perform a task of socio-cultural recognition and so represent a form of social legitimacy.

Political language, more than any other language, is a social device that 'legitimises' a system of values and an ideology that contribute to building the existing power relations. There is a close link between the political language, in the precise sense of political discourse, and the identity of the people. This space, in which we define the contours of psychological and cognitive identity, establishes the boundaries of what is seen as legitimate, that is, according to the law, valid for the customs and shared values. In fact, the speakers use the word not only to communicate but, in many cases, for reasons related to their

Benedetta Baldi, Università di Firenze

https://doi.org/10.1515/9781501505201-004

social and cultural identity and their role in the complex of social interactions. Each linguistic expression is political because every word context implies negotiation, meaning and power relations. Stated differently, 'power is embedded in existing discursive practices' (Shapiro 1984: 15). Without reducing the policy to a political message, clearly there is a symbolic and communicative dimension of political reality, as the set of power relations underlying the social organization.

The mass media has further strengthened the discursive nature of politics, so that Edelman (1992: 98) can conclude that the political language of the mass media is the language of the political events, and, as such, it replaces the events themselves; in this sense, the audience gains experience of the meaning produced by the language that describes them. For this reason, political language is political reality itself and has always been the subject of moral investigation insofar as political communication is indeed a powerful factor in society: leaders either conquer or lose their power by whether or not they effectively use political language, and people are rendered powerless or gain strength, are deceived or informed, through these discursive strategies.

The policy seeks in language the way to obtain consent, legitimacy, the evocation of those symbolic models within which the word creates myths and 'myth can be anything that undergoes the laws of speech' (Barthes 2001[1957]). 'The ways of speaking [Barthes writes, referring to the technical language] differ from group to group, and each person is a prisoner of his own language: out of his social class, the first word reveals him, brings to light his social position and shows him with all his history. The man is laid bare, revealed by his speech, betrayed by a formal truth that escapes his interested and generous lies' (Barthes 1982: 59).

In this regard, it should be noted that languages are not devices organized by operating criteria for optimizing communication. The intrinsic nature of natural languages, on the basis of the mentalist framework that I assume, is that of a system of knowledge (language-internal), namely a biologically determined component of the speaker's mind / brain that allows him to produce and understand the sentences of his language (Chomsky 1995, 2000). In the language systems, the words do not denote persons, objects, or real-world events except that by virtue of the pragmatic conditions associated to the sentences they recur with. In other words, languages are not rigid nomenclatures, on the contrary they use the indeterminacy of meaning as the interpretive key device. The 'cognoscitive' nature of language is clearly explained by Chomsky (2004):

> We can add another insight of 17th and 18th century philosophy, with roots as far back as Aristotle's analysis of what were later interpreted as mental entities: that even the most elementary concepts of human language do not relate to mind independent objects by means of some reference-like relation between symbols and identifiable physical features of the external world, as seems to be universal in animal communication systems. Rather, they are creations of the "cognoscitive powers" that provide us with rich means to refer to the outside world from certain perspectives, but are individuated by mental operations that cannot be reduced to a "peculiar nature belonging" to the thing we are talking about, [...]. Those are critical observations about the elementary semantics of natural language, suggesting that its most primitive elements are related to the mind-independent world much as the internal elements of phonology are, not by a reference-like relation but as part of a considerably more intricate species of conception and action. (Chomsky 2004:6)

The linguistic units (words, sentences) are 'mental operations', i.e. a form of operating instructions, not directly connected to the outside world. So, a simplistic approach to the relationship between language and message appears indefensible, with the result that traditional ideas about the relationship between language and culture / thought are drastically downsized. The assignment of words to objects or events, will depend on the conditions of communication, including the characteristics and the situation in which the utterance is used. Communication and language, therefore, do not coincide to the extent that the speaker's language is just one of the means used for communication purposes.

Sperber and Wilson's (1996) analysis shows how the inclusion of oral or written statements in communicative contexts is just one of the factors that go into determining the meaning. However, the information transmitted in communication can't, in any case, be reduced to a set of propositions, as the pragmatic approaches tend to assume, which treat the meaning of a sentence as the combination of a proposition and a propositional attitude. Conversely, the communication includes the vagueness, understood as the production of 'cognitive effects' not necessarily unambiguously decidable and identifiable:

> Now we all know, as speakers and hearers, that what is implicitly conveyed by an utterance is generally much vaguer than what is explicitly expressed, and that when the implicit import of an utterance is explicitly spelled out, it tends to be distorted by the elimination of this often intentional vagueness. The distortion is even greater in the case of metaphor and other figures of speech, whose poetic effects are generally destroyed by being explicitly spelled out. [...] We see it as a major challenge for any account of human communication to give a precise description and explanation of its vaguer effects. Distinguishing meaning from communication, accepting that something can be communicated without being strictly speaking *meant* by the communicator or the communicator's behaviour, is a first essential step – a step away from the traditional approach to communication and most modern approaches. (Sperber and Wilson 1996: 56, 57–58)

2 Identity and legitimacy as cognitive constructs and identity as a background in political discourse

As noted by Berger and Luckmann (1991), the reality that surrounds each of us, including our own ways of life and our social order, represents a product of human activity that every person needs to internalize through the process of socialization. By socializing, the person internalizes the social order, including the micro and macro sociological components that make him participate in the symbolic universe, inspiring the society in which he lives. The identity and legitimacy are two components of the formation process of the social order and of its symbolic representation in all of us:

> Legitimation as a process is best described as a 'second-order' objectivation of meaning. Legitimation produces new meanings that serve to integrate the meanings already attached to disparate institutional processes. The function of legitimation is to make objectively available and subjectively plausible the 'first-order' objectivations that have been institutionalized. (Berger and Luckmann 1991: 110)

Berger and Luckmann's idea (1991) is that legitimation is established in the very moment that a semantic system, the language, conveys the human experience. Thus, the legitimacy, even in its most conscious forms such as the theories and traditions, translates in terms of language and symbolic representation, of the social and institutional organization and meanings that characterize the society surrounding the subject. Leeuwen (2008) characterizes this notion by reference to the factors that contribute to fix it, such as authority, the value system, cognitive validity and myths, which are understood as society's narrations and its rules.

The other side of legitimacy is identity, which in turn is understood as a construct due to social processes that establish the symbolic universe of the individual:

> Identity [...] stands in a dialectical relationship with society. Identity is formed by social processes. Once crystallized, it is maintained, modified, or even reshaped by social relations. The social processes involved in both the formation and the maintenance of identity are determined by the social structure. Conversely, the identities [...] react upon the given social structure, maintaining it, modifying it, or even reshaping it. (Berger and Luckmann 1991: 194)

It is in the dialectic between social order, the symbolic universe, and identity, that systems of values, beliefs and cognitive environment emerge that define the existential space within which people share ideas and behaviour. Legitimation / delegitimation of behaviour and persons is one of the constitutive properties of political discourse. We can wonder whether it is the political discourse that creates this particular system of meanings or, on the contrary, the political discourse occurs as a linguistic component within a cognitive system already present; the system of the values and meanings that make up the ideal agreement and the so-called consensus. The idea that I pursue in this article is that the (de)legitimation, specifically the recognition of shared values and meanings, is a linguistic and rhetoric construct that externalizes the identity, that is, the actual sharing of a cognitive space including social values and meanings. So I will focus upon the relationship between language and identity and between identity and social relationships; what I will try to highlight is the fact that the identity process is the primary component from which the political discourse as a mechanism of self-recognition can be developed.

Relations between individuals in society depend on the reciprocal position relevant to those who interact. They reproduce norms, rules and values related to the different aspects of living in common, such as customs, traditions, beliefs, etc. These rules are internalized by the members of the group and contribute to create what we call identity and at least some aspects of the personality. The identity of individuals is therefore built on the basis of a set of features that fix their membership in the social group. This set includes both inalienable traits, such as the age, the gender, the ethnicity, the language, and the acquired traits, such as the level of education, religion, moral convictions, political views, etc. The point is that this set of features is liable to vary in relation to the material conditions of life, or to the psychology and the experience of individuals. It is, definitely, a process of construction.

The identification process includes, at the same time, the linguistic, symbolic and non-verbal components, which play a primary role in the production of meanings as relevant factors for pragmatic interpretation. These paralinguistic factors are subject to phenomena of homogenization in a manner similar to those that may interest the languages. What is more, it is the specific linguistic system that has an crucial role in establishing the identity of individuals, insofar as it 'expresses' and together, it 'provides the means' to create the link between the individual identities and the social ones (Tabouret-Keller 1998). More generally, in the formation of identity and the symbolic processes introjected, language is the real 'depository of collective sedimentation'.

> Language becomes the depository of a large aggregate of collective sedimentations, which can be acqnired monothetically, that is, as cohesive wholes and without reconstructing their original process of formation. (Berger e Luckmann 1991: 84)

The uniqueness of the language reflects a particular social, legal or economic organization to which the speakers tend to refer. It is known that the correspondence generally accepted between national entities and language is a semantic construct related to the creation of the national state (Hobsbawm 1996; Anderson 2000) expressing the 'imagined community' which inspires national and ethnic ideologies (Anderson 2000).

Hence, the language, in addition to being itself a sign of identity for the social group, provides the differences (lexical, morphosyntactic and phonological) used to introduce the various identifications. For instance, in the recent cases of the formation of new states the recognition of an autonomous language represented a source of legitimacy. In this perspective, Gumperz (2000[1968]) speaks of 'linguistic loyalty' with reference to a linguistic variety felt as a symbol of a particular group or of a 'particular social movement'. 'Language loyalty' represents an excellent glue for the social classes and for the different local groups, whose members can continue to use vernacular language in their family and can become a political issue in a society in the process of modernization when the minorities socially isolated mobilize themselves.

Returning to the political language, it reflects the inclination to share opinions rather than any real interest in understanding facts. For this characteristic, it resembles other types of rhetoric relevance whose purpose is the persuasion (cf. Baldi 2006, 2007, 2012). As already noted, According to Edelman (1992: 98) the political language of the mass media provides the people with the experience and meaning of the facts describing them. In other words, the linguistic practices are the real political practices, given that the power in setting and structuring authority relations lies in the discursive practices (Corcoran 1990). It follows that the ability to master the political discourse is equivalent to the ability to exercise control of the thought, or at least to guarantee you are holding appropriate tools to do so.

Assuming a purely linguistic perspective, the political language is often analysed focusing on the syntactic and semantic features of the language that politicians use within a defined scope of relevance. But a sectorial perspective, understood as specificity, does not provide an exhaustive definition of the political speech, since it leaves aside the semantic and pragmatic components that accompany it. We prefer to speak of political discourse, which happens to be, intuitively more effective insofar as it includes the symbolic and ritual aspect. In this regard, Edelman (1987) notes that politics can't exist without the symbols and the rituals and a political system can never subsist if it is based only on rational principles, without any symbolic connotation. In essence, however, the political discourse refers mainly to rhetorical, textual, structural and stylistic aspects implicated in the use of language.

Linguistic expressions are interpreted on the basis of their ability to bring meaningful structures and cognitive contexts that the interlocutors can recognize precisely as they are part of their system of knowledge. The words that individuals or groups use and on which they rely to obtain certain responses or behaviours, can be traced to the conceptual frameworks of the culture in which they live. In this sense, the culture models the words and speech associating to it a specific meaning and a particular emotion that can differ, perhaps significantly, between one group and another, and also within the same group in relation to the social role. The words, and generally the symbolic devices, produce a strong emotional response only in those who are, by group membership or social role, sensitive to certain cues. In addition, the words have a different meaning for each of us if they are pronounced by an ordinary person or by a person who holds a strategic position in personal and social terms. The context within which the words are produced and the opportunity of the moment contribute to assign value and credibility to the propositions; a similar argument concerns the symbols and the opportunities associated with the values.

Some authors indeed see the system of meanings introduced by the current language as a conditioning factor on thinking and actions of the people; certainly, the language is the encoding mechanism of fundamental social meanings in the identity formation (cf. Berger and Luckmann 1991). This applies in particular to the ideologies imposed or otherwise accepted, occasionally or permanently, by a social group. Cultural tradition, conformist thinking, and ideological orientations related to economic interests and ethical and political beliefs, contribute to defining universes of reference for the symbolic interpretation of the speeches. In this, the role of the media as dominant orthodoxy interpreters is crucial (Said 1995 [1994]). As noted by Chomsky (1999), the major economic forces govern by controlling the means of production, trade, advertising and communication. The aspects of totalitarian policies are realized in different ways in the Western democracies, since they are based on the conscious manipulation of the organized habits and opinions of the masses through continuous and systematic propaganda by the intelligent minorities to gain public control (cf. Baldi and Savoia 2005).

The political discourse contextualizes the social practices (Leeuwen 2008), it narrates and expresses the contents underlying the shared symbolic universe. In political discourse, therefore, the pragmatic procedures have a decisive role associated with the production of meanings, as they represent the system of beliefs and convictions of the recipients. Although these procedures do not necessarily aim to construe self-identification, they certainly have the effect of introducing ideas, messages and content that enrich the shared cognitive space. The representation of the relationship of trust with the voter or, in general, with listeners has a central role in that shared values and a feeling of belonging to the same symbolic network produce particularly evident results. The interpretation of a sentence depends on the additional information provided by a number of other contents introduced by what we call the context (Sperber and Wilson 1996). The propositions themselves, once introduced in the context, can change the initial cognitive environment by creating additional elements and assumptions that contribute to defining the information communicated.

3 Persuasion or sharing?

Although the pragmatic perspective concerning the construction of meanings helps us to account for the way in which people interact by means of utterances in communicative situations, it is still true that there are uses of language, including political discourse, that show a particular status. Not surprisingly, the political discourse favours sharing beliefs rather than any interest for the understanding of the facts. The irrational nature of this type of discourse is outlined in a precise and acute way by Leibniz (1982) in New Essays on Human Understanding (1765) in which he considers 'the authority, the party, the custom' the cause of a 'kind of madness' that distorts the reasoning processes and identifies in the 'search for truth' the only possible solution. Of course this feature of political language is one of the traits studied by the Critical Discourse Analysis, as noted by van Dijk (2001: 357):

> [...] recipients tend to accept beliefs, knowledge, and opinions (unless they are inconsistent with their personal beliefs and experiences) through discourse from what they see as authoritative, trustworthy, or credible sources, such as scholars, experts, professionals, or reliable media.

However, there is a basic dimension in the political discourse that calls into question both the 'kind of madness' invoked by Leibniz and the sender's authority, in the sense of van Dijk. Chilton (2005), examining a propaganda text such as *Mein Kampf* asks himself 'How do the ideas get transferred from mind to mind?' and points out that the recipient has sufficient interpretive means to decide whether to believe or adhere to the assertions contained in a text:

> Of course, no-one *has* to accept as true any of the virtual worlds set up in discourse. But in so far as propositions come as social transactions claiming *prima facie* to be true, people are inclined to accept them as true, initially, [...]. Still, because human language users are also good at detecting deception, speakers may want to take preemptive measures. This means that speakers often seek to build in guarantees, authorisations and assurances as to their veracity, seeking to appeal to whatever they believe their interlocutors believe to be veracious. (Chilton 2005: 22)

Of course, the basic requirement in the exchange of information is that it is compatible with the human cognitive organization. In the last analysis, cognitive components underlying the organization of human cognition are involved:

> Some of the cognitive components that make up political ideologies are 'parasitic' on basic modular knowledge, [...] The cognitive components in question are both representational in nature and procedural. The representational part belongs to different modules – e.g., intuitive physics, intuitive biology, intuitive physiology modules. The procedural part has to do with the special way the human mind appears to generate imaginative representations by integrating representations from different domains processed by different modules. (Chilton 2005: 18)

Manipulation, i.e. to obtain in the recipient the development of 'mental representations' desired by the issuer, takes place in an only partially unconscious way. When we speak of manipulation of consciences by political propaganda, we must take into account that the recipient has no less intellectual and interpretive abilities than the sender:

> Texts are complex structures that prompt readers to construct conceptualisations. They draw on existing cognitive capacities and manipulate them. The effects on readers are not of course totally predictable – and readers, as we have said, are not absolutely manipulable. The cognitive ingredients that readers assemble are a kind of *bricolage* guided by the linguistic input. The cognitive structures are not *in* the texts, they are in people's heads. They can be transferred by texts, but once in people's heads they can be elaborated in variable ways, depending on social and psychological factors. [...] Possibly, the conceptual constructs themselves need to be already dormant in the social and psychological environment. (Chilton 2005: 39)

The activation of implicatures (Sperber and Wilson 1996) not directly linked to the context has the effect to expand, intentionally by the sender, the semantic potential of the message so as to go beyond the literal content of the message itself. It is this stylistic effect which widens the transmitted contents in the direction of a much broader and inclusive universe of feelings and experiences.

4 The speech as a semantic environment

The semantic structures evoked by the language constitute or rather reproduce the way of thinking and acting of people. In this sense, the political discourse expresses expectations and existing values in the cognitive heritage legitimizing them in speech and configuring the corresponding symbolic universe. Basically, people are living in society thanks to a continuous process of integration through the use of symbols in the form of linguistic expressions, discursive and pragmatic devices, conventional behaviours, etc., that shape their existence. Of course, these symbolic components are recalled by (means of) the language that identifies them with justice, reason, truth, destiny and with other fields of experience of the real world. Moreover, the assignment of a name to things is in itself a form of knowledge (cf. Dewey and Bentley 1974) that allows us to place them in a class of objects with which is it possible to compare them and to interpret them.

The political discourse, typically that of the media today, creates a representation of reality that affects the cognitive repertoires of the people to a greater or lesser extent depending on the direct experience about the relevant phenomenon and on the interpretation skills. Political language is inherently a metaphoric language that evokes the meanings that, while being not literal and hidden, are not less decisive in political communication. This occurs also, more subtly, through a 'slipped' use of literal meanings. The lexical choice of the media connotes, through a process of attribution of meaning, the semiotics of power by reproducing the principal meanings of the social blocks and of the legitimizing symbolic universes. The reality represented by the media gives rise to a symbolic reference framework that favours the representation of aspirations, sensitivities and instincts which are prevailing in the society, rather than the objective reality (Baldi 2006, 2007, 2012).

In this perspective it is possible to understand the lexical replacements that dot the experience of the various societies. The ability of the lexical occurrences, in particular the metaphoric uses, to project a system of semantic relations has the effect to create a new semantics substituting the old meanings, or, as Lakoff and Johnson (1999, 1998[1980]) note, conceal new interpretations of the world and society. The metaphor for Lakoff and Johnson (1998[1980]) has a central role in human thinking and language, hence in verbal communication and, more generally, in symbolic expression, as it is seen as the mechanism ordering an important part of our subjective experience:

> Metaphor allows conventional mental imagery from sensorimotor domains to be used for domain of subjective experience [...] Conceptual metaphor is pervasive in both thought and language. (Lakoff e Johnson 1999: 45)

Lakoff and Johnson argue that the metaphorical representation is actually the way in which we conceptualize and categorize abstract experiences. In their model all conceptual analogies underlying the metaphors and the idioms are not only automatically available, as present in the 'semantic memory', but invariably accessible to the speaker regardless of the context. Lakoff and Johnson (1998[1980]) also point out that the creation of *frames* and metaphors is related to space and time boundaries within which the interpreter shares with other users a given encyclopaedic competence linked to a specific socio-cultural network.

A direct correspondence between the values and the metaphorical concepts follows; this does not mean that all cultural values consistent with a metaphorical system actually exist, but only that those that do exist, and are deeply rooted, are all consistent with the metaphorical system (Lakoff and Johnson 1998 [1980]). Not surprisingly, the metaphor is central to the language and to the ideology of politics, where it can play an ambiguous role, implying opaque meanings or hidden systems.

The neo-semantics of the sort introduced by figured uses or by even only subtle, not literal lexical occurrences does not necessarily derive from the media. The media generally uses it for adhering to a collective imagination associated with a political-cultural line or uncritically repeat it. The representation of the events proposed by mass media, especially by television, tends to reflect the dominant symbolic universe, which incorporates shared images and linguistic expressions. In this sense, as highlighted by many authors, mass media favour a communication based on emotion, characterized by impressionistic and ideological discursive devices, rather than providing the tools for a rational or explicit manner of understanding of the reality (Simone 2000, Baldi and Savoia 2005, Loporcaro 2005).

Bowles and Gentner in their model (Bowdle and Gentner 2005, Bowdle and Gentner 2001, 2008) assume that the metaphor is the result of an analogical process that establishes correspondences between the partially isomorphic conceptual structures associated with two terms. In this sense, the metaphor is source of polysemy, as it generates an additional abstract meaning in addition to the literal meaning of a term. More precisely, the metaphor gives rise to an abstract category that includes both terms, with the result that this new category can be conceptualized separately from the original ones of the two terms.

Metaphorical and figurative uses of language form a continuum with the literal use. In other words, the metaphors do not behave differently from the normal processes of interpretation, whereby the interpretation is the result of the combination of words in the sentence and the established relationship with the context and the speaker's knowledge (cf. Baldi and Savoia 2009, 2010). The interpretation of any utterance, including metaphors, follows the same inferential procedures based on the relevance and does not imply special cognitive measures (Sperber and Wilson 1996, 2006). Sperber and Wilson (1996) treat the effects of rhetorical figures in a similar manner to as the poetic and stylistic effect, understood as the result of an expansion of the meaning. In particular, figures of speech can be seen as ways to induce the listener to look for the conditions in which the utterance is relevant:

> A good creative metaphor is precisely one in which a variety of contextual effects can be retained and understood as weakly implicated by the speaker. [...] metaphor and a variety of related tropes (e.g. hyperbole, metonymy, synecdoche) are simply creative exploitations of a perfectly general dimension of language use. [...] Metaphor thus requires no special interpretive abilities or procedures: it is a natural outcome of some very general abilities and procedures used in verbal communication. (Sperber and Wilson 1996: 236, 237)

What defines the metaphorical use is therefore the connection between two lexical semantic contents and the context in which they trigger the search for more information, especially about the intention of the speaker. The point is that figurative uses, new or unconventional ones, regularly enter speech, contributing to its interpretation. In other words, the figured uses do not seem to constitute a separate field of semantic phenomena from the normal way of creating and interpreting meanings. Surely, some communicative situations make recourse to them in a more systematic way, both in the case of certain styles or genres and in the case of political speech insofatr as it aims to evoke and bring to the surface intentions and beliefs.

5 Textual procedures in the political discourse of Palmiro Togliatti

In this paragraph, discourse procedures and communication strategies will be examined in the speeches of a political leader in correspondence with the particular historical and political significance of the situations. Specifically, our interest focuses on the contrast between delegitimization of the opponent as a means for enhancing the legitimization sentiment and the identity recognizability of his own people (cf. Baldi and Franco 2014, 2015, Vinciguerra 2016). Let us briefly consider some of the speeches of Palmiro Togliatti, the secretary of the Italian Communist Party, in the period following the Italian general election in 1948 (Baldi and Franco 2015). It is important to take into account that the Communist Party was a political and socio-economic reality strongly rooted in Italian society; in particular it presented itself as the heir to the ideals of the Resistance and anti-fascism.

As Baldi and Franco (2015) noted, Togliatti's speeches aim to 'regain legitimacy after a political failure'; in them the personal legitimacy and the delegitimation of the political and cultural opponent appear indissolubly bound together. In fact, the elections of 1948 saw the victory of a widespread conservative conscience, strongly linked to Catholic thought and doctrine; on the contrary, as noted by Smith (2000 [1997]) the Communists and the Socialists did not convince the population of having really accepted the democratic rules.

Baldi and Franco (2015) point out the systematic use of linguistic procedures that conceals practices of delegitimation endowed with a strong perlocutionary effect. In particular, Togliatti has recourse to the denotational use of metaphors denoting, as in the following two passages, where the choice of the lexical entries *spectrum* and *chameleon* directly introduces the reference to political opponents. The recourse to dehumanizing and alienating metaphors is a procedure that significantly characterizes the political discourse insofar as it intends to reshape the symbolic universe of the persons or bring to light a hidden perception of things. Moreover, the metaphors used as referential expressions induce the current value system to be removed and drive the person described to a sort of no man's land, devoid of values. In (1a, b) the participant designed by the intensional properties of *spectrum* and of *chameleon* is initially treated as a subject / agent; then, the semantic structure is reversed, and the two metaphors are introduced as predicates, depicting the two referents in terms of non-human qualities, so restoring the true logical order.

(1) a. quando tra i presenti a un'assemblea si muove uno **spettro**, è inevitabile che **quello spettro** attiri l'attenzione e ad esso ci si rivolga. **Onorevole Tesauro**, lei qui è lo **spettro del regime fascista** [...]. (8/12/1952)
"when among those who are present in the Assembly, there is a ghost it is inevitable that that ghost draws attention, so that we talk directly to it. Mr. Tesauro, here you are the ghost of the fascist regime."
b. Lascerò da parte le volgarità, gli articoli come quelli che scriveva l'altro giorno un *illustre camaleonte*, il signor Mario Missiroli, domandandosi che cosa c'è sotto all'atteggiamento dei comunisti [...] proprio lui che, per esaltare i Patti del Laterano, scrisse un intiero volume che, si dice, ebbe il personale plauso di Mussolini! *È evidente che lezioni di etica da un camaleonte non le prendiamo.* (27/3/1947)
"I will leave aside vulgarity, such as the articles that were written the other day by an illustrious chameleon, Mr. Mario Missiroli, wondering what's underneath the attitude of the Communists [...] the same man who wrote a full volume to exalt the Lateran Pacts, a volume that, it is said, had the personal approval of Mussolini! It is clear that we do not take ethics lessons from a chameleon."

As I noted, the metaphor – the figurative device – has important effects of sense. It is able to bring new meanings, different to both the source and the target, to the people's conceptual system, as underlined by Chilton (2005):

> Metaphor is primarily seen as a cognitive operation, in which different domains of knowledge and experience are brought together. [...] Target domains, on the other hand, tend to be more abstract, understructured or problematic conceptual areas or subjective experiences – such as understanding, affection, life, time, society, causality. Important ideological or quasi-ideological beliefs are often understood in terms of one or more primary source domains. (Chilton 2005: 22)

Thus, the metaphors such as those discussed above in the Togliatti speeches introduce new meanings in the semantic space of language increasing the symbolic universe of the individuals by means of new interpretive nuances that make deep sentiments and perceptions surface. In fact, as discussed in preceding paragraph, the *chamaleon* in its association with a human being is different both from the term for the animal and generic terms such as *opportunistic*, etc. It introduces a dehumanizing effect that recalls other similar uses of terms of animals applied to humans. An interesting case is that of the metaphors of *parasites* and *noxious bacillus* selected, in Mein Kampf, by Hitler for describing the Jews (Chilton 2005). The procedure that exploits a dehumanizing reading of the referents seems related to strong ideological motivations, without of course wanting to compare the Nazi ideology with that of the Togliatti communism. These motivations invite to declass the opponents to levels of non-human existence, that is an existence irreducible to the new man pursued by totalitarian approaches to policy.

Togliatti is conscious of the fact that he is turning to a political part and a thought well-rooted in the society; it is no accident that the rhetoric he uses is that of the activation of expectations and of a semantic system that responds to a broad identitary representation. It is in the linguistic process, in its lexical and pragmatic choices that the identity of the working class is expressed. Thus, Togliatti may foreshadow a future goal, in terms generally valid in the presence of a strong and wide sharing of identity, as in his speech in Modena in 1950, where the promise and the act of commitment establishe the borders of the self-legitimation. The speaker knows that large parts of the working class and of intellectuals identify with 'the healthy forces of the Italian people', in opposition to the interests, often obscure, of liberal forces and of economic powers:

(2) Come partito dì avanguardia della classe operaia e del popolo italiano, coscienti della nostra forza che ci ha consentito di conchiudere vittoriosamente cento battaglie, **ci impegneremo ad una nuova, più vasta lotta**, in difesa della esistenza, della sicurezza, degli elementari diritti civili dei lavoratori. **Ci impegniamo a svolgere un'azione tale**, di propaganda, di agitazione, di organizzazione, che raccolga ed unisca in questa lotta **nuovi** milioni e milioni

di lavoratori, tutte le forze sane del popolo italiano. Ci impegniamo a preparare e suscitare un movimento tale, un sussulto proveniente dal più profondo stato di cose che grida vendetta al cospetto di Dio. (9/1/1950)

"As a vanguard party of the working class and of the Italian people, aware of our strength that allowed us to successfully conclude a hundred battles, we are committed to a new, broader struggle in defence of life, safety, the basic civil rights of the workers. We will engage in such an action, propaganda, agitation, organization, gathering new millions and millions of workers in this fight, all the healthy forces of the Italian people. We are committed to prepare and launch a movement which rises from the deepest state of affairs, that cries out to heaven for vengeance."

The linguistic representation couples the delegitimization of the opponent to the legitimation of themselves as guarantors and defenders of the values threatened by the adversary. Not surprisingly, the pragmatic and morphosyntactic organization mechanisms generally reflect the polarization, for example by means of sharing, using *I / we / you*, or the opposition, contrasting *we vs. they / you*, as in Togliatti's strongly identitary speeches that we just examined. The topicalization and focusing processes distribute sentential / eventive content in order to associate them to the desired information flow. The topic conveys shared content, '*Come partito di avanguardia della classe operaia e del popolo italiano...*', although the focus, in turn, does not introduce real alternatives but meanings internal to the cognitive system on which the speech is built '*...una nuova, più vasta lotta..*', '*... un'azione tale...*', '*... nuovi milioni e milioni...*'. The morphosyntactic structures exploit the elementary thematic relations of the linguistic codification of the events and their participants in a way functional to the symbolic structure driving the discourse.

6 Conclusions

As we saw, legitimization as a cognitive mechanism is based on identitary features and meanings. It is the shared identity that legitimizes the values system which people identify with. Complementarily, it delegitimizes what is felt as extraneous or contrasting, namely alternative symbolic universes, that could undermine the complex cognitive construction inspiring the dominant social and conceptual order. Delegitimization can be understood as the symbolic process (linguistic and pragmatic) that highlights the difference and hence the extraneousness from the system of shared values.

The discourses we have examined in the preceding discussion uncover an aspect that helps us to understand their real informational scope. The situations in which these narrations are inscribed indeed show that the idea, often supported, that the fundamental intention driving political language of persuading the addressee is already inadequate on an empirical level. In fact, the discourses we have considered, with the partial exception of the electoral ones, are pronounced either in Parliament or in demonstrations. In these contexts persuasion seems to be only a marginal perlocutory effect in comparison with the semantic core of these discourses, which, on the contrary, are directed to evoke and elaborate its cognitive base, the symbolic universe they imply.

All things considered, political discourse has the evident nature of ritualized communication, reproducing and representing the shared conceptual contents and values, the beliefs and the experiences of what we can think of as a common identity system by means of linguistic formulas – i.e. lexical, morphosyntactic and pragmatic devices. Its effect is to control the reciprocal disposability and accessibility between the speaker and the addressees.

Of course, what is observed by van Dijk (2001) cannot be denied, whereby:

> Language users as social actors have both personal and social cognition: personal memories, knowledge and opinions, as well as those shared with members of the group or culture as a whole. Both types of cognition influence interaction and discourse of individual members, whereas shared "social representations" govern the collective actions of a group. We have seen that among many other resources that define the power base of a group or institution, *access to* or *control over* public discourse and communication is an important "symbolic" resource, as is the case for knowledge and information. [...] If controlling discourse is a first major form of power, controlling people's minds is the other fundamental way to reproduce dominance and hegemony. (van Dijk 2001: 355, 357)

Using public discourse is a powerful symbolic tool for controlling the people's mind. What I have tried to highlight is that public discourse is able to verify the reciprocal accessibility not as it imposes new or specific systems of content but as it expresses and externalizes a thinking order and a social order depending on dominant contents, conceptual structures, beliefs and culture in a certain social group. In this sense the analysis of political discourse appears to be a more delicate and countercurrent task: its real target is not only the politician or the powerful person but the system that created her/ him, i.e. the responsibility of consciences.

References

Anderson, Benedict. 2000. *Comunità immaginate. Origini e fortuna dei nazionalismi*. Roma: Manifestolibri.
Argyle, Michael. 1974[1972]. *Il comportamento sociale*. Bologna: Il Mulino.
Baldi, Benedetta. 2006. *Opinione pubblica: un potere fragile. Introduzione alla comunicazione politica*. Alessandria: Edizioni dell'Orso.
Baldi, Benedetta. 2007. *La politica lontana*. Roma: Bulzoni.
Baldi, Benedetta. 2012. *Pensieri e parole nel linguaggio politico*. Alessandria: Edizioni dell'Orso.
Baldi, Benedetta and Ludovico Franco. 2014. Sanctions, fate and (de)legitimization: the speeches of Benito Mussolini during the italo-ethiopian war (1935–1936). *Studi Italiani di Linguistica Teorica e Applicata*. XLIII(3): 387–422.
Baldi, Benedetta and Ludovico Franco. 2015. (De)legitimization strategies in the 'austere prose' of Palmiro Togliatti. *QULSO – Quaderni di Linguistica e Studi Orientali* 1: 139–158.
Baldi, Benedetta and Leonardo M. Savoia. 2005. I media e la formazione dell'opinione pubblica. Alcune riflessioni sul rapporto tra informazione e globalizzazione. *Quaderni del Dipartimento di Linguistica dell'Università di Firenze*. 15: 255–279.
Baldi, Benedetta e Leonardo M. Savoia. 2009. *Lingua e comunicazione. La lingua e i parlanti*. Pisa: Pacini.
Baldi, Benedetta e Leonardo M. Savoia. 2010. Metafora e ideologia nel linguaggio politico. In Massimo Arcangeli (ed.), *Lingua Italiana d'Oggi*. 119–165. Roma: Bulzoni.
Barthes, Roland. 1982. *Il grado zero della scrittura*. Torino: Einaudi.
Barthes, Roland. 2001[1957]. *Miti d'oggi*. Milano: Fabbri.
Berger, Peter and Thomas Luckmann. 1991. *The Social Construction of Reality*. Harmondsworth, England: Penguin.
Bourdieu, Pierre. 2001. *Language & Symbolic Power*. Cambridge, MA: Harvard University Press.
Bowdle, Brian and Derdre Gentner. 2001. Convention, form, and figurative language processing. *Metaphor and Symbol*, 16: 223–247.
Bowdle, Brian and Derdre Gentner 2005, The Career of Metaphor. *Psychological Review*, 112, 1: 193–216.
Bowdle, Brian and Derdre Gentner. 2008. Metaphor as structure-mapping. In Raymond Gibbs (ed.), *The Cambridge Handbook of Metaphor and Thought*, 109–128. Cambridge: Cambridge University Press.
Chilton, Paul. 2005. Manipulation, memes and metaphors: The case of Mein Kampf. In Louis de Saussure. Peter Schulz (eds), *Manipulation and Ideologies in the Twentieth Century: Discourse, Language, Mind*, 15–43. Amsterdam: John Benjamins.
Chomsky, Noam. 1995. *A minimalist program*. Cambridge, Mass: MIT Press.
Chomsky, Noam. 1999. *Sulla nostra pelle*. Milano: Tropea Editore.
Chomsky, Noam. 2000. *New Horizons in the Study of Language and Mind*. Cambridge: Cambridge University Press.
Chomsky, Noam. 2004. The biolinguistic perspective after 50 years. *Quaderni del Dipartimento di Linguistica dell'Università di Firenze* 14: 3–12.
Corcoran, Paul E. 1990. *Language and Politics*. In David Swanson, Dan Nimmo (eds.). *New Directions in Political Communication*, 51–85. Newbury Park: Sage.
Dewey, John and Arthur F. Bentley 1974, *Conoscenza e transazione*. Firenze: La Nuova Italia.

Dijk, Van Teun. 2001. Critical Discourse Analysis. In Deborah Schiffrin, Deborah Tannen, Heidi E. Hamilton (eds.), *The Handbook of Discourse Analysis*, 352–371. Oxford: Blackwell.
Edelman, Murray. 1987. *Gli usi simbolici della politica*. Napoli: Guida.
Edelman, Murray. 1992. *Costruire lo spettacolo politico*. Torino: Nuova Eri.
Fishman, Joshua A. 1972. *The sociology of language; an interdisciplinary social science approach to language in society*. Rowley. Mass.: Newbury House.
Glucksberg, Sam. 2003. *The psycholinguistics of metaphor*. Trends in cognitive sciences 7(2): 92–96.
Gumperz, John J. 2000[1968]. *La comunità linguistica*, In Pierpaolo Giglioli and Giolo Fele (eds.), *Linguaggio e contesto sociale*, 171–183. Bologna: Il Mulino:
Hobsbawm, Eric J.E. 1996. *L'invenzione della tradizione*. Torino: Einaudi.
Lakoff, George and Mark Johnson. 1999. *Philosophy In The Flesh: the Embodied Mind and its Challenge to Western Thought*. New York: Basic Books.
Lakoff, George and Mark Johnson 1998 [1980]. *Metafora e vita quotidiana*. Milano: Bompiani.
Leeuwen Van, Theo. 2008. *Discourse and practice: new tools for critical discourse analysis*. Oxford: Oxford University Press.
Leibniz Gottfried W. 1982. *Nuovi saggi sull'intelletto umano*. Roma: Editori Riuniti.
Loporcaro, Michele. 2005. *Cattive notizie*: Milano: Feltrinelli.
Noelle-Neumann, Elisabeth. 1984. *The spiral of silence: public opinion, our social skin*, Chicago-London: University of Chicago Press.
Said, Edward W. 1995[1994]. *Dire la verità. Gli intellettuali e il potere*. Milano: Feltrinelli.
Shapiro, Michael. 1984, Language and Political understanding: an assessment. A paper presented at the conference on political linguistics: precursors and prospects, Toronto: York University.
Simone, Raffaele. 2000. *La Terza fase: forme di sapere che stiamo perdendo*. Roma-Bari: Laterza.
Sperber, Dan. 1996. *Explaining Culture: A Naturalistic Approach*. Oxford: Blackwell.
Sperber, Dan and Deirdre Wilson. 1996. *Relevance. Communication and Cognition*. Oxford: Blackwell.
Sperber, Dan and Deirdre Wilson. 2006. A deflationary account of metaphor. *UCL Working Papers in Linguistics* 18: 171–203.
Smith Denis Mack. 2000[1997]. *Storia d'Italia*. Roma-Bari: Laterza.
Tabouret-Keller Andrée. 1998. Language and identity. In Florian Coulmas (ed.). *The Handbook of Sociolinguistics*, 315–326. Oxford: Blackwell.
Vinciguerra Antonio. 2016. La delegittimazione dell'avversario politico nei discorsi di Alcide De Gasperi per la campagna elettorale del 1948. *Lingua e Linguaggi* 16: 277–296.

Josef Bayer
Why doubling discourse particles?

1 Introduction

In this chapter, I want to extend my earlier work on discourse particles as functional heads by providing new evidence from particle doubling. I will argue that the German data on doubling that I will present are explained in a natural way within the unificational theory of focus particles as well as discourse particles developed in Bayer (1996, 1999, 2012, 2018) and in Bayer and Obenauer (2011), Bayer and Trotzke (2015) as well as in Bayer, Häussler and Bader (2016). Particle doubling lends new support to this theory which defends the view that particles of the relevant sort are functional heads.

2 The particle problem in syntax

Particles, focus particles as well as discourse particles, have remained a controversial issue in linguistic theory for many years. On one side, they have much in common with adverbs, on the other side, they differ from adverbs by showing both more constrained and more relaxed word orders. Focus particles (FP) like *only* and *even* and their correspondents in other languages are usually taken to be adverbs. Especially in the semantic literature not too much attention is given to their syntactic status. Since they are (supposed to be) optional, they are adjoined. Since they are semantically propositional operators, they must be adjoined to sentential domains (*v*P, TP or CP). In cases like *He adores only ROSSINI*, this is obviously not the case. So it needs some acrobatics to arrive at the LF "For every composer x that he adores, x equals Rossini". Various proposals have been made, which I cannot discuss here in

---

Notes: This work was supported by grant BA 1178/9-1 of the DFG (German Research Council). My thoughts benefitted from discussions with Sjef Barbiers, Alex Grosu, Rita Manzini, Andreas Trotzke, Yvonne Viesel, Michael Wagner, George Walkden and participants of the 2015 workshop on *Freezing* held in Tübingen. Written comments by Michael Wagner, Yvonne Viesel, and an anonymous reviewer were of great help. Thanks to Uwe Braun, Marc Meisezahl and Verena Simmler for technical support. Any insufficiencies are in my responsibility.

Josef Bayer, University of Konstanz

https://doi.org/10.1515/9781501505201-005

detail. Investigations of FPs in German have resulted in roughly two proposals, the "adverb theory" and the "mixed theory". The former, see Jacobs (1983) and Büring and Hartmann (2001), assumes a syntax in which FPs are adjoined sentential operators. Phrases like [$_{DP}$ *only ROSSINI*] are a big problem, and their existence has even been denied. The latter, see Reis (2005) and Barbiers (2010, 2014), assumes an extension by which FPs can also be adjoined to non-sentential major constituents such as DP, PP etc. Rochemont (2018), following Bayer (1999), uses the term "constituent *only*" which he distinguishes from "adverbial *only*". In these aproaches, it remains to be seen how the syntax to semantics mapping works.

With respect to discourse particles (DiP), the dominant theory is also the "adverb theory" by which a DiP is adjoined to a propositional domain. In studies of German, where most of the research on DiPs comes from, DiPs are assumed to be adjoined to *v*P i.e. a propositional domain. For Italian, researchers are split. Some argue for adverb status, see Manzini (2015), or a special category of "weak adverbs", see Cardinaletti (2011) and Coniglio (2008), others have argued that DiPs are heads which occupy the C-domain, see Munaro and Poletto (2003), Poletto (2000), Poletto and Vanelli (1995), and for criticism Manzini (2015). For German, a straight adverb account is hard to defend. If DiPs are adverb-like, they have undergone grammaticalization and, as a result, have become weak and immobile.[1] Unlike adverbs, they can, for example, not be displaced, see Thurmair (1989). The projective status of DiPs has been discussed within X-bar theory. Meibauer (1994) finds that various facts speak in favor of head status, but ultimately he leaves the issue undecided.

In my work on FPs, (see Bayer 1996; 1999; 2018), as well as in my work on DiPs (see Bayer 2010; 2012; 2018; Bayer and Obenauer 2011; Bayer and Trotzke 2015), I have continuously argued for an account in which particles have the status of functional heads. Before I will provide new evidence for this hypothesis in section 4, I will give in section 3 a summary of why I believe that this is the most adequate theory, at least for the German data under consideration.[2]

---

[1] According to Manzini (2015), Italian DiPs and adverbs occupy the same positions in the sentence and are not grammaticalized. If so, this would be in strong contrast with German, see Hentschel (1986).

[2] Bangla, as studied by Bayer and Dasgupta (2016) and Bayer, Dasgupta and Mukhopadhyay (2014), offers independent evidence for the functional head theory, and so seem to do many other languages. According to Li (2006: 64), the final particles of Mandarin are "heads of functional projections in the CP domain", similarly Endo (to appear) for Japanese. For Paul and Pan (2017), Chinese sentence-final particles are head-final complementizers.

3 Particles as functional heads

According to my earlier work, FPs as well as DiPs are not adverbs but syncategorematically introduced heads which project a so-called PARTICLE PHRASE (PrtP). In other words, particles import semantic but no categorial syntactic features. If their sister is of type vP, the resulting PrtP is also of type vP. Importantly, vP is a propositional domain, i.e. Prt takes scope over a proposition. The general observation is that in pre-vP position, Prt takes scope once and forever. In other words, the scope cannot be altered by further operations. To see this, consider the English example in (1a) with the structure in (1b).

(1) a. *We are required to only study SYNTAX*
    b. *We are required to* [$_{PrtP}$ *only* [$_{vP}$ *study SYNTAX*]]

Since *only* is syncategorematic, PrtP equals vP in terms of lexical syntactic category. The fact that it is in a scope position is reflected by the scopal non-ambiguity of the example.[3] There is an alternative analysis by which the particle undergoes merger with the DP. The result is what I call a SMALL PARTICLE PHRASE (SPrtP).

(2) a. *We are required to study only SYNTAX*
    b. *We are required to* [$_{vP}$ *study* [$_{SPrtP}$ *only* [$_{DP}$ *SYNTAX*]]]

A classical finding about examples of type (2) is that they can be ambiguous (see Klima 1964 on negation, and Taglicht 1984 and Rooth 1985, 1992 on FPs.) The point is that unlike in (1), the particle is not in a proper scope position. A traditional answer would be that it undergoes LF-movement to a scope position which can be the lower vP or – as a more marked case – the next higher vP while nothing of this sort happens in (1) due to the fact that the particle is already frozen in a proper scope position.

Notorious German examples with a SPrtP in first position as seen in (3)

(3) *Nur Florenz haben die Touristen besucht*
     only Florence have   the tourists   visited
     'It was only Florence that the tourists visited'

---

[3] Apart from this, *only* may quantify over properties (e.g. study syntax) or over individuals (e.g. syntax). Due to nuclear stress, this difference is phonetically undetermined. For reasons of space, I limit myself to vP and leave out the bigger generalization according to which some focused XP may also qualify if it is the predicate of a proposition as in small clauses. See Grohmann and Kallulli (2006), Frascarelli (2010), and for earlier discussions with respect to FPs Jacobs (1983) and Bayer (1996).

are no problem in this theory. The particle is not interpreted where it occurs phonetically but lower down in the clause. The first constituent is the SPrtP [*nur FLORENZ*].[4] This phrase is initially merged in *v*P as the direct object of *visit*. From there it moves to the specifier of a silent Prt-head which heads the regular PrtP associated with *v*P. This is the position where the particle finds its scope position. Spec-head agreement (SHA) with the particle head freezes its scope. The rest of the derivation affects the particle on the PF-side of the grammar but not on the LF-side. The topicalization we see in (3) has no effect on the semantic scope of the particle. The steps are summarized in (4); the scope of the particle is indicated with ✓

(4) a. [$_{vP}$ *die Touristen* [$_{VP}$ [$_{SPrtP}$ *nur FLORENZ*] *besucht*]]   = MERGE Prt =>
    b. [$_{Prt'}$ Prt [$_{vP}$ *die Touristen* [$_{VP}$ [$_{SPrtP}$ *nur FLORENZ*] *besucht*]]]
                                          = MOVE SPrtP & SPECHEAD AGREEMENT =>
    c. [$_{PrtP}$ [$_{SPrtP}$ *nur FLORENZ*] [$_{Prt'}$ Prt✓ [$_{vP}$ *die Touristen* [$_{VP}$ {$_{SPrtP}$ *nur FLORENZ*} *besucht*]]]]
        ┖────── SHA ──┚
                                                              = further steps =>
    d. [$_{Fin'}$ *haben* [$_{TP}$ ... [$_{PrtP}$ [$_{SPrtP}$ *nur FLORENZ*] [$_{Prt'}$ Prt✓ [$_{vP}$ *die Touristen* [$_{VP}$ {$_{SPrtP}$ *nur FLO-RENZ*} *besucht*]]]]]]
                                                                  = MOVE SPrtP =>
    e. [$_{FinP}$ [$_{SPrtP}$ *nur FLORENZ*] [$_{Fin'}$ *haben* [$_{TP}$ *die Touristen* [$_{PrtP}$ {$_{SPrtP}$ *nur FLORENZ*} [$_{Prt'}$ Prt✓ [$_{vP}$ *die Touristen* [$_{VP}$ {$_{SPrtP}$ *nur FLORENZ*} *besucht*]]]]]]]

As one can see, raising of the SPrtP to the immediate pre-*v*P position derives a semantically interpretable structure in which the Prt-feature on the SPrtP is interpretable and ceases to be syntactically active. We express this in terms of SHA à la Rizzi (1991/1996).[5] The second raising of this phrase that we see in the transition from (4d) to (4e) has no relevance for the particle. The particle is simply pied-piped along.[6]

---

[4] Since the particle does not impose a syntactic category, the phrase structure of the SPrtP looks like an adjunction construction: [$_{DP}$ *nur* [$_{DP}$ *Florenz*]]. For the sake of readability, this structure will remain implicit in the following.

[5] Barbiers (2010: 26), who shares with me and others the basic difference between the particle's scope and its associated focus, makes a very similar proposal by which a NumP prefixed with a particle raises to the specifier of a particle that is prefixed to TP or VP. The latter position defines the scope domain. Referring to Haegeman (1995), he proposes SHA as the mechanism that "fuses" the two occurrences of the particle syntactically.

[6] Approaches to FPs in which the FP can freely team up with non-propositional XPs and nevertheless find its way to propositional scope have been suggested by Barbiers (2014) and by Smeets and Wagner (2017).

Assume next that the grammar of DiPs works more or less in the same way. We assume that a DiP is merged with *v*P (or an "extension" of it, for example a NegP). In this case, the DiP is in an irreversible scope position. The question is then how the DiP can be made dependent on the clause type and ultimately on the speech act type of the sentence. As argued extensively in Bayer and Obenauer (2011) and in Bayer, Häussler and Bader (2016), the DiP does not undergo LF-movement to the left periphery; it rather enters a probe-goal agreement relation with whatever represents the clause type and ultimately the speech act in the upper left periphery. Since the DiP is merged in a proper scope position, there is no need for it to move away. This explains why in the core cases we do not find displacement of DiPs.

Unlike FPs, DiPs do not seem to enter alternative constituentships.[7] There is at least one exception though: In *wh*-interrogatives, DiPs can team up with a *wh*-phrase. In German, a somewhat marked but fully legitimate and in fact rather frequent alternative to (5a) could be (5b).[8]

(5) a. *An wen könnte er sich denn gewandt haben?*
    at who could he REF DENN turned have
    'Who could he have turned to after all?'
    b. *An wen denn könnte er sich gewandt haben?*
    At who DENN could he REF turned have

The interpretation of (5b) is almost the same as in (5a), the difference being that (5b) is a more emotionally loaded, more emphatic question with a more exclamative flavor. The construction has been studied in Meibauer (1994), Bayer and Obenauer (2011) and then in Bayer and Trotzke (2015) and more recently in Bayer (2018). Trotzke and Turco (2015) as well as Trotzke (2017) provide experimental evidence that the *wh*-phrase in (5b) has a specific phonetic signature that could be identified as a typical property of emphatic speech. The syntactic assumption is that the DiP may undergo merger with a *wh*-phrase forming again a SPrtP, [$_{SPrtP}$ Prt *wh*P]; this *wh*P moves to the specifier of the SPrtP where it values a feature for emphasis that the DiP has been endowed with in the

---

[7] A plausible reason for this could be that DiPs do not associate with a focus-bearing constituent in the way FPs do. DiPs separate the topic domain from the (information) focus domain but they do not induce focus alternatives.
[8] The DiP *denn* (lit. then) is restricted to interrogatives and imports a quasi anaphoric relation to the discourse in which the question is uttered. *Denn* means something like "after all", "under the actual circumstances".

numeration. The result of this operation is [$_{SPrtP}$ whP [Prt ~~whP~~]].⁹ The unavoidable conclusion is that wh and DiP can form a constituent, and that this constituent undergoes wh-movement, pied-piping the DiP along just like in the case of the FPs we considered above. As shown by the works quoted above, there is strong evidence that in this case the DiP is not interpreted where we see it but rather in the place of the copy that the SPrtP has left behind in the specifier of the particle phrase that is already familiar from our discussion of the syntax of FPs. An immediate idea could be that the DiP is merged with vP and is then picked up by the wh-phrase once it moves out of vP.

(6) a. ... [$_{PrtP}$ Prt [$_{vP}$ ... whP ...]]] =>
    b. ... [$_{PrtP}$ [Prt whP] [$_{vP}$ ... ~~whP~~ ...]]] =>
    c. ... [$_{PrtP}$ [$_{SPrtP}$ whP [Prt ~~whP~~]] [$_{vP}$ ... ~~whP~~ ...]]] =>
    d. [$_{SPrtP}$ whP [Prt ~~whP~~]] ... [$_{PrtP}$ [$_{SPrtP}$ ~~whP [Prt whP]~~] [$_{vP}$ ... ~~whP~~ ...]]] ...

However, this is not a viable solution. As pointed out in Bayer and Trotzke (2015), the step from (6a) to (6b) violates the Extension Condition, see Chomsky (1995: 248), which requires that "Merge always applies at the simplest possible form: at the root". Notice also that the on-line formation of a SPrtP would prevent the whP from c-commanding its trace/copy in vP. The alternative is to generate the SPrtP in a separate work space and merge it in vP.¹⁰ In this case, the derivation works along the lines of (4): on its way out of vP, the SPrtP cycles through the specifier of a particle phrase that has been created by merger of a silent particle, and in which it undergoes SHA. Let us see in (7) how the derivation of example (5b) proceeds; once again, the scope of the particle is indicated with ✓.

(7) a. [$_{vP}$ er [$_{VP}$ sich [$_{SPrtP}$ an wen denn ~~an wen~~] gewandt haben könnte]]
                                                                    = MERGE Prt =>
    b. [$_{Prt'}$ Prt [$_{vP}$ er [$_{VP}$ sich [$_{SPrtP}$ an wen denn ~~an wen~~] gewandt haben könnte]]]
                                                      = MOVE SPrtP & SPECHEAD AGREEMENT =>
    c. [$_{PrtP}$ [$_{SPrtP}$ an wen denn] [$_{Prt'}$ Prt✓ [$_{vP}$ er [$_{VP}$ sich [$_{SPrtP}$ ~~an wen denn~~] gewandt
       └─── SHA ───┘
       haben könnte]]]]   = further steps =>
    d. [$_{Fin'}$ könnte [$_{TP}$ er sich ... [$_{PrtP}$ [$_{SPrtP}$ an wen denn] [$_{Prt'}$ Prt✓ [$_{vP}$ ~~er~~ [$_{VP}$ ~~sich~~
       [$_{SPrtP}$ ~~an wen denn~~] gewandt haben]]]]]]   = MOVE SPrtP =>

---

9 The simplest assumption about [$_{SPrtP}$ whP [Prt ~~whP~~]] is that Prt has an uninterpretable feature for emphasis, and that an emphatically marked whP moves into its specified where it agrees and deletes this uninterpretable feature. For further details see Bayer and Trotzke (2015).
10 The inner structure of theSPrtP is as in [$_{SPrtP}$ [an wen] [$_{SPrt'}$ denn [~~an wen~~]]; again we oppress this structure in the following derivation for reasons of readability.

e. [FinP [SPrtP *an wen denn*] [Fin' könnte [TP er sich ... [PrtP [SPrtP ~~an wen denn~~] [Prt' Prt✓ [vP ~~er~~ [vP ~~sich~~ [SPrtP ~~an wen denn~~] gewandt haben]]]]]]

The step from (7b) to (7c) freezes the scope of *denn* by SHA, and *denn* is deactivated. The raising of the SPrtP we see in the transition from (7d) to (7e) is nothing else but regular *wh*-movement by which *denn* is pied-piped along, a movement step that has no relevance for the semantic interpretation of *denn*.

This derivation is technically feasible and serves as input to further processes of agreement between the DiP and the higher left periphery's features of clause type and speech act. These are not relevant in the present context; interested readers are referred to Bayer, Häussler and Bader (2016) and to my previous work on this issue. The advantage of the account is obvious: (i) it rests on processes which are known from the paradigm case of *wh*-movement or the syntax of negation. (ii) it unifies the syntax of FPs and DiPs to a maximal degree, a result that is conceptually desirable. The account depends crucially on the assumption that DiPs as well as FPs are functional heads. Standard adjunction does not create the positions into which a SPrtP moves, and the formation of a SPrtP itself is hard to imagine if the particle is an adjunct. Thus, we have a strong argument in favor of the "head theory" and against the "adverb theory". There is one point though which might be seen as a technical trick to get the derivation running. This is the merger of a silent particle. In the rest of this chapter, I want to comment on this point with novel data.

4 Doubling discourse particles

It is known from the work of Thurmair (1989) and following work that in German DiPs can be stacked. It is less known that they can also be doubled[11]. Consider the following example in (8).

(8) Vor was denn ist er denn geflüchtet?
 from what DENN is he DENN fled
 'What on earth did he flee from?'
 http://www.trennungsschmerzen.de/verlassen-mit-baby-wer-noch-t604.html (24.01.2016)

---

[11] This section has benefitted in particular from comments by Michael Wagner.

The repetition of the particle *denn* could in principle be a speech error which by some accident made it onto a web page. This would in a sense trivialize the example. But it is unlikely that this would count as an explanation. Examples like those in (9), in which another constituent is doubled, appear to be rare if not inexistent. # should signal an uncertain deviation from the standard.

(9) a. #*Vielleicht ist er vielleicht ins Kino gegangen*
    perhaps is he perhaps in.the movie gone
    'Perhaps he went to the movies'
   b. #*Gerade sind sie gerade nach hause gekommen*
    just are they just to home come
    'They just came home.'
   c. #*Er ist er vielleicht ins Kino gegangen*
    he is he perhaps in.the movie gone
    'Perhaps he went to the movies'
   d. #*Was für Leuten passiert für Leuten so etwas*
    what for people happens for people so something
    'What kind of people does something like that happen to?'

(9a,b) show that regular adverbs are unlikely to be echoed. (9c) shows that pronouns, i.e. comparably short and unstressed element, are unlikely to be echoed. (9d) shows that phrases which are attached to *wh*-words are equally unlikely to be echoed. In addition, if some part of speech is repeated as a result of lack of processing capacities, the distance between the two occurrences would hardly be as close as the distance between the occurrences of *denn* in (8). (10a) shows a frequently observed blending in running speech, but (10b) sounds unrealistic because the distance between the doubled parts is extremely small.

(10) a. *Der ist doch schon vor zwei Jahren für einen Monat*
     he is DOCH already before two years for one month
     in Florenz gewesen ist der
     in Florence been is he
     Literally: 'He has been in Florence for one month already two years ago, don't you rember?'
     Suggestive question: 'Hasn't he already been in Florence for one month two years ago?'
    b. #*Der ist hier ist der*
     he is here is he
     'He is here.'

According to these considerations, an explanation of (8) in terms of speech errors or processing overload appears to be inadequate. Importantly, the example seen in (8) is not an isolated case. The examples that follow in (11) through (14) are a collection of internet finds on the doubling of different DiPs which can co-occur with *wh*P in SPrtPs.[12] The numbers in square brackets refer to the sources listed in the appendix.

(11) Examples with *denn*
    a. *Wer **denn** hat **denn** merkel gewählt???* [1]
       'Who has voted for Merkel after all?'
    b. *Hab das jetzt schon öfters gelesen, dass eben nicht Brecko den Wagen gefahren haben soll, aber wer **denn** hat **denn** nun hinter dem Steuer gesessen?* [2]
       'I've read this a couple of times that Brecko did not drive the car but who on earth was behind the stirring wheel then?'
    c. *Wer **denn** hat **denn** noch Interesse* [3]
       'Who is still interested after all?'
    d. *Wer **denn** will **denn** nach Berlin?* [4]
       'Who wants to go/move to Berlin after all?'
    e. *Wie **denn** ist **denn** der Kontakt zu den Reutlinger Banater Schwaben zustande gekommen?* [5]
       'How then did the contact with the Reutlingen Banat Swabians come about?'
    f. *Wie **denn** wäre er **denn** „vorgegangen" gegen den Lehrer, der den Islam nicht nach Weisung der Moslems darstellt?* [6]
       'How would he have "acted" then against the teacher who did not represent islam according to the rules of the muslims?'
    g. *Wie **denn** könnten wir **denn** besser unsere Einheit im Grund, der gelegt ist in Christus, bekunden?* [7]
       'How then could we better express our unity on the foundation that is defined by Christ?'

---

[12] I am indebted to Verena Simmler, who compiled this list of examples. For reasons of space, the examples are not glossed but simply translated in an intuitive way to the extent that a halfway realistic translation is possible. Orthography largely retains the original form. What is relevant is the structure. I provide the entire collection as it will become relevant when we discuss their underlying structure. References to work on the particles *denn, nur, schon* and *wohl* can be found in Bayer and Obenauer (2011) and in various other publications.

h. *Wie **denn** könnten **denn** unsere Politiker solche Firmen ertragen, weiter Waffen verkaufen, wenn sie nicht die Gabe des „weisen Marabu" hätten?* [8]
 'How after all could our politicians tolerate such companies (and?) continue to sell weapons, if they did not have the gift of the "wise maraboo"?'
i. *Wie **denn** sollten sie **denn** auch gehandhabt werden?* [9]
 'How should they be handled then?'
j. *Vor was **denn** ist er **denn** geflüchtet?* [10] = (8)
 'What on earth did he flee from?'
k. *Bitte erleuchten Sie mich, was **denn** sind **denn** die Pyramiden und auf welchen Forschungen beziehen Sie ihr Wissen?* [11]
 'Please enlighten me, what are the pyramids after all, and from which research do you derive your knowledge?'
l. *Was **denn** sind **denn** deine Favoriten?* [12]
 'What are your favorites then?'
m. *Nun mal Butter bei de Fische, was **denn** sind **denn** diese Spiele?* [13]
 'Don't try to evade my question, what are these games really?'
n. *Vor allem, was **denn** hätte **denn** Schlimmeres passieren können?* [14]
 'Above all, how could things get worse after all?'
o. *Oh, wo **denn** ist **denn** nochmal der Frosch hin?* [15]
 'Oh, where again did the frog disappear then?'
p. *Wo **denn** ist **denn** hier nur dieser komische empfehlen-knopf...?* [16]
 'Where after all is this funny recommendation button?'
q. *Und wo **denn** sind **denn** all Eure Rechtsantworten auf eingereichte Strafanzeigen von mir, Herrn Moritz Günthert, meinen Mandanten oder meinen behandelten Ärzten geblieben?* [17]
 'And where please have all your juridical responses to declarations been left that have been filed by myself, Mr. Moritz Günthert, my clients or my doctors?'
r. *Seit wann **denn** ist **denn** das thema Sex für u18 nicht erlaubt?* [18]
 'Since when is the topic "Sex" not allowed for those under 18?'
s. *Seit wann, Schrammel, seit wann **denn** hast du **denn** 'nen Krankenschein?* [19]
 'Since when, Schrammel, since when do you have a sick report?'
t. *Warum **denn** hat **denn** die Fee den Drachen nicht gestreichelt...?* [20]
 'Why after all did the fairy not caress the dragon?'
u. *Warum **denn** sollte ich **denn** was von dir behalten?* [21]
 'Why on earth should I keep stuff that belongs to you?'
v. *Warum **denn** sollte ich **denn** in einen Wert engagiert sein, wenn ich ihn erwähne?* [22]
 'Why after all should I be engaged in a value that I do not mention?'

w. *Vom wem **denn** bin ich **denn** der beste Freund, ...?* [23]
   'Whose best friend am I after all?'
x. *Wen **denn** hast du **denn** alles so lieb?* [24]
   'Who all are dear to you then?'

(12) Examples with *nur*
   a. *Wer **nur** könnte **nur** hinter den ausgeklügelten Überfällen stecken?* [25]
      'Who on earth could be responsible for these sophisticated attacks?'
   b. *Was **nur** ist **nur** mit denen los?* [26]
      'What the hell is going on with them?'
   c. *Warum **nur** bin ich **nur** so langsam?* [27]
      'Why the hell am I so slow?'
   d. *Warum **nur** bin ich **nur** so spät hier?* [28]
      'Why the hell am I here at this late hour?'
   e. *Warum **nur** bist Du **nur** gegangen?* [29]
      'Why on earth did you leave?'
   f. *Warum **nur** bist du **nur** so scharf drauf das Saugrohr zu wechseln?* [30]
      'Why the hell are you so keen to change the suction-pipe?'
   g. *Warum **nur** ist er **nur** so schweigsam?* [31]
      'Why on earth is he so reserved?'
   h. *Warum **nur** seid ihr **nur** so wie ihr seid?* [32]
      'Why on earth are you as you are?'
   i. *Warum **nur** seid ihr **nur** soo gehässig?* [33]
      'Why the hell are you so malicious?'
   j. *Aber warum **nur** sind **nur** so viele Familienbande, Freundschaften der Deutschen nach Jahren der zwangsweisen Trennung und des Zusammenhaltes, auch einer Solidarität über das berühmte Westpaket, einfach so zerbrochen???* [34]
      'But why on earth did so many family ties and German friendships break apart just like this after years of forced separation and unity, also solidarity concerning the celebrated parcel from the west?'
   k. *Warum **nur** war ich **nur** immer so schrecklich unkreativ?* [35]
      'Why the hell was I always so terribly un-creative?'
   l. *Warum **nur** war er **nur** nicht schneller da gewesen?* [36]
      'Why the hell did he not show up earlier?'
   m. *Warum **nur** war er **nur** so unerreichbar für mich?* [37]
      'Why on earth was he so unreachable for me?'
   n. *Warum **nur** habe ich **nur** das Gefühl, Sie hätten absolut keine Ahnung wie der Wissenschaftsbetrieb funktioniert...* [38]

'Why on earth do I have the feeling that you have absolutely no idea how the science business works?'

o. *Warum **nur** haben wir **nur** trotzdem immer das Gefühl, als Schnorchler von Tauchern immer so von oben herab behandelt zu werden?* [39]
'Why on earth do we as snorkelers nevertheless always have the feeling to be treated by divers in a condescending manner?'

p. *Warum **nur** habt ihr **nur** Merkel gewählt?* [40]
'Why the hell did you vote for Merkel?'

q. *...warum **nur** habt ihr **nur** zugelassen, dass sich Ville bis zum Leberversagen betrinkt?* [41]
'Why the hell did you permit Ville to drink his liver away?'

r. *Warum **nur** haben Sie **nur** solange gewartet auf die Antwort der Menschlichkeit!* [42]
'Why on earth did you wait so long for an answer of humanity!'

s. *Aber warum **nur** hattest du **nur** diesen komischen Gesichtsausdruck?* [43]
'But why the hell did you have this funny expression?'

t. *Warum **nur** hatte sie **nur** diese Empfindungen?* [44]
'Why on earth does she have these sensations?'

u. *Warum **nur** können **nur** manche Leute den Tod nicht akzeptieren?* [45]
'Why on earth can certain people not accept death?'

v. *Warum **nur** musste ich **nur** laut lachen als ich las wer die Leitung übernimmt.* [46]
'Why the hell did I have to laugh loudly when a read who takes over the leadership.'

w. *Warum **nur** musstest Du **nur** zu Ihr gehen?!* [47]
'Why the hell do you have to go to her?!'

x. *Warum **nur** musstest du **nur** mein Leid ertragen?* [48]
'Why on earth did you have to suffer my pain?'

y. *Warum **nur** musste er **nur** so rennen?* [49]
'Why the hell did he have to run so fast?'

z. *Warum **nur** musste **nur** jedes rothaarige Mädchen Kimberly Ane heißen?* [50]
'Why on earth had every red-haired girl to be named Kimberly Ane?'

The particle *nur* can be used both as a DiP and as an FP. It is important to notice that in some of the examples the FP reading is excluded for principled reasons. This is, for instance, the case in (12o). Provided that the FP *nur* cannot associate with the non-contastable element *trotzdem* ("however"), the assertive version **Gerlinde und Rosa haben **nur** trotzdem immer das Gefühl, ...* ("G. and R. have only however always the feeling ..." is predicted to be impossible. Therefore, the lower *nur* in (12o) can only be a DiP. However, all of the examples are naturally interpreted with all occurrences of *nur* as DiPs. This suggests that we are really dealing with the doubling of the DiP and not with a mix of DiP and FP.

(13) Example with *schon*
Auch von Tissie Andere erfuhr er nichts, denn wer **schon** hätte **schon** Lust gehabt, seine Freunde zu verpfeifen. [51]
'Also from Tissie Andere he didn't learn anything because who would have liked to betray his friends [certainly nobody].'

(14) Examples with *wohl*
    a. Wer **wohl** ist **wohl** der Typ mit dem Doppelkinn, und der spärlichen Frisur. [54]
    'Who is the guy with the double chin and the scanty hair style, I'm wondering.'
    b. Und wer **wohl** hat **wohl** am meisten von diesem Produktionszuwachs profitiert? [55]
    'Guess who has profitted the most from this increase in production.'
    c. Warum **wohl** ist er **wohl** Mitglied bei „BT-go"? [56]
    'Why, you may ask, is he a member of "BT-go"?'
    d. Warum **wohl** sind sie **wohl** gelöscht worden? [57]
    'Why, I'm wondering, have they been deleted?'
    e. Warum **wohl** ist **wohl** in dem anderen Auto niemand gestorben? [58]
    'Why, I'm wondering, did nobody die in the other car?'
    f. Und warum **wohl** ist **wohl** die Kundeninfo von YEG (...) nicht mehr direkt auf der Homepage von Heino verlinkt? [59]
    'And why, tell me, is the customers' information not any longer linked to Heino's homepage?'
    g. Warum **wohl** sind **wohl** die Kandidaten bei GNTM, am Ende dann KEINE Topmodels...? [60]
    'Guess why the candidates at GNTM are no top models in the end.'
    h. Warum **wohl** waren **wohl** GULAGs notwendig? [61]
    'Why were GULAGs necessary after all?'
    i. Warum **wohl** habe ich **wohl** nach den Aufbau der bestehenden Steuerung gefragt...? [62]
    'Guess why I asked about the set-up of the existing control.'
    j. Warum **wohl** habe ich **wohl** 3 Shure M 91 mit DN 330 genommen? [63]
    'Guess why I took 3 Shure M 91 with DN 330.'

k. *Warum **wohl** haben wir **wohl** in der Quali erst gegen Tschechien gewonnen und dann verloren?* [64]
'Why, do you think, did we first win and then lose in the qualification against the Czech Republic?'
l. *Warum **wohl** hat **wohl** das deutsche Verkehrsministerium von all dem nichts gewusst?* [65]
'Why did the German Ministry of Transport not know about all of this?'
m. *Warum **wohl** hat **wohl** Horst Seehofer im Interview gesagt, dass „die, die tatsächlich entscheiden, nicht gewählt sind und die, die gewählt sind, nichts zu entscheiden haben"?* [66]
'Why, for heaven's sake, did Horst Seehofer say in the interview that those who decide are not elected and those who are elected have nothing to decide?'
n. *Warum **wohl** haben **wohl** auch die regierungskritiker den kopf geschüttelt.* [67]
'Why, do you think, even the government critics shook their head?'
o. *Warum **wohl** haben **wohl** gute Ladegeräte und auch der viel zitierte Stirling-Regler eine Anschlußmöglichkeit für einen Temp.-Fühler?* [68]
'Why after all do solid chargers and also the much-mentioned Stirling regulator have a connection option for a temp.sensor?'
p. *Warum **wohl** könnte ich **wohl** Firefox 1.0 x erwähnen wollen?* [69]
'Why for heaven's sake could I be inclined to mention Firefox 1.0 x?'
q. *Und warum **wohl** sollte ich **wohl** das deutsche youtube bemuehen?* [70]
'And why, do you think, should I rely on the German youtube?'
r. *Warum **wohl** sollten sie **wohl** Waffen in den Händen halten, wenn sie sie nicht benutzen?* [71]
'Why on earth should they hold weapons in their hands if they don't use them?'
s. *Warum **wohl** sollten sie **wohl** die Zahlen zurückhalten, wenn die gut wären?* [72]
'Why after all should they withhold the numbers if they were ok?'
t. *Warum **wohl** sollte **wohl** beispielsweise ein Ochs grade bis 2010 verlängern, der wohl zweifelsfrei den Anspruch haben dürfte, um etwas mehr als den Klassenerhalt zu spielen?* [73]
'Why, for example, should an Ochs prolong his contract exactly until 2010 given that he is undoubtedly ready to play for more than just class maintenance?'
u. *Warum **wohl** hat **wohl** niemand in Deiner Aussage das Erkennen und schon gar nicht das Verwenden von irgendwas erkannt?* [74]

'Why, for heaven's sake, did nobody recognize in your statement the perception, let alone the use of something?'
v. *Warum **wohl** sollten **wohl** die Eltern ihren Kindern das mit dem Sex beibringen, hm?* [75]
'Why should, do you think, parents teach their children about sex, huh?'

Within the theory that has been sketched so far, there is a straightforward explanation for the doubling of DiPs. Reconsider the derivation of the question *An wen denn könnte er sich gewandt haben?* in (7). The doubling construction is already there. After the SPrtP *an wen denn* had been merged in VP/vP, a silent Prt-head was merged with vP, and the SPrtP was attracted to its specifier. The only change we need to assume now is that instead of a silent particle an OVERT particle is merged. Since there is Spec-Head agreement, the overt particle and the Prt-head of the SPrtP have to match, i.e. the Prt-head and the head of the SPrtP must be identical. This is the case. For the rest, the derivation remains the same as the one we have seen in (7). The result of (7), namely (7e), is then as in (15).[13]

(15) [FinP [SPrtP *an wen denn*] [Fin' *könnte* [TP er sich ... [PrtP [SPrtP ~~an wen denn~~]
 [Prt' [Prt *denn*]✓
 [vP ~~er~~ [VP ~~sich~~ [SPrtP ~~an wen denn~~] *gewandt haben*]]]]]]]

The lower *denn* is the DiP which determines the scope and is thus the semantically relevant one. The *denn* in the SPrtP has an extra feature for emphasis by which the *wh*-phrase moves to its left. If so, there is no redundancy. The two lexical occurrences of the DiP are the reflex of spelling out the lower head position. It is a matter of PF.

This looks like an attractive solution, and I will, in fact, stay with it. Nevertheless, there is a slight complication. The question is: can we exclude the possibility that the preposed SPrtP reconstructs into another potential particle projection, one that is independent of the spelled-out DiP? Since we can be sure that the preposed SPrtP cannot be interpreted in the high position where we see it in the output, the question is whether there can be particle doubling also in the middle field. The answer depends on data, of course. We know that different DiPs can line up in German, see Thurmair (1989) and Coniglio (2011). But are there also data in which the same particle recurs? We know that the same particle can recur if one is a FP and the other one is a DiP.

---

13 Prosodically, the example shows two peaks, one which results from the emphatic accent on the *wh*P, the other, on the verb *gewandt*, obviously from the lower DiP which has a focusing function although it is not a FP. For an interesting approach to capture the relation between DiP and focus see Egg and Mursell (2017).

(16) *Wer hat schon   schon   überlegt   ob   er/sie in*
     who has SCHON SCHON considered whether he/she in
     Ketose ist [76]
     ketosis is
     'Who after all has already thought about whether he/she is in the fat burning mode? – Nobody!'

Here, the first *schon* is the DiP that gives rise to the interpretation as a rhetorical question; the implicature is that, in fact, nobody has deliberated whether p is the case. The second one is a scalar FP which corresponds to the temporal operator "already". The question is whether identical DiPs can recur which allow no ambiguity with respect to their FP/DiP status. To be sure, we need to look for recursion of *denn* and *wohl*, both of which cannot be FPs. There are indeed such examples.

(17) a. *Wer sind denn   denn   die „gegen Toleranz wetternden*
        who are DENN   DENN   the against tolerance raving
        Kreise"? [77]
        circles
        'Who are those circles raving against tolerance?'
     b. *Wer hat Euch   denn   das denn   bitte   empfohlen?* [78]
        who has you.PL DENN this DENN please suggested
        'Who has, pardon me, suggested this?'

(18) *Und warum hat der Bundestag wohl   den Stgb*
     and why   has the parliament WOHL the penal.code
     §129 wohl   so formuliert [79]
     §129 WOHL so formulated
     'And why has the German parliament formulated §129 if the penal code in such a way?'

These examples show that it is in principle possible that the very same DiP recurs. If we can exclude speech errors, there should be a difference. Nevertheless, it is difficult to tell the difference between the two positions. Intuitively, it looks as if the first occurrence is the more general one which reshapes or modifies the illocutionary force whereas the second is in the service of information structure and interacts with the focus inside the predicate. At this moment, this is pure speculation; thus, I leave the issue pending. For the question of doubling, the conclusion must be that reconstruction of the SPrtP into the specifier of a PrtP whose DiP is spelled out is not the only analysis.

The SPrtP we see in (14) could in principle have cycled through a SEPARATE projection where its DiP-head agrees with the empty particle of a particle phrase that is independent of the spelled out DiP.

There is a reason why a reduction of the examples we see in (11) through (14) to this explanation seems problematic. Notice that the in-situ doubling cases are usually like in (19)

(19) *Wer hat nur diesen linksrotgrünfaschistischen Idioten nur so viel*
    who has NUR these left.red.green.fascist idiots NUR so much
    Macht verliehen, dass die ihre geisteskranken Visionen in
    given given that they their mind.sick visions in
    die Tat umsetzen können? [80]
    the deed transform can
    'Who on earth gave these leftist red and green fascist idiots so much power that they can turn their sick visions into reality?'

There is a high DiP which follows the finite verb and a low DiP near *v*P which is preceded by given information. Taking the option of multiple in-situ occurrences of the same DiP as a basis, consider now again movement of the SPrtP out of *v*P. The SPrtP would agree and take scope in the lowest criterial position before it moves on to the *wh*-destination. Skipping the low position followed by agreeing and scoping in the high position cannot arise as it would violate Relativized Minimality, see Rizzi 1990.[14] Turning now to the collection of data in (11) through (14), we see, however, that the spelled-out DiP in situ is always in a rather high position. In roughly 50%, it follows the finite verb directly; in the other 50%, it is separated from the finite verb only by a

---

14 Yvonne Viesel (p.c.) notes this reasoning is not fully conclusive. The multiple DiPs could in principle differ from each other in their respective function, say, by virtue of their information structural role. If the SPrtP reflects these differences, it could be primed to skip the low position because this low position would be featurally incompatible with the features of the SPrtP. Unfortunately, I have no idea how to test this and will therefore leave it as an unresolved problem. In connection with (15), we suggested that the DiP of a SPrtP has an extra feature for emphasis by which the *wh*-phrase moves to its left. As Bayer and Trotzke (2015: §3.3) point out, the feature for emphasis is likely to be checked in the upper left periphery. SPrtPs in lower position appear to be awkward. This is reminiscent of findings about *the-hell* questions in English, see Pesetsky (1987) and den Dikken and Giannakidou (2002). If so, the SPrtP is not a featural unity, and its Prt and its Emp-feature will be checked in distinct functional positions. No conflict with Relativized Minimality can arise.

pronoun.[15] In the face of this, movement of the SPrtP through a low specifier position with a silent Prt-head is – at least quantitatively – not supported by the data.

The derivation that converges immediately is the one that has been proposed in (15). In (15), doubling arises by means of an SPrtP that passes through a single criterial position whose head is spelled out with the same DiP that heads the SPrtP. In the face of this, my conclusion is for the time being that DiP doubling as seen in (11) through (14) should not be reduced to agreement in Prt-projections with a SILENT head. It is rather agreement in Prt-projections with an OVERT head. If my conclusion is on the right track, the doubling data lend new support to my theory as it has been developed in my previous publications.

5 A note on focus particle doubling

It is widely known that focus particles (FP) can be doubled in the sense of double acts of quantification.

(20) **Only** John ate **only** vegetables

There are two distinct *only*s, and the reading is that for nobody else than for John it was true that he ate nothing else but vegetables. From (20) it follows that people other than John ate – perhaps in addition to vegetables – also fish or meat or pasta or bread. This is not surprising. We are all familiar with stacked negation as in *Nobody ate no vegetables at all*, which amounts to 'Everybody ate at least some vegetables'.

In rarer cases, one can, however, also find examples in which logical cancellation is unlikely. Consider the following internet finds:

(21) a. *they are solid options for the wireless speaker fan, even if they **only** support **only** the original AirPlay.* [81]

---

15 As long as the pronoun does not bear contrastive stress, this ordering is exceptionless. The fact that no examples were found with the in-situ DiP in a lower position is surprising. According to my intuitions, examples like (i) still sound quite natural.

(i) *Warum* **denn** *bist du gestern*
     why   DENN did you yesterday
     denn *nicht gekommen?*
     DENN   not come
     'Why the hell didn't you come yesterday?'

b. *the stakes have never been higher as he **only** has **only** 48 hours to find someone to take care of his young daughter* [82]
c. *He doesn't love me at all; he **only** thinks **only** of himself.* [83]

These examples come across like a blend of (1a) and (2a). The pre-*VP only* is in an irreversible scope position whereas the lower *only* is the one that needs to raise to the scope position or needs to be probed from the scope position. In the context of my account of DiP doubling, these data receive a straightforward explanation: There is a SPrtP in situ, headed by *only*, and there is a pre-verbal PrtP with a spelled-out head *only*. Unlike in (20), the two particles are two ocurrences of the same operator. The two phonetic occurrences are linked by an agreement relation. Semantically, there is only a single occurrence of *only*. (21c) means the same as "He only thinks of himself" with *(of) himself* being the focus associate. FP-doubling seems to rest on the same mechanism as negative concord. This can be seen in the standard Italian example *non ho visto nessuno*, in which *non* occupies the scope position and *nessuno* is according to my theory a "small negation phrase" (SnegP).

To return to the continental Germanic side, Barbiers (2010, 2014) observes doubling of FPs in colloquial Dutch, especially with the FP *maar* ('only'). Consider (22).

(22) **Maar** een student ken ik **maar**
MAAR one student know I MAAR
'I know only one student.'

The preferred reading of (22) seems to be that of all numbers of students I know, this number is exhausted by one. One could imagine also another reading by which there are two *maars* involved. Of all persons I know, this set of persons is exhausted by not more than a single student. There would be one *maar* base-generated in pre-*v*P scope position, and a second *maar* in the DP, the scope of which would be confined to the scale of natural numbers excluding those that go beyond 1. This meaning is hard to compute, and it is clearly not how the Dutch speaking majority would understand (22). According to my reasoning so far, the structure of (22), before V2 and movement to SpecCP, would be as in (23).

(23) ... ik [$_{PrtP}$ [$_{SPrtP}$ *maar een student*] [$_{Prt'}$ *maar* [$_{vP}$ ~~ik~~ {$_{SPrtP}$ ~~maar een student~~} *ken*]]]

Strangely, finding convincing examples of FP doubling turns out to be hard in German. The closest I could find in a cursory search was (24).

(24) Die Verlage   haben nie   etwas   beanstandet, **nur**
      the publishing.houses have never something criticized   only
      einer hat mich **nur** einmal ganz ganz höflich auf meine
      one has me   only once   very very politely to my
      Flüchtigkeitsfehler aufmerksam gemacht ... [84]
      careless.mistakes   attentive made   ...
      'The publishers never criticized anything. Only one of them, very politely, once drew my attention to my slips of the pen ...'

Here, one cannot exclude a reading with two distinct representations of *nur*. Nevertheless, it seems to be easy enough to understand (24) with only a single interpretation of *nur* as in ... **nur** *einer hat mich einmal ganz ganz höflich auf meine Flüchtigkeitsfehler aufmerksam gemacht* or ... *einer hat mich* **nur** *einmal ganz ganz höflich auf meine Flüchtigkeitsfehler aufmerksam gemacht*.

This brief digression into the realm of *only/maar/nur* FPs can clearly not do justice to the theoretical complexities of FP-constructions. It could show, however, that my account of doubling DiPs may stand a good chance of being extendable to the domain of FPs. Given there is a silent head in scope position and an overt head in a SPrtP, it is not unreasonable to expect that the silent head may occasionally be spelled out.

6 Conclusions

The syntax of focus particles as well as the syntax of discourse particles in German allows a much more unified account than has been possible so far if certain well motivated assumptions are adopted. These assumptions include i. that particles are functional heads, ii. that they not only merged into scope positions but may also be co-constituents of non-propositional phrases such as PP and DP. iii. Phrases of the latter kind – "Small Particle Phrases" – must cycle through designated positions in which they can discharge their scope potential via agreement. iv. The derivation calls for spec-head agreement configurations in combination with the copy-theory of movement. v. While in the standard cases, they agree with a silent matching head, we have presented new data which show that this head can also be spelled out. Both the data and the theoretical account give support to theories in which particles, focus as well as discourse particles, are functional heads along with standard functional heads that are assumed in the grammar of German and many other languages. If focus particles and discourse particles are adverbs and therefore purely lexical

XPs, as the majority of researchers assume to date, it is impossible to arrive at the generalizations that are now in reach.

Appendix

Sources of internet data and time of finding in parentheses

[1] https://propagandaschau.wordpress.com/2015/05/13/wdr-verbreitet-erneut-aus-dem-kanzleramt-finanzierte-pr/ (23.01.2016)
[2] http://forum.express.de/showthread.php?t=17396&page=57 (23.01.2016)
[3] http://de.comp.os.unix.apps.kde.narkive.com/Jd9YV1b5/deutsche-anleitung-zu-qt-designer-kdevelop (23.01.2016)
[4] http://www.spiegel.de/forum/wirtschaft/flughafen-berlin-brandenburg-brandschutzexperten-waren-keine-experten-thread-376461-16.html (23.01.2016)
[5] http://www.gea.de/region+reutlingen/reutlingen/banater+schwaben+feiern+kirchweih+in+betzingen.4339490.htm (23.01.2016)
[6] http://paolohor.blogspot.de/2015/10/ein-schulmeister-aus-deutschland-mobbt.html (23.01.2016)
[7] http://www.kirche-koeln.de/aktuell/2391 (23.01.2016)
[8] http://www.tageswoche.ch/de/2014_09/schweiz/647092/ (23.01.2016)
[9] http://www.sta-forum.de/theologie/christentum-und-konfessionen/siebenten-tags-adventisten/3654-freiheit-statt-gesetz/index2.html (23.01.2016)
[10] http://www.trennungsschmerzen.de/verlassen-mit-baby-wer-noch-t604.html (24.01.2016)
[11] http://www.spiegel.de/forum/wissenschaft/wissenschaft-den-medien-dafuer-sind-sie-zu-bloed-thread-129376-14.html (24.01.2016)
[12] http://www.arrcade.de/im-interview-horisont/ (24.01.2016)
[13] http://www.joyclub.de/forum/t302788-165.sex_wie_lange_ist_es_bei_euch_so.html (24.01.2016)
[14] https://books.google.de/books?id=d3o1AwAAQBAJ&pg=PT11&lpg=PT11&dq=%22was+denn+h%C3%A4tte+denn%22&source=bl&ots=sKiz4TiNEi&sig=MjFimbAEgitD_DPSMw0ldnWzRHg&hl=de&sa= X&ved=0ahUKEwiOy5Gdq8LKAhXJiywKHek2AJUQ6AEIHTAA#v=onepage&q=%22was%20denn%20h%C3% A4tte%20denn%22&f=false (24.01.2016)
[15] http://www.urbia.de/archiv/forum/th-4367193/unsere-nachbarn-rufen-bestimmt-bald-die-polizei-wenn-wir-haare-waschen.html (24.01.2016)
[16] http://rebellmarkt.blogger.de/stories/2210381/ (24.01.2016)
[17] http://forum-swiss.blogspot.de/2012_03_01_archive.html (24.01.2016)
[18] http://www.bsmparty.de/forum/thread/751 (24.01.2016)
[19] https://books.google.de/books?id=DvgygAAQBAJ&pg=PA76&lpg=PA76&dq=%22wann+denn+hast+du+denn%22&source=bl&ots=l83eBpC6ik&sig= QPewIact0o838uahgLLeg9L6kPU&hl=de&sa=X&ved= 0ahUKEwi1oNrni8PKAhVC1iwKHVYRD0kQ6AEIHjAA#v=onepage&q=%22wann%20denn %20hast% 20du%20denn%22&f=false (24.01.2016)

[20] http://www.poetry.de/showthread.php?t=44833 (24.01.2016)
[21] http://www.bunnx-exzurück.de/print-id-1725-page-1.html (24.01.2016)
[22] http://www.wallstreet-online.de/diskussion/1122456-19631-19640/blockbuster-bei-grant-life (24.01.2016)
[23] http://diskussionen.die-fans.de/nordostfussball/21821-der-vorstellungsthread/5.html (24.01.2016)
[24] https://ask.fm/SchenheitenAusDemLahnDillKreis (24.01.2016)
[25] http://www.film-rezensionen.de/2016/01/point-break-gewinnspiel/ (24.01.2016)
[26] http://forum.golem.de/kommentare/security/landesdatenschuetzer-bei-dashcam-nutzung-drohen-hohe-geldstrafen/was-nur-ist-nur-los-mit-denen/85300,3837972,3837972,read.html (24.01.2016)
[27] https://books.google.de/books?id=WZgsAQAAQBAJ&pg=PA365&lpg=PA365&dq=%22warum+nur+bin+ich+nur%22&source=bl&ots=tizxsedb4t&sig=Cm2sfeSz9iaZ6zi6ywc8zRFV5U&hl=de&sa= X&ved=0ahUKEwiJg9_D88TKAhUFkywKHcz7AE0Q6AEIHDAA#v=onepage&q=%22warum%20nur%20bin%20ich%20nur%22&f=false (25.01.2016)
[28] http://resisweissewelt.blogspot.de/2014/12/leise-rieselt-der-schnee.html (25.01.2016)
[29] http://www.almac.de/forum/archive/index.php/t-13250.html (25.01.2016)
[30] http://www.sciroccoforum.de/forum/archive/index.php/t-326704.html (25.01.2016)
[31] https://books.google.de/books?id=FJexCgAAQBAJ&pg=PT4&lpg=PT4&dq=%22warum+nur+ist+er+nur%22&source=bl&ots=k0zcNnki7w&sig=Rn3Cv3MQzyvi5_c1eXJGkBv_SwE&hl=de&sa=X&ved=0ahUKEwiK8ZnO9MTKAhUG1iwKHT2-Ax4Q6AEIHDAA#v=onepage&q=%22warum%20nur%20ist%20er%20nur%22&f=false (25.01.2016)
[32] https://de.answers.yahoo.com/question/index?qid=20090221025612AA4WRZa (25.01.2016)
[33] http://www.purkersdorf-online.at/komm/_da.php?ar=7&num=02046-00001-00001-00002-00001-00001-00000-00000-00000-00000 (25.01.2016)
[34] http://www.forum-ddr-grenze.de/t12633f70-Die-Geschichte-n-der-Wende-2.html (25.01.2016)
[35] https://books.google.de/books?id=gEe7SW5WcbEC&pg=PT89&lpg=PT89&dq=%22warum+nur+war+ich+nur%22&source=bl&ots=z25A_12W1u&sig=gpaJeZqQdwn6vLWFkQfGUs9xAw&hl=de&sa=X&ved=0ahUKEwjk1YPb9cTKAhXDkywKHWa5DG8Q6AEIHDAA#v=onepage&q=%22warum%20nur%20war%20ich%20nur% 22&f=false (25.01.2016)
[36] https://books.google.de/books?id=XFvCgAAQBAJ&pg=PT87&lpg=PT87&dq=%22warum+nur+war+er+nur%22&source=bl&ots=RIqxLp4IDD&sig=-1qSN3kzXHKsQ738mtopjFaP9X4&hl=de&sa=X&ved=0ahUKEwj-m-D_9cTKAhWDWiwKHS9-Dk4Q6AEIHDAA#v=onepage&q=%22warum%20nur%20war%20er%20nur %22&f=false (25.01.2016)
[37] https://www.wattpad.com/78507062-i-wish-larry-german-au-kapitel-19 (25.01.2016)
[38] http://blog.gwup.net/2014/12/12/globale-erwarmung-leugner-sind-keine-skeptiker/ (25.01.20
[39] http://www.taucher.net/edb/SUB_AQUA_DiveCenter_Utopia_Beach_b113_bericht11874.html (25.01.2016)
[40] https://m.facebook.com/CDU/posts/10153194594340415?comment_id=10153194605140415&offset=0&total_comments=51&comment_tracking={%22tn%22 3A%22R0%22}%20 (25.01.2016)

[41] http://www.myfanfiction.net/de/t/132389/him/last_love.haben_wir_nicht_schon_alles_gespuert.710713.html (25.01.2016)
[42] https://meta.tagesschau.de/id/102198/merkel-will-in-heidenau-mit-fluechtlingen-sprechen (25.01.2016)
[43] http://www.fanfiktion.de/s/4f53ed0a000215a20c903a98/1/Sie-hat-mir-dein-Herz-gestohlen (25.01.2016)
[44] http://www.fanfiktion.de/s/42f66a9700001837067007d0/1/Just-Love-Me- (25.01.2016)
[45] http://www.welt.de/vermischtes/article139978959/Eltern-lassen-an-Krebs-verstorbene-Zweijaehrige-einfrieren.html (25.01.2016)
[46] https://twitter.com/kc__dc/status/671766956152856576 (25.01.2016)
[47] http://www.trendmile.de/gedichte/Herz_Schmerz72.php (25.01.2016)
[48] http://forum.rotetraenen.de/index.php/Thread/24789-schauspieler/?pageNo=2 (25.01.2016)
[49] https://www.google.de/url?sa=t&rct=j&q=&esrc=s&source=web&cd=1&ved=0ahUKEwjw5srahMXKAhVIfywKHQiEB1AQFggfMAA&url=https%3A%2F%2Fwww.fanfiction.net%2Fs%2F2379536%2F2%2FSnapes-Girl&usg=AFQjCNF9e1VmNLIW0-iFowGNCOel-BoDeg (25.01.2016)
[50] https://www.wattpad.com/63478826-mps-slow-updates-14-kill-the-leader-gewalt/page/3 (25.01.2016)
[51] https://books.google.de/books?id=r4QhCwAAQBAJ&pg=PT1870&lpg=PT1870&dq=%22wer+schon+h%C3%A4tte+schon%22&source=bl&ots=WlLJ9Odk19&sig=qQwFZxfSvc4qpJc4kee052vyK8U&hl=de&sa=X&ved=0ahUKEwiX8vLkjMDKAhWEGCwKHcqxDnAQ6AEIHzAA#v=onepage&q=%22wer%20schon%20h%C3%A4tte%20schon%22&f=false (23.01.2016)
[52] http://www.wrestling-infos.de/board/showthread.php?t=25441 (23.01.2016)
[53] http://politik-forum.eu/viewtopic.php?p=2455063 (23.01.2016)
[54] http://www.nordbayerischer-kurier.de/nachrichten/merk-erbe-verlangt-entschuldigung-von-specht_99446 (23.01.2016)
[55] http://m.lifeline.de/expertenrat/frage/Forum-Wechseljahre/-Alle-?threadId=185124&pageNumber=3 (23.01.2016)
[56] http://www.welt.de/regionales/hamburg/article119623046/Schwerer-Unfall-auf-der-A-23-Totgeglaubte-lebt.html (23.01.2016)
[57] http://www.rc-network.de/forum/archive/index.php/t-308057.html (23.01.2016)
[58] https://de-de.facebook.com/DSDS/posts/10153151543198221 (23.01.2016)
[59] http://www.chefduzen.de/index.php?action=printpage;topic=12793.0 (23.01.2016)
[60] http://homematic-forum.de/forum/viewtopic.php?t=28480&p=254238 (24.01.2016)
[61] http://www.dual-board.de/index.php?thread/15178-auswirkung-der-zarge-auf-den-klang/ (24.01.2016)
[62] http://www.rp-online.de/sport/fussball/em/dfb/deutschland-am-boden-aid-1.476221 (24.01.2016)
[63] http://www.heise.de/forum/heise-online/News-Kommentare/Abgas-Skandal-VW-Umruestungsplan-verblueftt-Experten/Re-Wirklich-Betrug-bei-VW/posting-23962919/show/ (24.01.2016)
[64] http://www.essenspausen.com/die-pharma-mafia-lebensmittel-und-hormone/ (24.01.2016)
[65] http://derstandard.at/1348284457159/Rebellen-greifen-Armeestuetzpunkt-in-Aleppo-an (24.01.2016)

[66] https://www.boote-forum.de/showthread.php?t=12621 (24.01.2016)
[67] http://www.computerbase.de/forum/showthread.php?t=331054&page=2 (24.01.2016)
[68] http://www.spiegel.de/forum/politik/kritik-westerwelle-borniertester-aussenminister-seit-von-ribbentrop-thread-34151-44.html (24.01.2016)
[69] http://www.1000steine.de/de/gemeinschaft/forum/?entry=1&entrylink=1&id=186334&PHPSESSID=f6e17f27968b4568933119b9d416b169 (24.01.2016)
[70] http://www.wallstreet-online.de/diskussion/500-beitraege/112858-1-500/uvgi-neuer-thread (24.01.2016)
[71] http://community.eintracht.de/forum/diskussionen/12216?page=3 (24.01.2016)
[72] http://uhrforum.de/seiko-snke01k1-bezugsquelle-oder-fuer-seiko-allgemein-t189992 (24.01.2016)
[73] http://www.20min.ch/talkbacks/story/17700456 (24.01.2016)
[74] http://www.radarforum.de/forum/index.php/topic/49737-verkehrskontrolle-mit-rest-thc-im-blut/page-2 (13.12.2018)
[75] https://www.20min.ch/community/storydiscussion/messageoverview.tmpl?stryid=17700456&type=1&l=0&channel=de/schweiz (03.12.2018)
[76] https://wuerzedeinleben.wordpress.com/category/ketonix/ (16.06.2016)
[77] https://blog.campact.de/2014/01/danke-baden-wuerttemberg/ (16.06.2016)
[78] https://forum.hirntumorhilfe.de/neuroonkologie/erfahrung-mit-ttf-8386.html (16.06.2016)
[79] http://www.pi-news.net/2014/12/bargeldverbot-bedeutet-verlust-der-freiheit/ (16.06.2016)
[80] http://www.pi-news.net/2014/04/inklusion-2-henri-geistig-behindert-will-ans-gymnasium/ (16.06.2016)
[81] https://appleinsider.com/articles/18/07/02/review-marshall-multi-room-speakers-sound-great-but-lack-airplay-2 (20.11.2018)
[82] https://www.dailydot.com/upstream/netflix-original-movies-2018/ (20.11.2018)
[83] https://alliesinrecovery.net/2015/12/coping-with-negative-feelings-around-a-loved-ones-addiction/ (20.11.2018)
[84] https://literaturgefluester.wordpress.com/category/literaturbetrieb/ (05.12.2018)

References

Barbiers, Sjef. 2010. Focus particle doubling. In Jan-Wouter Zwart & Mark de Vries (eds.), *Structure Preserved: Studies in Syntax for Jan Koster*, 21-29. Amsterdam: John Benjamins.
Barbiers, Sjef. 2014. Syntactic doubling and deletion as a source of variation. In M. Carme Picallo (ed.), *Linguistic Variation in the Minimalist Framework*, 197-223. Oxford: Oxford University Press.
Bayer, Josef. 1996. *Directionality and Logical Form: On the Scope of Focusing Particles and Wh-In-Situ*. Dordrecht: Kluwer.
Bayer, Josef. 1999. Bound focus in German or how can association with focus be achieved without going semantically astray?. In Georges Rebuschi & Laurice Tuller (eds.), *The Grammar of Focus*, 55-82. Amsterdam: John Benjamins.
Bayer, Josef. 2010. Wh-drop and recoverability. In Jan-Wouter Zwart & Mark de Vries (eds.), *Structure preserved: Studies in Syntax for Jan Koster*, 31-39. Amsterdam: John Benjamins.

Bayer, Josef. 2012. From modal particle to interrogative marker: a study of German *denn*. In Laura Brugè, Anna Cardinaletti, Giuliana Giusti, Nicola Munaro & Cecilia Poletto (eds.), *Functional heads* (The Cartography of Syntactic Structures 7), 13-28. Oxford: Oxford University Press.

Bayer, Josef. 2018. Criterial freezing in the syntax of particles. In Jutta Hartmann, Marion Jäger, Andreas Kehl, Andreas Konietzko & Susanne Winkler (eds.), *Freezing: Theoretical Approaches and empirical domains*, 225-263. Berlin & New York: Mouton de Gruyter.

Bayer, Josef, Jana Häussler & Markus Bader. 2016. A new diagnostic for cyclic *wh*-movement. Discourse particles in German questions. *Linguistic Inquiry* 47(4). 591-629.

Bayer, Josef & Probal Dasgupta. 2016. Emphatic topicalization and the structure of the left periphery: Evidence from German and Bangla. *Syntax: A Journal of Theoretical, Experimental and Interdisciplinary Research* 19. 309-353.

Bayer, Josef, Probal Dasgupta & Sibansu Mukhopadhyay. 2014. Functional structure and the Bangla discourse particle *to*. *30th South Asian Languages Analysis Roundtable* (SALA 30), University of Hyderabad, 6-8 February 2014. [handout].

Bayer, Josef & Hans-Georg Obenauer. 2011. Discourse particles, clause structure, and question types. *The Linguistic Review* 28. 449-491.

Bayer, Josef & Andreas Trotzke. 2015. The derivation and interpretation of left peripheral discourse particles. In Josef Bayer, Roland Hinterhölzl & Andreas Trotzke (eds.), *Discourse-oriented Syntax*, 13-40. Amsterdam: John Benjamins.

Büring, Daniel & Katharina Hartmann. 2001. The syntax and semantics of focus-sensitive particles in German. *Natural Language & Linguistic Theory* 19. 229–281.

Cardinaletti, Anna. 2011. German and Italian modal particles and clause structure. *The Linguistic Review* 28. 493–531.

Chomsky, Noam. 1995. *The Minimalist Program*. Cambridge, MA: MIT Press.

Coniglio, Marco. 2008. Modal particles in Italian. *University of Venice Working Papers in Linguistics* 18. 91–129.

Coniglio, Marco. 2011. *Die Syntax der deutschen Modalpartikeln: Ihre Distribution und Lizensierung in Haupt- und Nebensätzen*. Berlin: Akademie-Verlag.

Dikken, Marcel den & Anastasia Giannakidou. 2002. From *hell* to polarity: "Aggressively non-D-linked" *wh*-phrases as polarity items. *Linguistic Inquiry* 33. 31-61.

Egg Markus & Johannes Mursell. 2017. The syntax and semantics of discourse particles. In Josef Bayer & Volker Struckmeier (eds.), *Discourse particles: Formal approaches to their syntax and semantics*, 15-48. Berlin & Boston: De Gruyter.

Endo, Yoshio. to appear. Exploring right/left peripheries: Expressive meanings in questions. In Josef Bayer & Yvonne Viesel (eds.), *Clause typing and the syntax-to-discourse relation in head-final languages* University of Konstanz. Arbeitspapiere des Fachbereichs Linguistik.

Frascarelli, Mara 2010. Narrow Focus, clefting and predicate inversion. *Lingua* 120. 2121-2147.

Grohmann, Kleanthes & Dalina Kallulli. 2006. A case study in syntax-semantics isomorphy: Some thoughts on existential bare plural subjects. *QDLF Università di Firenze*. 1-15.

Haegeman, Liliane. 1995. *The Syntax of Negation*. Cambridge: Cambridge University Press.

Hentschel, Elke. 1986. *Funktion und Geschichte deutscher Partikeln. Ja, doch, halt und eben*. Tübingen: Niemeyer.

Jacobs, Joachim. 1983. *Fokus und Skalen*. Tübingen: Niemeyer.

Klima, Edward. 1964. Negation in English. In Jerry A. Fodor & Jerrold J. Katz (eds.), *The structure of language: Readings in the philosophy of language*, 246-323. Englewood Cliffs, NJ: Prentice-Hall.

Li, Boya. 2006. *Chinese Final Particles and the Syntax of the Periphery*. Leiden: LOT dissertation 133.
Manzini, Rita M. 2015. Italian adverbs and discourse particles: between recategorization and ambiguity. In Josef Bayer, Roland Hinterhölzl & Andreas Trotzke (eds.), *Discourse-oriented Syntax*, 93-120. Amsterdam: John Benjamins.
Meibauer, Jörg. 1994. *Modaler Kontrast und konzeptuelle Verschiebung: Studien zur Syntax und Semantik deutscher Modalpartikeln*. Tübingen: Niemeyer.
Munaro, Nicola & Cecilia Poletto. 2003. Ways of clausal typing. *Rivista di Grammatica Generativa* 27. 87–105.
Paul, Waltraud & Victor Pan. 2017. What you see is what you get: Chinese sentence-final particles as head-final complementizers. In Josef Bayer & Volker Struckmeier (eds.), *Discourse particles: Formal approaches to their syntax and semantics*, 49-77. Berlin & Boston: De Gruyter.
Pesetsky, David. 1987. Wh-in-situ: Movement and unselective binding. In Eric J. Reuland & Alice G. Ter Meulen (eds.), *The representation of (in)definiteness*, 98-129. Cambridge, MA: MIT Press.
Poletto, Cecilia. 2000. *The higher functional field*. Oxford: Oxford University Press.
Poletto, Cecilia & Vanelli, Laura. 1995. Gli introduttori delle frasi interrogative nei dialettiitaliani settentrionali. In Emanuele Banfi, Giovanni Bonfadini, Patrizia Cordin & Maria Iliescu (eds.), *Italia settentrionale: Crocevia di idiomi romanza*, 145-158. Tübingen: Niemeyer.
Reis, Marga. 2005. On the syntax of so-called focus particles in German – A reply to Büring and Hartmann 2001. *Natural Language & Linguistic Theory* 23. 459–483.
Rizzi. Luigi. 1990. *Relativized Minimality*. Cambridge, MA: MIT Press.
Rizzi, Luigi. 1991/1996. Residual verb second and the Wh-Criterion. In Adriana Belleti & Luigi Rizzi (eds.), *Parameters and Functional Heads*, 63-90. New York: Oxford University Press.
Rochemont, Michael. 2018. *Only* syntax. In Jutta Hartmann, Marion Jäger, Andreas Kehl, Andreas Konietzko & Susanne Winkler (eds.), *Freezing: Theoretical Approaches and empirical domains*, 264-283. Berlin & New York: Mouton de Gruyter.
Rooth, Mats. 1985. *Association with Focus*. Amherst, MA: University of Massachusetts Ph.D. dissertation.
Rooth, Mats. 1992. A theory of focus interpretation. *Natural Language Semantics* 1. 75-116.
Smeets, Liz & Michael Wagner. 2017. The syntax of focus association in Dutch and German: Evidence from scope reconstruction. *West Coast Conference on Formal Linguistics (WCCFL)* 34. 470-480.
Taglicht, Joseph. 1984. *Message and emphasis: On focus and scope in English*. London: Longman.
Thurmair, Maria. 1989. *Modalpartikeln und ihre Kombinationen*. Tübingen: Niemeyer.
Trotzke, Andreas. 2017. *The Grammar of Emphasis. From Information Structure to the Expressive Dimension*. Berlin & New York. Mouton de Gruyter.
Trotzke, Andreas & Giuseppina Turco. 2015. The grammatical reflexes of emphasis: evidence from German *wh*-questions. *Lingua* 168. 37-56.

Adriana Belletti
(Reflexive) *Si* as a route to passive in Italian

1 Introduction

The present article explores the hypothesis that some Italian sentences involving the reflexive clitic *si* may represent a possible route to access the passive computation in the course of acquisition. This hypothesis builds on results from experimental studies on the acquisition of passive carried out in collaboration with Claudia Manetti, which indicate that young children in the age range 4;1 – 5;11 sometimes respond with a reflexive construction to questions that typically give rise to a (copular or *venire*) passive answer in Italian speaking adults. For instance, a sentence like (1)A can be produced as the answer to the patient oriented question (1)Q, asking what happens to the elephant in a picture in which the bear is washing it:

(1)   Q: Che cosa succede al mio amico l'elefante?
            what happens to my friend the elephant
       A: Si lava
            it washes itself   (Olmo, 4;1 y.o.)

Similarly, in a slightly different discourse condition involving two topic patients an answer like (2)A can be produced referred to a picture in which the cat is washing the dog and the rabbit is dressing/drying the bear:

(2)   Q: Che cosa succede ai miei amici il cane e l'orso?
            what happens to my friends the dog and the bear
       A: Il cane si lava e l'orso si sta asciugando
            the dog is washing itself the bear is drying itself   (Leonardo, 4;2 y.o.)

In both cases the answer refers to a transitive action not to a reflexive action. The external argument of the verbs (*wash* and *dry*) is thus suppressed in the

---

Note: The research presented here was funded in part by the European Research Council/ERC Advanced Grant 340297 SynCart – "Syntactic cartography and locality in adult grammars and language acquisition".

Adriana Belletti, University of Geneva – University of Siena

https://doi.org/10.1515/9781501505201-006

answers that are provided. Answers of this type were produced by the children of the younger 4 year-old group tested in up to 9% of the cases. I will refer to these structures here as reflexive passive.[1]

As discussed in previous work (Contemori and Belletti 2014, Belletti and Manetti 2016, Belletti 2017), in elicitation experiments[2] young children's first passive type productions in Italian are realized in the form of a causative passive involving reflexive *si* and the causative verb *fare* in a *fare-da* causative; (3) offers an example from the same experiment in which (1)A and (2)A have been found; (3) answers the patient-oriented question referred to a picture in which the cat is washing the dog; answers of this type were produced by the children of the 5 year-old group in up to 17% of the cases:

(3) Il cane si fa   lavare   dal gatto
    the dog – makes itself – wash   – by the cat   (Neri, 5 y.o.)

Sentences like (1)A and (2)A produced as the answer to patient-oriented questions (what happens to the DP?), are less and less present (only up to 5%) in older children's responses after age 5, in favor of the causative passive of the type in (3), which is in contrast seldom present (only up to 2%) in the productions of the younger group before age 5 (copular passive is completely absent and *venire* passive is also virtually absent in the two groups of children investigated, 4;1 – 4;11 and 5 – 5;11, an interesting fact *per se*, which cannot be addressed here). For detailed discussion and precise presentation of the relevant experimental results and some of their implications, the reader is referred to Belletti & Manetti (2018). In this article, I will concentrate on some basic aspects of a possible (morpho-)syntactic analysis, which makes explicit the common properties shared by the *si*-causative passives of the type in (3) and the reflexive

---

[1] The largely preferred answer provided by children of both 4 and 5 year-old groups in this experiment contained either a pronoun or a Clitic Left Dislocated/CLLD structure (up to 52%; see also Volpato et al. 2015 for similar results). This aspect of the results is discussed at length in Belletti and Manetti (2018); I will not address it here, as it would diverge the attention from the focus of the present discussion. Indeed children's performance significantly diverged from that of adults who preferred to answer the very same patient-oriented question with a (copular or *venire*) passive sentence. Children (especially in the 5 y.o. group) only marginally answered with a passive, and always with a *si*-causative passive (cfr. section 2.2). The 9% of children's answers with a reflexive as in (1) and (2) can naturally be seen as a first step toward the more typical passive answer.

[2] Similarly in the priming experiments discussed in Manetti and Belletti (2015), utilizing the priming technique adapted to Italian by Manetti (2012, 2013) from the design first created by Messanger et a. (2008).

passive sentences of the type in (1)A,(2)A, also involving *si*. The latter can thus be viewed as a first possibly explored route to access the passive computation, paving the way to the *si*-causative passive, in which all arguments of the lexical verb are expressed, including its external argument through a *by*-phrase. *Si*-causative passive can in turn be seen as a further step toward productive access to the passive computation (involving passive auxiliaries, e.g. in Italian the copula and *venire*).[3]

2 On the derivation of reflexive passive and of si-causative passive

A crucial assumption of the analysis defended here is that the clitic *si* present in both (1)A -(2)A and in (3) is indeed the same reflexive clitic, much in the spirit of the unified analysis of the diverse types of *si* of Italian first developed in Manzini (1986) (Cinque 1988 for a comprehensive analysis of different types of Italian *si*, consistent with this view). In a (originally) *kaynian* perspective, I assume *si* to be an external argument in both reflexive passive and *si*-causative passive structures. As such, it fills the specifier position of (a) little *v*.[4] Let us now consider the reflexive passive structure first.

2.1 Reflexive passive

The schema in (4) illustrates the essential ingredients of the analysis: *si* is the external argument of the lexical verb (*wash* or *dry* of the examples above), filling the specifier position of the functional little *v* head, the introducer of the external argument. The computation then runs as follow: *si* head-moves to the head which participates in the assignment of accusative Case in the clause functional structure, which I label Acc for clarity; *si* further moves to the head hosting clitics, which, simplifying the picture, I identify with T in (4). Since Acc has been taken by *si*, little *v* cannot participate in the assignment of accusative Case to the direct object DP, in the internal argument (IA) position. Thus, as a consequence of the morphosyntax of *si*, the DP/IA cannot be assigned Case as

---

[3] In Belletti (2017a) a hypothesis is put forward as to why the *si*-causative passive could have this possibly privileged status in terms of labeling. A presentation of this proposal here would take the present discussion too far afield and will not be pursued.
[4] D'Alessandro (2008) on related analysis of impersonal *si*.

a direct object. It then moves into the subject position. In this position nominative is available. The result is a well-formed structure. This derivation shares two crucial properties with passive: lack of Accusative for the direct object internal argument and its promotion as a subject, a preverbal subject in the derivation illustrated in (4). *Si* is consequently co-indexed with the DP subject, with which it enters agreement. This would yield the reflexive interpretation in the adult grammar. Presumably, in the young children's early productions of the type in (1)A and (2)A this interpretation is not necessarily triggered, as children appear to understand the pictures proposed to them, in which the depicted action is transitive and not reflexive.[5] Thus, *si* appears to be exploited as a way to eliminate the external argument of the verb and the availability of Accusative case for the object. In this way, presence of *si* is what allows promotion of the internal argument into subject position through a derivational mechanism shared with structures involving Burzio's (1986) so called "ergative" *si* (as in e.g. *La luce si è spenta/the light went off*), and more generally with structures involving so called "middle" *si* (as in e.g. *Questo vestito si lava facilmente/this suit washes easily,* Cinque 1988: 87a; Ruwet 1972 for French):

(4)

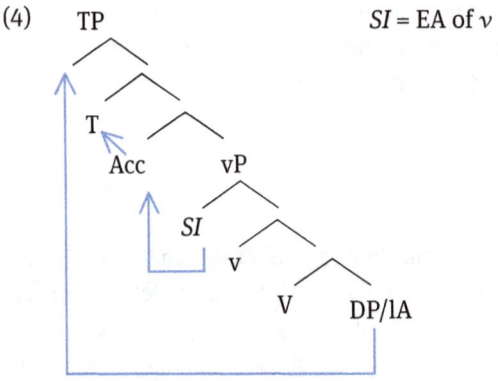

SI = EA of v

As illustrated in (4), I assume that movement of the DP/IA takes place directly from the vP-internal position. In current analyses of copular-type passive inspired by Collins (2005) *smuggling* approach, movement of the internal argument into subject position does not take place directly form the vP-internal position, but is preceded by movement of a chunk of the vP containing (at least) the verb/past participle and the internal argument. The chunk is attracted

---

5 Following a reviewer's suggestion, the co-indexation may just not operative in the children's grammar, favored by lack of agreement features on *si*.

by some component of the passive voice. This derivation allows extraction of the DP/IA from the position where the verbal chunk has moved and no locality violation is produced; a violation of Relativized Minimality (Rizzi 1990, 2004) would otherwise occur, as it is always the case when extraction of an internal argument crosses the hierarchically higher intervening external argument. In (4) I assume, instead, that no intervention problem is created by presence of *si* in the movement of the internal argument crossing it. The reason for this is that *si* does not count as an intervener for movement of DP/IA as it has a reduced internal structure, lacking e.g. a D layer, along the lines recently proposed in Holmberg and Roberts (2013). The reduced structure makes it dissimilar in the sense relevant in the computation of intervention for the moved full DP/IA; since the attracted element in the A-chain is a DP, only an intervening DP would determine a locality violation. Hence no *smuggling* is needed in this case, in contrast with, e.g., copular passive. Let us now turn to *si*-causative passive.[6]

2.2 *Si*-causative passive

Si-causative passive can be analyzed along the lines in (5). As in (4) illustrating the reflexive passive, also in (5) *si* is an external argument. In this case, however, it is the initiator (Ramchand 2008; Folli & Harley 2007 for related ideas) external argument of the semi-functional verb *fare*, which I assume to be selected by a causative voice (Belletti 2017a for detailed discussion). The morphosyntactic computation of *si* is exactly the same in (5) as the one in (4). In the derivation in (5) I illustrate the hypothesis that the causative voice attracts into its specifier a chunk of the verb phrase containing the verb and its internal argument (Belletti & Rizzi 2012; Belletti 2017a). This is an instance of the *smuggling* operation overtly moving a chunk of the verb phrase, as extensively discussed in the references quoted. As *si* blocks assignment of accusative Case, the DP/IA moves and is promoted as the subject of the clause; as such, it agrees with the (third person) reflexive *si*.

---

6 The status of the *si*-causative passive with respect to *smuggling* is addressed in detail in sections 2.2.1 and 3. The fact that *smuggling* is not at work in the reflexive passive in (4) may contribute to explain why this form of passive could count as a simpler route to target-like passives in development, as young children do not easily access *smuggling* (Snyder and Hyams 2015). This point is taken up again in sections 2.2.1 and 3 mentioned above.

(5) Il bambino si fa   pettinare dalla mamma
     the kid   – makes himself – comb – by the mum

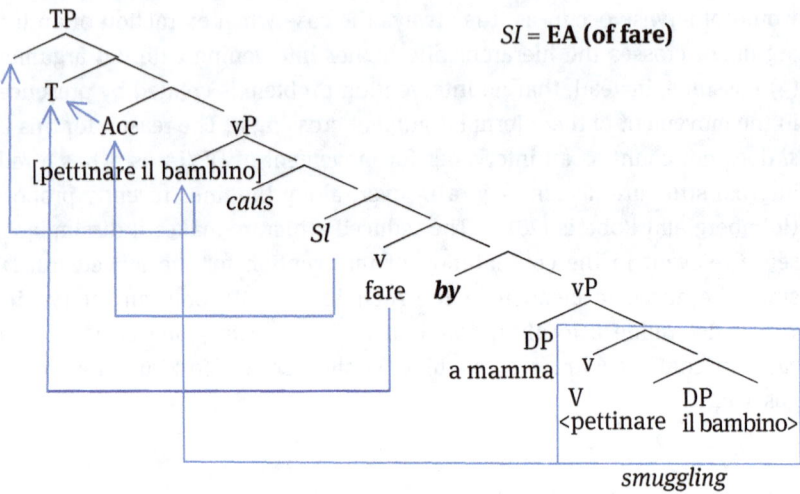

In sum the derivation proceeds as follows:
1. V+DP/IA chunk is *smuggled* into Spec-caus voice
2. *Si* moves to Acc (the functional head participating in the assignment of structural accusative), thus blocking availability of accusative for DP/IA; *Si* moves to T, as any clitic
3. DP/IA moves into subject position

The properties in 2 and 3 are shared with other types of passives: lack of accusative, movement of the internal argument into subject position. Step 2. is shared with reflexive passive above.

2.2.1 On the status of the by-phrase in *si*-causative passive and movement of the verbal chunk

In (5) *by* is analyzed as an expletive preposition, much as it is in copular passive. Indeed, as in copular passive *by* does not contribute to the thematic interpretation of its DP complement and the *by*-phrase has exactly the same interpretation as the external argument/subject in the corresponding active sentence containing the same verb, a fundamental property of the active-passive alternation. In this respect, the same preposition *by* has a different status in *si*-causative passive than in active *fare da* causatives (Hanno fatto pettinare il bambino dalla mamma/ they-made-comb-the-child-by-the mother), where it contributes to a clear agentive interpretation of its DP complement. As a way to account for this property, in Belletti (2017a) I have proposed that in (active) *fare da* causatives the preposition incorporates (head to head) the *caus* head, whence its agentive interpretation clearly illustrated by the incompatibility of *fare da* causatives with psych-verbs involving an experiencer non-agentive external argument (6b below). In (5) it is assumed that this process does not take place in *si*-causative passive: *by* stays low in the *si*-causative passive and does not incorporate the *caus* voice; it thus preserves its expletive status, whence its compatibility with a non-agentive external argument (6a below), in contrast with the active *fare da* causative construction. The contrast in (6) illustrates the ungrammaticality of the active *fare da* causative with a psych predicate whose external argument is an experiencer and the possibility of the same verb in the *si*-causative passive, with the experiencer complement of preposition *da/by*:

(6) a   Maria si fa   capire   da tutti
        Maria – makes herself – understand – by everybody
    b   * Questa spiegazione ha fatto   capire   il problema
        this explantion   – has made   – understand – the problem
        da tutti
        – by everybody

Thus, the *si*-causative passive appears to be only partly related to the active *fare da* causative: the status of the *by*-phrase is very different in the two cases. This may suggest that early access by children to the *si*-causative passive may not be directly linked to a possible early access to the *fare da* active causative (e.g. accessed earlier than *fare a*, Guasti's 2016 conjecture, discussed and confirmed for French in Borga and Snyder 2016).

Borga and Snyder (2016) have recently suggested that active *fare da* does not (necessarily) involve *smuggling* in its derivation, moving the relevant chunk of the verb phrase. Rather, the lexical vP may be reduced in *fare da* and only involve the verb and the DP/IA with the external argument introduced as an adjunct PP; this analysis is inspired by the original proposal in Guasti (1993). A related proposal has been put forth in Folli and Harley (2007), in which the reduced constituent is analyzed as a nominal constituent; this gives further plausibility to the introduction of the external argument as a PP adjunct by directly assimilating the process to the one operative in derived nominals (Sheehan and Cyrino 2016 for a recent cross-Romance overview). Details aside, according to this hypothesis the relevant portion of the structure of *fare da* causatives would be as in (7) (same sentence as in 5):

(7)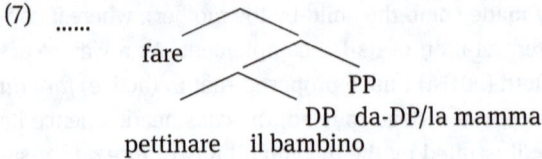

If the *fare da* portion in (7) is embedded below the *caus* voice as in the *si*-causative passive in (5), this would open up the possibility of a derivation in which the DP/IA could move directly from the object position into the subject position of the clause; recourse to *smuggling* would not be necessary, with movement of the chunk of the verb phrase illustrated in (5). This is precisely the hypothesis suggested in Borga & Snyder (2016), based on similar data from French. The relevant structure and the direct movement of the DP/IA are schematically illustrated in (8) (all other processes remain the same as in (5) and are not illustrated in (8) for clarity):

(8)   *SI* = **EA (of *fare*)** Il bambino si fa pettinare dalla mamma
                                                               the kid makes himself comb by the mum

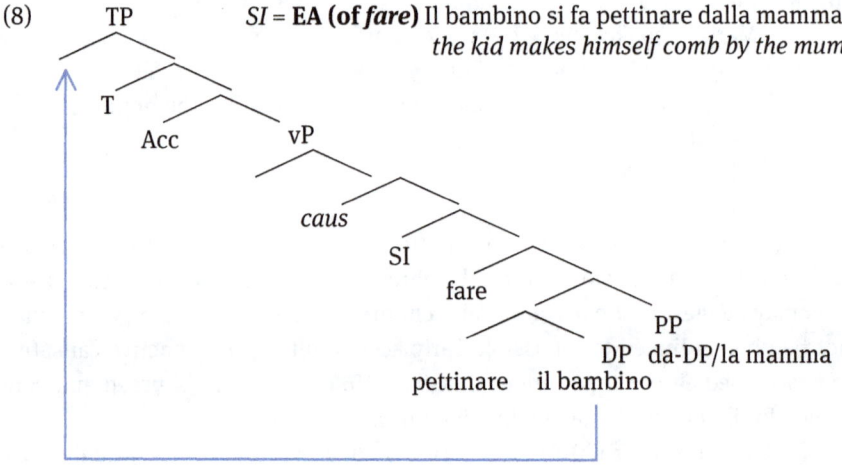

Given the different status of the *by*-phrase in active *fare da* and in *si*-causative passive clearly illustrated in (6), I leave it as an open question whether the better representation of the derivation of *si*-causative passive should be along the lines in (5) or along the lines in (8). If (5) is assumed, the conclusion must be drawn that young children between age 4 and 5 can access the process of *smuggling* moving a chunk of the verb phrase, at least to some extent (Snyder and Hyams 2015 for a partly different view); if (8) is assumed, as no *smuggling* is involved this would be compatible with the stricter hypothesis that the young children tested either still do not smuggle the verbal chunk or have an extended freezing effect, so that the DP/IA could not be extracted from the smuggled position (Snyder and Hyams 2015); yet they could access the *si*-causative passive because it does not require *smuggling* altogether. In the latter view, an explanation should be found as to why the status of the *by*-phrase is different in *si*-causative passive and in *fare da* causative, given that the latter structure is assumed to be part of the former in (8).

3 From reflexive passive to *si*-causative passive

Given the analysis developed in section 2, the crucial difference between reflexive passive and *si*-causative passive is that only in the latter can the external argument of the lexical verb be present, whereas in the former it is taken up by *si*. Another possible difference is lack of *smuggling* in reflexive passive and its possible presence in the computation of *si*-causative passive, depending on the considerations at the end of the previous section. Let us discuss the two properties in turn: from the resulting picture the way how (/the reason why) the reflexive passive could plausibly constitute a first route to passive should emerge.

Both the Case properties and the promotion of the internal argument to the subject position are properties which the reflexive passive shares with different types of passives in Italian, and cross-linguistically, as noted. Interestingly, the fact that the passive morphology may correspond to/contain the reflexive morphology is also a well-attested fact cross-linguistically. Hence, it is tempting to speculate that in the course of acquisition, Italian-speaking young children exploit a grammatical possibility, by entertaining the hypothesis that also Italian allows for a reflexive passive; as pointed out above, the hypothesis is also supported by other passive-like uses of *si* in Italian, such as in particular middle *si* and the *si* marker of several unaccusatives. Belletti & Manetti's (2018) results describe a developmental path from age 4;1 to age 5;11 according to which the reflexive passive option is abandoned by the children of the older group in favor of the *si*-causative passive. This path finds a natural explanation in the need to introduce a further argument different from *si* expressing the external argument of the lexical verb (this was required in the elicitation condition of the experiment, as described in the introduction). Recall that in the *si*-causative passive an independent external argument of the lexical verb is present, which is expressed through the *by*-phrase in the way illustrated in (5). In the reflexive passive, in contrast, since the external argument of the lexical verb is *si*, no other external argument is possible hence no *by*-phrase is possible in turn. Thus, the possibility to introduce an external argument of the verb is available in the *si*-causative passive through the expression of a *by*-phrase, but it is not available in the reflexive passive, which typically does not allow for the expression of a *by*-phrase.[7]

But why should the reflexive passive come first? If the proposed characterization of the developmental path is on the right track, one should ask: why should children entertain the hypothesis that Italian allows for a reflexive passive to start with? As pointed out in Belletti (2017, fn. 10) presence of the reflexive may in principle play some role in favoring this route, as reflexive anaphors are known to be mastered rather early by young children (Hamann 2011 for a general overview; Snyder and Hyams 2015 on French/Italian acquisition of reflexive clitics *se/si*). We can further speculate that, given the structure in (4) with *si* the external argument of the lexical verb, the proposed derivation could represent a less demanding path to directly promote the DP/IA into subject position, one crucial feature of the passive computation; specifically, blocking accusative Case through clitic *si* could constitute a more direct hence simpler way to access this aspect of the passive morphosyntax, the first necessary step to promote DP/IA as a subject.

In the analysis developed in (4) a further crucial property of the reflexive passive is that it allows for movement of DP/IA directly from IA object position without recourse to *smuggling*; no movement of a chunk of the verb phrase is needed as impoverished *si* does not count as an intervener, as suggested above. This aspect of the computation of reflexive passive could give a further reason as to why this type of passive should have a privileged status for young children. Following Snyder and Hyams (2015), *smuggling* is a costly operation for young children, who may be just unable to smoothly access it in early stages of acquisition (before age 5). Then, if a passive-type derivation can be put into work without any need of *smuggling*, it is not surprising that young children entertain this option first.

How about *si*-causative passive, the preferred option of older children (5–5;11)? It seems natural to propose that it may constitute a natural way to introduce the external argument of the lexical verb, while still implementing passive

---

[7] The possibility to express a *by*-phrase in a reflexive passive may be limited cross-linguistically to cases in which the reflexive is a grammaticalized marker of the passive voice. As noted in Cinque (1988, fn. 11) reporting observations by Lepschy (1986) for Italian and Ruwet (1972) for French, in special rhetorical registers the *by*-phrase is allowed to appear in some *si(/se)* sentences. As Cinque observes the examples mentioned in the quoted references were all cases of middle *si*, which could precisely count as a grammaticalized marker of the passive voice as suggested above or as "non-argument" *si* in the terms of Cinque's typology of different types of Italian *si*. Interestingly, in Belletti and Manetti's (2018) data only one child expressed the *by*-phrase in one reflexive passive sentence only once.

through *si*, which is the external argument of *fare* in this case according to the analysis in (5).

In section 2.2.1 we have left open the question whether the *smuggling* operation is necessarily implemented in *si*-causative passive. If it is not, as suggested in Borga and Snyder (2016) according to which this passive contains a *fare da/faire par* causative (as in structure 8, for Italian), then in this respect the *si*-causative passive should be as accessible to young children like a reflexive passive is, the only difference between the two being the possible systematic presence of the external argument of the lexical verb in *si*-causative passive. We have pointed out in 2.2.1 a crucial clear difference in the nature of the *by*-phrase in the *si*-causative passive compared to active *fare da*: only in the latter is *by*-phrase strongly agentive, thus suggesting a different status of the *by*-phrase in the two constructions. However, from the available data and results we are not in a position to determine whether children at the relevant ages do make the relevant distinction between the *by*-phrases in the *si*-causative passive and in the *fare-da* causative. Since all the experimental sentences involved an agentive external argument of the verb phrase, they are compatible with both a reduced structure along the lines in (8), hence a derivation not implying *smuggling* of the chunk of the verb phrase, and a complete structure along the lines in (5) implying the *smuggling* operation along the lines described. It is impossible to tease apart what derivational option children would take on the basis of the available evidence so far.

It seems that the following scenario could fit the known results: the tested children are precisely in the age in which they start trying out *smuggling* more and more productively (as types of passive appear to be better mastered); at the younger age 4 they still have this possibility only marginally (Snyder and Hyams 2015 for similar considerations). Sometimes they fail, and resort to the reflexive passive, which unambiguously does not involve the *smuggling* operation. Later, at age 5, they abandon this construction, as they need to describe a transitive action not a reflexive one. They resort then to *si*-causative passive, which, in the experimental conditions (in which all external arguments are agentive) allows for both a derivation with no *smuggling* (as in 8) and one with movement of the verbal chunk (as in 5).[8]

---

[8] Clearly, if *smuggling* is necessarily at work in *si*-causative passive also in children's grammar, then one can think that this extra step is what makes the *caus* passive a bit more complex and then come after the reflexive passive. Note however, that some causative passives are present also in the productions of the children of the younger 4 year-old group, but to a very limited extent, as noted (2%).

We can further speculate that *smuggling* through causative *fare* could be readily accessible to children – hence somewhat privileged by them – also due to the overtness of the moved

4 Conclusion

In this paper we have explored the idea that Italian-speaking children adopt a reflexive passive route involving the reflexive clitic *si* as a step toward access to (other forms of) passive. We have speculated that this route may count as simpler for the younger children of the reported study (aged 4;1–4;11) both because it involves the reflexive clitic and because it does not involve the *smuggling* operation moving a chunk of the verb phrase. The reflexive passive is then abandoned in favor of a systematic access to the *si*-causative passive in the reported results from older children (5–5;11). The somewhat privileged status of *si*-causative passive in children confirms previous findings and can be interpreted as being due to the fact that this type of passive combines the reflexive passive computation with the causative computation, which allows for the introduction of an independent external argument of the lexical verb. Since the age between 4 and 5 is the one in which children get to properly master *smuggling* moving a chunk of the verb phrase, access to *si*-causative passive may be favored (at least in part, footnote 8) by the possibility of analyzing it either through a *smuggling* derivation or not; this possibility arises in the experimental conditions described since all relevant external arguments were agentive in the stimuli utilized, hence they were possibly realized either in a *by*-phrase of the active *fare da* causative type or in a *by*-phrase of the *si*-causative passive type. Digging more on this issue is one question left to future research.

References

Belletti, Adriana. 2017. "On the acquisition of complex derivations with related considerations on poverty of the stimulus and frequency". In *Syntactic Complexity from a Language Acquisition Perspective*, ed. by Elisa Di Domenico. Newcastle-Upon-Tyne: Cambridge Scholars Publishing, 28–44.

Belletti, Adriana. 2017a. "Labeling (Romance) causatives". In *Elements of Comparative Syntax: Theory and description*, ed. by Enoch Aboh et al. Berlin: De Gruyter, 13–46.

---

chunk in Italian/French type causatives. Cfr. the structure in 5 and the underscored phrase of the active *fare-da* causative in i.:

i. Ho fatto <u>pettinare il bambino</u> dalla mamma
    (I) made <u>comb the child</u> by the mother
    I made the mother comb the child

Manetti and Belletti (2015) for a proposal along these lines.

Belletti Adriana, and Luigi Rizzi. 2012. "Moving Verbal Chunks in the Low Functional Field." In *Functional Heads. The Cartography of Syntactic Structures*, vol.7, ed. by Laura Brugè, Anna Cardinaletti, Giuliana Giusti, Nicola Munaro, Cecila Poletto. Oxford: Oxford University Press, 129–137.

Belletti, Adriana and Claudia Manetti. 2018. "Topics and Passive in Italian speaking children and adults", *Language Acquisition*, DOI: 10.1080/10489223.2018.1508465

Borga, Jason, and William Snyder. 2016. "Acquisition of Causatives and Experiencer verbs in French", paper presented at Romance Turn 8, Barcelona September 2016.

Burzio, Luigi. 1986. *Italian Syntax. A Government-Binding Approach*. Dordrecht: Reidel.

Cinque, Guglielmo. 1988 "On *si* constructions and the theory of Arb". *Linguistic Inquiry* 19: 521–581.

Collins, Chris. 2005. "A smuggling approach to the passive in English". *Syntax* 8: 81–120.

Contemori, Carla, and Adriana Belletti. 2014. "Relatives and passive object relatives in Italian-speaking children and adults: Intervention in production and comprehension". *Applied Psycholinguistics* 35(6): 1021–1053.

D'Alessandro, Roberta. 2008. *Impersonal si constructions*. Berlin: Mouton De Gruyter.

Folli, Raffaella, and Heidi Harley. 2007. "Causation, obligation, and argument structure: On the nature of little *v*". *Linguistic Inquiry* 38: 197–238.

Guasti, Maria Teresa. 1993. *Causative and perception verbs. A comparative study*. Torino: Rosenberg & Sellier.

Guasti, Maria Teresa. 2016. "Voice alternations (active, passive, middle)". In *The Oxford Handbook of Developmental Linguistics*, ed. by Jeffrey Lidz, William Snyder, and Joe Pater, Oxford: Oxford University Press.

Hamann, Cornelia 2011. Binding and coreference. Views from child language". in: , *Handobook of Generative Approaches to Language Acquisition*, edited by Jill De Villier and Thomas Roeper, 247-290. Berlin: Springer.

Holmberg, Anders, and Ian Roberts. 2013. "The syntax-morphology relation". *Lingua* 130: 111–131.

Lepschy, Giulio C. 1986. "Aspects of Italian constructions with *si*". *The Italianist* 6: 139–151.

Manetti, Claudia. 2012. *The acquisition of passives in Italian. Evidence from comprehension, production and syntactic priming studies*. Ph. D. dissertation, University of Siena.

Manetti, Claudia. 2013. "On the production of passives in Italian: evidence from an elicited production task and a syntactic priming study with preschool children". *Online Proceedings of the 37th Annual Boston University Conference on Language Development. Online Proceedings Supplement*.

Manetti, Claudia, and Adriana Belletti. 2015 "Causatives and the acquisition of the Italian passive". In *Language Acquisition and Development*, ed. by C.Hamann & E. Ruigendijk eds. (Selected proceedings of Gala-2013 – University of Oldenburg). CSP, 282–298.

Manzini, M. Rita. 1986. "On Italian 'si'. In *The syntax of pronominal clitics. Syntax and Semantics* vol. 18, ed. by Hagit Borer, New York: Academic Press, 241–262

Messenger, K., Branigan, H.P., McLean, J.F. & Sorace, A. 2008. "English-Speaking Children's Early Passives: Evidence from Syntactic Priming". In *Proceedings of the 32nd Aannual Boston University Conference on Language Development*, ed. by H. Chan, H. Jacob & E. Kapia, 275–286. Sommerville, MA: Cascadilla Press.

Ramchand, Gillian. 2008. *Verb Meaning and the Lexicon: A first Phase Syntax*. Cambridge: Cambridge University Press.

Rizzi, Luigi. 1990 *Relativized Minimality*. Cambridge, Mass.: The MIT Press.
Rizzi, Luigi. 2004. "Locality and Left Periphery". In *Structures and Beyond. The Cartography of Syntactic Structures*, vol.3, ed. by Adriana Belletti. New York: Oxford University Press.
Ruwet, Nicholas. 1972. "Les constructions pronominales neutres at moyennes". In *Théorie syntaxique et syntaxe du français*, Paris: Editions du Seuil.
Sheehan, Michelle and Sonia Cyrino. 2016. "Variation and change in the Romance *faire-par* causative", to appear in LSRL Proceedings.
Snyder, William, and Nina Hyams. 2015. "Minimality effects in children's passives". In *Structures, Strategies and Beyond*, ed by Elisa Di Domenico, Cornelia Hamann, and Simona Matteini. Amsterdam: John Benjamins, 343–368
Volpato, Francesca, Verin, Laura and Anna Cardinaletti. 2015. The comprehension and production of verbal passives by Italian preschool-age children, *Applied Psycholinguistics*, http://dx.doi.org/10.1017/S0142716415000302

Andrea Calabrese
Irregular verbal morphology and locality

The irregular Latin perfect forms, their Proto-Indo-European ancestors and their Romance outcomes

1 Introduction

In several recent papers, summarized and reanalyzed in Calabrese (2016a), I argued that in Italian irregular verbal morphology conditioned by root information is governed by locality and can occur only in athematic verbal forms, i.e., when the root and the target morpheme are adjacent.

In this paper, I will try to show that the same locality principle governs the development of perfective forms from Proto-Indo-European (PIE) to modern Italo-Romance through Latin. The assumption is that by investigating how morphological systems change, we can achieve a better understanding of the principles that govern their structure: "Like an animal standing against the background of a forest, the outlines of a grammar can be thrown into sudden relief when something changes. (Anderson 1988: 324)." The present paper thus provides further diachronic support to the growing body of synchronic and typological evidence showing that morphemic interactions in morpho-syntactic structures are governed by Locality Principles (cf. Bobaljik 2012, Embick 2010, Moskal 2015, a.o.).

The article is organized as follows. In section 2, I will deal with the general issue of the conditions under which irregular morphology, in particular root-conditioned contextual allomorphy, is possible, and argue that the root diacritics necessary for the application of the rules accounting for the irregularity can be accessed only in local configurations involving adjacency. Thus, root-conditioned allomorphy in Italian perfect and past participle forms occurs only when the root and the relevant aspect/tense node are adjacent, i.e., when these forms are athematic. In section 3 we will see that irregular Latin perfect forms are governed by the same locality principle. Root conditioned irregular allomorphy of the aspectual node occurs only when the root and the aspect node are adjacent. The same structural condition also governs aspect allomorphy in PIE (sect. 4) and is active in the development of irregular Latin perfect forms from PIE (sect. 5) and in the development of irregular Italo-Romance forms from Latin (sect. 6). A brief conclusion will close the article.

Andrea Calabrese, University of Connecticut

https://doi.org/10.1515/9781501505201-007

2 Irregular morphology

When we talk of irregular morphology, we are dealing with morpheme-specific morphology, i.e., with situations in which morphological operations are dependent on morpheme specific information. In (1) I contrast a case of irregular morphology with a case of regular morphology. On the one hand, we have the Italian Imperfect marker, which is regular in being always the same across verbs. On the other hand, we have the irregular Italian perfect marker /s/ which appears only with certain verbal roots. In the case of this marker, we need a special vocabulary item that includes reference to root information in the structural description. No such contextual restrictions are needed for regular morphology.

(1)   Regular morphology   Irregular morphology
        Italian Imperfect marker   Italian perfect marker /s/
        amavo/battevo/partivo   *persi*
        /-v-/ <--> [+imperfect]   /-s-/ <--> [+perfect]/ root^s ___ (root^s =perd, etc.)

As for the cases of irregular morphology, one of the most typical ones involves morphological operations dependent on root specific information, as the one mentioned above. Morpheme exponence dependent on root specific information can be referred to as root conditioned contextual allomorphy. Root-conditioned contextual allomorphy is accounted for by: vocabulary items (VI) and morphophonological (MP) rules[1] including root-information in their structural description. In this article, I will be dealing with root-conditioned contextual allomorphy.

In my work on irregular Italian perfect and past participle forms, I have observed a striking correlation between presence vs. absence of regular morphology and presence vs. absence of thematic vowels, respectively.

(2)   Irregular: vs.   Regular:
        [[[[perd]$_{root}$__]$_V$ -s-]$_T$ i]$_{AGR}$ [[[part]$_{root}$ -**i**$_{TV}$-]$_V$ -∅-]$_T$-sti]$_{AGR}$
        pérsi 'lose-Perf-1sg'   *partisti* 'leave-Perf-1sg'
        [[[[perd]$_{root}$__]$_V$ -s-]$_T$ o]$_{AGR}$ [[[part]$_{root}$ -**i**$_{TV}$-]$_V$ -t-]$_T$-o]$_{AGR}$
        perso 'lose-PstPart-MscSg'   *partito* 'leave-PstPart-MscSg'
        Athematic   **Thematic**

---

[1] As in Calabrese (2016b) I will refer to morpho-syntactically conditioned phonological rules with the term MP rules, instead of readjustments rules, the term usually used in Distributed Morphology.

It appears that root-conditioned contextual allomorphy is observed only in athematic morphology. I have accounted for this basic fact by assuming, following Embick (2010, 2013), that the transmission of information necessary for morphological operation application, and more generally any morpheme-to-morpheme interaction, can occur only in a local configuration at the morphological level, where locality involves adjacency, as stated in the principle below:

(3) a. Node α morphologically interact with node β iff α, β are local.
b. α, β are local if no node intervenes (Adjacency).

Now, whereas in the case of thematic perfect/ past participle we have the structure in (4), in the case of the athematic perfect/past participle we have the structure in (5), where I assume that the thematic vowel (TV) has not been inserted (see below for discussion).

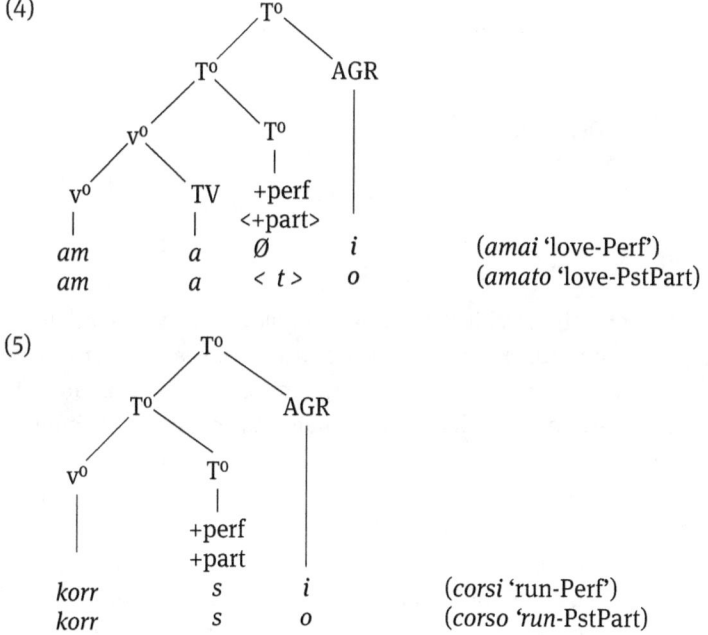

Given (3), the tense morpheme can interact with the root in the structure in (5) but not in the structure in (4). As shown diagrammatically in the configurations in (6), root information can be accessed only in the former structure (see (6)a) where root and T node are adjacent, but not in the latter (see (6)b)). Given that root information cannot be transmitted across the thematic vowel, only default, regular morphology can appear in this case.

(6) a.   Athematic   b.   Thematic

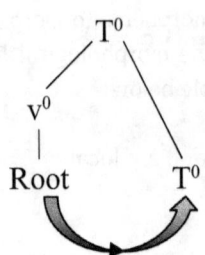
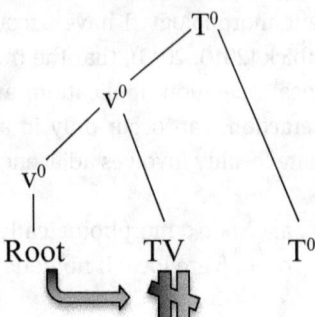

(7) /s/ <--> [+Perf]_T/ Roots ___ (where Roots = *korr, val, perd, met*, etc.)

The analysis developed in this paper adopts Distributed Morphology (DM; Halle & Marantz 1993). DM proposes a piece-based view of word formation, in which the syntax/morphology interface is as transparent as possible

(8)   The Grammar
                (Syntactic Derivation)

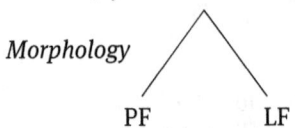

  Morphology

        PF   LF

DM crucially incorporates hierarchical structure into morphology; essentially, it assumes the input to morphology to be syntactic structure. Features (or feature bundles) are distributed over nodes forming morphemes, which in turn are subject to Vocabulary Insertion rules that add phonological material (exponents) to these morphemes.

The derivation of all morphological forms takes place in accordance with the architecture given in (8). Roots and other morphemes are combined into larger syntactic objects, which are moved when necessary (Merge, Move). The basic morpho-syntactic structure of Italian verbs is generated by root raising to v^0, verb raising to T^0 and AGR insertion (see Halle and Marantz (1993)). Note that head-movement here generates a morphological word (m-word), i.e., a (potentially complex) head not dominated by further head-projections (Embick and Noyer 2001).

(9)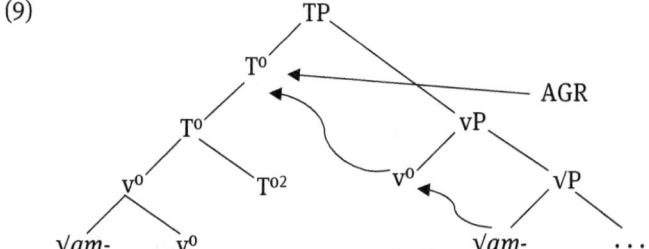

The basic morphosyntactic structure of Italian verbs derived as above is given in (10):

(10)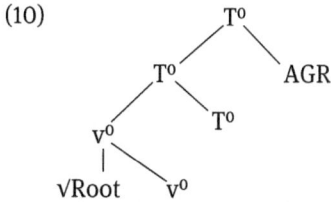

Embick (2010) proposes that non-overt category defining (lexical) nodes are pruned away by the rule in (11). I will assume this operation here.

(11)
```
      XV
     /  \
   root  X⁰
```
(with X⁰ crossed out)

Application of (11) to (10) will generate (12):

---

2 A morphosyntactic change occurred in the development of the Romance languages as can be seen in (i), where I compare the Latin pluperfect subjunctive in (ia) with the form that historically derived from it in Italian, i.e., the Imperfect subjunctive (ib):
(i)   a.   laud - a: + u-i   + s   + s-e: + mus   'praise-PlprfSubj1pl.'
      b.   lod -a-   +ss-i-   + mo   'praise-ImpSubj1pl.'
In Italian, functional categories such as aspect, tense and mood are no longer represented as independent morphological pieces as they were in Latin. Instead, a single morpheme appears in their place. I will simply assume that the Asp, Tense and Mood nodes are fused together in Italian (i.e., T=Aspect+Tense+Mood).

(12)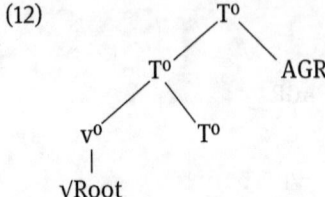

As proposed by Oltra-Massuet and Arregi (2005), Embick and Halle (2005), every functional/lexical projection in Latin and Romance has a Thematic Vowel. Thematic Vowels (TV) are special "ornamental" morphological elements adjoined to certain functional heads in morphological structure by the rule in (13)[3]:

(13) X^0 → X^0 [X^0 TV]

After thematic vowel insertion, the structure in (12) is changed into that in (14).

(14)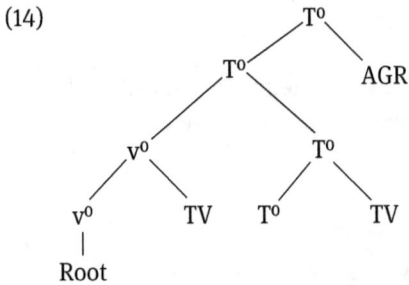

(14) accounts for the morphological structure of the imperfect forms in (15):

(15) **Italian imperfect indicative**
AMARE 'love':
am-a-v-o am-a-v-i am-a-v-a am-a-v-a-mo am-a-v-a-te am-a-v-a-no
BATTERE 'beat':
batt-e-v-o batt-e-v-i batt-e-v-a batt-e-v-a-mo batt-e-v-a-te batt-e-v-a-no
PARTIRE 'leave':

---

3 In Italian, but not in Latin, the functional head must have an overt exponent, cf. Italian (23) vs. Latin (55). I assume that this is due to an independent condition governing (13) in Italian. I will not discuss this point further here.

part-i-v-o	part-i-v-i	part-i-v-a	part-i-v-a-mo	part-i-v-a-te	part-i-v-a-no
1	2	3	1	2	3
Singular			Plural		

In the simplest case, Morphology linearize the hierarchical structure generated by the syntax by adding phonological material to the abstract morphemes in a process called *Vocabulary Insertion*. During this process, the (abstract) morpho-syntactic representation is the input to a morphological component that assign phonological realizations to the terminal nodes (Late Insertion). In particular, individual *Vocabulary Items* – rules that pair a phonological *exponent* with a morphosyntactic context – are consulted, and the most specific rule that can apply to an abstract morpheme applies (in the so-called Elsewhere (Subset, Paninian) ordering).

(16) Elsewhere condition:
Where more than one mutually exclusive rule may apply, (only) the most highly specified rule applies.

The vocabulary items needed to account for verbal inflections in the Italian imperfect tenses of regular verbs are given below. (In the case of the thematic vowels in (17), the Head can include a root or the head of a functional projection (cf. (19)). This accounts for the parallel behavior between roots and inflectional heads; so both the root /am-/ and imperfect tense have /-a-/ as a thematic vowel.):

(17) TV --> /-a-/ Head $_a$ _____
/-e-/ Head $_e$ _____
/-i-/ Head $_i$ _____

(18) AGR Suffixes:
    a. /-mo/ <--> [+author, +plural]$_{AGR}$
    b. /-te/ <--> [+participant, +plural] $_{AGR}$
    c. /-no/ <--> [+plural] $_{AGR}$
    d. /-o/ <--> [+author]$_{AGR}$ / [-subjunctive] $_T$ _____
    e. /-i/ <--> [+participant] $_{AGR}$ / [-subjunctive] $_T$ _____
    f. /Ø/ <--> [-participant] $_{AGR}$

(19) Tense Exponents (the subscript -$_a$ indicates that the imperfect Thematic Vowel is /a/ By (11)):
   a. /-v$_a$-/ <--> [+imperfect] $_{tense}$

Application of Cyclic vocabulary insertion to (14) generates (20).[4]

(20)
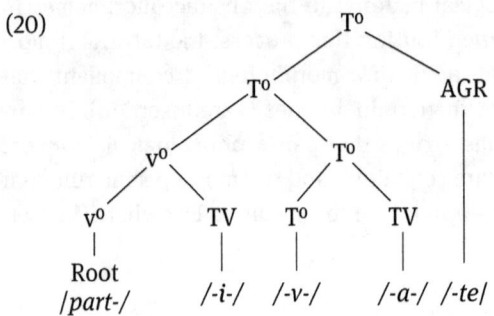

Let us turn to the perfect of regular verbs Also in this case, no overt independent exponent for Tense and the associated thematic vowel are present.

(21) AMARE 'love':
   am-a-i   am-a-sti   am-o~   am-a-mmo   am-a-ste   am-a-ro-no
   BATTERE 'beat':
   batt-e-i   batt-e-sti   batt-e~   batt-e-mmo   batt-e-ste   batt-e-ro-no
   TEMERE 'be afraid':
   tem-e-i   tem-e-sti   tem-e~   tem-e-mmo   tem-e-ste   tem-e-ro-no
   PARTIRE 'leave':
   part-i-i   part-i-sti   part-ì   part-i-mmo   part-i-ste   part-i-ro-no

Given that both the present and the perfect display a null exponent, we can assume that this is the elsewhere tense VI[5]:

---

[4] In order to account for word surface phonological form of words, in addition to VI, we need the application of morpho-phonological and phonological rules. In the present article I will focus only on vocabulary insertion rules (see Calabrese (2016a,b, forthcoming) for discussion of morpho-phonological rules). In the same way, I will not discuss the stress patterns of verbal forms (again see the quoted works for discussion).

[5] In Calabrese (2012) following Oltra-Massuet and Arregi (2005), I assumed that T and AGR are fused in this case. This leads to derivational complications discussed in Calabrese (2015) where I adopt the analysis presented here. This issue is irrelevant in the present article and will not be considered further here.

(22) VI for Perfect:
/-Ø-/ <--> [ ]$_{tense}$

(23)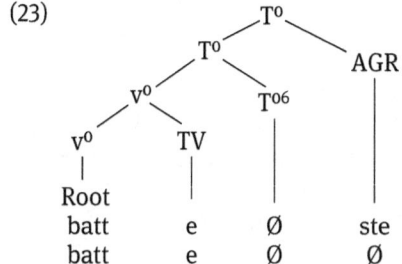

The vocabulary items for the AGR terminal node in the Perfect are given in (24):

(24) VIs for the AGR morpheme in the Perfect.
[+round]
|
a.   <--> [+perfect] /TV$_a$]$_V$ _____ [-participant, -plural] $_{AGR}$
b.   /-mmo/   <--> [+author, +plural]$_{AGR}$ / [+perfect] _____
c.   /-ste/   <--> [+participant, +plural]$_{AGR}$ / [+perfect] _____
d.   /-sti/   <--> [+participant, -author]$_{AGR}$ / [+perfect] _____
e.   /-i/   <--> [+author] / [+perfect] $_{AGR}$ _____
f.   /-ro/[7] <--> [-participant, +plural] $_{AGR}$ / [+perfect] _____
g.   /-Ø/   <--> [-participant] $_{AGR}$ = ((18) f)

We can now discuss irregular perfect forms. They show an overt morpheme for this tense.[8]

(25) val-e   val-s-e   'be worth'
     ettſell-e   ettſell-s-e [ettſelse] 'excel'

---

[6] As proposed in Footnote 3, in Italian a thematic vowel is not inserted if the functional head is null.

[7] The suffix /-no/ that appears in the 3rd pl. of regular Perfect forms is due to an operation fissioning [+plural] in [-part, +plural, +Perf] in the context TV]$_V$ ___. Subsequent application of (18)c insert the default [+plural] /-no/ (see Halle 1997), Noyer 1992) on morphological fission).

[8] In this article, I focus only on the distribution of the vocabulary items, /-s/ in this case. I will not discuss all other morpho-phonological adjustments needed to account for the surface allomorphy of the forms in (25), See Calabrese (2016a) for detailed discussion.

korr-e   korr-s-e [korse]   'run'
speɲɲ-e   speɲɲ-s-e [spense]   'turn off'
perd-e   perd-s-e [perse]   'lose'
vold3-e   vold3-s-e [volse]   'turn'

These forms have the constituent structure in (26):

(26)
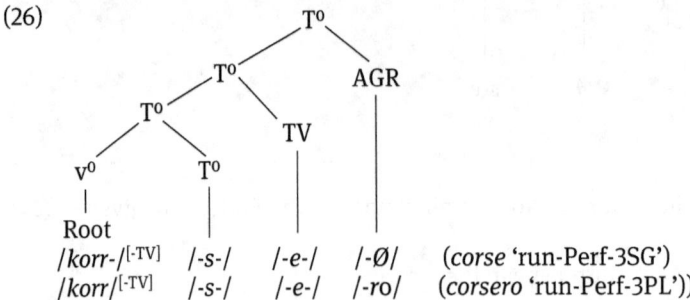

/korr-/[-TV]   /-s-/   /-e-/   /-Ø/   (*corse* 'run-Perf-3SG')
/korr/[-TV]   /-s-/   /-e-/   /-ro/ (*corsero* 'run-Perf-3PL'))

As discussed in Calabrese (2016a), the crucial aspect of the structure in (26) is the absence of the Verb Thematic Vowel, cf. Regular [[[[batt]$_V$ -e]$_{ThV}$ Ø]$_T$ -i]$_{AGR}$ vs. Irregular [[[[corr]$_V$ -s]$_T$ -i]$_{AGR}$ / [[[[perd]$_V$-s]$_T$ -i]$_{AGR}$. To account for this, I assume that these verbs are exceptions to the TV insertion rule. In particular, the roots in these verbs are assigned a special diacritic [-TV] indicating that the rule in (13) does not apply when the verbal head contains one of these roots and T is [+perfect]. In these cases, therefore, the verbal TV is absent.⁹

The exponent /-s-/ for the [+past] Tense of some of the irregular perfect forms is inserted by the Vocabulary Item in (27), which is crucially sensitive to the root diacritic /^{s}/:

(27) /-s-/ <--> [+Perf] T / Roots^s ____ (where Root^s = *corr, val, perd, met*, etc.)

As discussed above, the hypothesis is that morpheme-to-morpheme interactions are local (see Embick 2010, 2013):

(28) a. Node α morphologically interacts with node β iff α, β are local.
     b. α, β are local if no node intervenes (adjacency).

---

9 In addition to /-s-/ (cf. *val-e/val-s-e* 'be worth pres/Perf'), irregular forms of the perfect display other exponents such as those observed in *venne*, root *ven* 'come', *kadde* root *kad* 'fall' *nokkʷe*, root *nok* harm', *vide* root *ved* 'see' (see Calabrese (2016a) for detailed analysis and discussion). Here I will focus only on the exponent /-s-/.

As observed above, the basic observation is that there is correlation between presence vs. absence of regular morphology and presence vs. absence of thematic vowels in perfect forms. Root based contextual allomorphy occurs only when the thematic vowel is absent.

(29) **Irregular= Athematic** vs. **Regular=Thematic**
[[[perd]root__]v -s-]T] i]AGR   [[[part]root -iTV-]v -Ø-]T-i]AGR
persi 'lose-Perf-1sg'   *partii* 'leave-Perf-1sg'

(30) Athematic   Thematic

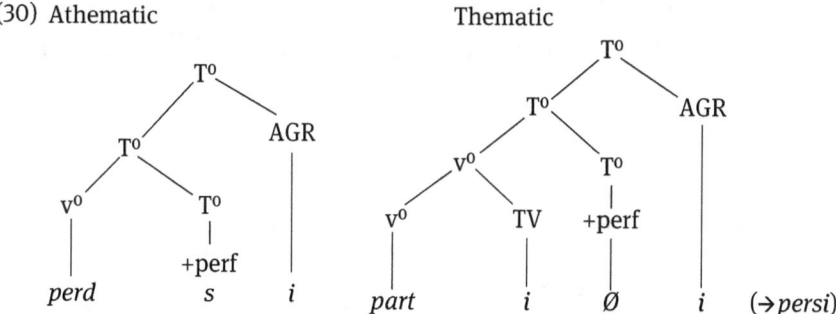

My proposal here is that VI in (27) crucially refers to root information and therefore can apply only in a node adjacent to it. If this adjacency is disrupted by the presence of a Thematic Vowel, only regular unmarked morphology will occur, i.e., only the VI in (27) can apply.

(31)   Athematic   Thematic

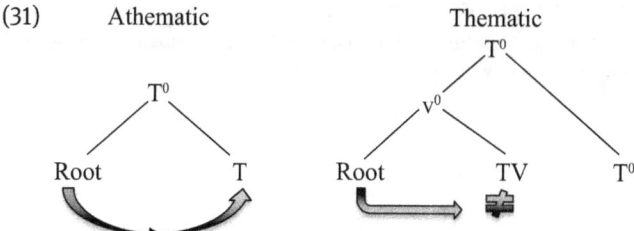

Given the linear adjacency requirements, (29) can apply only when the Thematic Vowels are missing. Thus, it can apply in the structure in (30) but not in (31) where the TV is present:

(32) a. [[[korr^S]root +Perf]T +part,-+auth, -pl] AGR
     b. [[[korr^S]root   s]T   i   ]AGR
        kor-s- i

(33) a. [[[korr^S]$_{root}$ TV] +Perf]$_T$ +part,-+auth, -pl]$_{AGR}$
 b. [[[korr^S]$_{root}$ e] s]$_T$ i]$_{AGR}$
 *korr-e-s-i

In contrast, regular morphology is not dependent on root information and does not need to appear in a local configuration with the root. Only root conditioned irregular morphology like the VI in (27) does.[10,11,12]

It is to observe that the analysis developed above is not possible in Affixless theories (Anderson 1992a, Aronoff 1976, 1994, Maiden 2004, Matthews 1972, Stump 2001 a.o) where the forms of words are derived by operations that apply to representations consisting of roots and matrices of features as in (34) (Embick (2013: 160))

---

10 A crucial aspect of the analysis developed in this paper is the assumption that thematic vowels are generated in an independent morphosyntactic node. Therefore, morphological segmentations that do not recognize the thematic vowel as an autonomous piece are unable to account for locality effects in contextual allomorphy. In particular, TVs are not considered to be independent pieces under the following two analyses

1. The TV is considered to be integral part of the piece including the root (=the stem, cf. Bermudez-Otero (2013):
 ama-i, batte-i, parti-i vs. kor(r)-s-i, vid-i, etc.

2. The TV is considered to be integral part of the desinence (cf. traditional grammars, also Maiden (2010):
 am-ai, batt-ei, part-ii vs. kor(r)-s-i, vid-i, etc.

Under both analyses, there is no way to account for locality effects in contextual allomorphy, all roots/stems should behave in the same way:

11 See Calabrese (2012, 2016) for extensive discussion of the person-number conditioned alternations (i.e., irregular: korsi/korse/korsero 'run-1stSG/3SG./3PL', vs. regular: korremmo/korreste 'run-1stPL, 2PL') characterizing the Italian perfects.

12 Note that the correlation between presence vs. absence of regular morphology and presence vs. absence of thematic vowels appears to be relevant also in the case of derivational morphology in the case of nominalizations such as the following: regular thematic: *portatore/venditore/spaccatura/battitura* 'bearer/seller/cleaving/threshing' vs. irregular athematic: *direttore/divisore/rottura/chiusura* 'director/divisor/breaking/closing'. See Calabrese (2015) for a preliminary analysis.

(34) Affixless theories

$$\text{Root} \begin{pmatrix} \pm W \\ \pm X \\ \pm Y \end{pmatrix}$$

As observed by Embick (2013), affixless theories make no predictions about the locality of morpho-phonological interactions since all of the features are equally local in representations like (34).

3 The Latin perfect forms

Latin is traditionally described as having four conjugations characterized by different thematic vowels as shown in (35). The thematic vowel may be absent in specific morphological categories such as irregular perfects or past participles and in specific verbs (e.g., *su-mus/es-se*).:

(35)
Traditional Label	Theme Vowel	Example 1st Pl	Infinitive
Conj. I	-ā-	laud-ā-mus	laud-ā-re
Conj. II	-ē-	mon-ē-mus	mon-ē-re
Conj. III	-e-	dūc-i-mus	duc-e-re
Conj. III(i)	-i-	cap-i-mus	cap-e-re
Conj. IV -	-ī-	aud-ī-mus	aud-ī-re

The Latin verbal system is characterized by a basic aspectual opposition between imperfective and perfective forms (*Infectum* vs. *Perfectum*) (The semantic characterization of this opposition will not be dealt with here). Tense distinctions are found in each of these aspectual categories, as shown below:

(36)
Infectum			vs.	*Perfectum*[13]		
[-perfect]				[+perfect]		
[-past]	[+past]	[+future]		[-past]	[+past]	[+future]
Present	Imperfect	Future		Present	Pluperfect	Future Perfect
amō	amābam	amābo		amāvī	amāveram	amāverō

---

[13] The *perfectum* is the conflation of PIE Aorist and Perfect as we will see later.

Morpho-syntactic structure of Latin Verb forms is given below (Embick and Halle 2001) (See Calabrese (2019) for detailed discussion of the realization of voice in Latin:

(37) *laud - a: + u-i + s + s-e: + mus* 'praise-Perf-Past-Subj-1st pl.'

(38)
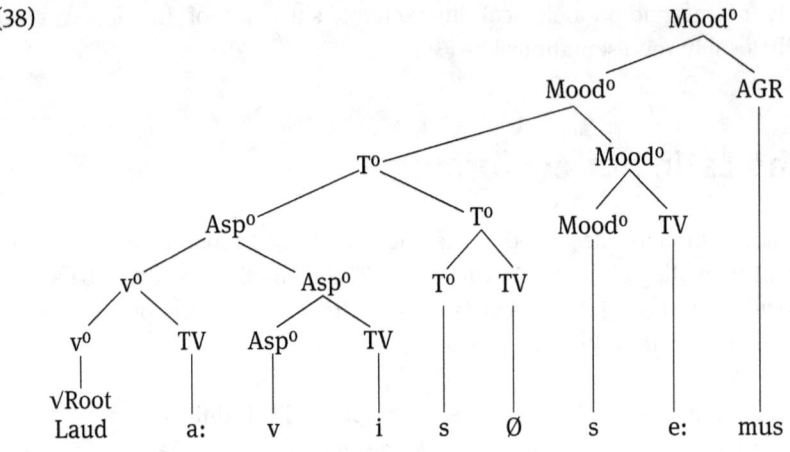

However, following Embick and Halle (2001), I assume that unmarked functional categories such as [-passive]$_{Voice}$, [-perfect]$_{Asp}$, [-past]$_T$, [-subjunctive]$_{Mood}$ are either pruned away in the morphology, or simply not projected in the syntax. So, the perfect (*perfectum*) present indicative has the structure in (39):

(39)
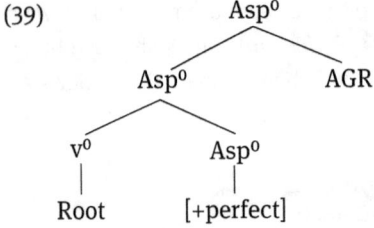

Aronoff (1994) shows that thematic vowels must be analyzed as pure structural elements, ornamental morphology. In particular, they cannot be treated as derivational suffixes, i.e., exponents of category-defining v-heads in the DM perspective adopted here. In Latin, there are many of these suffixes. Each of them has a particular meaning and selects a different Thematic vowel.

(40) Derivational verb suffixes

Suffixes	Thematic vowel	Meaning	Example	Gloss
-ur-	ī	Desiderative	ēs-ur-ī-re	'be hungry'
-it-	ā	iterative	vīs-it-ā-re	'see often'
-fic-	ā	causative	ex-carn-ific-ā-re	'flesh out'
-ic-	ā	iterative	mors-ic-ā-re	'bite continually'
-ess-	e	intensive	cap-ess-e-re	'seize'
-Ø-	ā	intensive	iact-Ø-ā-re	'throw hard'

Because all these suffixes are associated with a dedicated thematic vowel, under the analysis of the thematic vowel as a v head, each one of them would have to be analyzed as complex, consisting of a v head with a clear functional meaning, followed by the "thematic vowel", another v-head but without a functional meaning. The theme vowel would essentially be a "redundant" v head as in (41):

(41)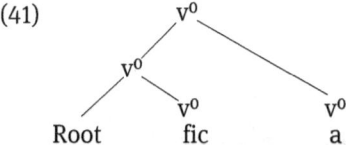

According to Aronoff, the most adequate analysis is one in which the theme vowel is considered a pure structural element, ornamental morphology.[14] In the theory adopted here, this structural element is inserted by Oltra-Massuet and Arregi's (2005) rule in (13)(repeated here in (43)), as in (42):

(42)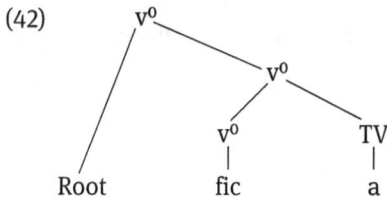

(43) X^0 →

---

[14] But see Bertocci (2017, forthcoming) who argues that there are common morpho-syntactic properties shared by the ā-conjugation involving a voice feature.

After thematic vowel insertion, the structure in (39) is changed into that in (44).

(44)
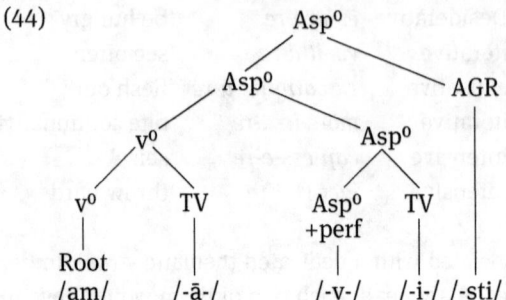

The VIs for the Regular Perfect forms are given below:

(45) TV --> /-ā-/ Head $_a$ ____
         /-ē-/ Head $_e$ ____
         /-ī-/ Head $_i$ ____

(46) AGR Suffixes:
    b. /-stis/ <--> [+participant, +plural] $_{AGR}$ / [+perfect]$_{ASP}$ ____
    e. /-sti/ <--> [+participant] $_{AGR}$ / [+perfect]$_{ASP}$ ____
    a. /-mus/ <--> [+author, +plural]$_{AGR}$
    d. /-Ø/ <--> [+author]$_{AGR}$ / [+perfect]$_{ASP}$ ____
    c. /-unt/ <--> [-participant, +plural] $_{AGR}$
    f. /-t/ <--> [-participant] $_{AGR}$

(47) Regular Perfect (the subscript -i indicates that the perfect Thematic Vowel is / i- /:
/-v$_i$-/ <--> [+perfect] Asp

We thus have an account for perfect regular morphology:

(48) **Present**   **Perfect**
    laud-ā-mus laud-ā-v-i-mus 'praise'
    aud-ī-mus   aud-ī-v-i-mus 'hear'

(49)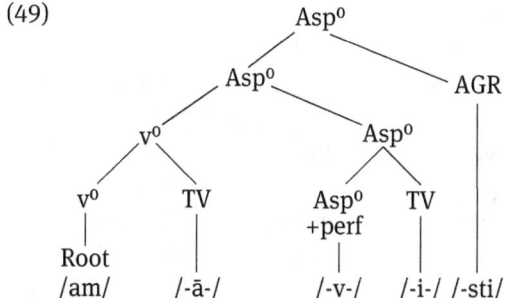

Irregular perfect morphology is the standard case in Conjugations II and III. It is also found, although unusually, in Conjugations I and IV. As already mentioned, irregular morphology is found only in athematic constructions.

(50) Allomorphy in Latin Perfects (from Embick and Halle (2004))

	Conj.	Verb	Perfect	Gloss.	Type
a.	I	laud-ā-mus	laud-ā-v-ī	'praise'	Thematic + -v-
b.	I	crep-ā-mus	crep-u-ī [15]	'rattle'	Athematic + v-
c.	I	iuv-ā-mus	iūv-ī	'help'	Athematic + -Ø-
	I	–	–	–	Athematic + -s-
	I	–	–	–	Athematic + -Ø-+ Reduplication
d.	II	del-ē-mus	del-e-v-ī	'destroy'	Thematic + -v-
e.	II	mon-ē-mus	mon-u-ī	'warn'	Athematic + -v-
f.	II	sed-ē-mus	sēd-ī	'sit'	Athematic + -Ø-
g.	II	man-ē-mus	man-s-ī	'remain'	Athematic + -s-
h.	II	mord-ē-mus	mo-mord-ī	'bite'	Athematic + -Ø-+ Reduplication
i.	III	pet-i-mus	petī-v-ī	'seek'	Thematic + -v-
j.	III	vom-i-mus	vom-v-ī	'vomit'	Athematic + -v-
k.	III	vert-i-mus	vert-ī	'turn'	Athematic + -Ø-
l.	III	dūc-i-mus	dūc-s-ī	'lead'	Athematic + -s-
m.	III	cad-i-mus	ce-cid-ī	'fall'	Athematic + -Ø-+ Reduplication
n.	III(i)	cup-i-mus	cup-ī-v-ī	'desire'	Thematic + -v-
o.	III(i)	rap-i-mus	rap-u-ī	'seize'	Athematic + -v-

---

[15] The alternation [u]/[v(=w)] is due to syllable structure: [u] appears after consonants, [v] after vowels. For the sake of simplicity, I assume that the underlying form of the suffix is /v/ instead of a syllabically unspecified /U/.

p.	III(i)	cap-i-mus	cēp-ī	'take'	Athematic + -Ø-
q.	III(i)	-spic-i-mus	spec-s-ī	'peer'	Athematic + -s-
r.	III(i)	par-i-mus	pe-per-ī	'bring forth'	Athematic + -Ø-+ Reduplication
s.	IV	aud-ī-mus	aud-ī-v-ī	'hear'	Thematic + -v-
t.	IV	aper-ī-mus	aper-u-ī	'open'	Athematic + -v-
u.	IV	ven-ī-mus	vēn-ī	'come'	Athematic + -Ø-
v.	IV	farc-ī-mus	far-s-ī	'stuff'	Athematic + -s-
	IV	–	–	–	Athematic + -Ø-+ Reduplication

The basic cases are given below:

(51) Perfect forms:
    a. *mon-u-i-mus* 'remind'   Athematic forms with -v-
    b. *dūc-s-i-mus* 'lead'   Athematic forms with -s-
    c. *prand-Ø-i-mus* 'take breakfast'   Athematic forms with -Ø- (+ablaut)
    d. *to-tond-Ø-i-mus* 'shear'   Athematic forms with -Ø- +reduplication
       (pres. tond-ē-mus)

No surface phonological generalization can account for the distribution of the different allomorphs of the perfect. The exponent /-v-/ is found both after vowels and consonants, e.g. *delēvī, monuī* . The exponent /-s-/ is found both after vowels and consonants: *divīsī, scrīpsī*

Generalizations can be captured only if the underlying morphosyntactic configuration is accessed. Once this is done, one can observe that /-s-/ and /-Ø-/ are found only after consonants. However, saying this is essentially saying that these exponents are directly attached to a root, i.e., they occur in an athematic construction.[16] Furthermore, one also observes that only the exponent /-v-/ appears after thematic vowels, whereas a variety of perfect exponents is found in athematic conditions.

---

[16] And still no root phonological property can select between them, and we still need to resort to a root diacritic to do this.

(52) Distribution of Perfect exponence
　　　Perfect　　　　　　　-v-　　　　　　　/ Thematic __
　　　　　　　　　　　　　-v-　　　　　　　/ Athematic __
　　　　　　　　　　　　　-Ø-
　　　　　　　　　　　　　-s-
　　　　　　　　　　　　　-Ø-+ Reduplication

We can now proceed to an analysis of Latin perfect forms. The absence of the root thematic vowel is accounted for as before in Italian. Athematic verbs are exceptions to TV insertion when Asp⁰ is [+perfect]:

(53) root$^{[-TV]}$ = curr, ed, scrib, leg, ser, etc.

Regular verbs, together with verbs such as those in (51)a0, form the Perfect with the suffix /-v-/, which can be considered the elsewhere case. The verbs in (51)b) form the Perfect with the suffix /-s-/, whereas those in (51)c,d) take the suffix /-Ø-/. In (51)d) there is also root reduplication. Each of these [+perf]$_{Asp}$ exponents is followed by the vowel -i-, which I assume is the realization of a TV position attached to Asp⁰:

(54) a. /-Ø-/ <---> Perfect / Root^{Ø} ___, root^{Ø} = leg, etc
　　 b. /-s-/ <---> Perfect / Root^{s}- ___, root^{s} = scrib, etc.
　　 c. /-v-/ <---> Perfect

(55)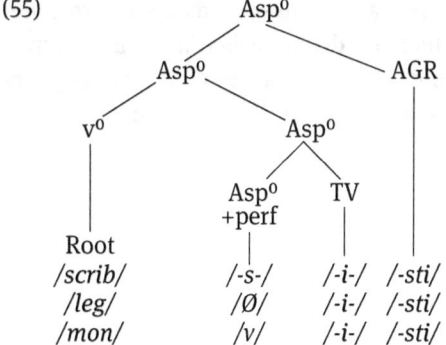

Reduplication is due to a special Morpho-Phonological rule which is not discussed here. Also, I will not discuss the other Morpho-Phonological and phonological rules needed to derive surface Latin irregular perfect forms (see Calabrese (2013, forthcoming).

(54)a,b) require access to root diacritics. Therefore, they can apply only in condition of locality with the root, i.e., in nodes that are adjacent to it. Therefore, as in Italian, irregular aspectual morphology can occur only in athematic constructions where this adjacency is found, as shown in (56).

(56) Locality in Latin Verbs

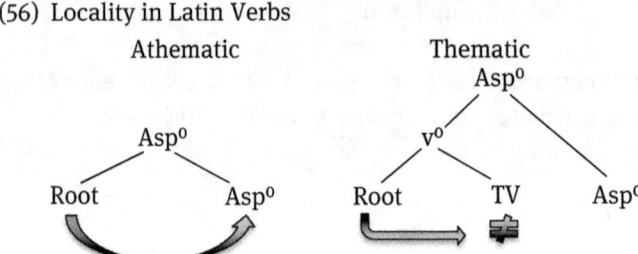

This explains the distribution of the perfect exponents in (50). It also follows that complex ASP allomophy, i.e., a situation in which Asp^0 is realized with different exponents, can be found only in athematic constructions.

4 PIE verbal morphology

I will now consider the development of Latin perfects from the reconstructed verbal morphology of PIE.

PIE verbs are traditionally described as being organized into 'systems' based on the different "stem" forms. The basic stem systems are the so-called Present, the Perfect and the Aorist, which are distinguished in terms of aspectual features. Here I will be unable to discuss the semantic differences of the different aspect forms, and will simply assume that they are characterized by the following features:

(57)
	Present	Aorist	Perfect
perfective	–	+	+
stative	–	–	+

Other traditional stem systems are the Future, the Passive, the Causative, the Desiderative, the Denominative and the Intensive/Frequentatives. Some of them will be considered later.

Each system includes mood distinctions: indicative, subjunctive, optative, imperative.

(58)

Aspect	Present				Aorist				Perfect			
Perfective	–				+				+			
Stative	–				–				+			
Mood	Ind	Subj	Opt	Imp	Ind	Subj	Opt	Imp	Ind	Subj	Opt	Imp
irrealis	–	+	+	–	–	+	+	–	–	+	+	–
desiderative	–	–	+	+	–	–	+	+	+	+	+	+

The basic verbal morpho-syntactic structure of PIE verbs can be observed in the following forms from Vedic Sanskrit and Classical Greek, where one observes that voice and subject agreement Phi-features (person and number) are realized as a single exponent, which also includes tense distinctions (+/-Past):

(59) a. *kṛṇuyā́ta* 'make-Imperfective-Optative-Active-2PL   Root: kar
        [[[[kar]_{root} nau]_{Aspect} yā]_{Mood} ta]_{Tense+Voice+AGR}
        δεικνύοιτε 'point-Imperfective-Optative-Active-2PL   Root: deik
        [[[[deik]_{root}nu]_{Aspect}oi]_{Mood} te]_{Tense+Voice+AGR}
   b. *kṛṇávadhve* 'make-Imperfective-Subjuntive-Middle-2PL
        [[[[kar]_{root} nau]_{Aspect} a]_{Mood} dhve]_{Tense+Voice+AGR}
        δεικνύητε 'point-Imperfective-Subjuntive-Middle-2PL
        [[[[deik]_{root}nu]_{Aspect} e:]_{Mood} te]_{Tense+Voice+AGR}

I therefore assume that the basic morphosyntactic structure of PIE verbs, which is essentially maintained in Sanskrit and C. Greek, is that in (60):

(60)
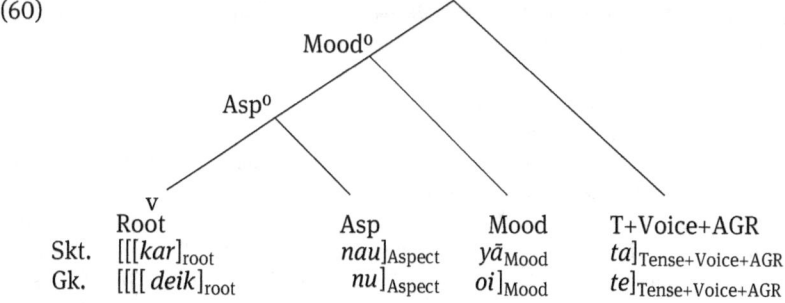

Present (imperfect) aspect displays a wide variety of affixes (based on Ringe (2006: 27–28), see also Rix et al. (1986), Szemerenyi (1996)).[17,18]

(61) Root presents. There is no overt suffixal element
  *$h_1$és-Ø- ~ *h_1s-Ø-* 'be', Root: h_1es *$h_1$éd-Ø- ~ *$h_1$éd-Ø-* 'eat', Root: h_1ed
Presents with no overt suffixal element and reduplication with *Ce
  *d^hé-$d^h eh_1$-Ø- ~ *d^hé-$d^h h_1$-Ø-* 'be putting', Root: $d^h eh_1$
Presents with no overt suffixal element and reduplication with with *Ci
  *$stí$-$steh_2$-Ø- ~ *$stí$-sth_2-Ø-* 'be getting up (in a standing position), Root: $steh_2$
Presents infixed with *né - *n:
  *li-$né$-k^w- ~ *li-n-k^w-* 'be leaving behind', Root: $leik^w$
Presents with suffix *néw - *nw/nu:
  *$tṇ$-néw- ~ * $tṇ$-nu-* 'be stretching', Root: ten
Present with accented suffixal -e-[19]:
  *$wṛg$- é - 'work', Root: $werg/wṛg$
Present with suffixal -e- and root accent:
  b^hér-e- 'bring', Root: $b^h er/b^h ṛ$
Present with suffixal -e- and reduplication with reduplicated with *Ci-
  si-sd-$é$- 'be sitting down', Root: sed
Presents in *-yé-
  $wṛg$-yé- 'be working', Root: $werg$
Presents in *-yé (with accent on the root)
  g^{wh}éd^h-ye- 'keep asking for', Root: $g^{wh}éd^h$

---

17 Some of these affixes may have had different non-aspectual functional or derivational properties originally in pre-PIE stages, cf. the causative flavor of the *ne*-affix (Bertocci, forthcoming, Meiser 1993). Such properties can no longer be clearly identified at the PIE stage (see Burrow 1955: 302). At this stage, these suffixes can only treated as aspectual markers.

18 I will not deal with accent and zero-grade alternations that are fundamental to understand the complex morpho-phonology of the ancient IE language (see Calabrese (2019) for an analysis of these alternations in Vedic Sanskrit). I will also put aside the so-called *o*-grade by which vowel *-e- became -o- in determined morpho-phonological environment. For the sake of simplicity, I will refer to this vowel as just /-e-/ in the examples.

19 In Calabrese (2019) I show that suffixal "thematic" /-a-/ of Sanskrit is just one of the exponents of the ASP node like -nau-, -na- etc. not an ornamental "thematic" vowel like in Latin. I assume that it is the same for PIE. As mentioned above, see also Calabrese (2019) for discussion of the accentual and zero grade properties of this vowel: it is always accented – unless preceded by another accented syllable, in which case it is the latter syllable to get ictus – and never undergoes zero grade, whereas aspectual suffixes such as /-new-/, /-ne-/, even if they can be assigned accent, may lose it, and then undergo zero grade, when followed by an accented suffix.

Therefore, I propose that that the present allomorphs that form the different classes mentioned above involve root dependent realizations of [-perfect] aspect:

(62) Sanskrit   PIE   cf. Greek
     [[bhav]$_{Root}$ - a]$_{Aspect}$ *- e]$_{Aspect}$ - e]$_{Aspect}$
     [[raudh]$_{Root}$ - na]$_{Aspect}$ *- ne]$_{Aspect}$ - ne]$_{Aspect}$
     [[pas]$_{Root}$ - ya]$_{Aspect}$ *- ye]$_{Aspect}$ - ie]$_{Aspect}$
     [[star]$_{Root}$ -nau]$_{Aspect}$ *- new]$_{Aspect}$ -nü]$_{Aspect}$
     [[ad]$_{Root}$ - Ø]$_{Aspect}$ *- Ø]$_{Aspect}$ - Ø]$_{Aspect}$

Given (62), one can propose that [-perfect] aspect is realized through the different root dependent VI listed below:

(63) a. /*-e-/   <--> [-perfect]$_{Aspect}$ / Root $^{-a-}$____
     b. /*-ye-/   <--> [-perfect]$_{Aspect}$ / Root $^{-ya-}$____
     c. /*-ne-/   <--> [-perfect]$_{Aspect}$ / Root $^{-na-}$____
     d. /*-new-/   <--> [-perfect]$_{Aspect}$ / Root $^{-nau-}$____
     e. /*-Ø-/   <--> [-perfect]$_{Aspect}$ / Root $^{-Ø-}$____

In (63), we have a complex system of root-conditioned contextual allomorphy in present aspect. Observe that the different VIs in (63) can apply only if they have access to root-based information (root -diacritics). Therefore, they can apply only when the root and the aspect node are adjacent, i.e., in a local configuration that allows morphemic interactions:

(64) Locality in PIE Verb:

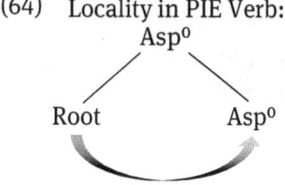

In contrast, mood and AGR suffixes never shows complex root-conditioned allomorphy: they only show a single exponent, i.e., subjunctive /*-e-/; optative /*-yeH$_1$-/, as expected since they are not in a local configuration with the root. Exponent variation in this case can only be conditioned by Aspect.

(65)

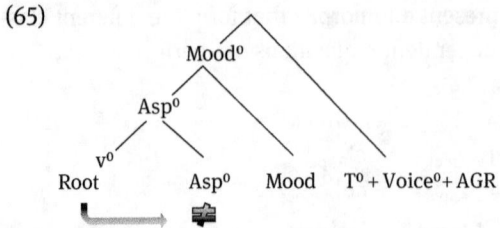

We can now consider the perfect and aorist system. There are two types of perfect: root perfects and reduplicated perfects:

(66) a. Root perfects:
*woyd-Ø- ~ *wid-Ø-   'know' (root: weid)
b. Reduplicated perfects:
*me-món-Ø- ~ *me-mn-Ø-   'remember' (root: men)

The aorist system stem has different formations. The simple aorist is taken directly from the root stem. The s-aorist is formed with the suffixation of /-s-/ to the stem. The "thematic" aorist is formed with suffixal /-e-/ The reduplicating aorist involves reduplication and suffixal /-e-/[20]:

(67) a. The root aorist with no overt suffixal element:
*gʷém-Ø- ~ *gʷm̥-Ø-   'step' (root: gʷem)
*bʰuh₂-Ø-   'become' (root: bʰeuh₂)
b. The /-s-/ aorist.
*déyk'-s-   'point out' (root: deik')
*wég̑ʰ-s-   'transport' (root: wegʰ)
c. The /-é-/ aorist (traditionally called the thematic aorist)
*h₂ludʰ-é-   'arrive' (root: h₂leudʰ)
Reduplicating aorist
*wé-wk-e-   'say' (root wek)

I assume that the perfect and aorist have the morpho-syntactic structures in (68):

---

20 Some Indo-European languages such as Sanskrit and Greek display a prefixal vowel, the so-called augment (Gr. ε-/ Skt. a-), in past tenses such as the aorist and the imperfect. Since it is irrelevant in the analysis presented here, I will not consider it.

Irregular verbal morphology and locality — 111

(68)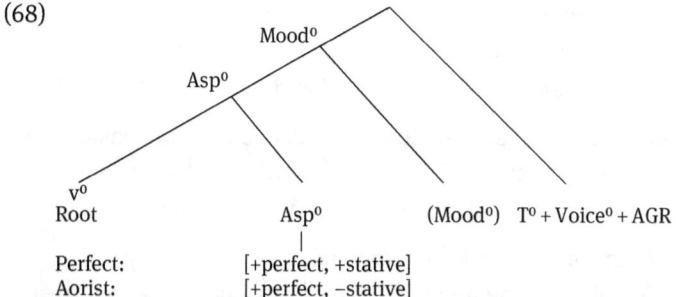

Perfect: [+perfect, +stative]
Aorist: [+perfect, −stative]

The VIs are given below. Reduplication is due to special MP rules which are not discussed here.

(69) Perfect:
/*-Ø-/ <--> [+Perf. +stat]

(70) Aorist:
/*-Ø-/ <--> [+perfect, −stative]   /   Root^Ø ___
/*-s-/ <--> [+perfect, −stative]   /   Root^s ___
/*-e-/ <--> [+perfect, −stative]   /   Root^e ___

As in the case of the present, in the case of the perfect and of the aorist there is a complex system of root-conditioned contextual allomorphy. I assume that this is possible because the root and aspect node are adjacent

(71) Locality in PIE Verbs

Asp⁰
/   \
Root   Asp⁰
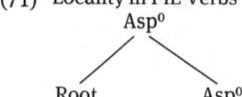

To understand the development of the Latin conjugation system, one must consider PIE derived stems. We have the following derived verbs:

(72) Statives in -eh_1-
h_1rudh-éh_1-   'be red'   (h_1rewdh-   'red')
Factitives in -eh_2-
$néwe$-h_2-   'renew'   ($newo$ 'new')

Causatives and iteratives in *-éye- (with o-grade root) from basic roots:
*sod-éye- 'seat (someone)' (*sed 'sit down')
*bhor-éye- 'be carrying around' (*bher 'carry')

Desideratives in *-sé, with and without reduplication Ci from basic roots,
*wéid-se- 'want to see' (*weyd 'catch sight of')
*k'i-k'l̥-se- 'try to conceal' (*k'el 'hide')

Denominatives in -yé- formed from nominals:
*h₂k'h₂ows-yé- 'be sharp-heared (*h₂ek 'sharp' and *k'h₂éw-es 'hear')

Factitives in *-yé- formed from adjectives:
*pr̥kto-yé- 'frighten' (*pr̥kto- 'afraid')

Originally verb-forming suffixes were associated with present (imperfect) aspect and were incompatible with other aspectual markers (see Ridge (2006: 26–35), Sihler (1995: 494) for discussion and possible historical motivation for this situation). Probably this indicates that the v⁰-node under which these derivatives were inserted and the Asp⁰ node were originally fused together (see Calabrese (2019) for discussion). But evidence from Vedic Sanskrit (a few cases (73)) and Classical Greek (the regular situation (74)) show that verb-forming derivative suffixes must have been able to co-occur with aspectual suffixes already in later stages of the Proto-language:

(73) Aorist denominative/Causative in Vedic Sanskrit
 pāp -ay-iṣ- from pāpa-ya- (denominative /-ya-/) 'lead into evil (pāpa)'
 vyath-ay-is- from vyath-aya- (causative /-aya-/) 'disturb'
 dhvan-ay-is- from dhvan-aya- 'envelope'

(74) Aorist denominative/Causative in Greek (just stem, no augment)
 -οἰκ-η-σ- <*woik-eye-se 'inhabit' (Denominative from οἰκος 'house')
 -φορ- η-σ- <bhor-eye-se- 'carry about/wear' (Causative from φερω 'bring')

We can then assume that at later stages of proto-language the v⁰ node was no longer fused with Asp⁰, and that these derivatives were independently generated under the v⁰ node. The derived verbs in (72) had thus the morphosyntactic structure in (75):

(75)
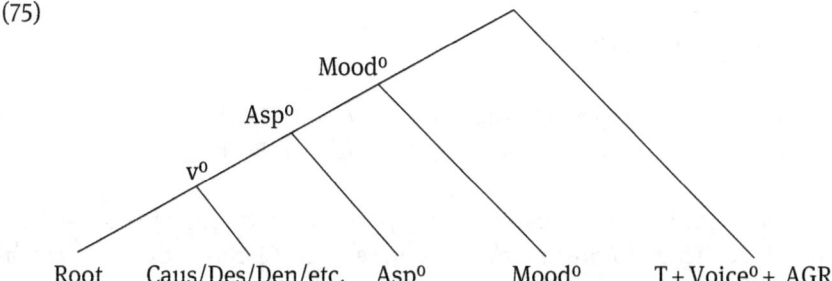

This is the situation that can be reconstructed for pre-Latin, as discussed below.

5 The development of the Latin perfect system

The major change in the development of Latin Verbal System was the conflation of the PIE aorist and Perfect. In this paper, I will not deal with the reasons of this change or with its syntactico-semantic consequences, but only with its implications for the verbal morphology of Latin.

As we saw in sect., the perfectum exponents of Latin are those in (76):

(76) a. /-Ø-/ <---> Perfect / Root^Ø ___, root^Ø = vert, etc
 b. /-s-/ <---> Perfect / Root^s- ___, root^s = scrib, etc.
 c. /-v-/ <---> Perfect

The exponent /-v-/ cannot be traced back to PIE, is not found in other Italic languages and is peculiar to Latin.[21] /-s-/ and /-Ø-/ can instead be traced back to PIE. They, in fact, are etymologically related to the PIE VIs in (69) and (70), repeated in (77):

---

[21] According to Sihler (1995: 585), the default exponent /-v (=[w])-/ for Aspect [+perf, +stat] may have originally developed as a hiatus filler between the thematic vowel and vocalic endings. If this is correct, one must assume that at one point there was a general use of /-Ø-/ as the default exponent of ASP. Once the hiatus breaking /-w-/ was reanalyzed as an exponent of ASP, as proposed by Sihler, /-Ø-/ became the exponent of ASP for roots not taking /-s-/. See Sihler (1995: ibid.) for discussion of other accounts of the development of this exponent.

(77) a. Perfect:
    /*-Ø-/ <--> [+Perf. +stat]
   b. Aorist:
    /*-Ø-/ <--> [+perfect, -stative]   /   Root^Ø ___
    /*-s-/ <--> [+perfect, -stative]   /   Root^s ___

Latin /-s-/ directly derives from PIE Aorist /-s-/. Latin /-Ø-/ instead derives from both PIE Perfect and Aorist /-Ø-/. So we have perfect forms with reduplication that underwent changes such as the following[22] *sēd-Ø-ī < *se-sd-Ø-*> 'sit' (Sihler (1995: 582). At the same time, we have aorist forms that were preserved in Latin: *fīd-Ø-ī* < *bh^{h}eid-Ø-, Infectum present *findō* 'split' (cf. Skt. *bhinátti* 3sg pres. vs. *bhét* /bháit-Ø-t/ 3sg. aor.), *līqu-Ø-ī* <*leik^w*, Infectum present *linquō* 'leave' (cf. Skt. *riṇakti* 3sg pres. vs. *riktám* /rik-Ø-tam/ 2du Aor.)(see Sihler (1995: 581–2) for more examples and detailed discussion).

The PIE derived verbs discussed above played a major role in the development of Latin Verbal System and formed the bases for the regular verbal conjugations. In contrast, the original underived PIE verb forms became a closed, relic class and gave rise to the third irregular conjugation.

In Pre-Latin, as in Greek, verb-forming derivatives were inserted under the v^0-node independently of Asp^0 suffixes as in (75). Therefore, there could be an overt suffixal piece such as the *-eye-* characteristic of causatives in PIE, the *-ye* of denominatives, the *-eH$_1$-* characteristic of statives, etc., between root and ASP in all forms of the verb. In Latin, this overt piece became the thematic vowel appearing between root and aspect in all forms of the verb, including in the *Perfectum* forms (Ernout 1989, Sihler 1995).

The *-ā-* conjugation developed mostly from denominatives in *-ye-* whose bases were the nominal stems of the *-ā-*(<*-eH$_2$-) declension: /-ā-/ < *-eH$_2$-ye: e.g. *curō* 'cure' (cf. *curā* 'cure').

The *-ē-* conjugation developed mostly from the stative suffix *-ē-*(<*-eH$_2$-), or from causatives in -*eye-(with o-grade of root): /-ē-/<*-eH$_1$: e.g., *sedeō* 'I am sitting' (<*sed-eH$_1$- (cf. *sīdo* (*si-sd-) 'I sit down', /-ē-/<*-eye: e.g. *moneō* 'I warn' (<*mon-eye-*) (cf. *re-min-isc-or*, root: *men*)

The *-ī-* conjugation developed mostly from from denominatives in -*ye-, /-ī-/ <*-denominative -*ye: e.g. *f īnio* 'limit' (cf. *f īnis* 'end'). But also original stems in -*ye-: *venio* 'come' (<*g^{w}en-ye-).

---

[22] The presence of /-Ø-/ is usually associated with root vowel lengthening. The reasons for this and the relevant morpho-phonological rule governing this process are not discussed here (see Sihler (1995: 582, Calabrese (2013, 2019) for discussion).

In this way, thematic perfects such as those in (78) developed[23]:

(78) am-ā-v-ī
fīn-ī-v-i

Assuming that the thematic vowels were just ornamental phonology as discussed above, a crucial development in the history of Latin is then the change by which the v-forming derivatives such as /-*eye-/, /-*ye-/, /-*eH₁-/, etc., lost their functional motivation as exponents of v⁰ and became purely structural elements representing "ornamental" pieces inserted by the rule in (13)/(43):

(79)

In contrast, in the case of PIE underived verbs, there was no overt piece between root and aspectual exponent in all forms of the verb. These are the verbs that as mentioned above gave rise to the third (irregular) conjugation. What appears to have happened in the case of these verbs is that they acquired a thematic vowel unless there was a root conditioned exponent in Asp⁰. So, the verbs of the third conjugation have a thematic vowel in the forms such as the following[24]:

---

23 The thematic vowel /-ī-/ was shortened after roots such *cap*, giving rise to the third i-conjugation. I will not discuss this process here.
24 Morr Halle (2018) observes that the thematic vowel that appears in the infectum forms of the third conjugation shares properties both with the vowel /- ā-/ of the first conjugation and with the vowel /-ī-/ of the fourth conjugation and of the third i-conjugation. On the one hand, like /- ā-/, it deletes before initial suffixes (*am-ā-ō→amō*, cf. *duc-TV-ō →ducō*, vs. *mon-ē-ō→moneō*, *aud-ī-ō →audiō*, *cap-ī-ō →capiō*). On the other hand, like /-ī-/, it triggers the insertion of an ornamental piece /-ē-/ in the imperfect indicative (*aud-ī-ē-bam →audiēbam*, *cap-ī-ē-bam →capiēbam*, cf. *duc-TV-ē-bam →ducēbam*, vs. *am-ā-bam*, vs. *mon-ē-bam*) and it selects /-ē-/ as an exponent of the future. Halle proposes the following rules to account for the phenomena just discussed:
(i) TV deletion:
[-cons, +back]→Ø/ [__]ₜᵥ -V
(ii) Imperfect Augment:
Ø→ ē / [+high]ₜᵥ __ [b-, -perf., +past]
(iii) Future exponents
/-ē-/ <--> [+fut]/ [+high]ₜᵥ __
/-b-/ <--> [+fut]

(80) dūc-i-mus   dūc-ē-bāmus   dūc-ē-mus   dūc-ā-mus   dūc-e-rēmus   dūc-i-te
Pres. Ind. Imperf. Ind. Fut. Ind. Pres. Subj Imperf. Subj. Imper
dūc-e-re
Inf.

However, a thematic vowel was never inserted if there was a root conditioned exponent in Asp⁰.

(81) Athematic Perfects
dūc-s-īmus   dūc-s-erāmus   dūc-s-erimus   dūc-s-erīmus   dūc-s-issemus
(dūximus)[25]   (dūxerāmus)   (dūxerimus)   (dūxerīmus)   (dūxissemus)
lēg-Ø-i   lēg-Ø-erāmus   lēg-Ø-erimus   lēg-Ø-erīmus   lēg-Ø-issemus

If the thematic vowel had been inserted in this case, the adjacency required for these exponents would have been lost, and they would have been replaced by the regular A exponent /-v-/. Given that this did not happen, we have to assume that roots of third conjugation verbs were analyzed as having the diacritic [-TV]; therefore, they were considered to be exceptions to the TV insertion rule in the Perfect.

These innovations from PIE to Latin lead to a situation in which there was irregularity in the athematic forms and regularity in the thematic forms. The presence of the TV involved regular morphology. The thematic vowel appears in all cases where there is no root-conditioned contextual allomorphy. If there is root-conditioned contextual allomorphy, then there is no TV. Again, we can assume that this follows from the fact that only in this case, the aspectual node can access the root diacritics needed for the application of the specific VIs.

Note that forms were not simply preserved in the passage from PIE to Latin. There was a major redistribution of exponents so that the use of /-s-/ was extended to new verbs. For example, this is what we find in the following cases

---

The special behavior of the third conjugation thematic vowel can be captured if it involves a [+high] and [+back] vowel, i.e. [ɨ], which would be deleted by (i) and triggers the application of (ii) and (iii). When it occurred before a consonant, and therefore it was not deleted, this would be fronted by the rule in (iv) (cf. *dūcimus, dūcite*; the /e/ in *dūceremus, dūcere* is accounted for by an independently needed rule lowering short [i] before rhotics.:
(iv)   [-round]→[-back]/ [__, -low]
If this analysis is correct, one can propose that the verbs of the third (irregular) conjugation acquired the thematic vowel [ɨ] in the *infectum*.
25 The diacritic [-TV] was extended to the most of the roots of second and third i- conjugations and also to some roots of the other conjugations (cf.(50)). The reasons for this extensions are unclear to me. Further research is needed on this point.

where the Ø-allomorph of the Perfect aspect is replaced by the /-s-/, especially when there is a prefixal element. Crucially the redistribution occurred only in athematic constructions:

(82) Redistribution of the exponents in athematic contexts:
    a. *iungō* *iunxī*   (<*iugī*, cf. *vincō/vicī, frango/frēgi, rumpo/rūpī*)
       pingō *pinxī*   (<*pigī*)
       fingō *finxī*   (<*figī*)
       pangō *panxī/pepigī*

If there was a prefixal element:
    b. *momordī* *praemorsī* (< *prae-mord-*)
       peperci   *compersī*   (< *con-perd-*)
       pupugī   *compunxī* (< *con-pung-*)
       pepulī   *expulsī*   (< *ex-pulg-*)
    c. *ēmī*   *dempsī*   (< *de-em-*)
       iēcī   *amixī*   (< *ami-iac-*)
       lēgī   *intellexī* (< *inter-leg-*)

Observe that given that verbal derivatives such as /-*eye-/, /-*ye-/, /-*eH₁-/, etc., could occur with aspectual exponents, if root adjacency did not matter, one could expect the development of forms in which a root conditioned allomorph such as /-s-/ could appear with a derivative, and eventually a TV. No such a development took place in Latin. Whereas there are cases in which regular /-v-/ can be found in athematic contexts, there are no cases in which /-s-/ was extended to thematic contexts, despite the presence of surface forms that display the sequence ī-s-ī (cf. *divīsī* <*divid-s-ī*), *mīsī* (<*mitt-s-ī*), *rīsī* (<*rid-s-ī*)[26]:

(83) *moneō* *monuī*
      volō   *voluī*
      domō   *domuī*
      saliō   *saluī*
      aperiō *aperuī*
      rapiō   *rapuī*

(84) †*sal-ī-s-ī*, †*trap-ī-s-ī*

---

26 † indicates that such forms were never attested.

Notice that nothing in principle could have prevented /-s-/ to appear with a thematic vowel. However, the prediction is that if that had happened, /-s-/ also should have become a regular, non-root conditioned exponent.[27] This did not happen. The exponent /-s-/ remained root-conditioned, and therefore its presence required a local configuration, i.e., node adjacency. It follows that it could be found only in athematic forms

(85) Locality in Latin Verbs

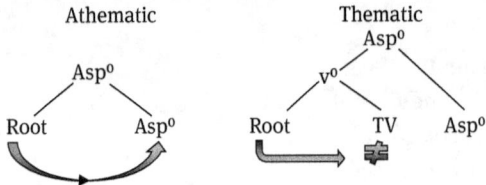

This holds also for /-Ø-/. It thus also follows that allomorphic complexity, the possibility of multiple root conditioned exponents for ASP is restricted to cases in which ASP is adjacent to the root node, i.e. in athematic contexts.

Note that in all of these diachronic developments, the actual forms changed, they were not preserved: there was no preservation of actual forms, what was preserved, however, was a structural property: complex root-conditioned allomorpy was possible only under adjacency with the root.

6 From Latin to Romance perfects

As shown in Calabrese (2016a), the changes leading to the Romance perfects appear to respect this principle. Putting aside the case in which athematic verbs became thematic, i.e., regular, (86), the following changes occurred in Italian (87)

(86) A number of verbs lost the diacritic preventing TV insertion. Thus they became thematic, and displayed regular morphology in the past.

exigere	*exēgī*	-->	*esigere esigei/esigetti*
potere	*potuī*		*potere potei*
debere	*debuī*		*dovere dovei/dovetti*
etc.			

---

[27] This may have actually happened in Classical Greek (see Calabrese (2019)).

(87) Morphological Changes:
a. Redistribution of the exponents of the vocabulary items – where the exponent
/-Ø-/ was replaced by either /-s-/ or /-v-/

accendere	accend-Ø-ī	-->	accend-s-i	Italian: accesi
legere	lēg-Ø-ī	-->	leg-s-i	lessi
absolvere	absolv-Ø-ī	-->	absol-s-i	absolsi
respondēre	respond-Ø-ī	-->	respond-s-i	risposi
movēre	mōv-Ø-ī	-->	mov-s-i	mossi
venīre	vēn-Ø-ī	-->	ven-u-i	venni
bibere	bib-Ø-ī	-->	bib-u-i	bevvi,

etc.

b. Loss of MP Rules. Reduplication was eliminated .The null exponent /-Ø-/ characteristic of the reduplicated forms was replaced by /-s-/ or /-v- /

mordere	momordī	-->	morsi
currere	cucurrī	-->	cursi
cadere	cecidī	-->	cadui

In the same way, new creations with suffixal /-s-/[28] are found in all other Italo-Romance varieties that have synthetic perfect forms. Crucially, if a new form is created, /-s-/ is attached directly to the root in an athematic construction. For example, one has developments such as the following ones:

(88) Tuscan dialects: *volsi* (< *vol-s-i*) 'turn', *salsi* (< *sal-s-i*) 'clim', *ʃersi* (< *ʃeʎ-s-i*) 'choose', *sensi* (< *sent-s-i*) 'feel', *morse* (< *mor-s-i*) 'die', *viense*, (< *ven-s-i*) 'come'

Umbrian: *krese* (< *kred-s-i*) 'believe', *tienzi* (< *ten-s-i*) 'hold', *morze* (< *mor-s-i*) 'die'

Salentino: *wesi/ose*(< *ol-i*) 'want', *krise* (< *kred-s-i*) 'believe', *morse* (< *mor-s-i*) 'die'.

From what we see in (87) and (88), we can conclude that irregular morphology in Italo-Romance varieties is restricted only to athematic constructions, as expected in the theory developed in this paper. Only in these type of constructions, in fact, do we have the local structural configuration that allows root-

---

[28] See Calabrese (2016a), for examples involving the other root-conditioned exponents of the Latin perfect in other Italo-Romance varieties. As expected they appear only in in athematic constructions.

conditioned contextual allomorphy. Therefore, only regular morphology is possible when the verbal thematic vowels is present.

It is important to observe that there are indeed cases in which the special suffix /-s-/ is found in thematic constructions. Crucially in this case, it has become the regular exponent of the perfect (Rohlfs (1968)) Thus, the suffix /-s-/ is found with regular verbs such as 'eat', 'sing', and 'think' in these varieties:

(89) Colle Sannita:
    vənize 'he came'
    morize 'he died'
    təneze 'he kept'
    fatʃeze 'he did'
    maɲɲaze 'he ate'

Melfi: kantaze 'he sang'

San Bartolomeo in Galdo: fatʃeze 'he did'
    ditʃeze 'he said'
    penzese 'he thought'
    vendikeze 'he avenged'

Despite the phonological diversity, we observe preservation across Romance[29] of the morphological system of Latin. Thus, in the development of Romance perfect forms there is essentially preservation of the morphological properties of the Latin perfect system: Irregularity in the athematic forms/ regularity in the thematic forms. Crucially, we are not dealing with a preservation of forms, but of structural properties: contextual allomorphy is found only in local configurations. Despite all of the morphological restructuring we have observed in 4 millennia of history from PIE to Romance, root-conditioned contextual allomorphy in verbal forms has remained possible only in positions adjacent to the root.

7 Conclusions

As discussed by Kiparsky (1986), historical changes in grammatical structures provide the best "window" on the actual composition of these structure in so far as we expect that the components of the structures play a role in the changes.

---

[29] In fact, this is not restricted to Italo-Romance. As argued in Calabrese (2016a), the dichotomy: irregularity in the athematic forms/ regularity in the thematic forms is a characteristic feature of all Romance varieties.

The morphological changes we observe in the historical development of the Perfect from PIE to Romance are most adequately accounted when analyzed in terms of morphosyntactic structures involving morphemes such as roots, thematic vowels, aspect and tense whose interactions are governed by a simple locality principle involving adjacency. If this analysis is correct, it provides further support to theories stating that all morphological interactions are local (cf. Bobaljik (2012), Embick (2010), Moskal (2015), a.o.).[30] Obviously only further research on other branches of Indo-European, on other phenomena and other language families will show that adjacency truly governs allomorphic interactions.

References

Anderson, Stephen. 1992a. *A-Morphous Morphology*. Cambridge: Cambridge University Press

Anderson, Stephen. 1992b. Morphological Change. In Frederick Newmeyer (ed.), *Linguistics: The Cambridge Survey*. Cambridge: Cambridge University Press. 324–363.

Aronoff, Mark. 1976. *Word Formation in Generative Grammar*. Cambridge, MA: MIT Press.

Aronoff, Mark. 1994. *Morphology by-Itself: Stems and Inflectional Classes*. Cambridge, MA: MIT Press.

Bermúdez-Otero, Ricardo. 2013. The Spanish lexicon stores stems with theme vowels, not roots with inflectional class features. *Probus* 25(1):3–103.

Bertocci, Davide. Forthcoming. Quasi-thematic stems in Latin: towards a syntactic analysis of the Latin verbal classes. Ms. University of Padova.

Bertocci, Davide. 2017. Latin 1st class -ā- verbs as thematic formations: on the deficiency of IE roots. In *Proceedings of the 18° International Conference on Latin linguistics, Toulouse 2015*. In "Pallas. Revue d'études antiques", 2017.

Bobaljik, Jonathan David. 2000. The ins and outs of contextual allomorphy. In Kleanthes K. Grohmann & Caro Struijke (eds), *Proceedings of the Maryland Mayfest on Morphology 1999*, 35–71. University of Maryland Working Papers in Linguistics 10.

Bobaljik, Jonathan David. 2012. *Universals in Comparative Morphology: Suppletion, Superlatives and the Structure of Words*. Cambridge, MA: MIT Press.

Burrow, Thomas. 1955. *The Sanskrit language*. London: Faber and Faber.

Calabrese, Andrea. 2008. On absolute and contextual syncretism. Remarks on the structure of paradigms and on how to derive it. In Andrew Nevins and Asef Bachrach (eds.), *The bases of Inflectional Identity*, 156–205. Oxford: Oxford University Press.

Calabrese, Andrea. 2011. Investigations on Markedness, Syncretism and Zero Exponence in Morphology. *Morphology* 21(2): 283–325.

Calabrese, Andrea. 2012. Allomorphy in the Italian Passato Remoto: A Distributed Morphology Analysis. *Language and Information Society*, 1–75. Sogang University, Korea.

---

[30] These theories may vary with respect to the exact conditions under which locality occurs (see Calabrese (2019) for an attempt to account for all known cases of local morphemic interactions in terms of adjacency)

Calabrese, Andrea. 2013. The irregular forms of the Italian "Passato Remoto": A synchronic and diachronic analysis. In Sergio Bauuw, Frank. Drijkoningen, Luisa Meroni and Manuela Pinto (eds), *Romance Languages and Linguistic Theory 2011. Selected Papers from "Going Romance" Utrecht 2011*, 17–58. Amsterdam: John Benjamins.

Calabrese, Andrea. 2015. Locality effects in Italian Verbal Morphology. In Di Domenico, E., Hamann, C. & Matteini, S. (eds.), *Structures, Strategies and Beyond: Studies in honor of Adriana Belletti*. Amsterdam: John Benjamins, 97–132.

Calabrese, Andrea. 2016a. Irregular Morphology and Athematic Verbs in Italo-Romance. *Isogloss* 1: 71–102.

Calabrese, Andrea. 2016b. On the morphophonology of Metaphonic Alternations in Altamurano. In Francesc Torres-Tamarit, Kathrin Linke and Marc van Oostendorp (eds.), *Approaches to Metaphony in the Languages of Italy*. Berlin: Mouton De Gruyter.

Calabrese, Andrea. 2019. *Morphophonological Investigations* Ms., University of Connecticut.

Embick, David. 2010. *Localism versus Globalism in Morphology and Phonology*. Cambridge, MA: MIT Press.

Embick, David. 2013. Morphemes and Morphophonological Loci. In Ora Matushansky and Alec Marantz (eds), *Distributed Morphology Today. Morphemes for Morris Halle*, 151–166. Cambridge, MA: MIT Press.

Embick, David and Morris Halle. 2004. The Latin conjugation. Ms., University of Pennsylvania and MIT.

Embick, David and Morris Halle. 2005. On the status of stems in morphological theory. In Twan Geerts, Ivo van Ginneken and Haike Jacobs (eds), *Romance languages and linguistic theory 2003*, 59–88. Amsterdam: John Benjamins.

Embick, David and Rolf Noyer. 2001. Movement Operations after Syntax. *Linguistic Inquiry* 32 (4): 555–595.

Embick, David, and Alec Marantz. 2008. Architecture and blocking. *Linguistic Inquiry* 39(1): 1–53.

Ernout, Alfred. 1989. *Morphologie historique du Latin*. Paris: Klincksieck.

Halle, Morris. 1997. Impoverishment and fission. PF: Papers at the Interface. In Benjamin Bruening, Yoonjung Kang, and Martha McGinnis (eds.), *MIT Working Papers in Linguistics 30*, 425–450. Cambridge, MA: MITWPL.

Halle, Morris. 2018. Aspects of the morphophonology of the verb in Latin and in German and English. Linguistic Inquiry. 50.1: 3–12.

Halle, Morris & Marantz, Alec. 1993. Distributed Morphology and the pieces of inflection. In Kenneth Hale & Samuel Jay Keyser (eds.), *The view from Building 20: Essays in linguistics in honor of Sylvain Bromberger*, 111–176. Cambridge, MA: MIT Press.

Kiparsky, Paul. 1986. *Explanation in Phonology*. Dordrecht: Foris.

Maiden, Martin. 2004. Morphological Autonomy and Diachrony. *Yearbook of Morphology* 2004: 137–175.

Maiden, Martin. 2010. Morphophonological Persistence. In Martin Maiden, John Charles Smith, Adam Ledgeway (eds), *The Cambridge History of the Romance Languages*, Vol. 1, 155–215. Cambridge: Cambridge University Press.

Marantz, Alec. 2007. Phases and words. In Sook-Hee Choe (ed.), *Phases in the theory of grammar*, 191–222. Seoul: Dong In.

Matthews, Peter H. 1972. *Inflectional Morphology. A Theoretical Study Based on Aspects of the Latin Verb Conjugation*. Cambridge: Cambridge University Press.

Meiser, Gerhard. 1993. Zur Funktion des Nasalpräsens im Urindogermanischen. In Gerhard Meiser (ed.), *Indogermanica et Italica. Festschrift für H. Rix*, 289–313. Innsbruck: IBS.
Moskal, Beata. 2015. *Domains on the Border: Between Morphology and Phonology*, PhD Dissertation, University of Connecticut.
Noyer, Rolf. 1992. *Features, Positions, and Affixes in Autonomous Morphological Structure*, PhD dissertation, MIT, Cambridge, MA.
Oltra-Massuet, Isabel and Karlos Arregi. 2005. Stress by Structure in Spanish. *Linguistic Inquiry* 36(1): 43–84.
Ringe, Don. 2006. *From Proto-Indo-European to Germanic*. Oxford: Oxford University Press.
Rix, Helmut. 1986. *Zur Entstehung des Urindogermanisches Modussystems*. Innsbruck: IBS.
Rix, Helmut et al. 2001. *Lexicon der indogermanischen Verben*. Wiesbaden: Reichert.
Sihler, Andrew. 1995. *New Comparative Grammar Greek and Latin*. Oxford: Oxford University Press.
Stump, Gregory. 2001. *Inflectional Morphology. A Theory of Paradigm Structure*. Cambridge: Cambridge University Press
Szemerényi, Oswald. 1990. *Introduction to Indo-European Linguistics*. Oxford: Oxford University Press.

Anna Cardinaletti and Giuliana Giusti
Multiple agreement in Southern Italian dialects

1 Introduction

In Southern Italian varieties of Sicily, Calabria and Apulia, motion verbs enter multiple agreement constructions like the ones listed in (1), in which V1 and V2 are inflected for the same Person and Tense features[1]:

(1) a. vɔ 'maɲdʒə   (Martina Franca, Apulia, Manzini & Savoia 2005: 690)
        go.1p.sg eat.1p.sg
    b. va[japp]igghio u pani   (Marsala, Sicily, Cardinaletti & Giusti 2003: 32)
        go.1p.sg *a* fetch.1p.sg the bread
    c. vinni mu ti viju   (Southern Calabria, Rohlfs 1969: 103)
        come.past.1p.sg *mu* you.cl eat.1p.sg
    d. vau ku m'maɲdʒu   (Mesagne, Apulia, Manzini & Savoia 2005: 692)
        go.1p.sg *ku* eat.1p.sg

As noted since Rohlfs (1969: §761, §788, §789), the three connecting elements in (1b–d) have a different diatopic distribution. *A* is attested in Sicily and Apulia,[2] *mu* and its variants *mi, ma, u* and *i* are restricted to north-eastern Sicily and Calabria,[3] while *ku* is restricted to Apulia.

---

[1] We report the data as they are found in the literature. The transcription of the examples will therefore not be consistent throughout the paper.
[2] Rohlfs (1969: §761) reports that the inflected construction has a wider distribution across the dialects of Italy, especially in the imperative. This is outside the scope of this paper.
[3] The following examples illustrate some variants of the linker *mu*:
(i) a. vaju i pigghiu u pani   (Roghudi, Calabria, Maesano 2016)
        go.1p.sg *i* fetch.1p.sg the bread

Note: This paper is dedicated to Rita, a senior sister linguist for us. We have known Rita's name since our very first year of classes, as her paper on control was part of the syllabus of our introduction to linguistics at Ca' Foscari, 1980–81, taught by Guglielmo Cinque. Reading and trying to understand that paper was probably our first experience of theoretical argumentation; and knowing that it was by an Italian, and a young woman, was certainly of stimulus for us to entertain our own professional career.

Anna Cardinaletti and Giuliana Giusti, Ca' Foscari University of Venice

https://doi.org/10.1515/9781501505201-008

In their broad account of Italian dialects, Manzini & Savoia (2005) discuss all constructions in (1) and treat (1a–b) as "aspectual constructions with finite verbs" (see Volume 1: 688–701) and (1c–d) as "subjunctive in place of infinitives" (see Volume 1: 650–673). Other authors have limited their attention to one of the constructions. Cases like (1b) are analysed by Cardinaletti & Giusti (2001, 2003) for Sicilian and Ledgeway (2016) for Apulia; cases like (1c) are analysed by Chillà (2011) for Calabrian; cases like (1d) are analysed by Calabrese (1993) for Salentino. Cases like (1a) are mentioned in all works.

In all of these works, two generalizations emerge. First, it is often the case that more than one construction in (1) can coexist in one and the same variety (often together with the infinitive on V2). For instance, Cardinaletti & Giusti (2003: 374) note that the Sicilian dialect of Milazzo displays both *a* and *mi*; Manzini & Savoia (2005: 691–2) provide examples from the Apulian dialect of Mesagne where both *a* and *ku* are possible. Second, the constructions in (1) have a different degree of restructuring: when tested against the properties in (2), (1a–b) display monoclausal behaviour, while (1c–d) have a biclausal structure:

(2) a. Restricted class of V1
    b. Restrictions on Person and Tense
    c. Possible reduced morphology on V1 or on V2
    d. Presence / absence of arguments of V1
    e. Anaphoric vs. disjoint reference of the subject of V2
    f. Presence / absence of clitic climbing onto V1

The aim of this paper is to apply the diagnostics in (2) in order to distinguish systematically among the constructions in (1) from a structural point of view, as outlined in (3). As in Cardinaletti & Giusti (2001: 374), we call (3a) the "Inflected construction" to capture the fact that V1 is parasitically inflected on the features of V2 (which we express by suggesting that V1 is merged in *t*, a head immediately higher than T), and (3b) the "Finite construction" to capture the fact that V1 selects a reduced subordinate clause (FinP) with an independent TP (parallel to the type of subordinate clause found in Balkan

---

    b.   vaju u cattu u pani   (Siderno, Calabria, Maesano 2016)
         go.1p.sg *u* fetch.1p.sg the bread
    c.   vaju mi pigghiu u pani   (Milazzo, Sicily, Cardinaletti & Giusti 2001: 374)
         go.1p.sg *mi* fetch.1p.sg the bread

languages which replaces infinitival constructions, cf. Calabrese 1993). Multiple agreement thus arises in different ways in the two constructions[4]:

(3) a. [$_{tP}$ V1 [a [$_{TP}$ V2 [$_{VP}$ ~~V2~~   (Inflected construction)
    b. [$_{TP}$ V1 [$_{VP}$ ~~V1~~ [$_{FinP}$ mu / ku [$_{TP}$ V2 [$_{VP}$ ~~V2~~   (Finite construction)

Our second aim is to provide a more general picture of their diatopic distribution and observe how the structures in (3) can be entered by other verbal elements such as aspectuals and modals.

The connecting element in (1b) triggers Raddoppiamento sintattico (RS) on V2. This has also been discussed for the Apulian dialects by Ledgeway (2016), as in (4a). When the connecting element is absent, its presence can be detected by the presence of RS, as in (4b):

(4) a. vok a ffattsə   (Putignano, Apulia, Ledgeway 2016)
       go.1p.sg *a* do.1p.sg
    b. lu va ffazzu   (Mesagne, Apulia, Ledgeway 2016)
       it.cl go do.1p.sg

In (1a), no RS on V2 is found. Thus, the connecting element is truly missing. The presence of *a* can be optional, as is the case of Enna. *A* in (5a) triggers RS; in (5b) *a* is absent, and no RS is found[5]:

(5) a. vaju / vignu a ppigliu u pani.   (Enna, Sicily, Di Caro 2015: 84)
       go.1p.sg / come.1p.sg *a* fetch.1p.sg the bread
    b. vaju / vignu pigliu u pani   (Enna, Sicily, Di Caro 2015: 84)
       go.1p.sg / come.1p.sg fetch.1p.sg the bread

Absence of the connecting element as in (1a) will be shown to arise in either construction in (3).

---

[4] As discussed in detail by Cardinaletti & Giusti (2001, 2003) and Ledgeway (2016), the Inflected construction is not a coordination structure although the connecting element *a* is diachronically related to the Latin conjunction AC. Cardinaletti & Giusti (2001: 374, 409, fn. 3) also exclude that the Inflected construction is a serial verb construction because of the lack of object sharing between V1 and V2 and the presence of the connecting element *a*. Manzini and Savoia (2005: 701) envisage the possibility that the Inflected construction be a serial verb construction (also see Cruschina 2013).

[5] In the dialect of Marsala, lack of *a* without RS is only found in the imperative form (Cardinaletti & Giusti 2001: 412, fn. 19).

2 Lexical and morphological restrictions

2.1 Restrictions on V1

Being merged in one and the same clause as the lexical verb V2, V1 in the Inflected construction qualifies as a functional verb. Its functional status correlates with a restriction on the type of verbs that can appear as V1. In western Sicily, the Inflected construction is possible with the most basic andative verbs (6a). In central Sicily, the Inflected construction also allows for two aspectual verbs, (6b). The most restricted distribution is found in Apulia where the Inflected construction is limited to *go, stand* and *want* (6c)[6]:

(6) a. Marsala (Western Sicily) (Cardinaletti & Giusti 1998, 2001, 2003):
motion verbs: go, come, send, come by.
b. Delia (Central Sicily) (Di Caro 2015):
motion verbs: go, come, send, come by, come back;
aspectual verbs: come back (= do again), start.
c. Apulia (Manzini & Savoia 2005: 689; Ledgeway 2016):
motion verbs: go (rarely come).
aspectual verbs: go, stand.
modal verbs: want.

The Finite construction is much more productive in that many more verbs can appear as V1, as already noted by Calabrese (1993) for Salentino and Manzini & Savoia (2005) for Calabrian. In the detailed overview of three geographically adjacent Southern Calabrian dialects (in the province of Reggio Calabria), Maesano (2016) reports that the Finite construction can be selected by most motion verbs and, in addition, by most aspectual and modal verbs (7a). For the Finite construction with *ku* in the Apulian dialects, Manzini & Savoia (2005) provide examples with verbs of the three classes listed in (7b):

(7) a. Galati/Roghudi (Southern Calabria) (Maesano 2016):
motion verbs: go, come, send, come by, come back, go out, go down, go up, run, come in, jump, arrive, stretch out, hurry up;
aspectual verbs: start, begin, finish, try, keep;
modal verbs: want, can, must.

---

[6] Cardinaletti and Giusti (2001: 372) define motion verbs occurring in the Inflected construction as "semi-lexical", namely "lexical categories merged as functional heads". This is to capture the fact that they preserve the andative meaning while losing the goal argument (*ibid.*: 392f).

b. Alliste, Carmiano, Copertino, Mesagne, Nociglia, Torre Santa Susanna (Apulia) (Manzini & Savoia 2005: 653–656, 692–695):
motion verbs: go, come, sit;
aspectual verbs: begin, stay, try;
modal verbs: want, must.

As already noted by Calabrese (1993) for Salentino (8), the Finite construction is also possible as the complement of lexical verbs and alternates with the full finite clause introduced by *ka* 'that'. The same is true for Calabrian dialects (9) with *mi*:[7]

(8) a. speru lu Karlu ku bbene kray   (Salentino, Apulia, Calabrese 1993: 46)
hope.1p.sg the Karlu *ku* come.3p.sg tomorrow
b. speru ka lu Karlu ene kray   (Salentino, Apulia, Calabrese 1993: 46)
hope.1p.sg *ka* the Karlu come.3p.sg tomorrow

(9) a. pensu mi partu dumani.   (Roghudi, Calabria, D. Maesano, p.c.)
think.1p.sg *mi* leave.1p.sg tomorrow
b. pensu ca partu dumani.   (Roghudi, Calabria, D. Maesano, p.c.)
think.1p.sg *ca* leave.1p.sg tomorrow

The restrictions seen in (6), which are typical of functional verbs, support the peculiar monoclausal analysis proposed in (3a). In each variety, only a few verbs are lexically marked for the possibility of being merged as the head of *t*P, a functional projection higher than TP whose head copies the featural specification of T, which we take to be a bundle of features including subject Agreement (Agr).[8] The full productivity of the Finite construction in (7)–(9) supports the biclausal analysis proposed in (3b).

---

[7] The finite construction is also found in other environments, such as adverbial and relative clauses, which will not be discussed here (also see Chillà 2011).

[8] Ledgeway (2016) criticizes Cardinaletti & Giusti (2003) by saying that their hypothesis of a low AgrP is in conflict with hypotheses on the location of AgrP in current syntactic theory (Cinque 1999). In that paper on page 36, we show that the lexical verb V2 raises to its usual surface position preceding floating quantifiers and adverbs (Agr/T, which in Sicilian is as high as in Italian) and suggest that the motion verb is first-merged immediately higher than that position. No low AgrP is suggested in Cardinaletti & Giusti (2003) (or here). On the contrary, a high merger of V1 parasitically copying the Agr/T features of V2 is proposed by us. Ledgeway's criticism actually applies to his own proposal which will be provided in (28b) below, where V2 carrying [+Agr] remains inside VP and the Agr position in the clause is filled by V1 which actually carries a [-Agr] feature.

Strong support for this analysis comes from the observation that the Finite construction refers to two different events, while the Inflected construction has single event interpretation. By stating (10a) with the Inflected construction, the speaker not only claims that she goes to buy chicory but, crucially, that she actually buys it every day. For this reason, the continuation which implies that the event of buying has not taken place is ungrammatical. This is not the case in the infinitival construction in Marsalese (10b) and in the Finite construction in Leccese (10c), where the two verbs have separate Tenses (also cf. Cardinaletti & Giusti 2001: 386–8)[9]:

(10) a. Vaju a accattu a cicoria gnignornu (*ma unn'a trovu mai).
(Marsala, Sicily)
go.1p.sg *a* buy.1p.sg the chicory every day (but not it.cl find.1p.sg never)
b. Vaju a accattari a cicoria gnignornu (ma unn'a trovu mai).
(Marsala, Sicily)
go.1p.sg to buy.inf the chicory every day (but not it.cl find.1p.sg never)
'I go to buy chicory every day, but I can never find any.'
c. Au cu cattu le cecore ogne giurnu (ma nu le trou mai).
(Lecce, Apulia, D. Cesiri p.c.)
go.1p.sg *ku* buy.1p.sg the chicories every day (but not them.cl find.1p.sg never)

2.2 Restrictions on person and tense

The Inflected construction displays Person and Tense restrictions which are not found in the Finite construction.

Cardinaletti & Giusti (1998, 2001, 2003) note for the dialect of Marsala that the Inflected construction is possible in the three persons singular (11a,b,c) and in the 3rd person plural of the present indicative (11f) and the 2nd person singular of the imperative (11g). The 1st and 2nd person plural of the indicative (11d, e) and the 2nd person plural of the imperative (11h) are ungrammatical[10]:

---

[9] Manzini & Savoia (2005: 698) observe that the events of the two verbs of the Inflected construction share the same time reference; they however assume a biclausal analysis of the Inflected construction, different from our hypothesis in (3a).
[10] In the dialect of Marsala, as in most other Sicilian dialects, the Inflected construction coexists with the infinitival construction also found in Italian. The persons which are ungrammatical in the Inflected construction can only express the andative meaning with the infinitive on V2, while the other persons display both the Inflected and the infinitival construction.

(11) a. vaju / vegnu / passu / mannu a pigghiu u pani
 b. vai / veni / passi / manni a pigghi u pani
 c. va / vene / passa / manna a pigghia u pani
 d. *imu / *vinimu / *passamu / *mannamu a pigghiamu u pani
 e. *iti / *viniti / *passati / *mannati a pigghati u pani
 f. vannu / vennu / passanu / mannanu a pigghianu u pani
 g. va pigghia u pani
 h. *iti pigghiati u pani
 go / come / come by / send *a* fetch the bread

There are more liberal Sicilian dialects which display the Inflected construction with other persons and tenses. For the dialect of Modica (Sicily), Manzini & Savoia (2015) provide the full pattern in the present and imperfect indicative, and Cruschina (2013: 274, fn. 9) reports to have personally checked that "the paradigm is actually complete". However, he does not provide examples, neither does he specify whether the alleged complete paradigm refers to all moods (including subjunctive / conditional, infinitival and gerund) and all tenses (including compound tenses). If the dialect of Modica presents the same situation as Di Caro (2015) reports for the dialect of Aci, another eastern Sicilian variety, Cruschina's complete pattern should be intended as being limited to simple finite tenses.[11]

The general picture obtained from these works is that the Inflected construction manifests a mechanism of Person and Tense feature sharing between V1 and V2 which display different morphological patterns in different dialects.

Cruschina (2013: 273) claims that "no morphosyntactic restrictions or semantic principles can be considered responsible for the irregular distribution" of the Inflected construction and reduces the defective paradigm of the Marsalese Inflected construction to a manifestation of Maiden's (2004) N-pattern, which is typical of the morphological organization of verbal paradigms in Romance languages (also see Dressler & Thornton 1991, Thornton 2007). This account is not incompatible with the hypothesis put forth by Cardinaletti & Giusti (2001: 407–409 and 2003: 44) that the less marked forms of the verbal paradigm enter the Inflected construction in Marsalese: 1st, 2nd, 3rd person singular and 3rd person plural of the present indicative plus 2nd person singular of the imperative. In fact, the N-pattern sorts out

---

[11] An Inflected construction with a non-finite V1 is logically possible even if it cannot be detected in Marsalese (cf. Cardinaletti & Giusti 2003: 48, fn. 19). For Apulian dialects, Ledgeway (2016) provides examples with reduced infinitive *sci'* instead of *scire* and reduced past participle *sciu'* instead of *sciuta*, which can only occur when a V2 is also present; thereby, providing a case for the Inflected construction in the infinitive and participle moods.

morphologically less marked forms built on the bare stem of the verb from more marked forms built on the theme and in more complex ways (cf. Thornton 2007).[12]

Many questions arise in Cruschina's purely morphological account. First, since many verbs in Marsalese display the N-pattern, why don't other verbs (e.g. 'go out' or 'stay' and 'sit') enter the Inflected construction as V1? (Note that this is indeed possible in other varieties, see (6) above). Second, why do regular verbs such as *passari* 'come by' and *mannari* 'send' only enter the Inflected construction in the same persons and moods as the verbs which have the morphological N-pattern and not in the whole paradigm (see (11) above)? Third, what is the parameter that allows the complete paradigm in dialects like Modicano (and thus also the persons and tenses outside the N-pattern) but still limits the Inflected construction to very few selected V1s? We believe that a syntactic account is still needed and should complement a morphological account, as also suggested by Corbett (2015: 179–180), who brings the Inflected construction as an example of externally relevant morphological irregularity in a paradigm.

Other issues are raised by the application of morphomic patterns to the Inflected construction across dialects. In the Sicilian dialects of Marsala (12a) and Delia (12b), *viniri* 'come' displays an L-pattern in Maiden's (2005) terms (only 1st person indicative and all persons in the present subjunctive).[13] Yet, the person split in the Inflected construction with this verb singles out the same persons and moods as in the N-pattern in both Marsalese (cf. (11)) and Deliano (Di Caro 2015):

---

[12] "Morphomic paradigms" are classified by Maiden (2004) with the letters of the alphabet that most resemble the shape resulting by highlighting cells of the paradigm realized by a certain allomorph. The 1st, 2nd, 3rd person singular and 3rd person plural of the present indicative plus 2nd person singular of the imperative form an N:

	indicative						imperative	
	1st sg	2nd sg	3rd sg	1st pl	2nd pl	3rd pl	2nd sg	2nd pl
	vaju	vai	va	imu	iti	vannu	va	iti

For the graphic representation of other patterns, see fn. 14 and fn. 15.

[13] The L-pattern is exemplified by Portuguese *poder* 'be able' (Maiden 2004: 149):

	1st sg	2nd sg	3rd sg	1st pl	2nd pl	3rd pl
Indicative	posso	podes	pode	podemos	podeis	podem
Subjunctive	possa	possas	possa	possamos	possais	possam

Note that present subjunctive is independently absent in the dialects of Marsala (Cardinaletti and Giusti 2001: 410, fn. 9), and Delia (Di Caro 2015). Thus, in these dialects, the L-pattern only includes the 1st singular person of the present indicative.

(12) a. vegnu, veni, veni, vinimu, viniti, vennu
   b. vjignu, vjini, veni, vinjimmu, viniti, vjinnu
      come.1p.sg, come.2p.sg, come3p.sg, come.1p.pl, come.2p.pl, come.3p.pl

Furthermore, the aspectual verbs *turnari* 'do again' and *accuminciari* 'begin' in Deliano display different morphomic patterns from one another, yet they enter the Inflected construction only in the 1st person singular and 3rd person plural indicative. These two persons remind us of Maiden's (2005) U-pattern, if we consider that present subjunctive is independently absent in this dialect (see fn. 11)[14]:

(13) a. tuirnu / accuminciu a ddicu
   b. *tuirni / *accuminci a ddici
   c. *torna / *accumincia a ddici
   d. *turnammu / *accuminciammu a ddiciimmu
   e. *turnati / *accuminciati a ddiciti
   f. tornanu / accumincianu a ddicinu
      return / start *a* say

Lack of straight correspondence between the morphomic patterns of the paradigms and the person restrictions in the Inflected construction shows that the former cannot be the only and direct trigger of the latter.

In all the cases discussed above, the verb relevant for morphomic considerations is V1. The dialect of Delia lets us uncover another morphological restriction on the Inflected construction which is unexpected in Cruschina's morphomic account. In Delia, the Inflected construction is also possible in the simple past. However, it undergoes different restrictions from those observed for the present indicative. It is limited to 'go' and 'come' as V1 and is possible in the 1st and 3rd persons singular and plural. This person split is not discussed in Maiden's (2005) overview of morphomic patterns in Romance. Following Di Caro and Giusti (2016), we call it the W-pattern:

---

[14] The U-pattern is exemplified by Old Tuscan *potere* 'be able' and other Central Italian varieties (Maiden 2004: 149):

	1st sg	2nd sg	3rd sg	1st pl	2nd pl	3rd pl
Indicative	posso	puoi	può	potemo	potete	possono
Subjunctive	possa	possa	possa	possiamo	possiate	possano

(14) a. jivu / vinni a bbitti
    b. *jisti / *vinìsti a bbidìsti
    c. ji / vinni a bbitti
    d. jammu / vìnnimu a bbìttimu
    e. *jìstivu / *vinìstivu a bbidìstivu
    f. jiru / vìnniru a bbìttiru
       go / come *a* see

Di Caro (2015) also observes that the Inflected construction in the past is only possible in Deliano when both V1 and V2 are "rhyzotonic", namely when the main stress falls on the root. Thus, the morpho-phonological properties of V2 are also relevant:

(15) a. *jivu a mmangiàvu
    b. *jisti a mmangiàsti
    c. *ji a mmangià
    d. *jammu a mmangiàmmu
    e. *jìstivu a mmangiàstivu
    f. *jiru a mmangiàru
       go *a* eat.

Note that the stress on the root also characterizes the relevant forms in the N-pattern. Building on this as well as other properties, Thornton (2007) suggests that the N-pattern should be extended to regular verbs, where the three persons of the singular and the 3rd person plural have a stressed verbal root, while the 1st and 2nd person plural are "arhyzotonic", namely they have an unstressed root. In this hypothesis, any verb can in principle enter the Inflected construction in those varieties that display it. Since this is trivially not the case, further specifications in the lexicon of each variety must be assumed as regards which forms of V1 have the capacity to check their features parasitically on the Tense+Agr features of V2.

In conclusion, the Sicilian facts discussed in this section argue against Cruschina's (2013: 273) assumption that "no morphosyntactic restrictions or semantic principles can be considered responsible for the irregular distribution" of the Inflected construction and suggest that an intricate interaction between syntax and morpho-phonology is at stake.

Whatever the correct syntactic analysis of the peculiar restrictions on V1 (and V2, see (15) in Deliano) in the Inflected construction should be, it is crucial to note that no such restrictions have been pointed out for the Finite Construction in Calabrian and and Apulian dialects (Calabrese 1993, Manzini & Savoia 2005,

Ledgeway 2016, Maesano 2016). This is expected in the biclausal analysis of the Finite construction, in which the superordinate and the subordinate clauses have independent Tenses (see (3b) and (18) below). When the two verbs share the same Agreement features, this is because the subject of V2 is anaphoric to the subject of V1. But the two subjects may also be different, as in (8) above, in which case V1 and V2 expectedly display different person agreement morphology. At this point, it should be clear that in the Finite construction, multiple agreement is only apparent. This is further supported by cases like (16), where the superordinate clause contains an infinitival V1 which displays no agreement at all, while V2 is a subjunctive-like form, namely *u* + indicative:

(16) pozzu iri u'ccattu u pani   (Siderno, Calabria, Maesano 2016)
      can.1p.sg go *u* buy.1p.sg the bread

2.3 Invariant or reduced forms of V1 or V2

V1 and V2 do not always display full inflection for Tense and Agreement. In some dialects, it is possible / obligatory to find reduced inflection on either verb. The Inflected construction allows for a reduced or invariant form of V1 and has full Tense+Agr realization on V2 (17), while the Finite construction allows for a reduced T (but full Agr) on V2 and has full Tense+Agr realization on V1 (18):

(17) a. (Tu) vai/va a pigghi u pani.   (Marsala, Sicily, Cardinaletti & Giusti 2001: 383)
         (you) go.2p.sg/go *a* fetch.2p.sg the bread
     b. lu sta f'fattsu / f'fatʃi / etc.   (Mesagne, Apulia, Manzini & Savoia 2005: 691)
         it.cl stay do.1p.sg / do.2p.sg / etc.
     c. ti sta rispun'nia   (Copertino, Apulia, Manzini & Savoia 2005: 693)
         you.cl stay answer.past.1p.sg

(18) a. u'lia ku 'maɲtʃu   (Alliste, Apulia, Manzini & Savoia 2005: 695)
         want.past.1p.sg *ku* eat.1p.sg
     b. potiva i pigghiu u pani   (Galati, Calabria, Maesano 2016)
         can.past.1p.sg *i* fetch.1p.sg the bread

The patterns in (17) are expected under Cardinaletti & Giusti's (2001, 2003) hypothesis that in the Inflected construction, Agreement and Tense features are checked parasitically by V1 sitting in *t* onto V2 sitting in T, as in (3a) above. If V1 does not have autonomous Tense and Agreement features, it is not implausible that V1 has a more reduced feature realization than V2.

Cardinaletti and Giusti (2001, 2003) report that the only reduced V1 in Marsalese is *va* 'go'. More accurate field work, however, reveals that *viniri* 'come', *passari* 'come by', and *mannari* 'send' also display reduced forms, as represented in the following paradigms which distinguish between elided and invariant forms. Note that in some persons, the two forms cannot be distinguished phonologically, but we have inserted them for completeness. Note also that the invariant forms are not possible in the 1st and 2nd person plural, which never allow the Inflected construction in this dialect, see (11d,e) above:

(19) a. vegn(u) /*ven a pigghiu u pani
　　b. ven(i) / ven a pigghi u pani
　　c. ven(a) / ven a pigghia u pani
　　d. *imu / *ven a pigghiamu u pani
　　e. *iti / *ven a pigghia u pani
　　f. venn(u) /ven a pigghianu u pani

(20) a. pass(u) / pass a pigghiu u pani
　　b. pass(i) / pass a pigghi u pani
　　c. pass(a) / pass a pigghia u pani
　　d. *passam(u) / *pass a pigghiamu u pani
　　e. *passat(i) / *pass a pigghiati u pani
　　f. passan(u) /pass a pigghianu u pani

In both paradigms, it is clear that phonological elision of the ending vowel of V1 triggered by adjacency with the vocalic connecting element *a* is always possible. In the 2nd and 3rd person singular forms of *viniri* in (19b,c) and in the three persons singular of *passari* in (20a,b,c), the elided forms are homophonous to the bare stem, *ven-* and *pass-*, respectively. However, the 1st person singular of *viniri* (19a) shows that only the elided form is possible and not the bare stem. Differently from this, the 3rd person plural forms display both possibilities (19f) and (20f). These data clearly show that phonological reduction should be kept distinct from invariant forms, and that both may be possible in the same persons of the verbal paradigm in one and the same variety. Thus, invariant forms cannot be taken as the final step of grammaticalization due to "inflectional attrition" (Ledgeway 2016) or "phonological erosion" (Cruschina 2013).

The impossibility of the invariant form in (19a) also shows that the availability of invariant / uninflected forms in the dialect is independent of their use in the Inflected construction. This is further confirmed by empirical evidence going in both directions. On the one hand, the dialect of Marsala displays uninflected forms for the present perfect auxiliary *ha* 'have' and the progressive auxiliary *sta* 'stay' (cf. Cardinaletti & Giusti 2001: 384–5); however, *sta* does not enter the Inflected construction. On the other hand, the dialect of Delia displays an invariant form only for the progressive auxiliary *sta* 'stay' and not for *va* 'go' in the Inflected construction (Di Caro 2015). This means that the overt realization of parasitic agreement is mandatory in some dialects (e.g. Delia), optional in others (e.g. Marsala), and impossible in those dialects in which the Inflected construction is only found with the invariant form of 'go' and 'stay' (e.g. Mesagne (17b), cf. Manzini & Savoia 2005: 691–2).

The Finite construction presents a very different picture. As shown in (18), not only is the reduced form on V2 and not on V1, but it is also of a different nature in that it only regards Tense features while Person features are fully realized. The patterns in (18), where V1 is past indicative and V2 is present indicative, are expected if the V2 clause contains a Tense anaphoric to the Tense on V1, as is the case of subjunctives (cf. Calabrese 1993: 46–48 and Manzini & Savoia 2005: 652), and if this anaphoric tense is formed analytically with the morpheme *ku/mu* preceding the forms of the indicative, as suggested by Manzini & Savoia (2005).

Note finally that the patterns in (18) can also be found in the absence of *ku*. Example (18), repeated in (21a), forms a minimal pair with (21b):

(21) a. u'lia ku' maɲtʃu   (Alliste, Apulia, Manzini & Savoia 2005: 695)
         want.past.1p.sg *ku* eat.1p.sg
     b. u'lia 'maɲtʃu   (Alliste, Apulia, Manzini & Savoia 2005: 695)
         want.past.1p.sg eat.1p.sg

The optional realization of *ku* in (21) reminds us of the optional realization of the complementizer in Italian when the subordinate clause contains a subjunctive (or conditional or future indicative) verb (22) (Poletto 2001, Cardinaletti 2004: 129–131, Giorgi & Pianesi 2004):

(22) Credo (che) lo incontri domani.
     think.1p.sg (that) him.cl meet.3p.sg tomorrow

This analysis will be supported by clitic placement discussed in section 3.3.2 below.

3 Syntactic properties

So far, we have illustrated the different morphological properties which characterize V1 in the Inflected construction: we have seen that in some dialects, V1 respects morphomic patterns and that in other dialects, different patterns are found in this construction. We have also seen that V1 may appear in reduced and invariant forms. In what follows, we show that independently of the morphology of V1, the Inflected construction is a unitary syntactic phenomenon that reacts consistently to syntactic diagnostics to detect monoclausal structures (2d–f) and it is different from the Finite construction.

3.1 Presence / absence of arguments of V1

If the Inflected construction is monoclausal with a single VP and a single TP, unlike the Finite construction which has two independent VPs and two independent TPs (see (3)), we expect that V1 behaves like an auxiliary and cannot project its argument structure. This is in fact the case. The Inflected construction does not allow for arguments of V1 (such as locative arguments in (23) and clitic clusters selected by the lexical motion verb 'go' in (24)), while they are possible in the Finite construction (25)–(26)[15]:

(23) a. Va (*agghiri a casa) a mangia.   (Marsala, Sicily, Cardinaletti & Giusti 2001: 377)
go.3p.sg (towards to home) *a* eat.3p.sg
b. Va (*alla scola) ffatìa.   (Lecce, Apulia, Ledgeway 2016)
go.3p.sg (to-the school) work.3p.sg

(24) a. (*Minni) vaju a mangiu.   (Marsala, Sicily, Cardinaletti & Giusti 2001: 377)
(me.cl-from-it.cl) go.1p.sg *a* eat.1p.sg
b. (*Se nde) va ccanta.   (Lecce, Apulia, Ledgeway 2016)
(self.cl-from-it.cl) go.3p.sg sing.1p.sg

---

[15] Daniela Cesiri (p.c.) points out that the form *va* in (23b) and (25b) is not used in the town of Lecce, which displays *ae*, as in (i), but it is used in other Salentino varieties:
(i) a.   Ae (*alla scola) ffatìa.   (Lecce, Apulia)
b.   Ae alla scola cu ffatìa.   (Lecce, Apulia)
go.3p.sg to-the school *ku* work.3p.sg

(25) a. Va a scola i/mi lavora.   (Galati/Roghudi, Calabria, D. Maesano, p.c.)
       go.3p.sg to school *i/mi* work.3p.sg
   b. Va alla scola cu ffatìa.   (Lecce, Apulia, Ledgeway 2016)
       go.3p.sg to-the school *ku* work.3p.sg

(26) a. Sinni va a scola i/mi lavora.   (Galati/Roghudi, Calabria, D. Maesano, p.c.)
       self.cl-from-it.cl go.3p.sg to school work.1p.sg
   b. Se nde va cu ffatìa.   (Salentino, Apulia, D. Cesiri, p.c.)
       self.cl-from-it.cl go.3p.sg *cu* work.1p.sg

It is incorrect to assume a biclausal structure in all cases in which V1 is fully inflected. We thus disagree with Ledgeway's (2016) analysis of Apulian dialects. He claims that in the northern dialects, the inflected V1 (*stoc* in (27a)) selects a CP, as shown in the structural representation in (28a), while in Salentino, the invariant V1 (*sta* in (27b)) gives rise to a monoclausal structure as in (28b):

(27) a. stoc' a ffazzu   (Northern Apulian, Ledgeway 2016)
       stay.1p.sg *a* do.1p.sg
   b. sta ffazzu   (Salentino, Ledgeway 2016)
       stay do.1p.sg

(28) a. [$_{IP}$ AgrP$_i$ STAND/GO$_{[+Agr_i]}$] [$_{v\text{-}VP}$ ~~STAND/GO~~ [$_{CP}$ *a* [$_{IP}$ AgrP$_j$ V$_{[+Agr_j]}$]]]]
   b. [$_{IP}$ AgrP$_i$ STAND/GO$_{[-Agr]}$ [$_{v\text{-}VP}$ V$_{[+Agr_i]}$]]

If the correct analysis of (27a) were (28a), we would expect V1 *stoc* to behave as a lexical verb and therefore occur with its arguments on a par with (25)–(26), something which Ledgeway does not illustrate and to our knowledge is unattested. We analyze both (27a) and (27b) as instances of the Inflected construction, with a monoclausal structural analysis as in (3a) above. This analysis is supported by the clitic placement facts discussed in Section 3.3.1 below.

3.2 Anaphoric vs. disjoint reference of the subject of V2

As already observed in (8), the *ku* construction has an independent subject position, which can but does not have to be anaphoric to the subject of the main predicate:

(29) a. oyyu ku mme ne bbau (Salentino, Apulia, Calabrese 1993: 44)
       want.1p.sg *ku* me.cl from-it.cl go.1p.sg
    b. oyyu ku bbene krai (Salentino, Apulia, Calabrese 1993: 34)
       want.1p.sg *ku* come.3p.sg

Different subjects and hence different agreement morphology on V1 and V2 are never possible in the Inflected construction, even in the case of 'send' as V1, whose causative meaning implies that the causer is necessarily different from the external argument of V2:

(30) a. mannu a pigghiu u pani (Marsala, Sicily, Di Caro & Giusti 2016)
       send.1p.sg *a* fetch.1p.sg the bread
    b. *mannu a pigghia u pani
       send.1p.sg *a* fetch.3p.sg the bread

The grammaticality is reversed in the Finite construction in (31). Coreference of the two subjects is impossible due to the meaning of 'send' (31a); V1 and V2 necessarily display different subjects and hence different agreement morphology in (31b)[16]:

(31) a. *mandu cu pigghiu lu pane (Lecce, Apulia, D. Cesiri, p.c.)
       send.1p.sg *ku* fetch.1p.sg the bread
    b. mandu figghiama cu pigghia lu pane (Lecce, Apulia, D. Cesiri, p.c.)
       send.1p.sg daughter-my *ku* fetch.3p.sg the bread

Cliticization in (32) shows that *figghiama* 'my daughter' in (31b) is the accusative object of V1, confirming that V1 in the Finite construction has full argument structure (see section 3.1)[17]:

(32) la mandu cu pigghia lu pane (Lecce, Apulia, D. Cesiri p.c.)
     her.cl send.1p.sg *ku* fetch.3p.sg the bread

---

16 If the external argument of V2 is not expressed, the infinitival construction should be used:
(i)   Mandu pigghiare lu pane (Lecce, Apulia, D. Cesiri, p.c.)
      send.1p.sg fetch.inf the bread

17 In (32), *cu* may be missing, as already noted for the complement of 'want' in (21) above:
(i)   La mandu pigghia lu pane. (Lecce, Apulia, D. Cesiri p.c.)
      her.cl send.1p.sg fetch.3p.sg the bread

Note that (32) with 'send' crucially differs from (33) with 'want'. In (33), the strong pronoun *iḍḍa* 'she' is the subject of V2 and not the object of V1, hence it cannot be cliticized (33b):

(33) a. oyyu iḍḍa ku bbene krai   (Salentino, Apulia, Calabrese 1993: 36)
         want.1p.sg she *ku* come.3p.sg tomorrow
     b. *la oyyu ku bbene krai   (Salentino, Apulia, Calabrese 1993: 36)
         her.cl want.1p.sg *ku* fetch.3p.sg the bread

Note that the position of the subject of V2 in (33) is above *ku* (34a). This makes the Finite construction different from the embedded clause introduced the complementizer *ka*, which occurs above the subject position (see (8) above). The same holds of Calabrian *(m)u* in (34b):

(34) a. oju {lu Maryu} ku {*lu Maryu} bbene   (Salentino, Apulia, Calabrese
                                                    1993: 34)
         want.1p.sg {the Maryu} *ku* {the Maryu} come.3p.sg tomorrow
     b. vogghiu {Giuvanni} u {*Giuvanni} parta   (Calabrian, Chillà 2011: 25)
         want.1p.sg {Giuvanni} *u* {Giuvanni} come.3p.sg tomorrow

Following Calabrese (1993: 36), we take the subject to be in the usual preverbal subject position, where it receives nominative case (see the ungrammaticality of (33b)). The connecting element *ku* / *mu* thus occurs in a position of the IP field, which Roberts & Roussou (2003) takes to be MoodP, the same position as infinitival *to* in English and subjunctive *na* in Greek.

3.3 The position of object clitic pronouns

Since clitic pronouns target the first T-layer above them, they provide a good diagnostics of the presence or absence of an independent T. The diagnostics works only in one direction: if we find clitic climbing onto V1, we can be sure that there is no intervening T in the path, as in Italian (35a). If we do not find climbing however, we have no direct indication that there is a lower independent T, as the pronoun may cliticize on the lower verb V2 even in monoclausal constructions, as is the case of infinitival constructions in Italian according to Cinque (2006); see (35b):

(35) a. [TP lo vado [subito [andP V [a [VP prendere
       it.cl go.1p.sg immediately to fetch.inf
    b. [TP vado [subito [andP V [a [VP prenderlo
       go.1p.sg immediately to fetch.inf it.cl

3.3.1 Cliticization on V1

Clitic placement onto V1 only occurs in the Inflected construction with or without the overt connecting element *a*, as in (36a)–(37a) and (36b)–(37b), respectively:

(36) a. u vaju a pigghiu   (Marsala, Sicily, Cardinaletti & Giusti 2001: 388)
       it.cl go.1p.sg *a* fetch.1p.sg
    b. u 'vəju 'cəmu   (Umbriatico, Calabria, Manzini & Savoia 2005: 695)
       it.cl go.1p.sg call.1p.sg

(37) a. lu 'vɔɟɟ a v'veku   (Monteparano, Apulia, Manzini & Savoia 2005: 692)
       it.cl want.1p.sg *a* see.1p.sg
    b. nɔl lu 'vɔɟɟu 'fattsu c'cui   (Torre S. Susanna, Apulia, Manzini & Savoia 2005: 693)
       not it.cl want.1p.sg do.1p.sg any-more

Clitic climbing is possible with both agreeing (36)–(38) and invariant V1 (39)–(40):

(38) a. u vok a f'fattsu   (Putignano, Apulia, Manzini & Savoia 2005: 689)
       it.cl go.1p.sg *a* do.1p.sg
    b. u stok a f'fattsə
       it.cl stay.1p.sg *a* do.1p.sg

(39) u va pigghiu   (Marsala, Sicily)
    it.cl go.1p.sg *a* do.1p.sg

(40) a. lu va ffattsu   (Mesagne, Apulia, Manzini & Savoia 2005: 691)
       it.cl go.1p.sg do.1p.sg
    b. lu sta ffattsu   (Mesagne, Apulia, Manzini & Savoia 2005: 691)
       it.cl stay.1p.sg do.1p.sg

The parallel behavior of agreeing and invariant forms confirms that the two cases must be unified under the same syntactic analysis and is further evidence against Ledgeway's biclausal analysis of sentences like (27a) with agreeing forms of V1, as depicted in (28a) above.

3.3.2 Cliticization on V2

In the Finite construction (41), the pronoun follows the connecting element and procliticizes onto V2:

(41) a. vegnu i vi sconzu (Galati, Calabria, Maesano 2016)
come.1p.sg *i* you.cl disturb.1p.sg
b. vi'nia ku llu fattsu (Mesagne, Apulia, Manzini & Savoia 2005: 692)
come.past.1p.sg *ku* you.cl do.1p.sg

(42) a. 'stannu ku sse s'karfane 'l akkwa (Nociglia, Apulia, Manzini & Savoia 2005: 694)
stay.3p.pl *ku* refl.cl warm.3p.sg the water
b. 'vɛnɛ ku llu 'viðe (Nociglia, Apulia, Manzini & Savoia 2005: 694)
come.3p.sg *ku* him.cl see.3p.sg

Apulian dialects provide cases where the connecting element is absent and the clitic pronoun is on V2:

(43) u'lia llu 'fattsu (Carmiano, Apulia, Manzini & Savoia 2005: 693)
volevo lo faccio

This is clearly an instance of the Finite construction because V1 is fully inflected for Agreement and (past) Tense, while V2 appears in the present form, following the pattern seen above in section 2.2. We therefore hypothesize that (43) is a Finite construction without an overt connecting element parallel to what we have independently observed in (21) above for the Apulian dialect of Alliste.

In other cases, however, cliticization on V2 occurs with an invariant V1, which characterizes the Inflected construction and differentiates it from the Finite construction (see section 2.3). Our hypothesis forces us to take the cases in (44) as instances of the Inflected construction:

(44) a. ʃta llu ca'mati (Melissano, Apulia, Manzini & Savoia 2005: 695)
b. 'va lli 'kuntu 'jɔu (Maglie, Apulia, Manzini & Savoia 2005: 694)

Thus, clitic climbing is not an obligatory feature of the Inflected construction but depends on the properties of the language. As seen above in section 3.3.1, clitic climbing is obligatory in Marsalese, but both options are possible in Apulian dialects where microvariation is indeed observed. In particular, while the Salentino dialects south of Lecce (Maglie, Nociglia, Alliste, Melissano) quite robustly show procliticization on V2 (Manzini & Savoia 2005: 694–5), as in (44), the main town Lecce requires climbing to V1 (Daniela Cesiri, p.c.).

This is not unwelcome as it may appear at first sight because optionality of clitic climbing is found in monoclausal constructions in many Romance varieties including Italian as in (44) (cf. Cardinaletti & Shlonsky 2004):

(45) a. lo ha dovuto andare a prendere
        it.cl has had.to go to fetch
    b. ha dovuto andarlo a prendere
        has had.to go it.cl to fetch
    c. ha dovuto andare a prenderlo
        has had.to go to fetch it.cl

In the dialect of Brindisi (Apulia), the modal verb 'want' with the connecting element *a* displays such an optionality. Note that *a* is present in both cases, suggesting that both cases are instances of the Inflected construction:

(46) a. lu vɔl(i) a m'maɲdʒa.   (Brindisi, Apulia, Manzini & Savoia 2005: 693)
        it.cl want.3p.sg *a* do.3p.sg
    b. vɔl(i) a ssi lu 'maɲdʒa   (Brindisi, Apulia, Manzini & Savoia 2005: 693)

Other cases of procliticization on V2, where *a* is missing and V1 and V2 share identical Agreement and Tense morphology, could in principle be ambiguous in those varieties that have both the Inflected and the Finite constructions:

(47) a. 'sta tʃi s'karfa 'l akkwa   (Nociglia, Apulia, Manzini & Savoia 2005: 694)
        stay.3p.sg. there.cl refl.cl warm.3p.sg the water
    b. 'vɛnɛ llu 'viðe   (Nociglia, Apulia, Manzini & Savoia 2005: 694)
        come.3p.sg him.cl see.3p.sg
    c. vu'limu lu vi'timu   (Mesagne, Apulia, Manzini & Savoia 2005: 691)
        want.1p.pl it.cl see.1p.pl

Note finally that the causative verb 'send', which unambiguously enters the Inflected construction in Marsala and unambiguously enters the Finite construction in Calabrian and Apulian, behaves consistently with respect to the diagnostics of clitic climbing. In Marsalese, the object of V2 must procliticize on V1 (48a), while in Calabrian, the object of V2 remains on V2 (48b) (and the obligatory object of V1 procliticizes on V1, see (32) above):

(48) a. u mannu a pigghiu   (Marsala, Sicily, Di Caro & Giusti 2016)
         it.cl send.1p.sg *a* fetch.1p.sg
     b. a mandu m'u pigghia   (Galati/Roghudi, Calabria, D. Maesano p.c.)
         her.cl send.1p.sg *mi* it.cl fetch.3p.sg

4 Conclusions

The data discussed in this paper clearly show that in Southern Italian dialects, there are two different multiple agreement constructions, which Cardinaletti & Giusti (2001) call the Inflected construction and the Finite construction, respectively.

The Inflected construction is a monoclausal / monoeventive structure where V2 carries the fully fledged bundle of Tense and Agreement features and V1 is parasitic on V2. This accounts for the occurrence of a connecting element (*a* < AC) which points to a conjunction of events, a restricted number of verbs which can occur as V1, full Tense+Agr realization on V2, the possibility of reduced and invariant forms as V1, lack of arguments of V1, and clitic climbing onto V1.

The Finite construction is a biclausal / bieventive structure where V1 carries the fully fledged bundle of Tense and Agreement features and allows for a reduced T on V2. This construction is similar to an independent infinitive in Italian or subjunctive in Balkan languages. V1 selects for a clause introduced by a complementizer typical of reduced CPs (FinP in Rizzi's 1997 terms), shows full Tense+Agr realization and cannot be reduced, has arguments, and does not allow for clitic climbing.

Nothing prevents that the two constructions co-occur in one and the same sentence. The Inflected construction can indeed occur in the embedded clause of a Finite construction, as in (49):

(49) E ssu' sciuti cu bba ffatìanu.   (Matino, Apulia, Ledgeway 2016)
      and are.3p.pl gone.ms.pl *cu* go worked.3p.pl

In (49), the fully inflected lexical verb 'go' (in the present perfect with agreeing past participle *sciuti*) selects for the Finite construction introduced by *cu*, which contains an instance of the Inflected construction with invariant 'go' (*bba*) as V1 and the fully agreeing lexical 'work' (*ffatìanu*) as V2.[18]

In conclusion, we hope to have somehow clarified the complex set of multiple agreement data found in Southern Italian dialects. Much remains to be explained, among which the microvariation observed in the intricate interplay of syntactic and morpho-phonological properties which allows a specific verbal form to enter the Inflected construction.

References

Calabrese, Andrea. 1993. The sentential complementation of Salentino: A study of a language without infinitival clauses. In Adriana Belletti (ed.), *Syntactic Theory and the Dialects of Italy*, 28–98. Torino: Rosenberg & Sellier.
Cardinaletti Anna. 2004. Toward a cartography of subject positions. In L. Rizzi (ed.), *The Structure of CP and IP, The Cartography of Syntactic Structures, Volume 2*. New York: Oxford University Press, 115–165.
Cardinaletti, Anna and Giuliana Giusti. 1998. Motion verbs as functional heads. *GenGenP* 6.1: 50–60.
Cardinaletti Anna and Giuliana Giusti. 2001. 'Semi-Lexical' Motion Verbs in Romance and Germanic. In N. Corver and H. van Riemsdijk (eds.), *Semi-lexical categories. On the function of content words and content of function words*. Berlin: Mouton de Gruyter, 371–414.
Cardinaletti, Anna and Giuliana Giusti. 2003. Motion verbs as functional heads. In Christina Tortora (ed.), *The Syntax of Italian Dialects*. New York: Oxford University Press.
Cardinaletti Anna and Ur Shlonsky. 2004. Clitic positions and restructuring in Italian. *Linguistic Inquiry* 35.4: 519–557.
Chillà, Leonida. 2011. *Variazioni sintattiche in alcune varietà meridionali estreme: le strutture a controllo e la selezione dell'ausiliare*. PhD dissertation. University of Florence.
Cinque, Guglielmo. 1999. *Adverbs and Functional Heads*. New York-Oxford: Oxford University Press.
Cinque, Guglielmo. 2006. *Restructuring and Functional Heads, The Cartography of Syntactic Structures, Volume 4*. New York: Oxford University Press.
Corbett Greville G. 2015. Morphosyntactic complexity: A typology of lexical splits. *Language* 91: 145–193.
Cruschina, Silvio. 2013. Beyond the Stem and Inflectional Morphology: an Irregular Pattern at the Level of Periphrasis. In Cruschina, Silvio, Martin Maiden, and John Charles Smith

---

18 This analysis is different from Ledgeway's account of (49): he takes the double occurrence of 'go' to show that the first instance *sciuti* has dethematicized and can therefore enter a sentence with the lexical version of 'go' without any "pleonastic repetition". In support to our analysis in (49), contrast the full forms of the past participle to the reduced forms found in the Inflected construction (see fn. 10).

(eds.) *The Boundaries of Pure Morphology*, 262–283. New York-Oxford: Oxford University Press.

Di Caro Vincenzo N. 2015. *Syntactic constructions with motion verbs in some Sicilian dialects: a comparative analysis*, Ma Thesis, Ca' Foscari University of Venice.

Di Caro Vincenzo N. and Giuliana Giusti. 2016. Dimensions of variation: the Inflected construction in the dialect of Delia. Paper delivered at the 42nd IGG, February 2016, Lecce; at the 46th LSRL, May 2016, Stony Brook, NY.

Dressler Wolfgang U. and Anna Thornton. 1991. Doppie basi e binarismo nella morfologia italiana. *Rivista di Linguistica* 3: 3–22.

Giorgi Alessandra and Fabio Pianesi. 2004. Complementizer Deletion in Italian. In L. Rizzi (ed.), *The Structure of CP and IP, The Cartography of Syntactic Structures, Volume 2*, New York: Oxford University Press, 190–210.

Ledgeway Adam. 2016. From Coordination to Subordination: The Grammaticalisation of Progressive and Andative Aspect in the dialects of Salento. In A. Cardoso et al. (eds), *Coordination and Subordination. Form and Meaning*. Newcastle: Cambridge Scholars Publishing

Maesano, Deborah. 2016. *Inflected Construction in Southern Calabrian Dialects*, BA Thesis, Ca' Foscari University of Venice.

Maiden Martin. 2004. When lexemes become allomorphs. On the genesis of suppletion. *Folia Linguistica* 38: 227–256.

Maiden Martin. 2005. Morphological autonomy and diachrony, in G. Booij and J. Van Marle (eds), *Yearbook of Morphology 2004*, 137–175.

Manzini, M. Rita and Leonardo Maria Savoia. 2005. *I dialetti italiani e romanci. Morfosintassi generativa*. Alessandria.

Poletto Cecilia. 2001. Complementizer Deletion: Edizioni dall'Orso and Verb Movement in Standard Italian, in G. Cinque and G. Salvi, eds., *Current Studies in Italian Syntax. Essays Offered to Lorenzo Renzi*, Elsevier, Amsterdam, 265–286.

Rizzi Luigi. 1997. The fine structure of the left periphery, in L. Haegeman (ed), *Elements of Grammar*. Dordrecht: Kluwer, 281–337.

Roberts Ian and Anna Roussou. 2003. *Syntactic change. A minimalist approach to grammaticalization*. Cambridge: Cambridge University Press.

Rohlfs Gerhard. 1969. *Grammatica storica della lingua italiana e dei suoi dialetti*, vol. 3: *Sintassi e formazione delle parole*. Torino: Einaudi.

Thornton Anna. 2007. Is there a partition in the present indicative of Italian regular verbs?, *Annali Online di Ferrara – Lettere* 2, 43–61.

Carlo Cecchetto and Caterina Donati
Relabeling participial constructions

1 Introduction

Participial relatives show a considerable degree of morphosyntactic variation crosslinguistically, with different structures and forms corresponding to different syntactic derivations (Doron & Reintges 2007). The most well-known type is that of past participial relatives in Romance, which display typical unaccusative/passive diagnostics in only allowing object relatives without an external argument (Burzio 1986). In Italian, for example, past participle reduced relatives are acceptable with passives (1) and unaccusatives (2) but unacceptable with active (3) and unergative verbs (4).

(1) Il ragazzo rimproverato (era arrivato tardi)
     The boy   reproach-PAST PART had arrived late

(2) Il ragazzo arrivato tardi (sarà rimproverato)
     The boy   arrive-PAST PART late will-be reproached-PAST PART

(3) * Il professore mangiato   il panino
     The professor   eat-PAST PART the sandwich

(4) * Il professore telefonato   ieri
     The professor   phone-PAST PART yesterday

We will explain these facts thanks to an extension of the (re)labeling analysis proposed in Donati and Cecchetto (2011) and Cecchetto and Donati (2015) (C&D) for other more articulated relative structures. In order to do so, we will first briefly summarize C&D's relabeling analysis (section 2); we will then review other analyses that have been proposed for reduced relatives clauses, and discard them (section 3). Going back to participial relatives, we will show how the

---

Note: The two of us met Rita in different moments and different situations, but since then we have been both convinced that she is one of the smartest and most unpredictable linguist in our field. Discussing with her is always extreme fun, enormously inspirational, even if it can be very hard. Thanks Rita for your enthusiasm and for you sharp intelligence, and for the many more exhausting discussions still ahead of us.

Carlo Cecchetto and Caterina Donati, SFL (CNRS & Paris 8) and University of Milan-Bicocca– LLF/Labex EFL/Paris 7*

https://doi.org/10.1515/9781501505201-009

relabeling approach can account for their properties (section 4). This approach will allow us to predict the existence of a minimally different structure, namely absolute participial clauses (Section 5).

2 The relabeling analysis of relativization

The starting point of C&D is the observation that a word, intended as the output of the morphology module, plays a crucial role in labeling determination. Uncontroversially, a word "projects" (provides the label) in head-complement configurations. C&D claim that the same happens when various types of relatives are formed, modulo the fact that labeling takes place after movement of the "head".

In free relatives as in (5), for example, 'what', being a word, can provide the label. If it does, the structure ends up being a DP, i.e. a free relative.

(5) I like what you read

Alternatively, C, being the probe of the *wh*-movement of 'what', can provide the label, and the structure ends up being an interrogative clause.

(6) I wonder what you read

This potential labeling conflict explains the systematic ambiguity of the string 'what you read'. Crucially, no ambiguity arises when a phrase is moved. In (7) only the target C is bound to project. The reason is that only words have a relabeling power, and 'what book' is a phrase (we refer to Cecchetto and Donati 2015: section 3.2 for an analysis of a class of *ever*-relatives, as "I will buy whichever book you will buy", which prima facie seem free relatives resulting from phrasal *wh*-movement).

(7) a. I wonder what book you read
     b. *I read what book you read.

We now illustrate the relabeling analysis for the wh-relative in (8):

(8) The book which John read

The derivation of (8) involves two movement steps: first, 'which book' moves as a phrase to a dedicated position in the left periphery. This is an instance of phrasal *wh*-movement (copies are indicated by strikethrough).

(8') [~CP~ which book John read ~~which book~~]

Second, the noun 'book' moves out of the phrase 'which book' and projects, giving the N label to the structure. The movement of 'book', with its relabeling property, derives the defining feature of relative constructions: that of involving a clause with a nominal distribution.

(8") [~NP~ book [~CP~ which ~~book~~ John read ~~which book~~]]

Finally, the external determiner selects the NP resulting from the relabeling movement of the head noun.

(8''') The [~NP~ book [~CP~ which ~~book~~ John read ~~which book~~]]

An obvious problem arises in cases like (9), where the antecedent of the relative clause 'destruction of the city' should not be able to re-label the structure, since in C&D's approach only words (not phrases) have a relabeling property.

(9)   *the destruction of the city which you witnessed*

C&D assume that whatever material modifies the head noun, crucially including so-called complements of the noun ('of the city' in 9), can (and must) be late-merged after the head noun has moved and has "relabeled" the structure. See C&D (but also Adger 2013) for an articulated defence of the view that nouns do not take complements the way verbs do.

The relabeling analysis can be straightforwardly expanded to an Italian *that*-relative like (10), under the assumption that, as proposed by Manzini & Savoia (2003, 2011), the counterpart of 'that' (*che*) is a wh-determiner, not a complementizer.

(10)   *Il libro   che Gianni legge*
       The book   that Gianni reads

Under this assumption, the analysis of *that*-relatives, illustrated in (10') is minimally different from the analysis of *wh*-relatives.

(10') Il [~NP~ libro [~CP~ che ~~libro~~ Gianni legge ~~che libro~~]]

An advantage of this analysis of relative clauses is that it dissociates the raising of the head from a specific feature or a specific cartographic position: what defines relative clauses is the nature of the movement operation itself, which, involving a word, can relabel, and thus nominalize the structure. We will capitalize on this feature of the relabeling analysis when it comes to participial relative clauses.

3 Participial relative clauses are reduced, but not from full-fledged structures

Let us now turn to briefly review the analyses that have been proposed for participial relative clauses. Historically, the term "reduced relatives" comes from the first analyses that were proposed in generative grammar, by which these structures were literally seen as reduced (elided) versions of full relative clauses (cf. Jacobs and Rosenbaum 1968: 204; Baker 1978: 12–3, a.o.). A variant of this analysis is illustrated in (11), an Italian reduced relative.

(11) Il ragazzo [~~che è~~ arrivato   tardi]
      the boy   ~~that is~~ arrive-PAST PART late

At the other extreme, we find another line of though, inaugurated by Burzio (1986: 150), where reduced relatives are identified with various kinds of small clauses (see also Pesetsky 1995: 296). In Burzio's analysis, for example, a reduced relative involves a null PRO, as in (12).

(12) il ragazzo [PRO arrivato tardi]
      the boy   arrive-PAST PART late

In more recent times, the idea of a full-fledged clausal structure assimilated to finite relative clauses has been revived. Participial relatives are analyzed as involving a relative operator which is licensed in the specifier position of a functional projection headed by a complementizer-like functional head, as illustrated in (13).

(13) il [ragazzo] $_{[FP}$ Op$_i$ F° t$_i$ arrivato   tardi]
      the boy   arrive-PAST PART late

Under this approach, the only peculiarity of participial clauses would be that they do not contain a tense node. In Kayne (1994), the functional head is identified with C; in Siloni (1995, 1997) it is identified with D.

This recent revival of the literally reduced approach is partly related to the cartographic framework, whereby structures are defined by dedicated functional projections: the defining feature of relativization is identified with a functional projection hosting an operator (or the raising head in Kayne's terms): since participial relatives are relatives, they must contain this position.

The relabeling approach we just summarized in the previous section is very different, since it identifies the essence of relativization in the derivation itself, more specifically in the relabeling movement, no matter whether it happens in a full-fledged structure, as in full inflected relative clauses, or in a constituent as small as a VP. We shall return to this.

Going back to previous accounts, an obvious problem with Kayne's proposal is that it does not explain why complementizers are systematically banned from participial relatives. Furthermore, this incompatibility does not hold only in Romance, but is robustly attested across languages and is indeed a well-established typological observation (see Doron and Reintges 2013, and the reference quoted therein and Manzini et al. 2016 for a related construction in Punjabi). Another problem with a full-fledged structure for participial relatives is that it does not explain Burzio (1986)'s observation, namely why these relatives are only possible with unaccusatives and passives. This is why we think that a relabeling approach might be worth trying.

4 Participial reduced relative clauses are relabeled

All that is needed under the relabeling approach in order to build a relative structure is a relabeling movement, i.e. the movement of a nominal head.

Consider as an illustration the structure in (14), containing a participial relative with a passive verb (unless indicated differently, examples are in Italian).

(14) Conosco [$_{DP}$ il [$_{NP}$ ragazzo [$_{VP}$ rimproverato ~~ragazzo~~]]]
    (I) know   the boy   reproach-PAST PART

Here the head of the reduced relative ('ragazzo') is external since it precedes the verb, much like the head noun in full relatives. As in full relatives, we claim that it is the movement of N which "relabels" the structure, and provides the external determiner with the NP it needs to select. This amounts to saying that the derivation in (14) is parallel to the derivation of a full relative but for two aspects:

- the landing site of N movement is a position in the VP periphery in reduced relatives, while it is in the CP area in full relatives[1];
- in (14) there is no manifestation of a D inside the relative. Participial relatives never contain wh-determiners such as 'which' or the complementizer 'che', which we analyzed as a wh-determiner following Manzini and Savoia's work.

We take the absence of a D inside the reduced relative at face value, and we assume that in (14) the participle 'rimproverato' ("scolded") is merged directly with the bare noun 'ragazzo'. This assumption plays a crucial role in explaining Burzio's facts.

If the verb does not need to check/assign accusative as in passive and unaccusative constructions, nothing goes wrong: the noun 'ragazzo' gets a thematic role from the past participle and gets a case from the main verb 'conosco' together with the external D after the noun has moved and has relabeled the structure. Under this analysis, theta role assignment is *not* restricted to DPs, as the past participle assigns a theta-role to the bare noun 'ragazzo'. This is not problematic, since there is independent evidence that nouns can receive theta roles: this happens with adjectives.

In languages like Italian bare singular nouns do not get case (DPs do). Therefore, an object past participle reduced relative as (15) is predicted to be impossible: (15) is a case violation because the verb 'eat' needs to (but cannot) assign accusative.[2]

(15) *Il [NP panino [vP Gianni mangiato ~~panino~~]]
 The sandwich Gianni eate-PAST PART

Let us now turn to subject relatives. Consider (16), an ungrammatical participial relative with a transitive active verb.

(16) *Incontrerò [DP il [NP professore [v [vP visto il ragazzo]]
 (I) will-meet the professor see-PAST PART the boy

---

[1] We will not try to detail further what exact position in the vP/VP area this should be. According to Alcázar and Saltarelli (2008) what they call adnominal participial clauses are as small as VP, not vP.

[2] The derivation (15) also involves a locality violation, since the movement of the object noun 'panino' skips a c-commanding N, the subject 'Gianni', in a typical Relativized Minimality violation configuration. See Cecchetto and Donati (2015: Chapter 4) for a detailed discussion of intervention effects in object relative clauses in a relabeling framework.

A first derivation is illustrated in (17'): the bare noun 'professore' becomes the label when it is merged with the structure headed by v.

(17') [$_{NP}$ professore [v [$_{VP}$ visto il ragazzo]]]

The problem with (17') is that, if v does not provide the label, the configuration for the Agent theta role assignment is not created (informally, the noun is not in Spec,vP). Therefore, a theta violation occurs and the structure is out. In other words, the relabeling configuration is incompatible with that for theta assignment: as a result subject relatives with a transitive verb as (17'), where the two configurations coincide, are ungrammatical. In principle, a different derivation might be the source of the reduced relative in (16), namely (17'').

(17'')[$_{NP}$ professore [v ~~professore~~ [v [$_{VP}$ visto il ragazzo]]]]

In (17'') the noun 'professore' moves and relabels the structure after it has received a theta role in Spec,vP. However, this derivation would be a case of vacuous movement and, crucially, it would also violate anti-locality. The anti-locality principle is a corollary of Last Resort that establishes that movement is allowed only if it creates a configuration in which some condition can be satisfied that could not be satisfied before movement took place (cf. Abels 2003 and Grohmann 2000 for discussion about different versions of the anti-locality principle). For example, anti-locality rules out movement of the complement of some head to the specifier of that very same head. The reason for this is that the head-complement configuration is the closest relation that can be established between two categories in syntax, so all feature checking that involves these two categories should be satisfied in the head-complement configuration. As a consequence, movement to the specifier position of the same head is excluded because "useless", since it does not allow any further feature checking. We propose that the same rationale applies to a case like (17''): the noun "professore" might have labeled the structure before movement (although ultimately this would have caused a theta-violation, as in 17'). So, it cannot move to create a relabeling configuration that was already possible without movement.[3] The same reasons that blocks the derivations (17') and (17'') blocks (18), with an unergative verb: in a nutshell, (18) either involves a theta violation or an anti-locality violation. All in all the structure is out.

---

[3] An alternative account, which might not be incompatible with the one proposed here, is to assume that participial relatives are as reduced as VPs, therefore they do include the external argument position: see Alcázar and Saltarelli (2008) for a detailed argumentation.

(18) *Incontrerò [DP il [NP ragazzo [v [VP telefonato]]
    (I) will-meet the boy phoned

Notice that auxiliary selection does not play any role in this account of past participle reduced relatives. This explains why reduced relatives are possible with passives but also with unaccusatives in English (cf. 19) and Spanish (cf. 20), even if unaccusatives do not select for the auxiliary *be* in these languages.[4]

(19) *The people recently arrived from the South*

(20) *Las chicas recién llegadas a la estación son mis hermanas.*
    the girls recently arrived at the station are my sisters.

5 Absolute participial constructions

An interesting feature of the relabeling approach is that it predicts a number of structural ambiguities due to labeling, such as the ones we briefly discussed in Section 1 in relation to free relatives. Let us start considering the minimally different structures in (21) and (22). (21) contains a reduced relative with a past participle while (22) contains an absolute participial construction.

(21) *Il ragazzo arrivato   tardi (non si scusò neppure)*
    The boy arrive-PAST PART late (not himself apologized even)
    'The boy who arrived late did not even apologize'

(22) *Arrivato   il ragazzo (Gianni se ne andò)*
    Arrive-PAST PART the boy   Gianni left
    'Since the boy arrived, Gianni left'

In (21) we have a *preverbal* noun and a relative clause distribution of a participial structure. In (22) we observe a a *postverbal* DP and a clausal (absolute) distribution of a participial structure. This alternation between reduced relatives (nominal structures) and absolute participial constructions (clausal structures) is expected under the relabeling hypothesis, as well as their word order

---

4 We acknowledge however that past participle reduced relatives with unaccusatives are not fully productive at least in English, unlike what happens in languages like Italian. We do not have an explanation for this.

difference: what turns a verbal category (or a clause) into a nominal structure is the relabeling movement of the noun and word order shows that noun movement takes place in (21), not in (22).

Interestingly, as observed by Belletti (1990;1991) absolute participle constructions, just like reduced relatives, are possible with unaccusatives (21-22) and impossible with unergatives (23-24).

(23) *Il ragazzo telefonato   tardi (non si scusò neppure)
     The boy call-PAST PART   late (did not even apoligize)

(24) *Telefonato   il ragazzo (Gianni se ne andò)
     Call-PAST PART the boy (Gianni left)

As for unergative subjects, we already offered an account for why they are impossible in reduced relatives (cf. 18 above). As for the ungrammaticality of the absolute participle construction (24), we claim now that the structure does not include the Focus position in the vP periphery dedicated to postverbal subjects, which has been identified by Belletti (2004).[5] That this position is not available is suggested by the fact that 'il ragazzo' in (25) cannot be interpreted as the postverbal subject of a passive verb,[6] namely (25) cannot mean "Having the boy been scolded...".

(25) Rimproverato   il ragazzo (Gianni si mise a piangere)
     Scold-PAST PART the boy,   Gianni started to cry
     'Having scolded the boy, Gianni burst into tears'

The only interpretation for (25) is with 'il ragazzo' interpreted as the object, and a null subject, arguably PRO, controlled by 'Gianni'.

(25') PRO rimproverato il ragazzo, Gianni si mise a piangere

The difference is here that PRO can sit in the preverbal position of the absolute clause (arguably Spec, vP), where a lexical subject is disallowed.

---

[5] As for why this low focus position is not available in this construction, we speculate that it is related to because the fact that absolute small clauses as a whole express given information, as indicated by translation ("having scolded the boy......").
[6] This assumes that the postverbal subject of a passive verb does not surface in its argumental position (the sister position of the verb) but must move to a dedicated position in the vP periphery.

More generally, interesting questions arise concerning Case assignment in absolute participial constructions. The well-formedness of (22) repeated here as (26), indicates that Case is correctly assigned/checked in this type of structure.

(26) *Arrivato il ragazzo (Gianni se ne andò)*

We know however that 'arrivare' is an unaccusative verb. In fact, we relied on *lack* of case assignment by unaccusatives in the relabeling analysis of the related reduced relative construction. So, what is the case of 'il ragazzo' and where does it come from in (26)?

As extensively discussed by Belletti (1990; 1992) there is evidence that the subject of an unaccusative verb receives *nominative* case in the absolute participle construction: the contrast in (27) shows that the Case assigned to the postverbal lexical NP is nominative, which is visible in the personal pronouns of first and second person singular, where the distinction nominative/non-nominative is morphologically realized (Belletti 1990).

(27) a. *Arrivato   io/tu,   Gianni tirò un sospiro di sollievo.*
         arrive-PAST PART I/you,   Gianni was relieved
         'Since I/you arrived, Gianni was relieved'
    b. **Arrivato   me,   Gianni tirò un sospiro di sollievo.*
         arrive-PAST PART meACC   Gianni was relieved

Belletti claims that nominative assignment is evidence that V raises to C, by sticking to the idea that a clausal structure needs a C to be a proper clause. It has indeed been argued by Rizzi (1982) for Italian, and by Raposo (1987) for Portuguese, that a nominative Case assigner can be present in the left periphery of some nonfinite clauses in these languagse, on the basis of facts like those illustrated in (28).

(28) a. *Avendo Gianni/io chiuso   il dibattito, la riunione è finita prima*
         Having Gianni/I close-PAST PART the debate, the meeting ended early
         'Since Gianni/I closed the debate, the meeting ended early.'
    b. *O Manel pensa terem os omigos   levado   o livro*
         Manel thinks   have(3PL) the friends take-PAST PART the book
         'Manel thinks the friends have taken the book.'

We will not commit to this V to C analysis, since we believe there is no evidence for the presence of a complementizer in these reduced structures. In addition, if we assumed a full CP structure, it would become more difficult to explain why absolute participial constructions are not possible with unergatives. However, we do assume that the participle moves to a functional head in the middle-field from where it can assign nominative into a position to its right. Crucially, we assume this position to be lower than the one that hosts preverbal subjects.[7]

Let us take stock: in our account both Italian reduced relatives and absolute participial constructions are reduced in a structural sense (or are truncated structures, following a terminology used in slightly different contexts). A reduced relative is a *v*P in which a noun (crucially, not a full DP) is generated. The noun moves to the *v*P periphery, relabels the structure (which becomes an NP) and is selected by the external determiner. An absolute participial constructions is also truncated. The internal argument is a full DP, unlike what happens in reduced relatives. It receives nominative from the participle that moves out of the *v*P, no relabeling movement occurs and the structure maintains a clausal (not a nominal) distribution.

The situation is slightly different in French. Belletti (1990) observes that the structure equivalent to (22) is impossible, as illustrated in (29).

(29) *Arrivée Marie,   la fête commença
     Arrive-PAST PART Marie, the party started

Belletti explains the ungrammaticality of (29) as a Case filter violation, ultimately due to the Head Movement Constraint: the French V does not move into the Agreement position involved in participial agreement, so it cannot further move to C. This prevents the Verb from accessing the position where the exceptional mechanism of nominative assignment takes place. We will stick to the part of the explanation which does not commit ourselves to assuming a complementizer in this structure: simply, we will say that in French the verb cannot move in the position where it can assign nominative Case to its right.

What Belletti does not discuss in much detail, though, is another possibility, which indeed seems available in French. This alternative is illustrated in (30).

(30) *Le train parti, on se dépêcha de sortir*
     The train left, we hurried up and exited
     'After the train left, we quickly went out'

---

[7] The portion of the *v*P layer in the participle construction is big enough to include enclitics.
(i)   *Accusatolo,   Gianni scoppiò a piangere*
       Accused-him,   Gianni started to cry
       'Having accused him, Gianni started to cry'

The difference here is that the DP is preverbal, not postverbal. This entails that French displays the genuine ambiguity that we expect given the relabeling approach. The very same string, repeated in (31) can either be interpreted as a (reduced) relative or as a (reduced) clause, depending on labelling.

(31) *Le train parti*
   a. (On a pris) [$_{DP}$ le [$_{NP}$ train [$_{VP}$ parti ~~train~~]]
      (We have taken) the train left
   b. P [le train [$_{VP}$ parti ~~le train~~]], (on se dépêcha de sortir)
      the train left (we hurried up and exited)

In one case (31a), the Noun alone moves in order to get Case and relabels the structure. It shares Case with the external Determiner, and the result is a complex NP, a relative.

In the other structure (31b), the entire DP moves in order to get case without relabeling the structure. It gets case at the edge of the structure, probably from some kind of a silent preposition, as in *avec le train parti'* ('with the train left') in (32).

(32) *Avec le train parti, on peut aller prendre une bière*[8]
     With the train left, we can go get a beer

The difference between the two structures in (31) does not stem from cartography or configuration, but from their derivation: in (a) N moves, and labels the structure, relativizing it; in (b) a phrase moves and does not label the structure, with remains a (small) clause. Case is also assigned consequently: in (a) the structure receives case as every NP does, through agreement with a determiner; (b) is a configuration of exceptional case marking, probably from a null preposition.[9] All in all the difference between Italian and French participial constructions

---

8 As expected, the subject of an absolute participial clause in French displays the case (accusative) normally assigned by a preposition, as shown in (i), which contrasts with (ii) in Italian.
(i)   *(avec) moi parti, mes enfants   s'amusent beaucoup.*
      (with) me left   my kids   have a lot of fun
(ii) *Partita io, i miei figli si divertono molto*
      Left I,   my kids   have a lot of fun

9 In fact, the absolute participial construction of the French type is marginally available in Italian as well:
(i)   *Con il treno   partito, possiamo prenderci una birra*
      With the train left,   we can   go get a beer

reduces to the case assigner: in Italian the Nominative case assigner is the past participle itself, which moves to a dedicated functional position in the middle field. In French, a possibly null preposition assigns Accusative.

6 Conclusion

The account of Romance reduced relatives proposed here has three welcome features:
- it is minimally different from the analysis of full relatives but it does not stipulate a fully-fledged silent clausal structure.
- it derives straightforwardly the impossibility of past participle reduced relatives with active transitive verbs and ergative verbs.
- it predicts the existence of a minimally different structure, the absolute participial construction, that obeys the same constraints but has a clausal distribution.

To the best of our knowledge, no alternative account exists that combines all these three features.

References

Abels, Klaus. 2003. Successive cyclicity, anti-locality, and adposition stranding. Doctoral Dissertation. University of Connecticut.
Baker Carl. 1978. *Introduction to Generative-Transformational syntax*. Englewood Cliffs: Prentice-Hall.
Adger, David. 2013. *A syntax of substance*. Cambridge, MA: MIT Press.
Alcázar, Asier and Mario Saltarelli. 2008. Argument structure of participial clauses: the unaccusative phase. In Joyce Bruhm de Garavito and Elena Valenzuela (eds.), *Selected Proceedings of the 10th Hispanic Linguistics Symposium*, Somerville, MA: Cascadilla Proceedings Project.
Belletti, Adriana. 1990. *Generalized Verb Movement. Aspects of Verb Syntax*. Turin: Rosenberg and Sellier. Reprinted in Belletti 2009.
Belletti, Adriana. 1992. Agreement and Case in Past Participial Clauses in Italian. In Tim Stowell and Eric Wehrli (Eds.), *Syntax and Semantics, vol. 26, Syntax and the Lexicon*, 21-44. New York: Academic Press. Reprinted in Belletti 2009.
Belletti, Adriana. 2004. Aspects of the low IP area. In Luigi Rizzi (ed.), *The structure of CP and IP. The cartography of syntactic structures*, Vol. 2, 16–51. New York: Oxford University Press.
Belletti, Adriana. 2009. *Structures and strategies*. London: Routledge.

Bianchi, Valentina. 1999. *Consequences of Antisymmetry: Headed Relative Clauses.* Berlin: Mouton de Gruyter.
Burzio, Luigi. 1986. *Italian Syntax.* Dordrecht: Reidel.
Cecchetto, Carlo and Caterina Donati. 2015. *(Re)labeling*, Cambridge, MA: MIT Press.
Donati, Caterina and Carlo Cecchetto. 2011. Relabeling Heads. A Unified Account for Relativization Structures. *Linguistic Inquiry* 42(4): 519-560.
Doron, Edit. and Chris Reintges. 2007. On the syntax of participial modifiers. Unpublished, manuscript. University of Jerusalem/ LLF CNRS.
Grohmann, Kleanthes. 2000. Prolific Peripheries: A Radical View from the Left. Doctoral Dissertation. University of Maryland, College Park.
Jacobs, Roderick and Peter Rosenbaum. 1968. *English Transformational Grammar.* Waltham, MA: Blaisdell.
Manzini, M. Rita and Leonardo Savoia, 2003. The nature of complementizers. *Rivista di Grammatica Generativa* 28: 87-110.
Manzini, M. Rita and Leonardo Savoia. 2011. *Grammatical Categories.* Cambridge: Cambridge University Press.
Manzini M. Rita, Leonardo Savoia and Ludovico Franco 2016. Suffixaufnahme, oblique case and Agree, manuscript, University of Florence/Universidade Nova de Lisboa.
Pesetsky, David. 1996. *Zero syntax: experiencers and cascades* .Cambridge, MA. MIT Press.
Raposo, Eduardo. 1987. Case Theory and Infl-to-Comp: The Inflected Infinitive in European Portuguese. *Linguistic Inquiry* 18: 85-109.
Rizzi, Luigi. 1982. Issues in Italian Syntax. Dordrect: Foris.
Siloni, Tal. 1995. On participial relatives and complementizer D°: a case study in Hebrew and French. *Natural Language and Linguistic Theory* 13: 445-487.

Noam Chomsky
Puzzles about phases

I will assume here the framework of Chomsky (2013, 2015), and consider two related puzzles that appear in the two major (perhaps only) phases considered in this approach: CP and v*P. In the former, a relation is established between C and T (grounding Aux-raising), providing T with φ-features inherited from C, followed by raising of the external argument EA to SPEC-T (in informal terminology). But that series of operations is counter-cyclic, and requires a complex substitution operation that is a sign of an error. The v* phase exhibits a puzzle that traces back to Postal's (1974) work on "raising to object." Lasnik and Saito (1991) provide a straightforward analysis in which the embedded subject raises to SPEC of the matrix verb, which then raises to v*, yielding the empirical facts. The puzzle is that the operations are not forced (as they should be) and pose a hopeless learnability problem: they restore the original order while changing the hierarchy, and the learner has no evidence for this strange process. Both puzzles are resolved if the generative process adheres more strictly to principles of minimal computation, abandoning common assumptions about triggering of operations.

I would like to consider two puzzles that have been lurking in one or another form for many years, and that arise in a particularly clear way within the framework of Chomsky (2013, 2015), which I will assume here, including the analysis of EPP-ECP and the analogues for the verb phrase, the discussion of head movement, and the general principles proposed there: in particular, the labeling theory and the phase-theoretic interpretation of strict cyclicity, with at least (perhaps at most) two phases, CP and v*P, marked by the unvalued features at the phase head. The core structures, then, are (1a, b) (R an uncategorized root in the sense of Hagit Borer and Alex Marantz):

(1) (a) [C [$_\alpha$T XP]]
     (b) [v* [$_\alpha$R, XP]]

Assume further that the features of the phase head are inherited by the next lowest head, T and R respectively; that is where they are externalized and under the labeling theory, enter into establishing the subject-predicate relation and its VP analogue.

In passing, it should be noted that the existence of unvalued features is rather surprising. Why should language have redundant features that do not contribute to interpretation at the conceptual-intentional interface CI? One possibility is that their role is just to identify the phases, hence determining at which points in a derivation what has been generated is "closed," not subject to further modification, a significant contribution to reducing computation, arguably a "third factor" property.

In both CP and v*P phases, there is raising to SPEC-α (EPP and its v*P analogue).[1] In both cases the operation is problematic.

One problem is that raising to SPEC-α appears to be counter-cyclic. Thus in CP, C is merged to TP, its features are inherited by T, and then the probe T finds the external argument EA, triggering raising of EA to SPEC-α. In the case of v*P, analogously, v* is merged to RP, its features are inherited by R, and then the probe R triggers raising of a nominal phrase to SPEC-α.

Counter-cyclicity requires new and complex operations, a matter discussed by Epstein et al. (2012), who also offer an ingenious solution, though I think a simpler one is possible, outlined below. Another question is why EA raises instead of remaining in situ, yielding long-distance agreement, as in "there will [men [read books]]," analogous to unaccusatives; the same question arises with (2). Still another question is how the resulting structure is labeled so that it is legitimate at CI.

A particularly interesting case is ECM constructions, such as (2):

(2)   John expects [$_\beta$ Bill to win]

Here the subject *Bill*, the EA of β, functions within the matrix clause, the phenomenon of raising-to-object, explored by work tracing back to (Postal 1974). One reason why this case is important is that the evidence is quite subtle, surely unavailable in acquisition, so it serves as a particularly striking example of poverty of stimulus (POS).[2] In all POS cases, a methodological problem arises. Insofar as the rule is unlearnable, the results must follow from rules that independently exist and are learnable (or belong to UG or are "third factor" properties). For that reason, POS problems are particularly enlightening as to the nature of language. One task, then, is to show that this methodological condition can be satisfied for raising-to-object.

A significant step in this direction was taken by Lasnik and Saito (1991). Consider (3), the underlying structure of v*P in (2), R = *expect*:

---

[1] Using the conventional term SPEC informally, meaning sister-of XP or of the head X of XP = {X, YP}.

[2] Contrary to what is often believed, the problem is ubiquitous, but I will leave that aside here.

(3) v* [ₐ R [Bill [to win]]]

Keeping to independently existing rules, *Bill* raises to SPEC-α and R raises to v*, yielding the new structure but with linear order unchanged, posing the POS problem in a sharp form: why should this happen, given the lack of empirical evidence for the language learner, and the restructuring with order unchanged?

In accord with the probe-goal triggering mechanisms just discussed, first v* is merged to α and then R inherits the features of v* triggering the raising of its goal *Bill* to SPEC- α. The rules are the familiar ones, analogous to EPP in CP. Hence the methodological problem of POS is overcome. But we face the problems that arise for EPP in CP: counter-cyclicity, explaining why the rules operate, and accounting for the legitimacy of the resulting structures.[3]

Let us first consider the question why raising takes place in CP and v*P. In both cases, we have an XP-YP structure: {EA, v*P} and {EA, to-VP}, respectively. These are unlabelable, so one or the other of XP, YP must raise. In both cases, raising of YP yields an unlabelable structure (even under further successive-cyclic movement), so it must be XP that raises; that is, EA in both cases.[4] That accounts for the necessary raising of XP, but it leaves the other problems unresolved.

Consider next counter-cyclicity. The problems arise because of the assumption that Internal Merge IM ("Move") is triggered by a probe-goal relation. While conventional, it has always been clear that the assumption cannot be correct, if only because of successive-cyclic movement.[5] The intuition behind the assumption is that the end result must be what Luigi Rizzi calls a "criterial position." Restated within the labeling theory assumed here, a criterial position is an XP-YP structure where the labels of XP and YP agree: subject-predicate, wh-interrogatives, etc.[6]

---

[3] The remaining distinction between CP and v*P is the necessary raising of R to v*, an independent matter – and one that raises quite interesting questions, along with head-raising generally, an operation that does not fall within the traditional theory of movement, or the radically simplified Merge system. See Chomsky (2015).

[4] I put aside here the possibility that EA may remain in situ, with other modifications, brought up (but not pursued) in Chomsky (2015).

[5] Other reasons have to do with the "Activity Condition," dubious for reasons discussed in Nevins (2005). Thus the natural analysis of Topicalization does not assign an unvalued feature to the topicalized phrase, which gains the interpretation as topic from the target position so there is no probe-goal relation, as in the intermediate cases of successive-cyclic movement.

[6] Note that the associated condition of criterial freezing seems dispensable: see Chomsky (2015). The condition of agreement in addition to mere match, motivated there, might be overcome by a more careful analysis of the relevant features, a matter I will put aside here.

The guiding intuition can be preserved if we drop the triggering assumption, and simply assume that Merge (both IM and EM) applies freely, like all rules. Free application of rules can yield deviant expressions, but that is unproblematic, in fact required. Deviant expressions should be generated with their interpretations for reasons that go back to Chomsky (1956) and have been amplified in subsequent years.[7] It would radically complicate the generative procedure if, for example, EM were required to yield non-deviant structures[8]; redundantly, because the distinctions are made in any event at CI, and incorrectly, as just noted. There is no more reason to suppose that IM always must yield non-deviant structures.

Dropping the triggering assumption, we eliminate the problems posed by counter-cyclicity along with the failures of probe-goal triggering just mentioned. Rules apply cyclically. First, EA is raised to SPEC-α in both CP and v*P phases. The resulting EA-YP structure is unlabelable, a problem that must be overcome before transfer at the phase level, and it is. EM introduces the phase head (C, v*). AGREE then applies between the phase head and EA, by minimal search, as usual. The features of the phase head are then inherited (by T, R, respectively). The structure EA-α is now labelable by shared and agreeing φ-features, with the EA in its criterial position.

The puzzles raised earlier are now resolved. In both CP and ECM constructions, raising to SPEC-α is forced and its outcome is labeled, hence legitimate. The rules are cyclic, so the counter-cyclicity problem is overcome. There are no new rules required for ECM, overcoming the severe POS problem posed by raising-to-object.

Note that under this analysis, raising-to-object is obligatory. There are, I think, other reasons to suppose that this is the case, among them the obligatory application in ECM constructions of Principle B of the Binding Theory (under whatever interpretation one gives to the phenomenon), which should be a clause-mate condition under this analysis. However, there have been arguments to the contrary (see Lasnik 2002). Hence a problem still remains.

A related question has to do with optional/obligatory raising of direct object. Still assuming the same general framework, the question turns on whether R is analogous to "weak" T as in English-type languages that require EPP. If it is, then object-raising is obligatory to satisfy labeling requirements; if not, then

---

[7] Among other reasons, in the highly productive study of varying kinds of deviance: subjacency vs. ECP violations, for example.
[8] Even assuming that the concept can be defined in absolute terms, which has never been obvious.

object can remain in-situ, unlike the ECM constructions. The empirical question has been debated.

Though these and many other questions remain unsettled, we can, it seems, take some further steps towards approaching the Strong Minimalist Thesis SMT.

References

Chomsky, Noam. 1956. *Logical Structure of Linguistic Theory*, ms. Plenum, 1975; Chicago, 1975.

Chomsky, Noam. 2013. Problems of Projection. *Lingua* 130: 33–49.

Chomsky, Noam. 2015. Problems of Projection: Extensions. In Elisa Di Domenico, Cornelia Hamann and Simona Matteini (eds.), *Structures, Strategies and Beyond: Studies in honour of Adriana Belletti*, 1–16. Amsterdam: John Benjamins.

Epstein, Samuel, Hisatsugu Kitahara, T. Daniel Seely. 2012. Structure Building That Can't Be. Myriam Uribe-Etxebarria and Vidal Valmala (eds.), *Ways of Structure Building*, 253–270. Oxford. Oxford University Press.

Lasnik, Howard. 2002. Clause-mate Conditions Revisited. *Glot International* 6(4): 94–96.

Lasnik, Howard & Mamoru Saito. 1991. On the subject of infinitives. In Lise M. Dobrin, Lynn Nichols, and Rosa M. Rodriguez (eds.), *Proceedings of the 27th annual meeting of the Chicago Linguistic Society (CLS 27), vol. 1: The General Session*, 324–343. Chicago, IL: Chicago Linguistic Society.

Nevins, Andrew. 2005. Derivations without the Activity Condition. In Martha McGinnis and Norvin Richards (eds.), *Perspectives on phases: MITWPL 49*, 287–310. Cambridge MA.

Postal, Paul. 1974. *On Raising: One Rule of English Grammar and its Theoretical Implications*. Cambridge, MA: MIT Press.

Guglielmo Cinque
On the double-headed analysis of "Headless" relative clauses

1 Introduction

A particular challenge for the generalized double-headed analysis of relative clauses (RCs) proposed in Cinque (2003, 2008)[1] is posed by "Headless" (or Free) RCs, especially under the analysis which takes the wh-pronoun to be in the Spec, CP of the RC, the so-called 'COMP analysis' convincingly argued for in Groos and Riemsdijk (1981), Hirschbühler and Rivero (1983), Harbert (1983), Borsley (1984), Grosu (1986/87, 1994, 2003a,b), Kayne (1994), Pittner (1995), Grosu and Landman (1998), Benincà (2007, 2012), Gračanin-Yüksek (2008), and others.[2]

---

[1] What is proposed there is that the different types of RCs attested in the languages of the world (externally headed post-nominal, externally headed pre-nominal, internally headed, double-headed, headless (or 'free'), correlative, and adjoined – cf. Dryer 2005) can all be derived from a single, *double-headed*, universal structure via different, independently justified, syntactic operations (movement and deletion), under both a "Raising" and a "Matching" derivation. See Cinque (to appear) for refinements and more detailed discussion. Under the assumption argued for there that RCs are merged pre-nominally (arguably like every other modifier and head of the extended projection of a lexical category – Cinque 2009) also the "Matching" derivation is fully compatible with Antisymmetry (Kayne 1994).

[2] The alternative 'Head analysis' which takes the *wh*-phrase to be outside of the RC CP, in the external Head position (Bresnan and Grimshaw 1978, Larson 1987, 1998, Bury 2003, Citko 2002, 2008, 2009, among others), cannot account for the extraposition facts of German (and Dutch) "Headless" RCs pointed out in Groos and Riemsdijk (1981), for the Case mismatches in certain languages (Pittner 1991,1995, Grosu 1994), nor for the Croatian reconstruction and clitic facts discussed in Gračanin-Yüksek (2008). It also cannot easily account for such cases as (i) in English, where the "NP$_{matrix}$ is coreferential with *whoever*, but *whoever* is embedded in the larger NP *whoever's woods: [Whoever's woods are these] is a good judge of real estate*" (Andrews 2007, 214). As Andrews points out, such sentences are less problematic if the phrase is preposed within the RC than it would be if it were in the external Head position (also see fn. 28 below). For additional arguments against the 'Head analysis' see Borsley (1984), Grosu (1994,Study I, Chapter 4) and Jacobson (1995), among others. The obligatory presence of an overt antecedent in German when the extraposed "Headless" RC is part of a PP (*Der Reporter hat sich auf *(das) gestürzt [was man*

Note: For discussion and/or comments to a previous draft of the paper I wish to thank Paola Benincà, Chiara Branchini, Roland Hinterhölzl, Richard Kayne, Andrew Radford, Adam Szczegielniak and an anonymous reviewer.

Guglielmo Cinque, University of Venice

https://doi.org/10.1515/9781501505201-011

In following this analysis, which takes the CP containing the wh-pronoun to be embedded in a larger DP structure, I specifically suggested in Cinque (2003) that such a structure is a full DP with the RC CP merged in a specifier that modifies a portion of the nominal extended projection which constitutes the external Head 'matching' the internal one, as in every other RC type. Cf. (1)[3]:

(1)
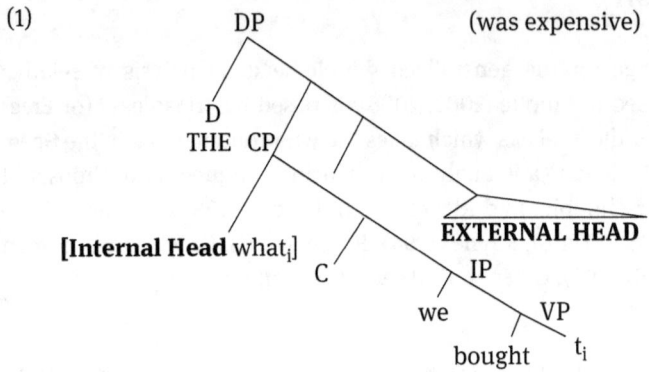

If so, the question arises as to the nature of the external Head in "Headless" RCs.[4]

2 Languages lacking "Headless" RCs

A first step toward answering the question of the nature of the external Head in (1) is the observation that in many languages the 'construction' isn't

---

ihm zeigte] 'The reporter jumped on what one showed to him' – Haider 1988,120) may suggest that a silent DP is not sufficient to avoid a violation of the ban on preposition stranding.

3 Capitals indicate silent elements.

4 In the case of '–ever' "Headless" RCs, which occur either as arguments (as in *I'll do [whatever you do]*) or as clausal adjuncts (as in *I won't change my mind, [whatever you do]*) only in the former does the question arise. As shown in Izvorski (2000), where they are dubbed 'Free adjunct free RCs', the latter are just CPs with no external Head. Setting these CP adjuncts aside, the bare CP analysis of all "Headless" RCs suggested in Åfarli (1994), Rooryck (1994), Vogel (2001) and others does not seem tenable. Their DP nature is clearly indicated by a number of properties, which make them differ from both Free adjunct free RCs, and indirect questions, pointing to a [$_{DP}$ [$_{CP}$ ...]] structure: e.g., same distribution as DPs (Grosu 1994, 3f) and strong island sensitivity (Alexiadou and Varlokosta 1996, §6, Branchini 2014, 77f). For further properties distinguishing standard "Headless" RCs from Free adjunct free RCs see section 6 below and for differences between them and indirect questions Rizzi (1982, 75f, note32), Daskalaki (2005), Benincà (2010, 2012) and Bertollo and Cavallo (2012, §4).

Headless at all. In structures corresponding to the "Headless" RCs of English or Italian several languages display an overt Head taking the form of one of the functional/light nouns/classifiers 'thing', 'person', 'place', 'time', etc. This is the case of the Gbe languages (see (2) from Gungbe, (3) from Gengbe, and, for Fongbe, Lefebvre and Brousseau 2002,164)[5]; this is also the case of many languages of the Nilo-Saharan family[6]; and the same is true of several Papuan languages (see, e.g., (4) from Makasae, and Berry and Berry 1990,157ff for Abun, and Davies 1989,§1.1.2. 3.6 for Kobon); of the Niger-Congo languages Obolo ((5)) and Mambay (to judge from Anonby 2011,§10.2.2.3), of the Austronesian language Rapanui,[7] and of Somali (Cushitic)[8]:

(2) Nú ḍĕ à ná mì w`ɛ nǎ yí
    thing REL 2SG give 1SG FOC 1SG.FUT take
    'I will take whatever you give me.' (Gungbe – Enoch Aboh, p.c.)

(3) Ame-ke gbe dzi be ye la ple gbɔ, yi-na asi ya me
    person-REL ever desire that 3SG FUT buy goat go-CNT market that in
    'Whoever wants to buy goats comes to this market.'
    (Gengbe – Huttar, Aboh and Ameka 2013, 118)

---

5 Enoch Aboh, p.c., conjectures that this may be a larger Kwa characteristic, pointing out the case of Akan. See Saah (2010, §5.5), where examples like the following are reported:
(i) a. Nea [ɔ-kɔ́ nsú] na ɔ-bɔ́ ahiná.
       person (that) 3SG-go water FM 3SG-break.PRES pot
       "He who fetches water breaks the pot."
To judge from Soubrier (2013, §15.5.2) for Ikposso and Obeng (2008, Chapter 12) for Efutu, indeed this property is shared by other Kwa languages.
6 See Hutchison (1976) for Kanuri: "In this sort of ["Headless"] construction, relative clauses headed by the following set of nouns are used: *kam* 'person' (who), *awo* 'thing' (what), *sa* 'time' (when), *na* 'place' (where), *dalil* 'reason' (why), *futu/delfu* 'way' (how)." (p. 90f). For Lango, Noonan (1992), giving examples like (i), explicitly states: "there are no 'headless' relatives in Lango. [...] In Lango an overt noun must be present" (p. 220).
(i) márô gìn àmê cámô
    3s.like.hab thing rel+part 3s.eat.hab
    'He likes what he eats'
Also see Walters (2015,§8.2.3.1) on Dazaga, Christiansen-Bolli (2010,§4.5) on Tadaksahak, and Heath (1999,§8.3) on Koyra Chinii.
7 Du Feu (1996) states that in Rapanui "Headless relatives are not found. Instead a dummy head is used: *me'e* 'thing or person', *hora* 'time', *kona* 'place', *aŋa* 'action'"(p. 47).
8 See Lecarme (2008,§2.4), especially fn. 23.

(4) Anu   wa'a ana   gi   seluku ma   rau ena   ere bada
    person REL   people other MRK   good see DEM   friend MRK
    na'u baunu
    many
    'Whoever treats others well will have many friends'
                                            (Makasae – Correia 2011, 157)

(5) Ḿkpó géèlék (èyí) îfùk (bé)   (Ek(-mé)) ìkâmá
    thing all   (Rel) 3PSCPread (Rel)   3PS.NEG.like
    'Whatever she read, he didn't like'   (Obolo – Faraclas 1984, 45)

The cases so far are all examples from languages with externally Headed **post**-nominal RCs. "Headless" RCs with functional/light Heads are also attested in languages with externally Headed **pre**-nominal RCs (see (6), from Afar – Cushitic), in languages with Internally Headed RCs (see (7), from Lakhota – Siouan), and in languages with double-headed RCs (see (8) from the Tibeto-Burman language Ronghong Qiang – Huang 2008 – and (9) from the Chadic language Mina – Frajzyngier and Johnston 2005).

(6) a'nu ge'd-a-kke   'isin t-amaa'too-n-u   'ma-dud-d-a-n
    I   go-impf-place   you   you-come-pl-juss neg-able-you-impf-pl
    'Where I am going you are not able to come'   (Afar – Bliese 1981, 29)[9]

(7) [[Mary [taku]   kağe] ki] ophewathų
        Mary something make the I.buy
    'I bought what Mary made'   (Lakhota – Williamson 1989, 188, note 4)[10]

(8) a. [[zəp   iɕtɕimɑqɑ zɑwɑ   tshu-tshu]$_{RC}$(-tɕ)   zəp   tha-kua]$_{NP}$
       [[**place** usually rock   drop-REDUP(-GEN)]   **place** that-CL]
    '(the place) where rockslides often occur'

---

[9] Functional nouns include 'place', 'time', 'reason', 'something', 'amount', 'manner' (Bliese 1981, Chapter 2).

[10] Lakhota may in fact also drop the indefinite pronoun. Compare (10) with (i)

(i)   [[Mary [e]   kağe] ki] ophewathų (Lakhota – Williamson 1989,189note4)
          Mary   make   the I.buy
      'I bought what Mary made'

For other such cases, see Culy (1990, 249f).

b. [[**mi** qɑ nə-xeˈ-m]_{RC} **mi**]_{NP}-le: kə-ji
    [[**person** 1SG DIR-scold-NOM] **person**]-DEF:CL go-CSM
    '(the person) who scolded me has gone'

    (Ronghong Qiang – Huang 2008, 761, 762)

(9) [**skə̀n** [nàm dzán **skə̀n** syì]] há diyà gáy kà
    [**thing** [1DU find **thing** COM]] 2sg put spoil POS
    'The thing we found, you are ruining it'

    (Mina – Frajzyngier and Johnston 2005, 433)[11]

3 The double-headed structure of "Headless" RCs

I take such functional nouns to also be present, if unpronounced, in the "Headless" RCs of English (and English-type languages), as shown in (10).[12] In English each *wh*-pronoun is associated with a specific functional noun: *what* with THING (or AMOUNT, or KIND), *who* with PERSON, *where* with PLACE (Kayne 2004), etc.[13]

---

[11] Frajzyngier and Johnston (2005) explicitly say that "[t]he relativized object may be coded twice, once at the beginning of the clause as the head of the relative clause, and the second time after the verb, in the position of object." (p.432f). Mina has also externally headed pre- and post-nominal RCs.

[12] Even though the argument may be more suggestive than conclusive, as Andrew Radford (p.c.) points out (in that one could argue that languages lacking free relatives will resort to headed relative structures, as semantically rather than syntactically equivalent), and even though a single-headed analysis with "Raising" in a [$_{DP}$ D° [$_{CP}$]] structure is conceivable for the examples from (2) to (9), as well as for (10), I will sketch here what a double-headed analysis with "Raising" would look like for them.

[13] Possibly all NPs are *always* merged as modifiers of one such (silent) functional/light noun, whether the NP contains a proper name or a common noun: [John [PERSON]], [dog [ANIMAL]], [table [THING]], etc. – cf. Kayne's (2007 Appendix) theoretical arguments. This is rendered additionally plausible by the existence of languages where some such functional/light nouns/classifiers are actually pronounced (see, e.g., (i), from the Australian language Yidiɲ):

(i) bama:l yabuɾuŋgu miɲa gangu:l wawa:l (Dixon 1977, 480)
    Person-erg girl-erg animal-abs wallaby-abs see.past
    Lit. 'the person girl saw the animal wallaby' ('the girl saw the wallaby')

(10) a. (We gave him) [$_{DP}$ THE [$_{CP}$ what THING$_i$ [C [we bought t$_i$]]] (SUCH) THING]
b. (He weighs) [$_{DP}$ THE [$_{CP}$ what AMOUNT$_i$ [C [you weigh t$_i$]]] (SUCH) AMOUNT]
c. (I hate) [$_{DP}$ THE [$_{CP}$ who(ever) PERSON$_i$ [C [t$_i$ does that to me]]] (SUCH) PERSON][14]
d. (This is) [$_{DP}$ THE [$_{CP}$ where PLACE$_i$ [C [they slept P t$_i$]]] THERE PLACE][15]
e. (He was born) [$_{DP}$ THE [$_{CP}$ when TIME$_i$ [C [I was born P t$_i$]]] THEN TIME]
f. (This is) [$_{DP}$THE [$_{CP}$ how MANNER$_i$ [C [we would like him to behave P t$_i$]] (SUCH) MANNER]

The structures in (10) represent the double-headed structure of Merge of "Headless" RCs in English. Within the (pre-nominal) RC the internal Head moves to Spec,CP, licensing the non-pronunciation of the external Head in what amounts to a 'Raising' derivation, the external Head remaining in situ.[16]

---

14 Bare *who* "Headless" RCs are generally quite marginal, if possible at all. Richard Kayne, p. c., tells me that for him the otherwise impossible **I'll invite who you want me to invite* improves if *exactly* is added (?*I'll invite exactly who you want me to invite*). The normal way is to use a 'light-headed' RC: *he who…* For recent discussion see Patterson and Caponigro (2016). In certain languages the 'functional' noun PERSON associated with the interrogative pronoun 'who' is actually pronounced. See the case of the Western Malayo-Polynesian language Bih:
(i) Sei   mnuih hiar lăm nei? (Nguyen 2013, §6.2.1.1)
     who person cry   LOC PROX
     'Who has cried in here?'
15 See again Bih for the pronunciation of the 'generic/functional' noun PLACE:
(i) ti anôk ŏng dôk? (Nguyen 2013, §6.2.1.5)
     where place you stay
     'Where are you?'
For arguments that *where, when, how* are necessarily merged with a silent preposition stranded by *wh*-movement, see Caponigro and Pearl (2008, 2009). They assume that preposition stranding may be possible with silent prepositions even in languages like Italian that do not allow it with overt (non-axial) prepositions. This may be confirmed by sluicing cases such as *Stava parlando con qualcuno. Non so chi/con chi* 'He was talking with someone. I don't know who/with whom'.
16 In the 'Matching' derivation of post-nominal externally Headed RCs, the external Head raises to a position to the left of (above) the RC CP (a consequence of the general head-initial word order property that raises constituents containing the lexical NP to the left (above) its modifiers), licensing the total (*that* relatives) or partial (*wh*-relatives) non pronunciation of the internal Head. There is some similarity here with "VP-Deletion", except that one of the two Heads has in most languages to be silent. In some the two Heads can however be both pronounced. See Cinque (2011).

The overt part (*what*, etc.) of the Head (*what* THING, etc.) is a *wh*-proform (also used in interrogatives and other constructions – see Caponigro 2003,Chapter 3 for the specific semantic contribution compatible with all of its uses) which does not need a c-commanding antecedent in contrast with relative *wh*-proforms.

In certain languages, the silent determiner of (10) is pronounced, as in Yucatec Maya (cf. (11), from Gutiérrez-Bravo 2013, 29)[17]:

(11) [**le** [ba'ax k-in tsikbal-t-ik-Ø te'ex]-a'
     det what HAB-ERG-1SG chat-TRNS-IND-ABS.3SG 2PL-CL
     'This (thing) which I'm telling you about'

I take the structures in (10) to underlie both *definite* "Headless" RCs (*Il mese prossimo sposerò proprio chi(*-unque) mi hai presentato l'anno scorso* 'Next month I will marry precisely who(*-ever) you introduced to me last year', '..the very person who..'; *Sarà ammesso alla festa solo chi(*-unque) porterà una bottiglia di vino* 'Only he who brings a bottle of wine will be admitted to the party';

See section 4 below for possible evidence, from Polish and Croatian, that a "Matching" derivation is needed (in addition to a "Raising" one). 'Raising' derivations in RCs are typical of amount/maximalizing RCs (for the maximalizing nature of "Headless" RCs, see Carlson 1977, Grosu 1994,§3.2, Grosu and Landman 1998, Caponigro 2003). The non existence of non-restrictive uses of "Headless" RCs (Emonds 1979, 232, Kayne 1994, 114) is taken here to be related to their maximalizing (hence "Raising") nature and to the exclusively "Matching" nature of non-restrictive RCs (Cinque to appear).

17 Also see Chomsky (2013, 46) on the presence in Spanish and French "Headless" RCs of a determiner possibly reduced in English (*ce que*..'what..'; *ce à quoi*.. 'to what..'). Nakamura (2009, 342) cites one example from English (cf. (i) below) in which an *overt* determiner co-occurs with Free relative *what*, but Andrew Radford, p.c., and other speakers find it completely unacceptable:

(i) Florence Griffith-Joyner's death is a stark warning of **the what** drugs do (The Observer, Sep 27, 1998).

In other languages the determiner is present while both the external and the internal Heads can be silent, as in the Lakhota example (i) of fn.10. In still others the determiner and the two Heads can all be silent. See (ii)a. and b. from Sinhala (Indo-Aryan) and Turkish Sign Language, respectively (in (ii)b. capitals stand for the corresponding signs):

(ii) a. [redi hodənə] Nuwanwə tarahə æwisuwə (Walker 2005, 170)
     clothes wash-PRES-REL Nuwan-ACC anger induce-PST
     'The one washing the clothes made Nuwan angry.'
  b. [ENGLISH KNOW] PRIZE WIN (Branchini 2014, 166)
     'the one who knows English won the prize'

Also see de Vries (2002, Chapter 2, §6.3).

I left when Daniel arrived '.. at the very time that..')[18] and *universal/free choice* "Headless" RCs (*I see him when(ever) I can* '..every time I can') (Dayal 1997, von Fintel 2000, Caponigro 2003, Riemsdijk 2005,§5.2).[19]

For a discussion of the interpretational possibilities of bare and '-ever' "Headless" RCs, see Larson (1987), Jacobson (1995), Grosu (1994,1996), Dayal (1997), Pancheva Izvorski (2000), von Fintel (2000), Caponigro (2003), Tredinnick (2005) and references cited there.

As to Modal Existential *wh* Constructions like (12) (Grosu 1994, 2004) they differ from standard "Headless" RCs in several respects. They are not maximalizing, they do not require category and Case matching, they disallow complex *wh*-'ever' phrases, they allow multiple *wh*-fronting in languages which allow it in questions,[20] and they are not strong islands. See Izvorski (1998), Pancheva Izvorski (2000,Chapter 2) and Grosu (1994, Study I, Chapter 5; 2004), where they are in fact analyzed as bare CPs (even if there is possibly a silent object, THING, PERSON, etc., of 'have', 'there is'). Also see Šimík (2011).[21]

---

18 A 'definite' *what* as the associate of a *there* existential construction in English is in general impossible: **There is what you ordered on the desk* (Wilder 1999,686). When possible (*There is what you need: wine in the cellar and food in the fridge*) it may be compatible with Kayne's (2016) analysis if the definite determiner is actually embedded within the associate, as in some of the cases that he discusses (*There is* [THE what KIND] THING(S) *you need*).

19 That the definite reading is made impossible by the presence of '-ever' is pointed out in Dayal (1997), who gives contrasts like the following (also see Jacobson 1995, Caponigro 2003, 112 and Tredinnick 2005, 2):

(i) What(*ever) Mary bought was Barriers. (Dayal 1997, 103)
(ii) What(*ever) Mary is cooking, namely ratatouille, uses onions. (Dayal 1997, 109)

For the possibility that the apparent universal/free choice reading of wh- and wh-'ever' reduces to a maximal (plural) definite reading, see Jacobson (1995, §5).

20 For multiple *wh*-pronouns also in the standard "Headless" RCs of Bulgarian, which has no special '-ever' *wh*-forms, see Dimova (2014) and references cited there.

21 The conclusion that they are distinct from standard "Headless" RCs may find some support from Italian, at least that spoken in the Northeast of Italy, where *che cosa* 'what thing', or *che* 'what', or *cosa* 'thing', have interrogative but no standard "Headless" RC usages (Cinque 1988,497; Benincà and Cinque 2010,§4.5; Bertollo and Cavallo 2012,§3, Cecchetto and Donati 2015,48f). The reason is that in such irrealis/existential "Headless" RCs, *cosa* sounds possible (just as in *wh*-interrogatives):

(i) a. Finalmente avrei cosa fare
        Lit.: At last I would have what to do
     b. Per noi, adesso, ci sarebbe cosa dire
        Lit.:For us now there would be what to say

(in other regional varieties of Italian *cosa*, or *che* can apparently be used in standard "Headless" RCs as well -cf. Caponigro 2003,26 and Manzini 2010,171).

As for the 'identifier' of the particular functional noun postulated in (10)/(11), I follow Grosu (1986/87, 47) in taking the *wh*-phrase of the "Headless" RC to be "the only reasonable candidate for the role of formal identifier [of the external Head]".[22]

(12) a. Maria are [cu cine să voteze]   (Grosu 1994, 138)
   Maria has with whom SUBJ vote
   'Maria has (someone) for whom to vote'
  b. Ima koj kâde da me zavede   (Pancheva Izvorski 2000, 41)
   have.3sg who where Part$_{subj}$ me take.3sg
   'I have someone to take me somewhere'
  c. Non ha con chi parlare   (Caponigro 2003, Chapter 3)
   not he.has with whom to talk
   'He doesn't have anyone to talk to'

4 The phrasal nature and the position of the *wh*- in "Headless" RCs

The present analysis, which takes the *wh*- to be a phrase in the Spec of the RC CP, is not compatible with Donati's (2006), Donati and Cecchetto's (2011), Cecchetto and Donati's (2015, Chapter 3) proposal (see fn. 3 of their 2011 article for precedents of this idea) that "Headless" RCs only involve a bare (X-bar) head which raises and projects, as a determiner, to DP[23]:

There is another indication that they may be just CPs. As noted in Rizzi (1982,75f,note32) embedded interrogative CPs but no standard "Headless" RCs (which are DPs) permit Gapping. Interestingly, Modal Existential *wh* Constructions, like embedded interrogative CPs allow Gapping: *C'è chi preferisce la pasta e chi il riso*, lit.'there is who prefers pasta and who rice'.
22 Also see van Riemsdijk's (2005, 363) and Assmann (2013).
23 In their system if C rather than the raised *wh*- projects the result is a standard interrogative CP rather than a "Headless" RC, which leaves to be seen how best to capture Benincà's (2007, 2012) finding that despite the morphological similarity of the *wh*-forms in the two constructions, the target of the *wh*- in (Italian) "Headless" RCs is higher (above Topics) than that of the *wh*- in interrogatives (below Topics).

(13)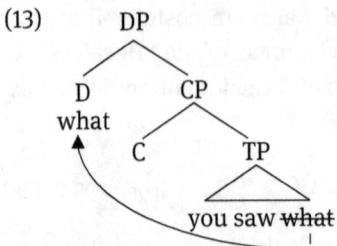

For one thing, as already mentioned, some languages provide direct evidence that the *wh*-phrase in "Headless" RCs is within the RC CP, not outside. In particular, a structure like (13) would lead one to expect that the corresponding German *wh*-free relative pronouns could not extrapose together with the rest of the "Headless" RC, contrary to fact.[24] Secondly there are two constructions which appear to front to Spec, CP complex *wh*-phrases; the 'paucal' relatives in sentences like (14), and the *wh*-'ever' relatives in sentences like (15)[25]:

(14) a. **What beer** we found was flat (Andrews 1975, 75)
 b. Fred hid **what (few) weapons** were on the table (Andrews 1975, 76)
 c. We gave him **what little money** we had (Kayne 1994, 154 note13)
 d. [I]t begins to fit with **what little** we know about history (Chomsky 2015, 74)[26]

(15) a. I shall visit **whatever town** you will visit (Donati and Cecchetto 2011, 552)
 b. I'll read **whatever book(s)** he tells me to read (Jacobson 1995, 451)

---

[24] Cable (2005 and 2010, §6.3) acknowledges that this is a serious challenge for the Move-and-Project analysis though he also advances some speculations on how it could be resolved.

[25] The discussion in Andrews (1975, §1.1.2.2) provides evidence that what he calls 'paucal' (free) relatives cannot be taken to be *wh*-'ever' relatives with a silent '-ever'. Apart from their special meaning of insufficiency, 'paucal' (free) relatives, as opposed to *wh*-'ever' phrases, can only be used with mass or plural nouns (*Fred hid what weapon was on the table* vs. *Fred hid whatever weapon was on the table*). Also, they are compatible with paucal modifiers like *few* and *little*, but not with multal or numeral quantifiers (**I saw what many/three people arrived early*), while exactly the opposite holds for *wh*-'ever' phrases (**I greeted whatever few people came to the door* vs. *I hid the coats of whatever three people he brought*). Should they co-occur with a different ('paucal') silent element (possibly LITTLE/FEW), this would likely be within CP, like '–ever', given the German extraposition facts to be mentioned below concerning the German *w- immer auch* phrases (the analogues of *wh-ever* phrases in English), which necessarily extrapose with the rest of the "Headless" RC.

[26] Which we take to be: .. *with* [THE [*what little* AMOUNT (THAT) *we know* ...] (SUCH) AMOUNT]. In the next page, the following variant is used: ... *with the little that we know* (i.e.,...*with* [*the* [(WHAT) *little* AMOUNT *that we know*] (SUCH) AMOUNT]. For the degraded status of overt *that* if *what* is also overt see footnotes 28 and 30.

Donati and Cecchetto (2011) may be right in suggesting that in some languages (some) *wh-*'ever' phrases can also be Heads of Headed RCs (see the Italian – *unque* case in (16)a, from Battye 1989, 230, where such sentences are dubbed 'pseudo-free relatives', and the English '-ever' case in (16)b, from Chierchia and Caponigro 2013, 7)[27]:

(16) a. Chiunque a cui tu avessi parlato ti avrebbe dato la stessa risposta
'Whoever to whom you had spoken would have given you the same reply'
b. John would read whichever book that he happened to put his hands on

There are however indications that the same does not hold for other languages and possibly for other *wh-* forms in English (for some speakers). Citko (2008, 930ff) points out three phenomena with respect to which RCs with *wh-*'ever' phrases pattern with standard "Headless" RCs (with bare *wh*-words in COMP) rather than with Headed RCs. They are: incompatibility of most forms with overt 'complementizers' in English (cf. (17)),[28] strict Case matching in Polish (cf. (18)),[29] and RC extraposition in German (cf. (19)).

---

27 The contrast between (16)a, grammatical with a slight pause between *chiunque* and *a cui*, and its English translation, ungrammatical, is to be related to the possibility of using *chiunque*, but not *whoever*, as an indefinite pronoun (= *anyone*). See *Parlerebbe con chiunque* 'He would speak with anyone (lit. whoever)' – Cecchetto and Donati 2011 Appendix) vs. **He would speak with who(m)ever*. For the special status of *–unque* "Headless" RCs in Italian and their Romanian analogues, see Caponigro and Fălăuș (2016).

(16)a–b should be kept distinct from the apparently similar cases found in 'doubly-filled COMP' languages like Middle English (Benincà 2007,§5.2) and Paduan (Benincà 2012,36f), where both the *wh-*phrase and the 'complementizer' are within the (split) CP. Indeed it remains to be seen whether (16)b isn't also a case of a doubly filled COMP if the same speakers who accept it also accept *that* with an interrogative *wh-*phrase, as Andrew Radford does (see fn. 30 below).

28 On the general inability of bare *wh-*'ever' phrases to be ordinary arguments in Head position in English, see Jacobson (1995,460). Also see Groat's (2012) example *I'd like to meet whoever's books (*that) sell over a million copies*. For such cases Groat assumes that it is the *wh-* at the edge that enters into an agree relation with the external antecedent. One can get even deeper embedding:

(i) [[Whoever's father's family] has a lot of money] will get rich.

The problematic status for the Head analysis of these examples (and that in fn. 2 above) is also pointed out in Jacobson (1995, 462). The relation between *whoever* and the external silent antecedent in (i) appears to be the same as that holding between *whose* and the overt antecedent in cases like *The boy [[whose father's family] has a lot of money] will get rich.* Also see Citko (2009, 61f).

29 Wh–*kolwiek* (*wh-*'ever') RCs require Case matching, like simple "Headless" RCs, and unlike Headed RCs.

(17) a. We'll hire whichever man (*that) you recommended to us
 (Citko 2009, 931)[30]
 b. I'll read whatever book (??that/which) you'll read
 (Jacobson 1995, 461)

(18) a. Zatrudnimy [któregokolwiek studenta nam polecisz t_ACC]_ACC
 Hire.1PL whichever.ACC student.ACC us recommend.2SG
 (Citko 2008, 931)
 'We'll hire whichever student you recommend to us'
 b. *Zatrudnimy [któremukolwiek studentowi ufamy t_DAT]_ACC
 hire.1PL whichever.DAT student.DAT trust.1PL
 (Citko 2008, 931)
 'We'll hire whichever student we trust'
 c. *Zatrudnimy [któregokolwiek studenta [ufamy t_DAT]]_ACC[31]
 hire.1PL whichever.ACC student.ACC trust.1PL
 'We'll hire whichever student we trust'

(19) a. Der Hans hat zurückgegeben [**welches Geld auch immer**
 The Hans has returned which money even ever
 er gestohlen hat]
 he stolen has
 'Hans has returned whatever money he has stolen'

---

30 The same is true of 'paucal' "Headless" RCs. See (i), from Andrews (1975, 78),

 (i) I drank what beer (*that) was on the table/we found.

though he finds the ungrammaticality of (i) less severe than that with ordinary free relatives with *that* (*I ate what that he brought*). Andrew Radford, p.c., who generally accepts both *wh-*'ever' and paucal *wh-* followed by a nominal to co-occur with *that* (see exercise 7.4 of Radford 2016), still finds a difference between *What little beer that was left, he drank* (perfect) and the much worse *What (little) that was left, he drank*. The fact that he has a similar contrast in *wh*-interrogatives (*I wonder what *(kind of celebration) that he has in mind*) may suggest that even in the Free RC construction the *wh-*'ever' or paucal phrase and *that* are for him both in CP.

31 Which should be good, given the well-formedness of

(i) Zatrudnimy [tego człowieka_ACC [któremu ufamy t_DAT]_ACC (Citko 2008, 931)
 hire.1PL this.ACC man.ACC whom.DAT trust.1PL
 'We'll hire the man that we trust.'

b. *Der Hans hat **welches Geld   auch immer** zurückgegeben
   The Hans has which   money even ever   returned
   [er gestohlen hat]³²
   he stolen has

Borsley (1984, 11f) discusses another case from Polish which suggests that *wh*-'ever' phrases, like bare *wh*-pronouns, and unlike the Head of Headed RCs, are located in Spec,CP.

The possessive anaphor *swój* must occur in the same local domain (IP/CP) as its antecedent. When inside the *wh*-phrase of an embedded interrogative it can only be bound (under reconstruction) by an antecedent inside the embedded interrogative (cf. (20)a.), and cannot be bound by an antecedent in the matrix clause (cf. (20)b.). When inside the Head of a Headed RC *swój* must instead be bound from an antecedent located in the matrix clause (cf. (21)a.), not by one located in the relative clause (cf. (21)b.)³³:

(20) a. Jan   zapytał [[którą ze   swoich$_i$ piosenek]$_k$ pro$_i$ lubisz t$_k$]
        John   asked   which from self.poss songs   you.like
        'John asked which of your songs you liked'
     b. *Jan$_i$ zapytał [[którą   ze swoich$_i$ piosenek]$_k$ lubisz t$_k$]
        John   asked   which from self.poss   songs   you.like
        'John asked which of his songs you liked'

(21) a. Jan$_i$ zaśpiewa [[każda ze swoich$_i$ piosenek] jaką$_k$ wybierzesz t$_k$]
        John will.sing each from self.poss songs   which you.will.choose
        'John will sing each of his songs that you choose'
     b. *Jan zaśpiewa [[każda ze swoich$_i$ piosenek]$_k$, jaką ty$_i$ wybierzesz t$_k$]
        John will.sing each from self.poss songs   which you.will.choose
        'John will sing each of his songs that you choose'

---

32 Also see the following, provided by Henk van Riemsdijk, p.c.:
(i) a. [[Wessen Buch auch immer] von Reich Ranicki gelobt wurde]
         whose book even ever   by Reich Ranicki praised was
         hat sich immer sehr gut verkauft
         has REFL always very well sold
         'Whoever's book was praised by Reich Ranicki always sold very well'
     b. **[Wessen Buch auch immer] hat sich immer sehr gut verkauft, von Reich Ranicki gelobt wurde

33 This appears to show that the RC Head cannot reconstruct inside the RC pointing to the presence of a "Matching", rather than a "Raising", derivation in (21).

Crucially, when *swój* is contained inside the *wh*'-ever' phrase of a "Headless" RC, it can**not** be bound by an antecedent in the matrix clause (cf. (22)a.); it can only be bound by one within the RC (under reconstruction) (cf. (22)b.), as when it is contained within a *wh*-phrase in the Spec,CP of an embedded interrogative clause (cf. (20) above).

(22) a. *Jan$_j$ zaśpiewa [[którąkolwiek ze swoich$_j$ piosenek]$_k$
John will.sing whichever from self.poss songs
pro$_i$ wybierzesz t$_k$]
(you) will.choose
'John will sing whichever of his songs you choose'

b. Jan zaśpiewa [[którąkolwiek ze swoich$_i$ piosenek]$_k$
John will.sing whichever from self.poss songs
pro$_i$ wybierzesz t$_k$]
(you) will.choose
'John will sing whichever of your songs you choose'

This clearly suggests that *wh*'-ever' phrases (in Polish) are in the COMP of the "Headless" RC, not in an external Head position.[34]

The same pattern is displayed by the Croatian possessive anaphor *svoj* (Gračanin-Yüksek 2008). When *svoj* is within the *wh*-phrase of an embedded *wh*-question it can only be bound by an antecedent within the embedded *wh*-question (under *total* reconstruction), not by one in the matrix clause:

(23) Ivan$_k$ ne zna koje je svoje$_{j/*i/*k}$ slike Vid$_i$ mislio
Ivan not know which Aux self's pictures Vid thought
da je Dan$_j$ poslao na natječaj
that Aux Dan sent on contest

---

[34] For Citko (2009, §3.3) 'however many' *wh*-phrases in Polish free relatives also allow for non-reconstructed interpretations. Adam Szczegielniak informs me that for certain speakers *swój* can also function as a pronominal, so that for them no comparable clear contrasts should be expected to exist. Nonetheless he himself finds the contrast between a headless RC ((i)a) and a headed one ((i)b) striking:

(i) a. Jan$_n$ zaśpiewa [[którąkolwiek ze swoich$_{i/*n}$ piosenek]$_k$ pro$_i$ wybierzesz t$_k$]
John will.sing whichever from self.poss songs (you) will.choose
'John will sing whichever of your songs you choose'
b. Jan$_n$ zaśpiewa [którąkolwiek ze swoich$_{*i/n}$ piosenek] [[którą$_k$ pro$_i$ wybierzesz t$_k$]
John will.sing whichever from your songs which (you) will.choose
'John will sing whichever of your songs which you choose'

'Ivan$_k$ doesn't know which pictures of himself$_{j/*i/*k}$ Vid$_i$ thought Dan$_j$ sent to the contest'

The opposite holds in Headed RCs. *Svoj* can only be bound by an antecedent in the matrix clause, not by one within the RC. See (24)[35]:

(24) Vid$_i$ će negraditi ono svoje$_{i/*j}$ dijete koje Dan$_j$ preporuči
     Vid will reward that self's   child which Dan recommends
     'Vid$_i$ will reward the one of his$_{i/*j}$ children that Dan$_j$ recommends'

Wh-'ever' phrases of "Headless" RCs behave like *wh*-phrases in *wh*-questions. The possessive anaphor *svoj* contained within them can only be bound (under total reconstruction) by an antecedent within the RC, not by one in the matrix clause (thus pointing to their location in the Spec,CP of the "Headless" RC)[36]:

(25) Vid$_i$ će negraditi koje god svoje$_{j/*i}$ dijete Dan$_j$ preporuči
     Vid will reward which ever self's child Dan recommends
     'Vid$_i$ will reward whichever of his$_{j/*i}$ children Dan$_j$ recommends'

Other languages show that even *Definite* "Headless" RCs (those that plausibly do not involve a silent '-ever', as seen above) can be introduced by complex *wh*-expression *who/what/which* + NP.

One such case is provided by Chuj (a Mayan language from Guatemala) (see (26), from Kotek and Erlewine (2015, §5.2.3), who explicitly say that they "may include overt nominal domains" (p. 34).[37]

---

35 "[R]econstruction of the head NP into the relative clause is impossible. The head NP and the matrix subject seem to belong to the same clause." (Gračanin-Yüksek 2008, 281) (which, as noted, points to a "Matching" rather than "Raising" derivation). The only exception is "H[eaded] R[elative]s denoting degrees" (Gračanin-Yüksek 2008, fn. 8) (which since Carlson 1977 are taken to involve a "Raising" derivation).
36 The clitic second syntax of Croatian also shows conclusively that they cannot have raised out of Spec,CP (Gračanin-Yüksek 2008, §3), and that "move-and-project analyses [...] cannot be the right account of Croatian FRs" (Gračanin-Yüksek 2008, fn. 22).
37 Another appears to be Melchor Ocampo Mixtec (Caponigro, Torrence and Cisneros 2013, §4.3 and §5.6).
    Cecchetto and Donati (2015, 51) point out that there appear to be no "Headless" RCs with in-situ *wh*-pronouns (cf. also Kayne 1994, 158note30) and that this follows from the need for the free relative CP to project into a DP via raising of the *wh*-pronoun/determiner (a case in point could be French: *[*Tu as rencontré qui*] *est malade* 'who you have met is sick' vs. *Tu as rencontré qui?* 'Who have you met?'). In the present context this might instead be related to

(26) a. Ix-Ø-w-ilelta [FR **mach** (**winh unin**) ix-Ø-ulek'-i].
       PRFV-B3-A1S-meet who (CL.MASC boy) PRFV-B3-come-ITV
       'I met (the boy) who came.'
   b. Ko-gana [FR **tas** (**libro-al**) ix-Ø-s-man waj Xun].
       A1P-like what book-NML PRFV-B3-A3-buy CL.NAME Juan
       'We like the book that Juan bought.'

Thus, a raising and projection of the *wh*-form in "Headless" RCs does not seem viable.

5 The lack of "Headless" reduced RCs

"Headless" reduced RCs appear not to be possible. See (27), explicitly noted in Jacobson (1995, 460) (and confirmed by other speakers):

(27) a. *What(ever) lurking outside my windows scares me.[38]
   b. *What(ever) displayed in this windows will be sold by midnight.
   c. *Whatever house cheaper than mine will sell quicker.

The pattern follows if no Case is assigned to Spec,IP as a consequence of the lack of finite Tense within the reduced RC (cf. Kayne 1994, §8.4), and

---

the non existence in French (and languages like French) of in-situ relative *wh*-pronouns (whatever the principle is that forces their movement). The ban on in-situ "Headless" *wh*-phrases may not be completely general if the correlative structures of Burushaski (isolate) ((ii)a.) and Koṇḍa (South-Central Dravidian) ((ii)b.) (and other Dravidian languages) are left dislocated "Headless" RCs with in-situ *wh*-pronouns:

(ii) a. šon gukúr   biṭáne   bésan   sénuma   ke   ité
        Shon-Gukur   shaman.ERG   what.indef.sg.abs say-adjvlz=Q LINK   that.abs
        sahíi   maními   (Yoshioka 2012, 199)
        correct   become.NPRS.3rdsg
        'What Shon Gukur had said turned out to be true'
   b. maa kiidu   inika manadoo daani peru veRtu   (Lakshmi Bai 1985, 185)
      our in.hands what to.be   its name tell
      'Tell us the name of what we have in our hands'

38 The ungrammaticality of (27)a should be contrasted with the grammaticality of *Anything lurking outside my windows scares me* (Andrew Radford, p.c.).

if there is no other way of assigning Case to the *wh*-phrase from the outside.[39]

The same seems true for Italian:

(28) *Chi invitato alla festa dovrà portare una bottiglia
 who invited to the party will have to bring a bottle.

Apparent exceptions, like (29), can be accounted for if, as suggested in Donati and Cecchetto (2011, Appendix), *qualunque cosa* and *chiunque* can be external Heads, which receive Case in the matrix clause (see (30), where they stand by themselves):

(29) a. Qualunque cosa persa da uno di voi non verrà ricomprata
 whatever thing lost by one of you will not be bought again
 b. ?Chiunque sorpreso a rubare verrà multato
 whoever caught stealing will be fined

(30) a. Farei qualunque cosa per aiutarti
 I would do whatever thing to help you
 'I would do anything to help you'
 b. Parlerebbe con chiunque
 (S)he would talk with whoever
 '(S)he would talk with anyone'

---

39 On the IP nature of reduced RCs see Cinque (2010,§4.2 and §5.1), where evidence from Fanselow (1986) is cited for the presence of a PRO subject with both present and past participles (pace Siloni 1995). The fact that "Headless" reduced RCs appear not to be possible even where no Case licensing is plausibly at issue (cf. (i)), may suggest that they contain no CP capable of hosting a *wh*-phrase:
(i) a. *Il lavoro sarà recensito dove pubblicato.
 the paper will be reviewed where published
 b. *Quando addormentata Gianna si mise a russare.
 when fallen asleep, Gianna started snoring
(vs. Appena addormentata,... 'Once fallen asleep,..', where *appena* is an AdvP plausibly in IP).
The absence of a CP in reduced RCs should also account for the impossibility of *the book which recently sent*... (cf. Kayne 1994, 98). Also see Siloni (1995) for the different structure to be attributed to present and past participle reduced RCs in French and Italian, IP and ParticipialP, respectively. If she is right that these categories are contained within an extra DP layer, no 'government' issues should arise for the presence of a PRO.

For the same reasons we take *newspapers* in (31)a–b to be an external Head, assigned Case in the matrix clause. If it could receive, in Spec,CP (or Spec,IP), the Case assigned by the matrix Tense to the matrix DP containing the CP (IP), we would expect the "Headless" RCs in (27) and (28) to also be possible, contrary to fact.[40]

(31) a. The [newspapers [recently arrived]] were eagerly read by everyone
     b. The [[recently arrived] newspapers] were eagerly read by everyone

6 Wh-'ever' in argument and in adjunct clausal position

As mentioned in fn.4, there are reasons to distinguish argument 'Headless' RCs from Free adjunct free RCs (Izvorski, 2000, Riemsdijk 2005, §5.1, Rawlins 2008), which are close in meaning to *no matter* clausal adjuncts (even if the two may share a common semantics at a more abstract level – cf. Hirsch to appear).

As noted in Riemsdijk (2005, §5.1) argument "Headless" RCs (as opposed to Free adjunct Free RCs) do not yield natural paraphrases with *no matter* concessive clauses (cf. *This dog attacks whoever/?*no matter who crosses its path*.).[41] Free adjunct Free RCs also differ from standard argument "Headless" RCs in requiring '–ever'(*Co**(kolwiek) się stanie, jedziemy jutro do Paryża/ What*(ever) happens,we are going to Paris tomorrow* – Citko 2010, 238).[42]

Here are listed a few additional phenomena which show that *wh'-*ever' phrases in argument and adjunct positions behave differently.

---

[40] By the same reasoning, differently from Cinque (2010, 56), the Head *headway* of a reduced RC like *The headway made so far is not negligible* must be an external Head (the coindexed PRO within the reduced RC perhaps satisfying the idiom requirements). See Cinque (to appear) and references cited there for the doubtful diagnostic nature of idiom chunks for "Raising".

[41] He also notes that there is no standard argument "Headless" RC that corresponds to *no matter whether* Free Adjunct Free RCs (such as *No matter whether Carl talks or not, he will be convicted*). Andrew Radford, p.c., however, finds *This dog attacks no matter who crosses its path* grammatical.

[42] Among the "Headless" *wh*-phrases of Italian *quant-* 'what,who.pl' cannot take the '-ever' suffix *–unque* (cf. Donati and Cecchetto 2011, 552) and, as opposed to those that do, they cannot be used in Free adjunct Free RCs (**Quanto succederà, noi ce ne andremo* 'What will happen, we will leave').

6.1 No relative pronouns in Free adjunct free RCs

Although –*unque wh*-phrases in Italian "Headless" RCs may (also) be external heads followed by a relative pronoun, as seen in (16) above, they cannot be followed by a relative pronoun in Free adjunct free RCs. This is expected if these are bare CPs, with no external Head:

(32) *Qualunque cosa di cui lui si vanti, noi non ci lasceremo impressionare

Whatever thing of which he may boast, we won't let ourselves be impressed (vs. *Di qualunque cosa lui si vanti, noi non ci lasceremo impressionare* 'Of whatever thing he may boast, we won't let ourselves to be impressed')

6.2 German Free adjunct free RCs in Vorvorfeld

To judge from German, Free adjunct free RCs also appear to occupy positions different from the positions occupied by arguments, where standard "Headless" RCs are internally merged. While the latter, as DPs, target ordinary DP positions, argument or topic and focus positions in the left periphery, counting as occupiers of the first position and yielding V2 (cf. (33)), Free adjunct free RCs occupy an adverbial position higher than topics and foci, forcing the finite verb to be in third position (cf.(34)), like other 'conditionals of irrelevance' ((35))[43]:

(33) Wen auch immer du einlädst, wird Maria gut erhalten
     Who also ever you invite, will Maria welcome

(34) a. Wen auch immer du einlädst, Maria wird nicht kommen
       Who also ever you invite, Maria will not come
       (d'Avis 2004,141)
   b. *Wen auch immer du einlädst, wird Maria nicht kommen
       (d'Avis 2004, 148)

(35) Ob es regnet oder nicht, wir gehen spazieren   (d'Avis 2004, 141)
     Whether it rains or not, we go for a walk

---

[43] I thank Roland Hinterhölzl for discussing this point with me.

6.3 Free adjunct free RCs in Appalachian English

In Appalachian English (AppE) the '-ever' of Standard American English (SAE) precedes the *wh*-phrase (see Johnson 2015), rather than following it[44]:

(36) a. You should return ever-what you have finished reading to the library. (AppE)
   b. You should return what-ever you have finished reading to the library. (SAE)

This ordering is however banned in Free adjunct free RCs. Cf. (37):

(37) *You will win the competition, ever-who judges the final round.

7 (Morphological) Case (mis)match in "Headless" RCs

The (morphological) Case matching requirement holding of "Headless" RCs has been the object of intensive research, which has come to distinguish essentially three types of languages: (1) fully matching languages (like Polish, English, Italian, etc. – Grosu 1994, Citko 2000) where the Case of the *wh*-phrase in Spec, CP and the Case assigned to the external DP have to exactly match,[45] (2) nonmatching languages where case conflicts between the internal and external Case are resolved in favor of the internal Case (certain varieties of German – Pittner 1991, 1995, sometime referred to as German B – Vogel 2001), and (3) nonmatching languages where case conflicts are resolved in favor of the external Case (like Classical Greek, Gothic, etc. – Harbert 1983). See the discussion

---

[44] We may take Standard English *wh-ever* phrases to be complex phrases derived by raising of the *wh-* part, from a structure essentially like the Appalachian English *ever-wh* (which possibly is itself complex: AT ever(y) TIME *wh-*) across *–ever*. Thinking of Kayne's (1994) analyses of 's and *-ever*, *Whoever's pictures* would be derivable from [ever [who ['s [pictures with *who* raising above *–ever*. *Whosever pictures,* in those variants that prefer it to *whoever's pictures,* could be derived from the same structure with *pictures* raising above *who[*'s before the merger of *–ever* followed by remnant movement of *who[*'s above *–ever*. Thanks to Richard Kayne for relevant discussion.
[45] Andrew Radford (2016, 468), however, reports cases of non-matching like (i) even in English:
(i) [*Whomever* you elect] will serve a four-year term.

and references in the above works as well the general discussions in Grosu (1994) and Riemsdijk (2005), Daskalaki (2011).

Here I won't add to these discussions except for a proposal meant to derive, in addition to the matching ones, the generalization holding of the *nonmatching type 2)* (where the Case conflict is resolved in favor of the internal Case).[46] The nonmatching type 2) appears to obey the following generalization: when different from the Case assigned externally, the *wh*-phrase can bear the Case assigned within the relative clause (as expected if it is in Spec,CP) *provided that such Case is lower in the Case hierarchy* (NOM > ACC > GEN > DAT > OBL) *than the Case assigned externally* (cf. Pittner 1995,211).[47] (38) and (39) provide some illustrative examples from German B:

(38) a. Sie lädt ein$_{\rightarrow Acc}$[$_{FR}$ wem$_{Dat}$ sie zu Dank verplichtet ist]
  she invites to.whom she to thanks obliged is
  (Pittner 1995, 208) (ACC [$_{FR}$DAT]])
  'She invites who she is obliged to'
 b. Jeder muss tun, wofür er bestimmt ist
  everybody must do what-for(PP) he destined is
  (Pittner 1995, 208) (ACC [$_{FR}$BENEF])
  'Everybody must do what he is destined for'
 c. [$_{FR}$Wen$_{Acc}$ Maria$_{Nom}$ mag$_{\rightarrow Acc}$]$_{Nom}$ wird eingeladen
  who.acc Maria likes is invited
  (Vogel 2001, 903) (NOM [$_{FR}$ACC])
  'Who Maria likes gets invited.'

(39) a. *Er zerstört $_{\rightarrow Acc}$ [$_{FR}$ wer$_{Nom}$ ihm begegnet]
  he destroys   who   him meets
  (Vogel 2001, 904) (ACC [$_{FR}$NOM])
  'He destroys he who meets him'

---

46 For type 3), and its complexities, see Harbert (1983) and especially Grosu (1994, Study I, Chapter 4) in terms of Case Attraction, which in some languages also holds of the corresponding Headed RCs.

47 The generalization appears to hold independently of the differences which may exist among the selective nonmatching languages with respect to which structural positions admit nonmatching: left dislocated positions (in German but not French – Harbert 1983, §4), subject positions, if distinct from clitic left dislocated positions in null subject languages (Spanish and Catalan – Hirschbühler and Rivero 1982 – but not Italian).

This recalls the possibility of Inverse Case Attraction in Headed RCs in left dislocated and subject positions in certain languages (Farsi varieties and Albanian dialects), analysed as "Raising" relatives in Cinque (2007, 99ff) and references cited there.

b. *Ich vertraue →Dat [FR wen_Acc ich einlade]
   I   trust   who   I invite
                                   (Vogel 2003, 283) (DAT [FR ACC])
   'I trust whom I invite'

In a double-headed configuration like, say, V_matrix [DP D [CP [XP *what* THING]$_i$ V_embedded t$_i$] (SUCH) THING]], the matrix V assigns Case to DP (which percolates to the external Head (SUCH) THING). The internal Head, [*what* THING] instead receives Case from the embedded V.

Such double-headed configuration allows one to derive the full matching case and the nonmatching case where the Case conflict is resolved in favor of the internal Case without having to resort to non-local relations spanning over two maximal projections, DP and CP.

The parametric variation between fully matching languages like English (but see fn.45), Polish, or Italian and nonmatching languages like German B appears to be expressible in terms of Caha's (2009, §1.6) Universal (Case) Containment (40), which is motivated by Case syncretism and other generalizations:

(40) Universal (Case) Containment
   a. In the Case sequence, the marking of Cases on the right can morphologically contain Cases on the left, but not the other way around.
   b. The Case sequence: NOM – ACC – GEN – DAT – INS – COM

Each Case in the sequence contains the Cases to its left though not those to its right, NOM being the poorest, for ex.: [AccP ACC [NomP NOM]].

In fully matching languages the raised internal Head licenses the nonpronunciation of the external Head, which it c-commands (under Kayne's 1994 definition), only if the category and (morphological) Case of the two Heads are identical. In German B type languages, the licensing is less strict. For the nonpronunciation of the external Head it is enough (for identification) that the internal Head, which c-commands it, has a Case which contains the Case of the external Head.[48]

---

[48] (38)a–c are thus fine as DAT/BENEF contains ACC (and NOM) and ACC contains NOM. If the opposite is the case ((39)a–b), an ungrammatical result obtains, presumably for lack of Case recoverability. See Assmann (2013) for a similar treatment in terms of Case features containment, though she takes Nominative to be "richer" than Accusative, which is richer than lower Cases.

Within analyses which do not assume an external Head (as in [DP D [CP]]) it is not clear why in the selective nonmatching cases it is enough for the Case of the *wh*-phrase (say, DAT) to

8 By way of conclusion

Evidence was reviewed above that renders it at least plausible to conceive of a double-headed analysis even for "Headless" RCs, where the external Head of the bare *wh*-forms (*what, who,* etc.), or, for that matter, complex *wh*-'ever' forms, is one of the functional/light nouns/classifiers THING, AMOUNT, PERSON, PLACE, TIME, etc., also silently present with the *wh*-forms (*what* THING, *whatever book* THING) raised to the Spec,CP of the RC.

References

Alexiadou, Artemis and Spyridoula Varlokosta. 1996. The Syntactic and Semantic Properties of Free Relatives in Modern Greek. *ZAS Papers in Linguistics* 5. 1–31.
Andrews, Avery Delano III. 1975. *Studies in the Syntax of Relative and Comparative Clauses.* Ph.D. Dissertation, MIT.
Andrews, Avery Delano III. 2007. Relative Clauses. In T. Shopen, ed., *Language Typology and Syntactic Description. Volume II: Complex Constructions* (Second Edition). 206–236. Cambridge: Cambridge University Press.
Anonby, Erik J. 2011. *A Grammar of Mambay: an Adamawa language of Chad and Cameroon.* Köln: Köppe.
Assmann, Anke. 2013. Three Stages in the Derivation of Free Relatives. In F. Heck & A. Assmann, eds. *Rule Interaction in Grammar* (Linguistische Arbeitsberichte 90). 203–245. Universität Leipzig, Leipzig. http://www.uni-leipzig.de/~asw/lab/lab90/LAB90_07_anke.pdf
Battye, Adrian. 1989. Free relatives, pseudo-free relatives, and the syntax of CP in Italian. *Rivista di Linguistica* 1.219–250 http://linguistica.sns.it/RdL/1.2/Battye.pdf
Benincà, Paola. 2007. Headless Relative clauses in Old Italian and some related issues. Handout of a paper presented at the Université de Paris VIII, 13.12.2007.
Benincà, Paola. 2010. Headless Relatives in Some Old Italian Varieties. In R. D'Alessandro, A. Ledgeway and I. Roberts, eds., *Syntactic Variation. The Dialects of Italy.* 55–70. Cambridge: Cambridge University Press.
Benincà, Paola. 2012. Lexical Complementizers and Headless Relatives. In L. Brugè et al., eds., *Functional Heads. The Cartography of Syntactic Structures, Vol. 7.* 29–41. New York: Oxford University Press.
Benincà, Paola and Guglielmo Cinque. 2010. La frase relativa. In G. Salvi and L. Renzi, eds., *Grammatica dell'italiano antico.* Vol. I., 469–507. Bologna: Il Mulino.
Bertollo, Sabrina and Guido Cavallo. 2012. The syntax of Italian free relative clauses: an analysis. *Generative Grammar in Geneva* 8. 59–76.

---

contain the Case of D (say, NOM), but not viceversa (why couldn't the Case of D contain the Case of the *wh*-, with D DAT and the *wh*- NOM?).

Bliese, Loren F. 1981. *A Generative Grammar of Afar*. Dallas: Summer Institute of Linguistics and Arlington: The University of Texas. http://www.sil.org/resources/archives/8559

Borsley, Robert D. 1984. Free relatives in Polish and English. In J. Fisiak, ed., *Contrastive Linguistics. Prospects and Problems*. 1–18. Berlin: Mouton Publishers.

Branchini, Chiara. 2014. *On Relativization and Clefting. An Analysis of Italian Sign Language*. Berlin: Mouton de Gruyter and Preston: Ishara Press.

Bresnan, Joan and Jane Grimshaw. 1978. The Syntax of Free Relatives in English. *Linguistic Inquiry* 9. 331–391

Bury, Dirk. 2003. *Phrase structure and derived heads*. Ph.D. Dissertation, University College, London. https://www.phon.ucl.ac.uk/home/deleted_22_09_10/dirk/PSderivedheads.pdf

Cable, Seth. 2005. Free Relatives in Lingít and Haida: Evidence that the Mover Projects. Unpublished ms., MIT, Cambridge, Mass.

Cable, Seth. 2010. *The Grammar of Q. Q-Particles, Wh-Movement, and Pied Piping*. New York: Oxford University Press.

Caponigro, Ivano. 2003. *Free not to ask*. Ph.D. dissertation, University of California, Los Angeles. http://idiom.ucsd.edu/~ivano/Papers/2003_dissertation_revised_2015-8-13.pdf

Caponigro, Ivan and Anamaria Fălăuş. 2016. Free Choice Free Relative Clauses in Italian and Romanian. Ms., University of California at San Diego.

Caponigro, Ivano and Lisa Pearl. 2008. Silent Prepositions: Evidence from free relatives. In A. Asbury et al., eds., *Syntax and Semantics of Spatial P*. 365–385. Amsterdam: John Benjamins.

Caponigro, Ivano and Lisa Pearl. 2009. The nominal nature of *where, when*, and *how*: Evidence from free relatives. *Linguistic Inquiry* 40. 155–164

Caponigro, Ivano, Harold Torrence and Carlos Cisneros. 2013. Free Relative Clauses in Two Mixtec Languages. *International Journal of American Linguistics* 79. 61–96

Cecchetto, Carlo and Caterina Donati. 2015. *(Re)labeling*. Cambridge, Mass.: MIT Press.

Chierchia, Gennaro and Ivano Caponigro. 2013. Questions on questions and free relatives. Handout of a paper presented at *Sinn und Bedeutung*, Vitoria, Basque Country.

Chomsky, Noam. 2013. Problems of projection. *Lingua* 130. 33–49.

Chomsky, Noam. 2015. A Discussion with Naoki Fukui and Mihoko Zushi (March 4, 2014). In N. Fukui, ed., *Noam Chomsky. The Sophia Lectures*. 71–97 (*Sophia Linguistica. Working Papers in Linguistics* 64). Tokyo: Sophia University.

Christiansen-Bolli, Regula. 2010. *A grammar of Tadaksahak: a Berberised Songhay language (Mali)*. Köln: Köppe.

Cinque, Guglielmo. 1988. La frase relativa. In L. Renzi, ed., *La Grande Grammatica di Consultazione*. Vol. I. 443–503. Bologna: Il Mulino.

Cinque, Guglielmo. 2003. The prenominal origin of relative clauses. Paper presented at the NYU Workshop on Antisymmetry and Remnant Movement, Oct. 31–Nov. 1 2003.

Cinque, Guglielmo. 2007. A Note on Linguistic Theory and Typology. *Linguistic Typology* 11. 93–106 (also in G.C. *Typological Studies. Word Order and Relative Clauses*. London: Routledge, 2013).

Cinque, Guglielmo. 2008. More on the indefinite character of the Head of restrictive relatives. In P. Benincà, F. Damonte and N. Penello (eds.), *Selected Proceedings of the 34th Incontro di Grammatica Generativa*, Unipress, Padova (Special issue of the *Rivista di Grammatica Generativa*, vol. 33, 3–24) (also in G.C. *Typological Studies. Word Order and Relative Clauses*. London: Routledge, 2013).

Cinque, Guglielmo. 2009. The Fundamental Left-Right Asymmetry of Natural Languages. In S. Scalise, E. Magni, A. Bisetto, eds., *Universals of Language Today*. 165–184. Dordrecht: Springer. (also in G.C. *Typological Studies. Word Order and Relative Clauses*. London: Routledge, 2013). http://lear.unive.it/jspui/handle/11707/99

Cinque, Guglielmo. 2011. On double-headed relative clauses. *Linguística. Revista de Estudos Linguísticos da Universidade do Porto* 6. 67–91.

Cinque, Guglielmo. 2014. Extraction from DP in Italian revisited. In E.O. Aboh, M. T. Guasti and I. Roberts, eds., *Locality*. 86–103. New York: Oxford University Press.

Cinque, Guglielmo. To appear. *The Syntax of Relative Clauses. A Unified Analysis*. Cambridge University Press.

Citko, Barbara. 2000. *Parallel Merge and the Syntax of Free Relatives*. Ph.D. Dissertation, State University of New York at Stony Brook.

Citko, Barbara. 2002. (Anti)reconstruction effects in free relatives: A new argument against the Comp account. *Linguistic Inquiry* 33. 507–511

Citko, Barbara. 2004. On headed, headless, and light-headed relatives. *Natural Language and Linguistic Theory* 22. 95–126.

Citko, Barbara. 2008. Missing labels. *Lingua* 118. 907–944

Citko, Barbara. 2009. What don't *wh*-questions, free relatives, and correlatives have in common? In A. Lipták, ed., *Correlatives Cross-linguistically*. 49–79. Amsterdam: Benjamins.

Citko, Barbara. 2010. On the distribution of –*kolwiek* 'ever' in Polish Free Relatives. *Journal of Slavic Linguistics* 18. 221–258

Citko, Barbara. 2011. *Symmetry in syntax: merge, move and labels*. Cambridge: Cambridge University Press.

Correia, A.J.G. 2011. *Describing Makasae: A Trans-New Guinea Language of East Timor*. Ph.D. Dissertation, University of Western Sydney.

Culy, Christopher Douglas. 1990. *The Syntax and Semantics of Internally Headed Relative Clauses*. Ph.D. Dissertation, Stanford University.

Daskalaki, Evangelia. 2005. The external category of free relatives: Evidence from Modern Greek. *Cambridge Occasional Papers in Linguistics* 2.87–107

Davies, John. 1989. *Kobon*. London: Routledge.

d'Avis, Franz Josef. 2004. In front of the prefield – inside or outside the clause? In H. Lohenstein and S.Trissler, eds., *The Syntax and Semantics of the Left Periphery*. 139–177. Berlin: Mouton de Gruyter.

Dayal, Veneeta. 1997. Free relatives and *ever*: Identity and free choice readings. In *Proceedings of Semantics and Linguistic Theory* 7.99–116. Ithaca, NY: CLC Publications, Cornell University.

Dimova, Elena. 2014. A New Look at Multiple Free Relatives: Evidence from Bulgarian. Paper given at the 9th Slavic Linguistics Society Annual Conference, University of Washington, Seattle, September 19–21, 2014

Dixon, R.M.W. 1977. *A Grammar of Yidiɲ*. Cambridge: Cambridge University Press.

Donati, Caterina. 2006. On *wh*-movement. In L. Cheng and N. Corver, eds., Wh-*movement: Moving on*. 21–46. Cambridge, Mass.: MIT Press.

Donati, Caterina and Carlo Cecchetto. 2011. Relabeling Heads: A Unified Account for Relativization Structures. *Linguistic Inquiry* 42. 519–560

Dryer, Matthew. 2005. Order of Relative Clause and Noun. WALSonline http://wals.info/chapter/90

Emonds, Joseph. 1979. Appositive Relatives Have No Properties. *Linguistic Inquiry* 10. 211–243
Faraclas, Nicholas. 1984. *A Grammar of Obolo*. Bloomington: Indiana University Linguistics Club.
Fintel, Kai von. 2000. Whatever. *Proceedings of SALT 10*. 27–39. Ithaca, NY: CLC Publications, Cornell University.
Frajzyngier, Zygmunt and Eric Johnston (with Adrian Edwards). 2005. *A Grammar of Mina*. Berlin: Mouton De Gruyter.
Gračanin-Yüksek, Martina. 2008. Free Relatives in Croatian: An Argument for the Comp Account. *Linguistic Inquiry* 39. 275–294.
Groat, Eric. 2012. Headhunting at the Edge of the C: A Probe-Goal Analysis for Free Relative Clauses. Oberseminar, Universität Frankfurt.
Grosu, Alexander. 1986/87. Pied Piping and the Matching Parameter. *The Linguistic Review* 6. 41–58.
Grosu, Alexander. 1994. *Three Studies in Locality and Case*. London: Routledge.
Grosu, Alexander. 1995. Free Relatives with "Missing Prepositions" in Rumanian and Universal Grammar. In G. Cinque and G. Giusti, eds., *Advances in Roumanian Linguistics*. 127–160. Amsterdam: Benjamins.
Grosu, Alexander. 1996. The proper analysis of 'missing-P' free relative constructions. *Linguistic Inquiry* 27. 257–293
Grosu, Alexander. 2003a. 'Transparent' free relatives as a special instance of 'standard' free relatives. In M. Coene, Y. D'Hulst and L. Tasmovski, eds., *The structure of DPs*. Amsterdam: Elsevier North-Holland.
Grosu, Alexander. 2003b. A unified theory of 'standard' and 'transparent' free relatives. *Natural Language and Linguistic Theory* 21. 247–331.
Grosu, Alexander. 2004. The syntax-semantics of modal existential wh constructions. In O. M. Tomić, ed., *Balkan Syntax and Semantics*. 405–438. Amsterdam: Benjamins.
Grosu, Alexander and Fred Landman. 1998. Strange Relatives of the Third Kind. *Natural Language Semantics* 6. 125–170
Gutiérrez-Bravo, Rodrigo. 2013. Free relative clauses in Yucatec Maya. *Sprachtypologie und Universalien Forschung/Language Typology and Universals* 66.22–39.
Haider, Hubert. 1988. Matching Projections. In A. Cardinaletti, G. Cinque and G. Giusti, eds., *Constituent Structure. Papers from the 1987 Glow Conference*. 101–121. Dordrecht: Foris.
Harbert, Wayne. 1983. On the nature of the matching parameter. *The Linguistic Review* 2. 237–284
Heath, Jeffrey. 1999. *A Grammar of Koyra Chiini: The Songhay of Timbuktu*. Berlin: Mouton de Gruyter.
Hirsch, Aron. To appear. A compositional semantics for *wh-ever* free relatives. In *Proceedings of Sinn und Bedeutung 20*.
Hirschbühler, Paul and Maria Luisa Rivero. 1983. Remarks on Free Relatives and Matching Phenomena. *Linguistic Inquiry* 14. 505–520.
Huang, Chenglong. 2008. Relativization in Qiang. *Language and Linguistics* 9.735–768.
Hutchison, John Priestley. 1976. *Aspects of Kanuri Syntax*. Ph.D. Dissertation, Indiana University.
Huttar, George L, Enoch O. Aboh, and Felix K. Ameka. 2013. Relative clauses in Suriname creoles and Gbe languages. *Lingua* 129. 96–123
Izvorski, Roumyana. 1995. (Non-)Matching Effects in Free Relatives and pro-Drop. In M. Przezdziecki and L. Whaley, eds., *Proceedings of ESCOL* 12. 89–102 (Cornell University).

Izvorski, Roumyana. 1998. Non-indicative wh-complements of existential/possessive predicates. *Proceedings of the 28th Meeting of the North East Linguistics Society.* 159–173. University of Massachusetts, Amherst.

Izvorski, Roumyana. 2000. Free adjunct free relatives. In R. Billerey and B. Lillehaugen, eds., *Proceedings of the 19th West Coast Conference in Formal Linguistics (WCCFL 19).* 232–245. Somerville, MA: Cascadilla Press.

Jacobson, Pauline. 1995. On the Quantificational Force of English Free Relatives. In E. Bach, E. Jelinek, A. Kratzer and B. H. Partee, eds., *Quantification in Natural Language.* 451–486. Dordrecht: Kluwer.

Johnson, Greg. 2015. The Morphosyntax of *Whatever* in Free Relatives: Variation and optionality in Appalachian English. Handout of LSA talk. Ms., Graduate Center, CUNY.

Kayne, Richard S. 1994. *The Antisymmetry of Syntax.* Cambridge, Mass.: MIT Press.

Kayne, Richard S. 2004. Here and There. In C. Leclère, E. Laporte, M. Piot & M. Silberztein, eds., *Syntax, Lexis and Lexicon-Grammar. Papers in Honour of Maurice Gross.* 253–273. Amsterdam: Benjamins (reprinted in Kayne 2005).

Kayne, Richard S. 2005. *Movement and Silence.* New York: Oxford University Press.

Kayne, Richard S. 2007. On the Syntax of Quantity in English. In J. Bayer, T. Bhattacharya and M.T. Hany Babu, eds., *Linguistic Theory and South Asian Languages: Essays in honour of K. A. Jayaseelan.* 73–105. Amsterdam: Benjamins (also in Kayne 2005).

Kayne, Richard S. 2016. The Unicity of *There* and the Definiteness Effect. Ms. NYU.

Kotek, Hadas and Michael Yoshitaka Erlewine. 2015. Non-interrogative *wh*-constructions in Chuj. Paper presented at *21st Workshop on Structure and Constituency in Languages of the Americas* (WSCLA 2016), Université du Québec à Montréal (UQAM), Montréal, Canada, April 1–3, 2016. http://hkotek.com/Kotek-ChujPaper.pdf

Lakshmi Bai, B. 1985. Some Notes on Correlative Constructions in Dravidian. In V.Z. Acson and R.L. Leed, eds., *For Gordon H. Fairbanks.* 181–190. Honolulu: University of Hawai'i Press.

Larson, Richard. 1987. Missing prepositions and the analysis of English free relative clauses. *Linguistic Inquiry* 18.239–266.

Larson, Richard. 1998. Free relative clauses and missing Ps: Reply to Grosu. Unpublished ms., State University of New York at Stony Brook.

Lefebvre, Claire and Anne-Marie Brousseau. 2002. *A Grammar of Fongbe.* Berlin: Mouton de Gruyter.

Manzini, M. Rita. 2010. The Structure and Interpretation of (Romance) Complementizers. In E. P. Panagiotidis, ed., *The Complementizer Phase. Subjects and Operators.* 167–199. Oxford: Oxford University Press.

Nakamura, Taichi. 2009. Headed Relative Free Relatives, and Determiner Headed Free Relatives. *English Linguistics* 26.329–355

Nguyen, Tam Thi Minh. 2013. *A Grammar of Bih.* Ph.D. Dissertation, University of Oregon.

Obeng, Samuel Gyasi. 2008. *Efutu Grammar.* München: Lincom Europa.

Pancheva Izvorski, Roumyana. 2000. *Free relatives and related matters.* Ph.D. Dissertation, University of Pennsylvania. http://repository.upenn.edu/dissertations/AAI9965537

Patterson, Gary and Ivano Caponigro. 2016. The puzzling degraded status of *who* free relative clauses in English. *English Language and Linguistics* 20. 341–352.

Pittner, Karin. 1991. Freie Relativsätze und die Kasushierarchie. In E. Feldbusch, R. Pogarell and C. Weiss, eds., *Neue Fragen der Linguistik.* 341–347. Tübingen: Niemeyer.

Pittner, Karin. 1995. The Case of German relatives. *The Linguistic Review* 12. 197–231

Radford, Andrew. 2016. *Analysing English Sentences. 2nd Edition*. Cambridge: Cambridge University Press.

Rawlins, Kyle. 2008. *(Un)conditionals: An investigation in the syntax and semantics of conditional structures*. Ph.D. Dissertation, University of California, Santa Cruz.

Rizzi, Luigi. 1982. *Issues in Italian Syntax*. Dordrecht: Foris.

Saah, Kofi K. 2010. Relative Clauses in Akan. In E.O. Aboh and J. Essegbey, eds., *Topics in Kwa Syntax*. 91–107. Dordrecht: Springer.

Siloni, Tal. 1995. On Participial Relatives and Complementizer D°: A Case Study in Hebrew and French. *Natural Language and Linguistic Theory* 13.445–487

Šimík, Radek. 2011. Modal existential *wh*-constructions. Ph.D. Dissertation, Rijksuniversiteit Groningen.

Smits, R.J.C., 1989. *Eurogrammar. The Relative and Cleft Constructions of the Germanic and Romance Languages*. Dordrecht: Foris.

Soubrier, Aude. 2013. *L'ikposso uwi. Phonologie, grammaire, textes, lexique*. Thèse de doctorat, Université Lumière Lyon 2.

Sportiche, Dominique. 2015. Relative Clauses are Matchless. Ms., UCLA.

Tredinnick, Victoria A. 2005. *On the Semantics of Free Relatives with –ever*. Ph.D. Dissertation, University of Pennsylvania.

van Riemsdijk, Henk. 2005. Free relatives: A syntactic case study. In M. Everaert and H. van Riemsdijk, eds., *The Blackwell Companion to Syntax*. Oxford: Blackwell.

Vogel, Ralf. 2001. Case Conflict in German Free-Relative Constructions: An Optimality-Theoretic Treatment. In G. Müller and W. Sternefeld, eds., *Competition in Syntax*. 341–375. Berlin: Mouton de Gruyter.

Vogel, Ralf. 2002. Free Relative Constructions in OT-Syntax. In G. Fanselow and C. Féry, eds., *Resolving Conflicts in Grammars: Optimality Theory in Syntax, Morphology, and Phonology*. 119–162. Hamburg: Buske.

Vogel, Ralf. 2003. Surface Matters. Case Conflict in Free Relative Constructions and Case Theory. In E. Brandner and H. Zinsmeister, eds., *New Perspectives on Case Theory*. 269–299. Stanford,CA: CSLI Publications.

Vries, Mark de. 2002. *The Syntax of Relativization*. Ph.D. Dissertation, University of Amsterdam.

Walker, Benjamin R. 2005. Relative Clauses in Sinhala. *Santa Barbara Papers in Linguistics* 17.163–171

Walters, Josiah Keith. 2015. *A Grammar Sketch of Dazaga*. M.A. Thesis, Graduate Institute of Applied Linguistics. http://www.gial.edu/documents/Theses/Walters_Josiah-thesis.pdf

Wilder, Chris. 1999. Transparent Free Relatives. In Shahin, K. N., S. Blake & E.-S. Kim, eds., *Proceedings of the Seventeenth West Coast Conference on Formal Linguistics*. 685–699.

Yoshioka, Noboru. 2012. *A Reference Grammar of Eastern Burushaski*. Ph.D. Dissertation, Tokyo University of Foreign Studies.

Gloria Cocchi
Bantu class prefixes: Towards a cross-categorial account

Abstract: Bantu verbal forms are notoriously complex from a morphological point of view, in that they consist of several morphemes, some of which are obligatorily present, and others optionally. Nominal forms, on the contrary, look much simpler and less structured.

Following a long line of research which started from Abney (1987), the aim of the present paper is to devise a strict parallelism between the structure of Bantu nouns and verbs, which is crucially based on the important role played by class prefixes. Moreover, in line with Manzini and Savoia's recent work (e.g. 2008, 2011), I will argue that the same set of inflectional projections are to be assumed at both syntactic and morphological levels; indeed Bantu languages, which feature a very rich morphology, are the perfect candidates to show how morphology mirrors syntax.

Finally, I will briefly investigate adjectives and (some) prepositions, as also these categories – even the latter – present functional projections which involve agreement.

1 Introduction

Descriptive works on Bantu languages (cf. Guthrie 1967–71; Van Bulck 1952; Alexandre 1981; see also Cocchi 2014) assume that most Bantu words are formed by agglutination, according to a fixed prefix + root + suffix pattern. The root is invariable and generally has a CVC structure. Some roots are bi-functional and can form either a verb or a noun stem,[1] depending on the inflectional suffix that is added at the end of the word; others are, however, mono-functional and can only perform one of these functions. Prefixes are crucial for instantiating agreement relations, either between a verb and its

---

[1] The two notions of *stem* and *root* are often used as synonyms. In this paper, with *root* we will intend the basic, indivisible lexical morpheme, while with *stem* we will indicate the root + the final inflection, which generally consists of a single vowel (indeed, in the literature on Bantu, it is often referred to as *final vowel*).

Gloria Cocchi, Università di Urbino

https://doi.org/10.1515/9781501505201-012

subject (pronominal prefixes), or between a noun and its modifiers, determiners and adjectives (nominal prefixes).

This brief description, besides highlighting the morphological complexity of Bantu words, already contains an important insight, which has received a growing attention in the Generative literature since the seminal work of Abney (1987), i.e. the strict parallelism in the structure of nouns and verbs and their extended functional projections. It is exactly on this parallelism that we will speculate in the present work, also extending the proposal to other categories, like adjectives and prepositions, and showing that even for them we can assume the existence of similar extended functional projections.

This work proceeds as follows. In section 2 we will describe the main aspects regarding the morphological structure of the different categories of words in Bantu languages. In section 3 we will discuss some interesting phenomena that emerge from the data, which deserve a further investigation. In section 4 we will try to analyse the structure of Bantu verbs and nouns within Manzini and Savoia's (2005, 2008, 2011) framework, which seems to be the most adequate to account for these data, given the many similarities that can be traced between Bantu and Romance languages, as already suggested by Cocchi (2000a) and related work. Finally, in section 5 we will tentatively extend the proposed analysis also to adjectives and prepositions.

When not indicated otherwise, we will discuss data from Tshiluba, a core Bantu language spoken in the Kasayi region of Congo-Kinshasa.[2]

2 The morphological structure of Bantu words

2.1 Verbs

Verbal forms are often more complex than the basic pattern indicated in the Introduction above, and generally involve a higher number of morphemes. According to Alexandre (1981: 361), a Bantu verb may comprehend as many as the following elements:
– Pre-prefix
– Pronominal prefix (also known as subject prefix)
– Tense/aspect infix

---

[2] Data from Tshiluba are in part personally collected, and in part drawn from Willems (1949) and Burssens (1946, 1954). We have discussed several aspects of this language in previous work; see the References section.

- Object infix(es)
- ROOT
- Verbal extension(s)
- Inflectional suffix
- Post-suffix

Besides the root, two of these elements are (almost) always present: the subject prefix[3] and the inflectional suffix; however, also the tense/aspect (T/A) infix appears in most finite forms, though in some languages we may find an unmarked form which lacks it, usually corresponding to a present or generic tense.

Object infixes emerge when a (direct or indirect) object is expressed by a pronoun[4]; in some languages – the so-called asymmetrical languages, like Swahili – only one object infix may be present at a time, while in other languages – the symmetrical ones, like Tshiluba – we may have the co-occurrence of two or even more object infixes in marked constructions, such as the applicative sentence given in (1)[5]:

(1) a. *mukaji   u-sumb-il-a   muana   tshimuma*
       cl.1-woman   cl.1-buy-appl   cl.1-boy   cl.7-fruit
       'the woman bought fruit for the boy'
    b. *mukaji   u-tshi-mu-sumb-il-a*
       cl.1-woman   cl.1-cl.7-cl.1-buy-appl
       'the woman bought it for him'

Verbal extensions are used when required to form derivates, such as causative, applicative, reciprocal or passive (cf. Schadeberg 1982; Cocchi 2009); they are infixed between the root and the final inflection, as also shown in (1a-b) above.

---

3 The subject prefix is absent only in imperatives; besides, it is substituted by a nominal prefix in infinitives and in forms, which Willems (1949) calls *nominal forms*, roughly corresponding to our participles.

4 Not only direct or indirect objects can be expressed by an object affix, but also the causee in causative constructions and the applied object (beneficiary) in applicative constructions; see, among the many, Baker (1988). On locatives, see the discussion later on.

5 Bresnan and Moshi (1990) call *symmetrical* the languages like Kichaga (which they investigated) or Tshiluba, where the two (or more) objects in a dative shift, causative or applicative construction behave in the same way (e.g. all objects can be substituted by a pronominal infix, even two or more at the same time, or become the subject of the corresponding passive clause), and *asymmetrical* those languages – like Swahili or Chichewa – where, in the mentioned contexts, only one of the objects exhibits the mentioned properties, while the 'second' object (generally the patient/theme) loses them.

There may be more inflections at the same time, e.g. if an applicative sentence like (1a) is passivized.

Finally, other morphemes appear in a very restricted number of cases, i.e. the pre-prefix mainly emerges in negative verbal forms, and the post-suffix in the plural imperative, as well as – in symmetrical languages – in order to express a second object pronoun, or even a post-verbal subject pronoun.

2.2 Nouns

Bantu noun morphology is generally regarded to be much simpler, in that a noun generally consists only in a stem (root + final vowel) preceded by a class prefix. All nouns are in fact divided in classes, which nowadays simply represent different agreement patterns, without any semantic correlation, except for classes 1/2 which contain nouns indicating humans.[6]

In Table 1 below we see the complete scheme of class prefixes/classifiers in Tshiluba (from Burssens 1954, also reported in Cocchi 2014); in the left column we find prefixes for singular nouns (or classes containing nouns which admit no plural), and in the right column the corresponding plural prefixes[7]:

The prefix represents part of the noun and it is inseparable from the stem: while adjectives or verbs change their prefixes according to, respectively, the noun or subject they agree with, nouns do not change their prefix; in fact, in dictionaries (e.g. De Clercq 1937; Willems 1960) nouns are listed according to the prefix, while verbs and adjectives are listed according to the stem. Nonetheless, there are several nominal stems which are compatible with more prefixes, and their meaning remains constant. For example, the stem -*luba* indicates one person or more people belonging to the Luba ethnic group when preceded by 1/2 class prefixes (*muluba/baluba*), but it indicates the language spoken by such a group when preceded by class 7 prefix (*tshiluba*); analogously, the stem -*bote*

---

6 Indeed in Proto-Bantu there was a clearer semantic division according to classes, which has virtually gone lost in modern languages, except for classes 1/2 which homogeneously indicate humans. Traces of such a division, however, remain, e.g. classes 9/10 contain many nouns indicating animals, and classes 7/8 many nouns of inanimate beings. See Der-Houssikian (1974) for more details.

7 For classes 9/10 prefixes are traditionally indicated with N, which means that the words begin with a nasal sound, which, according to the consonant that follows, is spelled out as [n], [m] or [ŋ].

Table 1: Class prefixes in Tshiluba.

Class	nom. pref.	pron. pref.	Class	nom. pref.	pron. pref.
1	mu-/ø	u-	2	ba-	ba-
3	mu-	mu- (u-)	4	mi-	i-
5	di-	di-	6	ma-	a-
7	tshi-	tshi-	8	bi-	bi-
9	N-/mu-	u-	10	N-/mi-	i-
11	lu-	lu-	10	N-/mi-	i-
13	ka-	ka-	12	tu-	tu-
14	bu-	bu-	6	ma-	a-
15	ku-	ku-			
16	pa-	pa-			
17	ku-	ku-			
18	mu-	mu-			

indicates banana(s) if preceded by class 7/8 prefixes (*tshibote/bibote*), and banana tree(s) when preceded instead by class 5/6 prefixes (*dibote/mabote*).[8]

2.3 Adjectives

Adjectives are formed out of a stem preceded by a nominal prefix, which means that the prefix of the noun they modify is copied onto the adjective, which always follows the noun: e.g. *tshibote tshinene* 'big banana'.

However, pure adjectival roots are very limited in number: Willems (1949: 10–11) lists only 15. Many adjectives are indeed formed out of a verbal root preceded by a nominal prefix instead of a pronominal one, like -*kole* 'strong', which derives from the verb *kukola* 'to grow up, to get stronger'. Notice that the final inflection is -*e* rather than -*a*, and this roughly corresponds to the participial -*ed* inflection. The form thus obtained, in fact, roughly corresponds to a past participle: *muntu mukole* [cl.1] 'strong man' < 'a man who has grown stronger'. Indeed, even in European languages, participles are traditionally considered as the "adjectival" forms of verbs.

---

[8] As regards Tshiluba class prefixes, in this work we will follow Burssens's (1954: 58) classification, which follows the traditional Bantu numbering system and partially differs from Willems (1949: 8).

Also demonstratives, possessives, numbers and indefinite quantifiers follow the noun (with few exceptions) and agree with it by means of a nominal prefix. Definite or indefinite articles are absent in Bantu languages.

2.4 Prepositions and locative markers

Finally, a brief description of prepositions, as some cases are particularly interesting to discuss.

To start with, there is a widely used prepositional element, more or less corresponding to English *of*, which descriptive works on Bantu call "connective" or "associative", in that it links two nouns, often – but not always – expressing possession. This is rendered with *-a* preceded by a pronominal prefix; thus the preposition agrees with the noun that precedes, as if it were a verb agreeing with its subject. In other words, the preposition agrees with the owned thing/person, and not with the possessor:

(2) a. *tshimuma tshia mfumu*
    cl.7-fruit cl.7-of cl.1-chief
    'the fruit of the chief'
  b. *bana ba mukaji*
    cl.2-boy cl.2-of cl.1-woman
    'the woman's children'

Another interesting case is represented by locatives. This type of relation is in fact generally expressed by means of (one or different) prepositions, but, in Bantu languages, locatives are typically expressed by class prefixes, i.e. they behave as nominal elements (cf. Stucky 1976; Cocchi 2000b). Three specialized locative classes have been reconstructed for Proto-Bantu (Guthrie 1967–71), and in Tshiluba they are perfectly preserved: cl. 16 *pa-*, 'on, above'; cl. 17 *ku-* 'at, by, towards', and cl. 18 *mu-* 'in, inside'. The peculiar fact concerning locatives is that the locative prefix virtually "demotes" the original prefix of the noun, and governs all agreement relations in its place. Crucially, a locative noun can even represent the subject of a clause and agree in class (the locative class) with the inflected verb, as in the following example:

(3) *mu nzubu mudi bantu*
    cl.18 cl.9-house cl.18-be cl.2-person
    'at home there are people'

In (3), indeed, the copula *-di* 'be', not only does not agree with cl.2 *bantu* 'people' (as it does in English, cf. translation), but agrees with cl.18 locative prefix, rather than with the cl.9 regular prefix of the noun *nzubu* 'house'. Therefore, it looks uncertain whether to classify locative prefixes as prepositions, in line with the relation they express, or as nominal elements, as their morphology would suggest.

A similar consideration can be made for the Tshiluba preposition *ne* 'with', which, once associated to the copula *-di*, yields 'have', similarly to the well-known Latin construction *mihi est* (cf. Benveniste 1966), as in (4a) below. Interestingly in Swahili, where the copula is reduced to the invariant form *ni*, which is used (in the present tense) for all persons, we witness the corresponding preposition, *na*, directly adjoined to the subject prefixes (with no trace of the copula) to yield 'have', as in (4b):

(4) a. *muana udi   ne   mukanda* (Tshiluba)
        boy   cl.1-be   with book
        'the boy has (< is with) a book'
   b. *mtoto ana   kitabu* (Swahili)
        boy   cl.1-with book
        'the boy has a book'

3 Considerations on the data: categorial ambiguity

The data described above point to some interesting considerations.

To start with, roots do not seem to be clearly divisible into lexical categories. We have already mentioned the fact that many adjectives are formed out of verbal roots. Much work on Bantu also mentions the existence of roots which can be either nominal or verbal; for instance, Alexandre (1981: 360) reports an example from Lingala, where the root *-sal-* 'work' can be used both as a verb and as a noun, if merged with different prefixes and inflectional suffixes. For Swahili, Perrott (1957: 134–35) maintains that many verbs and nouns share the same root, and reports some ways of forming nouns out of verbs by affixing a nominal prefix to the stem and sometimes changing the final inflection from *-a* to *-i*[9]:

---

[9] Though Swahili has fewer noun classes with respect to Tshiluba, we maintain the traditional Bantu numbering system, given for Tshiluba in Table 1. Thus infinitives are homogeneously

(5) a. *kupika*
cl.15-cook
'to cook'
b. *mpishi*
cl.1-cook
'a cook'

Besides, we could speculate on the role of infinitives, which also traditional grammars consider as the "nominal" forms of verbs.[10] This is even more evident in Bantu languages, where infinitives, from a morphological point of view, are at the same time verbs – as they can be formed out of any verbal stem – and nouns – since such stems are preceded by a specialized nominal prefix (in Tshiluba it is class 15, *ku-*), which can govern subject agreement.

This is not an original result, as similar phenomena emerge in most languages; see e.g. the many English roots like *love*, which are at the same time nominal and verbal: the distinction into categories is indeed often determined by syntactic distribution, as well as by morphological considerations, i.e. which inflectional elements are associated with the root.

The latter criteria is however only partially valid in Bantu, given that not only roots, but also inflections can be categorially ambiguous. First of all, identical prefixes are often used for nouns/adjectives on the one side, and verbs on the other. In other words, the so-called nominal and pronominal prefixes have the same morpho-phonological shape in most classes. Indeed, in Tshiluba, out of 18 agreement classes (see Table 1 above), 12 exhibit identical prefixes for nominal and pronominal functions. Only prefixes which start with a nasal sound – [m], [ŋ] or [n] – tend to lose this sound when employed as subject prefixes in verbal forms, while they maintain it on nouns and all of their agreeing modifiers (adjectives, demonstratives, possessives, etc.): *mu-* vs. *u-* [classes 1 and 3]; *mi-* vs. *i-* [cl. 4]; *ma-* vs. *a-* [cl. 6]; *N-* vs. *u-* [cl. 9]; *N-* vs. *i-* [cl.10].[11]

However, this is nothing more than a tendency, as there are exceptions. For instance, the initial *m-* does not get lost in the locative subject prefix *mu-* [cl.

---

class 15, even if Swahili lacks classes 12 and 13, while classes 11 and 14 merge into a single class prefixed by *u-*.

Besides, in (5b) palatalization has applied, turning [k] + [i] into [ʃ]. Similar phonological phenomena are common across Bantu; see also Cocchi (2014) for similar effects in Tshiluba.

10 Indeed, in languages like Italian, they can be preceded by an article.

11 The morpho-syntactic value linked to this initial nasal sound, which gets lost in pronominal prefixes, certainly deserved a more detailed investigation, that is however postponed to future work.

18], as seen in (3) above. Besides, for class 3, though the older descriptions of the language only report the form *u-* as a pronominal prefix (cf. also Willems 1949), in nowadays' language the form *mu-* tends to be used in its place; mother tongue speakers report (p.c.) that this is due to the necessity to distinguish class 1 (humans) and class 3 (non-humans) subject prefixes.

Furthermore, as regards the final inflection, i.e. the element which converts a root into a stem, in the vast majority of inflected words (nouns, verbs and adjectives) this is homogeneously represented by an *-a*, or sometimes another vocalic morpheme (generally *-e*), with few exceptions.

Last but not least, when we hinted at the existence of post-suffixes, which are employed to form the plural imperatives (cf. 2.1. above), there may be something similar (and sometimes homophonous) which attaches to nouns: for instance, in Swahili, the same post-suffix *-ni*, which forms the plural imperative, also attaches to a noun stem to express the locative (Perrott 1957: 25; 46), since locative class prefixes have disappeared in this language:

(6) a. *nyumba* 'house' vs. *nyumbani* 'at home'
    b. *soma* 'read! (2.sg.)' vs. *someni* 'read! (2.pl.)'

Finally, as concerns prepositions, which are generally uninflected elements across languages, they do not exhibit a homogeneous behaviour in Bantu, as seen above: together with a few invariant elements, on the one side we have connective/associative *-a*, which is inflected with a pronominal prefix, as if it were a verbal root; on the other we have locative class prefixes (*pa-*, *ku-* and *mu-*), hence nominal elements, which behave as prepositions, or perhaps as locative Case markers, though Bantu languages are generally regarded as caseless varieties.

4 Bantu verbal forms: how morphology mirrors syntax

Much work in the generative tradition, ever since Abney (1987), has reflected on the strict parallelism in the structure of verbs and nouns and their extended functional projections, with the determiner which plays for the noun the same role performed by inflection for the verb. The data on Bantu that we have just presented, and crucially the fact that, on the one side, not all roots have a categorial specification, and, on the other, the same (or very similar) prefixes are employed to provide grammatical information to both verbal and nominal (as well as adjectival) elements, seem to point in the same direction.

More recently, Manzini and Savoia (2008, 2011) further speculate on such a parallelism in the structure of nouns and verbs. Moreover, they assume that "the same structures and categories underlie both syntax and morphology" (2011: 152). This means that the inflectional elements which combine with a root (with predicative content) in morphology correspond to the arguments which are projected by the same root in syntax.[12]

4.1 Subject pronouns

This parallelism between morphology and syntax clearly emerges in null subject languages like Italian, where verbal inflection has six differentiated forms which encode person and number features. We can thus assume, in line with Manzini and Savoia (1997 and subsequent work), that the verb has morphologically incorporated the subject pronoun; hence there is even no need to posit the existence of an empty category like *pro* to saturate the verb's argument structure[13]: verbal inflection itself *is* the subject.[14]

In more recent work, Manzini and Savoia (2011: 153-155) further reflect on the internal structure of Italian verbs and assume that, in a transitive sentence like *lavo la macchina* 'I wash the car', the root *lav-* combines with an inflection, *-o*, notated as D, as it represents the incorporated 1st person singular subject pronoun *io* 'I', hence a D°, even though the two elements may not be morpho-phonologically related.[15] The inflectional suffix thus represents the (external) EPP argument. The internal argument of the verb is instead the DP *la macchina* 'the car', where the root *macchin-* (which has no intrinsic nominal properties, according to these authors) combines with the nominal inflection *-a*, which provides the categorial specification N. In turn, this nominal is turned into an argument of the verb by the determiner *la* (which agrees with the noun, in that it also contains the 'nominal' morpheme *-a*). Thus the two D's saturate the argument structure of the predicate, as in (7):

---

[12] On the parallelism between syntax and morphology, and its effects on Bantu, see also Baker's (1985, 1988) Mirror Principle.
[13] On the null subject pronoun *pro*, see Jaeggli and Safir (1990) and related work.
[14] In this framework agreement is thus a result of incorporation, rather than a feature checking process in the sense of Chomsky (1995 and related work).
[15] Indeed the same derivation would work also for a form like *lavi* 'you (sg.) wash', where there does not seem to be any morpho-phonological relation at all between the inflection *-i* and the covert subject pronoun *tu*.

(7)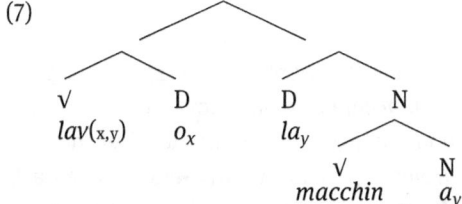

Crucially, Bantu languages add further empirical evidence to such a theory. Indeed, they are also null subject varieties, where tonic subject pronouns are very seldom used.[16] Hence, in a transitive sentence like *usumba mukanda* 's/he buys the book', we can assume that the verb has incorporated the subject, as any finite verb shows six inflected forms, differentiated by the subject prefix, or better many more than six, as there are as many third person subject prefixes as there are noun classes.[17]

Moreover, in Bantu verbs the subject prefix, which performs the same role as the final inflection in Italian, is indeed morphologically connected to the nominal subject it replaces, or better to its class prefix, which can be seen as its functional part, thus its D-extended projection. We have in fact noticed, in section 3, how most subject prefixes are identical – or very similar – to the nominal prefixes of the corresponding nouns. The final inflection, on the contrary, does not have argument status in Bantu, but it has the important role of converting a root (which is not intrinsically belonging to any category) into a verbal stem, hence we will notate it as V.

The structure of an inflected verbal form like *usumba* 's/he buys' will thus have the following structure:

(8)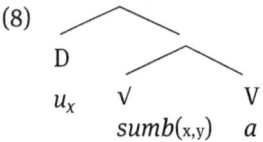

Therefore, as in the Italian example in (7), the verb has incorporated its EPP-argument (external argument in the two cases at hand).

---

16 Bantu languages have tonic pronouns, which are used mainly in focussed or left-dislocated structures. In Tshiluba they are: *meme* (1st sg.), *wewe* (2nd sg.), *yeye* (3rd sg.), *tuetu* (1st pl.), *nuenu* (2nd pl.), *bobo* (3rd pl.). However, if the 3rd person pronoun does not refer to a (/more) human being(s), different pronouns formed out of the subject prefixes of the various classes will be used instead; cf. Willems (1949: 44–45).
17 Notice however that, in Bantu, human subjects (and sometimes even animals) take the subject prefixes corresponding to classes 1/2 (*u-* / *ba-*) even when they belong to different classes.

4.2 Object pronouns

As concerns the internal argument, *mukanda* 'the book', the derivation hypothesized by Manzini and Savoia for *la macchina*, seen above, can be easily adapted. Indeed, as said above, Bantu languages have no articles, but the class prefix can be seen as the extended projection of the noun stem, thus as a D. Hence we can assume that, analogously to the Italian example, the inflectional suffix -*a* adds nominal categorization to the root -*kand*- (which is not intrinsically nominal), while the class 3 prefix *mu*-, attached to the nominal stem, represents the D-head, through which the noun gets argument status. Thus the direct object *mukanda*, together with the subject prefix *u*-, saturates the argument structure of the predicate, as in (9) [cf. (7) above]:

(9)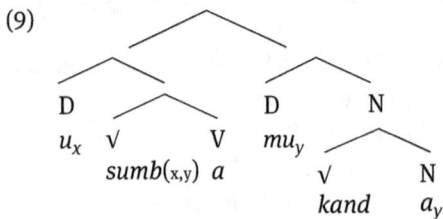

Furthermore, as described in 2.1, a direct object in Bantu can be replaced by an object infix. Therefore, in a complex verbal form like (10) below, the transitive verb has morphologically incorporated both arguments, not only the EPP one, and can be structured as in (11):

(10) u-mu-sumb-a
 cl1.su-cl3.obj-buy-infl
 's/he buys it'

(11)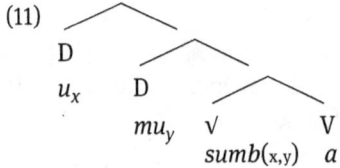

Indeed, also in Italian we may have something comparable to (10–11), once we replace the direct object with a clitic pronoun, as in *la lavo* 'I wash it'. In previous work (Cocchi 2000a), we have already speculated on the strict parallelism between Bantu bound affixes and Romance free clitics: though the latter, unlike the former, are independent words from a morphological point of view, they are nonetheless unstressed elements which form a single phonological word together with the verb they cliticize onto. Thus, they do not behave very differently from Bantu affixes, which are morphologically bound, and the two groups of elements can be accounted for with a unitary analysis.

Building on Sportiche's (1996) original intuition, Manzini and Savoia (2004, 2005 and related work) crucially assume that Romance clitics are not generated in argument positions within VP (i.e. where we would find the corresponding DPs), but rather they are directly merged where we see them, i.e. in specialized inflectional positions above VP. In this way we can better account for the attested restrictions in co-occurrence, as well as for the fixed order they exhibit, which may differ from the order of post-verbal DP-arguments.

Bantu languages give further empirical support to this thesis: since object infixes are bound morphemes rather than independent words, it would be much more logical to assume that they are morphologically generated within the verbal form rather than moving there; furthermore, even Bantu infixes show restrictions in co-occurrence and have a fixed order.[18] The Tshiluba structure in (12a), thus, corresponds to the Italian one in (12b), though in Tshiluba the direct object infix obligatorily precedes the indirect object one, like in French (*je la lui donne* 'I give it to him'), while Italian exhibits the reverse order of the two clitics:

(12) a. *u-tshi-mu-sumb-il-a* (*muana*) (*tshimuma*)
 1.su-7.do-1.io-buy-appl-infl (cl.1-boy) (cl.7-fruit)
 's/he buys it for him (the fruit for the boy)'
 b. *gliela compra* (*la frutta*) (*al ragazzo*)
 3sg.io-3sg.do buys the fruit to.the boy
 's/he buys it for him (the fruit for the boy)'

Hence, the complex verbal form in (12a-b) has incorporated all of the three arguments: the subject, the direct object and the indirect/applied object. In Romance languages, clitic pronouns are assumed to be D-heads which (more or less) coincide with the articles of the DPs they substitute (cf. (7) above); similarly, in Bantu, pronominal affixes (more or less) coincide with the class prefixes of the nouns they substitute. Thus, in both groups of languages, these elements are to be analysed as determiners when attached to a nominal stem, and arguments when affixed/cliticized onto a verbal stem.

---

[18] Obviously this is valid only for symmetrical languages like Tshiluba, where two object infixes may co-occur.

Indeed in Tshiluba, as in Italian, infixes/clitics and full DP-objects are mutually exclusive; when present, the DP-objects in a sentence like (12a) are to be intended as right-dislocated elements, as in the corresponding Italian sentence (12b).[19] A similar situation has been reported to hold for other Bantu languages, like Chichewa (cf. Bresnan and Mchombo 1987; Labelle 2008). In this case the object infix can rightfully be analysed as the internal argument of the verb.

However, a problem may arise in other Bantu languages, like Swahili, which are said to admit object infix-doubling; for instance, Perrott (1957: 38–40) assumes that the object infix must be expressed, in the presence of the DP-object, whenever the object is definite; cf. (13a) vs. (13b). Anyway, Perrott herself underlines the fact that, in the spoken language, "doubling" object infixes tend to be omitted, even with definite objects; they are mainly used only when we want to emphasize a particular thing, and their use becomes obligatory when the object is mentioned first, as in (13c):

(13) a. *umeleta*   *kitabu* ?
      2nd.su-T/A-bring-infl cl.7-book
      'have you brought a book?'
   b. *umekileta*   *kitabu* ?
      2nd.su-T/A-7.do-bring-infl cl.7-book
      'have you brought the book (the particular one I wanted)?'
   c. *kitabu*   *changu*   *umekileta* ?
      cl.7-book cl.7-my 2nd.su-T/A-7.do-bring-infl
      'my book, have you brought it?'

Thus, also a language like Swahili preferably admits the co-occurrence of the object infix and the full DP-object when the latter is emphasized and regarded as a topic, i.e. a left- or right-dislocated element, exactly as in Tshiluba; in non-marked constructions the object infix tends instead to be omitted "especially where the object is a thing" (Perrott 1957: 40). In this we may see a parallelism with Spanish, a language which, unlike Italian, allows clitic-doubling, but this phenomenon is generally restricted to human objects.[20]

---

19 Also full DP-subjects, which always co-occur (when present) with subject prefixes, can be analysed as topics; such an account has been proposed also for null subject languages like Italian. This assumption is reinforced by the fact that Bantu tonic subject pronouns are always topics; cf. fn. 16 above.
20 On clitic doubling see Anagnostopoulou (2006), which discusses the main theories on this phenomenon.

Therefore, though many more data on different languages would be necessary, we may provisionally conclude that Bantu languages, exactly like Romance ones, diverge on the acceptability and restrictions on clitic/affix-doubling. The availability of doubling seems thus to be a matter of parameter setting. However, if we want to offer a unitary analysis for all Bantu (as well as Romance) languages, we may assume, following Sportiche (1992) and related work, that the clitic/infix – generated in the extended projection of V, as in (11) above – always represents the incorporated internal argument of the verb and, in 'doubling' languages, the full DP – generated VP-internally in argument position – undergoes covert movement to the clitic/infix specifier position.[21]

5 Extending the analysis to other categories

We will now try to extend the analysis sketched in section 4 to some of the interesting cases that we have described in sections 2 and 3 above. Of course a more detailed investigation will be needed, but it is our opinion that the line of research we have pursued till now looks promising.

5.1 Adjectives

As we have seen, adjectives always agree in class with the noun they refer to. Besides verbs, adjectives can be predicates too; however, there may be a copula or not between the noun and the predicative adjective. In Tshiluba, the copula is formed out of the invariable root *-di* preceded by a subject prefix. Indeed, when the copula is absent, the adjective can be interpreted either as an attribute or as a predicate[22]:

(14) a. *muntu   udi   munene*
        cl.1-man 1.su-be   cl.1-big
        'the man is big'

---

[21] This analysis, thus, differs from Uriagereka (1995), which assumes that the clitic is a D°-head generated VP-internally in argument position, while the doubled DP is generated in its specifier, and gets stranded by clitic movement to inflection.
[22] The zero option of the copula is limited to the present / generic tense (default case). In other tenses the copula will be present, but it cannot be formed out of the root *-di*, which is invariant (it comes from the Proto-Bantu defective verb *li*, cf. Guthrie 1967-71), but rather out of the root of the verb *kuvua* 'to become'. On copulas in Bantu see also Cocchi (2003).

b. *muntu   munene*
   cl.1-man cl.1-big
   'the big man / the man is big'

Thus we can assume that also adjectives are composed of a root, a final inflection and a functional part, the prefix, which has argument status in case the adjective is used as a predicate. Moreover, if we consider the so-called deverbal adjectives, such as *mukole* 'strong', discussed in 2.3., we confirm the thesis that adjectives are formed out of an unspecified root which merges with a specialized inflectional suffix (different from the one employed when the root functions as a verb), which gives it categorial specification, and with a nominal prefix, as in (15):

(15)
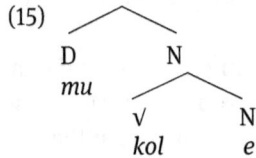
```
        D       N
        mu
             V       N
             kol     e
```

Notice that, in (15), we have assumed that the final inflection is categorially N, rather than A. Indeed, in this work we will posit that the basic categorial features are only N and V, as also traditional analyses assumed.[23] Furthermore, also Bantu descriptive works (e.g. Willems 1949) call "nominal forms" those obtained when a verbal stem combines with a nominal prefix.

5.2 Preposition-like elements

As regards the connective *-a*, which attaches to a subject prefix to form possessive (or similar) constructions, we can analyse it as a verb-final inflection, thus as a morpheme which is intrinsically verbal (cf. (11) above), like the final inflection which attaches to an unspecified root in order to convert it into a verbal stem; not accidentally, most verbs have an *-a* morpheme as an inflection, at least in the infinitive and in the present tense.

---

[23] Beside nouns [+N; -V] and verbs [-N; +V], adjectives were analysed as [+N; +V] and prepositions as [-N, -V], thus all main categories were rephrased in terms of ±N and ±V. This underlines how N and V were assumed to be the most "primitive" categories.

The structure of the connective, given in (7a) above, would thus be the following:

(16)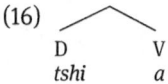
  D V
  tshi a

The fact that the connective -*a* requires a pronominal rather than a nominal prefix underlines its verbal nature: if it were simply to be analysed as a noun modifier, we would expect a nominal prefix instead, as for adjectives, demonstratives, etc. The pronominal prefix in (16), thus, qualifies as an EPP argument.

An analysis along the same lines might perhaps be extended to the Swahili *have*-construction seen in (4b) above. Indeed, also in this case a pronominal prefix attaches to what is otherwise considered as a preposition, *na*. However, since there is no trace of the copula anymore (which survives in the more conservative Tshiluba language), we could even assume that the particle *na* has reanalysed (in Baker's 1988 terms) as a verb, hence the use of a pronominal prefix.[24]

As for locatives, we have seen that, in most Bantu languages, the element encoding the locative information does not behave as an independent preposition,[25] but rather as a nominal prefix: it attaches to a noun stem, controls subject agreement, and can be used as an object infix too. In this, again, we see a parallelism with Romance languages, where we find locative clitics (e.g. Italian *ci* 'there') together with direct and indirect object ones, with the possibility of clustering. For this reason, Manzini and Savoia (2004 and subsequent work) assume the existence of a specialized Loc projection within the inflectional layer above VP, where locative clitics are merged.

Indeed, an element like *mu nzubu* 'at home', discussed in 2.4, behaves as a real DP-argument: it can be a clause subject, which agrees with the verb, as in (3) above, or a 'direct' object, in which case it can even appear as an object infix. Therefore, we tentatively propose the following structure, which also underlines the fact that the locative prefix has demoted the original noun class prefix:

---

24 Indeed, verbs and prepositions have often been assumed to have something in common, as they are case assigners, while nouns and adjectives are not.
25 Willems (1949: 177) states that Tshiluba does not have prepositions like European languages; the information these elements generally convey in our languages are rendered with the connective -*a*, locative prefixes, the applicative construction or other devices. Notwithstanding, we can find some invariant words, which recall our prepositions, like the mentioned *ne* 'with', or *bua* 'for'.

(17)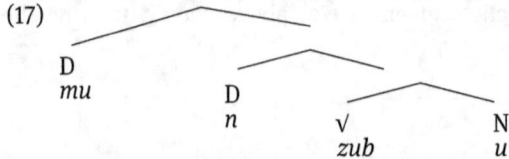

More difficult to account in these terms is the Swahili locative construction *nyumbani* 'at home', which makes use of a post-suffix instead of a locative prefix, as locative classes have disappeared in this language. However, in Manzini and Savoia's framework (2004 and subsequent work), the whole set of clitic projections posited for Romance languages is assumed to occur recursively in different domains, not only in the inflectional one. In his regard, in previous work on Bantu (Cocchi 2003), we have argued that post-verbal subject or object affixes in Tshiluba may occupy such specialized positions in the predicative layer, i.e. below inflection. Thus, we tentatively assume that the Swahili locative post-suffix, which is a D° like the Tshiluba locative prefix in (17), may occur in such an environment as well, though this phenomenon certainly deserves further investigation.

6 Conclusions

In this work we have discussed several interesting phenomena which characterize Bantu languages, and especially what concerns class prefixes, i.e. elements which are strictly connected with nominal stems and control agreement on verbs, adjectives, as well as (what might be called) prepositions.

We have come to the conclusion that class prefixes are D°-elements which, when merged with a noun stem, have the same function of the (definite) articles that we find in other languages, and which Bantu typically lacks; on the other side, these elements can be interpreted as pronouns, when they attach instead to verbal stems, in the form of a subject prefix or an object infix. In this we see a parallelism with Romance determiners, which can be interpreted either as definite articles (as in the Italian example *la* macchina '*the* car') or as clitic pronouns (*la* lavo 'I wash *it*'). Indeed, the many connections between Romance clitics and Bantu affixes have already been noticed since Cocchi (2000a).

In this perspective, a theoretical framework like Manzini and Savoia's (2008, 2011), which argues that the same set of inflectional projections are to be assumed at both syntactic and morphological levels, seem to provide the most adequate answers for the complex set of Bantu data. Indeed,

Bantu class prefixes have at the same time a morphological function (as they are inflectional affixes) and a syntactic one (since they have argument status).

Finally, an analysis of this type could also help overcome the traditional subdivision of words into lexical categories, as most roots prove to be categorially unspecified, and even affixes may have a multiple function. Therefore the structures that we assume in order to analyse the extended projections of nouns and verbs, and even adjectives and prepositions, are substantially the same.

References

Abney, Steve. 1987. *The English noun phrase in its sentential aspect*, Ph.D. Thesis, MIT.
Alexandre, Pierre. 1981. [Les langues bantoues,] Tableau d'ensemble. In Jean Perrot (ed.), *Les langues dans le monde ancien et moderne*, 353–375. Paris : CNRS.
Anagnostopoulou, Elena. 2006. Clitic doubling. In Martin Everaert and Henk van Riemsdijk (eds.), *The Blackwell Companion to Syntax*, Volume I, Ch. 14, 519–580. Oxford: Blackwell.
Baker, Mark. 1985. The Mirror Principle and morphosyntactic explanation. *Linguistic Inquiry* 14. 373–415.
Baker, Mark. 1988. *Incorporation*. Chicago and London: The University of Chicago Press.
Benveniste, Emile. 1966. *Problèmes de Linguistique Générale*. Paris: Gallimard.
Bresnan, Joan and Sam Mchombo. 1987. Topic, pronoun and agreement in Chicheŵa. *Language* 63. 741–782.
Bresnan, Joan and Lioba Moshi. 1990. Object asymmetries in comparative Bantu syntax. *Linguistic Inquiry* 21. 147–185.
Burssens, Amaat. 1946. *Manuel du Tshiluba*, Kongo-Overzee Bibliotheek III, Anvers: De Sikkel.
Burssens, Amaat. 1954. *Introduction à l'étude des langues bantoues du Congo Belge* (Kongo-Overzee Bibliotheek VIII). Anvers: De Sikkel.
Chomsky, Noam. 1995. *The Minimalist Program*, Cambridge MA: The MIT Press.
Cocchi, Gloria. 2000a. Free clitics and bound affixes: towards a unitary analysis. In Birgit Gerlach and Janet Grijzenhout (eds.), *Clitics in phonology, morphology, and syntax*, 85–119. Amsterdam: John Benjamins.
Cocchi, Gloria. 2000b. Locative constructions in Bantu. *Quaderni del Dipartimento di Linguistica dell'Università di Firenze* 10. 43–54.
Cocchi, Gloria. 2003. Copulas in Bantu: Hints for verb movement. *Quaderni del Dipartimento di Linguistica dell'Università di Firenze* 13. 1–14.
Cocchi, Gloria. 2009. Bantu verbal extensions: a cartographic approach. In Vincenzo Moscati and Emilio Servadio (eds.), *Proceedings of the "XXXV Incontro di Grammatica Generativa"* (STiL – Studies in Linguistics 3), 91–103. Siena: CISCL. Distributed by MIT Working Papers in Linguistics, Cambridge MA.

Cocchi, Gloria. 2014. Considerazioni per uno studio delle lingue bantu. *Linguæ&* 13(1). 53–73. http://www.ledonline.it
De Clercq, Auguste. 1937. *Dictionnaire Luba (Luba-Français – Français-Luba)*. Leopoldville: Missions de Scheut.
Der-Houssikian, Haig. 1974. The semantic content of class in Bantu and its syntactic significance. *Linguistics* 124. 5–19.
Guthrie, Malcom. 1967–1971. *Comparative Bantu*, 4 vols. Farneborough, Hants: Gregg International Publishers.
Jaeggli, Osvaldo and Ken Safir (eds.). 1989. *The Null Subject Parameter*. Dordrecht: Kluwer.
Labelle, Marie. 2008. Pronominal object markers in Romance and Bantu. In Cécile De Cat and Katherine Demuth (eds.) *The Bantu-Romance connection. A comparative investigation of verbal agreement, DPs and information structure* (Linguistik Aktuell / Linguistics Today 131), 83–109. Amsterdam: John Benjamins.
Manzini, Maria Rita and Leonardo M. Savoia. 1997. Null subjects without *pro*. *UCL Working Papers in Linguistics* 9. 303–313.
Manzini, Maria Rita and Leonardo M. Savoia. 2004. Clitics: Cooccurrence and mutual exclusion patterns". In Luigi Rizzi (ed.), *The structure of CP and IP*, 211–250. New York: Oxford University Press.
Manzini, Maria Rita and Leonardo M. Savoia. 2005. *I dialetti italiani e romanci. Morfosintassi generativa*. 3 vols. Alessandria: Edizioni dell'Orso.
Manzini, Maria Rita and Leonardo M. Savoia. 2008. *Worknotes on Romance Morphosyntax – Appunti di morfosintassi romanza*. Alessandria: Edizioni dell'Orso.
Manzini, Maria Rita and Leonardo M. Savoia. 2011. (Definite) denotation and case in Romance. In Janine Berns, Haike Jacobs and Tobias Scheer (eds.), *Romance Languages and Linguistic Theory 2009*, 149–165. Amsterdam: John Benjamins.
Perrott, Daisy Valerie. 1957. *Teach Yourself Swahili*, 2nd edn. Sevenoaks, Kent: Hodder and Stoughton.
Schadeberg, Thilo. 1983. *Manuel Bantu*. Ms. Tervuren: Bibliothèque du Musée Royal de l'Afrique Centrale.
Sportiche, Dominque. 1992. Clitic constructions. Ms. University of California, Los Angeles.
Stucky, Susan. 1976. Locatives as objects in Tshiluba: a function of transitivity. *Studies in the Linguistic Sciences* 6. 174–202.
Uriagereka, Juan. 1995. Aspects of the syntax of clitic placement in Western Romance. *Linguistic Inquiry* 26. 79–123.
Van Bulck, Gaston. 1952. Les langues bantoues. In Antoine Meillet and Marcel Cohen (eds.), *Les Langues du Monde* – Nouvelle Edition, 847–904. Paris, CNRS.
Willems, Emile. 1949. *Le Tshiluba du Kasayi pour débutants*, 2nd edn. Hemptinne St. Benoit (Congo). Mission de Scheut.
Willems, Emile. 1960. *Dictionnaire Tshiluba-Français*, Nouvelle Edition. Leopoldville (Congo): Société Missionaire de St. Paul.

Marcel den Dikken
Differential object marking and the structure of transitive clauses

The functional structure of a transitive clause accommodates a position for the object outside VP, lower than the lowest structural position for the external argument, and mapped outside the nuclear scope of the object. This is the position for specific and generic objects, available, in languages with differential object marking, only for those objects that have the appropriate formal marking. The relation between differential object marking and specificity/genericity is not a biunique one, however. Following the long trail of the literature on *a*-marking of objects in Spanish, and taking important cues from Manzini & Franco's (2016) recent analysis of differential object marking, this paper *(a)* pinpoints the location of the low VP-external position for objects, *(b)* specifies the connection between occupancy of this position, the presence of differential object marking, the semantics of specificity/genericity, and the syntax of secondary predication, *(c)* explains why differential object markers are absent in passives, and *(d)* derives a link between the status of the differential object marker as a preposition or as inflectional material and the distribution of object agreement in DOM constructions.

Nominal objects of verbs are often inside VP. For non-specific ones, this is the object position *par excellence.* But specific and generic objects like to be outside the minimal VP, outside the domain of existential closure (Diesing 1992). If there is precisely one domain of existential closure in the structure of the clause, this leads to paradoxes of the following sort.

As first observed by Ter Beek (2008: 68), a 'scrambled' object can be within the nuclear scope for the subject quantifier, but can nonetheless receive a specific or generic interpretation even when the subject is clearly non-specific. One of Ter Beek's Dutch examples is reproduced in (1a) (along with the context that she provides for it); I have added another example of the same type, and from the same language, in (1b). Both examples have a bare-plural or existentially quantified subject that is the associate of expletive *er* and therefore necessarily stands within the domain of existential closure, and a bare-plural object that has 'scrambled' across an adverb (*meteen* 'immediately', *hartgrondig* 'wholeheartedly'; I do not have space to address the syntax of adverbial modification — see

---

Marcel den Dikken, Department of English Linguistics • SEAS • Eötvös Loránd University Research Institute for Linguistics • Hungarian Academy of Sciences

https://doi.org/10.1515/9781501505201-013

Cinque 1999) and is interpreted generically, that is, outside the domain of existential closure.

(1) a. [a dangerous virus has been discovered, spread by insects looking like mosquitoes]
   dat   er   mensen muggen   meteen   doodslaan kan ik me
   that   there people mosquitoes immediately dead.hit   can I   me
   dus   goed   voorstellen
   therefore well   imagine
   'I can well imagine, therefore, that some people kill mosquitoes right away'
b. ik vrees dat   er   altijd   wel   iemand   generativisten
   I   fear   that   there always   AFF   someone   generativists
   hartgronding   zal   verachten
   wholeheartedly   will   despise
   'I fear that there will always be someone who despises generativists wholeheartedly'

If there were just a single bipartition of the clause into a nuclear scope and a restrictor, and this bipartition were made at the juncture between TP and *v*P, as is customary, it would be hard to imagine how (1a,b) could support the particular interpretations that they do: how could the object be lower than (hence to the right of) the subject, which is interpreted inside the domain of existential closure, yet itself be interpreted outside the domain of existential closure?

There are two logically possible responses to this. One would be to reject the Diesing-style 'zonal' approach to the mapping of syntax onto interpretation, and to adopt instead an outlook in which there are no fixed zones (see e.g. Reinhart 2006): scrambling of the object is what induces its specific or generic interpretation; the fact that the subject in (1) has not moved leads it to be interpreted non-specifically. The alternative is to revise the zonal approach by abandoning the hypothesis that there is just a single cut-off point between *v*P and T to mark the split between the nuclear scope and the restrictor, for all quantificational expressions in a sentence: instead, there are separate bipartitions into a nuclear scope and a restrictor for subjects and for objects. In this short essay, I will explore the feasibility and merits of an approach along the latter lines.

If there is to be a designated position for specific/generic objects, that position must be independent of the position earmarked for objects that measure out or delimit the event: the specific/non-specific distinction for objects is not co-extensive with the telic/atelic distinction for events (i.e., specific objects do not only occur in telic constructions). On the plausible assumption that event delimitation is the province of *v*P, and that objects that measure out the event are in Spec*v*P, it follows that the position of specific/generic objects cannot be Spec*v*P: it must be lower.

If the verbal root can itself accommodate a specifier position for the object to be merged in, (2a) will provide SpecVP as the position for specific/generic objects, with the division between the restrictor and the nuclear scope lying, for the object, between SpecVP and the rest of the VP. But if the projection of the verbal root cannot harbour a specifier (for instance, if the root is not a RELATOR in the sense of Den Dikken 2006), we need some head to project a phrase between *v* and VP, with the head's specifier position serving as the location for specific/generic objects, and with the nuclear scope/restrictor division made at the juncture between VP and H in (2b).

(2) a. [TP ⟨SUBJECT⟩ [T [VoiceP ⟨SUBJECT⟩ [Voice [*v*P *v* [VP ⟨OBJECT⟩ [V ⟨OBJECT⟩)]]]]]]
   b. [TP ⟨SUBJECT⟩ [T [VoiceP ⟨SUBJECT⟩ [Voice [*v*P *v* [HP ⟨OBJECT⟩ [H [VP V ⟨OBJECT⟩)]]]]]]]

Selection of the option in (2b) raises the nature of the head 'H' as an interesting research topic. The syntax of differential object marking (DOM) is highly relevant in this connection. Manzini & Franco (2016) argue that certain types of objects are dependent on a functional that mediates a predicational relationship of set inclusion (usually ⊆ but occasionally ⊇). This head is by its nature a RELATOR in the sense of Den Dikken (2006). In Manzini & Franco's structures for DOM datives, their head 'Q(⊆)' projects in the complement of V and takes the object as its complement — which easily accounts for the linear order found in DOM constructions (as in Spanish (3b), below, with Q(⊆) spelled out as a *a*), but does not let the head establish a relation between two terms. Placing the head *outside* VP, in the position of 'H' in (2b), and accommodating the DOM-object in SpecHP has two advantages: it gives the head two terms to relate (the VP in its complement and the object in its specifier), and it structurally assimilates the treatments of the subject and the object — for both, the structurally higher position is the specifier of a functional head. If differential object markers such as Spanish *a* were literally the spell-outs of the head in question, the placement of this head outside VP would raise the same linearity and constituency questions that Kayne's (2004) 'prepositions as probes' hypothesis does. Instead, for languages in which they clearly form a constituent with the object, I treat these markers as belonging directly to the object; the connection between H and the marker is that only those objects that bear the marker have the licence to occupy the specifier of H.

Adapting Manzini & Franco's (2016) proposal along these lines, I will identify the head 'H' as a RELATOR of the set-inclusion (part-whole) relationship between the object and the VP. I will label it '$R_\subseteq$', for 'RELATOR of an inclusion relation'. I thus update (2b) as in (2b').

(2b') [$_{TP}$ ⟨SUBJECT⟩] [T [$_{VoiceP}$ ⟨SUBJECT⟩] [Voice [$_{vP}$ v [$_{RP}$ ⟨OBJECT⟩] [$R_\subseteq$ [$_{VP}$ V ⟨OBJECT⟩]]]]]]]

The projection of what I am calling $R_\subseteq$ in DOM constructions is 'required by the referential properties of the internal argument' (Manzini & Franco 2016:219) — their animacy, their person specification, their specificity, or a combination of these. DOM in Spanish (see Jaeggli 1982, Torrego 1999, *i.a.*) specialises towards [+human] objects, and exhibits a distribution with intensional verbs such as *buscar* 'seek, look for' that points in the direction of a connection between the differential object marker *a* and a [+specific] reading for the object: in the absence of *a*, as in (3a), we find only a *de dicto* reading; the *de re* interpretation for the object (i.e., there is a particular secretary that Juan is looking for) requires the presence of the differential object marker *a* on the object in (3b).

(3) a. *Juan busca una secretaria*
    Juan seeks a   secretary
  b. *Juan busca a   una secretaria*
    Juan seeks DOM a   secretary
    both: 'Juan is looking for a secretary'

The waters seem to be muddied by the fact that (3b) is not categorical in its *de re* reading for the object: a non-specific reading is possible as well. This is shown particularly clearly by the distribution of mood in a relative clause modifying the object (Jaeggli 1982: 56, Brugè & Brugger 1996: 31f.). While indicative mood in the relative clause signals specificity, subjunctive mood forces a non-specific reading. With this in mind, consider (4).

(4) a. *Juan busca una secretaria que {hable/   *habla}   francés*
    Juan seeks a   secretary that speaks.SUBJ/ speaks.INDIC French
  b. *Juan busca a   una secretaria que {hable/   habla}   francés*
    Juan seeks DOM a   secretary that speaks.SUBJ/ speaks.INDIC French

In (4a) the distribution of mood is exactly as expected if in the absence of *a* the object is in the VP and if this position is correlated with a non-specific interpretation: the indicative is excluded. But the grammaticality of (4b) with subjunctive mood indicates that it is possible for an *a*-marked object to be assigned a non-specific reading.

The ambiguity of (3b) regarding specificity need not deter us from pursuing the path we set out on in (2b′), however: as long as it is possible to derivationally link the two object positions (i.e., as long as it is possible for an object situated in the VP-external SpecRP position to bind a lower copy in the VP), the fact that (3b) supports a non-specific reading for the object can be accounted for in the same way that Diesing (1992) accounts for the well-known ambiguity of English (5) — via reconstruction. We thus conclude that (6) is a grammatical representation: the object in the 'DOM position' can bind a copy inside the VP.

(5) *firemen are available*

(6) [$_{VoiceP}$ Voice [$_{vP}$ *v* [$_{RP}$ OBJECT [$R_{\subseteq}$ [$_{VP}$ V ~~OBJECT~~]]]]]

Placing the object in the DOM position (whether via Internal Merge, as in (6), or via External Merge, with $R_{\subseteq}$ as the RELATOR of the minimal VP predicate and the object) allows it to be interpreted outside the nuclear scope. For Spanish, the element that makes placement of the object in SpecRP possible is a preposition: dative *a*. But when the verb selecting the object is passivised, the object is promoted to subject and the dative marker does not show up.[1] This is very much unlike what we find in the case of goal datives, in ditransitive constructions: these cannot be promoted to subject; the dative marker never disappears in passives of ditransitives. This contrast between DOM datives and goal datives is one of the puzzles (by no means specific to Spanish) that Manzini & Franco (2016) highlight prominently in their discussion of DOM.

---

[1] Manzini & Franco (2016: 220–1) contrast (ib) (an ungrammatical attempt at constructing an impersonal passive with a DOM dative, *mi*) and (ii) (a grammatical impersonal *si*-construction). Apparently the non-periphrastic impersonal construction allows for a DOM dative clitic; but the periphrastic passive never does.

(i) a. io   vengo colpito
       I   am   hit
    b. *mi   è   stato   colpito
       me   is   been   hit
(ii) mi   si   colpisce
     me   SE   hits
     'one hits me/I am hit'

They themselves say in this connection that the constraint that requires certain objects to combine with what they call 'Q(⊆)' (as distinct from the 'P(⊆)' of ditransitives, which is required for structural reasons) does not apply when movement of those objects to SpecTP takes place: the copy left behind by such movement is just a bound variable at LF (the level at which the constraint in question is assumed to be active), and this bound variable lacks the properties that would force 'Q(⊆)' to be present. But this does not yet explain how the properties of the object that, in the active, require 'Q(⊆)' to be merged are licensed when this object is promoted to subject in the passive.

From the perspective on DOM and specificity unfolded here, the absence of a differential object marker in the passive falls out if in the passive, the functional structure outside *v*P takes proper care of the licensing of the deep object, and the distinction between specific and non-specific objects can be made at the T/*v*P juncture in the way familiar from Diesing's (1992) work. There are (at least) two subject positions in the structure: one outside VoiceP (SpecTP), and one further down the tree (SpecVoiceP for unergative and transitive predicates, and a position inside the complement of Voice for unaccusatives and passives). In the passive, the special quantificational properties of DOM objects are associated with SpecTP; there is no need to call upon a head projecting between *v* and VP to license these properties of the object in the passive: (7) is sufficient.

(7) [TP OBJECT [T [VoiceP Voice [vP *v* [VP ... O̶B̶J̶E̶C̶T̶ ...]]]]]

If R⊆ is to the object what T is to the subject of the clause, parallels in distribution between preverbal subjects (in SpecTP) and DOM objects are naturally expected to manifest themselves. Such parallels do indeed exist. Take, for instance, the restrictions known to exist on bare-plural subjects in Spanish: they resist the preverbal structural subject position unless they are restrictively modified. The contrast in (8) (Leonetti 2003; cf. Laca 1996) illustrates this. What is relevant for our purposes here is that a parallel contrast presents itself in the object domain: (9), again from Leonetti (2003), illustrates that a bare-plural object can be *a*-marked only if it has a restrictive modifier.

(8) {^{??}/*guerilleros*/ ✓*guerrilleros de las FARC fuertemente Armados*}
    guerillas   guerillas   of the   FARC strongly   armed
    atacaron   *ayer*   *un puesto de*   *policia*
    attacked   yesterday   a post of   police
    'heavily armed FARC guerillas attacked a police post yesterday'

(9) conocemos   a   {??profesores/ ✓profesores que se pasan
     we.know   DOM   teachers/   teachers   that SE pass
     el   fin de semana trabajando}
     the   weekend   working
     'we know teachers who spend the weekend working'

Even more interesting is the fact that the distribution of DOM in Spanish has an effect on the interpretation of constructions in which the object is followed by an agreeing adjective. For instances of V that allow both nominal and small-clause complements and for instances of A that are stage-level, the string in (10) is ambiguous in Spanish between a reading in which the AP is mapped into the object as an attributive modifier (Spanish has postnominal attributive adjectives), as in (10a), and one in which it is a secondary predicate of the object, which is depicted in (10b).

(10) V N A
   a. V [DP D [NP AP]]
   b. V [DP D [NP]] [AP]

Because *inteligente* 'intelligent' is an individual-level predicate, it does not make a parse of the string in (11) as in (10b) possible; so all of *una mujer muy inteligente* 'a very intelligent wife' has to be mapped into a DP, as in (10a). Manzini & Franco (2016: 225) suggest that (11) is ungrammatical with *a* because *tener* and *a* would play the same role (of marking set inclusion) twice, redundantly: *tener* is itself a relator of predicational set inclusion (part-whole) relations; so *a* is not needed.

(11) Juan tiene (*a) una mujer muy inteligente
     Juan has   DOM a wife very intelligent
     'Juan has a very intelligent wife'

Assuming that possessive *tener* is a relator of a predicational set inclusion relation, between the possessor (i.e., the subject) and the possessum, we expect that the latter must usually be mapped onto the complement-of-V position with possessive *tener*, and DOM is impossible. Now consider what happens when the object of *tener* is marked with *a* and must sit in the higher object position. This should be grammatical provided that something other than the object gets placed in the complement of V. The projection of a stage-level predicate such as *enfermo* 'sick' in (12) should be a candidate.

(12) *Juan tiene a   un hermano enfermo*
     Juan has DOM a   brother sick
     'Juan has a brother sick'

This is exactly right: when *tener* grammatically co-occurs with the differential object marker *a*, a (10b)-type parse is forced (Laca 1987, Leonetti 2003); to get a (10a)-type parse, the object must not be adorned with *a* (as in (11)). When *enfermo* is inside the DP of *hermano*, and this DP is marked with *a* and occupies the higher object position, as in (13a), the complement-of-V position remains empty, and *tener* fails to play its relator role. But with the AP of *enfermo* mapped onto the complement-of-V position (as in Larson's 1988 and Hale & Keyser's 1993 approach to (certain) cases of secondary predication), as in (13b), (12) converges with *un hermano* in the higher object position, introduced by *a*, and *tiene enfermo* as a complex predicate. Thus, combining *tener* with DOM is in fact grammatical, but the result only allows a reading along the lines of (10b), with the stage-level adjective as a secondary predicate of the *a*-marked object.

(13) a. *[$_{vP}$ v [$_{RP}$ *a un hermano enfermo* [R$_\subseteq$ [$_{VP}$ *tiene*]]]]
     b. [$_{vP}$ v [$_{RP}$ *a un hermano* [R$_\subseteq$ [$_{VP}$ *tiene* [$_{AP}$ *enfermo*]]]]]

While possessive *tener* is inherently a relator of a predicational set inclusion (part-whole) relation, and therefore is in need of a complement, other verbs are not. So it is not predicted that we should find the effects shown for *tener* with every verb in the lexicon. It is also not necessarily expected that the presence of a secondary predicate will irrevocably force specificity onto the object (and, in DOM languages, force it to be combined with the relevant marker). The syntax of secondary predication is appreciably more complex than the few remarks made in the previous paragraph might lead one to suspect.

    In light of the structural discussion of DOM and specificity laid out above, one would expect that whenever the object cannot arrive in SpecRP via movement but can only be base-generated there, reconstruction of the object into the VP should be impossible and the specific/generic reading should be the only one available. This expectation arises in the context of Diesing's (1992) discussion of the difference between stage-level and individual-level predicates — the difference, that is, between the ambiguity of (5) and the generic-only interpretation of (14).

(14) *firemen are intelligent*

For Diesing, the subject of an individual-level predicate is externally merged in SpecTP; it does not bind a lower copy of itself further down the tree, so reconstruction is impossible and no existential reading can arise for *firemen* in (14). When we transplant this to the object domain, we expect that whenever the VP portion of the structure cannot harbour a lower copy for the object, only a specific or generic reading should be available for the object, and the object should be marked with *a* whenever it is [+human]. This is certainly true for (15), with individual-level *inteligentes*, where the bare-plural noun phrase gets a generic interpretation and *a*-marking is obligatory.

(15) considero inteligentes *(a) profesores que trabajan el fin de semana
      I.consider intelligent   DOM   teachers   that work   the weekend

But *a*-marking is also obligatory in stage-level (16) (Luis López, p.c.), which supports an existential interpretation on a par with English *I consider firemen available* or (5). Just as in (3b), the presence of *a* on the [+human] accusative noun phrase does not in itself force a specific or generic interpretation: whenever a position lower in the structure is available in which a silent copy of the noun phrase can be postulated, reconstruction can deliver the existential reading.

(16) considero disponibles *(a) profesores que trabajan el fin de semana
      I.consider available   DOM   teachers   that work   the weekend

What does this tell us about the relationship between the marker *a* and the head 'R$_\subseteq$' in the structure outside VP in (2b′)? The presence of the marker is what makes it possible for an object to be realised in the VP-external SpecRP position for specifics and generics. The distribution of *a* is not co-extensive with that of R$_\subseteq$: *a* is not itself the spell-out of R$_\subseteq$. But when R$_\subseteq$ is present and a [+human] object occupies its specifier position, that object must be marked with *a*: the head R$_\subseteq$ in (2b′) is not what licenses *a*; it is the presence of *a* that licenses the placement of a [+human] object in SpecRP. So for [+human] objects in Spanish, placement in SpecRP in (2b′), outside the domain of existential closure for the object, is legitimate only in the presence of the marker *a*.

This marker *a* is formally a preposition, projecting a PP. PPs are well known to differ from DPs in not triggering φ-feature agreement with a predicate head. For Spanish, verifying that the *a*-marked object of a DOM construction behaves like a *bona fide* PP in this respect is impossible: even DP-objects fail to agree with the verb in the language. But in Hindi, the PP-status of a DOM object can be tested and confirmed.

The suffix -*ko* in the Hindi DOM example in (17b) is usually treated as a case particle. But Ahmed (2006) (from whose paper the example in (17b) was taken) credits Beames (1872–79) with the observation that the earliest attestions of -*ko* (which in turn probably originates from a noun) involved the marking of the recipient goal of ditransitive verbs — very much like Spanish *a*. The marker -*ko* still serves this function in Hindi today. Taking the marker of the goal of a ditransitive construction to be a P (see Den Dikken 1995), I translate this observation into the statement that -*ko* is a P. So *saddaf-ko* in (17b) is a PP — one whose distribution is tied to the head labelled 'R$_\subseteq$' in (2b'). Concretely, *saddaf-ko* in (17b) occurs in the higher object position, SpecRP, in (2b'). Participle agreement is often (though by no means exclusively) controlled from specifier positions, so *saddaf-ko* is in the right kind of syntactic position to bring about φ-feature agreement with the participle. But because it is a PP rather than a DP, and since PPs cannot control φ-feature agreement, the participle does not take on the feminine singular specification of *saddaf*. While the 'plain' object in (17a) agrees with the perfect participle, the object marked with -*ko* in the DOM case in (17b) does not; the participle bears default masculine singular inflection.

(17) a. *anil-ne   kitaabē   becī*
      Anil-ERG book.FPL sell.PRF.FPL
      'Anil sold (the) books'
   b. *anjum-ne   saddaf-ko   dekhaa*
      Anjum.FSG-ERG Saddaf.FSG-DOM see.PRF.MSG
      'Anjum saw Saddaf'

There are languages closely related to Hindi but differing fom it in having the DOM object control φ-feature agreement with the predicate head. Manzini & Franco (2016: 232–3) mention the Rajasthani dialects of Indo-Aryan as a case in point. Though I cannot pursue the matter in detail due to a lack of relevant information, what is interesting here is that the so-called differential object marker in these dialects (-*nai*) shows a clear resemblance to the ergative particle of Hindi (-*ne*), and in at least one Rajasthani dialect (Harauti) is used as a *factotum* particle that adorns ergative and experiencer subjects, DOM-objects, and indirect objects (Verbeke 2008, via Phillips 2014: 107). While it is possible that all of these functions are marked with the aid of a P, the discussion in the present paragraph and the previous one leads us to surmise that Harauti's generalised marker -*nai* is not of the category P, but instead is an inflectional element that leaves DP's categorial status untouched and hence does not interfere with the relationship between the object-DP and the predicate head. If this conjecture can be substantiated, the fact that in the Rajasthani dialects of Indo-Aryan the DOM object controls φ-feature agreement with the predicate head is unsurprising.

Manzini & Franco (2016) treat the Italian first and second person object pronouns *mi* and *ti*, for the singular, and *ci* and *vi*, for the plural, uniformly as datives, instead of assuming syncretism for accusative and dative in the first and second person. If their analysis is correct, then Italian has systematic DOM for first and second person objects. The fact that past participle agreement for number is grammatical (though not obligatory) with *ci* and *vi* when these serve as direct objects (as in (18), taken, along with (19), from Manzini & Franco 2016: 234) then indicates that these first and second person objects behave nominally, not like PPs: unquestionable PP-uses of *ci* and *vi* never give rise to participial agreement (see (19)).

(18) a. ci   ha   colpito/colpiti
     us   he.has hit.MSG/MPL
   b. vi   ha   colpito/colpiti
     you_PL he.has hit.MSG/MPL

(19) a. ci   ha   parlato/*parlati
     us   he.has talked.MSG/MPL
   b. vi   ha   parlato/*parlati
     you_PL he.has talked.MSG/MPL

Italian, then, is another language in which DOM objects (restricted in this language to first and second person) are nominal. Indeed, there is nothing about the form of the clitics *ci* and *vi* that suggests that they are PPs.[2] But pan-Romance *a* is indubitably a P. So for dialects of Italian that *(a)* extend DOM to full third-person DPs (such as the Sasso di Castalda dialect mentioned in the introduction of Manzini and Franco's paper) and *(b)* have past participle agreement, I would expect it to be case that an object can trigger participial agreement only when *not* marked with *a*.

If this is confirmed, it tells us that in languages in which the differential object marker is a P-element that forms a constituent with the object, this P is

---

[2] I assume that the fact that the form *ci* also occurs in Italian as a locative proform glossed as 'there' is a historical accident, a true case of accidental homophony, not compelling us to a locative treatment of the *ci* glossed as 'us'.

not the spell-out of the functional head (labelled 'R⊆' in (2b′)) that licenses the DOM object but instead the projector of a PP containing the object, licensed in a structural relationship (Spec-Head agreement) with the head that introduces the higher object position.

> *I offer this paper to Rita Manzini on the occasion of her 60th birthday, in great appreciation of the profoundly original and insightful analytical and descriptive work that she has enriched generative linguistic theorising with for decades.*

References

Ahmed, Tafseer. 2006. Spatial, temporal and structural uses of Urdo *ko*. In Miriam Butt & Tracy Holloway King (eds.), *Proceedings of the LFG 06 Conference*, 1–13. Stanford: CSLI Publications. http://web.stanford.edu/group/cslipublications/cslipublications/LFG/11/pdfs/lfg06.pdf

Beames, John. 1872–79. *A comparative grammar of the Modern Aryan languages of India*. Delhi: Munshiram Manoharlal. Republished 1966.

Beek, Janneke ter. 2008. Dutch indefinites, word order, and the mapping hypothesis. *Groninger Arbeiten zur Germanistischen Linguistik* 46. 55–72.

Brugè, Laura & Gerhard Brugger. 1996. On the accusative *a* in Spanish. *Probus* 8. 1–51.

Cinque, Guglielmo. 1999. *Adverbs and functional heads*. Oxford/New York: Oxford University Press.

Diesing, Molly. 1992. *Indefinites*. Cambridge, MA: MIT Press.

Dikken, Marcel den. 1995. *Particles: On the syntax of verb-particle, triadic, and causative constructions*. Oxford/New York: Oxford University Press.

Dikken, Marcel den. 2006. *Relators and linkers*. Cambridge, MA: MIT Press.

Hale, Kenneth & S. Jay Keyser. 1993. On argument structure and the lexical expression of syntactic relations. In Kenneth Hale and S. Jay Keyser (eds.), *The view from Building 20: Essays in linguistics in honor of Sylvain Bromberger*, 53–110. Cambridge, MA: MIT Press.

Jaeggli, Osvaldo. 1982. *Topics in Romance syntax*. Dordrecht: Foris.

Kayne, Richard S. 2004. Prepositions as probes. In Adriana Belletti (ed.), *Structures and beyond*, 192–212. Oxford: Oxford University Press.

Kratzer, Angelika. 1996. Severing the external argument from its verb. In Johan Rooryck & Laurie Zaring (eds.), *Phrase structure and the lexicon*, 109–137. Dordrecht: Kluwer.

Laca, Brenda. 1987. Sobre el uso del acusativo preposicional en español. In C. Pensado (ed.), *El complemento directo preposicional*, 61–91. Madrid: Visor.

Laca, Brenda. 1996. Acerca de la semántica de los plurales escuetos del español. In Ignacio Bosque (ed.), *El sustantivo sin determinación. La ausencia de determinante en la lengua Española*, 241–68. Madrid: Visor.

Larson, Richard. 1988. On the double object construction. *Linguistic Inquiry* 19. 335–391.

Leonetti, Manuel. 2003. Specificity and object marking: The case of Spanish *a*. In Klaus von Heusinger & Georg Kaiser (eds.), *Proceedings of the workshop 'Semantic and Syntactic Aspects of Specificity in Romance Languages'*, 67–101. Konstanz: Fachbereich Sprachwissenschaft der Universität Konstanz.

Manzini, M. Rita & Ludovico Franco. 2016. Goal and DOM datives. *Natural Language & Linguistic Theory* 34. 197–240.
Phillips, Maxwell. 2014. Book review of Verbeke (2008). *Journal of South Asian Languages and Linguistics* 1. 103–10.
Reinhart, Tanya. 2006. *Interface strategies: Optimal and costly computations*. Cambridge, MA: MIT Press.
Torrego, Esther. 1999. El complemento directo preposicional. In Ignacio Bosque & Violeta Demonte (eds.), *Gramática descriptiva de la lengua española, Vol. II*, 1779–1805. Madrid: Espasa-Calpe.
Verbeke, Sjaantje. 2008. *Alignment and ergativity in New Indo-Aryan languages*. Berlin: Mouton de Gruyter.

Elisa Di Domenico
Countability and the /s/ morpheme in English

1 Introduction

It is well known that English inflection/agreement employs the /s/ morpheme, in various syntactic environments[1]:

(1) a. three books
 b. John loves Mary
 c. Mary's in the garden
 d. Mary's going home
 e. Mary's got two dogs
 f. John's book
 g. That book is yours
 h. A book of John's
 i. His book

If we strictly adhere to a tradition first systematized in the *Téchnē Grammatikḗ* by Dionysios Thrax, (170–90 B.C) in his *parepómena* (concurrent features), the English /s/ morpheme expresses quite different feature values in these environments, such as 'plural number', as in (1.a), 'third person singular present', as in (1.b), (1.c), (1.d), (1.e) 'genitive case', as in (1.f), (1.g), and (1.h), (1.i).

A first possibility is to think that different syntactic/semantic features happen to be spelled out in an identical fashion (morphological syncretism), i.e. through a unique, extremely opaque, morpho- phonological exponent.

---

[1] I will consider /s/ subsuming both its –s and 's variant, leaving open the possibility that these variants are not merely orthographic but reflect a difference in the derivation of the syntactic structure to which they pertain. Adopting Borer's (2005) terminology, I will consider /s/ an f- morph with a morphologically free and a morphologically bound variant.

Note: I thank an anonymous reviewer for helpful comments and suggestions. All errors and shortcomings are of course my own.

Elisa Di Domenico, Università per Stranieri di Perugia

Another possibility, the one pursued in this work, is to think that the /s/ morpheme in English is instead the expression of a unique feature heading its own functional projection. This feature, that has to be identified perhaps beyond traditional labels, can be thought of as a sort of lowest common denominator of the feature values that can be ascribed to /s/ following traditional labels. This functional head will have the further characteristics of being present in different syntactic domains, /s/ having different merging sites, as shown in (1): various kinds of simple and complex DPs, various kinds of clauses.

Two interrelated problems must be solved to maintain this perspective:
- a first problem is to demonstrate the equivalence, at the syntactic-interpretive level, of the various kinds of /s/ in (1. a – i). This will allow us to maintain the view that /s/ is the exponent of one and the same functional head.
- a second problem is to properly identify the underlying featural content of the functional head expressed by /s/.

The proposal which I will outline in what follows, in line with a suggestion that Rita Manzini (p. c.) made for the Latin –s morpheme, is that the /s/ morpheme in English expresses [countability]. I will further argue that the expression of this feature is a necessary requirement of DPs and clauses in inflectional languages, whenever person is not expressed. I will discuss previous linguistic analyses confined or not to the English /s/ morpheme, (Kayne 1989, 1993, 1995; den Dikken 1998,1999; Bernstein and Tortora, 2005; Manzini and Savoia 2011), as well as data coming from the acquisition of English as a first (Brown, 1973) and second (Di Domenico, 2013) language. In Section 2 I'll start examining Kayne's (1989; 1993) proposals, which establish an equivalence among the various occurrences of /s/ in (1.b – g) under the assumption that /s/ is an agreement morpheme expressing singular number. A problem with this analysis (i.e. the compatibility of 'genitival' /s/ with both singular and plural antecedents) will be the starting point of Section 3, where acquisitional evidence strengthening the 's = is equivalence will be introduced, previous proposals to solve the 'singular/ plural compatibility' problem will be discussed, and the idea that /s/ expresses a feature which can characterize only non- first/non- second person arguments, but connected to number, will be sketched. In Section 4, Manzini and Savoia's (2011) work on the Latin –s morpheme will be briefly summarized, in order to shed light (through relevant comparative data and their analysis) on some aspects of the English /s/ morpheme, to which I will go back in Section 5. In Section 6 I'll draw some conclusions and I'll mention some residual problems to be left for further research.

2 Genitival, copular, auxiliary and verbal /s/

That *have* (auxiliary and main verb) should be analyzed as *be* plus an abstract (dative) preposition, is a familiar, widely shared conception after Kayne's (1993) seminal work on auxiliary selection.[2] Kayne's analysis starts from the assumption that possessive DPs are included in possessive sentences with *have*.[3] Possessive sentences such as:

(2) John has three sisters/a sister

contain, at D-structure, a copula (BE) with a single DP complement, inside which is the possessor:

(3) BE [$_{DP}$Spec D°] [DP$_{poss}$]][4]

Further detailing the possessive DP, Kayne (1993) argues that the English *'s* is akin to AGR°, followed by NP or QP. Thus, the fuller D- structure of a possessive sentence in English will be:

(4) BE [$_{DP}$ Spec D° [DP$_{poss}$ [AGR°QP/NP]]]
              John   's   three sisters/sister

He suggests that *'s* is not only AGR but actually substantially the same as the morpheme *–s* found on verbs and that, like the latter, it requires a singular antecedent.[5]

---

2 Kayne follows Benveniste (1966) for the idea that (the evolution of) auxiliary *have* and main verb (i.e. possessive) *have* should be thought of in parallel fashion, and Freeze (1992) for the idea that *have* should be analyzed as an instance of *be* to which an abstract preposition has been incorporated.
3 'If a proper understanding of auxiliary *have* depends on a proper understanding of main verb *have*, then it is essential to have a clear idea of the syntax of possessive constructions' [Kayne,1993:3]. For possessive constructions, Kayne (1993) draws on the essentials of Szabolcsi's (1981; 1983) analysis of Hungarian possessive constructions.
4 The structure in (3) is thought of as 'intuitively clear to an English speaker given the almost acceptable sentence' in (i):
(i)   There is (exists) a sister of John's
5 In Kayne (1989) the value attributed to *-s* is indeed 'singular number'. We'll come back more in detail to this proposal, noting for the moment that for Kayne (1993) this explains the incompatibility of *'s* with (regular) plural possessors as in (i):
(i)   *The kids's mother

Kayne notes that when D° is definite, it must be phonetically unrealized in English (*the John's sister*), for reasons that are not clear.

When D° is indefinite, English moves QP/NP to Spec and inserts an overt preposition under D° to Case license DP$_{poss}$:

(5) BE [$_{DP}$ Spec   D° [DP$_{poss}$ [AGR°QP/NP]]]
       three sisters/a sister   of John   's[6]

English has a non-overt prepositional (oblique) D° in possessive constructions, represented as D/P$_e$, to whose specifier DP$_{poss}$ is allowed to move, after D/P$_e$ has incorporated to BE[7]:

(6) DP$_{poss/i}$ D/P$_{e/j}$+BE [$_{DP}$ [e$_i$] [$_{D/P}$ e]$_j$ [[e$_i$]...

D/P$_e$ + BE is spelled out as HAVE:

(7) John$_i$ has [$_{DP}$ [e$_i$] D/P° [[e$_i$] [AGR° 3 sisters]]]

Auxiliary *have* is essentially the same as possessive *have*, the difference lying in the fact that auxiliary *have* has a DP complement containing a participial substructure, whereas possessive *have*, as we have seen, has a DP complement containing a QP/NP structure.

Let's now go back to the content of 's. As we saw above, for Kayne (1993) 's is akin to –s, which in turn, following Kayne (1989), is specified for 'singular number'. Kayne (1989) further argues that -s contains no specification of person (contrary to what commonly assumed).

He first considers the contrast in (8):

A problem with this account, as we shall see, is however the full acceptability of 's with irregular plural possessors:
(ii)   The children's mother
6 Kayne assumes that the indefinite article *a* must be of category Q, and not of category D as the definite article *the*. Ungrammaticality of:
(i) * the sister of John's
follows, with *the* and *of* competing for the same position.
  It is unclear to me, however, why, under this analysis, you can have:
(i)   John's three sisters
but not:
(ii) John's a sister
7 As a result of incorporation to BE, its Spec becomes an A-position, hence a position where DP$_{poss}$ can move.

(8) a. You sing well
    b. He sings well

Assuming *you* to be grammatically plural, the contrast between *sing* and *sings* can be taken to be one between plural and singular, that is, to be one of number.

He then considers *I* and the fact that it does not take the –*s* form despite having singular reference. His suggestion is that English treats *I* as being grammatically unmarked for number. From this, the conclusion is made that the –*s* form occurs with grammatically singular NP subjects, while the bare form occurs elsewhere.

Turning to the verb *be*, he assumes that *is* can then be taken to be 'singular number' like the –*s* form of all other verbs. He further argues that *are* is not marked as 'plural', but is an elsewhere form which occurs whenever *is* and *am* cannot be used.

From this brief examination of Kayne (1993) and Kayne (1989) we can conclude that if 's = -s (Kayne, 1993) and *is* = -s (Kayne, 1989), it must also be that 's = *is*:[8]

(9) 's = -s = *is*

All instances of /s/ in (9) have, according to Kayne, the value 'singular number', i.e. require a singular antecedent.

As far as 's is concerned, however, there are some reasons to doubt on this characterization of its featural content. Let's consider the examples below:

(10) Those children's mother[9]

(11) Two friends of theirs

(12) Jack and Jill's brothers

In these cases 's appears indeed to be compatible with a plural antecedent.

Perhaps a solution can be found assuming that the value of 's is not exactly singular number and then extending this characterization to the other instantiations of /s/. This would allow us to maintain the equivalence proposed by Kayne (1993; 1989) with respect to the various instantiations of /s/ in (9), and could have

---

8 Furthermore, assuming (7), we are also led to take *has* to be *have* + 's.
9 Kayne's (1993: fn.9) example. Kayne observes that an open question is why plurals unmarked with -s are compatible with 's but not with the verbal –s.

the further advantage of leaving more space to the possibility of including the –s in (1.a) (apparently indicating plural number), as well as the -s in (1.i), as part of the family.

3 The 's = *is* Hypothesis and the content of 's

In Di Domenico (2013) I have presented some data coming from the acquisition of English as a second language that indicate that the 's in Genitive constructions and copular *is* (in its contracted form 's) are considered as one and the same element by the experimental subjects. This suggested the 's = *is* Hypothesis in (13):[10]

(13) *Is* and 's are allomorphs of one and the same morpheme that can be merged DP internally and clause internally

In discussing about the content of this element, and in order to overcome the problems in (10), (11), (12) I have proposed (Di Domenico, 2015) that 's is not specified for number (neither singular nor plural) but for (third) person only. This explains not only its compatibility with plural and singular antecedents, but also the fact that 's Genitive constructions always have third person (non – pronominal) possessors. In all other cases, a possessive pronoun is employed:

(14) a. John's book
 b. my book
 c. your book etc.

My account for the presence of a person feature in possessive DPs was the following. Starting from Benveniste's generalization, i.e. the observation that a person

---

10 Work from den Dikken (1998, 1999) draws the explicit conclusion that the 's found in English Saxon Genitive constructions is indeed a copula, in turn the expression of a functional projection FP, whose specifier is the target of possessor movement in prenominal possessive constructions. A detailed comparison of Kayne's and den Dikken's analysis of English 's Genitive constructions in connection with Hungarian possessive constructions, however, would lead us too far afield. Support for the 's = *is* Hypothesis comes also from the acquisition of English as a first language, where, as from Brown's (1973) seminal work, possessive and (non contractable) copular /s/ are acquired at nearly the same MLU (Mean Length of Utterances): 6.33 and 6.50 respectively.

feature is present in verbs and in pronominal DPs, [11] I proposed, a long time ago, what I called the Denotation Principle:

(15) Every lexically expressed argument (be it a noun phrase or a sentence) must be denoted. The expression of denotation is the person feature [Di Domenico, 1994:5]

While a person feature is expressed in pronouns, in non- pronominal DPs the determiner (or raising to D for proper names, as in Longobardi, 1994) performs the same role: making the nominal expression argumental (Longobardi, 1994) or referential (Rizzi, 1986), or, in Higginbotham's (1983) terms, discharging its theta role.

In subject-verb agreement the person feature (correlated to a tense feature, Guéron and Hoekstra, 1992) discharges the Eventive variable (Higginbotham, 1983) of the sentence. I further argued, in Di Domenico (2004), that the tense/person indication in finite sentences, as well as the person feature on pronouns (or the determiner in non-pronominal DPs) has the function of placing the sentence/argument with respect to the speech event.[12] Let's then reformulate (15) as (15)':

(15)' Every lexically expressed argument (be it a noun phrase or a sentence) must be denoted/placed with respect to the speech event.[13] The expression of denotation/placement is the person feature.

In English 's Genitive constructions, as I argued in Di Domenico (2015), the person/denotation feature of these complex DPs is expressed by 's, which, coherently, is in complementary distribution with the determiner of the possessum (i.e. the head noun):

(16) *the John's house

If (third) person is the content of 's, and 's=is, then is as well expresses (third) person.

The extension to the –s of the verbal domain can follow without further stipulations.

---

[11] "Le verbe est, avec le pronom, la seule espèce de mots qui soit soumise à la catégorie de la personne" [Benveniste, 1966:225]
[12] Expressing what the relation is between what is said and the speech event, in turn related to the possibility of implementing Displaced Reference in human language, is not required in imperative clauses. See Di Domenico (2004) for further details.
[13] At the sentence level, as we said, person is connected to tense.

Indirect support to this view, as we shall see in Section 4, also comes from work by Manzini and Savoia (2011) which assume that the Latin and Romansh –s ending (in traditional terms, a case ending) is associated with denotational operator properties.

We are left now with the following situation:
- when /s/ is realized as 's it is compatible with singular and (irregular) plural antecedent, but not with regular plural antecedents (* *the kids's mother*)
- when /s/ is realized as –s it is compatible only with singular (third person) antecedents, and alternates with a bare morpheme
- when /s/ is realized as *is* it is compatible with singular (third person) antecedents and alternates with a plural form (*are*) and with a form for first person singular (*am*).

These problems have been solved in different ways by different authors. As for den Dikken (1998,1999), which considers 's and *is* only, assuming (see fn. 10 above) an identity between the two (i.e. assuming that 's is indeed a copula), the cases in which 's is compatible with plural antecedents are considered instances of anti- agreement, characterizing non-pronominal DPs but not pronouns, as in Welsh clauses (Rouveret, 1991): [14]

(17) a. the man's ill
     b. the men are ill

(18) a. he's ill
     b. they're ill

(19) a. the man's illness
     b. the men's illness

(20) a. he's (→his) illness
     b. they're (→their) illness

Bernstein and Tortora (2005) assume instead that 's is not a copula, but a singular number morpheme akin to –s, the copula having two different forms, one for the singular (*is*) and one for the plural (*are*). A copula is present instead, according to

---

14 The same full DPs/pronouns asymmetries in anti- agreement is found in Hungarian possessive constructions, with the same difference between possessive constructions and full clauses attested in English.

the authors, in possessive pronouns, which have a singular and a plural form.[15] In their analysis, however, the compatibility of 's with irregular plural antecedents (as in (10) – (12)), is admittedly still a problem.

As for Kayne (1989; 1993), as we have seen, the equivalence 's = –s= *is* is made under the assumption that their value is singular number. With respect to 's, Kayne (1993: fn.9) argues that an open question is why plurals unmarked with –s are compatible with 's. Perhaps, he suggests, this is related to the fact that 's does not alternate with a zero morpheme as –s.[16]

The fact that 's is compatible with irregular plurals remains thus an open question if we assume that it expresses singular number (Kayne 1993; Bernstein and Tortora, 2005); this question has been solved by den Dikken (1998) assuming cases like (19) above to be an instance of anti-agreement. As Bernstein and Tortora (2005) argue, however, this does not explain why regular plurals are incompatible with 's.

My proposal (i.e. 's (= –s = *is*) as (third) person, unspecified for number) allows us to dispense with anti- agreement to solve the puzzle of the compatibility of 's with both singular and irregular plural antecedents.[17]

The incompatibility of 's with regular plurals, at this point, still remains a problem for my analysis.

In this respect, Bernstein and Tortora (2005) convincingly show that the incompatibility of 's with regular plural antecedents, like (21) below, cannot be due to phonological or morphological reasons:

(21) * The kids's mother

They report that for many speakers (22.b) is worse than (22.a), although in (22.b) the plural marker is separated from the possessive marker by other material:

(22) a. the kid from New York's mother
     b. ?* the kids from New York's mother

---

15 We'll come back to possessive pronouns in Section 5.
16 Kayne (1989) assumes that –s alternates with a bare form. The latter is free to co-occur with any subject NP, but given a choice between an inflected form and a bare form, the inflected form must be taken. As for the verb *be*, where *is* (+sg as –s) in the present tense alternates with *am* and *are*, while *am* is assumed to be specified for first person, *are*, which might appear to be +plural, is considered in the spirit of the article, as unmarked, hence usable whenever *is* or *am* are not.
17 As I argued in Di Domenico (2015) anti-agreement is problematic because what you really see is anti-agreement in number, but not in person.

The fact that (22.b) is felt deviant, thus, cannot be explained assuming a phonological or morphological incompatibility of the two instances of /s/.[18] Under their view, the incompatibility is due to the fact that the –s of *kids* is a plural marker, while *'s* expresses singular number.

I would like to pursue a different path, and assume that the two instances of /s/, in (21) as well as in (22.b), are incompatible because they express indeed the same featural content, which cannot be expressed twice. With this in mind, let's turn to the precise characterization of the feature in question.

On one side, for what we saw in Section 3, this feature must have denotational properties, i.e. must be connected to person. On the other side, however, this feature must be connected to number, since it differentiates singular from plural DPs (*the kid/the kids*). For this reason, following a suggestion that Rita Manzini (p.c.) made for the Latin and Romansh –s morpheme, I propose that the English /s/ morpheme expresses [countability].

Before examining how a characterization in terms of [countability] can account for the distribution of the English /s/ morpheme, we'll briefly examine Manzini and Savoia's (2011) characterization of the Latin and Romansh –s ending.

4 The Latin and Romansh –s as denotation

As we mentioned in Section 3, Manzini and Savoia (2011) assume that the Latin –s ending is associated with denotational operator properties, and does not indicate case, as in traditional accounts, since case is not a primitive of grammar (Chomsky, 2008; Pesetsky and Torrego, 2007). They observe that –s appears in different environments, as exemplified in (23) for the (non – neuter) third class, such as the nominative singular, the genitive singular and the nominative and accusative plural:

(23) a. Canis   currit
        dog.SG.NOM runs
        'The dog runs'
     b. canis cauda
        dog.SG.GEN tail
        'The dog's tail'

---

18 A morphological explanation has been proposed by Zwicky (1987) and Aronoff and Fuhrhop (2002).

c. Canes currunt/ video
   dogs.PL.NOM/ACC run/ I see
   'The dogs run/ I see the dogs'
   [adapted from Manzini and Savoia, 2011:154]

The fact that −s shows up as a plural (as in 23.c), leads the authors to postulate that −s can be identified with a quantificational feature Q, plurality being a quantificational property. This seems in contradiction with the occurrence of −s as a singular (23.a and b). This apparent contradiction is solved assuming (as in Pesetsky, 1985), that Q elements have scope properties: the plural reading of a Q element like−s corresponds to a noun internal quantificational scope; the singular reading of −s corresponds to a scope wider than the noun.

As for the genitive (23.b), Manzini and Savoia argue that it roughly corresponds to a quantificational inclusion relation: the scope of −s as a so-called genitive specification is the entire noun phrase: 'the genitive argument is interpreted as 'including' the referent of the head noun'. [Manzini and Savoia 2011: 156].

In the singular nominative (23.a), the scope of −s is sentential: agreement with the finite verb characterizes the nominative context, and the authors' proposal is that quantificational specifications are required to satisfy this syntactic context, involving the EPP argument: −s as a Q morphology is specialized for the satisfaction of the syntactic EPP environment.

The authors then consider −s in the Romansh variety of Vella (Lumnesia Valley, Grisons). In this variety −s, a nominative ending for masculine singular, characterizes masculine singular adjectives and participles in predicative contexts, but not in attributive contexts:

(24) a. kwai om ai kwərt-s
    that man is short- m.sg
    'that man is short'
  b. in om kwərt
    a man short
    'a short man' [adapted from Manzini and Savoia 2011: 159–160]

In contexts like (24.a) -s provides, according to the authors, the quantificational/definite closure for the argument slot that the adjectival base is associated with: the D/Q closure, provided by determiners and quantifiers when the adjectival base is embedded in a noun phrase (24.b), is not provided in predicative contexts as (24.a), and the −s thus provides it.

The similarity of the Latin −s and the English /s/ morpheme is extremely interesting, and the analysis provided by Manzini and Savoia (2011) for the

Latin –s is particularly revealing to characterize the English /s/ more in details. The conclusion that –s expresses a quantificational feature (Manzini and Savoia 2011) naturally leads to the suggestion that it expresses indeed [countability] (Rita Manzini, p.c), a suggestion which I will explore for the English /s/ morpheme in the following section.

5 The English /s/ morpheme as countability

Going back to English, in the light of what we saw in the previous sections, I can now reformulate (13) as (25):

(25) *Is*, *'s* and *–s* are allomorphs of one and the same morpheme /s/ that can be merged DP internally or clause internally. /s/ expresses [countability], a denotational feature.

Let us also keep in mind (15)', here repeated as (15)'' for convenience:

(15)'' Every lexically expressed argument (be it a noun phrase or a sentence) must be denoted/placed with respect to the speech event. The expression of denotation/placement is the person feature.

Following Benveniste (1966) and Bianchi (2006a), (see also Forchheimer, 1953), I will assume that pronouns are inherently specified for person. I will further assume, that [countability] is expressed, and with the same denoting/placing role, whenever person is not: personal referents are, in a peculiar sense, unique, non – replicable, hence they are not 'countable'.[19]

We can now derive the fact that /s/, at the sentence level, occurs where person is not expressed:

(26) a. I go to work by train
     b. John goes to work by train
     c. We go to work by train

---

[19] Harley and Ritter (2002) assume that there is no genuine first person plural, since we never speak in choruses. Wechsler (2004) extends a similar claim, together with some evidence, to second person. In Di Domenico (2004), I extended the claim to third person pronouns: 'they' does not mean 'several instances of (s)he', but rather '(s)he plus someone else'. See also Bianchi (2006b) for independent evidence setting apart pronominal and non-pronominal DPs in this respect.

d. You go to work by train
e. They go to work by train[20]

English so-called third person singular and plural pronouns seem to differ in this respect. While *they* seems to express person in that the sentence where it is the subject does not require /s/, singular third person pronouns do not, in that sentences where *he/she/it* are the subject do require /s/:

(27) He goes to work by train

So-called third person singular pronouns in English do not seem to express person also in other respects, as we shall see in a moment.

Considering the verb *be*, we can observe that *is* occurs where person does not occur:

(28) a. John *is* tall
b. She *is* tall

Let's take, with Kayne (1989), the position that *are* instantiates the 'elsewhere' form, which we now understand as the form that occurs with personal arguments.[21] Let's further assume, as in Bernstein and Tortora (2005), that possessive pronouns are personal pronouns plus a copula: here again we find the asymmetry mentioned above, with *he/it* taking the /s/ form,[22] and *they* (as *we*, *you*) taking the 'elsewhere' form:

(29) a. his
b. their
c. our
d. your

Accordingly, the paradigm of possessive constructions in English is derived: they contain either a specification of person or of [countability]:

---

20 A missing member in (26) is surely a sentence with a third person plural non-pronominal subject, such as:
(i) The kids go to school by train
We'll discuss such cases in (33) and fn. 23 below.
21 Why *I* does not take *are* remains a problem for my analysis.
22 As in Bernstein and Tortora (2005) we take possessive *her* (omophonous to the accusative form e.g. *I saw her*) to be a suppletive form.

(30) a. John's book
　　 b. my book
　　 c. your book
　　 d. his book
　　 e. their book

Let's go now to the contrast in (31) (where (31.a) corresponds to (30.c) and (31.b) to (1.g):

(31) a. your book
　　 b. That book is yours

I will assume, along the lines of Manzini and Savoia (2011) for the Romansh variety of Vella, that the predicative use of possessive pronouns requires an extra specification of denotation/placement with respect to their attributive use, and that this specification is provided by /s/, as in (31.b). This naturally extends to partitive genitives like (32.b) below, or (1.h) above, here repeated for convenience:

(32) a. your book
　　 b. a book of yours

(1.h)' A book of John's

As we said in Section 3, a determiner, at the DP level, can perform the role of denoting/placing it in non-pronominal DPs: this accounts for the incompatibility of determiners and 's in 's Genitive constructions which we have seen in (16) (here repeated for convenience as (16)':

(16)' *the John's house

In simple non- pronominal DPs denotation is expressed by a determiner or by /s/ (expressing countability): this is in turn related to the fact that 'plural' DPs in English can be bare.[23]

---

[23] They do not have to be bare, however. It seems to me, anyway, that when /s/ and a determiner co-occur, the determiner is devoid of its denotational function and expresses instead other features commonly associated to the D category, as in (i):

(i)　a.　This is not suitable for kids
　　 b.　This is not suitable for the kids

With this in mind, we can go back to /s/ at the sentence level, where either /s/ is expressed as a feature on the verb or on the subject DP:

(33) a. Dogs bark
b. The dog barks

If /s/ is one and the same morpheme, with a unique feature specification, we can account for why a double specification of /s/, as in (22), here repeated for convenience as (22)', discussed at the end of Section 3, is not grammatical:

(22)' * the kids's mother

6 Conclusions

In this work I have proposed that the various instantiations of the /s/ morpheme in English exemplified in (1) are not to be considered a case of syncretism: /s/ is one and the same morpheme (i.e. has the same featural content) in all cases. I have identified in [countability] the featural specification of /s/, following a suggestion that Rita Manzini (p.c.) made for the Latin –s ending. I have further argued that [countability] performs the same role that person /D performs: placing an argument (be it a DP or a CP) with respect to the speech event. In English, [countability] is expressed whenever person/D is not. This derives all instantiations of /s/ in (1) without further stipulations, and also accounts for the occurrence of other morphemes or of bare forms in different environments, as discussed in Section 5.

My analysis also predicts why cases like (22) and (16), problematic or unclear for other analyses (as we saw in Section 3 and Section 1 respectively) are ungrammatical. There are however some residual problems to solve.

An indefinite determiner (Q) like *a* seems sufficient to denote/place a simple DP like a definite determiner:

(34) a. A dog
b. The dog

Still, an indefinite determiner, or Q, seems compatible with /s/, as (32.b) and (1.h)' show, unlike a definite determiner, as (16) shows, in 's Genitive constructions. The incompatibility of a definite determiner with /s/ in 's Genitive constructions, furthermore, does not hold as a requirement, but just like a possibility, in simple DPs

(*The dogs*) as we noted in fn. 23 above. Perhaps a more fine-grained analysis of the Q, D, and [countability] features is needed, to solve these problems. I leave this issue to future research, and to future research I also leave a deeper concern with respect to the interesting analogies that the Latin *–s* and the English /s/ morpheme show. [24]

References

Aronoff, Mark & Nanna Fuhrhop. 2002. Restricting suffix combinations in German and English: Closing suffixes and the monosuffix constraint. *Natural Language and Linguistic Theory* 20: 451–490.
Benveniste, Émile. 1966. *Problèmes de linguistique générale*. Paris: Gallimard.
Bernstein, Judy & Christina Tortora. 2005. Two types of possessive forms in English. *Lingua* 115: 1221–1242.
Bianchi, Valentina. 2006a. On the syntax of personal arguments. *Lingua* 116: 2023–2067.
Bianchi, Valentina. 2006b. An asymmetry between personal pronouns and other DPs. *Snippets* 13: 5–6.
Borer, Hagit. 2005. *In Name Only: Structuring Sense Vol.1*. Oxford: Oxford University Press.
Brown, Roger. 1973. *A First Language: The Early Stages*. Cambridge, MA: Harvard University Press.
Chomsky, Noam. 2008. On Phases. In Robert Freidin, Carlos P. Otero & Maria Luisa Zubizarreta (eds.), *Foundational Issues in Linguistic Theory. Essays in Honor of Jean-Roger Vergnaud*, 133–166. Cambridge, MA: The MIT Press.
den Dikken, Marcel. 1998. (Anti-)agreement in DP. In Renée van Bezooijen & René Kager (eds.), *Linguistics in the Netherlands 1998*, 95–107. Amsterdam/Philadelphia: John Benjamins.
den Dikken, Marcel. 1999. On the structural representation of possession and agreement. The case of (anti-) agreement in Hungarian possessed nominal phrases. In István Kenesei (ed.), *Crossing Boundaries: Theoretic Advances in Central and Eastern European Languages*, 137–178. Amsterdam: John Benjamins.
Di Domenico, Elisa. 1994. *The Denotation Principle*. University of Geneva, Ms.
Di Domenico, Elisa. 2004. Placed, Non-Placed and Anaphorically Placed Expressions. *Italian Journal of Linguistics*, 16: 63–105.
Di Domenico, Elisa. 2013. Setting Parameters in L2A: On the English 's Morpheme. In Jennifer Cabrelli-Amaro, Tiffany Judy & Diego Pascual (eds.), *Proceedings of the 12th Generative*

---

[24] Last but not least, as an anonymous reviewer notes, it would be important to individuate the exact correlate of /s/ in terms of structural positions, at the sentence as well as at the DP level, and to explain what DPs and CPs have in common. While the latter issue is far beyond the scope of the present work, with respect to the former in Di Domenico (2004) I have proposed that a Placement P could be identified in the sentence inflectional (T/Agr-S) layer. Further work is needed to established whether a DP internal 'agreement' projection can be considered the DP internal analogue of the Placement P at the sentence level.

Approaches to Second Language Acquisition (GASLA 2013), 32–38. Somerville, MA: Cascadilla Proceedings Project.

Di Domenico, Elisa. 2015. Some Considerations on the 's Morpheme in English: Acquisition and Theory. *Quaderni di Linguistica e Studi Orientali/Working Papers in Linguistics and Oriental Studies*, 1: 105–127.

Forchheimer, Paul. 1953. *The Category of Person in Language*. Berlin: De Gruyter.

Guéron, Jaqueline & Teun Hoekstra. 1992. Chaînes temporelles et phrases réduites. In Hans G. Obenauer & Anne Zribi-Hertz (eds.), *Structures de la phrase et théorie du liage*, 69–92. Saint Denis: Presses Universitaires de Vincennes.

Harley, Heidy & Elizabeth Ritter. 2002. Hug a Tree: Deriving the Morphosyntactic Feature Hierarchy. *Language* 78:/3: 482–586.

Higginbotham, James. 1983. Logical Form, Binding and Nominals. *Linguistic Inquiry*, 14: 395–420.

Kayne, Richard. 1989 [2000]. Notes on English agreement. *Central Institute of English and Foreign Languages Bulletin* 1: 41–67. Re-appeared as Chapter 10 of Kayne, Richard, *Parameters and Universals*. New York: Oxford University Press.

Kayne, Richard. 1993. Toward a modular theory of auxiliary selection. *Studia Linguistica* 47: 3–31.

Longobardi, Giuseppe. 1994. Reference and Proper Names: A theory of N- Movement in syntax and Logical Form. *Linguistic Inquiry* 25: 609–665.

Manzini, M. Rita & Leonardo M. Savoia. 2011. (Definite) denotation and case in Romance: History and variation. In Janine Berns, Haike Jacobs & Tobias Scheer (eds.), *Romance languages and linguistic theory 2009. Selected papers from 'Going Romance' Nice 2009*, 149–165. Amsterdam: John Benjamins.

Pesetsky, David. 1985. Morphology and Logical Form. *Linguistic Inquiry* 16: 193–246.

Pesetsky, David & Esther Torrego. 2007. The syntax of Valuation and the Interpretability of Features. In Samin Karimi, Vida Samiian & Wendy K. Wilkins (eds.) *Phrasal and Clausal Architecture: Syntactic derivation and interpretation. In honor of Joseph E. Emonds*, 262–294. Amsterdam: John Benjamins.

Rizzi, Luigi. 1986. Null Objects in Italian and the Theory of *pro*. *Linguistic Inquiry*, 17: 501–556.

Rouveret, Alain .1991. Functional categories and agreement. *The Linguistic Review* 8: 353–387.

Szabolcsi, Anna. 1981. The Possessive Construction in Hungarian: A Configurational Category in a Non- Configurational Language. *Acta Linguistica Academiae Scientiarum Hungaricae* 3:261–289.

Szabolcsi, Anna. 1983. The possessor that ran away from home. *The Linguistic Review* 3: 89 –102.

Wechsler, Stephen. 2004. Number as Person. In Olivier Bonami and Patricia Cabredo Hofherr *Empirical Issues in Syntax and Semantics 5*, 255–274. http://www.cssp.cnrs.fr/eiss5

Zwicky, Arnold. 1987. Suppressing the Zs. *Journal of Linguistics* 23: 133–148.

Ludovico Franco
(Im)proper prepositions in (Old and Modern) Italian

1 Introduction

In this paper we will show that the structural (and terminological) partition operated within the set of Italian prepositions between proper/simple and improper/complex ones does not seem to presuppose an unspoiled syntactic reality. On the basis of syntactic tests and diachronic evidence, we will show that, within the subset of so called proper/simple preposition (Rizzi 1988, Salvi & Vanelli 2004, Tortora 2005, among others), two morphemes, specifically *su*, on, *tra* (*fra*), between/among, could be better characterized as Axial Parts (in the sense of Svenonius 2006; henceforth AxP), namely lexical items whose semantic function would be to identify a region (a set of points/vectors in space, cf. Zwart 1995; Kracht 2002), based on a Ground item (i.e. the complement DP of P, in a Figure/Ground configuration, Talmy 1991; 2000).[1] AxP has a somewhat mixed behaviour, sharing some properties with nouns - often AxP is homophonous with Relation Nouns (RelN) (as opposed to Sortal nouns, e.g. a child of someone *vs.* *a person of someone, cf. Jackendoff 1996, Hagege 2010: 162ff, Barker 1995, 2011), denoting body parts (Roy 2006) or other nominal items with spatial relevance.

Svenonius (2006), based on a set of diagnostics (e.g. AxPs contra homophonous RelNs commonly do not have articles, do not pluralize, do not take modifiers, can be specified by a measure phrase, etc.) argues against the idea that AxPs (items like *front, beside, behind* and so on) are nothing else but a subclass of nouns, precisely RelNs. It has been argued that AxP can be seen as an independent category, which is in between nouns and prepositions (cf. Pantcheva 2006, 2010, Fabregas 2007, Cinque 2010, Franco 2016, among many others).

---

[1] (Proto)typical AxParts refer to the front, back, top, bottom, sides, and middle of an object, though further zones projected by a pivotal Ground can be defined as well (cf. Zwart 1995, Roy 2006, Fabregas 2007, Svenonius 2008, Cinque 2010, Franco 2013, 2015, 2016 among others for ideas and taxonomies). Axial Part would be a grammatical category which identifies a specific part of the Ground (the reference landmark for a location), which in turn can be taken as a spatial axis to locate the Figure (an object whose location is at issue) (cf. Talmy 2000, Svenonius 2006).

Ludovico Franco, Università di Firenze

https://doi.org/10.1515/9781501505201-015

In Svenonius (2006), the AxP is located in a position within a functional layer which is immediately dominated by a locative preposition (Place) and is above the DP that introduces the Ground. Svenonius uses the descriptive label K(ase) to indicate the item linking the AxP to the Ground. He assumes what Borer (2005) calls 'Neo-constructivism', namely the working hypothesis that some dimensions of meaning are shaped by syntactic structure, while other dimensions come directly from the lexical content of the item introduced into the syntactic module. The AxP vs. RelN dichotomy is a case in point. An item like English *front* is ambiguos. Inserted under an N node in a syntactic derivation, front will express a noun, combining with plural morphology, determiners, etc. Inserted under an AxP node it will be possibly part of the functional skeleton of the extended projection of P (or an abstract Place N, according to Terzi 2008, Cinque 2010, cf. also Van Riemsdijk 1990). Basically, RelN and AxP enter different syntactic configurations, which following the representation given in Svenonius (2006), are illustrated in (1).

(1) (a). Axpart > *front*   (b). RelNoun > (*the*) *front*

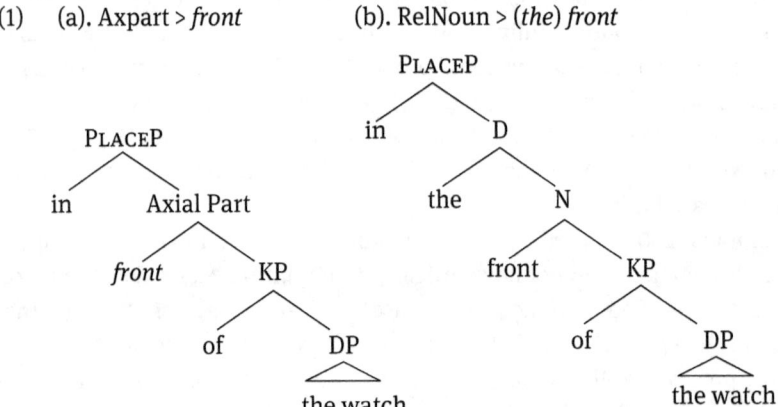

The present contribution is structured as follows. In the remaining part of this introductory paragraph, we will introduce the canonical partition operated in Italian -at the syntax-lexicon interface level- between proper and improper adpositions. In section 2, on the basis of synchronic and diachronic evidence, we will show that two members of the canonical set of proper/simple preposition might be actually 'improper' from the viewpoint of syntax, as they share the same syntactic structure/interpretive content with complex adpositions. Actually, we will see that *su* has all the morphosyntactic traits pertaining to a complex preposition while *tra/fra* shows a mixed behaviour. In section 3 we will provide a syntactic characterization of these empirical facts, based on a two-tiered syntax of adpositions (matching that of transitive VPs, in the spirit of Hale and Kayser 1993, Chomsky 1995). The conclusion follows.

Traditionally, in Italian, a partition between two distinct sets within the realm of adpositions has been operated. In fact, it is customary to distinguish between simple/proper and complex/improper prepositions (Rizzi 1988). Simple/proper adpositions include a small set of monosyllabic unstressed items ('di' *of,* 'a' *to,* 'da' *from,* 'in' *in,* 'con' *with,* 'su' *on,* 'per' *for,* 'tra/fra' *between*) that can be often 'inflected' by the determiner, which introduces a complement DP Ground (e.g. dalla spiaggia, *from.det.f beach,* sulla spiaggia, *on.det.f beach,* della spiaggia, *of.det.f beach,* etc.).

Complex adpositions in turn are at least bimorphemic, are stressed and form quite a big inventory (see Rizzi 1988, for an extensive description). They often require or optionally take a simple preposition in order to be linked to their DP complement, that is what we label here the DP Ground (see again Rizzi 1988, who precisely subdivides complex preposition into three classes, based on the obligatory, optional or impossible presence of a simple preposition, cf. Tortora 2005, Ursini 2015, Garzonio & Rossi 2016, for an interpretation of the distribution of the simple preposition in this precise configuration). Examples are 'davanti (a)', *in front of,* prima (di), *before of,* sopra (a/di), *above/on top of,* etc. Such items can be broadly classified as AxPs, as argued in Cinque (2010), specifying a relative frame of reference for the ground DP (cf. also Jackendoff 1996). In what follow, we will show that there is enough evidence to change the perspective on this dichotomy. In particular we will illustrate that the adpositions *su* and *tra/fra* in Italian, despite being monosyllabic like the other proper/simple prepositions, are actually far from being unequivocally proper/simple with respect to their syntactic behaviour.

2 Refining the partition: *su* and *tra/fra* as Axial Parts

There are many facts that show that *su* and *tra/fra* differ from the other components of the set of simple prepositions. First, they present a person split of sort, because contrary to the other members of their set allow (for some native speakers require) the presence of a (further) simple adposition (di, *of*) when introducing a pronominal DP Ground. Consider the examples provided in (2).²

(2) a. *di di noi   'of us'
    b. *a di noi   'to us'
    c. *da di noi   'from us'
    d. *in di noi   'in us'
    e. *con di noi   'with us'
    f. su di noi   'on/above us'
    g. *per di noi   'for us'
    h. tra/fra di noi 'between us'

From this viewpoint *su* and *tra/fra* pattern with complex adpositions, which allow/require the presence of a functional item sandwiched between them and the DP Ground (here a pronoun) they introduce, as illustrated in (3).

(3) a. sopra (di) noi   'above us'
    b. dentro ?(di) noi   'inside us'
    c. sotto ??(di) noi   'below us'

Personal pronouns are not the only items that are selected by a simple preposition following *su* and *tra/fra*. In some stages/registers of Italian also demonstratives (either pronouns or adjectives) are/have been introduced by means of this functional layered skeleton (4). In Contemporary Italian, according to our judgements, the use of *tra* in such context is quite marked, despite still attested, as shown in (4b).

(4) a. lo   spazio voto che tra   di quelle   rimarrebbe [...]
       the   space empty that between of that.f.pl remain.prs.cond.3sg
       'the empty space that between them would remain...'
                                              (Galileo Galilei, 1638)

---

2 Note that the same behaviour is attested for those complex adpositions which, according to Rizzi (1988), do not take simple preposition when introducing a Ground complement. Consider the examples in (i):

(i) a. dopo di me   vs. dopo *della/*alla/la partita
       'after me'   'after the macht'
    b. senza di te   vs. senza *della/*alla/la cucina
       'without you'   'without the kitchen'

b. Kurosawa è tra   di quei   pochi registi
    K.   is between of that.m.pl few.pl filmmakers
    che hanno   tentato [...]
    that have.prs.3pl tried
    'Kurosawa is one of the few filmmakers that have tried...'
    (retrieved from Google)
c. perché su di   quelle   l'   azione   del
    because on of   those.f.pl the action of.the
    Governo   si   può   esercitare...
    Government cl.refl can   practiced
    'because the action of the government can be practiced on those (things)...' (Giovanni Giolitti, 1901)
d. vorremmo   che si   esprimessero   su di quei
    want.prs.cond.1pl that cl.refl express.sbjv.3pl on of those.m.pl
    punti.
    points.m
    points.m 'we wish that they would take their stance on those points'
    (Matteo Renzi, 2014)

Note that in various stages of Italian the presence of *di* after *tra* (*fra*) and *su* was not restricted to personal pronouns and demonstratives, involving also bare DPs, as illustrated in (5a) with an Old Florentine example and in (5b) with an example dated back to the first half of the 19th century.

(5) a. Tra   di danari   e   di promesse di mercatanti
        between of money.pl and of promises of merchants
        'between the money and promises of merchants'
        (Giovanni Villani, *Cronica* 1348, L. 9, cap. 306)
    b. sostanze   sperimentate su di uomini sani
        substances   tested   on of men   healthy
        'substances tested on healthy men' (*Effemeridi di Medicina Omiopatica*, 1829)

A second test that provide us with some further evidence that the same syntax is involved when considering at least *su* and improper prepositions in Italian is that *su contra* other simple prepositions can be used intransitively, without the presence of an overt DP complement, as illustrated in (6).

(6) a. Vieni dietro, davanti, sopra
   'come behind/in front of/over'
   b. Vieni su/*per/* di/*in/*con/*da/* tra(*fra)/*a
   'come on/*for/*of/*in/*with/*from/*between/*to(at)'

Nevertheless, the fact that *tra/fra* does not allow an intransitive reading in Italian is not sufficient to set it apart from complex adpositions. Indeed, there are some complex items, which do not display a 'stand-alone' behaviour, as illustrated in (7).

(7) Vieni *presso/* durante/*verso
   'come near, during, toward'

More straightforward evidence comes from diachronic facts. In Old Italian (Old Florentine/Old Tuscan, cf. Salvi and Renzi 2010) complex prepositions were commonly sandwiched in a layered sequence, comprising a functional/simple preposition above and one below them (cf. also Delfitto and Paradisi 2009). Such constructions are still widely attested for some items of Contemporary Italian, e.g. 'in mezzo a', *in the middle of,* and they are widespread in dialectal varieties (e.g. Modena, M. Rita Manzini, p.c., *de dre a la ca*, 'behind the house'). Consider the Old Italian examples in (8) taken from the OVI (*Opera del Vocabolario Italiano*) database.

(8) a. **di** dietro **al** cavaliere (Tristano Ricc. XIII ex. Fior cap.44)
   of behind at.det.m. knight
   "behind the knight"
   b. **di** sotto **alla** tavola (Milione, tosc. XIV, cap. 80)
   of under at.det.f table
   "under the table"
   c. **in** sommo **de** la bocca (Dante, Commedia, Purgatorio. 6)
   in top of the mouth
   "on top of the mouth"
   d. **in** sovra **a** ciò (Alberto della Piagentina, 1322/32 fior. L. 1 Cap. 4)
   in above at this
   "on top of this"
   e. siede Rachel **di** sotto **da** costei (Dante, Commedia, Paradiso XXXII:8)
   sits Rachel of under from her
   "Rachel sits under her"

Crucially, the same behaviour is attested with *tra*, *fra*, and *su*, as reported in (9), but does not uphold for the other simple/proper prepositions.[3]

(9) a. **in** tra **di** sè medesimo
   in between of himself
   "to himself" Alberto della Piagentina, 1322/32 L. 5, cap. 6 (fior.)
   b. l' acqua **in** su **d'** ogni riviera
   the water in on of every coast
   "the water on every coast" Guinizzelli, Tosc. a. 13. V.4 1276

Comparing (8) and (9), it is quite clear that historical/variational evidence point to a similar syntactic status of complex preposition and the monosyllabic morphemes *tra/fra* and *su*. They can both enter a layered adpositional structure, in which they are sandwiched between two simple adpositions.

Also, consider that in Old Italian practically all simple/proper prepositions can be employed in the configuration sketched above, namely a simpleP-AxP-simpleP-Ground configuration, with the notable exception of *su* and *tra/fra*. Consider at this regard, the examples provided in (10) which show that an item like *in* (hence, not only *di*, *a*, *da*, cf. examples in (8)) can link a complex preposition to a Ground DP), and compare them with the ones in (11) and (12), for *tra/fra* and *su*, respectively. *Tra/fra* and *su* are never attested, according to the data we have collected from OVI, Opera del Vocabolario Italiano On-line (cf. gattoweb.ovi.cnr.it/), as simple Ps in a layered simpleP-AxP-simpleP-Ground configuration.

(10) a. arse dal Ponte vecchio **in** fine **in** Mercato vecchio.
   burn.pst.3sg from.the Ponte vecchio in until in Mercato vecchio
   "It burned from Ponte Vecchio to Mercato Vecchio" Gesta Florentin. (ed. Hartwig), XIV pm. (fior.)
   b. lo contado **in** fine **alle** mura
   the peasantry in until to.the walls
   "the peasantly up to the walls" Gesta Florentin. (ed. Hartwig), XIV pm. (fior.)

---

3 Note that tra/fra morphemes have been topped of by a simple preposition (most often the stative morpheme in, *in/at*) in various stages/registers of Italian, just consider the example in (i). Note also that often *intra/infra* are spelled out as a single word:

(i) Egli alto ride al vomero che splende in tra le brune zolle (Giosué Carducci, *Rime nuove*).
   "He smiles upon the plough-share, damp with dew, among brown earthern clods"
   English translation by Laura Fullerton Gilbert (1916).

c. assai **di** sotto **dal** Caucaso
    much of under from.the Caucasus
    "Much under the Caucasus" Bono Giamboni, Orosio, a. 1292 (fior.)
d. uno ramo di fuoco l' entrava **di** sotto **nel**
    a branch of fire cl.dat.3g.f enter.ipfv.3sg of under in.the
    corpo e rescivale per la bocca
    body and re-exit.ipfv.3sg.cl.dat.3g.f for the mouth
    "a tongue of fire entered in her body and went out again from her mouth" Conti morali (ed. Segre), XIII ex. (sen.)

(11) a. questa terra gli debbo rendere **in** fra **in**
     this.f land cl.dat.3sg must.prs.1sg give.back.inf in among in
     due years
     two anni
     "I must give back this land to him by two years" Cavalcanti 1315 (fior.)
  b. crede sia gioia stata **infra** **di** noi l'
     believe.prs.3sg be.subj.3sg joy been.f in.among of us the
     omo che vi savete
     man that you.pl know.prs.2pl
     "the man that you know believes that there has been joy between us" Neri de' Visdomini (ed. Panvini), XIII sm. (fior.)
  c. et queste cose farò **in fra** a uno mese
     and these things do.fut.1sg in between to a month
     "And I will do these things in a month" Stat. sen., 1309–10 (Gangalandi)

(12) a. li due re si pigliano per mano et
     the.pl two kings cl.refl take.prs.3pl for hand and
     assettansi **in** su 'n due ricche sedie d' avorio
     sit.prs.3pl.cl.refl in on in two rich.pl chair.pl of ivory
     "the two kings join their hands and sit on two rich ivory chairs" Tavola Ritonda (XIV sec., first half, Fior.)
  b. non puote trapassare e andare **in su** a la
     not can.prs.3sg trespass.inf and go.inf in on a the
     regione calda del fuoco
     region hot of fire
     "It cannot trespass and go into the hot region of the fire" Metaura volg., XIV s.-t.d. (fior.)

Furthermore, coming back to the synchronic evidence, at least the preposition *su* patterns with complex adpositions, when it follows the simple preposition *con*, as shown in (13). Here *tra* as shown in (13d) patterns with simple prepositions.[4]

(13) a. il   comodino   con su la   mensola
        the night.table with on the.f.sg shelf
        "the night table with the shelf on it"
    b. il   comodino   con sopra/davanti/dietro...   la mensola
        the night.table with above/in front of/behind... the shelf
        "the night table with the shelf above in front of/ behind it"
    c. il   comodino   con **in/*di/*per** la   mensola
        the night.table with *in/*of/*for   the shelf
        " the night table with the shelf in/of/for it"
    d. il   comodino   con *tra   la mensola
        the night.table with *between the shelf
        "the night table with the shelf between it"

Also, in Italian *su* may easily stand as a head noun as in the example in (14).

(14) il su del vestito
    'the upper-part of the dress'

Even if it is somewhat more marked, it not uncommon to find also *tra* as an head-noun, as in the example in (15).

(15) il tra dell'incontro
    (lit.) 'the between/among of the meeting'
    (Primavera Fisogno, *Incontro al dialogo*, Franco Angeli, Milano, 2012)

---

4 Con (with) may be seen as expressing a relation parallel to that of the verb have (cf. Harley 1995, Levinson 2011). Franco and Manzini (2017) have recently assumed that with-like items express, cross-linguistically, a relation which is the mirror image to that of genitives/datives. This behaviour seems to be maintained in the spatial domain. Consider the symmetrical sentences in (i), where the preposition *con* (ia) alternates with the dative *a* in (ib):

(i) a. il comodino **con** sopra la mensola
        'the night table with the shelf on it'
    b. la mensola sopra **al** comodino
        'the shelf above (to) the night.table'

This behaviour is very common for improper prepositions (cf. *il sopra del vestito*, the upper-part of the dress matching example (14)), as predicted for items functioning as AxPart (cf. the discussion in section 1 on the similarities between RelNs-AxPs), while it is impossible for simple preposition. Consider (16) below:

(16) i pro e i contro della riforma /* i per e i contro della riforma
    'the ups and down of the reform' (literally 'the for and against of the reform')

Normally *per* and *contro* stand as opposites in Italian, as in the pair in (17):

(17) a. ho votato per lui
        'I voted for him'
    b. ho votato contro di lui
        'I voted against him'

Nevertheless, *contro*, being a complex preposition, can be easily turned into a nominal item, while the simple preposition *per* cannot be employed as a nominal element. This is the reason that we find the item *pro*, which is never used as a preposition in Italian, and not *per* in the example in (16).

Moreover, *su* patterns with complex prepositions in allowing terms of DP complement cliticization, as illustrated in (18)-(19):

(18) a. è   seduto su di lui/lei/un sasso
        be.prs.3sg seated on of him/her/a stone
        "He is seated on him/her/a stone"
    b. gli/le/ci   è   seduto su
        cl.dat.m/cl.dat.f/cl.dat.n be.prs.3sg seated on
        "He is seated on him/her/it"

(18') anima vene   in corpo come taula lavata, che nulla cosa
      soul come.prs.3sg   in body like table cleaned that no   thing
      elli   su
      is.cl.dat.3sg on
      "the soul comes into the body like a cleaned table, on which there's nothing" Old Florentine (Ar. Orl. 13, 42, 1308)

(19) a. è seduto sopra   di lui/lei/un sasso
        is seated on/over of him/her/a stone
        "He is seated on/over him/her/a stone"

b. gli/le/ci   è   seduto sopra
   cl.dat.m/cl.dat.f/cl.dat.n be.prs.3sg seated on/over
   "He is seated on/over him/her/it"

Concerning this diagnostics, *tra* behaves again like simple Ps and disallow extraction, as shown in (20) and (21).

(20) a. ho   una casa   tra   gli ulivi
        have.prs.1sg a   house   among the olive trees
        "I have a house among the olive trees"
     b. *ci/*gli   ho   una casa   tra
        cl.dat.m/cl.dat.f/cl.dat.n have.prs.1sg a   house   between

(21) a. ho votato per lui
        "I have vote for him"
     b. ho votato contro di lui
        "I have voted against him"
     c. *gli ho votato per
        cl.dat.m have.prs.1sg voted for
     d. gli   ho   votato contro
        cl.dat.m have.prs.1sg voted   against
        "I have voted against him"

Finally *tra/fra* and *su* have a quite fixed semantic range when compared with the other simple preposition in Italian.[5] Just to give an example, consider for instance a rough sketch (cf. Franco & Manzini 2017) of the range of fundamental meanings associated with Italian *con* 'with'. These include possession in (22a), the comitative in (22b), ambiguous in that *Maria* can be with the speaker or *Maria* can be with *Gianni*; the same is true in (instrumental/possession) sentences of the type *The boy saw the girl with the binoculars*, as is well known in psycholinguistics (Frazier and Fodor 1978, and subsequent literature). The example in (22c) illustrates the instrumental meaning of *con*, (22d) illustrates the cause meaning. In (22e) *con* introduces a manner adverbial and can be effectively paraphrased by a sentence including the manner adverb *efficacemente* 'efficaciously'.

---

[5] Note that Andreose (2009) argues that in Old Italian (up to Dante's Commedia) the semantic values expressed by *tra* and *fra* do not overlap, namely *tra* expressed only a sub-set of the values of *fra*, who was e.g. the only lexical item capable to convey the temporal meanings 'within', 'by'. Such distinction is now completely lost.

(22) a. Ho incontrato un ragazzo **con** gli occhiali
"I have met a boy with the eye-glasses"
b. Ho incontrato Gianni **con** Maria
"I have met Gianni with Maria"
c. Mangio la pizza **con** le posate
"I eat the pizza with the cutlery "
d. Gianni ha perso il lavoro **con** la crisi
"Gianni has lost his job with the crisis"
e. Gli antibiotici agiscono **con** efficacia
"Antibiotics act with efficacy"

Conversely, *su* and *tra/fra* have a more fixed meaning, being roughly interpreted as 'above'/'over/on' and 'between/among' respectively, despite non-literal uses are widely attested (as is the case also of complex prepositions).[6] Consider some examples of *tra* in (23):

(23) a. abito   in una casa   *tra*   gli   ulivi
     live.prs.1sg in a   house between the   olive.trees
     "I live in a house surrounded by olive trees"
b. gli   studenti   torneranno   presto *tra*   (di) noi
   the.pl students come.back.fut.3pl soon   among   of   us
   'the students will soon come back among us'
c. il   pranzo   sarà   pronto   *tra* dieci   minuti.
   the   lunch   be.fut.3sg. ready   in   ten   minutes
   "the lunch will be ready in ten minutes"
d. è   il   più   bravo   *tra*   (di)   noi
   be.3sg the   most good   among   of   us
   "He is the best among us"

Despite it could be possible to propose a functionalist taxonomy for the examples in (23), *tra* seems to have a basic 'medial' value, as in (23a,b), where the state *vs.* motion axis is determined by the verbal predicate (see section 3 below, cf. Wood 2015). Note that meaning shifts from space to time, as illustrated in (23c), are common in the realm of temporal complex prepositions, as illustrated in Haspelmath (1997), Roy and Svenonius (2009), Franco (2013, 2015).

---

6 In Italian for instance, "essere/stare *vicino* a qualcuno" "to be near/close to someone" can either have a literal meaning, which indicates that the Figure DP is located in the proximity of the Ground DP (qualcuno "someone") or it can have a figurative meaning having to do with "emotional closeness" between people.

Furthermore the partitive value that can be ascribed to (23d) might be easily expressed by means of 'medial' axial parts (e.g. *'è il più bravo in mezzo a noi'* "he is the best among (all) of us", (cf. Roy 2006, Dekany 2012). [7]

Another piece of evidence in support of our claim that (at least) *su* is best analysed in terms of Axial Parts comes from Italian dialects. In particular, in contemporary Sicilian *su* is not lexicalized. What we find instead is the corresponding prototypical Axial Part/complex preposition *supra* 'on/above' in all the relevant contexts where Standard Italian resorts to *su*.[8]

To sum up, we have tried to show that *su* and *tra (fra)* have the morpholexical/syntactic status of complex prepositions (Axial Parts). As for the mixed behaviour of *tra* 'between' we can only speculate that *tra* has undergone a process of grammaticalization (cf. e.g. Svenonius 2006 on Finnish adpositions) and this is the reason why it behaves in various contexts as a simple P in contemporary Italian.[9] In any event, the evidence we have examined seems to suggest that in synchrony both *su* (quite safely) and *tra* (more residually) retain their original (spatial) meaning. In this respect, they pattern with complex prepositions/Axial Parts.

---

7 A clear example of a morphologically transparent medial Axial Part conveying a partitive meaning is the English preposition *amid(st)*.

8 As pointed out by Giulia Bellucci (p.c.), in the Sicilian-Italian dictionary edited by Traina (1868) the equivalent *su* is attested; we find the basic forms form *susu* (matching old Italian item *suso*, that altenated with *su* in adverbial/intransitive contexts). *Nsusu* is also attested meaning 'upwards'. Nevertheless, the aforementioned lexical items are not present in the *Vocabolario Siciliano* edited by Piccitto (1977), only *supra* is attested in the relevant contexts. It is worth mentioning that our analysis of *su* in Italian as an Axial Part actually predicts the existence of a language like Sicilian. The fact that present-day Sicilian only resorts to the lexical item *supra* to express the same range of spatial meanings is not surprising if we assume that *su* 'up/on' on the one hand and *sopra* 'on/above' on the other hand are formally identical, namely they are both Axial Parts.

9 As suggested by an anonymous reviewer, some peculiarities of tra/fra can be a consequence of the fact that it defines a spatial relation with potentially more than one Ground: when there are two explicit Ground elements they are expressed by a coordination of DPs (and not PPs), as in (i):

(i) a. Tra noi e loro
    b. Tra (??di) noi e (*di) loro
    'between us and them'

This suggests that the lower part of the functional structure with tra/fra can be more complex. In English, for instance, the difference between a simple and a complex Ground corresponds to a different lexicalization of the AxPart item (*between* vs. *among*).

3 A Figure-Ground syntax and the position of *su* and *tra*: Axial parts and whole

In this paragraph we will introduce the syntactic configuration in which we assume that *su* and *tra*, given the evidence provided in the previous section, are couched. Before doing that we need to provide some background on the spatial concepts of Figure & Ground and the way they have been applied to syntactic investigation. The terms 'figure' and 'ground' have been introduced by Leon Talmy (1985, 1991) and were adopted following insight from Gestalt psychology (cf. Svenonius 2003: 433). Talmy (1985: 61) defines Figure & Ground as follows:

i). *The Figure is a moving or conceptually movable object whose path or site is at issue.*
ii). *The Ground is a reference-frame, or a reference-point stationary within a reference-frame, with respect to which the Figure's path or site is characterized.*

The concepts of Figure and Ground are relational, as originally assumed in Svenonius (2003, 2006, 2007). Indeed, Figure and Grounds are positioned with respect to each other and it is very likely to assume that the adpositions that connect them are sort of relators/predicates. For example, in the expression *the keys on the table*, *the keys* is the figure, and it is positioned with respect to the ground, *the table*, by the predication denoted by the adposition *on* (cf. Wood 2015: 173, from which the examples in (24) are taken). The figure can be in motion, as in (24a), or at rest, as in (24b).

(24) a. John threw the keys on the table.
    b. John saw the keys on the table.

In (24a), the keys, acting as the Figure, are understood to traverse a path, the endpoint of which is on the table, which acts as the Ground. In (24b), the keys are at rest in a position on the table. Still, their relational content is expressed by means of the adposition *on*.

Svenonius (2003, 2008, cf. also Levinson 2011, Wood 2015, among others) assumes that the Figure has properties reminiscent of external arguments, while the ground has properties reminiscent of internal arguments.[10] Svenonius (2003,

---

10 Many of these properties are comparable to the asymmetries tearing apart subjects and objects observed in the generative literature (at least from Marantz 1984). For instance, adpositions exhibit c-selectional restrictions on the ground and determine its case in a way that they do not with the figure (see also Svenonius 2002 on inherent case assignment to internal

2007) assume that figures are introduced by a functional head *p* in a way that is analogous to the introduction of external arguments by v, along the lines of Hale and Keyser 1993, Chomsky 1995 (or maybe Voice, according to Kratzer 1996).[11]

We propose here a simple refinement of this basic model, assuming that what are traditionally labelled as complex prepositions are best characterized as Axial-Parts, in the sense of Svenonius (2006, cf. Cinque 2010). We assume that the projection of such elements is the 'external argument' of the lower P projection responsible of introducing a Ground complement (in Italian normally, the genitive *di* or the dative *a*, in English commonly the genitive *of*, etc.). The relation between AxPart and the complement of the genitive predicate is a kind of 'part-whole' relationship (cf. Fabregas 2007), notated here as ($\subseteq$), following Manzini and Franco (2016), Franco et al. (2016), among others. This is precisely the same relation Manzini and Franco (2016) assume is entertained by the two internal arguments of a ditransitive structure, which can be conceived to be a possessum (Theme) – possessor (Goal) relation.

In a Figure/Ground configuration à la Talmy the Ground-complement of ($\subseteq$) is the possessor of the axis (axial Part P) taken to evaluate the location of the Figure, standardly introduced by means of the pP node. A rough sketch of the model we propose is represented in (25b) for example (25a).

---

arguments, cf. Manzini and Franco 2016, Garzonio & Rossi 2013, 2016). Furthermore the interpretation of the ground is much more dependent on the adposition than the figure is. For instance, *on* specifies that its ground be interpreted as a surface-ground, whereas *in* specifies a container-ground. Nevertheless, alternating between *on/in* has no interpretive effect at all on the figure (Wood 2015).

[11] The idea of a layered p-P structure matches the quite standard assumption that the PP domain is quite rich and articulated (cf. e.g. Koopman 2000, den Dikken 2010 on Dutch, Holmberg 2002 on Zina Kotoko, Svenonius 2004, 2007, 2010, crosslinguistically) comprising at least what can be labelled Place (associated with stative locational meanings) and what is commonly called Path (associated with directed motion) (cf. also Pantcheva 2011, Romeu 2013 for more layered ideas). Place elements would give information on the physical configuration of the relation between the Figure and the Ground (the reference landmark for the location of the Figure). This is illustrated in (2a), where the elephants are the Figure and the boat is the Ground. On the contrary, Paths would provide information about a trajectory; Path elements may specify whether a Place is a Goal (2b) or a Source (2c), and may also give information on the orientation of a trajectory (2d) (Pantcheva 2011). (Examples from Svenonius 2010).

(2) a. The elephants remained in the boat.
 b. They cast a wistful glance to the shore.
 c. The boat drifted further from the beach.
 d. Their ears sank down several notches.

(25)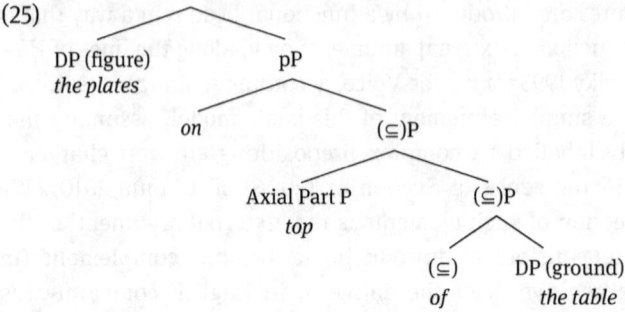

Note that Axial Part has been taken to be a semi-lexical or properly functional category (cf. Svenonius 2006, Franco 2015), but in many languages they retain full nominal properties (cf. John and Thurgood 2011 for Inuktitut and Uzbeki, Franco et al. 2016, for Uralic languages, Ursini and Long 2018 on Chinese). Hence it is quite reasonable that Axial Parts and Grounds may stand in a possessum-possessor configuration (see also the data in section 2 pointing to the possibility of employing the items under scrutiny as relational nouns, cf. (14)-(15)).[12]

Hence, our proposal here is that *tra/fra* and *su*, whose behaviour and syntactic configuration parallel those of complex/improper preposition in Italian, may be characterized as Axial Parts, potentially entering a relation with the Ground by means of a genitive/dative (⊆) device acting as a relator/elementary predicate. According to Manzini and Savoia (2011), which we follow here, the languages where dative is lexically different from genitive (including English *of* and *to*, Italian *di* 'of' and *a* 'to', etc.) display contextual sensitivity in the realization of the (⊆) category, which is externalized as dative 'to' when attached to sentential projections, while it is externalized as genitive 'of' when it is attached to nominal categories. Very interestingly the relation between AxPs and Grounds is instantiated in Italian by both *a* (e.g. sotto al fiume, 'below to-the river') and *di* (sotto di te, 'below of you'). This may be related to a sensitivity to the animacy hierarchy (i.e. *di* is the obligatory choice with pronouns) (cf. Fábregas 2015 a,b). When the relator is not spelled out (e.g. sotto il fiume, below the river) we simply assume here that we are dealing with a silent category, following Kayne (2004a,b, 2007 and subsequent works) (but see Tortora 2005, Garzonio and Rossi 2013, 2016 for principled explanations). The relevant

---

[12] Franco et al. (2016) have shown that in the Uralic family the device employed to link Axial Parts and grounds, and Part-whole/inalienable possession proper is consistently the same and may involve oblique case morphemes, juxtaposition, possessive inflections.

structure for *su* is illustrated in (26) for (9b). The same structure may be conceived for the complex adpositions of (Old and Modern) Italian.

(26)
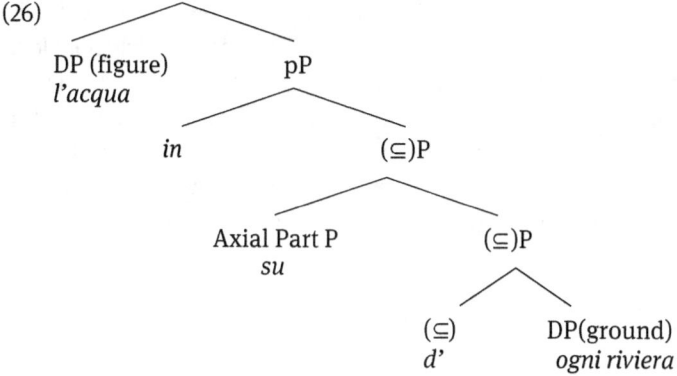

In short, we impute an interpretive content to the item which links Axial Parts and Grounds, which Svenonius (2006) descriptively characterizes as K (case). This content is predicative, and it can be realized by prepositions (Italian, English), or by nominal inflections (Uralic, Indo-Aryan, cf. Franco et al. 2016). The (⊆) content is primitive but it is not a case; it is an elementary predicate. The inflectional realization of the (⊆) predicate is conventionally called a case. But in present terms, case is definable at most as the crossing of the more elementary notions of atomic predicate and inflectional realization. As originally argued in Fillmore (1968), we see no differences between (oblique) case and adpositions.[13]

---

13 Actually oblique cases can be in principle reduced to Chomsky's (2001) agreement model of case, if we assume that there are abstract heads, such as Appl heads (Pylkkänen 2008), endowed with uninterpretable features and that oblique cases are a byproduct of Agree with these heads. However the morphosyntactic reality is that cases are uniquely represented in the morphology of nouns (and nominal constituents) and not on the verb or verbal constituents. Therefore, inspired by Manzini and Savoia (2011), Manzini and Franco (2016), we follow a different tradition of studies, represented in formal approaches originally by Fillmore (1968), in which oblique cases are inflectional counterparts of Ps, i.e. elementary predicates. Specifically, we take the basic oblique case of natural languages to correspond to the part-whole elementary predicate, notated (⊆); so a 'possessor' (genitive, dative) is essentially a 'whole' including a 'part' (the possessee). Following Belvin and den Dikken (1997), we assume possessors as 'zonally including' the possessee. The part-whole or zonal inclusion relation is wide-ranging, encompassing at least partitives, inalienable and alienable possession. We may construe locatives as a specialization of the part-whole relation, roughly 'x included by y, y a location', where different locatives introduce different restrictions on inclusion (cf. Franco et al. 2016). This could be the characterization of the Italian preposition *in*. Furthermore, this is compatible with the expression of (certain

For what concerns the syntactic layer above the Axial Part, we have maintained the descriptive characterization *p*, in a way that is analogous to the introduction of external arguments by *v*. We leave a more detailed characterization of the p layer for future research. Nevertheless, taking in consideration, for instance, the shape of the examples in (8)-(11) for Old Italian[14] the 'inclusion' layer appears to be 'reduplicated',[15] pointing to the idea that the node above the AxP may have the same morpho-lexical status of the lower P/K, namely that of an elementary predicate (⊆) (by which arguably the Figure is 'included' in the AxP-Ground predication by the means of this upper (⊆) elementary predicate), leading to a revised structure as in (27) for the representation provided in (26).

---

types of) possession as locations, for instance alienable possession in Palestinian Arabic according to Boneh and Sichel (2010).

14 Actually, this pattern, namely an AxP sandwiched between two (identical) (⊆)-like predicates is cross-linguistically widespread. Just consider the examples from Catalan (i) (Romance), Pashto (Iranian) (ii), Wandala (iii) (Chadic, Afro-Asiatic), Mongsen Ao (Sino-Tibetan) (iv).

(i) La rata va sortir **de** sota **de** la taula
 'the rat came out from under the table' *Catalan*, (Hualde 1992)

(ii) **də** mez-Ø **də** pās-a kitāb-una zmā
 of table-M.OBL of top-M.ABL book-PL.M.DIR 1SG.STR.POSS
 ná day
 NEG be.CONT.PRS.3SG.M 'The books on top of the table are not mine' *Pashto*, David (2014)

(iii) ká kàt **á-fk-á** ordinater
 2.SG be PRED-face-GEN computer
 'you are in front of computer' *Wandala* (Frajzyngier 2012)

(iv) nuksənsaŋ-pà? **nə** taŋ **nə** wa-lıkà?
 PN-M ALL side ALL go-CONTEMP
 'When [the son-in-law] had gone to Noksensangba?' Mongsen Ao (Coupe 2008)

15 As suggested by the preceding considerations (cf. fn. 10), we roughly assume that in natural languages, a locative may be construed as a specialization of the part-whole relation, roughly 'x included by y, y location'. We assume that the layer above the the AxP may be precisely a (locative specialization of) the elementary relator (⊆).Consider the trivial pair in (i).

(i) a. Sono *al* mare
 'I'm at the sea'
 b. Sono *in* mare
 'I'm in the sea'

We may dub in as proper inclusion (containment) and *a* as contact/vicinity-inclusion. But in any event both morphemes compete for the lexicalization of an inclusion relator (⊆) node.

Specifically, in the pair above, (ia) means that I'm zonally included by the sea, but not necessary contained by the sea; on the contrary, (ib) says that I'm zonally included by the sea, properly contained by it. Hence, we assume that Italian *a/di* and *in* express different flavours of the very same (⊆) relation.

Alternatively one may say that locative nouns-AxPs project, and a new inclusion relation is directly established between it (as a spatial *part* of the Ground) and the Figure.

(27)
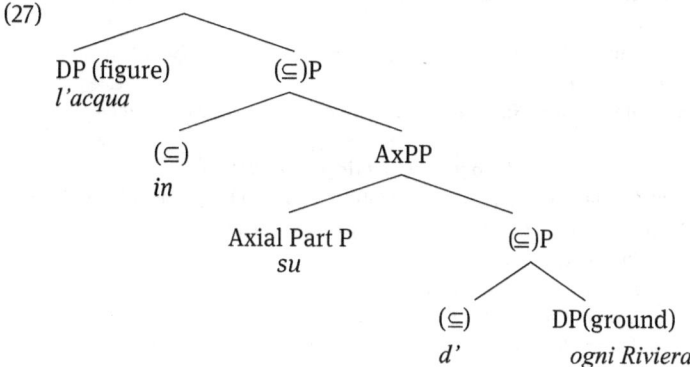

4 Conclusion

In this paper we have shown that the structural (and terminological) partition between proper/simple and improper/complex adpositions operated for Italian does not presuppose an unspoiled syntactic reality. Indeed, on the basis of syntactic tests and diachronic evidence, we have shown that – within the subset of so called proper/simple preposition (Rizzi 1988, Salvi & Vanelli 2004, Tortora 2005, among others) – two morphemes, specifically su, *on* and tra (fra), *between*, might be better characterized as Axial Parts (following Svenonius 2006 and subsequent literature), namely lexical items whose semantic function would be to identify a region (a set of points/vectors in space, cf. Zwart 1995; Kracht 2002) based on a Ground item (i.e. the complement DP of P, in a Figure/Ground configuration, cf. Talmy 1991; 2000), which is optionally introduced in Italian by means of a genitive/dative (i.e. oblique) relator/elementary predicate (Manzini & Savoia 2011, Manzini & Franco 2016).

References

Andreose, Alvise. 2009. It.A. Infra/ Intra,In Fra/In Tra: Preposizioni Polisillabiche o Preposizioni Doppie? *Laboratorio sulle Varietà Romanze Antiche* 3: 39–72.

Barker, Chris. 2011. 'Possessives and relational nouns', in Claudia Maienborn, Klaus von Heusinger, & Paul Portner (eds.), *Semantics: An international handbook of natural language meaning*, vol. 2, Berlin: Walter de Gruyter, 1109–1130.

Barker, Chris. 1995. *Possessive Descriptions*. Stanford: CSLI Publications.

Belvin, Robert, and Marcel Den Dikken. 1997. "'*There*, happens, *to, be, have*'" *Lingua* 101: 151–183.

Boneh, Nora, and Ivy Sichel. 2010. "Deconstructing possession." *Natural Language and Linguistic Theory* 28: 1–40.

Borer, Hagit, 2005. *In name only, Structuring sense, vol I*. Oxford: Oxford University Press.

Chomsky, Noam. 1995. *The minimalist program*. Cambridge, MA: MIT Press.

Cinque, Guglielmo, 2010. 'Mapping Spatial PPs: an Introduction', in Guglielmo Cinque & Luigi Rizzi (eds.), *Mapping Spatial PPs, The Cartography of Syntactic Structures*, Vol. 6, New York: Oxford University Press, 3–25.

Coupe, Alexander. 2008. *A Grammar of Mongsen Ao*. Berlin: Mouton De Gruyter:.

David, Anne. 2014. *Descriptive Grammar of Pashto and its Dialects*. Berlin: Mouton De Gruyter.

Delfitto, Denis, and Paola Paradisi. 2009. For a diachronic theory of genitive assignment in Romance. In Paola Crisma and Giuseppe Longobardi (eds.), *Historical syntax and linguistic theory*. Oxford, Oxford University Press, 292–310.

Den Dikken, Marcel, 2010. 'On the functional structure of locative and directional PPs', in Guglielmo Cinque & Luigi Rizzi (eds.), *Mapping Spatial PPs, The Cartography of Syntactic Structures*, Vol. 6, New York: Oxford University Press, 74–126.

Fábregas, Antonio. 2007. "(Axial) parts and wholes." *Nordlyd* 34: 1–32.

Fábregas, Antonio. 2015a. "Una nota sobre locativos y acusativos." *Archivum* LXV: 57–74.

Fábregas, Antonio. 2015b. "Direccionales con *con* y Marcado Diferencial de Objeto." *Revue Romane* 50: 163–190.

Fillmore, Charles J. 1968. "The case for case." In *Universals in linguistic theory*, edited by Emmon Bach and Robert T. Harms, 1–88. New York: Holt, Rinehart, and Winston.

Frajzyngier, Zygmunt. 2012. *A Grammar of Wandala*. Berlin: De Gruyter.

Franco, Ludovico, 2013. '*Before* strikes *Back* - an *ABA constraint on temporal expressions', *Acta Linguistica Hungarica* 60. 265–302.

Franco, Ludovico, 2015. "The case of (per) addietro in Old Florentine. When before was (apparently) based on back", *Onomázein* 31. 282–301.

Franco, Ludovico, and M. Rita Manzini. 2017. "Instrumental prepositions and case: context of occurrence and alternation with datives." *Glossa* 2(8): 1–37.

Franco, Ludovico. 2016. "Axial Parts, phi-features and degrammaticalization." *Transactions of the Philological Society* 114: 149–170.

Franco, Ludovico, Bellucci, Giulia, Dal Pozzo, Lena, and M. Rita Manzini. 2016. Locatives, Part and Whole in Uralic. *Olinco2016*, Olomouc, Czech Republic, 9-11/6/2016.

Frazier, Lyn, and Janet Dean Fodor. 1978. The Sausage Machine: A New Two-stage Parsing Model. *Cognition* 6. 291–325.

Freeze, Ray. 1992. "Existentials and other locatives." *Language* 68: 553–595.

Garzonio, Jacopo, and Silvia Rossi. 2013. The a/di/Ø alternation in Italian complex Ps: P selection or C selection? *43rd Linguistic Symposium on Romance Languages*, New York, 17-19.04.2013.

Garzonio, Jacopo, and Silvia Rossi. 2016. Case in Italian Complex PPs. In *Romance Languages and Linguistic Theory 10: Selected papers from 'Going Romance' 28, Lisbon*, ed. by

Ernestina Carrilho, Alexandra Fiéis, Maria Lobo and Sandra Pereira, 121–138. Amsterdam: John Benjamins.

Hagège, Claude. 2010. *Adpositions*. Oxford: Oxford University Press.

Hale, Kenneth, and S. Jay Keyser. 1993. "On Argument Structure And The Lexical Expression Of Grammatical Relations." In *The View From Building* 20, edited by Kenneth Hale and S. Jay Keyser, 53–109. Cambridge, MA: MIT Press.

Harley, Heidi. 1995. Subjects, Events and Licensing. PhD. Dissertation, Massachusetts Institute of Technology.

Haspelmath, Martin, 1997. *From space to time*. München: Lincom Europa.

Holmberg, Anders. 2002. "Prepositions and PPs in Zina Kotoko." In *Some Aspects of the Grammar of Zina Kotoko*, edited by Bodil Kappel Schmidt, David Odden, and Anders Holmberg, 162–174. Munich: Lincom Europa.

Hualde, José Ignacio. 1992. Catalan. (Descriptive Grammars.) London: Routledge.

Jackendoff, Ray. 1996. 'The Architecture of the Linguistic-spatial Interface', in Paul Bloom, Mary A. Peterson, Lynn Nadel, & Merrill F. Garrett (eds.), *Language and Space*, Cambridge, MA: MIT Press, 1–30.

Johns, Alana & Brigid Thurgood. 2011. "Axial Parts in Inuktitut and Uzbeki." *Proceedings of the 2011 annual conference of the Canadian Linguistic Association*.

Kayne, Richard, 2004a. 'Here and There', in Christian Leclère, Éric Laporte, Mireille Piot, & Max Silberztein (eds.), *Lexique, syntaxe, et lexique-grammaire (Syntax, Lexis, and Lexicon-Grammar): Papers in Honour of Maurice Gross* (Lingvisticæ Investigationes Supplementa, 24), Amsterdam: John Benjamins, 275–85.

Kayne, Richard, 2004b. 'Prepositions as Probes', in Adriana Belletti (ed.), *Structures and Beyond: The Cartography of Syntactic Structures*, vol. 3, New York: Oxford University Press, 192–212.

Kayne, Richard, 2007. 'A Short Note on Where *vs.* Place', in Roberta Maschi, Nicoletta Penello, & Piera Rizzolatti (eds.), *Miscellanea di studi linguistici offerti a Laura Vanelli da amici e allievi padovani*, Udine: Forum, 245–257.

Koopman, Hilda. 2000. "Prepositions, postpositions, circumpositions, and particles." In *The Syntax of Specifiers and Heads*, edited by Hilda Koopman, 204–260. London: Routledge.

Kracht, Marcus, 2002. 'On the Semantics of Locatives', *Linguistics and Philosophy* 25, 157–232.

Kratzer, Angelika 1996. Severing the External Argument from its Verb. In Johan Rooryck and Laurie Zaring (eds.), *Phrase Structure and the Lexicon*. Kluwer. Dordrecht. 109–137.

Levinson, Lisa. 2011. "Possessive with in Germanic: have and the Role of P." *Syntax* 14: 355–393.

Manzini, M. Rita, and Ludovico Franco. 2016. "Goal and DOM datives." *Natural Language and Linguistic Theory* 34: 197–240.

Manzini, M. Rita, Savoia, Leonardo M. 2011. 'Reducing 'case' to denotational primitives: Nominal inflections in Albanian', *Linguistic Variation* 11, 76–120.

Marantz, Alec. 1984. *On the Nature of Grammatical Relations*. Cambridge, MA: MIT Press.

Pantcheva, Marina, 2006. 'Persian Preposition Classes', *Nordlyd* 33, 1–25.

Pantcheva, Marina, 2010. 'The syntactic structure of locations, goals and sources', *Linguistics* 48, 1043–1081.

Pantcheva, Marina, 2011. Decomposing Path: The Nanosyntax of Directional Expressions. Doctoral dissertation, University of Tromsø.

Piccitto, Giorgio. *Vocabolario Siciliano*. Catania – Palermo: Centro di Studi Filologici e Linguistici Siciliani.

Pylkkänen, Liina. 2008. *Introducing Arguments*. Cambridge, MA: MIT Press.

Riemsdijk, Henk van, 1990. 'Functional prepositions', in Harm Pinkster, & Inge Genee (eds.), *Unity in Diversity: Papers Presented to Simon C. Dik on his 50th Birthday*, Dordrecht: Foris, 229–241.

Rizzi, Luigi, 1988. 'Il sintagma preposizionale', in Lorenzo Renzi (ed.), *Grande grammatica italiana di consultazione*, vol. 1, Bologna: Il Mulino, 508–531.

Romeu, Juan 2013. "The nanosyntax of Path." Ms. Madrid http://ling.auf.net/lingbuzz/

Roy, Isabelle, & Svenonius, Peter, 2009. 'Complex prepositions', in Francois Jacques, Eric Gilbert, Claude Guimier, & Maxi Krause (eds.), *Autour de la préposition. Actes du Colloque International de Caen* (20-22 septembre 2007), Caen: Presses Universitaires de Caen, 105–116.

Roy, Isabelle, 2006. 'Body part nouns in expressions of location in French', *Nordlyd* 33, 98–119.

Salvi, Giampaolo, and Renzi, Lorenzo (eds.). 2010. *Grammatica dell'italiano antico*. Bologna: Il Mulino.

Salvi, Giampaolo, and Laura Vanelli. 2004. *Nuova grammatica italiana*. Bologna: Il Mulino.

Svenonius, Peter. 2002. Icelandic case and the structure of events. Journal of Comparative Germanic Linguistics 5(1–3): 197–225.

Svenonius, Peter 2003. "Limits on p: filling in holes vs. falling in holes." *Nordlyd* 31: 431–445.

Svenonius, Peter, 2006. "The emergence of axial parts". *Nordlyd* 33. 1–22.

Svenonius, Peter, 2008. "Projections of P." In *Syntax and Semantics of Spatial P*, edited by Anna Asbury, Jakub Dotlačil, Berit Gehrke and Rick Nouwen, 63–84. Amsterdam: John Benjamins.

Svenonius, Peter. 2007. "Adpositions, particles and the arguments they introduce." In *Argument structure*, edited by Eric Reuland, Tanmoy Bhattacharya, and Giorgos Spathas, 63–103. Amsterdam: John Benjamins.

Svenonius, Peter, 2008. Projections of P. In Anna Asbury, Jakub Dotlačil, Berit Gehrke & Rick Nouwen (eds.), *Syntax and Semantics of Spatial P*, Amsterdam: John Benjamins, 63–84.

Svenonius, Peter. 2010. "Spatial P in English." In *Mapping Spatial PPs, The Cartography of Syntactic Structures, Vol. 6*, edited by Guglielmo Cinque and Luigi Rizzi, 127–160. New York: Oxford University Press.

Talmy, Leonard, 1985. 'Lexicalization patterns: semantic structure in lexical forms', in Timothy Shopen (ed.), *Language typology and syntactic description. Vol. 3: grammatical categories and the lexicon*, Cambridge: Cambridge University Press, 57–149.

Talmy, Leonard, 1991. 'Path to realization: a typology of event conflation', in Laurel A. Sutton, Christopher Johnson, & Ruth Shields (eds.), *Papers of the Seventeenth Annual Meeting of the Berkeley Linguistics Society*, Berkeley, CA: Berkeley Linguistics Society, 480–520.

Talmy, Leonard, 2000. *Toward a cognitive semantics. Concept structuring systems, Vol. 1*. Cambridge, MA: MIT Press.

Terzi, Arhonto, 2008. 'Locative Prepositions as Modifiers of an Unpronouced Noun', in Charles B. Chang, & Hannah J. Haynie (eds.), *Proceedings of the 26th West Coast Conference on Formal Linguistics*, Somerville, MA: Cascadilla Press, 471–479.

Tortora, Christina, 2005. 'The preposition's preposition in Italian: Evidence for boundedness of space', in Randall Scott Gess, & Edward J. Rubin (eds.), *Theoretical and Experimental Approaches to Romance Linguistics*, Amsterdam: John Benjamins, 307–327.

Traina, Antonino. 1868. *Nuovo vocabolario Siciliano-Italiano*. Palermo: Giuseppe Pedone Lauriel.

Ursini, Francesco-Alessio. 2015. "On the Syntax and Semantics of Italian Spatial Ps." *Acta Linguistica Hungarica* 63(1). 3–51.

Ursini, Francesco-Alessio, and Haiping Long 2018. "On spatial nouns and adpositions in Mandarin." *Language and Linguistics* 81: 193–226.

Wood, Jim. 2015. *Icelandic Morphosyntax and Argument Structure*. Dordrecht: Springer.

Zwarts, Joost, 1995. 'Lexical and Functional Direction', in Marcel den Dikken, & Kees Hengeveld (eds.), *Linguistics in the Netherlands 1995*, Amsterdam: John Benjamins, 227–38.

Jacopo Garzonio
Not even a crumb of negation: on *mica* in Old Italian

1 Introduction

In this article I compare the syntactic properties of the postverbal negation *mica* in Old and Modern Italian. According to many current analyses of the doubling stages of the Jespersen cycle, new negation markers start as lexical items bearing an uninterpretable Negative feature. Gradually these items become interpretable as Negative, which eventually allows them to replace the older sentence negation marker. I analyze the distribution of the postverbal negation *mica* in Old and Modern Italian and argue that the observed changes are not a consequence of a change in the interpretability of the Negative feature. Adopting the idea that negation is not directly represented in the syntactic spine, I analyze the diachronic development of *mica* in terms of a different parametric setting in the lexicalization and attraction properties of Focus and Existential projections.

The Jespersen cycle is a diachronic process where an originally nonnegative lexical item undergoes a grammaticalization path becoming a new marker of sentential negation. A classic example (Jespersen 1917) is found in the history of English, where the preverbal negative marker *ne* is at first accompanied by the reinforcer *not* (in origin a quantifier, *nāwiht* 'nothing'; cf. Willis, Lucas and Breitbarth (2013: 7)) and then replaced by it. In the original formulation, it was assumed that the position of *not* in Present-day English before the lexical verb (but under *do*) is the same position of Old English *ne*.

(1) a. *ic **ne** secge*   (Old English)
    b. *I **ne** seye **not***   (Middle English)
    c. *I say **not***   (Early Modern English)
    d. *I don't say*   (Present-day English)

It is now generally accepted that the processes that lead to the grammaticalization of new negative markers do not follow necessarily all the steps originally

---

To Rita, who has shown me how questions are more interesting even than (right) answers

Jacopo Garzonio, University of Padova

https://doi.org/10.1515/9781501505201-016

proposed by Jespersen. For instance, in some cases there is no evidence for the existence of a doubling stage where the combination NEG-V-NEG, as in (1b), is the standard sentential negation and not some type of emphatic construction (Larrivée 2011). Nevertheless, cases of discontinuous negation are not rare. The examples in (2) display some cases from Italo-Romance varieties and Celtic languages (Bernini and Ramat 1996: 18).

(2) a. *Sta donna ki la **nem** pyaz **miga**.* (Emilian)
 this woman here she=not=me pleases not
 'I do not like this woman.'
 b. *Kwela funna li **no** me pyas **miga**.* (Western Lombard)
 that woman there not=me=pleases not
 'I do not like that woman.'
 c. ...***ni** chyffroai ef **ddim**.* (Middle Welsh, Willis, 2011)
 not stir.3SG he not
 '...he didn't stir.'
 d. ***Ne** lavaro **ket** kement-se.* (Breton)
 not say.FUT.3SG not all-that
 'He will not say it.'

The analysis of doubling stages is crucial not only for a theoretical account of the Jespersen cycle, but more in general for a theory of negation (and polarity as a modal feature), the categorial status of negative items and the exact nature of n-words. A formal account of the Jespersen cycle in minimalist terms is offered by Roberts (2007: 64–80), who has considered negation in French. According to his proposal, the main change in the cycle regards the interpretability of a Neg-feature on the items involved in sentential negation. The preverbal marker *ne* "goes from having an interpretable Neg-feature to having an uninterpretable one, possibly via a period of variation. The postverbal element *pas* undergoes a partially reverse development, ultimately acquiring an interpretable Neg-feature" (Willis 2011: 95). According to this view the cases of discontinuous negation are not all the same. In some cases (the "older stage" looking at the cycle) the new negation is not intrinsically negative, while in other cases (the "more recent stage") it is the old negation that is not intrinsically negative, so that it becomes optional and then disappears.

In this article I take into exam the changes in the syntactic distribution of the item *mica*, generally considered a negative adverb (but see Manzini and Savoia 2002), occurred from Old Tuscan (or Old Italian) varieties to Modern Italian. In origin it was a quantity noun (derived from Latin *mica(m)* 'crumb'), presumably used in the direct object position of predicates, in order to express the smallest conceivable portion of the event.[1] This usage is already lost in the earliest attested stages of Tuscan varieties. The development of *mica* cannot be considered a standard example of the Jespersen cycle since it has not replaced the preverbal negation *non* as the standard negative marker. In fact, both in the Old Tuscan and the Modern Italian stages, *mica* is used to deny an explicit or implicit discourse assumption. In this sense it is called sometimes "presuppositional negation" (Cinque 1977) or "emphatic negation" (Wallage 2016). Nevertheless, Modern Italian displays cases where *mica* is the only negation and is found in preverbal position:

(3) *Mica ci vado.*
    not there=go.1SG
    'I'm not going there.'

Such examples can be interpreted as evidence of a complete cycle of *mica*. In other words, it seems that *mica* has become inherently negative and can appear in the same position of *non*. I will argue that a similar intuition is not on the right track. In what follows I will show that there are differences between the two stages taken into exam, but these differences are not a product of a change in the syntactic encoding of sentential negation, but rather in the "internal micro-morpho-syntax" (Déprez 2011: 222) of the negative item. More precisely, I will argue that *mica* is not inherently negative neither in Old Tuscan nor in Modern Italian.

For the Old Tuscan data I have used the database of the OVI project, a searchable collection of Italo-Romance texts from the first attestations to the beginning of the XV century.[2] I have searched for all the occurrences of the form *mica* (and the "northern" variant with intervocalic voicing *miga*) in texts tagged as Florentine, Sienese and generically Tuscan. As chronological limit of

---

[1] Minimizers are a very common source of new negative markers (see among many others Willis, Lucas and Breitbarth, 2013). For some Italo-Romance varieties there are early attestations of items derived from *mica(m)* used as quantity nouns both in negative and positive environments (cf. Parry 2013). The example in (i) shows the latter case for Old Milanese:

(i) On   sté   de scisceri   e   miga de vin   d'intrà
     one bushel of chickpeas and **miga** of wine of income
     'One bushel of chickpeas and a little of wine as income...'   (*Lancino Curti* 6.14)

[2] The OVI database (searchable online at https://artfl-project.uchicago.edu/content/ovi) has been created mainly for lexicographic research, so it allows only limited grammar-driven inquiries. Nevertheless, with 1960 texts, 22.3 million words and 456,000 unique forms it is a very rich textual resource.

the inquiry I have chosen the middle of the XIV century, since after that the language displays many substantial changes (like the loss of verb second syntax).

2 On the syntax of *mica* in Modern Italian

In Modern Italian, *mica* is not a marker of standard sentential negation. As shown by Cinque (1977), it is used to deny a presupposition and its distribution has pragmatic restrictions. The reasons why *mica* has not been reinterpreted as a neutral, non-emphatic marker of negation are beyond the goals of this paper (see Willis, Lucas and Breitbarth (2013: 22–23) on the possible reasons why the Jespersen cycle gets slower or stops). However, it can be argued that *mica* is not intrinsically negative. To put it simply, *mica* is an n-word (like for example the quantifier *niente* 'nothing' or the adverb *mai* 'never'), which means that in a language like Italian it is a free variable interpreted in the scope of a higher operator (on this, see among many others Rizzi 1982: 122; Acquaviva 1994). This operator can be a sentential negation, like in (4), but also an interrogative operator, like in (5), where no negative meaning is implied:

(4) a. *Non mangia mica.*
      not eats   not
      'S/he is not eating.'
   b. *Non mangia niente.*
      not eats   nothing
      'S/he eats nothing.'
   c. *Non mangia mai carote.*
      not eats   never carrots
      'S/he never eats carrots.'

(5) a. *Hai mica mangiato?*
      have.2SG not eaten
      'Have you eaten?'
   b. *Hai mangiato niente?*
      have.2SG eaten nothing
      'Have you eaten anything?'
   c. *Hai mai mangiato carote?*
      have.2SG never eaten carrots
      'Have you ever eaten carrots?'

The main argument to show that *mica* is an n-word is that, while in non-interrogative contexts it cannot surface after the verb without the preverbal negative marker *non*, a configuration that can be considered an instantiation of negative concord, in questions, as shown in (5a), postverbal *mica* is perfectly acceptable without *non*.[3]

A possible counterexample to the hypothesis that *mica* is not intrinsically negative is provided by examples like those in (6), where it is found in the preverbal space and no other negative element surfaces. From this position *mica* can license another n-word in postverbal position (7). It should be pointed out that this option is marginal for some speakers, but is nevertheless accepted.

(6) a. Mica mangio carote.
       not   eat.1SG carrots
       'I do not eat carrots.'
    b. Mica ci sono andato.
       not there=am gone
       'I have not gone there.'

(7) Mica ho   visto nessuno che parlava con lui.
    not have.1SG seen noone   that spoke   with him
    'I have not seen anyone speaking to him.'

However, from this point of view *mica* is not any different than other n-words, like *niente* or *mai*, which can surface before the verb as the only negative item in a sentence. Furthermore, contrary to other n-words, from the preverbal space it cannot license some polarity adverbs like *mai* 'never' or *ancora* 'yet'. This last property does not seem related to some kind of semantic clash, since *mica* can co-occur with these adverbs when it is postverbal:

---

3 As pointed out by Pescarini and Penello (2012) a polar question can display both *non* and *mica*:

(i) Non hai   mica mangiato?
    not have.2SG not eaten
    'Haven't you eaten?'

Reversing somehow their argumentation (since they discuss the optionality of *mica* in these cases), the presence of *non* in (i) does not influence the acceptability of the postverbal *mica*, but rather triggers the interpretation that the speaker considers less likely (and would be surprised by) a positive answer. I will not deal here with problems related to the polarity of yes/no questions (cf. Holmberg 2016).

(8) a. *?Mica ci sono   mai   andato.
        not there=am never gone
        'I have never been there.'
    b. *Mica l'ho   ancora fatto.
        not it=have.1SG yet   done
        'I have not yet done it.'
    c. Non ci sono mica mai andato.
    d. Non l'ho mica ancor fatto.

This suggests that preverbal *mica* cannot be considered simply as a pragmatically marked alternative to the standard preverbal negation *non*. There are two other facts pointing to this conclusion. With a modal verb, *non* can be interpreted both as scoping over and in the scope of the modal, while preverbal *mica* can be interpreted only as having scope over the modal (Pescarini and Penello 2012).

(9) a. Non deve   guidare.
        not must.3SG drive
        'It is not necessary that he drives.' (¬□)
        'It is necessary that he does not drive.' (□¬)
    b. Mica deve   guidare.
        not must.3SG drive
        'It is not necessary that he drives.' (¬□)
        *'It is necessary that he does not drive.' *(□¬)

Further evidence suggesting that preverbal *mica* is not like *non* comes from examples like the following ones:

(10)   A: Nella salsa che hai   preparato manca   qualcosa.
           in-the sauce that have.2SG prepared is-lacking something
           'The sauce you prepared lacks something.'
    a. B: Non il   sale... forse   il pepe.
           not the salt   perhaps the pepper
    b. B: Mica il sale... forse   il pepe.
           not the salt perhaps the pepper
        'Not the salt... perhaps the pepper.'

(11) a. Nella salsa ho   dimenticato **non** il sale, ma il pepe.
        in-the sauce have.1SG forgotten   not   the salt but the pepper
        'I forgot to add the pepper to the sauce, not the salt.'
    b. *Nella salsa ho dimenticato **mica** il sale ma il pepe.

In corrective focus constructions the negated constituent can be introduced by both *non* and *mica* if the structure is elliptical, like in (10). However, if the negated object is found in its position in a complete sentence, only *non* can be used. Following Manzini and Savoia (2011: 81), this distribution can be straightforwardly analyzed assuming that fragments like those in (10) are the product of ellipsis of a whole sentence. Interestingly, a constituent can be negated by *mica* if it is in the left peripheral focus position, so it is likely that (10b) is the elliptical version of (12).[4]

(12) **Mica il   sale ho   dimenticato.**
      not   the salt have.1SG forgotten
      'It is not the salt that I have forgotten.'

Summarizing, preverbal *mica* does not require the preverbal negative marker, exactly like focalized n-words like *niente* or *nessuno*; as a constituent negation it can only appear in focus position or in fragments; it has always scope over modals. All these properties can be accounted for assuming that preverbal *mica* always occupies a focus position (like FocusP in the CP, in Rizzi's (1997) terms, or one of the lower positions proposed by Benincà and Poletto 2004). Interestingly, the fact that it can license argumental n-words but not adverbs like *mai* or *ancora* can be considered evidence that its negative concord properties are computed at the vP level and not at the Tense/Aspect layer. In other words, it can interact with arguments, as expected if it is a nominal category (Manzini and Savoia 2002). In any case, focalized n-words only marginally can license adverbs like *mai* or *ancora* when they are not subjects:

(13) a. ?*Nessuno ho   mai   visto qui.
         nobody   have.1SG never seen   here
         'I have seen nobody here.'
     b. *Niente ho   ancora fatto.
         nothing have.1SG yet   done
         'I have done nothing yet.'

This distribution can be accounted assuming that *mica*, since it has to be licensed like other n-words, can either appear under the preverbal negative marker *non*

---

4 As Brunetti (2004, 111) argues, the movement to the left periphery of a non contrastively focused constituent is not explicitly visible, because ellipsis of post-focal material generally applies. The contrast between examples like (10), (11) and (12) is a possible clue that all elliptical chunks as those considered here are in fact the product of movement to the left periphery.

(14a) or surface in a left peripheral focus position (14b). The latter possibility is another case of the phenomenon labelled by Garzonio and Poletto (2015) as "syntactic parasitism": a lexical item with a given feature inventory (*mica* in this case) can surface in a structural position normally encoding one of the different features it is associated with (Focus in this case). As Garzonio and Poletto (2015: 147) point out discussing the grammaticalization of *neca* in Sicilian from negative cleft to CP negative marker, "across languages negation can be encoded by different lexical items and in different positions in the clause structure. This is not only true typologically but also at a micro-comparative level. This is a potential problem for any syntactic theory based on the idea that semantic features have a one-to-one structural counterpart. The case of *neca*, that is the case of an element associated with [focus] encoding negation, is one of many cases suggesting that negation is not a simple element (that is a simple [neg] feature or a unique NegP position) but a complex one, formed as the result of the interaction of several abstract processes."

(14) a. [*non* [T [*mica* [VP]]]]
    b. [$_{Focus}$ *mica* [T [VP]]]

The fact that *mica* can be used as constituent negation only in elliptical contexts (where T is not expressed and therefore there cannot be a preverbal *non*) or in the left periphery, but crucially not *in situ* under T, confirms this analysis. Again, *mica* is lexicalized in a focus position.

(15) [$_{Focus}$ *mica* [DP *il sale*]([T *ho* [VP *dimenticato*]]])

In the next section I will show how the behavior of *mica* in an earlier stage of Italian distributes according to similar factors.

3 On the syntax of *mica* in Old Tuscan texts

In this section I compare the syntactic behavior of Modern Italian *mica* to its counterpart *mica/miga* in Old Tuscan texts. In general, exactly like in Modern Italian, *mica* usually surfaces in postverbal position. As discussed by Mosegaard Hansen and Visconti (2009), there seem to be two competing forms: bare *mica* and *né mica*, which displays the same morpheme *ne-* found also in Old and Modern Italian forms like *neanche, nemmeno* 'not even', even if in this case it is usually written separate. This *ne-* is the same formant found on many n-words (like *nessuno* 'no one') and presumably derives from Latin *ně*, the older form of negation in Latin (already used in Latin in items grammaticalized as negative indefinites; see Gianollo 2016), or the negative coordinator *něc*. As pointed out by Mosegaard Hansen and Visconti (2009) *né mica* seems to be the older form, gradually substituted by the simple *mica*. This conclusion is based on the observation that the construction *non ... né mica* is found in the 48% of the earlier examples they have considered (while *non ... mica* is found in the 40%). In later texts *non ... mica* prevails: it is found in the 63% of the examples, while *non ... né mica* is found only in the 33% (and finally disappears after the XVI century). The two forms, however, seem to have a different distribution already in the earlier texts. In the corpus that I have considered, there are 40 instances of postverbal *mica* (16a) and 24 instances of postverbal *né mica* (16b) used in contexts where there is sentential negation.

(16) a. *La grandezza delle magioni non cessa mica la febbre,*
    the largeness of-the houses not extinguishes not the fever
    secondo che Orazio dice. (*Tesoro volgarizzato*, 7.68)
    as Horace says
    'The large size of a home does not extinguish the fever, as Horace says.'
 b. *Dio non ajuta nè mica per preghiera se l'opera*
    God not helps not due to prayer if the=deed
    non seguita la prieganza. (*Trattato di virtù morali*, 17)
    not follows the prayer
    'God does not help due to a prayer if there is no deed following it.'

In all these cases there is a preverbal negation, like *non* or the negative coordination *né*. Furthermore, there is one case where postverbal *né mica* appears in a conditional environment, without a preverbal negation, which is impossible with *mica* in Modern Italian.[5] In any case, this is further evidence that at this stage this item was not inherently negative, even when it appeared with the *né* prefix.

---

5 It should be pointed out that a comparable problem arises with other n-words in Modern Italian. While some speakers accept cases, like those in (i), where a postverbal n-word is licensed by the conditional operator, other speakers consider similar examples ungrammatical and can use only existential quantifiers in these contexts:

(i) a. *Se succede niente, chiamami.*
       if happens nothing call=me
       'If anything happens, call me.'
    b. *Se vedi nessuno di sospetto chiamami.*
       if see.2SG nobody of suspicious call=me
       'If you see anyone suspicious, call me.'

(17) se 'l   prenze dell'oste   di   questo [...] dottasse né mica
      if=the prince of-the=army about   this   doubted   not
      ch'elli   non fusse leale...   (*Reggimento de' principi volgarizzato*, 3.3.11)
      that=he not   was   loyal
      'If the leader of the army had any doubt about the loyalty of this man...'

However, a different picture emerges if the preverbal space is considered. In the whole corpus that I have taken into exam there is no instance of preverbal *mica*, while there are 5 examples of preverbal *né mica*, as in (18):

(18) a.   ...*che' defecti né mica son ne le donne viçi.*
          since   flaws   not   are in the women vices
          '...since vices are not a flaw in women.'
                                    (Francesco da Barberino, *Documenti d'Amore*, 1.12)
     b.   *Federigo di Stuffo   già   né-mica par*
          Frederick of Hohenstaufen already not   seems
          che si celi...   (Monte Andrea, *Rime*, tenz. 8, son. 1)
          that REFL=hides
          'It already seems that Frederick of Hohenstaufen is not hiding...'

This is a striking asymmetry considering that in Modern Italian and other Italo-Romance varieties *mica* can appear in preverbal position as the only marker of sentential negation. Even more interesting is the fact that in the corpus there are 17 cases of corrective structures (considered by Mosegaard Hansen and Visconti (2009) as the origin of the modern "presuppositional" meaning of *mica*) and all present either *né mica* or a complex form where *mica* is preceded by another negation (*non* or *no*)[6]:

(19) a.   *E   qui   s'intende   di riso   sfrenato   e   del*
          and here IMPERS=mean of laugh uncontrolled and of-the
          continovato, non miga   della faccia rallegrare
          not not   of-the face   amuse   continued

---

[6] In (19) all examples display both the negated constituent and the corrective chunk. There are also cases where only the negated part is explicit, like in (i). Again, in all these cases the form of the negation is either *né mica* or *no(n) mica*.

(i)   *extima   tuoi valor'   non mica   degni*
      prize.IMP your merits   not not   worthy
      'Do not consider adequate your merits.' (Francesco da Barberino, *Documenti d'Amore*, 8.1)

'And here one means uncontrollable and persisting laugh, not just brightening.'
(Francesco da Barberino, *Reggimento e costumi di donna*, 1.6)

b. sopr' un braccio del   chiaro ruscelletto,
over an arm   of-the clear   stream
tese   avean reti, e   non miga in pantano.
stretched had   nets and   not not   in bog
'They stretched the nets over an arm of the clear stream, and not in a bog.'
(Boccaccio, *Caccia di Diana*, 8)

c. quelli che vuole essere amato non dé   essere
that   that wants be.INF loved   not has-to be. INF
né mica avaro, ma molto largo
not   mean   but very prodigal
'Who wants to be loved must be very prodigal, not mean.'
(*Volgarizzamento del De Amore di Andrea Cappellano*, 1.13)

There are also a couple of cases where the form *né mica* is used as a negative focalizer, roughly corresponding to 'not at all', where the negated constituent is not contrasted but presented as an alternative:

(20) dond'elleno sono meno vergognose e   quasi   né mica   vergognose
so=they   are less shy   and almost not-at-all shy
'So that they are less shy or almost not shy at all.'
(*Reggimento de' principi volgarizzato*, 2.2.19)

As said in the methodological premise, I have not conducted a quantitative survey of the texts from the second half of the XIV century, but the tendency to have a complex form and not the simple *mica/miga* in corrective structures is very strong in later texts too.

(21) Pensa   e   stima   chi tu   se', e
think.IMP and prize.IMP who you are and
non mica dove   tu   fosti nato.
not not   where you were born
'Think about and prize who you are, not the place where you were born.'   (*Volgarizzamento della prima deca di Tito Livio*, 1.41)

The distribution of the different forms in Old Tuscan seems to be regulated by the same factors observed for the distribution of *mica* in Modern Italian, with an important difference. While even in the earlier texts the simple form *mica* is attested, it seems that it cannot be used before T. Similarly, it cannot be used as constituent negation unless it is preceded by another negation. The form *né mica* does not have these limitations. This state of things is represented in (22).

(22) a. [*non/né*   [T [(*né*) *mica* [VP]]]]
    b. [*(*né*) *mica* [T [VP]]]
    c. [*(*né/non*) *mica* [DP/PP/VP]]

Thus, it appears that in Old Tuscan it is the form *né mica* (or *non mica*) that has the same complete distribution of *mica* in Modern Italian. In the next section, building on this generalization I will propose an analysis for the development of the syntactic behavior of *mica* in Italian and, more in general, of its relation with the phenomena grouped under the label 'Jespersen cycle'.

4 Discussion

I will assume that *mica* is a quantificational polar item which takes scope over events when it appears in a sentence structure. The structural counterpart of this intuition is assuming that the standard post-verbal position of *mica* is an Existential projection.[7] More precisely, given that it has to precede all aspectual adverbs, this ExistP is located in the functional spine of the sentence structure and immediately dominates an AspectP (b)[8]:

(23) a. *Non ho   mica ancora mangiato.*
        not have.1SG not   yet   eaten
        'I have not eaten yet.'
    b. [*non* [T *ho* [$_{Exist}$ *mica* [$_{Aspect}$ *ancora* [VP *mangiato*]]]]]

---

7 I use the label Existential only to indicate that *mica* is a type of quantifier operating on the event (similarly to *ever* in English). Minimizers (and NPIs) have been analyzed in different ways concerning their quantificational nature (see Espinal 2000 on this), but since in Old Tuscan the argumental use of *(né) mica* is very marginal and it is a sentential element, I do not treat here the problem of its quantificational category.
8 Manzini and Savoia (2002) have pointed out that in some Italo-Romance dialects aspectual adverbs can precede postverbal negations similar to Italian *mica*. This variation could derive from a parametrized difference regarding the syntactic category selected by ExistP, but it can also be seen as evidence that items like *mica* are always generated in the VP and moved only in some varieties (like Italian) to a functional position in the sentence structure. Given the interactions between these negations and arguments (triggering of genitive objects, etc.) the latter hypothesis seems more likely.

This analysis is compatible with the standard cartographic theory of the split IP/TP layer (Cinque, 1999), where some of the Apectual specifiers can accommodate quantificational items (like *tutto* 'everything' in one the two Completive projections).

In Old Tuscan varieties the standard postverbal position is the only one that allows the free alternation of the form *mica* and the complex form *né mica*. Observable optionality can be considered a possible indication of a change in grammar (Kroch, 1989). As said in the previous section Mosegaard Hansen and Visconti (2009) argue that *né mica* is the older form. This can also be confirmed by the fact that there are some cases of *né mica* used as a quantifier (24), while there are not comparable cases with the simple *mica*. From this point of view *né mica* is similar to other items derived from a negated minimizer grammaticalized as negative quantifiers (like Old Lombard *negota* 'nothing', from *ne(c) gutta(m)* 'not a drop').

(24) *ellino mettarebbero il loro reame in pericolo*
 they would.put.3PL the their kingdom in danger
 *per piccola ragione o per **né mica**.*
 for small reason or for none
 'they would put their kingdom in danger for a little reason or none at all.' (*Reggimento de' principi volgarizzato*, 1.3.6)

In any case, at the earliest attested stage both *né mica* and *mica* can be found in the sentential ExistP projection. From a synchronic point of view, this alternation is reminiscent of similar alternations regarding the negative concord phenomenon. For instance, in some negative polarity contexts the direct object can be the bare item *cosa* 'thing', like in (25a-b), while in other cases *cosa* is paired to a negative quantifier, like in (25c).

(25) a. *...né mai non dissi **cosa***
 and-not never not said.1SG thing
 che disinore fosse di mio zio
 that shame was of my uncle
 'I never said anything that could disgrace my uncle.' (*Novellino*, 65b)
 b. *...ma elli non ardirà di pensare **cosa***
 but he not will-dare of thinking thing
 che no la possa predicare in palese.
 that not it=could.3SG teach in open
 '...but he will not dare to think about anything that he could not openly teach.' (*Fiori e vita di filosafi*)

c. ... *non temerai* **neuna cosa** *che induca la morte.*
   not   will-fear.2SG no   thing that brings the death
   'You will not fear anything that brings death.'   (*Fiori e vita di filosafi*)

The alternation in (25) is parallel to the *mica/né mica* alternation described above, with the difference that in the case of *mica/né mica* the optional negative quantification is expressed by *né*. As discussed in the previous section, the likely origin of this *né* is the Latin negative coordination particle *něc*, as straightforwardly shown by the fact that it is effectively homophonous with the Italian negative coordinator *né* 'neither'. I will take this etymological clue as an indication that *né* lexicalizes a negative additive Focus feature in the functional structure of *mica*.

(26) [Focus *né* [Exist *mica*]]

A similar analysis has been developed by Franco et al. (2015) for negative focalizers like *neanche* or *nemmeno* 'not even', formed by *ne-* plus *anche* 'too' and *meno* 'less', with a slightly difference: while they argue in the case of *neanche* that *anche* is found in a Focus position and *ne-* lexicalizes a coordination feature (the projection is labelled '&P'), I would rather propose that *ne-* (like *né* in *né mica*) is always the lexicalization of the negative additive Focus feature. It is well known from the typological literature that coordination particles are often used as additive focalizers (see König 1991: 63–64, who cites several cases[9]). In other words, negation cannot be expressed by the means of a neutral coordination, but can be derived from the semantic operation of negative addiction, which is a type of Focus (see also Hendriks 2004, on the idea that *either* and *neither* are not conjunctions but Focus particles). Furthermore, Old Tuscan displays many cases of *né* as the first item of a sentence even in contexts where there is no possible coordination interpretation. It is tempting to consider these instances of *né* as the negated counterpart of the coordinative particle *e* 'and' used as a pragmatic marker (see Poletto 2014: 22–27, on this).

The next point of my proposal is to explain the free alternation of *mica* and *né mica* in the postverbal ExistP position on the basis of two different licensing

---

9 "In many languages, the same expression can be used in both functions, i.e. in the sense of English 'also/too' and in the sense of 'and'. Examples are Lat. *et(iam)*, Gk. *kaí*, Russ. *i*, Norw. *og(så)*, Lezgian *-ni*, Manam *-be*, Zulu *na-*, Sesotho *le*, and Malayalam *-um*. This affinity may also show up in expressions of emphatic conjunction. English *both ... and* corresponds to expressions whose literal translation is *too ... too* in Amharic (*-mm ... -m*), Turkish (*de ... de*), Japanese (*mo ... mo*), Mandarin (*ye ... ye*), Hebrew and Kannada".

configurations: in the case of *né mica*, I assume that the preverbal negation agrees with the negative additive Focus (following Giannakidou's (1998) terminology, I call this case "anti-veridical" concord), while in the case of bare *mica* the preverbal negation can license the postverbal existential item like any other non-veridical operator.

(27) a. [*non* [T [Focus *né* [Exist *mica* [VP]]]]] Anti-veridical concord
 b. [*non* [T [Exist *mica* [VP]]]] Non-veridical licensing

This analysis entails the idea that negation *per se* is not a grammatical feature, but can be considered a composite of different combined features, among which there are at least Focus and Existentiality (Poletto 2008). A further consequence of this proposal is that negative concord could be seen as a complex phenomenon, comprising different types of concord, involving different types of features. I do not concentrate here on the preverbal negation *non*, but it has been argued by Manzini and Savoia (2011, 128ff.) that in Italo-Romance (and possibly in the whole Romance domain) the preverbal negation patterns with NPIs from many points of view and, therefore, it is the counterpart in the clitic space in T of postverbal negations in the verb domain. For this reason I do not use the label NEG in the syntactic representation of sentential negation. Nevertheless, the idea that *(né) mica* is not negative is compatible also with a more standard analysis where preverbal *non* corresponds to the negative operator (as, for instance, in Zeijlstra's (2004) model).

When used in corrective constructions or in preverbal position, the only possibility for Old Tuscan *mica* is to display the morpheme *né* or the standard constituent negation *non*. In other words, when *mica* is not in the scope of the preverbal negation and the constituent negation *non* is not used (as in 28a), the negative additive Focus head must be lexicalized, providing a non-veridical environment for the licensing of the Existential polar feature of *mica* (28b). It can be argued that in cases like (28a), which is the structure I propose for examples like (19a) or (21), Focus is expressed by syntax (Merge of *mica* with negation) and not by morphology, but here I leave aside the relation between Focus and the standard negative marker *non*.

(28) a. [*non* [Exist *mica* [T/DP/VP]]]
 b. [Focus *né* [Exist *mica* [T / DP /VP]]]

Consider now what happens in Modern Italian. As discussed above, the form *né mica* is absent in Modern Italian. From the point of view of the internal morpho-syntax of *mica* this development can be interpreted as a raising in the morpho-syntactic functional spine, a process involved in grammaticalization, as proposed by Roberts and Roussou (2003). So, the diachronic change consists in a different lexicalization, where *mica* surfaces in the Focus position in the internal functional layer:

(29) [Focus *mica* [Exist ~~*mica*~~]]

This explains why *mica* appears in Focus positions in the sentence structure (and in elliptical structures) and why in such case it does not need to be licensed by a separate constituent negation or by a morpheme like *né*. Compare (30) with (23).

(30) a. Mica ho   mangiato.
       not   have.1SG   eaten
       'I have not eaten.'
    b. [Focus [Focus **mica**] [T *ho* [Exist ~~*mica*~~ [VP *mangiato*]]]]

I leave open the problem of deciding if *mica* is generated in the postverbal space and then moved to the left periphery in examples like (30a), as represented in (30b), where it is moved through feature attraction, or is directly inserted in the surface position. However, in the case of elliptical chunks, if *mica* is analyzed as always generated under T, it must be argued that this type of ellipsis allows the PF cancellation of the base position of moved items (see van Craenenbroeck 2004 about two different types of sentential ellipsis). On the other hand, given that preverbal *mica* cannot license postverbal NPI adverbs like *ancora* 'yet', it can be assumed that it is not generated in [ExistP] but rather inside or at the edge of the verbal lexical layer.

The data I have considered in this article are empirically very interesting for the understanding of the Jespersen cycle. Minimizers are one of the main sources for new negative markers and at a first glance the evolution of *mica* could be seen as a prototypical case of the Jespersen cycle. However, it cannot be argued that *mica* has become inherently negative in Modern Italian, as it can appear in non-negative contexts like questions. Even more interestingly, cases where it seems to behave as a true negation (preverbal position, constituent negation in ellipsis) are already attested in Old Tuscan texts, where, however, it must be preceded by another constituent negation, or display the morpheme *né*, which I argued to be a marker of negative additive Focus. So, summarizing, what has changed in the history of *mica* is not the interpretability of a [Neg] feature, but the lexicalization properties of a Focus component present in the semantics of negative constructions.

This idea has some consequences for the analysis of the Jespersen cycle in general.

A first element to point out is that items like *mica* change their position independently from the expression of the negative feature. I have argued that both in Old and Modern Italian *mica* is normally found in postverbal position, but it can be optionally moved to the preverbal space, and that this option is not linked to negative semantics *per se*. A similar development can be assumed for varieties like the Southern Italian dialect of Rionero in Vulture: here *manco* (in origin a focalizer meaning 'not even'), has become obligatorily preverbal without a doubling stage and is now the standard negation. It can also license a postverbal emphatic negation similar to *mica*:

(31) Mankə hai   mica vistə i mii amica? (Garzonio and Poletto 2014: ex. 29)
     not   have.2SG not seen the my friends
     'You have not seen my friends by chance, have you?'

Similar facts strongly suggest that a "NegP free" approach is preferable for a formal analysis of the Jespersen cycle, as proposed by Breitbarth (2014).[10] In particular, it appears that the surface position of a negation correlates with other features, like Focus in the case discussed here.

Furthermore, the diachronic development of the distribution of *mica* is clearly related to the loss of the morpheme *né*. In this case, it seems that there is a cycle regarding the morphosyntactic expression of the semantic components of (emphatic) negation. This process, which is similar and is related to the standard Jespersen cycle, but is something different, can be observed in other cases, like in the development of the Latin preverbal negation *non* (from an unattested *ne oinom* 'not a single one'), or the Modern Greek *den*, from Classical Greek *u de hen* 'not even one' (Willmott, 2013). In general, there is a link between the internal morphosyntax of these items and their surface position in the clause structure, which again suggests that this position is not exclusively dedicated to the expression of negation or polarity.

Finally, even if there are some attestations in Old Tuscan of *né mica* as a negative quantifier, like in (24), this possibility has been lost: in the case of *mica* the grammaticalization process has begun when there was already an alternation between forms with and without the morpheme *né*. So, it seems that,

---

10 "Under an analysis without a functional projection NegP, the locus of cross-linguistic or historical variation in the expression of negation lies in the morphosyntactic properties of individual lexical items, not in the position, structure, or availability of a functional projection NegP" (Breitbarth, 2014, 127).

differently from other cases of postverbal negations developed from negative quantifiers (like English *not* or Piedmontese *nen*), the formation of a negative quantifier is not a key step of the cycle and, on the contrary, appears to be completely secondary.

References

Acquaviva, Paolo. 1994. 'The representation of operator-variable dependencies in sentential negation'. *Studia Linguistica* 48: 91–132.

Benincà, Paola and Cecilia Poletto. 2004. 'Topic, focus and V2: defining the CP sub-layers', in Luigi Rizzi (ed.), *The Structure of IP and CP. The Cartography of Syntactic Structures. Volume II*. Oxford/New York: Oxford University Press, pp. 52–75.

Bernini, Giuliano and Paolo Ramat. 1996. *Negative Sentences in the Languages of Europe. A Typological Approach*. Berlin/New York: Mouton de Gruyter.

Breitbarth, Anne. 2014. *The History of Low German Negation*. Oxford/New York: Oxford University Press.

Brunetti, Lisa. 2004. *A Unification of Focus*. Padova: Unipress.

Cinque, Guglielmo. 1977. 'Mica', *Annali della Facoltà di Lettere e Filosofia dell'Università di Padova* 1: 101–112.

Cinque, Guglielmo. 1999. *Adverbs and Functional Heads. A Cross-Linguistic Perspective*. Oxford/New York: Oxford University Press.

Déprez, Viviane. 2011. 'Atoms of negation: An outside-in micro-parametric approach to negative concord', in Pierre Larrivée and Richard P. Ingham (eds.), *The Evolution of Negation. Beyond the Jespersen Cycle*. Berlin: De Gruyter Mouton, pp. 221–272.

Espinal, M. Teresa. 2000. 'On the semantic status of n-words in Catalan and Spanish'. *Lingua* 110: 557–580.

Franco, Irene, Kellert, Olga, Mensching, Guido and Cecilia Poletto. 2015. 'A diachronic study of negative additives'. Paper presented at the GS Workshop on Negation, University of Goettingen, 18–19 September 2015.

Garzonio, Jacopo, and Cecilia Poletto. 2014. 'The negative marker that escaped the cycle: some notes on *manco*', in Carla Contemori and Lena Dal Pozzo (eds.), *Inquiries into Linguistic Theory and Language Acquisition. Papers offered to Adriana Belletti*, Siena: CISCL Press, pp. 181–197.

Garzonio, Jacopo, and Cecilia Poletto. 2015. 'On preverbal negation in Sicilian and syntactic parasitism', *Isogloss* 2, Special Issue on Italo-Romance morphosyntax: 133–149.

Giannakidou, Anastasia. 1998. *Polarity Sensitivity as (Non-)veridical Dependency*. Amsterdam: Benjamins.

Gianollo, Chiara. 2016. 'Negation and indefinites in Late Latin'. *Pallas* 102: 277–286.

Hendriks, Petra 2004. '*Either, both* and *neither* in coordinate structures', in Alice ter Meulen and Werner Abraham (Eds), *The Composition of Meaning: From Lexeme to Discourse*. Amsterdam: Benjamins, pp. 115–138.

Holmberg, Anders 2016. *The Syntax of Yes and No*. Oxford/New York: Oxford University Press.

Jespersen, Otto 1917. *Negation in English and Other Languages*. Copenhagen: A.F. Høst. Historisk-filologiske Meddelelser I, 5.

König, Ekkehard 1991. *The Meaning of Focus Particles: A Comparative Perspective*. London: Routledge.

Kroch, Anthony 1989. 'Reflexes of grammar in patterns of language change'. *Linguistic Variation and Change* 1: 199–244.

Larrivée, Pierre 2011. 'Is there a Jespersen cycle?', in Pierre Larrivée and Richard P. Ingham (eds.), *The Evolution of Negation. Beyond the Jespersen Cycle*. Berlin: De Gruyter Mouton, pp. 1–22.

Manzini, M. Rita and Leonardo Savoia. 2002. 'Negative adverbs are neither Adv nor Neg', in Masako Hirotani (ed.), *Proceedings of North East Linguistic Society 32*. Amherst: GLSA, University of Massachusetts, pp. 327–346.

Manzini, M. Rita and Leonardo Savoia. 2011. *Grammatical Categories: Variation in Romance Languages*. Cambridge: Cambridge University Press.

Mosegaard Hansen, Maj-Britt and Jacqueline Visconti. 2009. 'On the diachrony of "reinforced" negation in French and Italian', in Corinne Rossari, Claudia Ricci and Adriana Spiridon (eds.), *Grammaticalization and Pragmatics: Facts, Approaches, Theoretical Issues*. Leiden: Brill, pp. 137–171.

Parry, Mair 2013. 'Negation in the history of Italo-Romance', in David Willis, Christopher Lucas, and Anne Breitbarth (eds), *The History of Negation in the Languages of Europe and the Mediterranean*. Oxford/New York: Oxford University Press, pp. 77–118.

Pescarini, Diego and Penello, Nicoletta 2012. 'L'avverbio *mica* fra widening semantico e restrizioni sintattiche', in Valentina Bambini, Irene Ricci and Pier Marco Bertinetto (eds.), *Linguaggio e cervello - Semantica / Language and the brain - Semantics, Atti del XLII Convegno della Società di Linguistica Italiana (Pisa, Scuola Normale Superiore, 25-27 settembre 2008)*. Roma: Bulzoni. Volume 1.

Poletto, Cecilia. 2008. 'On negation splitting and doubling'. Paper presented at the NORMS Workshop on Negation, University of Oslo, 11–12 March 2008; <http://www.hf.uio.no/tekstlab/negasjon07/Poletto.pdf>.

Poletto, Cecilia. 2014. *Word Order in Old Italian*. Oxford/New York: Oxford University Press.

Rizzi, Luigi. 1982. *Issues in Italian Syntax*. Dordrecht: Foris.

Rizzi, Luigi. 1997. 'The fine structure of the left periphery', in Liliane Haegeman (ed.), *Elements of Grammar*. Dordrecht: Kluwer, pp. 281–337.

Roberts, Ian 2007. *Diachronic Syntax*. Oxford: Oxford University Press.

Roberts, Ian, and Anna Roussou. 2003. *Syntactic Change: A Minimalist Approach to Grammaticalization*. Cambridge: Cambridge University Press.

van Craenenbroeck, Jeroen. 2004. *Ellipsis in Dutch Dialects*. Utrecht: LOT Dissertation Series.

Wallage, Phillip. 2016. 'Identifying the role of pragmatic activation in changes to the expression of English negation', in Pierre Larrivée and Chungmin Lee (eds.), *Negation and Polarity: Experimental Perspectives*. Berlin: Springer, pp. 199–227.

Willis, David. 2011. 'A minimalist approach to Jespersen's Cycle in Welsh', in Dianne Jonas, John Whitman, and Andrew Garrett (eds.), *Grammatical Change: Origins, Natures, Outcomes*. Oxford/New York: Oxford University Press, pp. 93–119.

Willis, David, Lucas, Christopher and Breitbarth, Anne. 2013. 'Comparing diachronies of negation', in David Willis, Christopher Lucas, and Anne Breitbarth (eds), *The History of Negation in the Languages of Europe and the Mediterranean*. Oxford/New York: Oxford University Press, pp. 1–50.

Willmott, Jo. 2013. 'Negation in the history of Greek', in David Willis, Christopher Lucas, and Anne Breitbarth (eds), *The History of Negation in the Languages of Europe and the Mediterranean*. Oxford/New York: Oxford University Press, pp. 299–340.

Zeijlstra, Hedde. 2004. *Sentential Negation and Negative Concord*. PhD Dissertation, University of Amsterdam. Utrecht: LOT Publications.

Mirko Grimaldi
From brain noise to syntactic structures: A formal proposal within the oscillatory rhythms perspective

> ... *The whole burden of philosophy seems to consist in this, from the phenomena of motions to investigate the forces of nature, and from these forces to demonstrate the other phenomena.*
> Newton, 1687/1726

Abstract: The neurobiology investigation of language seems limited by the impossibility to link directly linguistic computations with neural computations. To address this issue, we need to explore the hierarchical interconnections between the investigated fields trying to develop an inter-field theory. Considerable research has realized that event-related fluctuations in rhythmic, oscillatory EEG/MEG activity may provide a new window on the dynamics of functional neuronal networks involved in cognitive processing. Accordingly, this paper aims to outline a formal proposal on neuronal computation and representation of syntactic structures within the oscillatory neuronal dynamics. I briefly present the nature of event-related oscillations and how they work on the base of synchronization and de-synchronization processes. Then, I discuss some theoretical premises assuming that reentrant (hierarchical) properties of synchronized oscillatory rhythms constitute the biological endowment that allow the development of language in humans when exposed to appropriate inputs. The main rhythms involved in language and speech processing are examined: i.e. theta, alpha, beta, and gamma bands. A possible formal representation of the syntactic structures on the base of these oscillatory rhythms is discussed: in this model, the theta-gamma rhythms are cross-frequency coupled into the alpha-gamma-beta and into the gamma-beta-theta rhythms to generate the sentence along reentrant cortico-thalamic pathways through Merge, Label and Move operations. Finally, I present few conclusive remarks within an evolutionary perspective.

Note: I thank Andrea Calabrese, Paolo Lorusso, Alec Marantz, Elliot Murphy, and Leonardo Savoia for their comments on previous versions of the manuscript.

Mirko Grimaldi, Centro di Ricerca Interdisciplinare sul Linguaggio (CRIL) – University of Salento (Lecce, Italy)

https://doi.org/10.1515/9781501505201-017

1 Introduction

The neurobiology investigation of language seeks to uncover the relation between the linguistic computations and its representations in the brain. In doing this, we need to coherently correlate linguistic ontologies – e.g., phoneme, syllable, morpheme, lexicon, syntax and their operations – with neurophysiological ontologies – e.g., neuron, dendrites, spines, synapses, action potentials and their operations. This is a not effortless task, since the two entities seem not directly commensurable. Furthermore, linguistic computation involves a number of fine-grained levels and explicit computational operations – that is how phonemes are combined together to form syllables and words, and how words are combined together to form sentences – whereas neuroscientific approaches to language operate in terms of broader conceptual distinctions (e.g., what areas of brain are deputed to phonology and what to syntax, etc.). These represent what Poeppel & Embick (2005) call, respectively, the Ontological Incommensurability Problem and the Granularity Mismatch Problem (see also Embick & Poeppel 2015; Grimaldi 2012). Thus, a direct reduction of the linguistic primitives into neurobiological primitives is a limitation in the progress of an integrated study of language and brain.

These issues may be solved if we assume that our description of the world is founded on various hierarchies. At one end we have concepts and words we use to capture some facts of the world, at the other end we have the fundamental laws of physics (Feynman 1967). For example, when we say 'heat', we are using a word for a mass of atoms which are jiggling, and when we say 'salt of crystal' fundamentally we are referring to a lot of protons, neutrons, and electrons. So, we may describe the world using ordinary language ignoring the fundamental laws. When we go higher up from this, we found words as 'phoneme' or 'syntax' to capture some computational properties of human language: (i) the fact that we use contrastively specific acoustic-articulatory features of sounds to generate words (as, for instance, the sounds [k] and [r] in ['kæt] *cat* vs. ['ræt] *rat*); (ii) and the fact that sentences are characterized by particular relation among words, also at long distance: e.g., *The book that was lying under all the other books is the most interesting*. As we go up in this hierarchy of complexity, we get words as 'neurons' and 'synapse' that refer to sophisticated chemical and electrical processes in the physical world and that control such computational properties of human language. In brief, we use different concepts and notions (or ontologies) to understand the world at an ever higher level.

How to correlate these different levels of the world knowledge? The best way is to investigate the world at various hierarchies, looking at the whole structural interconnection of the levels. So, we cannot draw carefully a line all the way from one end of the hierarchy to the other looking at the world in term of monolithic entities "[...] because we have only just begun to see that there is this relative hierarchy [...]. The great mass of workers in between, connecting one step to another, are improving all the time our understanding of the world, both from working at the ends and working in the middle, and in that way we are gradually understanding this tremendous world of interconnecting hierarchies" (Feynman 1967: 125–126).

I think this view presupposes the development of an inter-field theory that integrates and bridges fields rather than establishing one complete, unified theory. Inter-field theories can be generated when two fields share an interest in explaining different aspects of the same phenomenon in order to build solid knowledge and relations between the fields. This perspective advocates integration rather than reduction (see for example Murphy & Benitez-Burraco 2017). Accordingly, an inter-field theory should interconnect well-established linguistic computational primitives with neurophsysiological computations responsible for representational processes at the light of the knowledge reached within each research area. This demanding task will lead us to progressively create epistemological bridges between different disciplines. More precisely, the task ahead is to characterize this kind of linked computations and find out how they work in concert producing linguistic behaviors: and step by step it is probable that the 'neurobiology of language' may stand on its own feet integrating the two research traditions and producing an inter-theoretic framework.

Recently, considerable research has achieved that event-related fluctuations in rhythmic, oscillatory electroencephalography (EEG)/magnetoencephalography (MEG) activity may provide a new window on the dynamics of the coupling and uncoupling of functional neuronal networks involved in cognitive processing (Sauseng & Klimesch 2008; Canolty et al. 2010; Donner & Marcus 2011; Hanslmayr et al. 2016). This perspective, as we will see, offers the possibility to directly explore the interconnection between linguistic ontologies and neuronal ontologies. In this work, I aim to sketch a proposal on neuronal computation and representation of syntactic structures within the oscillatory neuronal dynamics along the line of previous studies (Murphy 2015a, 2016; Boeckx & Theofanopoulou 2014). Therefore, I will present and discuss a new representation of syntactic structures reinterpreting the classical tree-diagram according to oscillatory rhythms principles.

2 Electroencephalography, event-related potentials, and event-related oscillations

Electrodes placed in different areas of the scalp provide recording of the brain's electrical activity and noninvasive sensitive measures of brain functions in humans. Regardless of whether an individual receives sensory information or performs higher cognitive processes, the brain exhibit measurable electrical activity. By recording this activity with numerous electrodes, researchers have developed different approaches to determine when (and at least where) in the brain information processing occurs.

A first approach uses to monitor neural phenomena in the continuous EEG/MEG recording of brain activity when the subject is at rest and not involved in a task. It reveals the sum of the random activity of millions of neurons that have similar spatial orientation in the brain. This activity typically fluctuates in wavelike patterns, and depending on the frequency of these patterns, one distinguishes different brain waves called: delta (~0.5–4 Hz), theta (~4–10 Hz), alpha (~8–12 Hz), beta (~12–30 Hz), and gamma (~30–100 Hz) rhythms. Traditionally, variations in the patterns of these brain waves can indicate the level of consciousness, psychological state, or presence of neurological disorders.

A second approach consists to record the EEG/MEG while subjects are performing a sensory or cognitive task. Thereby stimuli are presented to subjects and markers are set into the EEG trace whenever a stimulus is presented. Then a short epoch of EEG/MEG around each marker is used to average all these segments. This is based on the logic that in each trial there is a systematic brain response to a stimulus. Practically, this means that one typically repeats a given experimental paradigm a number of times (say, >30 times), and then one averages the EEG/MEG recordings that are recorded time-locked to the experimental event. However, this systematic response cannot be seen in the raw EEG, as there it is overlaid by a lot of unsystematic background activity (which is simply considered as noise). By averaging all the single epochs that are time-locked to the experimental event, only the systematic brain response should remain (i.e., those generate neural action potentials related to the stimuli), but the background EEG/MEG should approach zero (Sauseng & Klimesch 2008). The noise (which is assumed to be randomly distributed across trials) diminishes each time a trial is added to the average, while the signal (which is assumed to be stationary across trials), gradually emerges out of the noise as more trials are added to the average. These brain responses are named event-related potentials (ERPs) and event-related magnetic fields (ERMFs) reflecting the summated activity of network ensembles active during the task.

ERPs/ERMFs are characterized by specific patterns called 'waveforms' (or 'components'), which are elicited around 50–1000 ms starting from the onset of the stimulus and show positive (P) and negative (N) oscillatory amplitudes (i.e., voltage deflections). For instance, P100, N100, P200, P300, N400, P600 are the principal components elicited during language processing starting from sound perception to semantic and syntactic operations. So, this technique provides millisecond-by-millisecond indices of brain functions and therefore provide excellent temporal resolution.

It is important to realize that the amplitude of an oscillation is, roughly speaking, the size of its (positive or negative) peak deflection relative to some baseline (that is, how big the oscillation is). There is, however, another notion that we need to consider: the phase of an oscillation. Roughly speaking, the phase is the slope (or direction) of the signal at a given one point in time, which is equivalent to the left–right shift of the oscillation. In this respect, ERPs are time- and phase-locked to the event (i.e., the experimental stimuli) that generated the oscillatory activity.

Although the ERP approach has opened an important window on the time course and the neural basis of speech and language processing, more than 100 years after the initial discovery of EEG activity, researchers are turning back to reconsider another aspect of EEG, that is the event-related oscillations. This is because an increasing number of researchers began to realize that an ERP only represents a certain part of the event-related EEG signal. Actually, there is another aspect of extreme interest for the study of cognitive functions: the event-related fluctuations in rhythmic, oscillatory EEG/MEG activity. This view, indeed, might provide a new window on the dynamics of the coupling and uncoupling of functional networks involved in cognitive processing (Varela et al., 2001). In fact, substantial literature now indicates that some ERP features may arise from changes in the dynamics of ongoing EEG rhythms/oscillations of different frequency bands that reflect ongoing sensory and/or cognitive processes (Başar 1998; Başar et al. 2001; Buzsaki 2006). More precisely, the EEG oscillations that are measured in a resting state become organized, amplified, and/or coupled during cognitive processes. It has been argued that ERP does not simply emerge from evoked, latency–fixed polarity responses that are additive to and independent of ongoing EEG (Sauseng et al., 2007): instead, evidence suggests that early ERP components are generated by a superposition of ongoing EEG oscillations that reset their phases in response to sensory input, (i.e., the external or internal stimuli generating cognitive activities). Therefore, event-related oscillation, further than to have the time-locked EEG information, permits to retrieve the non-phase locked EEG information related to the cognitive activity induced by the stimulus.

Within this perspective, ongoing cerebral activity can no longer be thought of as just relatively random background noise (the non-phase EEG activity) that must be removed in order to see the event-related responses, but as a whole containing crucial information on the dynamical activity of neural networks: thus, the EEG and ERP are the same neuronal event, as the ERP is generated because of stimulus-evoked phase perturbations in the ongoing EEG. A fundamental feature of the phase-resetting hypothesis is that following the presentation of a stimulus, the phases of ongoing EEG rhythms are shifted to lock to the stimulus. From this, it follows that during pre-stimulus intervals, the distribution of the phase at each EEG frequency would be random, whereas upon stimulus presentation, the phases would be set (or reset) to specific values (for each frequency). The resetting of the phases causes an ERP waveform to appear in the average in the form of an event-related oscillation (Makeig et al. 2002; Penny et al. 2002; Klimesch et al. 2004): cf. Fig. 1.

Unlike ERP (based on the analysis of components), event-related oscillation is based on the time-frequency analyses (e.g., Gross, 2014). One such method is wavelet analysis.

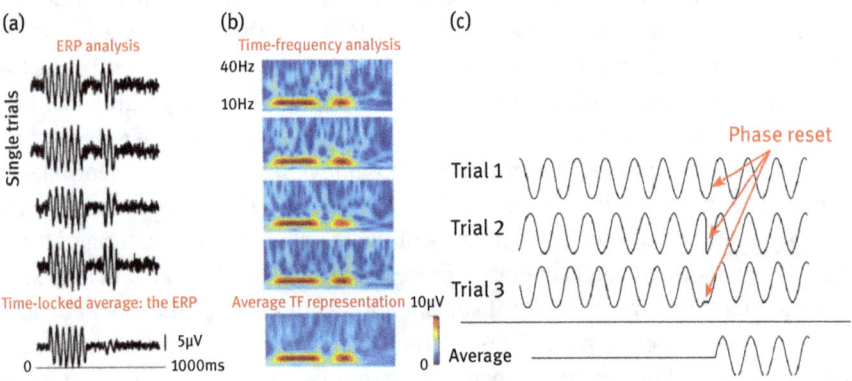

Fig. 1: Simulated EEG data illustrating the difference between phase-locked (evoked) activity and non-phase-locked (induced) activity. (A): Single-trial EEG time courses showing two consecutive event-related responses (an amplitude increase at 10 Hz). The first response is phase-locked with respect to the reference time-point (t = 0), and as a result this evoked response is adequately represented in the average ERP. The second response is time-locked, but not phase-locked to t = 0, and as a result this induced response is largely lost in the average ERP. (B): time-frequency (TF) representations of each single trial, with red colors coding for the amplitude increase at 10 Hz. Crucially, the average TF representation contains both the phase-locked and the non-phase-locked responses. (C): simulated data illustrating the principle of phase resetting. Three single trials are shown whose phases are not aligned initially. Red arrows indicate the point in time at which an event-induced phase reset occurs. The bottom trace shows what the average ERP would look like if a sufficient number of such trials (in practice >30 trials) are averaged. Adapted from Bastiaansen, Mazaheri & Jensen (2012).

The general idea is that not all relevant EEG activity is strictly phase-locked (or evoked) to the event of interest (Buszáki, 2006). Obviously, this activity shortly before stimulus onset is mostly not visible in ERPs due to cancellation; nevertheless, this pre-stimulus baseline activity may have a crucial impact on the observed ERPs (Klimesch, 2011). Time-frequency analyses enable us to determine the presence of oscillatory patterns in different frequency bands over time. Thus, with wavelet analyses, it can be established whether oscillatory activity in a specific frequency band, often expressed in power (squared amplitude), increases or decreases relative to a certain event, as represented in Fig. 1.

The importance in considering the non-phase locked event-related oscillations consists in the fact that, contrary to phase-locked responses as ERPs, they reflect the extent to which the underlying neuronal activity synchronizes. Synchronization and de-synchronization are related to the coupling and uncoupling of functional networks in cortical and subcortical areas of the brain (see, e. g., Varela et al., 2001). This aspect, of course, is related to how different types of information, which are stored in different parts of the network, are integrated during computational and representational processes. Importantly, elements pertaining to one and the same functional network are identifiable as such by the fact that they fire synchronously at a given frequency. This frequency specificity allows the same neuron (or neuronal pool) to participate at different times in different representations. Hence, synchronous oscillations in a wide range of frequencies are considered to play a crucial role in linking areas that are part of the same functional network. Importantly, in addition to recruiting all the relevant network elements, oscillatory neuronal synchrony serves to bind together the information represented in the different elements (Gray et al. 1989).

3 Theoretical premises

Inspired by Başar (2011), I assume that cognitive computational and representational processes are intrinsic to brain oscillatory activity. This oscillatory activity is characterized by coherent cooperation between distant structures through different oscillatory phases. Thus, according to Lasheley (1929), the brain operates as a "whole" thanks to rhythmic oscillations that are selectively distributed in the whole brain: it is the coordination and coherence of oscillations that generate parallel sensory-cognitive processing. Research has shown that neural population in cortical and subcortical areas (e.g., cortex, hippocampus or cerebellar cortex) are all tuned to the very same frequency ranges (Steriade et al., 1990; Başar, 1998). These findings support the hypothesis that all brain networks communicate by means of the same set of frequency codes of rhythmic oscillations. This presupposes that the intrinsic oscillatory activity of each single neuron shapes the natural frequencies of neural assemblies, that is the delta, theta, alpha, beta, and gamma frequencies.

As noted above, ERP components seem generated by a superposition of ongoing EEG oscillations that reset their phases in response to sensory input: this superposition principle suggests that there exists synergy between oscillations during performance of sensory-cognitive tasks. Accordingly, integrative brain function necessary for sensory-cognitive processing may be obtained through the combined action of multiple oscillations. Also, the superposition principle is crucial for memory functions directly correlated with all brain functions, and, in particular, with speech and language functions. This is a crucial point, because memory-related oscillations must have dynamic properties evolving in different hierarchical states that take place along a continuum where the boundaries of memory states integrate into each other. In line with Murphy (2015a), I assume that such property plays a key role in the basic computations that characterize the Faculty of Language: that is, Merge, Label, Move and its correlated Spell-Out operations (Chomsky 1995, 2001, 2013). Actually, these computational operations need that 'mnemonic objects' – concepts, words and related information determining, for example, agreement and case, etc. – are dynamically manipulated thanks to bidirectional exchange of signals along reciprocal axonal fibers linking two or more brain areas from thalamus to cerebral cortex and back.

According to Edelman (1989, 1993, 2004) a large and diverse body of evidence suggests that intermittent signaling along reentrant paths is critical to a variety of neural functions in vertebrate brains, ranging from perceptual categorization to motor coordination and cognition. Reentry takes on a variety of forms enabling many different processes. These processes facilitate the coordination of neuronal firing in anatomically and functionally segregated cortical areas. By these means they bind cross-modal sensory features by synchronizing and integrating patterns of neural activity in different brain regions. Reentrant signaling is a ubiquitous and dominant structural and functional motif of vertebrate telencephalons. Reentry has, conversely, rarely, if ever, been characterized in an invertebrate nervous system, and it may be a relatively recent evolutionary innovation. Reentrant processes are those that involve one localized population of excitatory neurons simultaneously both stimulating, and being stimulated by, another such population: the structural architecture that generates this process is likewise referred to as reentrant. Experimental evidence converges to indicates that processes of reentry play widespread and essential roles in vertebrate brain function, evolution, and development (Edelman & Gally 2011). The reciprocal exchange of signals among neural networks in distributed cortical and cortico-thalamic areas – when combined with appropriate mechanisms for synaptic plasticity – results in the spatiotemporal integration of patterns of neural network activity (cf. Fig. 2). This process may be considered a kind of neural recursion that allows the brain to categorize sensory input, remember and manipulate mental objects, generate motor commands and/or cognitive activity. In particular, it has been suggested that the hippocampal declarative memory system may control cognitive functions that require on-line integration of multiple sources of information, such as on-line speech and language perception and production processing (Duff & Brown-Schmidt 2012).

Within the cortico-thalamic pathway, the basal ganglia assume strategic function for speech and language processing. Thanks to the thalamus, the basal ganglia, the cerebellum, and the hippocampus interface with the cortex in a reciprocal fashion (Theofanopoulou & Boeckx 2016; Hickok 2012). The basal ganglia process information indirectly in a set of loops, whereby they receive input from the cortex and return it to the cortex via the thalamus. In that way, the basal ganglia modify the timing and amount of activity that leaves the cortex and travels down the pyramidal pathway effectively modulating the neural activity for motor and cognitive processes (cf. Fig. 2).

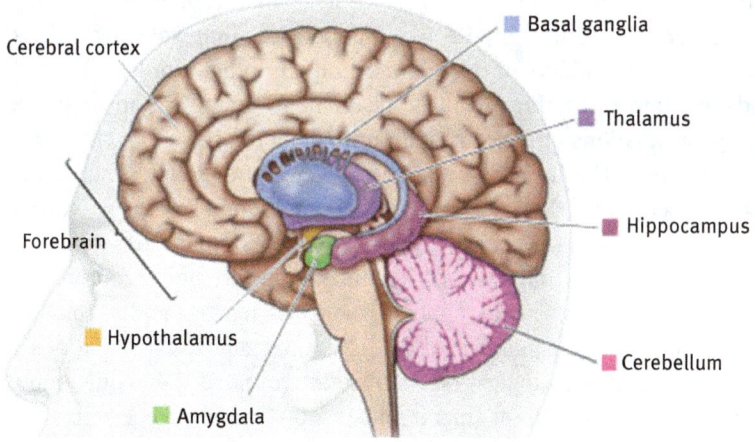

Fig. 2: Cortical and cortico-thalamic structures forming reentrant synchronized pathways. Adapted from http://www.proprofs.com/flashcards/story.php?title=intro-mind-and-brain–topic-2-foundation-brains.

In particular, basal ganglia dysfunction in humans can result in a subcortical dementia where an afflicted individual will perseverate, finding it difficult, in some cases impossible, to change the direction of a thought process (Flowers & Robertson 1985), or comprehend sentences that has moderately complex syntax (Lieberman et al. 1992). Furthermore, the basal ganglia are also involved in associative learning (Lieberman 2009). Although it is clear that basal ganglia are not directly involved in core semantic operations (their lesion does not generate semantic syndrome), they are recruited in the intention to retrieve lexical items during word generation regardless of the semantic category (Crosson, Benjamin, Levy 2007).

In generating sentences, we access to the knowledge system (KS): that is, the complex of processes represented by the long-term memory system together with the procedural and perceptual system (Klimesh 2012). The basic idea is that the KS interacts with the working memory (a multi-component system that holds and manipulates information in short-term memory) in a way that traces stored in the KS are used for short-term storage (Klimesch, Schack 2003). This is possible thanks to the synchronization property of neurons according to which different brain (cortical and sub-cortical) regions may be synchronized through phase amplitude cross-frequency coupling whereby phases of lower frequencies modulates the power of higher frequencies: for instance, the coupling between the phase of theta and the power of gamma (Hanslmayr et al. 2016).

I assume that synchronization reflects a basic computational principle that underlies the dynamic control of effective interactions along selective subsets of the anatomically possible neuronal connections. In other words, selectively distributed oscillatory rhythms act as resonant communication networks through large populations of neurons, with functional relations to memory and integrative functions. The implication is that the cross-frequency synchronization between oscillatory rhythms reflects the interaction between working memory and the KS. Thus, the access to the KS and the computations generated are a continuous process dynamically organized; furthermore, the memory functions from the simplest sensory memories to the most complex semantic and episodic memories are manifested in distributed multiple oscillations in the whole brain. On this biological mechanism is grounded the acquisition of natural languages. The reentrant (hierarchical) properties of synchronized oscillatory rhythms constitute the biological endowment that allow the development of grammar in human beings when exposed to some appropriate inputs. Inputs generating computations and representations are structured in memory according to universal biological constrains and some degrees of freedom (options) that the neural system presents: these optionality is at the basis of variation (and micro-variation) characterizing natural languages.

4 From oscillatory rhythms to syntactic structures

4.1 Functionality of rhythms for language and speech processing

Theta oscillations can be found in the human cortex, the hippocampus, and the hypothalamus. Theta oscillations seem to be important for a variety of cognitive functions. It was shown that hippocampal and cortical theta activity is associated with virtual navigation, declarative memory processes, successful memory encoding, the amount of information held in memory, and episodic memory processing (Sauseng & Klimesch 2008). Theta power increases during language processing have been related to the retrieval and encoding of lexical semantic information (Bastiaansen, et al. 2008; Bastiaansen & Hagoort 2015). Additionally, working memory-load-dependent increase of theta activity has been suggested: i.e., when the amount of encoded information increases, theta activity grows stronger (Jensen & Tesche 2002). Weiss et al. (2005) found higher anterior–posterior theta coherence over the left hemisphere during the processing of relative clauses and suggest it may be related to the initiation of linguistic analysis since coherence during linguistic analysis is higher in the left hemisphere. Thus, it seems that theta activity could be a correlate of control processes when multiple items have to be held in working memory to be managed or bound in comprehensive memory entry (Lisman & Idiart 1995). Indeed, recent studies suggest that higher gamma frequency oscillations can be nested into theta cycles. This seems to reflect organization of multiple items into sequential working memory representations or integration between sensory bottom-up and top-down memory representations (Sauseng et al. 2010).

Gamma oscillations, on the other hand, are cortically generated and arise from intrinsic membrane properties of interneurons or from neocortical excitatory-inhibitory circuits (Sauseng & Klimesch 2008). Actually, synchronization phenomena of this brain rhythm were related to binding of information. More recently, effects at human gamma frequency were also reported for the encoding, retention and retrieval of information independent of sensory modality. It has also been discussed that gamma binds large-scale brain networks (Kahana, 2006). Recently, Bastiaansen & Hagoort (2015) have clearly showed that gamma band neuronal synchronization is involved in sentence level semantic unification operations. This gamma-band effects have maxima over the left posterior temporal and the left frontal scalp, which is well compatible with the notion that semantic unification is a result of a dynamic interplay between left posterior superior/medial temporal gyrus and inferior frontal gyrus. Interestingly, a recent ECoG study (Rapela 2016) showed that rhythmic speech production (i.e., sequence of syllables) modulates the power of high-gamma oscillations over the ventral sensory motor cortex, a cortical region that controls the vocal articulators, and the power of beta oscillations over the auditory cortex (due to the auditory feedback necessary control acoustic-articulatory outputs). He found significant coupling between the phase of brain oscillations at the frequency of speech production and their amplitude in the high-gamma range (i.e., phase-amplitude coupling, PAC). Furthermore, the data showed that brain oscillations at the frequency of speech production were organized as traveling waves and synchronized to the rhythm of speech production.

The functional relevance of alpha oscillations is very widespread. There is strong evidence that alpha amplitudes are related to the level of cortical activation. A strong alpha activity is associated with cortical deactivation or inhibition, but it is also involved in highly specific perceptual, attentional, and executive processes functions in working memory processes as in responding selectively to semantic task demands (Klimesch et al. 2005; Bartsch et al. 2015). Actually, Klimesch (2012) argues that alpha-band oscillations reflect the temporal structure of one of the most basic cognitive processes, which may be described as 'knowledge-based consciousness' and which enables 'semantic orientation' via controlled access to information stored in the knowledge system. Furthermore, Benedek et al. (2011) found frontal alpha synchronization during convergent and divergent thinking only, under exclusive top-down control (high internal processing demands), suggesting that these rhythms are related to high internal processing demands which are typically involved in creative thinking. Finally, Strauß et al. (2015) demonstrated that alpha phase – both before and during the presentation of word or word-like stimuli – predicts the accuracy of lexical decisions in noise.

As alpha rhythms, also beta oscillations are cortically generated, due to their local strictness, although widespread cortical beta networks in humans have been shown (Gross et al. 2004). From a functional perspective beta oscillations have mainly been associated with motor activity, but beta has also been suggested to play an important role during attention or higher cognitive functions (Razumnikova 2004), as for binding mechanisms during language processing (Weiss & Mueller 2003). Indeed, it was also proposed that beta frequencies are used for higher-level interaction between multimodal areas involving more distant structures and the binding of temporally segregated events, which is especially important for language processing (Donner & Siegel 2011; Lam et al. 2016). Generally, it has been shown that target words for syntactically (Davidson & Indefrey 2007; Bastiaansen et al. 2010; Pérez et al. 2012; Kielar et al. 2014) and semantically (Luo et al. 2010; Wang et al. 2012; Kielar et al. 2014) acceptable sentences beta power was higher than target words resulted in syntactic or semantic incongruities. Accordingly, Lewis & Bastiaansen (2015) and Lewis et al. (2016) suggest that the increased beta activity reflects the active maintenance of the current neurocognitive network responsible for the construction and representation of the sentence-level meaning. It may also indicate a greater reliance on top-down predictions based on that sentence-level meaning (i.e., the increased activity may be related to greater weighting of the top-down signal based on the current generative model), in order to actively try to integrate the new linguistic input into the current sentence-level meaning representation. Along this line, beta synchronization has been correlated with the binding of semantic features of different lexical categories (Weiss & Mueller 2003). Crucially, Bastiaansen & Hagoort (2015) performed an elegant experiment showing that beta-band power is strictly related to syntactic structure building at the sentence level with a maximum around the vertex. Weiss et al. (2005), on the other hand, suggest that while theta changes may be associated with memory processes and gamma with attentional effort, beta bands may be activated with semantic–pragmatic integration.

All in all, (i) theta rhythms seem involved in retrieving lexical semantic information and controlling processes with multiple items. This process may be supported by the nesting of gamma frequency oscillations into theta cycles reflecting organization of multiple items into sequential working memory representations or integration; (ii) gamma-band neuronal synchronization on the one hand seems related to sentence level semantic unification, on the other hand to speech production; (iii) alpha phase acts not only in decisional weighting, but also in semantic orientation, in creative thinking, lexical decisions; (iv) beta synchronization serves to bind distributed sets of neurons into a coherent representation of (memorized) contents during language processing, and, in particular, to building syntactic structures. It is important to note that it is impossible to assign a single function to a given type of oscillatory activity (Başar et al. 2001). It is thus unlikely that, for instance, theta has a single role in language processing. In fact, theta's role and its varying patterns of coherence as a function of task demands may be better seen in its relationship to beta and gamma (and same thing is true for the other oscillatory rhythms). Accordingly, it may be important to consider the simultaneous changes in the coherence patterns in the different frequency ranges.

4.2 An inter-field model for syntactic structure generation

The challenge now is to develop an inter-field model that coherently interconnect and integrate neural computations (i.e., those intrinsic to oscillatory rhythms) with syntactic computations assumed as primitives within linguistic theory. The best candidate to sketch an interconnected neurobiological model is the fundamental structure-building operation of natural language syntax (Chomsky 1995, 2002, 2013): i.e., Merge and Label – or, according to Hornstein (2009) – Concatenation plus Label. Merge is an operation that takes a number of syntactic objects (lexical items) and join them together to form a unit. Merge strings together two elements when one selects the other and the element which projects (assigns the label to the whole structure) is the selector. The selector is also called the "head" of the construction. Note that Merge is recursive: so, we can string together multiple instances of Merge to create ever larger structures. For instance, image to realize the sentence in (1):

(1) *The cat lays on the carpet*

Merge takes the two lexical items *the* and *cat* and form a new object: [the cat]. The new unit has a label, which is inherited from one of the merged elements, i.e. the determiner, forming the Determiner Phrase (DP) [$_{DP}$ the cat]. The lexical items *on the carpet* fall on the same operation: in this case the element that assigns the label to the structure is the preposition *on* forming the Prepositional Phrase (PP) [$_{PP}$ on the carpet] which also contains the DP [$_{DP}$ the carpet]. The item *lays* is then merged with the PP [on the carpet] generating the Verbal Phrase (VP) [$_{VP}$ lays on the carpet]. The VP is merged with the DP [$_{DP}$ the cat]. Then the VP is merged with the Inflectional Phrase (IP) – a phrase that have inflectional properties – generating the sentence in (1): [$_{IP}$ [$_{DP}$ the cat [$_{VP}$ lays [$_{PP}$ on [$_{DP}$ the carpet]]]]].

According to the picture above outlined, I assume that cyclic, dynamic, and hierarchical oscillations cross-frequency coupling synchronize sub-cortical and cortical regions generating a functional neuronal network and ensuring bottom-up and top-down computations and communication. The strength of phase-amplitude cross-frequency coupling differs across brain areas in relation to cognitive processes accomplished: while high-frequency (beta, gamma) brain activity reflects local domains of cortical processing, low-frequency (theta, alpha) brain rhythms are dynamically entrained across distributed brain regions by both external sensory input and internal cognitive events. Thus, cross-frequency coupling may serve as a mechanism to transfer information from large-scale brain networks operating at behavioral timescales to the fast, local cortical processing required for effective computation and synaptic modification, integrating functional systems across multiple spatiotemporal scales (Canolty & Knight 2010).

In generating a sentence, I suggest the following neuronal operations controlled by oscillatory rhythms in generating syntactic structures:

- First of all, a speaker needs to access to the knowledge system where long-term memory interacts with working memory in retrieving conceptual objects (within the hippocampal and hypothalamic structures) mapping them onto lexical items (at the cortical level within fronto-temporal structures): this step is controlled by nested *theta-gamma* oscillations which organize multiple items into sequential representations between sensory bottom-up and top-down memory representations. So, following Jensen and Lisman (1998) and Murphy (2016a), I postulate that theta and gamma interact in the process of storing lexical representations in declarative memory.
- Cyclic coupling of *alpha-gamma-beta* rhythms are involved in merging and labelling lexical items. In particular, alpha oscillations (implicated in lexical decision) control what lexical items, selected to realize an appropriate sentence, may be grouped into units identifying phrases typologies; gamma rhythms, on the other hand, rule the overall process of merging and labelling (this process probably needs high frequency oscillation in order to rapidly control and concatenate a large number of lexical items, where also morphological information are computed); finally, beta bands control processes concerning inflectional properties of the syntactic structures generating a coherent representation of sentences. These rhythms are likely responsible for the Spell-Out transfer operation to conceptual-intentional (CI) interface.
- *Gamma-beta-theta* oscillations are deputed to supervise the Spell-Out transfer to sensory-motor (SM) interface. More precisely, this cross-frequency bands may control the production of sequence of syllables: they may have a crucial role in cyclic interacting with long-term memory and working memory. Actually, for what concerns speech perception processing, it has been suggested that a remarkable correspondence between average durations of speech units and the frequency ranges of cortical oscillations exists: phonetic features are associated with high gamma and beta oscillations, and syllables and words with theta oscillations (Giraud & Poeppel 2012). So, I hypothesize that the same mechanism can be reflected at the production level to control the speech perception-production interface (as recent data suggest: Rapela 2016). In other words, the conceptual objects retrieved by speakers from long-term memory – where I hypothesized the theta-gamma oscillation are involved – should contain not only lexical and morpho-syntactic information but also phonetic and phonological

information. At a certain point of the computational and representational processes the former are Spelled-Out to CI interface and the latter to SM interface resorting to cyclic cross-frequency synchronization.

For what concerns the SM interface, it should be interesting for future research to test whether also delta bands are involved a suggested by recent perceptive data (Giraud & Poeppel 2012). In fact, low-frequency oscillations at the delta (1–3 Hz) band seem to correspond to slower modulations such as phrase level prosody (Ghitza 2011). It is well known, indeed, that prosodic patterns drive the syntactic derivation and the formation of the prosodic representation in compliance with the T-model of grammar (e.g., see Bocci 2013; Hauser, Chomsky, Fitch 2002).

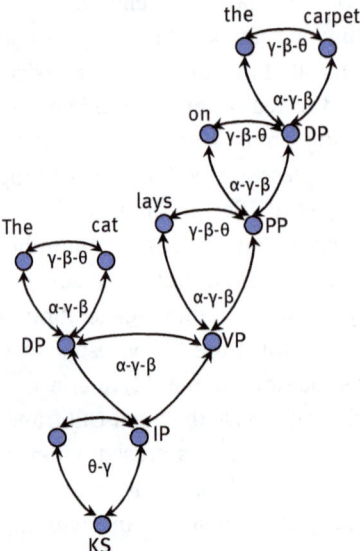

Fig. 3: Neuronal tree representation of the sentence *The cat lays on the carpet*. Hypothesized oscillatory rhythms involved in computational and representational processes are highlighted. KS = knowledge system; IP = Inflectional Phrase; DP = Determiner Phrase; VP = Verbal Phrase; PP = Prepositional Phrase. Starting from the KS, the θ-γ rhythms are cross-frequency coupled into the α-γ-β and into γ-β-θ rhythms to generate the sentence along reentrant cortico-thalamic pathways through Merge, Label and Move operations. The vertical arrows between the nodes indicate the ascending information conveyed by thalamic nuclei while the horizontal arrows between the nodes indicate the descending information from fronto-temporal cortical areas.

The formal proposal here outlined may be represented through a neuronal tree, as illustrated in Fig. 3. The hypothesis is that the neuronal tree has a bottom-up generation in line with the idea that sub-cortical oscillations are cyclically and selectively cross-frequency structured with upper cortical oscillations forming a neuronal network and allowing the brain to operate as a "whole" in real time: as above noted, this mechanism ensures bottom-up and top-down computations. If we want to develop an inter-field model aiming to integrate neural computation with those computations assumed to play a crucial role in syntactic structures, we need to link the neuronal primitives with the linguistic primitives as much as possible.

Accordingly, I propose to start representing the retrieval of the conceptual objects from the KS (in the thalamic nuclei) where cross-frequency coupling of theta-gamma oscillations evaluate and broadly organize them into lexical times. Then, phase resetting (cf. Fig. 2) synchronizes the coupling of alpha-gamma-beta rhythms generating Merge, Label and Inflectional computations together with the representation of the structure (a transfer to CI interface is possible at this point). Finally, a subsequent phase resetting into gamma-beta-theta rhythms projects syntactic structures to SM interface. The arrows in Fig. 1 represent the idea that computational and representational processes are guided by a cyclic principle that ensures ongoing communication between sub-cortical and cortical area along the entire process. The cyclic principle is also suitable to account for long-distance relations, movements and recursion.

5 Conclusion and further remarks

Based on the idea that language computational and representational processes are intrinsic to brain oscillatory activity, I developed a (preliminary) interdisciplinary formal proposal attempting to narrow the gap between linguistic and neuroscience for what concern the primitives assumed in syntactic computations (along the line of previous proposals: Murphy 2015a, 2016). This role assigned to oscillatory rhythms is justified by diverse body of evidence that signaling along reentrant cortical and cortico-thalamic areas paths is critical to cognition. Accordingly, within the model syntactic structures are derived by the specific functions assigned to cross-frequency coupled oscillatory rhythms: starting from the KS, the theta-gamma rhythms are cross-frequency coupled into the alpha-gamma-beta and into the gamma-beta-theta rhythms to generate the sentence along reentrant cortico-thalamic pathways through Merge, Label and Move operations. Crucially, this kind of model permits that both linguistic primitives and neurobiological primitives may be coherently investigated (an empirically tested) within a neurobiological perspective. The ultimate goal is to demonstrate whether cognitive brain functions are really represented by its oscillatory activity. This is probably the paradigm change that Mountcastle (1998) had announced for brain sciences toward the end of the last century, *pace* Chomsky (2000).

This perspective offers the basis to further reflect on the issue concerning what is special about language and its evolutionary genesis. Hauser, Chomsky

& Fitch (2002: 1573) suggest that the Narrow Language Faculty – the computational mechanism of recursion – is recently evolved and unique to our species (recursion referring to a procedure that calls itself, or to a constituent that contains a constituent of the same kind). They propose that Narrow Language Faculty comprises only the core computational mechanisms of recursion as they appear in narrow syntax and the mappings to the interfaces with conceptual knowledge (and intentions) and perception-production mechanisms (see Pinker & Jackendoff 2005 for a critical discussion). More precisely, what the authors suggested is that a significant piece of the linguistic machinery entails recursive operations (Merge at least), and that these recursive operations must interface with SM and CI (and thus include aspects of phonology, formal semantics and the lexicon insofar as they satisfy the uniqueness condition of Narrow Language Faculty). Thus, the hypothesis focuses on a known property of human language that provides its most powerful and unusual signature: discrete infinity (Fitch, Hauser & Chomsky 2005: 182). The question is: how this property emerged? Is it an adaptive phenomenon – shared with other species and underwent refunctionalization at a certain evolutionary stage – or is unique to human language faculty and emerged by evolutionary selection? According to Hauser, Chomsky & Fitcht (2002), the latter hypothesis seems the more plausible.

As I have above discussed (cf. Section 3), reentrant neuronal activity leads to a kind of neuronal recursion: this represents a fundamental feature of thalamo-cortical activity characterizing only vertebrate nervous system (that is humans and other species). Reentrant activity represents not simple feedbacks but functions in a network as recursive multiple pathways, which update iteratively and hierarchically on a time scale of tens to hundreds of milliseconds, rapidly converging to the dynamic core's synaptically connected neuronal network. It implies that computations in the brain assume primarily the form of interaction (if we accept early theoretical ideas that computation is interaction: Feynman 1996): i.e., intracellular interactions that generate recursive and integrated action potentials. Hence, it seems that recursive property is not exclusive to human brain and, most importantly, to human language.

If this primary mechanism is shared with non-human species, what is special to human language? What is absent in non-human vertebrate brains is the possibility to synchronize neuronal activity along a functional cortico-thalamic network: that is, for what concerns language computations, the synchronization of fronto-temporo-parietal cluster of neurons among themselves and with the thalamic nuclei (Edelman & Tononi, 2000). Reentrant activity per se is sufficient to generate primary conceptualization and categorization of the world (i.e., primary consciousness). However, high-order conceptualization and categorizations are possible only when long-term memory may be synchronously integrated with working memory to result in continuous computational and representational processes (i.e., secondary consciousness). This evolutionary specialization may be ascribed to functional synchronization and de-synchronization (coupling and uncoupling) of oscillatory rhythms that recursively bind together different conceptual objects (the words and all the relevant information) in a specie-specific recursive mechanism: that functional to build syntactic structures. So, some properties of the vertebrate brain may have been functionally reused during the emerging of unique cognitive abilities related to specific properties of natural languages: this may represent the Narrow Language Faculty recently evolved. While the hierarchy of brain rhythms themselves may be preserved, it is crucially their cross-frequency coupling relations which are at the basis of human language specialization (Murphy 2016b). I cannot address here the question whether Merge, Label or Concatenation plus Label (Hornstein 2009) represent the computational core of syntax computation, for which see Murphy (2015a,b; 2016a,b). But from the perspective outlined it seems problematic to exclusively assign to Merge the single computation operation, unique to language, to distinguishing it from other cognitive domains

To conclude, it is probable that synchronization of oscillatory rhythms has contributed to the emersion of a new connectivity that interconnected specific brain regions forming a fronto-temporo-parietal circuit that provides a more complete mechanism for richer representational capacities, viz. recursive capacities (Boeckx in press), together, of course, with the thalamo-basal ganglia loop.

References

Bartsch, Felix, Hamuni, Gilava, Miskovic, Vladimir, Lang, Peter J. & Keil Andreas 2015. Oscillatory brain activity in the alpha range is modulated by the content of word-prompted mental imagery. *Psychophysiology* 52(6). 727–735. http://doi.org/10.1111/psyp.12405.
Başar, Erol 1998. Brain Function and Oscillations: Vol. I. Integrative Brain Function. *Neurophysiology and Cognitive Processes*. Heidelberg: Springer-Verlag.
Başar, Erol 2011. *Brain-Body-Mind in the Nebulous Cartesian System: A Holistic Approach by Oscillations*. New York: Springer. 10.1007/978-1-4419-6136-5.
Başar, Erol, Başar-Erogluc, Canan, Karakaş, Sirel, Schürmann, Martin 2001. Gamma, alpha, delta, and theta oscillations govern cognitive processes. *International Journal of Psychophysiology* 39. 241–248.
Bastiaansen, Marcel & Hagoort, Peter 2015. Frequency-based Segregation of Syntactic and Semantic Unification during Online Sentence Level Language Comprehension. *Journal of Cognitive Neuroscience* 27(11). 2095–2107. doi:10.1162/jocn_a_00829.

Bastiaansen, Marcel, Magyari, Lilla, & Hagoort, Peter 2010. Syntactic unification operations are reflected in oscillatory dynamics during on-line sentence comprehension. *Journal of Cognitive Neuroscience* 22, 1333–1347.doi:10.1162/jocn. 2009.21283.

Bastiaansen, Marcel, Mazaheri, Ali & Jensen, Ole 2012. Beyond ERPs: Oscillatory Neuronal Dynamics. In Emily S. Kappenman & Steven J. Luck (Eds.), *The Oxford Handbook of Event-Related Potential Components*, 1–21. Oxford: Oxford University Press.

Bastiaansen, Marcel, Oostenveld, Robert, Jensen, Ole, & Hagoort, Peter 2008. I see what you mean: Theta power increases are involved in the retrieval of lexical semantic information. *Brain and Language* 106. 15–28.

Benedek, Mathias, Bergner, Sabine, Könen, Tanja, Fink, Andreas, Neubauer, Aljoscha C. 2011. Neuropsychologia EEG alpha synchronization is related to top-down processing in convergent and divergent thinking. *Neuropsychologia* 49(12). 3504–3511.

Bocci, Giuliano. 2013. *The Syntax–Prosody Interface A cartographic perspective with evidence from Italian*. Amsterdam / Philadelphia: Benjamins.

Boeckx, Cedric (in press), A conjecture about the neural basis of recursion in light of descent with modification. *Journal of Neurolinguistics*. http://dx.doi.org/10.1016/j.jneuroling.2016.08.003

Boeckx, Cedric & Theofanopoulou, Constantin 2014. A multidimensional interdisciplinary framework for linguistics: the lexicon as a case study. *Journal of Cognitive Sciences* 15. 403–420.

Buzsáki, Gyorgy 2006. *Rhythms of the Brain*. Oxford: Oxford University Press.

Canolty, Ryan T. & Knight, Robert T. 2010. The functional role of cross-frequency coupling. *Trends in Cognitive Sciences* 14(11). 506–515. doi:10.1016/j.tics.2010.09.001.

Chomsky, Noam 1995. The Minimalist Program. Cambridge (MA): The MIT Press.

Chomsky, Noam 2000. *New horizons in the study of language and mind*. Cambridge, MA: Cambridge University Press.

Chomsky, Noam 2001. Derivation by phase. In Michael Kenstowicz & Ken Hale (Eds.), *A Life in Language*, 1–52, Cambridege: MIT Press.

Chomsky, Noam 2013. Problems of projections. *Lingua* 130: 33–49.

Crosson, Bruce, Benjamin, Michelle, Levy, Ilana F. 2007. Role of the basal ganglia in language and semantics: Supporting cast. In John Hart J. & Michael A. Kraut (Eds.), *Neural Basis of Semantic Memory*, 219–243. New York: Cambridge University Press.

Davidson, Duglas J. & Indefrey, Peter 2007. An inverse relation between event-related and time-frequency violation responses in sentence processing. *Brain Research* 1158. 81–92. doi: 10.1016/j.brainres.2007.04.082.

Donner, Tobias. H. & Siegel, Marcus. 2011. A framework for local cortical oscillation patterns. *Trends in Cognitive Sciences* 15. 191–199.

Duff Melissa C. & Brown-Schmidt Sarah 2012. The hippocampus and the flexible use and processing of language. *Frontiers in Human Neuroscience* 6. 69.

Edelman, Gerald M. 1989. *The Remembered Present: A Biological Theory of Consciousness*. NewYork: Basic Books.

Edelman, Gerald M. 1993. Neural Darwinism: selection and reentrant signaling in higher brain function. *Neuron* 10, 115–125. doi:10.1016/0896-6273(93)90304-A.

Edelman, Gerald M. 2004. *Wider than the Sky*. New Haven: Yale University Press.

Edelman, Gerald M. & Gally, Joseph A. 2001. Degeneracy and complexity in biological systems. *Proceedings of the National Academy of Sciences U.S.A.* 98. 13763–13768. doi: 10.1073/pnas.231499798.

Edelman, Gerald M. & Tononi, Giulio 1999. Increased synchronization of neuro- magnetic responses during conscious perception. *Journal of Neuroscience* 19. 5435–5448.

Edelman, Gerald M., Tononi, Giulio. 2000. *A Universe of Consciousness. How Matter Becomes Imagination*, New York: Basic Books.

Edelman, Gerald M. & Gally, Joseph A. & Baars, Bernard J. 2011. Biology of consciousness. *Frontiers in Psychology* 2: 4. doi: 10.3389/fpsyg.2011.00004.

Embick, David, & Poeppel, David. 2015. Towards a computational(ist) neurobiology of language: correlational, integrated and explanatory neurolinguistics. *Language and Cognitive Neuroscience* 30. 357–366. doi:10.1080/23273798.2014.980750.

Feynman, Richard P. 1967. *The character of Physical low*. Cambridge, MA: The M.I.T. Press.

Feynman, Rychard P. 1996. *Feynman lectures on computation*. Reading, Massachusetts: Addison-Wesley Publishing Company, Inc.

Fitch, Tecumseh W., Hauser, Marc D. & Chomsky Noam 2005. The evolution of the language faculty: clarifications and implications. *Cognition* 97(2). 179–210.

Flowers Kim A., Robertson Carl 1985. The effect of Parkinson's disease on the ability to maintain a mental set. *Journal of Neurological and Neurosurgery Psychiatry* 48. 517–529. 10.1136/jnnp.48.6.517

Giraud, Anna Lise & Poeppel, David 2012. Cortical oscillations and speech processing: emerging computational principles and operations. *Nature Neuroscience*. 15. 511–517. doi:10.1038/nn.3063

Gray, Charles M., Engel, Andreas K., König, Peter & Singer, Wolf 1990. Stimulus-dependent neuronal oscillations in cat visual cortex: receptive field properties and feature dependence. *European Journal of Neuroscience* 2. 607–619.

Ghitza, Oded 2011. Linking speech perception and neurophysiology: speech decoding guided by cascaded oscillators locked to the input rhythm. *Frontiers in Psychology*, 2(130). 1–13.

Grimaldi, Mirko 2012. Toward a neural theory of language: Old issues and news perspectives. *Journal of Neurolinguistics* 24(5).304–327.

Gross, Joachim, Schmitz, Frank, Schnitzler, Irmtraud, Kessler, Klaus, Shapiro, Kimron, Hommel Bernhard & Schnitzler Alfons 2004. Modulation of long-range neural synchrony reflects temporal limitations of visual attention in humans. *Proceedings of the National Academy of Sciences U.S.A.* 101, 13050–13055. doi: 10.1073/pnas.0404944101.

Gross, Joachim 2014. Analytical methods and experimental approaches for electrophysiological studies of brain oscillations. *Journal of Neuroscience Methods* 228 (2014) 57–66. http://dx.doi.org/10.1016/j.jneumeth.2014.03.007.

Hanslmayr, Simon, Staresina, Bernhard P., Bowman, Howard 2016. Oscillations and episodic memory: Addressing the synchronization/desynchronization conundrum. *Trends in Neurosciences* 39.16–25. doi:10.1016/j.tins.2015.11.004.

Hauser, Marc D., Chomsky, Noam & Fitch, W. Tecumseh. 2002. The Faculty of Language: What Is It, Who Has It, and How Did It Evolve? *Science* 29822. 1569–1579.

Hickok, Gregory 2012. Computational neuroanatomy of speech production. *Nature Review Neuroscience* 13. 135–145. doi:10.1038/nrn3158.

Hornstein, Norbert. 2009. *A Theory of Syntax: Minimal Operations and Universal Grammar*. Cambridge: Cambridge University Press.

Jensen, Ole, Lisman, John E. 1998. An oscillatory short-term memory buffer model can account for data on the Sternberg task. *Journal of Neuroscience* 18. 10688–10699.

Jensen, Ole & Tesche, Claudia D. 2002. Frontal theta activity in humans increases with memory load in a working memory task. *European Journal of Neuroscience* 15. 1395–1399.

Kahana, Michal J. 2006. The cognitive correlates of human brain oscillations. *Journal of Neuroscience* 26. 1669–1672. DOI:10.1523/JNEUROSCI.3737-05c.2006.

Kielar, Aenta, Meltzer, Jed, Moreno, Sylvain, Alain, Claude & Bialystok, Eellen 2014. Oscillatory responses to semantic and syntactic violations. *Journal of Cognitive Neuroscience* 26. 2840–2862. doi: 10.1162/jocn_a_00670.

Klimesch, Wolfgang 1999. EEG alpha and theta oscillations reflect cognitive and memory performance: a review and analysis. *Brain Research Review* 29. 169–195.

Klimesch, Wolfgang & Schack, Bärbel 2003. Activation of long-term memory by alpha oscillations in a working memory task? *Behavioral and Brain Sciences* 26(6). 743–743. https://doi.org/10.1017/S0140525X03370165.

Klimesch, Wolfgang, Schack, Bärbel, Schabus, Manuel, Doppelmayr, Michael, Gruber, Williams, Sauseng, Paul 2004. Phase-locked alpha and theta oscillations generate the P1-N1 complex and are related to memory performance. *Cognitive Brain Research* 19. 302–316.

Klimesch, Wolfgang, Schack, Bärbel, Sauseng, Paul 2005. The functional significance of theta and upper alpha oscillations for working memory: a review. *Experimental Psychology* 52. 99–108.

Klimesch, Wolfgang 2011. Evoked alpha and early access to the knowledge system: the P1 inhibition timing hypothesis. *Brain Research* 1408: 52–71. doi: 10.1016/j.brainres.2011.06.003.

Klimesch, Wolfgang 2012. Alpha-band oscillations, attention, and controlled access to stored information. Trends in Cognitive Sciences, 16(12). 606–617. http://dx.doi.org/10.1016/j.tics.2012.10.007.

Lam, Nietzsche H.L., Schoffelen, Jan-Mathijs, Uddén, Julia, Hultén, Annika, Hagoort, Peter 2016. Neural activity during sentence processing as reflected in theta, alpha, beta, and gamma oscillations. *NeuroImage* 142. 43–54.

Lashley, Karl S., 1929. *Brain Mechanisms and Intelligence; A Quantitative Study of Injuries to the Brain*. Chicago: University of Chicago Press.

Lewis, A. G., Wang, Lin, & Bastiaansen, Marcel C. M. 2015. Fast oscillatory dynamics during language comprehension: unification versus maintenance and prediction? *Brain & Language* 148. 51–63. doi: 10.1016/j.bandl. 2015.01.003.

Lewis Ashley G., Schoffelen, Jan-Mathijs, Schriefers, Herbert & Bastiaansen, Marcel 2016. A Predictive Coding Perspective on Beta Oscillations during Sentence-Level Language Comprehension. *Frontier in Human Neuroscience*, 10 Article 85. doi: 10.3389/fnhum.2016.00085.

Lieberman Philip, Kako, Edward T., Friedman Joseph, Tajchman, Ggary, Feldman Liane S., Jiminez, Elsa B. 1992. Speech production, syntax comprehension, and cognitive deficits in Parkinson's disease. *Brain & Language* 43. 169–189.

Lieberman, Philip. 2009. *Human language and our reptilian brain: The subcortical bases of speech, syntax, and thought*. Harvard: Harvard University Press.

Lisman, John E. & Idiart Marco A. P. 1995. Storage of 7±2 short-term memories in oscillatory subcycles. *Science* 267. 1512–1515.

Luo, Yu, Zhang, Ying, Feng, Xuo & Zhou, Xiaolin 2010. Electroencephalogram oscillations differentiate semantic and prosodic processes during sentence reading. *Neuroscience* 169, 654–664.doi:10.1016/j.neuroscience.2010.05.032.

Makeig, Scott, Westerfield, Monte, Jung, Tzyy-Ping, Enghoff, Sonia, Townsend, John, Courchesne, Eric, Sejnowski, Terry J. 2002. Dynamic brain sources of visual evoked responses. *Science* 295. 690–694.

Mountcastle, Vernon, B. 1998. *Perceptual Neuroscience: The Cerebral Cortex.* Cambridge, MA: Harvard University Press.
Murphy, Elliot 2015a. The brain dynamics of linguistic computation. *Frontiers in Psychology* 6 1515. doi.org/10.3389/fpsyg.2015.01515.
Murphy, Elliot 2015b. Labels, cognomes, and cyclic computation: an ethological perspective. *Frontier in Psychology 6: 715.* doi: 10.3389/fpsyg.2015.00715.
Murphy, Elliot 2016a. The Human Oscillome and Its Explanatory Potential. *Biolinguistics*, 10. 6–20.
Murphy, Elliot. 2016b. A Theta-Gamma Neural Code for Feature Set Composition with Phase-Entrained Delta Nestings. *University College London Working Papers in Linguistics* (UCLWPL). 1–22.
Murphy, Elliot & Benitez-Burraco Antonio. 2017. The language oscillogenome. *bioRxiv.* doi: https://doi.org/10.1101/114033.
Newton, Isaac 1687/1726. *Philosophiae Naturalis Principia Mathematica.* Apud Guil. and Joh. Innys, Regiae Societatis Typographos, London.
Penny, Will D., Kiebel, Stefan J., Kilner, James M., Rugg, Michael D. 2002. Event-related brain dynamics. *Trends in Neuroscience* 25. 387–389.
Pérez, Alejandro, Molinaro, Nicola, Mancini, Simona, Barraza, Paulo & Carreiras, Manuel 2012. Oscillatory dynamics related to the Unagreement pattern in Spanish. *Neuropsychologia* 50. 2584–2597. doi: 10.1016/j.neuropsychologia.2012.07.009.
Poeppel, David & Embick, David 2005. Defining the relation between linguistics and neuroscience. In Anne Cutler (Ed.), *Twenty-First Century Psycholinguistics: Four Cornerstones*, 103–118. Mahwah, NJ: Lawrence Erlbaum.
Rapela, Joaquín 2016. Entrainment of traveling waves to rhythmic motor acts. *arXiv:1606.02372, Quantitative Biology – Neurons and Cognition.*
Razumnikova, Olga M. 2004. Gender differences in hemispheric organization during divergent thinking: an EEG investigation in human subjects. *Neuroscience Letters* 362. 193–195. doi: 10.1016/j.neulet.2004.02.066.
Rizzi, Luigi 2011. Core linguistic computations: How are they expressed in the mind/brain? *Journal of Neurolinguistics* 25. 489–499.
Sauseng, Paul, Hoppe, Julia, Klimesch, Wofgang, Gerloff, Christian, Hummel, Friedhelm C. 2007. Dissociation of sustained attention from central executive functions: local activity and interregional connectivity in the theta range. *European Journal of Neuroscience* 25. 587–593.
Sauseng, Paul & Klimesch Wolfgang 2008. What does phase information of oscillatory brain activity tell us about cognitive processes? *Neuroscience and Biobehavioral Reviews* 32. 1001–1013. doi:10.1016/j.neubiorev.2008.03.014.
Sauseng, Paul, Griesmayr, Birgit, Freunberger, Roman, Klimesch, Wolfgang 2010. Control mechanisms in working memory: A possible function of EEG theta oscillations. *Neuroscience and Biobehavioral Reviews* 34. 1015–1022 doi:10.1016/j.neubiorev.2009.12.006.
Steriade, Mircea, Gloor, Paul, Llinas, Rodolfo R., Lopes de Silva, Fernando H., Mesulam, Marcel M. 1990. Report of IFCN committee on basic mechanisms. Basic mechanisms of cerebral rhythmic activities. *Electroencephalography Clinical Neurophysiology* 76(6). 481–508.
Steven, Pinker, Jackendoff, Ray. 2013. The faculty of language: what's special about it? *Cognition* 95. 201–236.

Strauß, Antje, Henry, Molly J., Scharinger Mathias & Obleser Jonas 2015. Alpha Phase Determines Successful Lexical Decision in Noise. *The Journal of Neuroscience* 35(7). 3256–3262.

Theofanopoulou, Constantina & Boeckx, Cedric 2016. The central role of the thalamus in language and cognition. In: Koji Fujita, Cedric Boeckx, (Eds.), *Advances in Biolinguistics: The Human Language Faculty and Its Biological Basis*, 230–255. London: Routledge.

Varela, Francisco, Lachaux, Jean-Philippe, Rodriguez, Eugenio & Martinerie, Jacques 2001. The brain web: phase synchronization and large-scale integration. *Nature Review Neuroscience* 2. 229–239. doi:10.1038/35067550

Wang Lin, Jensen Ole, van den Brink Danielle, Weder Nienke, Schoffelen Jan-Mathijs, Magyari Lilla, et al. 2012. Beta oscillations relate to the N400m during language comprehension. *Human Brain Mapping* 33. 2898–2912. 10.1002/hbm.21410.

Weiss, Sabine & Mueller, Horst Martin 2003. The contribution of EEG coherence to the investigation of language. *Brain & Language* 85. 325–343.

Weiss, Sabine, Mueller, Horst M., Schack, Baerbel, King, Jonathan W., Kutas, Martha & Rappelsberger, Peter 2005. Increased neuronal communication accompanying sentence comprehension. *International Journal of Psychophysiology* 57. 129–141.

Kleanthes K. Grohmann
When *seem* wants to control

1 Introduction

The framework of Prolific Domains, which partitions the clause into three separate parts – relating to thematic, agreement, and discourse properties, respectively – makes a number of predictions for movement within a clause and across clause boundaries (Grohmann 2000 *et seq.*). One such prediction concerns the interaction of control and raising structures combined against the background of a PRO-less theory of control (e.g., Hornstein 1999, Manzini and Roussou 2000). This chapter revisits and expands earlier suggestions that an embedded raising predicate itself embedded in a control structure makes available a non-canonical thematic layer. Relating to the honoree of the present volume, the core of the paper addresses some central data for an alternative approach to control within the context of Prolific Domains, spanning over three decades of research since the seminal Manzini (1983).

Rita Manzini has been at the forefront of research on control and related phenomena for a very long time, covering at least the three decades between Manzini (1983) and Manzini (2009) – and she continues to be so (e.g., Manzini and Savoia 2016). This chapter revisits an issue first raised by myself (Grohmann 2000), around the time Manzini and Roussou (2000) appeared, which fell into a very productive period of formulating alternative approaches to the classic Control Theory of Chomsky (1981), such as Hornstein (1999) and a host of papers that came out of that research program (Hornstein 2003, 2007 but also precursors ranging from Bowers 1973 to Martin 1996 and O'Neil 1997) or Landau (1999). After a series of back-and-forths, the heated debates culminated, at least for the time being, in Boeckx et al. (2010) on the one hand (see also Hornstein and Polinsky 2010), and adverse views in Landau (2015) on the other (but see also Davies and Dubinsky 2007), with Manzini and Roussou (2000) perhaps somewhere in between (see also Bowers 2006). These perspectives, and many other issues, are also expertly illuminated in the research overviews by Davies and Dubinsky (2004) and Landau (2013), for example.

As Manzini (2009: 133) recaps, she originally suggested to reduce control to Binding Theory (Manzini 1983), "but le[ft] open the question as to why within a given domain an argument would be chosen as the obligatory controller

Kleanthes K. Grohmann, University of Cyprus

https://doi.org/10.1515/9781501505201-018

rather than another, yielding in particular subject vs. object control" (see also Manzini 1986, Manzini and Roussou 2000). She continues:

> Since Chomsky's (1995) minimalism adopts the GB theory of PRO and *pro*, it also inherits these problems. In addition to these, the ad hoc character of PRO and *pro* within minimalism, notably the fact that they are effectively empty lexical elements, endowed with such features as null Case has often been remarked upon (Manzini and Roussou (2000) on PRO, Manzini and Savoia (2005, 2007) on *pro*, and references quoted there).
>
> (Manzini 2009: 133)

Leaving aside Manzini and Savoia's (2005, 2007) and other authors' work on *pro* (recently summarized by Herbeck 2013, as cited by Landau 2015), a Manzini-style binding-theoretic approach identifies the controlled subject (obligatory PRO) "as a null anaphor, whose binding domain is the clause immediately dominating the nonfinite complement" (Landau 2013: 54). It thus requires neither PRO nor displacement, which would derive the controlled subject as a residue of movement.

Some of the existing approaches to control can be illustrated analytically with a straightforward structure such as *John hopes to win the race*, with copies/traces marked with strikethrough and CP left out. (1a) would arguably represent a modern version of classic Control Theory with a PRO subject (Chomsky 1995), (1b) a PRO-less alternative theory of construal (Manzini and Roussou 2000), (1c) the original movement theory of control (Hornstein 1999), and (1d) the alternative to the movement theory of control championed here (Grohmann 2000). A crucial ingredient of the movement theory of control is the possibility of argument movement into theta-positions (e.g., Bošković 1994), which will also be addressed briefly in section 2.

(1) a. [$_{TP}$ John$_i$ T [$_{vP}$ ~~John$_i$~~ hopes [$_{TP}$ PRO$_i$ to [$_{vP}$ ~~PRO$_i$~~ win the race]]]]
 b. [$_{TP}$ John$^{\theta\theta}$ T [$_{vP}$ __ $^\theta$hopes [$_{TP}$ __ to [$_{vP}$ __ $^\theta$win the race]]]]
 c. [$_{TP}$ John T [$_{vP}$ ~~John~~ hopes [$_{TP}$ ~~John~~ to [$_{vP}$ ~~John~~ win the race]]]]
 d. [$_{TP}$ John T [$_{vP}$ ~~John~~ hopes [$_{TP}$ __ to [$_{vP}$ ~~John~~ win the race]]]]

As somewhat of an outsider to the larger debate of control structures, I take as one core aspect underlying the rationale to rethink Control Theory the attempt to reduce rather than expand GB-style modules of the grammar. Thus, when Manzini (1983) proposed to integrate control within Binding Theory (also Manzini 1986), a welcome side effect was the abandonment of control as a separate module in a highly modular conception of the grammar, itself something of a literal adaptation of Fodor's (1983) modularity of mind to the theory of grammar. For further reflections, see the collection of papers in Webelhuth (1995) for early minimalist perspectives on the status of GB-modules as well as Hornstein (2001) and Hornstein et al. (2005) for slightly more recent discussion. In this line of reasoning falls also Hornstein's frequently expressed lamentation that a PRO-theory of control constitutes the last remnant of D-structure in minimalist analyses, most recently voiced on his *Faculty of Language* blog (http://facultyoflanguage.blog spot.com/2016/07/gg-re-education-camp.html). This gives just one flavor of reducing control to other parts of the grammar; additional models build on predication, movement, or the operation Agree within minimalist approaches, not to mention alternatives from other frameworks. And it is arguably a syntactico-centric approach; for an explicit syntax–semantics interface theory of obligatory control, see for example Landau (2015). Whatever the underlying motivation, it can be reasonably held that "there is no [single] 'theory of control', but rather, there are 'subtheories of control'" (Landau 2013: ix). It is in this sense that he later concludes that "the disintegration of 'the theory of control' is really the *advancement* of other grammatical theories" (Landau 2013: 258).

In this paper, I will add to that disintegration and advance one such alternative theory. Restricting myself to illustrate this idea with instances of obligatory control only, I will in particular consider the underlying derivations of the following pair:

(2) a. John seems to hope to win the race.
 b. John wants to appear to win the race.

In current terminology, (2a) could be described as an instance of an infinitival control structure (*to hope to win the race*) embedded under a finite raising verb (*seems*), and (2b) as an infinitival raising structure (*to appear to win the race*) embedded under a finite control verb (*wants*). In the generative context (starting with Rosenbaum 1967), such cases were discussed very early on by McCawley (1970), among others, to provide evidence for the 'cycle': The two relevant transformations, Equi-NP-deletion and Subject-raising, must be part of the cycle (as opposed to being pre- or post-cyclic rules). Moreover, "Subject-raising on a lower sentence must apply before Equi-NP-deletion on a higher sentence, and Equi-NP-deletion on a lower sentence must apply before Subject-raising on a higher sentence" (McCawley 1970: 287). Also, additional interactions may complicate the picture further, where raising ('Subject-raising') feeds control (Equi-NP-deletion) followed by further raising – as in (3a), which was also briefly discussed by McCawley – and where control feeds raising followed by further control – as in (3b), for example, which was not; more permutations can easily be thought up.

(3) a. John seems to hope to appear to win the race.
   b. John wants to appear to hope to win the race.

For reasons that will become obvious presently, the remainder of this brief chapter will address structures like (2), but also (3) to some extent, where subject control structures and other fully lexical verbs interact with apparent subject raising.

2 What's the issue?

When I originally considered cases like those in (2) and (3) above (Grohmann 2000 and subsequently published in Grohmann 2003a, 2003b), I did so in the context of the Anti-Locality Hypothesis (for a more recent exposition, see Grohmann 2011, which much of the present section is taken from; see also e.g. Putnam 2007, Boeckx 2008: chap. 5, Grohmann 2013, Funakoshi 2014, Haddad 2014). This framework is most dominantly expressed through the existence of very special 'cycles' in the syntactic derivation (as opposed to, say, phases of Chomsky 2000 *et seq.*): Prolific Domains (ΠΔs). A ΠΔ is a contextually defined part of the computational system which, on the one hand, provides the interfaces with the information relevant to that context and, on the other, consists of internal structure interacting with derivational operations (Grohmann 2007: 183).

Following from the Anti-Locality Hypothesis provided in (4), the framework is grounded in the ban on too-close movement within a relevant domain sketched abstractly in (5).

(4) *Anti-Locality Hypothesis* (Grohmann 2003b: 26)
    Movement must not be too local.

(5) *Ban on Domain-Internal Dependencies* (Grohmann 2007: 183)
    [$_{AP|α|}$ XP A^0$_{|α|}$ ... [$_{ZP|α|}$ ~~YP~~ ...]]

In other words, if XP and ZP in (6) belong to the same relevant domain, YP cannot move as indicated here (Grohmann 2011: 273):

(6) *[$_{XP}$ YP [$_{X'}$ X (...) [$_{ZP}$ ~~YP~~ [$_{Z'}$ Z ...]]]]

The notion of Prolific Domain then replaces the "relevant domain" from above. Restricting ourselves to the realm of clauses (for nominal structures, see Grohmann and Haegeman 2003), this leads to a formal tripartition with three such ΠΔs:

(7) *Clausal Tripartition* (Grohmann 2003b: 74)
   i. Θ-Domain: part of derivation where thematic relations are created
   ii. Φ-Domain: part of derivation where agreement properties are licensed
   iii. Ω-Domain: part of derivation where discourse information is established

Structures contained within each of these ΠΔs share that "common context" – i.e. |α| in (5) – where the specific context is |Θ|, |Φ|, or |Ω| for Theta-Domain (ΘΔ), Agreement-Domain (ΦΔ), and Discourse-Domain (ΩΔ), respectively. The resulting clausal structure is thus highly reminiscent of the traditional verbal projection line of V–Infl–Comp (i.e. VP–TP–CP; cf. Platzack 1991). *Thematic relations* correspond to the kinds of argument structure known to be created within vP and projections contained within it (at least VP, but possibly additional projections such as inner aspect or high and low applicatives). In turn, *agreement properties* correspond to the kinds of structural configurations known to be licensed within TP and projections contained within it (agreement, outer aspect, negation, and possibly other projections in a 'split Infl'). And, finally, *discourse information* corresponds to the kinds of semantically and/or pragmatically prominent elements, including quantification and other scope-relations, known to be established within CP and projections contained within it (such as TopP, FocP, and possibly further projections in a 'split Comp').

This yields a clausal tripartition into a finer articulated vP, a finer articulated TP, and a finer articulated CP, where I leave open for now the possibility of filling the "finer articulation" with additional projections (as just mentioned) or in some other way (such as multiple specifiers). Further details of the ΠΔ-driven framework are not relevant for present purposes, such as specific definitions of Spell-Out and Transfer assumed to make the Condition on Domain Exclusivity work, the postulation that any syntactic object in the phrase-marker must have an exclusive 'address identification' (roughly, one occurrence per ΠΔ), which then may give rise to Copy Spell-Out.

One relevant consequence of this framework, however, is the following. By assumption, the derivation unfolds successively by Prolific Domain. Thus, each occurrence of a displaced syntactic object in a given clause must have an address identification in the next lower ΠΔ, all the way down to its base-generated position. This assumption leads to a condition on clause-internal movement in (8), which can best be illustrated with *wh*-movement, as in (9), spanning all three ΠΔs:

(8) *Intra-Clausal Movement Generalization* (adapted from Grohmann 2003b: 251)
Movement within a clause must target the next higher Prolific Domain ΠΔ:
[$_{βΔ}$ XP ... [$_{αΔ}$ ... XP ...]], where β >> α

(9) [$_{ΩΔ}$ what did [$_{ΦΔ}$ John ~~what~~ [$_{ΘΔ}$ ~~John~~ read ~~what~~]]]

In more traditional clause-structural terms, the relevant derivational analysis would look as follows, where it does not matter here whether 'AgrOP' stands indeed for object agreement, an outer specifier of *v*P, or some other phrase (see Grohmann 2011 for further discussion); for a suggestion how *v*P could belong to both Θ-Domain and Φ-Domain, see Funakoshi (2014):

(10) [$_{CP}$ what did [$_{TP}$ John T [$_{AgrOP}$ ~~what~~ AgrO [$_{vP}$ ~~John~~ *v* [$_{VP}$ read ~~what~~]]]]]

Movement across clause boundaries leads to an extended reformulation of traditional successive cyclicity: A position within one clause is taken to be the stepping stone to movement to the same position one clause up, as in successive-cyclic *wh*-movement (SpecCP to SpecCP) or subject-to-subject raising (SpecTP to SpecTP), for example. But, it is argued, "same position" should better be understood as the same contextual type of position (i.e. same ΠΔ) – and this understanding of successive cyclicity should also be extended to the thematic layer. The arising generalization is given in (11):

(11) *Inter-Clausal Movement Generalization* (adapted from Grohmann 2003b: 253)
Movement across clauses must target the next higher ΠΔ of the same type:
[$_{αΔ}$ XP ... ǂ ... [$_{αΔ}$ ... XP ...]], where ǂ = clause boundary

An illustration of successive-cyclic movement into theta-positions, taking the cue from Hornstein (2001) and precursors that paved the way (Bošković 1994, Lidz and Idsardi 1998 within minimalism, but also Bowers 1973, 1981, 2006), comes from the movement theory of control (see especially Hornstein 1999, Boeckx et al. 2010, Hornstein and Polinsky 2010) – with the non-trivial proviso that the EPP can be dispensed with (as in Castillo et al. 1999, Grohmann et al. 2000 and references, including Manzini and Roussou 2000, Bošković 2002; see also Castillo et al. 2009 for a more recent update). As discussed in the works just cited, movement into theta-positions is not as wild an assumption as it may seem at first glance. After all, with the dispense of non-interface levels, especially D-structure, the Theta Criterion has a seriously outdated feel to it. In fact, neither the Theta Criterion nor classic Control Theory sit particularly well with the minimalist syntactician, as Norbert Hornstein never tires to highlight (Hornstein 1999 *et seq.*, but see also e.g. Bowers 2006). Thus, interclausal movement is not restricted to the familiar instances of successive-cyclic A- and A'-movement but may apply to successive-cyclic θ-movement as well. (12) provides one relevant derivation for a double control structure extending (1):

(12) [_TP John T [_vP ~~John~~ hopes [_TP to [_vP ~~John~~ try [_TP to [_vP ~~John~~ win the race]]]]]]

The subject moves from its base-generated thematic position in the most deeply embedded clause, receiving a θ-role from *win*, to the thematic subject position in the next higher clause where it gets a second θ-role from *try* and then to the main clause thematic subject position to be assigned a third θ-role from *hope*. After two steps of successive-cyclic θ-movement (inter-clausal movement), *John* then moves from the matrix Θ-Domain to the Φ-Domain (intra-clausal movement). Since only one copy can be spelled out under normal circumstances, it is the top-most copy of *John* that is pronounced but all lower copies are relevant for interpretation, providing the illusion of 'control' (see Grohmann 2013 for discussion on copy spell-out rules and further references).

As a side note, this conception of 'cycles' in clausal derivations is clearly different from Phase Theory (Chomsky 2000 *et seq.*), where each of the two clausal phases, headed by *v* and C, constitute a cycle. And in order to get out of one, the moving syntactic object must go through the edge of its current cycle – thus, "it is not only [inter]-clausal movement that is successive-cyclic, but also intra-clausal movement" (Keine 2015: 2). Whereas each phase is a cyclic structure, no such claim needs to be made for Prolific Domains (contra Grohmann 2003b: 236), though that also depends on how 'cycle' is defined and what such cycles do for the computation. It rather looks like Prolific Domains are much closer to the Williams Cycle (Gereon Müller, p.c.), referring to hierarchy-governed ordering (Williams 1974, 2003 but also Müller 2014 and then Georgi 2014), which would lead to a similar clausal partition as presently assumed: S' > S > Pred > VP or roughly CP > TP > vP > VP (and certainly subsuming ΩΔ > ΦΔ > ΘΔ). Concerning the relevance of intra- and inter-clausal movement for computational operations, Davies and Dubinsky (2003: 231) observe that Chomsky (1973) already "adopts the then-radical notion that derivational rules are not themselves marked as intra-clausal (e.g., passive) and inter-clausal (e.g., *wh*-movement)" and that instead "he proposes that rules may all, in principle, apply anywhere, and that they are 'conditioned' by the context of their application." Over the past five decades, the relevant contexts, conditions, and corollaries have arguably changed. Currently, the number of 'cycles' entertained alone ranges from two (Chomsky) or three (Grohmann) to four (Williams) – or as many as there are projections (Epstein and Seely 2002 but also Müller 2011 and related work).

Let us finally return to (2) and (3), repeated here for convenience.

(2) a. John seems to hope to win the race.
    b. John wants to appear to win the race.

(3) a. John seems to hope to appear to win the race.
    b. John wants to appear to hope to win the race.

First off, it should be noted that none of these constructions appear to pose a challenge to the contender theories of control exemplified in (1a–c). Classic Control Theory dissociates the different subject positions with the help of a phonetically empty PRO for each controlled subject which receives a theta-role (Theta Criterion) and moves to the grammatical subject position (EPP) – SpecIP (Chomsky 1981) or SpecTP ((13a); Chomsky 1995); this PRO can also move to the grammatical subject position in the raising clauses. In the PRO-less construal alternative to control, the only subject is one instance of *John* in the matrix SpecTP which attracts all theta-roles by construal, also without assuming the EPP ((13b); Manzini and Roussou 2000). And the original movement theory of control simply sees *John* move from theta- to subject- to theta-position, repeatedly and irrespective of there being a raising structure in between, in which case it would simply move successive-cyclically from SpecTP to SpecTP ((13c); Hornstein 1999). The three derivations are provided here for (2a):

(13) a. [$_{TP}$ John$_i$ T [$_{vP}$ ~~John$_i$~~ seems [$_{TP}$ PRO$_{1i}$ to [$_{vP}$ ~~PRO$_{1i}$~~ hope
       [$_{TP}$ PRO$_{2i}$ to [$_{vP}$ ~~PRO$_{2i}$~~ win the race]]]]]]
    b. [$_{TP}$ John$^{\theta\theta}$ T [$_{vP}$ seems [$_{TP}$ to [$_{vP}$ $^{\theta}$hope [$_{TP}$ to [$_{vP}$ $^{\theta}$win the race]]]]]]
    c. [$_{TP}$ John T [$_{vP}$ seems [$_{TP}$ ~~John~~ to [$_{vP}$ ~~John~~ hope
       [$_{TP}$ ~~John~~ to [$_{vP}$ ~~John~~ win the race]]]]]]

However, in the ΠΔ-driven framework, the following issue arises: If obligatory control is the result of movement from a position within the Θ-Domain of one clause to a position within the Θ-Domain of the next higher clause, and at the same time raising involves movement from a position within the Φ-Domain of one clause to a position within the Φ-Domain of the next higher clause, how can they be combined?

3 Can *seem* ever want?

A raising verb without a Θ-Domain embedding a fully lexical verb (see Kambanaros and Grohmann 2015 on this term), as in (2a), cannot easily interact with a thematic subject coming from the lower clause. So, the obvious answer to give is that a raising verb like *seem* just makes available a non-canonical thematic layer in the right non-canonical circumstances. Generalizing, a raising verb embedding a control structure comes equipped with a Θ-Domain to attract the controlled subject by movement.

Before exploring this further, (14) illustrates the present assumptions for simple control and raising structures:

(14) a. [TP John T [vP ~~John~~ hopes [TP __ to [vP ~~John~~ win the race]]]]   [cf. (1d)]
 b. [TP John T [vP __ seems [TP ~~John~~ to [vP ~~John~~ win the race]]]]

The theta-marked subject moves from the embedded Θ-Domain to the matrix Θ-Domain, skipping the embedded Φ-Domain (SpecTP, no EPP) before ending up in the matrix Φ-Domain (say, for case and agreement); due to the two theta-roles, it now counts as controller and controllee. Assuming that a simple raising verb does not have a full-fledged Θ-Domain to theta-mark a subject, the raised subject can only end up in the matrix Φ-Domain if it comes from the embedded Φ-Domain, hence the first movement step is from embedded Θ-Domain to embedded Φ-Domain. Without the EPP motivating this movement, it must be the Intra- and Inter-Clausal Movement Generalizations that are responsible. Without this movement step, the subject could not reach its final matrix position, a reasoning reminiscent of Lasnik's (1995) view of Greed as Enlightened Self-Interest: "Movement of α to β must be for the satisfaction of formal requirements of α or β" (Lasnik 1999: 128).

In turn, (15) provides the relevant assumed derivational histories for (2) and (3).

(15) a. [TP John T [vP __ seems [TP ~~John~~ to [vP ~~John~~ hope
     [TP __ to [vP ~~John~~ win the race]]]]]]
 b. [TP John T [vP ~~John~~ wants [TP __ to [vP ~~John~~ appear
     [TP __ to [vP ~~John~~ win the race]]]]]]
 c. [TP John T [vP __ seems [TP ~~John~~ to [vP ~~John~~ hope [TP __ to [vP ~~John~~ appear
     [TP __ to [vP ~~John~~ win the race]]]]]]
 d. [TP John T [vP ~~John~~ wants [TP __ to [vP ~~John~~ appear [TP __ to [vP ~~John~~ hope
     [TP __ to [vP ~~John~~ win the race]]]]]]

In order for the subject to target a matrix theta-position before ending up in matrix SpecTP, as in (15b,d), it must move through embedded theta-positions – and, by the Inter-Clausal Movement Generalization, *only* through embedded theta-positions: from embedded Θ-Domain to embedded Θ-Domain, all the way to the matrix Θ-Domain. If the raising predicate is in the matrix clause, this issue arises only partially, as in (15c), which also contains an embedded raising verb; in (15a), the subject *John* moves from the most deeply embedded Θ-Domain to the next higher Θ-Domain (by inter-clausal movement), then targets the Φ-Domain of that clause (intra-clausal movement) before landing in the matrix Φ-Domain (inter-clausal movement again).

The question that arises, then, is: Where does the full-fledged Θ-Domain around embedded raising verbs come from which makes available a thematic subject position here but is absent from regular raising structures? In other words: How can *seem* (or rather, *appear* in (15b–d)) ever look like *want*?

For starters, this type of intermingling inter- and intra-clausal movement is not problematic *per se*: Movement through SpecTP in infinitival environments of obligatory control is not ruled out by force – it is simply ruled out by economy considerations in the typical case. This movement step can only apply if needed for convergence, that is, when needed for locality reasons, and as such it *may* apply when necessary, as in (15a), for instance. While it may seem that the generalized conditions on successive cyclicity advocated here break down, this need not be so. If we consider the meaning expressed in the relevant structures more closely, we can observe that *seem* or *appear* act like a clear, pure raising predicate in (15a) – but perhaps not so in (15b–d). I used this point to address the following questions (from Grohmann 2003b: 261f.): What is a "pure raising predicate" – and how does it differ from an impure one? And how can *seem* be a pure raising predicate in one, but not the other case? After laying out my answers below and some additional musings, I will briefly consider the possibility of an independent test for raising purity at the very end.

To get a grip on these questions, consider the following paradigm, where (17a–f) are meant to be semantic equivalents to (16a–f):

(16) a. John seems to kiss Mary.
　　 b. John seems to be sick.
　　 c. John seems sick.
　　 d. John wants to seem sick.
　　 e. John wants to seem to be sick.
　　 f. John wants to seem to kiss Mary.

(17) a. It seems that John kisses Mary.
   b. It seems that John is sick.
   c. *It seems that John sick.
   d. *It seems that John wants sick.
   e. #It seems that John wants to be sick.
   f. #It seems that John wants to kiss Mary.

Aspects of these patterns are well known from Edwin Williams' work on predication structures (see Williams 1994: 1–2, 46–47 for brief discussion and further references), such as the relevance of *John seems sick* for issues relating to raising, control, and predication. Williams takes the complex [*seems sick*] as the relevant predicate, "by virtue of the predicate *sick*" (p. 2). In other words, *seem* does not serve a purely raising function void of any theta-structure, as opposed to *John seems to X*, as in (16a–b). One of the properties of such pure raising predicates, I take it, is allowing for an equivalent expletive structure, as shown in (17a–f). These are well-formed and semantically synonymous to (16a–b), but ungrammatical for (16c–d). The interesting case for present purposes concerns (16e–f): The expletive equivalents are grammatically well formed, but not synonymous. (A reviewer points out that "the scopal relations are inverted" in my (16e–f) and (17e–f), and, one could add, possibly (16d)/(17d) as well. The reviewer suggests to replace them with *John wants for it to seem that he is sick* and *John wants for it to seem that he kisses Mary*, respectively. This would add additional material, however, which I am not completely happy with as I briefly address at the end of this section.)

One way to interpret this state of affairs is to say that *seem* in (16e–f) is not a raising verb, but some other predicational element – possibly a control verb under the current understanding, in the sense that it makes available its own Θ-Domain. This is obviously the route I want to suggest for the cases in (15b–d) above: Just as *John* cannot be a 'seemer' in pure raising contexts, he may be a 'seemer' when embedded under a control predicate. This amounts to saying that *seem* has two lexical entries, one without an external argument (in which case the subject may be an expletive) and one with an external argument (in the relevant cases considered here, a 'seemer' or an 'appearer' of X is someone "who is trying to give the impression that X").

As a side note concerning the relation between (16f) and (17f), it looks to me as if *seem* embedded under *want* may actually constitute a possible performance issue when uttered. That is, when I found the quote in (18), my first interpretation was that Barrington meant to say (19):

(18) "Everybody wants to seem to crown me for no reason," Barrington said, via the Packers' official website. (http://www.nfl.com/news/story/0ap3000000499619/article/sam-barrington-everybody-wants-to-crown-me)

(19) It seems that everybody wants to crown me for no reason.

Now, of course, one could object to the preceding discussion and raise yet a different alternative. If raising verbs *can* have a full-fledged thematic layer, why do they not *always* have one? That is to say that the subject *John* could move from Θ- to Θ-Domain even in (15a,c) and only target the Φ-Domain in the very last step, in the matrix clause. The obvious answer would be the standard arguments for identifying raising predicates as special stemming from expletive insertion, preservation of meaning under passivization, or the ability to raise from idiom chunks (for a fuller list, see Landau 2013: 8–28). Still, as noted by a reviewer, there should be discourse-dependent instances of *John seems to be sick* with a 'control reading' of sick, with John the instigator of appearances or something like that.

In our attempt to rid the grammar of the EPP (see also Grohmann et al. 2000), Castillo et al. (1999) observed the following data (from the more and freely accessible Castillo et al. 2009: 97):

(20) a. The men seem to appear to want to leave.
    b. The men 'seemta' 'appearta' 'wanna' leave.

As we argued, "[i]f there are no traces in the specifiers of the intermediate non-finite T's (since there are, we claim, no such specifiers), then the contraction possibilities follow directly without having to make any stipulations about traces vs. PRO vs. Case-marked traces of *wh*-movement (e.g., **who do you wanna vanish?*)" (Castillo et al. 2009: 97). And indeed, in the present framework it can also be argued that the contraction in (20) is possible because nothing intervenes between each of the verb–*to* sequences – all the way down to the most deeply embedded control predicate *want to*. In the context of Hornstein (1999) vs. Manzini and Roussou (2000), we were also quick to state that "we actually have reason to favor the Manzini & Roussou account" (p. 99). Either way, (20) can also be accommodated in the present ΠΔ-driven framework.

In Grohmann (2003a), I pointed out that the present framework not only supports Bošković's (2002) approach to ridding the grammar of the EPP (see also Castillo et al. 1999, Grohmann et al. 2000, and references cited as well as Castillo et al. 2009 with more recent references), it also captures the following contrast:

(21) a. All the students seem to know French.
    b. All the students try to know French.

(22) a. The students seem all to know French.
    b. *The students try all to know French.

Regardless of the ultimate analysis of 'floating' quantifiers (see Bošković 2001 and especially Bobaljik 2003 for discussion and references), the possibility of 'stranding' *all* in the current context would point to only one state of affairs: The intermediate subject position, non-finite SpecTP, is involved in raising but not in control structures. Taking one popular approach, Sportiche's (1988) stranding analysis can be neatly applied to capture this difference – once we assume the Inter-Clausal Movement Generalization in (11): If the controlling subject starts out in the embedded Θ-Domain and moves in one fell swoop to the matrix Θ-Domain, as in (22b), the possibility of stranding the quantifier somewhere in between does not even arise. A raising subject, however, passes through one such position and may strand the quantifier, hence the grammatical (22a).

As Castillo et al. (1999) mentioned already, Manzini and Roussou (2000) can handle the contrast, too – however, they would need to analyze *all* as a floating rather than a stranded quantifier (see Castillo et al. 2099: 97 fn. 36 for references, starting with the seminal Postal 1974). It should be noted that under a less radical departure from traditional derivations, of the sort Bošković (2001, 2002) pursues, this contrast can arguably not be captured quite as easily, since it is not at all clear what happens to non-finite SpecTP in control environments (see also the relevant type of derivational history offered by Hornstein 1999 and related work within the movement theory of control). While floating quantifiers in raising structures can be accounted for without evoking the EPP, it is not ruled out for control structures. The present proposal does not face such complications.

In the current context of apparent interaction of raising and control structures, Hagstrom (2006) provides (23e) below, which "sounds to [him] about as bad as [(22b)]", though he hastens to add that "like [(22b)], its ungrammatical status would also follow from the traditional analysis of control with PRO" (Hagstrom (2006: 226). Note that the full paradigm in (23) certainly does receive a straightforward analysis in the present ΠΔ-based framework driven by the Intra- and Inter-Clausal Movement Generalizations:

(23) a. All the students try to seem to know French.
    b. The students all try to seem to know French.
    c. *The students try all to seem to know French.

d. The students try to all seem to know French.
e. *The students try to seem all to know French.
f. The students try to seem to all know French.

With all its faults, we now have ways to determine when apparent raising verbs make available a full Θ-Domain – though arguably with a post-hoc character, that is, there is no independent test for the purported control-character of raising verbs. A reviewer raised two interesting suggestions. I will not discuss the first one here, which relates to binding into experiencers (e.g., *John seems to himself to* ...), since I take the syntactic properties of and claimed concomitant independent evidence provided by experiencers problematic in this context (see e.g. Castillo et al. 2009: 93–96 for some critical discussion). But the reviewer's second suggestions strikes me as a good start for an independent test for the 'controlhood' or 'raising purity' of raising verbs: intentionality adverbs. Consider the two sentences in (24):

(24) a. John deliberately seems to be sick.
b. Mary intentionally appears to win the race.

As recently summarized by Migliori (2016: 66): "Non-agentive verbs are generally not compatible with adverbs expressing intentionality, typical of agentive contexts (Cinque 1999, Levin & Rappaport Hovav 2005)." In a raising reading, (24a–b) are out; acceptability requires an intentional subject, hence Θ-Domain.

4 Concluding remarks

Perhaps somewhat self-aggrandizing, though not meant to be, this brief contribution presented an old analysis of mine of interleaving raising and control structures from the framework perspective of Prolific Domains (Grohmann 2000 *et seq.*). As such, it was concerned with a topic that has been close to the honoree's linguistic heart for much longer, syntactic approaches to control at large (cf. Manzini 1983). Specifically, the discussion revolved around the analytical conundrum that a raising verb which embeds a control structure must make available a non-canonical thematic layer. While trying to justify this step, I would be equally happy, if not more so, to conclude that under an alternative, yet still PRO-less theory of control, this difficulty does not even arise. Thus, the core data that motivated this chapter may receive a perhaps more straightforward analysis under the theory laid out by Manzini and Roussou (2000) and developed in other work by this festschrift's jubilee ... #M.RitaManzini☺☙♥☀☙

References

Bobaljik, Jonathan. D. 2003. Floating quantifiers: Handle with care. In L. L.-S. Cheng and R. Sybesma (eds.), *The Second Glot International State-of-the-Art Book*, 107–148. Berlin: Mouton de Gruyter.

Boeckx, Cedric, Norbert Hornstein, and Jairo Nunes (2010). *Control as Movement*. Cambridge: Cambridge University Press.

Bošković, Željko. 1994. D-structure, theta criterion, and movement into theta positions. *Linguistic Analysis* 24: 247–286.

Bošković, Željko. 2001. Floating quantifiers and theta-role assignment. In M. Kim and U. Strauss (eds.), *Proceedings of NELS 31*, pp. 59–78. Amherst, MA: GSLA Publications, University of Massachusetts.

Bošković, Željko. 2002. A-movement and the EPP. *Syntax* 5: 167–218.

Bowers, John. 1973. *Grammatical relations*. Doctoral dissertation. Massachusetts Institute of Technology, Cambridge, MA. [Published by Garland, New York, 1986.]

Bowers, John. 1981. *The Theory of Grammatical Relations*. Ithaca, NY: Cornell University Press.

Bowers, John 2006. On reducing control to movement. *Syntax* 11: 125–143.

Castillo, Juan Carlos, John Drury, and Kleanthes K. Grohmann. 1999. Merge over move and the extended projection principle. In S. Aoshima, J. Drury, and T. Neuvonen (eds.), *University of Maryland Working Papers in Linguistics* 8, pp. 63–103. University of Maryland, College Park: Department of Linguistics.

Castillo, Juan Carlos, John Drury, and Kleanthes K. Grohmann. (2009). Merge over move and the extended projection principle: MOM and the EPP Revisited. *Iberia* 1: 53–114.

Chomsky, Noam. 1973. Conditions on transformations. In Stephen Anderson and Paul Kiparsky (eds.), *A Festschrift for Morris Halle*, pp. 232–286. New York: Holt, Rinehart and Winston.

Chomsky, Noam. 1981. *Lectures on Government and Binding: The Pisa Lectures*. Dordrecht: Foris.

Chomsky, Noam. 1995. *The Minimalist Program*. Cambridge, MA: MIT Press.

Chomsky, Noam. 2000. Minimalist inquiries: The framework. In R. Martin, D. Michaels, and J. Uriagereka (eds.), *Step by Step: Essays on Minimalist Syntax in Honor of Howard Lasnik*, pp. 89–155. Cambridge, MA: MIT Press.

Cinque, Guglielmo. 1999. *Adverbs and Functional Heads: A Cross-Linguistic Perspective*. Oxford: Oxford University Press.

Davies, William D. and Stanley Dubinsky. 2003. Raising (and control). *Glot International* 7, 230–243.

Davies, William D. and Stanley Dubinsky. 2004. *The Grammar of Raising and Control: A Course in Syntactic Argumentation*. Malden, MA: Blackwell.

Davies, William D. and Stanley Dubinsky. (eds.) (2007). *New Horizons in the Analysis of Control and Raising*. Dordrecht: Springer.

Epstein, Samuel D. and T. Daniel Seely (2002). Rule applications as cycles in a level-free syntax. In S. D. Epstein and T. D. Seely (eds.), *Derivation and Explanation in the Minimalist Program*, pp. 65–89. Blackwell, Oxford.

Fodor, Jerry A. 1983. *The Modularity of Mind*. Cambridge, MA: MIT Press.

Funakoshi, Kenshi. 2014. *Syntactic head movement and its consequences*. Doctoral dissertation, University of Maryland, College Park.

Georgi, Doreen. 2014. *Opaque interactions of Merge and Agree: On the nature and order of elementary operations*. Doctoral dissertation, University of Leipzig.

Grohmann, Kleanthes K. 2000. *Prolific peripheries: A radical view from the left*. Doctoral dissertation, University of Maryland, College Park.

Grohmann, Kleanthes K. 2003a. Successive cyclicity under (anti-)local considerations. *Syntax* 6: 260–312.

Grohmann, Kleanthes K. 2003b. *Prolific Domains: On the Anti-Locality of Movement Dependencies*. Amsterdam: John Benjamins.

Grohmann, Kleanthes K. 2007. Transfer vs. spell-out and the road to PF. *Linguistic Analysis* 33, 176–194.

Grohmann, Kleanthes K. 2011. Anti-locality: Too-close relations in grammar. In Cedric Boeckx (ed.), *The Oxford Handbook of Linguistic Minimalism*, 260–290. Oxford: Oxford University Press.

Grohmann, Kleanthes K. 2013. Spell-out rules. In H. Broekhuis and R. Vogel (eds.), *Linguistic Derivations and Filtering: Minimalism and Optimality Theory*, 316–352. Sheffield: Equinox.

Grohmann, Kleanthes K., John Drury, and Juan Carlos Castillo. 2000. No more EPP. In R. Billerey and B. D. Lillehaugen (eds.), *Proceedings of the Nineteenth West Coast Conference on Formal Linguistics*, pp. 153–166. Somerville, MA: Cascadilla Press.

Grohmann, Kleanthes. K. and Liliane Haegeman. 2003. Resuming reflexives. *Proceedings of the 19th Scandinavian Conference of Linguistics. Nordlyd: Tromsø University Working Papers in Language & Linguistics* 31: 46–62 [http://www.ub.uit.no/munin/nordlyd].

Grohmann, Kleanthes K. and Michael T. Putnam. 2007. Dynamic stress assignment. *Linguistic Analysis* 33: 326–363.

Haddad, Youssef. 2014. Attitude datives in Lebanese Arabic and the interplay of syntax and pragmatics. *Lingua* 145: 65–103.

Hagstrom, Paul. 2006. Book review [of Grohmann (2003b)]. *Journal of Comparative Germanic Linguistics* 9: 217–228.

Herbeck, Peter. 2013. PRO=*pro*. Ms., University of Salzburg.

Hornstein, Norbert.1999. Movement and control. *Linguistic Inquiry* 30, 69–96.

Hornstein, Norbert. 2001. *Move! A Minimalist Theory of Construal*. Malden, MA: Blackwell.

Hornstein, Norbert. 2003. On control. In R. Hendrick (ed.), *Minimalist syntax*, 6–81. Malden, MA: Blackwell.

Hornstein, Norbert (2007). Pronouns in minimal setting. In N. Corver and J. Nunes (eds.), *The Copy Theory of Movement*, pp. 351–385. Amsterdam: John Benjamins.

Hornstein, N., J. Nunes, and K. K. Grohmann (2005). *Understanding Minimalism*. Cambridge: Cambridge University Press.

Hornstein, Norbert and M. Polinsky (eds.) (2010). *Movement Theory of Control*. Amsterdam: John Benjamins.

Kambanaros, Maria, and Kleanthes K. Grohmann. 2015. More GAPs in children with SLI? Evidence from Greek for not fully lexical verbs in language development. *Applied Psycholinguistics* 36: 1029–1057.

Keine, Stefan. 2015. Locality domains in syntax: Evidence from sentence processing. Ms., http://ling.auf.net/lingbuzz/002473.

Landau, Idan. 1999. *Elements of control*. Doctoral dissertation, Massachusetts Institute of Technology, Cambridge. [Revised version appeared as Landau, I. (2000). *Elements of Control: Structure and Meaning in Infinitival Constructions*. Dordrecht: Kluwer.]

Landau, Idan. 2013. *Control in Generative Grammar: A Research Companion*. Cambridge: Cambridge University Press.
Landau, Idan. 2015. *A Two-Tiered Theory of Control*. Cambridge, MA: MIT Press.
Lasnik, Howard. 1995. Last Resort and Attract F. In L. Gabriele, D. Hardison, and R. Westmoreland (eds.), *Proceedings of the Sixth Annual Meeting of the Formal Linguistics Society of Mid-America*, pp. 62–81. Bloomington, IN: Indiana University Linguistics Club.
Lasnik, Howard. 1999. *Minimalist Analysis*. Oxford: Blackwell.
Levin, B. and M. Rappaport Hovav (2005). *Argument Realization*. Cambridge: Cambridge University Press.
Lidz, J. and W. J. Idsardi (1998). Chains and phono-logical form. *PLC 22 – University of Pennsylvania Working Papers in Linguistics* 5.1, 109–125.
Manzini, M. Rita. 1983. On control and control theory. *Linguistic Inquiry* 14: 421–446.
Manzini, M. Rita. 1986. On control and binding theory. In S. Berman, J.-W. Choe, and J. McDonough (eds.), *Proceedings of the 16th Annual Meeting of North Eastern Linguistic Society*, 322–337. Amherst, MA: GLSA Publications.
Manzini, M. Rita. 2009. PRO, pro, and NP-trace (raising) are interpretations. In Kleanthes K. Grohmann (ed.), *Explorations of Phase Theory: Features and Arguments*, 131–180. Berlin: Mouton de Gruyter.
Manzini, M. Rita and Anna Roussou. 2000. A minimalist theory of A-movement and control. *Lingua* 110: 409–447.
Manzini, M. Rita and Leonardo M. Savoia. 2005. *I dialetti italiani e romanci: Morfosintassi generativa*, 3 vols. Alessandria: Edizioni dell'Orso.
Manzini, M. Rita and Leonardo M. Savoia. 2007. *A Unification of Morphology and Syntax: Studies in Romance and Albanian Dialects*. London: Routledge.
Manzini, M. Rita and Leonardo M. Savoia. 2016. Finite and non-finite complementation, particles and control in Aromanian, compared to other Romance varieties and Albanian. Ms., http://ling.auf.net/lingbuzz/002874.
Martin, Roger. 1996. *A minimalist theory of PRO and control*. Doctoral dissertation, University of Connecticut, Storrs.
McCawley, James. D. 1970. English as a *VSO* language. *Language* 46: 286–299.
Migliori, Laura. 2016. *Argument structure, alignment and auxiliaries between Latin and Romance: A diachronic syntactic account*. Doctoral dissertation, Leiden University.
Müller, Gereon. 2011. *Constraints on Displacement: A Phase-Based Approach*. Amsterdam: John Benjamins.
Müller, Gereon. 2014. A local approach to the Williams Cycle. *Lingua* 140: 117–136.
O'Neil, John H. 1997. *Means of control: Deriving the properties of PRO in the minimalist program*. Doctoral dissertation, Harvard University, Cambridge, MA.
Platzack, Christer. 1991. Comp, Infl and Germanic word order. In L. Helland and K. Koch Christensen (eds.), *Topics in Scandinavian Syntax*, 185–234. Dordrecht: Foris.
Postal, Paul M. 1974. *On Raising: One Rule of English and Its Theoretical Implications*. Cambridge, MA: MIT Press.
Putnam, Michael T. 2007. *Scrambling and the Survive Principle*. Amsterdam: John Benjamins.
Rosenbaum, Peter. 1967. *The Grammar of English Predicate Complement Constructions*. Cambridge, MA: MIT Press.
Sportiche, Dominique. 1988. A theory of floating quantifiers and its corollaries for constituent structure. *Linguistic Inquiry* 19: 425–449.

Webelhuth, Gert (ed.) (1995). *Government and Binding Theory and the Minimalist Program*. Malden, MA: Blackwell.

Williams, Edwin S. 1974. *Rule ordering in syntax*. Doctoral dissertation, Massachusetts Institute of Technology, Cambridge.

Williams, Edwin S. 1994. *Thematic Structure in Syntax*. Cambridge, MA: MIT Press.

Richard S. Kayne
Some thoughts on *one* and *two* and other numerals

1 Introduction

The term 'numeral' is a familiar one. It gives the impression that *one, two, three* ..., etc. form a homogeneous class of elements. In this paper, I will try to show that numerals do not form a homogeneous class, and that there are three major subclasses. Numeral *one* is the only member of its subclass. Numeral *one* is associated with a classifier, and is necessarily accompanied by (a possibly silent counterpart of) *single* or *only*. With *two, three* and *four*, coordinate structures are involved. From *five* on up, a silent counterpart of *set* is necessarily present.

2 Only one *one* (anti-homophony)

In many languages, what we think of as numeral *one* has the same form as the indefinite article (e.g. French *un*). In English, though, what we think of as numeral *one* is distinct in form from the indefinite article *a(n)*. To apparently complicate things further, English prenominal *one* is itself not always numeral-like, as we can see from:

(1) John has written only one paper this year.

(2) Mary has just written one hell of a paper.

The numeral interpretation perceived in (1) is absent in (2). Other examples of a similarly non-numeral prenominal *one* are found in:

(3) There's one John Smithfield here to see you.

(4) One day, he'll realize that we were right.

(5) At one time, they were friends.

Richard S. Kayne, New York University

https://doi.org/10.1515/9781501505201-019

Perlmutter (1970) took prenominal *one* to be the same element in both (1) and (2). In support of Perlmutter's unified approach to these two instances of *one* is the fact that all of (1)-(5) are equally incompatible with plural nouns:

(6) *He's written only one papers this year.

(7) *She's just written one hell of papers.

(8) *There's one John Smithfields here to see you.

(9) *One days, he'll realize that we were right.

(10) *At one times, they were friends.

The fact that *one* is the same element in (1) as in (2)-(5) can itself be taken to follow from a general principle that bars homophones. The formulation given in Kayne (2017), originating in a discussion of English *there*, was (for languages with an English-type orthography)[1]:

(11) If X and Y are functional elements and are homophones, then X and Y cannot have the same spelling.

The appeal to orthography in (11) should be interpreted as a stand-in for an appropriate notion of abstract phonology.[2] For example, (11) allows English to have, as accidental homophones, *to* and *two*, which differ orthographically, but also almost certainly differ phonologically, given the -w- in *two*,

---

1 I am grateful to Thomas Leu for insightful discussion bearing on this questions. English *there* at first glance has (at least) four identities:
i)   There's a problem with your analysis. (expletive *there*)
ii) Don't go there! (locative *there*)
iii) That there book ain't no good. (deictic *there*, non-standard)
iv) They spoke thereof this morning. (referential non-locative *there*, productive in Dutch, German)

The proposal in Kayne (2004; 2017) takes all of (i)-(iv) to have the same *there*, with the apparent differences traceable to differences in the syntactic environment, including the presence of one or another silent element. The expectation is that all cases of merely apparent homophony will be amenable to similar treatment (as, for example, in Kayne (2010a) on English *that* and French/Italian *que/che*).

2 Cf. Chomsky and Halle (1968, 69, 184).

whose phonological presence is supported by its being pronounced in *twelve*, *twenty* and *twin*.[3]

It should be further noted that (11) leads to the conclusion that prenominal *one*, in addition to being one and the same element in all of (1)-(5), must be the same element as the *one* of both of the following:

(12) a blue one

(13) blue ones

The *one* of (1)-(5) and the *one* of (12)-(13) cannot be accidental homophones.[4]

3 *One* is a determiner

The *one* of (1)-(5) looks like a determiner of some sort. And Perlmutter (1970) and Barbiers (2005; 2007) did take there to be a close relation between prenominal *one* and the indefinite article. Perlmutter (1970: 234) more specifically took English to have, as a source for the indefinite article, "a rule which obligatorily converts unstressed proclitic *one* to *an*".[5]

Perlmutter's formulation/rule was not immediately able, as he himself noted, to account for generic-like *a/an*, given the absence of a comparable generic prenominal one that would be its source[6]:

---

[3] In addition, the non-pronunciation of the *w* in *two* is arguably a consequence of English never allowing word initial /twu.../ (and similarly for other stop consonants). The coexistence of *to* and *too* might be linked to their different spelling; alternatively the difference in spelling does not reflect any abstract phonological difference in this case and they are in fact the same element, as may be suggested by a link between *too* and (*in addition*) *to* (cf. German *dazu* ('there-to')).

[4] For evidence supporting this conclusion, see Kayne (2017).

[5] Left open by this reference to stress is the fact that English sometimes allows a stressed indefinite article, as in:

i) I can't give you the book (you want), but I can give you a book.

in which *a* rhymes with *say*. This stressed *a* does not license NP-ellipsis:

ii) *...but I can give you a.

suggesting that Borer's (2005, 111n) primarily phonological account of the impossibility of (ii) with unstressed *a* is not general enough.

[6] I am setting aside the reading in which *one spider* can correspond to *one type of spider*, arguably as 'one TYPE OF spider'.

Perlmutter suggests that generic *a/an* might perhaps derive from *any one*, but note:

(14) A spider has eight legs and many eyes.

(15) One spider has eight legs and many eyes.

The generic-like reading of (14) does not carry over in any exact way to (15).
The rule that Perlmutter suggested was meant to treat pairs like:

(16) That was a hell of a paper.

(17) That was one hell of a paper.

as involving, respectively, an unstressed and a (somewhat) stressed variant of the same element *a/one*, with the same interpretation. As just noted, the kind of pairing that holds for (16) and (17) does not hold for (14) and (15). In part similarly, the intended pairing breaks down for:

(18) too long a book

which has no counterpart with *one*[7]:

(19) *too long one book

A third such problem for Perlmutter's conversion rule lies in:

(20) a few books

(21) *one few books

where, again, the indefinite article has no *one* counterpart to serve as a plausible source. A fourth problem for the pairing of *a* and *one* can be seen in:

(22) They're selling one-drawer desks in the back of the store.

(23) *They're selling a-drawer desks in the back of the store.

---

i)   Any/*A spider whatsoever would be able to eat that insect.
ii) Hardly any/*a spider would eat that insect
iii) Not just any/*a spider could have done that.

7 Possibly related to this is:
i)   a half a day
ii) *a half one day.
On (i), see Wood (2002).

in which, this time, prenominal *one* is possible, but cannot be replaced by *a/an*. Despite these several discrepancies between *one* and *a/an*, I will, in partial agreement with both Perlmutter and Barbiers, take there to be a significant relation between *a/an* and *one*, to be broached in the next section.

4 *One* is a determiner associated with a classifier

Let me try to execute the idea that *a/an* is a reduced form of *one* in a different way from Perlmutter (and Barbiers). Let me start from the generic-like (14) and in particular from the fact that the contrast between (14) and (15) is reminiscent of a fact from Chinese. According to Cheng and Sybesma (1999, 533–534; 2012, 640), a singular classifier in Chinese cannot occur within a generic DP (whether or not *yi* ('a/an/one') is present).[8]

This leads me to think that *one* cannot occur in (15) with the generic-like reading of (14) for the same reason that singular classifiers are excluded from Chinese generic DPs. This leads in turn to the following proposal:

(24) An English DP with *one* contains a singular classifier. (Conversely, an English DP with *a/an* can (perhaps must) lack a classifier.)

The idea that *one* is always associated with a singular classifier has something in common with Perlmutter's idea that *a/an* is a phonologically 'reduced form' of *one*, though by reinterpreting the notion of 'reduction' as the more specific notion of the absence of a classifier, we are able to formulate an account of (14) vs. (15) that Perlmutter's less specific proposal was unable to do. More specifically put, the phrase *one spider* in (15) must, by (24), be associated with a singular classifier. But, judging from Chinese, singular classifiers are incompatible with generic readings. Therefore, (15) cannot be a generic type of sentence in the way that (14) can be.

---

[8] Cf. Simpson et al. (2011, 188) on Vietnamese; also Simpson and Biswas (2015, 7) on Bangla.

5 Back to *one* and its classifier

In Cardinaletti and Starke's (1999) terms, we might try to relate the fact that *one* is associated with extra syntactic material (the singular classifier) to the fact that *one* is morphophonologically 'bigger' than *a/an*. We could do this as follows. *One* is to be is to be understood as bimorphemic and in particular as 'w∧ + n', where w∧- is the classifier and *-n* an indefinite article.[9] The necessary pronunciation of the *n* of *one* even before a consonant, as opposed to the necessary dropping of the *n* of *an* before a consonant, might just be phonology. Or it might also be related to syntax, especially if the order 'classifier – indefinite article' ('w∧ + n)[10] is produced by leftward movement from a structure in which the indefinite article precedes the classifier.[11]

From this perspective, the additional contrasts (beyond the generic one) mentioned earlier between *one* and *a/an* look as follows. The contrast in:

(25) a. We have a few days left.
 b. *We have one few days left

could be attributed to a clash between the classifier w∧- that is part of *one* and the silent noun NUMBER (capitalization will indicate silence) that accompanies *few*.[12] That NUMBER is important here is supported by the existence of similar effects with overt *number*, as seen in:

(26) a. We have (only) a small number of days left.
 b. *We have (only) one small number of days left.

as well as in:

---

9 Consideration of ?*a whole another N* might support taking *-n* itself to be an indefinite article, as suggested to me a while back by Thomas Leu (p.c.), with subsequent questions about the status of *a*. An alternative that I will not pursue here would be to take *one* to be monomorphemic and to cooccur with a silent classifier.
10 Cf. Ghosh (2001, chap.3) on some Tibeto-Burman having 'CLF Numeral Noun' order.
11 Cf. Leu (2015, 116) on German *ein* being moved across.
12 Cf. Kayne (2002; 2005a); sometimes *few* can be accompanied by overt *number*, as in:
i) Of all the students, it's John who's written the fewest number of papers this year.

(27) a. Mary has written (quite) a number of papers this year.[13]
b. *Mary has written (quite) one number of papers this year.

In all of (25)-(27), *number*/NUMBER is not allowed to cooccur with the classifier associated with *one*. In the variants of (25)-(27) with *a*, there is no comparable classifer, just the indefinite article, and so no clash.[14] As for:

(28) too long (of) a book

(29) *too long (of) one book

it may be that the classifier in question blocks the preposing of the degree phrase.

Finally, the reverse type of restriction seen in:

(30) They're selling one-drawer desks in the back of the store.

(31) *They're selling a-drawer desks in the back of the store.

may be linked to:

(32) They're real Brooklyn-lovers.

(33) They're real (*the) Bronx-lovers.

via a prohibition against bare articles appearing within compound-like structures, with *one*'s classifier protecting it, in a way that remains to be spelled out, from this prohibition.[15]

In conclusion, then, *one*, always the same element, is associated with a (singular) classifier in all of its occurrences.

---

[13] In a rather different interpretation, one can to some extent have:
i) ?Mary has written one number of papers, John another
[14] The clash in question may in turn be related to the classifier-like status of *number*/NUMBER itself in these sentences – cf. Liao (2015).
[15] Why *one* acts differently here from demonstratives remains to be understood. Relevant to the formulation of the prohibition in question is:
i) two (beautiful) (*the) seventh inning home runs
vs.
ii) ?two (beautiful) top of the seventh inning home runs.

6 Numeral *one*

By (11), what we think of as numeral *one* must, since it is spelled the same and has the same (abstract) phonology, be the same element as the non-numeral prenominal *one* of (2)-(5) and the same element as the non-prenominal *one* of (12)-(13). Examples of numeral *one* are:

(34) John has written three papers. Two are on phonology and one is on syntax.

(35) There are three books on the table. Only one is worth reading.

In allowing its associated noun to remain silent, as in (34) and (35), numeral *one* behaves like other numerals. This may at first seem unsurprising, but Barbiers (2007) has emphasized that *one* is quite different from other numerals in some ways, in particular in not lending itself (in a great many languages) to regular ordinal formation:

(36) The first/*oneth chapter is the most interesting.

Similarly, in many Romance languages *one* is the only numeral that shows agreement in gender. In addition, in French complex numerals that are multiples of 100 (or 1000), *one* is the only numeral that cannot appear, as seen, for example, in:

(37) deux cents ('two hundred'), trois cents ('three hundred')...

(38) cent

(39) *un cent ('one hundred')[16]

French also displays a striking asymmetry between *one* and other numerals in that in the additive compound numerals 21, 31, 41, 51, 61, 71, an overt coordinating element *et* ('and') is necessary, e.g.:

---

[16] With 1000, French has:
i) (*un) mille linguistes ('a thousand linguists')
Possible, with a complex numeral containing *one* as a subpart, is:
ii) trente-et-un mille linguistes ('thirty and one thousand linguists')

(40) vingt-et-un livres ('twenty-and-one books')

whereas with 22, 23, ... 32, 33 ... no coordinating element appears, e.g.: [17]

(41) vingt-deux livres ('twenty-two books')

7 The analysis of numeral *one*

It may appear paradoxical that numeral *one* should be the same element as the non- numeral *one* of (2)-(5), repeated here as (42)-(45), insofar as numeral *one* and non-numeral *one* are felt to be distinct:

(42) Mary has just written one hell of a paper.

(43) There's one John Smithfield here to see you.

(44) One day, he'll realize that we were right.

(45) At one time, they were friends.

A proposal that comes to mind that dissolves this paradox is that sentences with numeral *one* such as:

(46) John has two brothers and one sister.

have the analysis:

(47) ...and one SINGLE sister.

with a silent adjective corresponding to *single*.[18] Whereas examples (42)-(45) do not contain SINGLE.

---

[17] Though there may be a silent *et* present, to judge by the obligatory pronunciation of the final consonant of *vingt* in 22, 23...
[18] There is a point of similarity here with Borer's (2005, 196) proposal that Hebrew *'exád* ('one') is an adjective interpreted as 'single'. In some cases, *one* is natural with a following overt *single*:
(i)   You haven't written one single paper this year.

The term 'numeral *one*' picks out those instances of *one* that occur in a syntactic context whose overall interpretation lends itself to contrast with other numerals. If (47) is correct, then that context will necessarily include an adjective like *single*/SINGLE. In some cases, *only* is very natural:

(48) John has two brothers but only one sister.

Silent ONLY might be present in other cases. Whatever the correct details, it seems extremely likely that the language faculty consistently treats numeral 1 as not being a primitive, and that something like (47) will hold for numeral 1 in all languages.

One is in fact in all its guises a complex determiner. It is always associated with a singular classifier. As a numeral, it is in addition accompanied by SINGLE or *single* (and/or by ONLY or *only*).

8 A note on ordinals

The idea that numeral *one* is to be understood as in (47) is in partial agreement with Barbiers's (2005; 2007) claim that *one* is very different from *two* and numerals higher than *two*. He took numeral *one* to be a stressed, focussed version of the indefinite article.[19] The present proposal doesn't rely directly on the notion of 'focus', using instead the presence of SINGLE.[20]

As mentioned earlier, Barbiers emphasized the relative systematicity of the cross-linguistic absence of a regularly formed ordinal based on *one*:

(49) Mary was the first/*oneth linguist to have proposed that.

From the present perspective, the impossibility of *oneth* must reflect the inability of ordinal – *th* to combine with '*one* SINGLE' (and similarly for other languages), as suggested by:

---

19 As mentioned in an earlier footnote, this view of *one* faces a challenge dealing with stressed *a*, as in:

(i) We don't need some chocolates, we need a chocolate.

with *a* pronounced to rhyme with *say*.

20 Presumably, the numerals from *two* on up (perhaps apart from complex numerals having 1 as a subpart) do not (necessarily) involve SINGLE.

(50) *the (one) single-th linguist

Why ordinal -th differs in this way from the suffixal -ce of *once*,[21] which can combine with numeral *one*, as in:

(51) We've been there only once.

remains to be elucidated.

9 *Two*: Introduction and proposal

If what we think of as numeral *one* is complex in the way outlined above and is not a syntactic (or a semantic) primitive, what about *two* (and *three* and *four* and *five*)?

In some varieties of English, *two* is paralleled by *both*, in cases like:

(52) the two of us

(53) the both of us

Although not as ordinary as (52), (53) seems to be fairly common. Quite a bit less common than (53), though attested, is:

(54) the both boys

in what appears to be the sense of:

(55) the two boys

The point of bringing in *both* here is that *both* also occurs in English with coordination:

(56) both this book and that book

A comparable use of *two* is not possible:

(57) *two this book and that book

---

21 On *once*, see Kayne (2014).

Consider, however, the following proposal. Although impossible in (57), *two* can occur in coordinate structures in a way that partially tracks *both*, but only with coordinated bare indefinites, as in:

(58) *two book and book

which is itself ill-formed, but becomes, in this proposal, well-formed if part of the coordinate structure is silent[22];

(59) two book AND BOOK

Now (59) gives the impression that English should allow *two book* rather than *two books*.
    In fact, English allows both types, depending on the syntactic environment:

(60) This file cabinet has two drawers.

(61) This is a two-drawer file cabinet.

In addition some speakers (myself not included) allow:

(62) You owe us two pound.

The proposal indicated in (59) should be interpreted as saying that (59) represents the only way in which *two* can combine with a noun. What we think of as simple phrases like *two book(s)* are actually instances of (minimal) coordination.

10 *Three* and *four*

There is no word in English that is to *three* as *both* is to *two*:

(63) both books; both Mary and John

---

22 Or perhaps 'two BOOK AND book'; in addition, classifiers will need to be integrated, as will the appearance of the preposition *de* in French in dislocation examples like (cf. Kayne (1975, sect. 2.7):
i)   Elle en a trois, de frères. ('she thereof has three, of brothers')
Something like this *de* appears in Moroccan Arabic even without dislocation – cf. Harrell (1962, 206); see also the discussion of Romanian in Kayne (2006).

(64) *t(h)roth books; *t(h)roth Mary and John and Susan

Therefore, the preceding discussion of *two* cannot be transposed mechanically to *three*. Let me instead try to get at *three* using *both* itself, in combination with *either*, which in some cases is, like *both*, clearly linked to *two*[23]:

(65) either of those two/*three books

Let me begin by constructing a three-argument coordinate counterpart to (56), using *both* and *either*:

(66) We should hire either Mary or both John and Bill.

This example is reasonably acceptable, and suggests the following picture for *three (books)*, modeled on (59) (and abstracting away from constituent structure)[24]:

(67) three book AND BOOK AND BOOK

Let me assume now that the well-formedness of (67) tracks the acceptability of (66) (even though (67) does not contain an overt *both* or an overt *either*), at least to the extent that the well-formedness of (67), and hence of *three book(s)*, depends on (66) not being strongly unacceptable.

In the spirit of (67), *four book(s)* can be thought of as:

(68) four book AND BOOK AND BOOK AND BOOK

whose well-formedness will depend on the (partial) acceptability of[25]:

(69) ??We should hire both Jim and either Mary or both John and Bill.

Similarly, *five book(s)* would potentially be:

---

23 As are suffixes indicating dual number, which at least in some languages seem clearly to be related to numeral 'two' itself – cf. Harlow (2006, 111) on Maori and Pearce (2015, 24) on Unua.
24 Following Kayne (1981; 1994), I take coordination to be built solely on binary branching structures.
25 Gertjan Postma (p.c.) notes that the following is more acceptable than the text example:
i)   We should hire either both John & Bill or both Mary and Sue.

(70) five book AND BOOK AND BOOK AND BOOK AND BOOK

with the well-formedness of (70) depending, however, on whether or not the following is acceptable at all:

(71) *We should hire either Ann or both Jim and either Mary or both John and Bill.

It seems to me that there is a sharp dropoff in acceptability from (69) to (71).[26] I conclude, needless to say, not that *five book(s)* is impossible, but rather that *five book(s)* does not and cannot have a coordinate-like derivation of the sort that is arguably available to *two book(s), three book(s)* and (to some extent) *four book(s)*.

If so, then the smooth generation of the set of natural numbers via Merge that was suggested by Chomsky (2008) (and Watanabe (2016)) is not appropriate for the language faculty, at least not for the case in which numerals are associated with nouns or noun phrases. (Conceivably, the language faculty might have a distinct counting mechanism, though that would depend on the non-obvious assumption that in counting there is no silent noun or noun phrase present.)

11 *Five* and up

One might wonder if smooth generation via Merge could hold for *five* and above even if not appropriate for the entire set of numerals. Let me address this question by jumping to *ten* and to the notion of numerical base.

Surely one of the most striking things about numerals in languages like English is how few there are that are monomorphemic. If the first part of this paper is on the right track, then *one* may well not be monomorphemic. *Two* may not be, either, if *tw-* is one morpheme (as seems virtually certain, given *twelve, twenty, twin*) and if *-o* is another. That leaves the numerals from *four to ten* as

---

[26] The deviance of the latter might perhaps, depending on its exact constituent structure, be linked to Chomsky and Miller's (1963) discussion of center embedding. For relevant discussion of the constituent structure of coordination, see den Dikken (2006). For a possible alternative to Chomsky and Miller (1963), see Kayne (2000a, chap. 15, Part III).

Sentences like *We should invite either J or M or S or A or P or...* may involve sentential, rather than DP, coordination. Luigi Rizzi (p.c.) raises the additional possibility that the cutoff between 3 and 5 might be linkable to subitization vs. counting, as discussed in Dehaene (2011).

very likely to be monomorphemic,[27] plus *hundred* and *thousand*. (*Twelve* is almost certainly not, given *tw-*; *eleven* is less clear, but the *-el(e)v-* that it shares with *twelve* suggests that it, too, may not be monomorphemic.) (*Million, billion, trillion* and the imprecise *zillion* suggest factoring out *-illion*, in which case none of them are monomorphemic, either.)

There are, then, approximately ten monomorphemic numerals. Why are there so few? A partial answer is that English has, starting at least with 13, composite numerals such as 423, based on addition and multiplication and powers of 10, instead of having a larger number of monomorphemic numerals. But why does English (and similarly for many other languages) have recourse to such composite numerals so soon? Why does it not wait until 100, say?

Part of the answer to this question must be related to the discussion above, to the effect that the coordinate strategy is available only as far as (*three* or) *four*.

Another part has to do, I think, with the question of the linguistic instantiation of the notion 'numerical base'. In earlier work,[28] I suggested that in a language in which the base is 10 (and similarly for languages with a different base), any multiple or power of 10 must have 10 (or that power of 10) accompanied by a silent counterpart of the noun *set* (silence will again be indicated by capitalization). Thus 306 is:

(72) three hundred SET and six

to be understood as 'three hundred-sets and six' or as:

(73) three sets of a hundred, plus six

In, say, 76, we have:

(74) seven ty SET AND six

in which *ty* is a form of 10 and *and* is silent, in addition to *set* being silent. (74), that is, 76, is then to be understood as:

(75) seven sets of ten, plus six

---

27 Guglielmo Cinque points out (p.c.) that the bimorphemic character of *three* may be supported by *thrice, thirteen, thirty*, all of which lack the *-ee* of *three*.
28 Cf. Kayne (2006).

When there is no 'and'-component to the numeral, we have, say for 70:

(76) seven ty SET

understood as:

(77) seven sets of ten

and we call these 'round numbers'.[29]

12 Semi-round numbers

Let me now jump to the hypothesis that there is a linguistically significant notion of semi- round number, based on half the numerical base. The semi-round numbers in English and in other languages with base 10 are, then:

(78) 5, 15, 25...

That semi-round numbers have a special status is supported by facts from French, which has a robust use of approximative expressions that correspond to some extent to English *hundreds of books*, which French readily allows in the singular: [30]

(79) une centaine de livres ('a 100-aine of books' = 'a hundred or so books')

(80) une soixantaine de livres ('a 60-aine of books' = 'sixty or so books')

The French numerals from 11 through 16 are arguably additive:

(81) onze, douze, treize, quatorze, quinze, seize

---

[29] In English, this term extends to additive numerals whose last part is 'round', e.g. 350.
[30] Though additive numerals in which the larger component comes first (e.g. in English thirty- one vs. thirteen) are subject to a restriction in French (brought to my attention by Michal Starke (p.c.)) that prohibits adding *-aine* to them (with the exact range of cases varying depending on the speaker):
(i) *une centdizaine de livres ('a 110-aine of books')
(ii) *une vingtcinquaine de livres ('a 25-aine of books')

with 10 expressed by the suffix -*ze*. If we abstract away from the special case of 12 (*douze*, special in English, too, given *dozen*), we can note a clear difference between semi-round 15 and its neighbors:

(82) une quinzaine ('a 15-aine')

(83) *une treizaine, *une quatorzaine, *une seizaine

With 15, the *-aine* form is straightforwardly acceptable as an approximative, as opposed to 13, 14 and 16.

Semi-round numbers thus have a special status. In languages with 10 as a numerical base, 5 and odd multiples of 5 (as in (78)) will have this special status. Let me now generalize the relevance of silent SET discussed above, as follows[31]:

(84) All round and semi-round numbers (and only those) are associated with silent SET.

This formulation is intended to cover 10 and 5 themselves, as well as higher multiples of 10 and 5.

If (84) is correct, then we find ourselves with an abrupt transition between 4 and 5. The numeral 4 has an analysis involving coordination, along the lines of (68). The numeral 5 does not have an analysis involving coordination. 5 is rather '5 SET'. (And 4 is not '*4 SET', since 4 is not round or semi-round.)

13 Semi-round vs. unround

In a language with numerical base 10, there will thus be a semi-round vs. unround distinction between 5 (semi-round) and 4 (unround). This brings to mind the well-known morphological case distinction found in Russian between 2,3,4 on the one hand, and 5,6,7 ... on the other.[32] With 5 and above,[33] the associated noun shows genitive plural, whereas with 2, 3 and 4, there is different case morphology, often called genitive singular. From the present perspective, we

---

31 Silent SET is to be kept distinct from the silent NUMBER discussed in section 5 above. For discussion relevant to whether NUMBER cooccurs with (some) numerals, see Zweig (2006).
32 For recent relevant discussion, see Pesetsky (2013).
33 6 will now be '5 SET AND ONE', with questions arising as to how the pieces are spelled out, and similarly for 7, 8, 9.

can say as a first approximation that Russian has genitive plural if the numeral is associated with SET.

Many French speakers make a similar cut with *tous* ('all'), in cases like the following (as already noted by Grevisse and Goosse (2011, §660bis))[34]:

(85) Tous deux/trois/quatre/*cinq ont réussi. ('all 2/3/4/*5 have succeeded')

For such speakers *tous* plus numeral is possible only in the absence of SET. (English readily allows *all five/seventeen of us*, in a way possibly related to *all five/seventeen books* vs. French **tous trois livres* ('all three books').) English has something similar in:

(86) twosome, threesome, foursome, *fivesome

with 'numeral + -*some*' possible again only in the absence of SET. For many speakers, there is also the fact that the series:

(87) bilingual, trilingual, quadrilingual

stops with 4. In addition, the denominator of fractions has an irregular form (without -*th*) only with 2,3,4:

(88) one half, one third, one quarter

14 Cutoffs near 4 vs. 5

On the other hand, there are French speakers who make the cutoff in (85) between 3 and 4, i.e. who accept *tous trois* but not *tous quatre*. This recalls English:

(89) once, twice, thrice, *fice

A cutoff between 3 and 4 (in a language with base 10) cannot be due solely to the presence vs. absence of SET, but must presumably involve some further sensitivity to complexity-like distinctions of the sort illustrated by the full acceptability of (66) vs. the lesser acceptability of (69). The same holds for cutoffs

---

34 Cf. Postma (2015) on Dutch.

between 2 and 3, as in colloquial English having only *once* and *twice*, but not *thrice*,³⁵ and similarly for:

(90) half the books; *third the books

as well as for the earlier mentioned:

(91) both books; *t(h)roth books.

15 Languages with few numerals

Distinctions of the sort seen in (85)-(91), as well as the Russian one alluded to briefly, recall the fact that some languages, such as Mundurucu,³⁶ have few numerals. From the present perspective, such languages (for reasons that remain to be elucidated) lack numerals based on silent SET, and lack a corresponding numerical base, though they appear to have numerals based on the coordination-related syntax seen earlier with 2,3,4.³⁷

16 Other species

Hauser, Chomsky & Fitch (2002, 1577) mention the existence of a precise number sense in non-human animals that is limited to 1,2,3,4. This limitation recalls the distinctions discussed above, both for languages like Mundurucu and within English-type languages, between low numerals and the higher ones starting with 5. This point of similarity between non-human animals and human language suggests in turn that some non-human animals may have coordination-like

---

35 Though there is a clear difference between:
i)   ?a thrice-held conference
and:
ii) *a conference that has been held thrice
36 Cf. Pica et al. (2004). On the question whether Mundurucu has number words that are exact, see Izard, Pica, Spelke and Dehaene (2008) and Pica and Lecomte (2008).
37 Pica and Lecomte (2008) emphasize the relevance of coordination (and reduplication) for Mundurucu numeral expressions.

derivations of low numerals, of the sort alluded to in the discussion of (56)-(71). If so, then those non-human animals must have access to Merge.[38]

The fact that non-human animals seem to lack other aspects of human language might then be attributed to their lacking verbs and other categories that take arguments. They could still have (simple) nouns as objects of coordination, if Kayne (2008) is correct to take nouns never to have arguments of any sort.[39]

17 Conclusion

Phrases of the form 'numeral + noun' never involve direct merger of numeral and noun. In every case, derivations are more complex than that. With *one*, there is, in addition to a classifier, the necessary presence of *single/only*, whether pronounced or silent. With 2-4, coordinate structures are involved. With 5 on up, silent SET is necessarily present (in addition to whatever structure is required to express addition and multiplication and powers of the numerical base).

*This paper is closely based on a talk presented at the Lorentz Center Workshop in Leiden in March, 2016.

References

Barbiers, Sjef. 2007. "Indefinite Numerals *One* and *Many* and the Cause of Ordinal Suppletion," *Lingua*, 117, 859–880.

Barbiers, Sjef. 2005. "Variation in the Morphosyntax of *One*," *Journal of Comparative Germanic Linguistics*, 8, 159–183.

Borer, Hagit. 2005. *In Name Only*, Oxford University Press, Oxford.

Cardinaletti, Anna, and Michal Starke. 1999. "The Typology of Structural Deficiency: A Case Study of the Three Classes of Pronouns," in Henk van Riemsdijk (ed.) *Clitics in the Languages of Europe*, Mouton de Gruyter, Berlin, 145–233.

Cheng, Lisa L.-S. and Rynt Sybesma. 1999. "Bare and Not-So-Bare Nouns and the Structure of NP," *Linguistic Inquiry*, 30, 509–542.

Cheng, Lisa L.-S. and Rynt Sybesma. 2012. "Classifiers and DP," *Linguistic Inquiry*, 43, 634–650.

Chomsky, Noam. 2008. "On Phases," in R. Freidin, C.P. Otero and M.L. Zubizarreta (eds.) *Foundational Issues in Linguistic Theory. Essays in Honor of Jean-Roger Vergnaud*, MIT Press, Cambridge, Mass., 133–166.

---

[38] Cf. Rizzi (2016).
[39] It would suffice for this point if some nouns lacked arguments. In addition, the status of *and* itself needs to be clarified.

Chomsky, Noam and Morris Halle. 1968. *The Sound Pattern of English*, Harper and Row, New York.
Chomsky, Noam. and George Miller. 1963. "Introduction to the formal analysis of natural languages," in R. Luce, R. Bush and E. Galanter (eds.) *Handbook of Mathematical Psychology, Vol 2*, Wiley, New York, 269–323.
Dehaene, Stanislas. 2011. *The Number Sense (2nd edition)*, Oxford University Press, New York.
Den Dikken, Marcel. 2006 "*Either*-Float and the Syntax of Co-*or*-dination," *Natural Language and Linguistic Theory*, 24, 689–74
Ghosh, Rajat. 2001. *Some Aspects of Determiner Phrase in Bangla and Asamiya*, Doctoral dissertation, Tezpur University, Assam.
Grevisse, Maurice and André Goosse (2011) *Le Bon Usage. 75 Ans*, De Boeck Duculot, Brussels
Harlow, Ray. 2006. *Māori. A Linguistic Introduction*, Cambridge University Press, Cambridge.
Harrell, R.S. (1962) *A Short Reference Grammar of Moroccan Arabic*, Georgetown University Press, Washington, D.C.
Hauser, Marc D., Noam Chomsky, and W. Tecumseh Fitch (2002) "The Faculty of Language: What Is It, Who Has It, and How Did It Evolve?," *Science*, 298, 1569–1579.
Izard, Véronique, Pierre Pica, Elizabeth S. Spelke and Stanislas Dehaene. 2008. "Exact Equality and Successor Function: Two Key Concepts on the Path towards Understanding Exact Numbers," *Philosophical Psychology*, 21, 491–505.
Kayne, Richard S. 1975 *French Syntax. The Transformational Cycle*, The MIT Press, Cambridge, Mass.
Kayne, Richard S. 1981. "Unambiguous Paths," in R. May and J. Koster (eds.) *Levels of Syntactic Representation*, Foris, Dordrecht, 143–183 (reprinted in Kayne (1984)).
Kayne, Richard S. 1984. *Connectedness and Binary Branching*, Foris, Dordrecht.
Kayne, Richard S. 1994. *The Antisymmetry of Syntax*, The MIT Press, Cambridge, Mass.
Kayne, Richard S. 2000a. "A Note on Prepositions, Complementizers and Word Order Universals", in Kayne (2000b).
Kayne, Richard S. 2000b. *Parameters and Universals*, Oxford University Press, New York.
Kayne, Richard S. 2002. "On Some Prepositions That Look DP-internal: English *of* and French *de*", *Catalan Journal of Linguistics*, 1, 71–115 (reprinted in Kayne 2005b).
Kayne, Richard S. 2004. "Here and There" in C. Leclère, E. Laporte, M. Piot & M. Silberztein (eds.) *Syntax, Lexis & Lexicon-Grammar. Papers in Honour of Maurice Gross*, John Benjamins, Amsterdam, 253–273 (reprinted in Kayne 2005b).
Kayne, Richard S. 2005a. "On the Syntax of Quantity in English", in Kayne (2005b) (also in J. Bayer, T. Bhattacharya and M. T. Hany Babu (eds.), *Linguistic Theory and South-Asian Languages. Essays in Honour of K.A. Jayaseelan*, John Benjamins, Amsterdam.), 73–105.
Kayne, Richard S. 2005b. *Movement and Silence*, Oxford University Press, New York.
Kayne, Richard S. 2006. "A Note on the Syntax of Numerical Bases", in Y. Suzuki (ed.) *In Search of the Essence of Language Science: Festschrift for Professor Heizo Nakajima on the Occasion of his Sixtieth Birthday*, Hituzi Syobo, Tokyo, 21–41 (reprinted in Kayne (2010b)).
Kayne, Richard S. 2008. "Antisymmetry and the Lexicon," *Linguistic Variation Yearbook*, 8, 1–31 (also in A.M. di Sciullo and C. Boeckx (eds.) *The Biolinguistic Enterprise: New Perspectives on the Evolution and Nature of the Human Language Faculty*, Oxford University Press, London, 329–353 (2011)) (reprinted in Kayne 2010b).

Kayne, Richard S. 2010a. "Why Isn't *This* a Complementizer?", in Kayne 2010b (also in P. Svenonius (ed.) *Functional Structure from Top to Toe: A Festschrift for Tarald Taraldsen*, Oxford University Press, New York, 2014), 188–231.

Kayne, Richard S. 2010b. *Comparisons and Contrasts*, Oxford University Press, New York.

Kayne, Richard S. 2014 "*Once* and *Twice*", in *Inquiries into Linguistic Theory and Language Acquisition. Papers offered to* Adriana Belletti, C. Contemori and L. Dal Pozzo (eds.), Siena, CISCL Press (also in *Studies in Chinese Linguistics* (2015) 36, 1–20).

Kayne, Richard S. (2017) "English *One* and *Ones* as Complex Determiners" G. Sengupta, S. Sircar, M.G. Raman and R. Balusu (eds.) *Perspectives on the Architecture and Acquisition of Syntax. Essays in Honor of R. Amritavalli*, Springer Nature, Singapore, 77–114

Leu, Thomas. 2015. *The Architecture of Determiners*, Oxford University Press, New York.

Liao, Wei-Wen Roger. 2015. "Once upon an Invisible TIME: On Frequentative Phrases in Chinese,"*Studies in Chinese Linguistics*, 36, 21–33.

Pearce, Elizabeth. 2015. *A Grammar of Unua*, De Gruyter Mouton, Boston.

Perlmutter, David M. 1970. "On the Article in English," in M. Bierwisch and K.E. Heidolph (eds.) *Progress in Linguistics*, Mouton, The Hague, 233–248.

Pesetsky, David. (2013) *Russian Case Morphology and the Syntactic Categories*, The MIT Press, Cambridge, Mass.

Pica, Pierre and A. Lecomte (2008) "Theoretical Implications of the Study of Numbers and Numerals in Mundurucu," *Philosophical Psychology*, 21, 507–522.

Pica, Pierre, Lemer, Cathy, Izard, Véeronique and Stanislas Dehaene. 2004. "Exact and Approximate Arithmetic in an Amazonian Indigene Group," *Science*, 306, 499–503.

Postma, Gertjan. 2015. "Numerals in Dutch Paucal Constructions. The Compositional Nature of Paucal Number," paper presented at the SLE-Workshop on the Syntax & Semantics of Numerals, Leiden.

Rizzi, Luigi. 2016. "Monkey morpho-syntax and merge-based systems," *Theoretical Linguistics*, 42, 139–145.

Simpson, Andrew. and Priyanka Biswas. 2015. "Bare Nominals, Classifiers and the Representation of Definiteness in Bangla," handout of talk presented at FASAL-5, Yale University.

Simpson, Andrew., Hooi L. Soh and Hiroki Nomoto (2011) "Bare Classifiers and Definiteness. A Cross- linguistic Investigation," *Studies in Language*, 35, 168–193.

Watanabe, Akira. 2016. "Natural Language and Set-Theoretic Conception of Natural Numbers", ms., University of Tokyo.

Wood, Johanna L. (2002) "Much about *Such*," *Studia Linguistica*, 56, 91–115.

Zweig, Eytan. 2006. "Nouns and Adjectives in Numeral NPs," in L. Bateman and C. Ussery (eds.) *NELS 35: Proceedings of the thirty-fifth annual meeting of the North East Linguistic Society*, 663–675.

Rosangela Lai
Stress shift under cliticization in the Sardinian transitional area

1 Introduction

Sardinian dialects display stress shift under cliticization in imperative and gerund forms. Differences can be found across dialects with respect to stress placement (Lai 2016). Up to three enclitic pronouns are acceptable and the combination thereof can generate different stress shift patterns. Here, I will focus on the behaviour of the Sardinian dialect of Villagrande Strisaili (Sard. *Biddamánna Strisáili*), from the eastern transitional area between Campidanese and Nuorese Sardinian. All combinations of enclitics will be taken into account to define the conditions under which stress shift applies in the Sardinian transitional area.

2 The eastern Sardinian transitional area

Sardinian is an endangered Romance language spoken on the island of Sardinia (Lai 2017a, 2018). Two main varieties can be find: Campidanese in the southern areas and Logudorese-Nuorese in Central-Northern Sardinia.[1] In this work, I will focus on the eastern transitional area, which roughly coincides with Northern and Central Ogliastra. More precisely, the patterns examined here are observed in a few villages that border the Nuorese to the north and the Campidanese varieties to the south. These transitional varieties differ from both macro-areas in peculiar ways. One peculiarity is their pattern of

---

1 See Wagner (1941), Virdis (1978). A brief account in English can be found in Lai (2013: 3–25).

Note: I would like to thank the editors for inviting me to contribute to this Festschrift. I am grateful to Laura Bafile and Leonardo M. Savoia for their valuable comments and efforts to improve the paper, as well as to Elisabetta Carpitelli, Jean-Pierre Lai, M. Rita Manzini, Lucia Molinu and Simone Pisano for helpful discussions. Special thanks go to my informants, Simona Mighela and her family. Finally, I would like to thank M. Rita Manzini for her constant encouragement and strong support. Any errors are my own.

Rosangela Lai, Georg-August-Universität Göttingen

https://doi.org/10.1515/9781501505201-020

stress shift under cliticization, which is different from Sardinian patterns observed elsewhere.[2]

3 Clitics in the eastern transitional area

3.1 A sketch of personal, locative and partitive clitics

Sardinian clitics, transitional area included, appear in a fixed order both in proclisis and enclisis. The eastern transitional area has personal, partitive and locative clitics.[3] The personal clitic forms are listed in Table 1.[4]

Table 1: Personal clitics in the eastern transitional area.

	1st p.s.	2nd p.s.	3rd p.s.			1st p.p.	2nd p.p.	3rd p.p.		
			m.	f.	refl.			m.	f.	refl.
acc.	mi	ði	ddu	dda	si	nosi/si	osi/si	ddos	ddas	si
dat.	mi	ði	ddi	ddi	si	nosi/si	osi/si	ddis	ddis	si

In addition to the personal clitic forms in Table 1, *Villagrande Strisaili* displays the following clitics: *(i)ntfe* and *(i)nde*. *(i)ntfe* is from Latin HINC while *(i)nde* derives from Latin INDE.[5] *(i)ntfe* is a locative while *(i)nde* is a partitive.[6]

3.2 Data: Enclisis and proclisis

Sardinian dialects display three different patterns of stress shift with pronominal enclitics (Lai 2016, 2017b; Bafile and Lai 2018). The southern areas (Campidanese Sardinian dialects) have a peculiar pattern in which some enclitics induce a stress

---

[2] An overview of the main patterns of stress shift in Sardinian is presented in Lai (2016) and Bafile and Lai (2018).
[3] Reflexive *si* patterns with 1st and 2nd person pronouns.
[4] It must be borne in mind that some speakers for the 3rd person clitics prefer a geminate voiced alveolar stop instead of a geminate voiced retroflex stop. Note also that the fricative [ð] is the result of intervocalic lenition.
[5] See Bentley (2004).
[6] See Jones (1993: 218) and Manzini and Savoia (2005, 2007) for further details. On the syntax of Old Sardinian clitics see Lombardi (2007).

shift to the final syllable of the verb-clitic sequence, while other clitics do so to the penultimate syllable. The central-northern areas handle single clitics differently compared to clitic clusters (Lai 2017b). The transitional area between southern and central-northern dialects has a consistent behaviour in which all enclitics, no matter their number or combination, cause stress shifts to the penultimate syllable. For space limitations, I will focus on the transitional area pattern, exemplified by Villagrande Strisaili. The same pattern is found in other villages of central-northern Ogliastra (i.e., Arzana, Talana and Urzulei), Lower Barbagia and Barigadu (Blasco Ferrer 1988; Pisano 2016: 51). The transitional area pattern is similar to the Lucanian pattern discussed in studies by Kenstowicz (1991), Monachesi (1996) and Manzini and Savoia (2017) and the Formenteran Catalan pattern analysed in Torres-Tamarit (2008) and Bonet and Torres-Tamarit (2011). The data reported in Tables 2 and 3. are the results of fieldwork conducted by the author herself and refer to Villagrande Strisaili. To understand the condition under which Villagrande Strisaili displays stress shift under cliticization, I take into consideration the kind of enclitics available in the dialect in question and all their possible combinations, reported in Table 2.

In the first column, I report the imperative form of *battire* ('bring to the speaker'). In the second column, I conflate 1st and 2nd p. accusative and dative clitics (i.e., *mi, ði*).[7] The third includes the locative and partitive clitics (i.e., *ntfɛ, ndɛ*, respectively). The fourth column hosts 3rd p. accusative and dative clitics (non reflexives), (i.e., *ɖɖa, ɖɖa(s), ɖɖu, ɖɖo(s), ɖɖi, ɖɖi(s)*).[8] For simplicity, I only exemplify one clitic in each column. In the second column, *mi* is the 1st p. accusative/dative clitic. In the third, *ndɛ* is a partitive.[9] In the fourth column, *ɖɖa* and *ɖɖu* are the 3rd p. accusative clitics (feminine and masculine clitics, respectively). We can find the same distribution for *ɖɖi* (3rd p. dative clitic) as well as for the plural forms *ɖɖas, ɖɖos* and *ɖɖis*. Every time a single clitic or a clitic cluster is added to the verbal host, stress shifts to the penultimate syllable of the sequence verb plus clitic(s), (e.g., *bátti + mi → battími*). The last column hosts a sample of combinations of clitics from different categories (e.g., 1st, 2nd p. clitics plus locative or partitive clitics; 1st, 2nd p. clitics plus 3rd p. clitics; locative or partitive clitics plus 3rd p. clitics, etc.).

---

7 Notice that the bilabial nasal [m] in the 1st person singular pronoun *mi* is usually pronounced long [mmi]. In the examples in Table 2, I have preferred the form *mi* over *mmi*, adopted by other authors, because consonantal length cannot be assessed by phonological criteria. See Lai (2015) for discussion.
8 For an analogous classification but from a syntactic point of view, see Manzini and Savoia (2005, 2007, 2017).
9 Cf. Jones (1993: 214), Manzini and Savoia (2005).

Table 2: Stress placement in enclisis.

host (imperative form)	1st, 2nd p. Acc./Dat.	Locative, Partitive clitics	3rd p. Acc., 3rd p. Dat.	Result (host+clitic(s))
one clitic				
bátti +	mi			battími bring.IMP.2SG=DAT.1SG
bátti +		ndɛ		battínde bring.IMP.2SG=LOC
bátti +			dda, ddu	battídda, battíddu bring.IMP.2SG=ACC.3SG
two clitics				
bátti +	mi		dda, ddu	battimídda, battimíddu bring.IMP.2SG=DAT.1SG-ACC.3SG
bátti +		ndɛ	dda, ddu	battindédda, battindéddu bring.IMP.2SG=LOC-ACC.3SG
bátti +	mi	ndɛ		battimínde bring.IMP.2SG=DAT.1SG-LOC
three clitics				
bátti +	mi	ndɛ	dda, ddu	battimindédda, battimindéddu bring.IMP.2SG=DAT.1SG-LOC-ACC.3SG

In Table 3 below, different kinds of proclitics and the distribution thereof are listed. As one can see by comparing Table 2 with Table 3, the clitic sequence and the stress assignment coincide both in the case of proclisis and in the case of enclisis.

In the first column (Table 3), we find the present indicative of the 3rd person singular of *battire* (i.e., (*b*)*áttiði* 'bring to the speaker'). In the 2nd, 3rd, and 4th columns the preverbal clitics are listed, whereas the last column indicates the proclitics (a single clitic or a clitic cluster) and the present indicative. It is also to be noted that in this area the order of the clitic string coincides both preverbally and post-verbally. There is also another peculiarity: proclitic clusters

Table 3: Stress placement in proclisis.

Host (present indicative, 3rd p. s.)	1st, 2nd p. Acc./Dat.	Locative, partitive clitics	3rd p. Acc., 3rd p. Dat.	Result (clitic(s)+host)
one clitic				
(b)áttiði	mi			mi attiði DAT.1SG=bring-PRES.IND.3SG
(b)áttiði		(i)ndɛ		indɛ attiði LOC=bring-PRES.IND.3SG
(b)áttiði			ɖɖa, ɖɖu	ɖɖa attiði, ɖɖu attiði ACC.3SG.F/M=bring-PRES.IND.3SG
two clitics				
(b)áttiði	mi		ɖɖa, ɖɖu	míɖɖa attiði, míɖɖu attiði DAT.1SG=ACC.3SG.F/M=bring-PRES.IND.3SG
(b)áttiði		(i)ndɛ	ɖɖa, ɖɖu	indɛ́ɖɖa attiði, indɛ́ɖɖu attiði LOC=ACC.3SG.F/M=bring-PRES.IND.3SG
(b)áttiði	mi	(i)ndɛ		míndɛ attiði DAT.1SG=LOC=bring-PRES.IND.3SG
three clitics				
(b)áttiði	mi	(i)ndɛ	ɖɖa, ɖɖu	mindɛ́ɖɖa attiði, mindɛ́ɖɖu attiði DAT.1SG=LOC=ACC.3SG.F/M=bring-PRES.IND.3SG

bear stress and the stress placement after cliticization coincides both in the case of enclisis and in the case of proclisis. Several cases of Romance languages that display stress shift under cliticization have been reported in the current body of literature. However, in most cases proclitics do not bear stress while enclitics do (Peperkamp 1997: 97).

4 Clitics and stress shift in the literature

In addition to Sardinian, stress shift with enclitics is also attested in other languages such as Balearic Catalan, Neapolitan, Lucanian and Occitan dialects. The resulting stress patterns are similar for sequences of clitics but differences emerge in the case of one a single clitic. Many authors have brought various stress shift patterns triggered by the adjunction of enclitics to the general attention of the research community. Nespor and Vogel (1986) claim that besides the traditional prosodic constituents, one further constituent called Clitic Group must be assumed in the prosodic hierarchy between the Prosodic Word (PW) and the Prosodic Phrase (PP). Clitics, they say, have the status of PWs. Together with their host, they form a clitic group.

Kenstowicz (1991) relies on metrical phonology and analyses the behaviour of a number of languages with respect to enclisis and stress shift, among these, Italian, Lucanian and Neapolitan dialects. Italian does not show stress shift, regardless of the number and nature of the enclitics adjoined to the host. Lucanian dialects have stress shift both with one clitic and a clitic cluster: stress always shifts to the penultimate syllable of the sequence verb plus clitic (s). Neapolitan only shows stress shift with clitic clusters, while with one enclitic the stress keeps its original position.

Neapolitan is also discussed in Bafile (1994). Bafile (1994) builds on the idea that clitics can be inserted into the prosodic structure via adjunction, either to the prosodic word or to the prosodic phrase. The difference between the two is that by the former the clitic is integrated into the metrical prosodic structure of the prosodic word, and thus induces stress shift. According to Bafile (1994), stress shift with two enclitics is due to a readjustment of sequences that are metrically ill-formed: in Neapolitan, the unmarked word stress pattern is the paroxytone one.

Monachesi (1996) proposes to do without the notion of a Clitic Group altogether, and that cliticization must be reduced in some cases to affixation and in others to morphological compounding. In comparing the Neapolitan and Italian data, Monachesi concludes that in the case of one clitic adjunction, the clitic and the host form one prosodic word. In the case of two or more clitics, these unite in a prosodic word, which then adjoins to the verb, in what resembles a compound.

Similarly, Peperkamp (1997) proposes that clitics can enter the prosodic structure in different ways. She proposes that whenever there is no stress shift, the clitics must be adjoined at the Prosodic Phrase level (the Italian case). When stress shift is observed, there are two subcases to consider. When one clitic induces stress shift (as in Lucanian dialects), it must have been incorporated at the Prosodic Word level. The Neapolitan pattern, in which only clitic clusters of two or more clitics cause the shift, is analysed by assuming that the clitics are adjoined recursively to the prosodic word.

Unlike Bafile (1994), Monachesi (1996) and Peperkamp (1997), Loporcaro (2000) rejects the idea that in languages without stress shift, clitics should be regarded as adjoined to the Prosodic Phrase. The lack of stress shift is not sufficient evidence to posit two different types of adjunction (to PW and to PP). Clitics can be thought of as always adjoining at the PW level, the result being a post-lexical prosodic word that includes the verb and the enclitics.

In Manzini and Savoia (2005: §7.3.1) different typologies of stress shift in enclisis are discussed. The authors cover a range of dialects from the following groups: Western Ligurian, Campanian, Provencal, Franco-Provencal, Corsican, Sardinian, Calabrian and Lucanian. Because the variation is remarkable, the authors focus on some differences between the paradigms of enclisis and proclisis that are observed in many dialects. Only some Romance languages have stress shift in enclisis. In order to explain the shift of some Sardinian dialects, the authors propose that 3rd person clitics must be endowed with a prosodic/stress-related feature that induces stress assignment to the preceding syllable. In the case of one enclitic, this amounts to stress reassignment to the final syllable of the host. In the case of two clitics, the prosodic feature stresses the first clitic. 1st and 2nd person clitics have different forms depending on the dialects. In some dialects, these clitics have intrinsically stressed forms, which are only used when they are the only enclitics. In clusters, their allomorphs are stressed only if followed by 3rd person or locative clitics, which are endowed with the above mentioned prosodic feature.

Ordoñez and Repetti (2006, 2014) claim that phonology cannot explain the whole range of stress shift data, so they resort to a syntactic explanation. In their analysis, pronouns widely regarded as clitics must be actually classified into two different categories: true clitics and weak pronouns (*contra* Manzini and Savoia 2014; Pescarini 2016). The observed patterns must then be reduced to a difference between clitics and weak pronouns. Weak pronouns affect stress assignment, while clitics do not.

Bonet and Torres-Tamarit (2011) compare and analyse data from three Catalan dialects: Central Catalan, Majorcan Catalan and Formenteran Catalan. Their analysis is formulated within the Optimality Theory framework. The two dialects from the Balearic Islands display stress shift, unlike Central Catalan. In Formenteran Catalan, clitics produce stress shift and the stress always moves to the penultimate syllable. In Majorcan Catalan, stress moves to the final syllable. In the former case, a moraic trochee is formed to the right of the clitic cluster, while in the latter case a moraic iamb is formed instead. According to their analysis, in cases of stress shift, the two Balearic varieties have a tendency to conform to these two metrical patterns.

Manzini and Savoia (2017) discuss in turn the alternations in enclisis and proclisis in Occitan, Lucanian, Corsican and Ligurian dialects. The presence of stress shift and lack thereof is one of the differences between enclisis and proclisis, respectively. The authors argue that these differences cannot be explained by phonology. The differences must be due to allomorphy. This allomorphy is connected with the interpretive properties associated to the enclisis, insofar as it externalizes imperative modality. In particular, they claim that stress properties are directly embedded in the enclitics. In Occitan varieties, they assume, enclitics are stressed. In Lucanian dialects, partially analogous to the Sardinian transitional area, they propose that stress assignment is due to a prosodic feature [FOOT]. This feature codifies a requirement that applies to a post-lexical domain that includes the verb plus the enclitics. The feature dictates that a final trochee (a leftward binary foot) be formed starting from the final vowel of the post-lexical string.

Compared to the literature surveyed so far, Kim and Repetti (2013) choose an entirely different methodology rooted in experimental phonetics. The so-called stress shift, they say, is not actually such: rather, a variation in pitch accent is responsible for the pattern.

5 Stress in Sardinian varieties

Sardinian is a language with variable stress. Differences can be found across dialects. In central-northern areas, for example Nuorese Sardinian, the stress system allows for paroxytone and proparoxytone words, with paroxytone words being the most common (Pittau 1972: 20 and J-P Lai 2002: 52). Thus, while central-northern areas accept paroxytone and proparoxytone words, in the southern areas most words are paroxytones. Bolognesi (1998) presents quantitative data on stress position in a random sample of items taken from a Campidanese dictionary (Porru 2002) and finds that 85.2% are paroxytones, 13.7% are proparoxytones and 1.1% are oxytones. Oxytones, though, are either loanwords or cultivated words. As already pointed out by a number of authors (Wagner 1941, Pittau 1972, Virdis 1978, Bolognesi 1998, among others), Southern Sardinian also shows a degree of aversion to oxytones. Historically, oxytone loanwords from Catalan, Spanish and Italian developed a paragogical vowel e.g., *caffè* (It.) → *caffei* (Sard.). There are no quantitative assessments of stress for the transitional area. It is fair to claim, though, that its stress system patterns more closely with the southern area, with a clear preference for paroxytone words.

6 Stress shift with clitics in the Sardinian transitional area

According to Spencer and Luís (2012), clitics lack inherent stress. However, clitics can receive stress when they attach to a host. This is the case of Sardinian and the other Romance languages mentioned in Section 4. From our data in Table 2, we can see that in the transitional area, clitics can trigger stress shift when in enclisis. In particular, when a single clitic (of any kind) or a clitic cluster (in any combination) is added to the host there is stress shift and the original primary stress of the hosting verb becomes a secondary stress. In the case of a single clitic, the stress moves to the right and it is the same verb that receives stress (e.g., *bátti* + *mi* → *battími*). In the case of a clitic cluster, the stress shifts to the cluster (e.g., *bátti* + *minde* → *battimínde*, *bátti* + *mindɛḍḍa* → *battimindɛ́ḍḍa*). Note that no difference is found with single clitics, two-clitic clusters or three-clitic clusters, in each case the resultant pattern is the paroxytone one. We can thus say that in the transitional area the reassignment of stress under cliticization replicates the prevalent stress pattern of the language: the paroxytone.

7 Prosodic representation of clitics

As for the representation of single clitics we will follow the assumptions and reasoning of Monachesi (1996), Peperkamp (1997) and Loporcaro (2000). Loporcaro (2000) argues that in all Romance languages clitics are adjoined to the prosodic word. The variation in terms of stress assignment depends on a parametric choice available in the grammar. In some languages, the grammar of clitics involves a postlexical re-assignment of the stress, while in others clitics have no effect on the stress of their verbal host. Stress re-assignment in stress shift varieties is presumably due to the need to avoid uncommon stress sequences (see Bafile 1994 for Neapolitan).

Let us now come back to our variety. We can say that the Sardinian transitional area is subjected to the postlexical stress re-assignment. We will adopt the representation in (1) as the representation for single clitics in the transitional area.

(1) *Representation of single clitics (adjunction to the PW)*

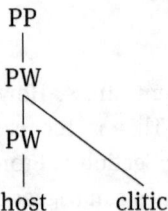

Clitic groups are characterised by a peculiarity that suggests that they might have a different prosodic representation. In Section 3, we mentioned the fact that our Sardinian variety displays both proclitics and enclitics. In the literature, several languages are attested in which enclitics can be stressed when attached to their host (cf. Section 4, this paper). However, to the best of our knowledge, the literature fails to report a peculiar phenomenon pertaining to this variety, namely that proclitics can receive stress as well. Another interesting aspect is that clitic clusters in the case of proclisis have the same stress pattern of clitic clusters when in enclisis (see Tables 2 and 3).

This peculiarity is of great importance in our analysis. An important objection to the idea that clitic clusters can constitute a prosodic word on their own is represented by the different stress behaviour of clitic clusters in proclisis and enclisis (Peperkamp 1997: 191). In fact, the languages studied in the literature are characterised by stressed clitics in enclisis, yet the same clitic sequence lacks stress when in proclisis. This discrepancy is regarded by Peperkamp (1997: 191) as evidence to reject the hypothesis stating that clitic sequences constitute an independent prosodic word on their own. Taking into account the data in Tables 2 and 3, it may be argued that the prosodic representation of our clitic clusters (both in the case of enclisis and in the case of proclisis) is as follows:

(2) *Representation of postverbal and preverbal clitic clusters*

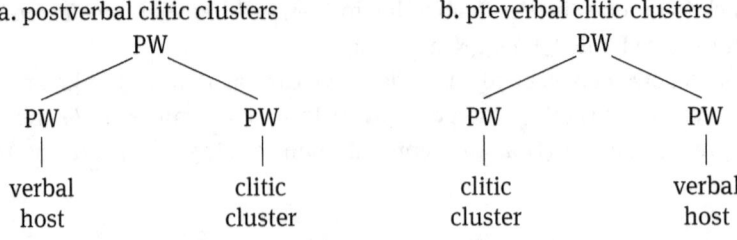

These representations are modelled after Monachesi (1996). Monachesi (1996) proposes that two clitics form an independent unit (a prosodic word on their own) and that this unit merges with the verbal host in a compound structure. As previously mentioned, Peperkamp (1997: 191) rejects the analysis in Monachesi by arguing that if clitic clusters formed a prosodic word, a symmetry between proclitics and enclitics is expected. This was however not the case for the data reported by Monachesi. An identical stress pattern in the case of preverbal and postverbal clitics may be found in association with the present data: Peperkamp's prediction is then borne out in the clitic clusters from the Sardinian transitional area.

However, in order to argue that the prosodic structures in (2) are the ones that best describe our data, we need to prove that clitic clusters are under stress. Kim and Repetti (2013: 267) suggest that in the case of Sardinian clitics there "is not a change in the word level stress, but variation in the association of the pitch accent". The authors present an experimental phonetic analysis of the sequences of verbs plus enclitics in Sardinian and conclude that, in spite of appearances, word stress stays *in situ*. It is furthermore argued that the so-called stress shift is not actually as such: rather, a variation in the pitch accent would be conducive to the pattern. We believe that this is not the case: Sardinian clitic clusters are actually under stress. Evidence is derived from a well-known phonological phenomenon that applies regularly to our enclitic clusters, namely the Sardinian metaphony.

Sardinian metaphony raises the mid-low vowels [ɛ] and [ɔ] to the mid-high vowels [e] and [o] respectively, when followed by high vowels, e.g., /bɔnu/ *good* (masc.) → [bonu] but /bɔna/ *good* (fem.) → [bɔna]. Metaphony only applies to stressed vowels. If word stress were *in situ*, as suggested by Kim and Repetti (2013), we would expect the following result: *báttindɛɖɖu*, in which the mid-low vowel /ɛ/ of the clitic is not raised. Nevertheless, the observed result is *battindéɖɖu* characterised by a regular application of metaphony. The presence of metaphony is indicative of the fact that the clitic is actually stressed.[10] For the purpose of this study, it is important to emphasise that metaphony applies regularly even in the case of proclitic clusters, e.g., *mindɛ́ɖɖa attidi* ('s/he brings it.FEM. there for me') but *mindéɖɖu attidi* ('s/he brings it.MASC. there for me') constitutes evidence that proclitic clusters are under stress. This supports the prosodic representations in (2) in the case of both enclitic and proclitic clusters.

---

10 Sardinian metaphony is a well-studied phenomenon, see Wagner (1941), Virdis (1978), Bolognesi (1998), Loporcaro (2005), Savoia (2015), among others. Works reporting Sardinian data indicative of stress shift in the case of enclisis include among others: Wagner (1941), Pittau (1972), Virdis (1978), Blasco Ferrer (1988), Jones (1993), Bolognesi (1998), Manzini and Savoia (2005, 2007), Ordoñez and Repetti (2014).

From a broader perspective, metaphony in proclitic clusters provides evidence for two conclusions. Firstly, it casts further doubt on the viability of Kim and Repetti's reduction of the facts to pitch accent association. Secondly, it makes it necessary to reconsider the commonly held view that enclisis and proclisis are fundamentally different and, most importantly, that no stress shift phenomena would exist in proclisis. Instead, the account of enclitic and proclitic clusters should preferably be as unified as possible (cf. Manzini and Savoia 2017).

8 Conclusions

In the Sardinian transitional area, if we focus on the combination of host plus clitic clusters and host plus clitic, a recurrent pattern may be identified indicating that the stress always falls on the penultimate syllable. It is widely known that in the case of Romance languages the stress obeys to the so-called 'three-syllable window': stress falls on one of the last three syllables of the word (cf. Spencer and Luís 2012: 84–85). The paroxytone pattern can be assumed to be the unmarked pattern in the Sardinian transitional area, judging by the fact that in the relevant dialects stress falls almost regularly on the penultimate syllable. Thus, we might assume that the stress shift is due to the adjustment of sequences that the speakers regard as being overly marked (cf. Bafile 1994). Thus, according to the analogous analyses of the Neapolitan and some Catalan and Lucanian dialects (Bafile 1994; Bonet and Torres-Tamarit 2011; Manzini and Savoia 2017), it may be argued that also in the case of the Sardinian transitional area, stress placement responds to a reassignment mechanism that generates a trochaic foot starting from the right edge of the word.

References

Bafile, Laura. 1994. La riassegnazione postlessicale dell'accento nel napoletano. *Quaderni del dipartimento di linguistica dell'Università di Firenze* 5. 1–23.

Bafile, Laura & Rosangela Lai. 2018. "Clitic stress allomorphy in Sardinian". In Mirko Grimaldi, Rosangela Lai, Ludovico Franco & Benedetta Baldi (eds.), *Structuring variation in Romance Linguistics and Beyond*, (Linguistik Aktuell/Linguistics Today 252), 195–213. Amsterdam: John Benjamins.

Bentley, Delia. 2004. Il partitivo inde nel siciliano e nel sardo delle origini. In Maurizio Dardano & Gianluca Frenguelli (eds.), *SintAnt. La sintassi dell'italiano antico*, 529–551. Roma: Aracne.

Blasco Ferrer, Eduardo. 1988. *Le parlate dell'Alta Ogliastra*. Cagliari: Edizioni Della Torre.
Bolognesi, Roberto. 1998. *The phonology of Campidanian Sardinian: A unitary account of a self-organizing structure*, (HIL dissertations 38). The Hague: Holland Academic Graphics.
Bonet, Eulàlia & Francesc Torres-Tamarit. 2011. Les formes d'imperatiu seguides de clític: Un cas de conservadorisme lèxic. In Maria-Rosa Lloret & Clàudia Pons-Moll (eds.), *Noves aproximacions a la fonologia i la morfologia del català*, 37–61. Alacant: Institut Interuniversitari de Filologia Valenciana.
Jones, Michael Allan. 1993. *Sardinian Syntax*. London & New York: Routledge.
Kenstowicz, Michael. 1991. Enclitic Accent: Latin, Macedonian, Italian, Polish. In Pier Marco Bertinetto, Michael Kenstowicz & Michele Loporcaro (eds.), *Certamen Phonologicum II: Papers from the 1990 Cortona Phonology Meeting*, 173–185. Torino: Rosenberg & Sellier.
Kim, Miran & Lori Repetti. 2013. Bitonal pitch accent and phonological alignment in Sardinian. *Probus* 25(2). 267–300.
Lai, Jean-Pierre. 2002. *L'intonation du parler de Nuoro*. Grenoble: Université Stendhal-Grenoble 3 dissertation.
Lai, Rosangela. 2013. *Positional Effects in Sardinian Muta cum Liquida. Lenition, Metathesis, and Liquid Deletion*. Alessandria: Edizioni dell'Orso.
Lai, Rosangela. 2015. Word-initial geminates in Sardinian. *Quaderni di linguistica e studi orientali* 1. 37–60.
Lai, Rosangela. 2016. Clitici e slittamento accentuale nelle varietà sarde: fra prosodia e allomorfia. In Benedetta Baldi & Leonardo M. Savoia (eds.), *La lingua e i parlanti. Studi e ricerche di linguistica*, 135–149. Alessandria: Edizioni dell'Orso.
Lai, Rosangela. 2017a. Orthography development in Sardinia: the case of Limba Sarda Comuna. In Mari C. Jones & Damien Mooney (eds.), *Creating Orthographies for Endangered Languages*, 176–189. Cambridge: Cambridge University Press.
Lai, Rosangela. 2017b. Stress shift under cliticization in Nuorese Sardinian. *Quaderni di linguistica e studi orientali* 3. 183–199.
Lai, Rosangela. 2018. Language Planning and Language Policy in Sardinia. *Language Problems and Language Planning* 42(1). 70–88. Amsterdam: John Benjamins.
Lombardi, Alessandra. 2007. Posizione dei clitici e ordine dei costituenti nella lingua sarda medievale. In Delia Bentley & Adam Ledgeway (eds.), *Sui dialetti italoromanzi. Saggi in onore di Nigel B. Vincent. The Italianist, Special supplement* 27. 133–147. Norfolk: Biddles.
Loporcaro, Michele. 2000. Stress stability under cliticization and the prosodic status of Romance clitics. In Lori Repetti (ed.), *Phonological Theory and the Dialects of Italy*, 137–168. Amsterdam: John Benjamins.
Loporcaro, Michele. 2005. Typological remarks on Sardinian: 1. Vowel harmony 2. Sardinian in a correlative typology of the Romance languages. *Sprachtypologie und Universalienforschung* 58(2–3). 210–227.
Manzini, M. Rita & Leonardo M. Savoia. 2005. *I dialetti italiani e romanci. Morfosintassi generativa*. Alessandria: Edizioni dell'Orso, 3 vols.
Manzini, M. Rita & Leonardo M. Savoia. 2007. *A unification of morphology and syntax. Studies in Romance and Albanian varieties*, London: Routledge.
Manzini, M. Rita & Leonardo M. Savoia. 2014. From Latin to Romance: Case loss and preservation in pronominal systems. *Probus* 26(2). 217–248.

Manzini, M. Rita & Leonardo M. Savoia. 2017. Enclisis/Proclisis Alternations in Romance: Allomorphies and (Re)Ordering. *Transactions of the Philological Society* 115. 98–136.

Monachesi, Paola. 1996. On the representation of Italian clitics. In Ursula Kleinhenz (ed.), *Interfaces in Phonology*. Studia Grammatica 41. 83–101. Berlin: Akademie Verlag.

Nespor, Marina & Irene Vogel. 1986. *Prosodic Phonology*. Dordrecht: Foris.

Ordóñez, Francisco & Lori Repetti. 2006. Stressed enclitics? In Jean-Pierre Montreuil & Chiyo Nishida (eds.), *New analyses in Romance linguistics*, 167–181. Amsterdam: Benjamins.

Ordóñez, Francisco & Lori Repetti. 2014. On the morphological restriction of hosting clitics in Italian and Sardinian dialects. *L'Italia dialettale* 75. 173–199.

Peperkamp, Sharon. 1997. *Prosodic Words* (HIL dissertations 34). The Hague: Holland Academic Graphics.

Pescarini, Diego. 2016. Non canonical enclitics are not weak pronouns. Paper presented at the 42th *Incontro di Grammatica Generativa*, University of Salento, 18–20 February.

Pisano, Simone. 2016. *Il sistema verbale del sardo moderno: tra conservazione e innovazione*. Pisa: Edizioni ETS.

Pittau, Massimo. 1972. *Grammatica del sardo nuorese*. Bologna: Pàtron.

Porru, Vincenzo Raimondo. 2002. *Nou dizionariu universali sardu-italianu*, Marinella Lőrinczi (ed.). Nuoro: Ilisso.

Savoia, Leonardo M. 2015. *I dialetti italiani. Sistemi e processi fonologici nelle varietà di area italiana e romancia*. Pisa: Pacini.

Spencer, Andrew & Ana R. Luís. 2012. *Clitics. An Introduction*. Cambridge: Cambridge University Press.

Torres-Tamarit, Francesc. 2008. *Stress shift in Formenteran Catalan verb plus enclitic(s) sequences: An Optimality Theory approach*. Barcelona: Universitat Autònoma de Barcelona MA thesis.

Virdis, Maurizio. 1978. *Fonetica del dialetto sardo campidanese*. Cagliari: Edizioni Della Torre.

Wagner, Max Leopold. 1941. *Historische Lautlehre des Sardischen*. Halle: Niemeyer.

Adam Ledgeway
The causative construction in the dialects of southern Italy and the phonology-syntax interface

1 Introduction

It is customary in typological studies on causatives (see Comrie 1985: 165–184) to distinguish on the one hand between analytic constructions such as the English example in (1a), where the causative predicate *make* and the verbal complement *fall* constitute two independent words, and morphological constructions such as the Chichewa example in (1b) on the other, where the causative morpheme *-ets-* is directly combined with the verbal root *-gw-* 'fall':

(1) a. *Mary **made** John **fall**.* (Eng.)
    b. *Mtsikana a-na-u-**gw**-**ets**-a*   *mtsuko.* (Chichewa)
       girl   ACC.SUBJ.-PST.-ACC.OBJ.-fall-CAUS-ASP jug
       'The girl made the jug fall.'

However, it is well known (cf. Kayne 1975; Zubizarreta 1985; Burzio 1986; Alsina 1992; 1996; Guasti 1993; Sheehan 2016) that within this typology most Romance varieties occupy an intermediate position between the analytic and the morphological types.[1] In particular, the Romance causative, although superficially of the analytic type transparently combining two independent predicates (cf. *fece* 'did' and *cadere* 'to fall' in 2a), nonetheless mimics the morphological type in that the causative predicate and lexical infinitive appear to form a single verbal complex (Vincent 2016: 43–44). As a consequence of the tight

---

[1] An obvious exception here is Romanian and many dialects of the extreme south of Italy where, due to the general avoidance of infinitival complementation, the causative is generally expressed by a bi-clausal structure involving a finite subjunctive complement (Ledgeway 2013, 2016b: 1023–1027; Ciutescu 2015; Squillaci 2017; Ledgeway, Schifano, and Silvestri in press).

Note: I would like to thank Rita Manzini for her insightful comments on an earlier oral version of this article presented at the 39th meeting of the Incontro di Grammatica Generativa held at the University of Modena and Reggio Emilia 2013. It is to her that I dedicate this article as a scholar of outstanding ability.

Adam Ledgeway, University of Cambridge

https://doi.org/10.1515/9781501505201-021

structural cohesion exhibited by both verbal components of the verbal complex, it proves impossible to interpolate material such as *Gianni* in (2b) and local operations such as clitic climbing from the embedded infinitive to the higher causative predicate are readily licensed (2c).[2]

(2) a. *Maria [ᵥ **fece cadere**] Gianni.* (It.)
    Maria made fall.INF Gianni
    'Maria made Gianni fall.'
  b. **Maria fece Gianni cadere.* (It.)
    Maria made Gianni fall.INF
  c. *Maria **lo** fece cadere(***lo**).* (It.)
    Maria him= made fall.INF=him
    'Maria made him fall.'

Furthermore, in analyses of the Romance causative it is standard, following the seminal work of Kayne (1975), to recognise two causative subtypes. In the so-called *faire-infinitif* construction (3a) we witness a complex predicate that selects for three arguments, the causer (*Marie*), the caused event (*nettoyer les toilettes*), and a composite argument (*Jean*) simultaneously realizing the Recipient of the causation and the Agent of the caused event which is marked either as a direct or an indirect object in accordance with the intransitive vs transitive nature of the lexical infinitive. In the *faire-par* construction (3b), by contrast, the complex predicate manifests just two arguments, the causer (*Marie*) and the caused event (*nettoyer les toilettes*). However, unlike the *faire-infinitif* construction, the infinitive in the *faire-par* construction assumes a passive reading, despite the absence of typical passive morphology, with backgrounding of the Agent which, if expressed, is introduced by an oblique *by*-phrase on a par with the canonical passive construction.

(3) a. *Marie fait nettoyer les toilettes à Jean.* (Fr.)
    Marie makes clean.INF the toilets to Jean
    'Marie makes Jean clean the toilets / Marie forces Jean to clean the toilets.'
  b. *Marie fait nettoyer les toilettes (par Jean).* (Fr.)
    Marie makes clean.INF the toilets by Jean
    'Marie has the toilets cleaned (by Jean).'

---

[2] Some Spanish and Catalan varieties also (optionally) allow a bi-clausal ECM structure in which clitics fail to climb and the infinitival subject intervenes between the causative and the infinitival verb (Sheehan 2016: 985–993). According to Davies (1995), the bi-clausal ECM option represents a relatively recent innovation in the history of Ibero-Romance.

If we now consider the dialects of southern Italy, these largely appear to pattern on a par with standard Romance varieties such as French and Italian (Lombardi 1997; Ledgeway 2009: 896–900). For instance, we can distinguish once again between the *faire-infinitif* (a examples) and *faire-par* (b examples) constructions, although there is some lexical variation across dialects, as in the canonical passive, in relation to the choice of preposition that introduces the demoted Agent (viz. DE+AB 'from, by' vs DE 'of').

Neapolitan
(4) a. *Papà facette accuncià 'a machina a Ciccio. (faire-infinitif)*
dad made repair.INF the car to Ciccio
'Dad made Ciccio repair the car.'
b. *Papà facette accuncià 'a machina ('a Ciccio). (faire-par)*
dad made repair.INF the car by Ciccio
'Dad had the car repaired (by Ciccio).'
c. *Papà **nce** 'a facette (*nce 'a) accuncià /Papà 'a facette*
dad to.him= it=made to.him= it= repair.INF dad it=made
(*l')accuncià ('a Ciccio).
it= repair.INF by Ciccio
'Dad made him repair it/had it repaired (by Ciccio).'

Cosentino (northern Calabria)
(5) a. *Maria fa pulizzà u cessu a Cicciu. (faire-infinitif)*
Maria makes clean.INF the toilet to Ciccio
'Maria makes Ciccio clean the toilet.'
b. *Maria fa pulizzà u cessu ('i Cicciu). (faire-par)*
Maria makes clean.INF the toilet of Ciccio
'Maria has the toilet cleaned by Ciccio.'
c. *Maria **cc'** 'u fa (*cc' 'u) pulizzà / Maria*
Maria to.him= it= makes to.him= it= clean.INF Maria
u fa (*u) pulizzà ('i Ciccio).
it= makes it= clean.INF of Ciccio
'Maria makes him clean it/has it cleaned (by Ciccio).'

Mussomelese (south-western Sicily)
(6) a. *Maria fa puliziari i gabbinetti a Giuwanni. (faire-infinitif)*
Maria makes clean.INF the toilets to Giovanni
'Maria makes Giovanni clean the toilets.'

b. *Maria si   fa   puliziari   i   gabbinetti*
Maria self= makes clean.INF the toilets
(di Giuwanni). (faire-par)
of Giovanni
'Maria has the toilets cleaned (by Giovanni).'

c. *Maria ci   -i   fa   puliziari(*ci-i)   /Maria s'*
Maria to.him= them= makes clean.INF=to.him=them Maria self=
'i   fa   (*'i)   puliziari   (di Giuwanni).
them= makes them= clean.INF of Giovanni
'Maria makes him clean them/has them cleaned (by Giovanni).'

Furthermore, in all the southern varieties above clitics dependent on the lexical infinitive are required once again to climb to the causative predicate (cf. c examples). In this respect, it is interesting to note that the usual Romance variation observed in the grammaticality or otherwise of clitic climbing (Kayne 1991; Manzini and Savoia 2005, III: 383–385; Cinque 2004, 2006; Tortora 2014: 135), as exemplified in the contrast between modern French and Italian in (7a-b), is systematically absent in the causative where in all varieties – though for some possible exceptions, see Tortora (2014: 150–153) and footnote 2 above regarding the Ibero-Romance ECM construction – clitics obligatorily climb to the causative predicate even in varieties such as modern French (8a-b).

(7) a. *Marc (*le) doit le corriger   tout de suite.* (Fr.)
    b. *Marco lo deve   correggere(lo) subito.* (It.)
       Mark it= must   it=correct.INF=it at.once
       'Mark must mark it at once.'

(8) a. *Marc le   fera   (*le) corriger   tout de suite.* (Fr.)
    b. *Marco lo   farà   correggere(*lo) subito.* (It.)
       Mark it= will.make   it=   correct.INF=it   at.once
       'Mark will have it corrected at once.'

Limiting ourselves just to the facts of clitic climbing, we interpret the otherwise exceptional obligatory nature of climbing in the Romance causative as a superficial reflex of a restructuring process (though see Cinque 2004 2006 for an alternative analysis), whereby an underlying biclausal construction consisting of two distinct predicates (9a) is transformed into a monoclausal construction superficially characterized by a single verbal complex (9b).

(9) a. [Luca fece + [Ugo aggiustare la macchina]] (It.) ⇒
   Luca made Ugo repair.INF the car
b. [Luca [ᵥ **fece aggiustare**] la macchina a Ugo] (It.)
   Luca made repair.INF the car to Ugo
   'Luca made Ugo repair the car.'

As a consequence of such restructuring, we observe that (i) the respective argument structures of the two predicates are merged into one (cf. dative marking of the logical subject of the infinitive *a Ugo* 'to Ugo' in 9b); (ii) with the exception of some VP-adverbs, nothing can intervene between the causative predicate and the lexical infinitive (cf. 2b); and (iii) clitic pronouns semantically dependent on the embedded infinitive must climb to the causative predicate (cf. 8a-b). In light of these facts, we now turn to examine the causative construction in the imperative, the principal focus of our discussion in the remainder of this article.

2 *Faire-infinitif* vs *faire-par* in the imperative

Beginning with Italian, we note that, on a par with the other paradigms observed hitherto, any clitics in the imperatival causative construction must also raise to the causative predicate (10a), and are not allowed to remain on the infinitive, either in proclitic or enclitic position (10b):

(10) a. Fate**mela** raccontare bene! (It.)
   make.IMP.2PL=me=it tell.INF well
b. *Fate **mela** raccontare bene! / *Fate raccontar**mela**
   make.IMP.2PL me=it= to.tell.INF well make.IMP.2PL tell.INF=me=it
   bene! (It.)
   well
c. 'Make/Let me tell it properly!' (*faire-infinitif*)
d. 'Have it told to me properly!' (*faire-par*)

Furthermore, as expected, we note a formal ambiguity in example (10a) between the *faire-infinitif* and *faire-par* interpretations. More specifically, the clitic *me* 'me' can be understood either as the Agent or the Recipient of *raccontare* 'to tell', respectively licensing the *faire-infinitif* (10c) and the *faire-par* (10d) readings.

Turning now to the dialects of southern Italy, we observe that, in some dialects at least, in the imperative clitics may continue to climb to the causative predicate (11a) or remain on the embedded infinitive (11b). This is unambiguously revealed in the Cosentino examples (11a-b) by the allomorphic alternation observed in the clitic clusters involving the third-person forms derived from ILLE: whereas the lateral is preserved in enclitic position (viz, *-mílla* '=me.DAT=it.F.ACC'), it is absent in proclitic position (namely, *m"a* 'me.DAT=it.F.ACC').

(11) a. *Facitimílla   cuntà   bbona!* (*faire-par*; Cos.)
        make.IMP.2PL=me=it tell.INF well
        'Have it told to me properly!' (??'Make/Let me tell it properly!')
    b. *Faciti   m"a   cuntà   bbona!* (*faire-infinitif*; Cos.)
        make.IMP.2PL me=it= tell.INF well
        'Make/Let me tell it properly!' (*'Have it told to me properly')

As the translations in (11) highlight, such variation in clitic placement is, however, not free, but serves to mark a formal distinction between the *faire-infinitif* and *faire-par* interpretations: when enclisis to the causative predicate obtains as in (11a), the argument encoded by *-mi-* can only correspond to the Recipient of *cuntà* 'to tell',[3] whereas when the clitic cluster attaches proclitically to the embedded infinitive as in (11b), the argument encoded by *m'* marks the Agent of *cuntà*.

Superficially, on the basis of these facts we might be tempted to conclude that, in contrast to the *faire-par* construction in which clitics regularly climb to the causative predicate following a restructuring process (12a), the *faire-infinitif* construction instantiates a case of failed restructuring in which, given a biclausal construction, clitics remain on the embedded infinitive (12b).

(12) a. [*Facitimílla   cuntà   bbona!*] (Cos.)
        make.IMP.2PL=me=it tell.INF well
    b. [*Faciti* +   [*m"a   cuntà   bbona!*]] (Cos.)
        make.IMP.2PL me=it= tell.INF well

---

[3] The *faire-infinitif* reading with clitics in enclitic position as in (11a) is not entirely excluded for some speakers, especially those of the younger generations, although even these consider it to represent the least natural and genuinely dialectal option. We therefore take this option to be due to influence from the grammar of Italian, in which younger speakers generally show a greater degree of active competence. Revealing in this respect is the observation that while these (typically younger) speakers do not entirely exclude the *faire-infinitif* reading in examples like (11a) in accordance with the corresponding Italian structure, they never associate the *faire-par* reading with structures like (11b) where pronouns appear in proclisis to the infinitive since this is an exclusively dialectal construction without any parallel in Italian.

In what follows, we present a complete description of the syntax of the southern Italian imperatival causative construction, a structure which to date has virtually gone unnoticed in the literature. On the basis of this description, we shall assess the evidence for the claim that the imperatival *faire-infinitive* construction involves a biclausal structure in which restructuring has failed to take place. In the final section we then outline a structural analysis of the southern Italian causative construction that is able to account for the structural distinction between the two causative constructions and the differences in clitic placement witnessed in the imperative.

3 Characteristics of southern causative in the imperative

3.1 Distribution

We begin by considering the lexical distribution of the southern Italian causative construction. Besides the prototypical causative predicate derived from FACERE 'make' (13a), many Romance varieties also license a monoclausal construction in conjunction with causative LAXARE 'let' (13b) and, to a lesser extent, with verbs of perception which, alongside a monoclausal construction (13c), also license a biclausal structure (13d).

(13) a. [*La*   feci   aprire   *a Ugo*]. (It.)
        it.F.ACC= I.made open.INF to Ugo
        'I made Ugo open it.'
    b. [*La*   lasciai aprire   *a Ugo*]. (It.)
        it.F.ACC= I.let   open.INF to Ugo
        'I let Ugo open it.'
    c. [*La*   vidi   aprire   *a Ugo*]. (It.)
        it.F.ACC= I.saw   open.INF to Ugo
        'I saw Ugo open it.'
    d. [*Vidi* [*Ugo aprirla*]].   (cf. also **Lo**   vidi   aprirla)
        I.saw Ugo open.INF=it.F.ACC   him= I.saw open.INF=it.F.ACC
        'I saw Ugo open it (I saw him open it).'

Judging by the facts of clitic placement alone, in the dialects of southern Italy, however, an apparently biclausal causative construction is found with reflexes of FACERE (14a) and LAXARE (14b), but never with verbs of perception (14c):

(14) a. *Facimu*   **'u**   *ricoglia!* (Cos.)
   make.IMP.1PL him= return.INF
   'Let's make him come back!'
   b. *Lassa*   **'u**   *dorma!* (Cos.)
   let.IMP.2SG= him= sleep.INF
   'Let him sleep!'
   c. *Guarda***lu**   *ballà* / **Guarda*   **'u**   *ballà!* (Cos.)
   watch.IMP.2SG=him dance.INF watch.IMP.2SG him= dance.INF
   'Watch him dance!'

As for its geographic distribution, investigations to date reveal that the biclausal causative construction is found in dialects of northern Calabria (15a–c; Ledgeway and Lombardi 2000) and the dialects of Campania 16a-c; Bichelli 1974: §191; Ledgeway 2009: 901–903).

(15) a. *Lassa*   **'i**   *sta*   *na picca!* (Cos.)
   let.IMP.2SG them= stay.INF a little
   'Let them be for a while!'
   b. *Faciti*   **cc"u**   *spiegà*   *chiru ca è succiessu!* (Cos.)
   make.IMP.2PL him=it= explain.INF that which is happened
   'Make him explain what happened!'
   c. *Facimu*   **'a**   *scinna*   *subbitu!* (Cos.)
   make.IMP.1PL her= descend.INF at.once
   'Let's make her come down at once!'

(16) a. *E facit'*   **'o**   *parlà!* (Nap.)
   and make.IMP.2PL him= speak.INF
   'And make him speak!'
   b. *'Ass'*   **'e**   *ffa'!* (Nap.)
   let.IMP.2SG them= do.INF
   'Let them do (it)!'
   c. *Facite*   **menn'**   *j'!* (Nap.)
   make.IMP.2PL me=thence= go.INF
   'Let me leave!'

The construction is not, however, universally available throughout the South, inasmuch as it appears to be absent from many other southern dialects including, for example, Abruzzese, Pugliese and Sicilian varieties such as Ariellese (17a–b), Barese (18a–b) and Mussomelese (19a–b)[4]:

(17) a. *Falle servì!* (Arielli (CH); *faire-infinitif/faire-par*)
 make.IMP.2sg=him serve.INF
 'Make him serve / Have him served!'
 b. *Facete**me**le accundà bbone!* (Arielli (CH); *faire-infinitif/faire-par*)
 make.IMP.2PL=me=it tell.INF well
 'Let/make me tell it properly! / Have it told to me properly!'

(18) a. *Facìt**ue** sèrve!* (BA; *faire-infinitif/faire-par*)
 make.IMP.2PL=him serve.INF
 'Make him serve! / Have him served!'
 b. *Fàmmela chend' bbune!* (BA; *faire-infinitif/faire-par*)
 make.IMP.2SG =me=it tell.INF well
 'Let/make me tell it properly! / Have it told to me properly!'

(19) a. *Faciti**lu** serviri!* (Mussomelese (CL); *faire-infinitif/faire-par*)
 make.IMP.2PL=him serve.INF
 'Make him serve! / Have him served!'
 b. *Fammìlla cuntari bbona!*
 make.IMP.2SG=me=it tell.INF well
 (Mussomelese (CL); *faire-infinitif/faire-par*)
 'Let/make me tell it properly! / Have it told to me properly!'

In what follows, however, we shall restrict our attention to the northern Calabrian dialect of Cosenza, since it is the variety for which we currently have most data, although the empirical and theoretical generalizations that hold for Cosentino appear *a priori* to hold of other northern Calabrian dialects and some Campanian varieties.

---

[4] I thank Roberta D'Alessandro, Luigi Andriani and Silvio Cruschina for supplying the Ariellese, Barese and Mussomelese data, respectively. It should not, however, be concluded on the basis of these superficial investigations that the apparently biclausal causative construction is systematically absent from all dialects of these regions. For example, Antonio Lupis (p.c.) informs me that the construction is found in numerous dialects spoken in the province of Bari.

3.2 Structural distinctions between *faire-par* and *faire-infinitif*

Having identified a formal distinction between the *faire-par* and *faire-infinitif* imperatival construction in Cosentino, we must now consider how this distinction is overtly manifested. As observed above, the most immediate formal indication of the distinction surfaces in the allomorphic variation witnessed in the third-person pronouns (< ILLE) which mark an overt distinction between enclitic and proclitic variants through the respective presence and absence of the lateral. This pronominal allomorphy is exemplified in Table 1 and the examples in (20)–(22):

Table 1: Allomorphic variation in clitic paradigms.

	Enclitic position	Proclitic position
1sg + 3 acc	V + -míllu / -mílla / -mílli	m"u- / m"a- / m"i + V
2sg + 3 acc	V + -tíllu / -tílla / -tílli	t"u- / t"a- / t"i + V
3 acc	V + -lu / -la / -li	'u- / 'a- / 'i- + V
3 dat + 3 acc	V + -ccíllu / -ccílla / -ccílli	cc"u- / cc"a- / cc"i + V
1pl + 3 acc	V + -níllu / -nílla / -nílli	n"u- / n"a- / n"i + V
2pl + 3 acc	V + -víllu / -vílla / -vílli	v"u- / v"a- / v"i + V

(20) a. *Facitila   serva!* (Cos.; *faire-par*)
       make.IMP.2PL=her   serve.INF
       'Have her served!'
   b. *Facit'   'a   serva!* (Cos.; *faire-infinitif*)
       make.IMP.2PL her= serve.INF
       'Make/Let her serve!'

(21) a. *Fannillu   vida!* (Cos.; *faire-par*)
       make.IMP.2SG=us=it see.INF
       'Have it shown to us!'
   b. *Fa   n"u   vida!* (Cos.; *faire-infinitif*)
       make.IMP.2SG us=it see.INF
       'Make/Let us see it!'

(22) a. *Lassalu   fà!* (Cos.; *faire-par*)
       let.IMP.2SG=it do.INF
       'Let it be done!'

b. *Lassa   'u   fà!* (Cos.; *faire-infinitif*)
   let.IMP.2SG him= do.INF
   'Let him do (it)!'

It follows from this that whenever the imperatival causative construction occurs in conjunction with the distinctive enclitic pronominal forms in Table 1, the Agent of the caused event can only be realized as a *by*-phrase (23a), while their proclitic variants only prove compatible with a *faire-infinitif* structure in which the Agent is variously realized as direct or indirect object in accordance with the transitivity or otherwise of the embedded infinitive (23b).

(23) a. *Facitila   serva   'i   Giuvanni!* (Cos.; *faire-par*)
       make.IMP.2PL=her serve.INF of Giovanni
       'Have her served by Giovanni!'
   b. *Facit'   'a   serva   (*'i   Giuvanni)!* (Cos.; *faire-infinitif*)
       make.IMP.2PL her= serve.INF of   Giovanni
       'Make/Let her serve (*by Giovanni)!'

The two constructions are further distinguished by the fact that in the causative construction unergative infinitives are compatible with the proclitic forms of the pronouns, but not their enclitic variants (24a–c). This observation finds an immediate explanation in the fact that the passive necessarily acts on the underlying direct object (internal argument), whereas we have seen that the enclitic pronominal form is identified with the *faire-par* causative, in essence a passive construction and hence incompatible with an intransitive infinitive which fails to select an internal argument. The presence of a proclitic pronoun, on the other hand, identifies, as we have seen, an active *faire-infinitif* structure whose compatibility with inergative infinitives is fully expected since the single external argument of the latter corresponds to the Recipient of the caused event.

(24) a. *Facit'   'a   ballà!   / *Facitila   ballà!* (Cos.)
       make.IMP.2PL her= dance.INF make.IMP.2PL =her dance.INF
       'Make/Let her dance! / *Have her danced!'
   b. *Facim'   'u   dorma!   / *Facimulu   dorma!* (Cos.)
       Make.IMP.1PL him= sleep.INF make.IMP.1PL=him sleep.INF
       'Let's make/let him sleep! / *Let's have him slept!'
   c. *Lassa   'i   cada!   / *Lassali   cada!* (Cos.)
       let.IMP.2SG them= fall.INF let.IMP.2SG =them fall.INF
       'Let them fall! / *Let them be fallen!'

Finally, another area in which the distinction between the two causative constructions surfaces regards anaphor binding (Burzio 1986; Sheehan 2016: 988–989). In Italian, for example, anaphors like the third-person singular anaphor *suo* 'his, her, its' can be bound by the Agent of the *faire-infinitif* causative construction (25b), but not by the Agent of the *faire-par* construction (26b) where the Agent is realized as an oblique *by*-phrase. As highlighted by the underlying structural representations in (25a, 26a), this distinction is a consequence of the fact that only in the *faire-infinitif* construction is the anaphor preceded by its antecedent *Ida* which occurs in an appropriate position from which it can c-command and bind the coreferential possessive.

(25) a. [Feci] + [[**Ida**]$_i$ chiamare il [**suo**]$_i$ avvocato] (It.)
       I.made Ida   call.INF the her   lawyer
   b. Feci   chiamare il [**suo**]$_i$ avvocato [a **Ida**]$_i$ (It., *faire-infinitif*)
      I.made call.INF the her   lawyer   to Ida
      'I made [Ida]$_i$ call [her]$_i$ lawyer'

(26) a. [Feci] + [chiamare il [**suo**]$_i$ avvocato [da **Ida**]$_i$] (It.)
       I.made call.INF the her   lawyer   by Ida
   b. *Feci chiamare il [**suo**]$_i$ avvocato [da **Ida**]$_i$ (It., *faire-par*)
      I.made call.INF the her   lawyer   by Ida
      'I had [her]$_i$ lawyer called [by Ida]$_i$'

In a similar vein, these same considerations hold for the Cosentino examples in (27) where we observe that the third-person possessive *sua* can be bound by a proclitic (viz. *cci* 'to her') that references the Agent of the *faire-infinitif* construction (27a), but not by an enclitic (viz. *nni* 'by her') which references the oblique Agent of the *faire-par* construction (27b).

(27) a. Faciti   [[**cc'**]$_i$ '*u*] chiamà a ll'avvucatu
        make.IMP.2PL to.her= him   call.INF to the.lawyer
        [**sua**]$_i$! (Cos.; *faire-infinitif*)
        her
        'Make/Let her call her lawyer!'
   b. *Faciti[[**nni**]$_i$ *llu*]   chiamà a ll'avvucatu
        make.IMP.2PL=by.her=him call.INF to the.lawyer
        [**sua**]$_i$! (Cos.; *faire-par*)
        her
        'Have by her her lawyer called!'

3.3 Properties and restrictions

Moving on to examine in greater detail other properties and restrictions of the Cosentino imperatival causative construction, we begin by observing that the formal distinction between the two causative subtypes surfaces in all three grammatical persons:

(28) a. *Faccíllu   dicia   ('i Maria)!* (Cos.; *faire-par*)
       make.IMP.2SG=to.him=it say.INF of Maria
       'Have him told it (by Maria)!'
   b. *Fa   cc"u   dicia!* (Cos.; *faire-infinitif*)
       make.IMP.2SG to.him=it= say.INF
       'Make/Let him say it!'

(29) a. *Facimula   cucinà ('i Maria)!* (Cos.; *faire-par*)
       make.IMP.1PL =it cook.INF of Maria
       'Let's have it cooked (by Maria)!'
   b. *Facimu   'a   cucinà!* (Cos.; *faire-infinitif*)
       make.IMP.1PL her= cook.INF
       'Let's make/let her cook!'

(30) a. *Facitila   vesta   ('i mamma)!* (Cos.; *faire-par*)
       make.IMP.2PL=her dress.INF of mum
       'Have her dressed (by mum)!'
   b. *Facit'   'a   vesta!* (Cos.; *faire-infinitif*)
       make.IMP.2PL her= dress.INF
       'Make/Let her get dressed!'

However, an important exception which concerns all three grammatical persons is the negative imperative where the distinction between the two causative constructions is neutralized, inasmuch as all clitics are invariably required to climb to the causative predicate:

(31) a. *Un cc"u   fa   (*cc"u)   dicia!* (Cos.; *faire-par / faire-infinitif*)
       not to.him=it= do.INF to.him=it say.INF
       'Don't have it told to him! / Don't make him say it!'
   b. *Unn' 'a   facimu   (*'a)*
       not it.F.ACC= make.IMP.1PL it.F.ACC=
       cucinà! (Cos.; *faire-par / faire-infinitif*)
       cook.INF
       'Let's not have it cooked! / Let's not let her cook!'

c. Unn' 'a faciti (*'a) vesta! (Cos.; *faire-par / faire-infinitif*)
   not her= make.IMP.1PL her= dress.INF
   'Don't have her dressed! / Don't let her get dressed!'

More generally, the distinction between the two causative constructions is not only neutralized in the negative imperative, but is also absent from all other paradigms outside of the positive imperative, witness the representative examples in (32a-c):

(32) a. 'U facìa (*'u) vesta. (Cos.)
     him= I.made him= dress.INF
     'I used to have him dressed.' (*faire-par*)/'I used to make him get dressed.'(*faire-infinitif*)
   b. **Cc"a** facissiru (*cc"a) cuntà bbona. (Cos.)
     to.him=it= they.would.make to.him=it tell.INF well
     'They would have it told to him properly.' (*faire-par*)/'They would make him tell it properly.' (*faire-infinitif*)
   c. 'A facìi (*'a) rapa. (Cos.)
     it= you.made him= open.INF
     'You would have it opened.' (*faire-par*)/'You made her open (it).' (*faire-infinitif*)

Another interesting restriction concerns unaccusatives which only generally prove compatible with the active *faire-infinitif* construction (33a), but not with the passive *faire-par* construction (33b). At first sight, this distribution seems somewhat puzzling given the obvious similarities between unaccusative and passive structures which might otherwise lead us to expect unaccusative predicates to actually favour the *faire-par* construction.[5]

---

[5] Among other things, in Romance both unaccusative (i.a) and passive (i.b) structures variously display non-Agentive subjects, unmarked postverbal position of the subject, selection of auxiliary BE, and participial agreement for number and gender with the surface subject (cf. Ledgeway 2012: 294–301):

i a **È** affondata la nave durante una burrasca. (It.)
      is sunk.FSG the.FSG ship.F during a storm
      'The ship sank during the storm.'
   b **Fu** fondata la nave dalla marina italiana. (It.)
      was sunk.FSG the.FSG ship.F by.the navy Italian
      'The ship was sunk by the Italian navy.'

(33) a. *Facit'*   *'u*   *trasa*   / *saglia*   / *scinna*   / *parta*
   make.IMP.2PL him= enter.INF ascend.INF descend.INF leave.INF
   / *nescia* / *vena!* (*faire-inf.*)
   exit.INF come.INF
 b?? *Faciti*   *lu*   *trasa*   / *saglia*   / *scinna*   / *parta*
   make.IMP.2PL =him enter.INF ascend.INF descend.INF leave.INF
   / *nescia* / *vena!* (*faire-par*)
   exit.INF come.INF
   'Make/Let him enter / go up / come down / leave / go out / come!'

In light of the preceding examination of the principal characteristics of the Calabrian causative and assuming clitic climbing to be an overt reflex of the application of restructuring, we might be tempted to conclude that the imperatival *faire-infinitif* construction in the dialects of southern Italy represents the result of a failed process of restructuring (cf. 12b), namely the superficial output of a biclausal structure along the lines of the English analytic causative in (1b). However attractive this analysis might initially seem, it would be rash to conclude that the absence of clitic climbing in such structures is the superficial reflex of a biclausal structure, as highlighted by the following considerations. First, if the relevant structures involved a biclausal, non-restructured construction, then we should expect the logical infinitival subject (namely, the Recipient of the causation and the Agent of the event) to be able to occur before the embedded infinitive not only when realized as a pronominal clitic (34a), but also when realized as a full lexical DP, contrary to fact (34b).

(34) a. *Facit'*   *'a*   *vesta!* (Cos.)
   make.IMP.2PL her= dress.INF
   'Make/Let her get dressed!'
 b. *Faciti   *a* **Maria** *vesta!*   (= *Faciti*   *vesta*   *a*
   make.IMP.2PL to Maria dress.INF make.IMP.2PL dress.INF to
   Maria!; Cos.)
   Maria
   'Make Maria get dressed!'

Second, whereas in declaratives (35a) and in imperatival *faire-par* structures (35b) pre-VP-adverbs such as *sempre* 'always' (Cinque 1999; Ledgeway in press a) can readily intervene between the causative predicate and embedded infinitive, it is surprising to observe that these same adverbs cannot be placed between the causative predicate and the embedded infinitive in the imperatival *faire-infinitif* construction (35c). Indeed, if in the positive imperative the *faire-infinitif* construction instantiates a biclausal construction (cf. 12b), then we should, on the contrary, expect the causative predicate situated in the higher clause to display an even greater degree of separability with respect to the embedded infinitive situated in the lower clause, including a concomitant greater accessibility of intervening adverbs. By the same token, given the presupposed monoclausal structure of examples such as (35a–b) we should also expect the causative predicate and embedded infinitive in such cases to exhibit a higher degree of structural cohesion.

(35) a. 'A faciti sempe serva. (Cos.) ⇒
　　　 her= you.make always serve.INF
　　　 'You have her always served.' (faire-par)
　　　 'You make/let her always serve.' (faire-infinitif)
　　b. Facitila sempe serva! (Cos.; faire-par)
　　　 make.IMP.2PL=her always serve.INF
　　　 'Have her always served!'
　　c. *Faciti sempe 'a serva! (Cos.; faire-infinitif)
　　　 make.IMP.2PL always her= serve.INF
　　　 'Make/Let her always serve!'

Finally, another observation which highlights that we are dealing with a monoclausal construction comes from a consideration of the case properties of the imperatival *faire-infinitif* construction. More specifically, in a biclausal causative construction like that exemplified in (36a) for English, the case of the logical subject of the infinitive and that of the object of the latter are licensed by two separate verbs, namely by the causative predicate *make* and by the infinitive *call*, respectively. This explains the presence of two accusative-marked arguments (viz. *him*) within the same sentence. In the Italian monoclausal construction (36b), by contrast, the case of the subject and that of the object are licensed compositionally by the single verbal complex [*fece+chiamare*]. As a consequence, the former is marked dative (*glie-*) and the latter accusative (*lo*) according to a pattern which obtains in all Italian causative constructions, not just in the imperative. In light of these observations, we cannot fail to note that the case properties of the southern causative construction in (36c) do not replicate those of the English biclausal structure in (36a) but, rather, those of the Italian monoclausal construction in (36b), inasmuch as the subject and object of the infinitive bear dative (*cc'*) and accusative (*'u*) case, respectively.

(36) a. *[Make **him** [call **him**]]!* (Eng.)
   b. *Fa**glielo**!*   *chiamare!* (It.)
      make.IMP=to.him=him call.INF
   c. *Fa*   ***cc"u***   *chiamà!* (Cos.)
      make.IMP to.him=him   call.INF

4 Structural analysis

Having excluded the possibility that in the case of proclisis to the infinitive the southern causative construction instantiates an underlying biclausal structure, we shall now sketch a structural analysis of the southern Italian causative which takes account of the formal distinction between the *faire-par* and *faire-infinitif* constructions in their imperatival uses. We begin by asking what is special about the nature of the positive imperative such that the formal distinction between the two causative constructions surfaces only in this particular context. The solution that we propose here rests on the idea widespread in the literature (Rivero 1994a,b; Graffi 1996; Zanuttini 1997; Manzini and Savoia 2005, III: 388) that imperatival clauses display a reduced functional structure. In particular, while declaratives are standardly argued to project a full array of functional projections associated with the T-domain (37a), imperatival clauses (37b) are assumed to lack this same series of functional projections (cf. also Tortora 2014: ch. 3, §6). Not by chance, the absence of T-related functional projections in second-person singular imperatival clauses is correlated with the frequent traditional observation that one of the most notable characteristics of the imperative is its absence of any inflectional marking or, at the very least, very minimal inflectional marking in accordance with a widespread cross-linguistic tendency (Pott 1859: 613; Bybee 1985: 173; Floricic 2008: 10; Ledgeway 2014; cf. however Auwera and Lejeune 2011). In theoretical terms and, in particular, in relation to phase theory discussed below, we can interpret the observed inflectional impoverishment of the imperative in terms of the mechanisms of feature transmission and inheritance (Chomsky 2007; 2008). Whereas phi-features that originate on the phase head, viz. C°, are usually 'transferred' down to T° in root declaratives, in the absence of T° in imperatives these same features fail to be passed down – or, to borrow Ouali's (2008) terminology are 'kept' – such that the imperatival verb is forced to raise to C° to licenses its inflectional features (see immediately below).

In the absence of the projection of T-related functional structure we therefore propose, following Manzini and Savoia (2005, III: 388), that the imperatival verb raises to the only available functional projection, namely the C° head (cf. also Rivero, 1994a,b; Rivero and Terzi 1995). As a consequence, any clitics are stranded *in situ* within the *v*-VP complex from where they subsequently encliticize, not syntactically, but phonologically at PF to the imperative verb now raised to C°. Not by chance, this structural analysis corresponds to the analysis of absolute participle constructions such as (37c) which display the same superficial properties as imperatives, in that they too fail to exhibit any TP structure and require the participial verb to raise to C° (cf. Belletti 1990, 2005; D'Alessandro and Roberts 2008: 485–488).

(37) a. (*So* [CP *che*) [TP *gli* *avete* [*v*-VP *servito la*
     I.know   that   to.him= you.have   served the
    cena]]]. (It.)
    dinner
    '(I know that) you served him dinner.'
  b. [CP *Servite* [*v*-VP *gli* ~~*servite*~~ *la cena!*]] (It.)
     serve.IMP.2PL   =to.him   the   dinner
    'Serve him dinner!'
  c. [CP *Servita* [*v*-VP *gli* ~~*servita*~~ *la cena*]], *cominciai*... (It.)
     served   =to.him   the dinner I.began
    'Having served him dinner, I began...'

Another important factor in our analysis concerns the active vs passive distinction which, we have seen, transparently surfaces in the distinction between the *faire-infinitif* and *faire-par* causative constructions. In current theory this voice distinction is generally understood in terms of phase theory (Chomsky 2000, 2008; Frascarelli 2006; Gallego 2010): in contrast to active *v*Ps which involve the projection of an external argument and hence are argued to be thematically and phi-complete, passive *v*Ps fail to project an external argument and are said to be defective in the relevant sense. From this it is argued that active *v*Ps are phases which constitute autonomous structural domains for the operation of phonosyntactic rules, whereas passive *v*Ps are non-phasal and are necessarily inserted in the phonosyntactic domain of the entire clause, namely the CP phase. This distinction can be transparently seen in the Abruzzese dialect examples from Arielli in (38a-b), where in the present perfect auxiliary BE is licensed in the first and second persons and auxiliary HAVE in the third persons (D'Alessandro and Ledgeway 2010; D'Alessandro and Roberts 2010) according to a pattern widespread in the dialects of central and southern Italy (Ledgeway 2012: 297–299, in press b). As Biberauer and D'Alessandro (2010) highlight, while in the passive example (38b) the passive auxiliary *si* 'are.2SG' licenses consonantal lengthening of the following passive participle *viste* (namely, [v:]*iste*), in (38a) the homophonous active auxiliary *si* fails to trigger consonantal lengthening of the following active participle, even though the auxiliary apparently continues to occur linearly adjacent to the participle.⁶

(38) a. [TP *Si*   [vP *viste* [vP ~~viste~~ la   *casa*]]]. (Ariellese)
         you.are   seen   the house
    'You have seen the house.'
   b. [TP *Si*   [vP *vviste* [vP ~~viste~~ *allà*]]]. (Ariellese)
         you.are   seen   there
    'You are seen there.'

Adopting a cyclical approach to Spell-Out in terms of the phase theory sketched above, these facts immediately find a natural explanation. In the active example (38a) consonantal lengthening fails to obtain because active auxiliary and participle are sent to PF in separate cycles: whereas the active participle is transferred to PF in the lower cycle upon completion of the lower *v*P phase, the active auxiliary raises to T° within the higher CP phrase from where it is sent to PF in the subsequent cycle. In the passive (38b), by contrast, both passive auxiliary and participle are contained within the same higher CP phase and are sent to PF together in the same cycle where the auxiliary, raised to T°, can license consonantal lengthening of the adjacent passive participle.

Similar considerations allow us to understand the observed distribution of enclisis and proclisis in conjunction with the imperatival uses of the *faire-infinitif* and *faire-par* causative constructions. In particular, we have established that in the absence of a T-domain the imperatival verb is forced to raise to the vacant C° head (39a), stranding any clitics within the *v*-VP complex (cf. Ledgeway and Lombardi 2005). Given the unmistakably active and passive values of the *faire-infinitif* and *faire-par* constructions, respectively, it is legitimate to assume that the *v*-VP complex constitutes a phase in the former case, but not in the latter. Structurally, therefore, in the *faire-infinitif* construction clitics necessarily surface proclitically to the infinitive within the *v*P (39b), since the infinitive and any clitics are sent to PF together in the lower cycle, while the causative predicate *facit'* under C° is spelt out subsequently in the higher phasal cycle. In the *faire-par* construction, by contrast, clitics surface

---

6 Cf. also D'Alessandro and Roberts' (2008) analysis of (Italo-)Romance participle agreement.

enclitically on the causative predicate under C° (39c) since they are sent to PF within the same single cycle.⁷

(39) a. [_CP_... [_TP_ **'a**   faciti   [_v-vP_ ~~(l)a~~ serva]]]. (Cos.)
            her=   you.do   serve.INF
       'You make her serve/have her served' (*faire-infinitif/faire-par*)
   b. [_CP_ *Faciti'*   [_vP_ **'a**   [_VP_ *serva!*]]] (Cos.; *faire-infinitif*)
            make.IMP.2PL   her=   serve.INF
       'Make her serve!'
   c. [_CP_ *Faciti*   [_vP_ **-la**   [_VP_ *serva!*]]] (Cos.; *faire-par*)
            make.IMP.2PL   =her   serve.INF
       'Have her served!'

Although unaccusatives are known to share many similarities with passive structures (cf. note 5), it will be recalled from examples (33a-b) that they prove incompatible with the *faire-par* construction. The evidence from the southern causative construction therefore highlights that there exist significant differences between unaccusatives and passives. According to the classic formulation, passivization involves the suppression and absorption of the external argument

---

[7] It remains to be explained why in this case clitics must encliticize phonologically to the causative predicate, but cannot procliticize phonologically to the infinitive. The phase theory presented in the text only excludes the possibility of enclisis in the imperatival uses of the *faire-infinitif* construction, but not the possibility of both enclisis and proclisis in the case of the *faire-par* construction. However, in the northern Calabrian dialect of Verbicaro (G. Silvestri p.c.), this prediction is in fact borne out, inasmuch as enclisis to the causative predicate (i.a) and proclisis to the infinitive (i.b) are both found in the *faire-par* construction:

i   a   *Faciətəla*   *sèrəvə!* (Verbicarese)
        do.IMP.2PL=it.F.ACC   serve.INF
    b   *Faciət*   *aa*   *serəvə!*
        do.IMP.2PL it.F.ACC=   serve.INF
    c   'Have her served!' (*faire-par*)
    d   'Make her serve!' (*faire-infinitif*)

Verbicarese also differs from Cosentino in that, alongside proclisis to the infinitive in (i.b), it also allows enclisis to the causative predicate (i.a) in the *faire-infinitif* construction (i.d), hence the double reading observed in (i.a-b) above. This possibility is predicted, though not forced, by the Phase Impenetrability Condition (PIC) which allows the raising of the clitic to the causative predicate on condition that it passes through the left edge of the infinitival phase. See also the discussion in note 11.

with obligatory movement (and/or co-indexation) of the internal argument to the surface subject position in the absence of accusative. Arguably, suppression of the external argument in the passive might be taken to indicate the failure of vP to project in line with our conclusion above that passive verb phrases are non-phasal, witness the modified representation of (39c) in (40a). By contrast, unaccusative structures are active, and not passive, and can legitimately be argued not to involve the suppression of the external argument position. Rather, unaccusative structures are characterized by an empty external argument position, hence the projection of the vP layer and their phasal status, as illustrated in (40b).

(40) a. [$_{CP}$ *Faciti* [$_{VP}$ *-la serva!*]] (Cos.; *faire-par*)
  make.IMP.2PL =her.ACC serve.INF
 b. [$_{CP}$ *Facit'* [$_{vP}$ *'a* [$_{VP}$ *serva!*]]] (Cos.; *faire-infinitif*)
  malke.IMP.2PL her.ACC= serve.INF

In this way, the absence vs presence of a vP layer and concomitant non-phasal vs phasal status now associated with the passive and unaccusative verb phrases in (40a-b) provides a straightforward explanation for the otherwise puzzling incompatibility of the *faire-par* construction with unaccusatives (41a) and their restriction to the *faire-infinitif* construction (41b).

(41) a. *[$_{CP}$ *Faciti* [$_{VP}$ *-la* trasa ~~la!~~]] (Cos.; *faire-par*)
  make.IMP.2PL =her.ACC enter.INF her.ACC
 b. [$_{CP}$ *Facit'* [$_{vP}$ *'a* [$_{VP}$ trasa ~~la!~~]]] (Cos.; *faire-infinitif*)
  make.IMP.2PL her.ACC= enter.INF her.ACC
  'Make/Let her come in!'

It now remains to explain our observation in (31a-c) above that proclisis to the embedded infinitive is excluded in the negative imperative, where the distinction between the *faire-par* and *faire-infinitif* constructions is neutralized through generalized enclisis to the causative predicate. This observation finds an immediate explanation in the presence of the sentential negator itself, a functional head whose presence in the clause necessarily forces the projection of the T-domain, otherwise absent in positive imperatives. As a consequence of the presence of the negator, negative imperatival clauses are therefore predicted to be inflectionally richer than affirmative imperatival clauses since they automatically come with T-related functional positions to host the inflected verb and any accompanying clitics, as exemplified by the Italian example in (42).[8]

(42) [_CP_... [_TP_ **Non la**   servite   [_v-VP_ ~~'a servite!~~]]] (It.)
          NEG her=   you.serve
   'Don't serve her!'

Further direct proof of this analysis can be seen in numerous Italian dialects where, in contrast to the positive imperative, the T° head is exceptionally lexicalized in the negative imperative through an overt auxiliary (Zanuttini 1994, 1997: 105–154; Manzini and Savoia 2005, III: §7.2). As illustrated in the following examples taken from Manzini and Savoia's (2005, III: 453–461) wide-ranging survey, this auxiliary may in accordance with dialect variation be a reflex of STARE 'stand' (43), IRE 'go' (44) or ESSE(*RE) (45).

(43) a. **sta**   mia   tʃa'mar-el (2sg; Revere, Mantua)
      stema mia   tʃa'mar-el (1pl; Revere)
      stɛ   mia   tʃa'mar-el (2pl; Revere)
      STARE   NEG   call.INF=him
   b. nɔn **sta**   l   tʃa'mɛ (2sg; Alfonsine, Ravenna)
      nɔn **sta'zeᵊ** l   tʃa'mɛ (1pl; Alfonsine)
      nɔn **sta'zi**   l   tʃa'mɛ (2pl; Alfonsine)
      NEG STARE   him= call.inf
   c. ni **stɛ**   l   tʃa'mɛ (2sg; Sassello, province of Savona)
      ni **stum**   le   tʃa'mɛ (1pl; Sassello)
      ni **stɛ**   l   tʃa'mɛ (2pl; Sassello)
      NEG STARE him= call.INF
   d. nu **ʃta**   lu   a   tʃa'ma (2sg; Favale di Malvaro, Genoa)
      nu **ʃtɛme** lu   a   tʃa'ma (1pl; Favale di Malvaro)
      nu **ʃtɛ**   lu   a   tʃa'ma (2pl; Favale di Malvaro)
      NEG STARE =him to call.INF

---

8 In this connection, consider also the distribution of *do*-support in modern English where, in contrast to affirmative declarative clauses (i.a), the presence of the negator *not* triggers the obligatory lexicalization of T° through the use of pleonastic *do* (i.b):

i   a   *She (*does) dance*
      b   *She *(does) not dance*

(44) a. nɔ   lu   ʃi   ca'mannə (2sg; Acerenza, Potenza)
       nɔ   lu   ʃəmə   ca'mannə (1pl; Acerenza)
       nɔ   lu   ʃətə   ca'mannə (2pl; Acerenza)
       NEG   him= IRE   call.GER
    b. nɔ   ɔ   ʃʃi   ca'mannə (2sg; Gravina di Puglia, Bari)
       nɔ   ɔ   ʃʃimə   ca'mannə (1pl; Gravina di Puglia)
       nɔ   ɔ   ʃʃitə   ca'mannə (2pl; Gravina di Puglia)
       NEG   him= IRE   call.GER
    c. nɔ   ɔ   ʃɛ   ca'mannə (2sg; Taranto)
       nɔ   ɔ   ʃəːmə   ca'mannə (1pl; Taranto)
       nɔ   ɔ   ʃəːtə   ca'mannə (2pl; Taranto)
       NEG   him= IRE   call.GER

(45) a. nɔ   ɔ   si   ca'mannə (2sg; Minvervino Murge, Barletta)
       nɔ   ɔ   simmə   ca'mannə (1pl; Minvervino Murge)
       nɔ   ɔ   sɛitə   ca'mannə (2pl; Minvervino Murge)
       NEG   him= ESSERE   call.GER
    b. na   wə   si   ca'mɛnnə (2sg; Giovinazzo, Bari)
       na   wə   seːmə   ca'mɛnnə (1pl; Giovinazzo)
       na   wə   seːtə   ca'mɛnnə (2pl; Giovinazzo)
       NEG   him= ESSERE   call.GER
    c. na   u   si   camannə (2sg; Ruvo di Puglia, Bari)
       na   u   sɔmə   camannə (1pl; Ruvo di Puglia)
       na   u   sɔːtə   camannə (2pl; Ruvo di Puglia)
       NEG   him= ESSERE   call.GER
       'Don't (let's) call him!'

In the light of this evidence, we can conclude that in the *faire-infinitif* construction (46) it is the presence of a TP projection in the negative imperative which, once introduced by the presence of the negator, obligatorily attracts any clitics (as well as the imperatival verb) which in the positive imperative (cf. 39b) otherwise remain within the lower *v*P phase in the absence of the projection of TP.

(46) [CP... [TP **Unn' 'a**   faciti   [*v*-VP ['a
               NEG   her= make.IMP.2PL
     serva]]] (Cos.; *faire-infinitif*(/-*par*))
     serve.INF
     'Don't have her serve(d)!'

4.1 Outstanding question

One final question which we still need to consider concerns the difference between northern Calabrian and Campanian dialects (47) on the one hand and all other Romance varieties (48)-(49) on the other which fail to formally distinguish between the *faire-par* and *faire-infinitif* constructions in the positive imperative.

(47) a. *Faciti**lu**   serva   'i ll'   atri!* (Cos.; *faire-par*)
        make.IMP.2PL=him serve.INF of the others
        'Have him served by the others!'
   b. *Facit'*   *'u*   *serva!* (Cos.; *faire-infinitive*)
        'make.IMP.2PL   him=   serve.INF
        'Make him serve!'

(48) a. *Faites-**moi***   (/*Laissez-**moi***) *servir*   (*par les autres*)! (Fr.)
        make.IMP.2PL=me   let.IMP.2PL=me   serve.INF by   the others
        'Have me (/Let me be) served by the others! (*faire-par*)
        'Make (/Let) me serve!' (*faire-infinitive*)
   b. **Faites*   (*/*Laissez*) **me**   *servir* (Fr.; *faire-infinitive*)
        make.IMP.2PL   let.IMP.2PL   me=   serve.INF

(49) a. *Faciti**lu***   *serviri!* (Mussomelese, Sicily; *faire-infinitif/faire-par*)
        make.IMP.2PL=him   serve.INF
        'Have/Let him (be) served! (*faire-par*)
        'Make/Let him serve!' (*faire-infinitive*)
   b. **Faciti*   *u*   *serviri!* (Mussomelese, Sicily; *faire-infinitif/faire-par*)
        make.IMP.2PL him=   serve.INF

The relevant facts can be explained by appealing to independently established differences in V-movement and clitic placement in the two groups of varieties. As argued in Ledgeway and Lombardi (2005) and Ledgeway (2009: 319–320; 2016a: 265), in southern varieties such as Calabrian and Campanian lexical verbs and clitics exhibit very low movement in that they remain in the lower adverb space (informally labelled here as *v*P) before the clitic can cliticize to the verb. This is shown in examples such as (50a) where: (i) the clitic and verb follow most low adverbs (Cinque 1999) such as *ggià* 'already' which mark the left margin of the verb phrase; and (ii) clitic and verb are separated from each other by the interpolation of lower adverbs of this same class such as *ammalappena* 'hardly' (for a different analysis of these facts, see Manzini and Savoia

2005, III: 537–541). In other varieties such as Italian (50b) and French (50c), by contrast, the lexical verb has to raise together with the clitic (which already cliticizes to the verb within the *v*P as shown by the ungrammaticality of interpolation structures) to T°, as shown by the fact that the verb and clitic must always precede all low adverbs.

(50) a. [_TP_ *Maria* Ø   [_vP_ g*già*   **mi** *ammalappena*
     b. [_TP_ *Maria* **mi**   *parla* [_vP_ *già*   *a malapena*
     c. [_TP_ *Maria* **me** *parle* [_vP_ *déjà*   *à peine*
          Maria me= speaks   already me hardly
     [_vP_   ***parra***   m̶i̶]]]. (Cos.)
     [_vP_ [m̶i̶ p̶a̶r̶l̶a̶]   m̶i̶]]]. (It.)
     [_vP_ [m̶e̶ p̶a̶r̶l̶e̶]   m̶e̶]]]. (Fr.)
          speaks
     'Maria already hardly speaks to me.'

Quite independently, these facts therefore highlight a significant structural difference concerning the nature of clitics in the two groups of languages: while clitics in languages like Italian and French must always vacate (together with the lexical verb) the *v*P to cliticize to a higher functional head, this is not the case in southern varieties like Cosentino where clitics usually remain within the *v*P.[9] It follows that also in the positive imperative of the *faire-infinitif* construction clitics in varieties such as Italian and French are forced to cliticize to a head above *v*P, namely the causative predicate under C° to which they phonologically encliticize from the left margin of the *v*P in accordance with the locality restrictions imposed by the Phase Impenetrability Condition,[10] whereas

---

9 In southern varieties such as Cosentino, clitics only vacate the *v*-VP complex if T° is lexicalized by a functional predicate (or by negation):
i a [_TP_ *Maria* **mi** *pò* / *addi* [_vP_ g*già*   m̶i̶ [_vP_ *parrà*   m̶i̶]]] (Cos.)
            Maria me=   can   must   already   speak.INF
   b [_TP_ *Maria* **m'** *a*   / *avìa* [_vP_ g*già*   m̶i̶ [_vP_ *parratu* m̶i̶]]] (Cos.)
            Maria me=   has   had   already   spoken
   c [_TP_ *Maria* **mi** *fa* / *facìa* [_vP_ g*già*   m̶i̶ [_vP_ *parrà*   m̶i̶]]] (Cos.)
            Maria me=   makes   made   already   speak.INF

10 The Phase Impenetrability Condition (Chomsky 2008) predicts that a constituent of a lower phase may only be available to, and feed, phonosyntactic processes of a higher phase if it targets, and possibly passes through, the left edge (Head or Specifier positions) of its own containing phase.

in Cosentino they legitimately continue to remain within the *v*P where they procliticize phonologically to the infinitive.[11]

5 Conclusions

In this article we have highlighted a phonosyntactic peculiarity of the Romance causative construction limited to the positive imperative which, in specific Calabrian and Campanian dialects of southern Italy, formally distinguishes between the *faire-par* and *faire-infinitif* constructions by means of an enclitic vs proclitic alternation of clitics on the causative predicate and embedded infinitive, respectively. Despite appearances, we have shown that proclisis in the case of the *faire-infinitif* construction is not the outcome of a process of failed restructuring but, rather, continues to represent to all intents and purposes a monoclausal structure. In particular, the enclitic vs proclitic alternation observed in the two causative constructions has been shown to relate to the voice distinction between the two constructions which, in turn, directly correlates with the structural architecture and possible opacity

---

[11] From this perspective, modern Verbicarese behaves, not like Cosentino, but more like Italian, such that any clitics usually raise, together with the lexical verb, to the T° head above *v*P (i.a-b; G. Silvestri p.c.). This observation explains, in part, the possibility of enclisis to the causative predicate in the Verbicarese *faire-infinitif* construction observed in note 7 above, whereas possible proclisis to the infinitive in the same context is most probably to be understood as a residue of a more archaic Cosentino-style Calabrian grammar in which clitics and verbs could remain within the *v*P. Indeed, given a grammar in which it is increasingly more natural for clitics to raise to T°, original proclisis to the infinitive in cases like (ii.a) can be readily reinterpreted as an example of enclisis to the causative predicate (ii.b) with concomitant reanalysis of originally exclusively proclitic forms such as *aa* 'her.ACC=' now also as (optionally) enclitic forms, namely '=her.ACC'.

i a [TP Maria **mə**   *chiamə* [vP *sempə* [vP [mə chiamə]]]] (Verbicarese)
          Maria me=   calls   always
   b [TP Maria **u**   *sapiva* [vP *ggià* [vP [u sapiva]]]] (Verbicarese)
          Maria him.ACC=   knew   already

ii a *Faciət*   [vP **aa**   *serəvə!*] (Verbicarese, *faire-infinitif*)
       make.IMP.2PL   her.acc=   serve.INF
   b *Faciət-aa*   [vP aa *serəvə!*] (Verbicarese, *faire-infinitif*)
       make.IMP.2PL=her.ACC   serve.INF
       'Make/Let her serve!'

of the verbal domain containing the infinitive and any clitics. On the one hand, the verbal domain of passive clauses is characterized by a reduced clausal structure, namely a simple lexical VP constituting a permeable phonosyntactic domain such that in the *faire-par* construction clitics dependent on the embedded infinitive are able to enter into a syntactic dependency with elements situated outside of the VP, witness the observed enclisis to the causative predicate. On the other, the verbal domain of active clauses involves the projection of a richer clausal structure, namely a vP constituting an impermeable phonosyntactic phasal domain, such that in the *faire-infinitif* construction clitics dependent on the embedded infinitive are unable to enter into syntactic dependencies with elements outside of the vP, hence the observed proclisis to the embedded infinitive. Finally, the distinction between these southern Italian dialects and other Romance varieties was interpreted as a consequence of an independent property regarding the low placement of clitics in northern Calabrian and Campanian which generally remain within the verbal domain.

References

Alsina, Alex. 1992. On the argument structure of causatives. *Linguistic Inquiry* 23. 517–555.
Alsina, Alex. 1996. *The role of argument structure in grammar*. Stanford: CSLI.
Belletti, Adriana. 1990. *Generalized verb movement*. Turin: Rosenberg & Sellier.
Belletti, Adriana. 2005. (Past-)Participle agreement. In Martin Everaert & Henk van Riemsdijk (eds.), *Blackwell companion to syntax. Volume 3*, 493–521. Oxford: Blackwell.
Biberauer, Theresa. & Roberta D'Alessandro. 2010. On the role of gemination in passives: The case of Abruzzese. *Snippets* 21. 4–6.
Bichelli, Pirro. 1974. *Grammatica del dialetto napoletano*. Bari: Pégaso.
Burzio, Luigi. 1986. *Italian syntax*. Dordrecht: Reidel.
Bybee, Joan L. 1985. *Morphology: A study of the relation between meaning and form*. Amsterdam: Benjamins.
Chomsky, Noam. 2000. Minimalist inquiries: The framework. In Roger Martin, David Michaels, & Juan Uriagereka (eds.), *Step by step. Essays on minimalist syntax in honour of Howard Lasnik*, 89–155. Cambridge Mass.: MIT Press.
Chomsky, Noam. 2007. Approaching UG from below. In Uli Sauerland & Hans-Martin Gärtner (eds.), *Interfaces + recursion =language?: Chomsky's Minimalism and the view from syntax-semantics*, 1–29. Berlin: Mouton.
Chomsky, Noam. 2008. On phases. In Robert Freidin, Carlos Otero, & Maria Luisa Zubizarreta (eds.), *Foundational issues in linguistic theory. Essays in honor of Jean-Roger Vergnaud*, 133–166. Cambridge, Mass.: MIT Press.
Cinque, Guglielmo. 1999. *Adverbs and functional heads. A cross-linguistic perspective*. Oxford: Oxford University Press.

Cinque, Guglielmo. 2004. "Restructuring" and functional structure. In Adriana Belletti (ed.), *Structures and Beyond. The Cartography of Syntactic Structures. Volume 3*, 132–91. Oxford: Oxford University Press.

Cinque, Guglielmo. 2006. *Restructuring and functional heads. The cartography of syntactic structures. Volume 4*. Oxford: Oxford University Press.

Ciutescu, Elena. 2015. Romance causatives and object shift. In Enoch Aboh, Jeannette Schaeffer & Petra Sleeman (eds.), *Romance languages and linguistic theory 2013. Selected papers from 'Going Romance' Amsterdam 2013*, 21–38. Amsterdam: Benjmains.

Comrie, Bernard. (1985). Causative verb formation and other verb-deriving morphology. Timothy Shopen (ed.), *Language typology and syntactic description* (vol. 3), 309–348. Cambridge: CUP.

Davies, Mark. 1995. The evolution of causative constructions in Spanish and Portuguese. In Jon Amastae, Grant Goodall, Mario Montalbetti, & Marianne Phinney (eds.), *Contemporary research in Romance linguistics*, 105–122. Amsterdam: John Benjamins.

D'Alessandro, Roberta & Ian Roberts. 2008. Movement and agreement in Italian past participles and defective phases. *Linguistic Inquiry* 39. 477–491.

D'Alessandro, Roberta & Ian Roberts. 2010. Past participle agreement in Abruzzese: Split auxiliary selection and the null-subject parameter. *Natural Language and Linguistic Theory* 28. 41–72.

Floricic, Frank. 2008. The Italian verb-noun anthroponymic compounds at the syntax / morphology interface. *Morphology* 18. 167–193.

Fracarelli, Mara. (ed.) (2006) *Phases of interpretation*. Berlin: de Gruyter.

Gallego, Ángel. 2010. *Phase theory*. Amsterdam: John Benjamins

Graffi, Giorgio. 1996. Alcune riflessioni sugli imperativi italiani. In Paola Benincà, Guglielmo Cinque, Tullio De Mauro, & Nigel Vincent (eds.), *Italiano e dialetto nel tempo. Saggi di grammatica per Giulio C. Lepschy*, 133–148. Rome: Bulzoni.

Guasti, Maria Teresa. 1993. *Causative and perception verbs. A comparative approach*. Turin: Rosenberg & Sellier.

Kayne, Richard. 1975. *French syntax: The transformational cycle*. Cambridge, MA: MIT Press.

Kayne, Richard. 1991. Romance clitics, verb movement and PRO. *Linguistic Inquiry* 22:. 647–686.

Ledgeway, Adam. 2009. *Grammatica diacronica del napoletano* (Beihefte zur Zeitschrift für romanische Philologie Band 350). Tübingen: Max Niemeyer Verlag.

Ledgeway, Adam. 2012. *From Latin to Romance. Morphosyntactic Typology and Change.* Oxford: Oxford University Press.

Ledgeway, Adam. 2013. Greek disguised as Romance? The case of southern Italy. In Mark Janse, Brian D. Joseph, Angela Ralli, & Metin Bagriacik (eds.), *Proceedings of the 5th International Conference on Greek Dialects and Linguistic Theory*, 184–228. Laboratory of Modern Greek Dialects, University of Patras.

Ledgeway, Adam. 2014. La morphologie flexionnelle de l'impératif des dialectes de l'Italie méridionale: La distribution de la métaphonie. In Jean Léo Léonard (ed.), *Morphologie flexionnelle et dialectologie romane: Typologie(s) et modélisation (s). Mémoires de la Société linguistique de Paris XXII*, 13–33. Louvain: Peeters.

Ledgeway, Adam. 2016a. The dialects of southern Italy. In Adam Ledgeway & Martin Maiden (eds.), *The Oxford Guide to the Romance Languages*, 246–269. Oxford: Oxford University Press.

Ledgeway, Adam. 2016b. Complementation. In Adam Ledgeway & Martin Maiden (eds.), *The Oxford Guide to the Romance Languages*, 1013–1028. Oxford: Oxford University Press.
Ledgeway, Adam. In press a. The verb phrase. In Giuseppe Longobardi (ed.), *The syntax of Italian*. Cambridge: Cambridge University Press.
Ledgeway, Adam. In press b. From Latin to Romance syntax: The great leap. In Paola Crisma & Giuseppe Longobardi (eds.), *The Oxford Handbook of Diachronic and Historical Linguistics*. Oxford: Oxford University Press.
Ledgeway, Adam. & Alessandra Lombardi. 2000. The *faire-par and faire-infinitive* causative constructions: Evidence from the Cosentino imperative', paper presented at the II *Incontro di dialettologia italiana*, University of Bristol, 14-15 September 2000.
Ledgeway, Adam. & Alessandra Lombardi. 2005. Verb movement, adverbs and clitic positions in Romance. *Probus* 17. 79–113.
Ledgeway, Adam, Norma, Schifano & Giuseppina Silvestri. In press. Variazione nella codifica degli argomenti verbali nelle varietà romanze e greche della Calabria meridionale: I costrutti causativi. In Patrizia Del Puente (ed.), *Atti del IV Convegno internazionale di dialettologia - Progetto A.L.Ba.* Rionero in Vulture: Calice Editore.
Lombardi, Alessandra. 1997. *The grammar of complementation in the dialects of Calabria*. University of Manchester: doctoral thesis.
Manzini, M. Rita & Leonardo Savoia. 2005. *I dialetti italiani e romanci. Morfosintassi generativa* (3 vols). Alessandria: Edizioni dell'Orso.
Ouali, Hamid. 2008. On C-to-T φ-feature transfer: The nature of agreement and anti-agreement in Berber. In Roberta D'Alessandro, Gunnar Hrafnbjargarson and Susann Fischer (eds), *Agreement restrictions*, 159–180. Berlin: Mouton.
Pott, August. 1859. *Die Personennamen, insbesondere die Familiennamen und ihre Entstehungsarten unter Berücksichtigung der Ortsnamen*. Leipzig: Brockhaus.
Rivero, Maria-Luisa. 1994a. Negation, imperatives and Wackernagel effects. *Rivista di linguistica* 6. 39–66.
Rivero, Maria-Luisa. 1994b. Clause structure and V movement in the languages of the Balkans. *Natural Language and Linguistic Theory* 12. 63–120.
Rivero, Maria-Luisa & Arhonto Terzi. 1995. Imperatives, V-movement and logical mood. *Journal of Linguistics* 31. 301–332.
Sheehan, Michelle. 2016. Complex predicates. In Adam Ledgeway & Martin Maiden (eds.), *The Oxford guide to the Romance languages*, 981–993. Oxford: Oxford University Press.
Squillaci, Maria Olimpia. 2017. *When Greek meets Romance. A morphosyntactic analysis of language contact in Aspromonte*. University of Cambridge: unpublished doctoral thesis.
Tortora, Christina. 2014. *A comparative grammar of Borgomanerese*. Oxford/New York: Oxford University Press.
van der Auwera, Johan & Lejeune, Ludo (with Umarani Pappuswamy & Valentin Goussev). 2011. The morphological imperative. 'In Matthew Dryer & Martin Haspelmath (eds.), *The world atlas of language structures online*, chapter 70. Munich: Max Planck Digital Library. (http://wals.info/chapter/70).
Vincent, Nigel. 2016. A structural comparison of Latin and Romance. In Adam Ledgeway & Martin Maiden (eds.), *The Oxford guide to the Romance Languages*, 37–49. Oxford: Oxford University Press.

Zanuttini, Raffaella. 1994. Speculations on negative imperatives. *Rivista di Linguistica* 6. 119–142.
Zanuttini, Raffaella. 1997. *Syntactic properties of sentential negation. A comparative study of Romance languages*. Oxford: Oxford University Press.
Zubizarreta, Maria-Luisa. 1985. The relationship between morphophonology and morphosyntax: The case of Romance causatives. *Linguistic Inquiry* 16. 247–289.

Paolo Lorusso
Lexical parametrization and early subjects in L1 Italian

1 Introduction

The distribution of overt/null subjects in Italian spontaneous is linked to the morpho-syntactic features of the lexical elements found in each sentence. Overt subjects in Italian are more likely to be found with unaccusative verbs (Lorusso 2017; Lorusso, Caprin and Guasti 2005) in postverbal position and with 3rd person indefinite subject (Lorusso 2014). We will propose and update the analysis of Lorusso (2017) on the distribution of the overt null subject as generated by the parametric variation across the lexical items that are inserted in the morpho-syntactic derivation (Chomsky 2001, Borer 1984, Manzini and Wexler 1987, Wexler and Manzini, 1987). Different interacting lexical parameters seem to be at work to account for the spontaneous speech of Italian children.

In this paper we will show that the distribution of overt subjects in Italian is linked to the morpho-syntactic features of the lexical elements found in each sentence. Italian allows subject drop, however overt subjects in Italian are more likely to be found with unaccusative verbs (Lorusso, Caprin and Guasti 2005) in postverbal position and with 3rd person indefinite subject (Lorusso 2017,2014). This pattern of distribution of overt subjects seems to be generated by the parametric variation across the lexical items that are inserted in the morpho-syntactic derivation (Chomsky 2001, Borer 1984, Manzini and Wexler 1987, Wexler and Manzini, 1987). The *Lexical Paremetrization Hypothesis* (Manzini and Wexler 1987, Wexler and Manzini, 1987) seems to be at work in the acquisition of Italian since the parametric variation between lexical items is acquired early on. We describe a corpus of spontaneous speech of four children and their parents and caregivers. Although the pro-drop parameter is set early on, different lexical and morpho-syntactic features influence the distribution of overt subjects. Indefiniteness has a central role within the different lexical parameters that interact in the determining the pattern of distribution of overt subjects. The definiteness of the subject DPs represents a subset condition for the postverbal subject with unaccusatives especially in child grammar. While in section 2 we resume the background studies on the characteristics of the *pro* drop parameter in Italian and its early settings, in section 3 we propose the general data about

Paolo Lorusso, IUSS, Scuola Universitaria Superiore Pavia the subject drop in the corpus of spontaneous speech. The dropped subjects are not found at the same rate in all sentences. There are pragmatic reasons, such as the informativeness and the recoverability of the subject DPs, that influence the pattern of omission in the spontaneous speech (Serratrice, 2005, Serratrice & Sorace, 2003). However, the pragmatic principles at work in the information structure operate within the boundaries imposed by grammar (Serratrice and Sorace, 2003). In section 4 we will show that the pattern of distribution of overt subjects depends on the lexical-syntactic class of the verbs they are found with. The loci of generation of the subjects within the VP shells (external /internal argument) influence the likelihood that a subject DP is overt. Furthermore, the person morphology (1st and 2nd person vs. 3rd person) and the definiteness of the subject DPs play a central role in the appearance of overt postverbal subjects. This will lead us to propose that a subset condition is at work with indefinite subjects, especially in the earliest stages of the acquisition of Italian in section 5. Section 6 is devoted to conclusive remarks: the Lexical Parameterization Hypothesis is internal structure of the grammar and represent a powerful cognitive mechanism in the acquisition of language.

2 Background on *pro drop* parameter in Italian

Italian is a null subject language. The central idea is that languages allow pro drop to the extent that their verbal agreement paradigm expresses the φ-features necessary for local recovery of the content of dropped arguments (see Taraldsen 1978, Rizzi 1986 among others). Italian allows null subjects due to the rich verbal morphology that permit their identification through the overt features of person and number.

Children from the very early stage correctly fix the pro-drop parameter (Lorusso et al. 2005, Serratrice 2005, Hyams 2007, Orfitelli 2008). Early null subjects in Italian have been a matter of investigation especially in a comparative perspective with English. It is well known (Hyams 1986, Bloom 1990, Valian 1991, Rizzi 1993/1994, among others) that young children learning English may omit referential subjects, albeit English is a non-pro-drop language, however the two types of subject drop are linked to different phenomena.[1]

---

[1] Valian (1991), for instance, compared the percentage of early null subjects in English with Italian productions. She found out that while in English early null subjects are the 30% in Italian they are the 70% . The difference in ratio between the two languages was taken by Valian as a proof of the fact that the two types of null subjects were linked to different phenomena.

Different studies have focused on the distribution of null subjects in the spontaneous speech of Italian learners (Lorusso et al., 2005, Serratrice 2005). Children from the very early stage correctly fix the pro-drop parameter. In Tab. 1 we report the data from Lorusso (2014) on the longitudinal corpus of spontaneous productions of four Italian children aged between 18 and 36 months (Calambrone corpus (Cipriani et al 1989): Diana, Martina, Raffaello, Rosa. CHILDES database, MacWhinney and Snow 1985): the production of null subjects is similar between adults and children (as also in Lorusso 2014, Serratrice 2005).

Tab. 1: General data about the distribution of Null /Overt subjects across children and adults (Lorusso, 2014).

	Null Subjects		Overt Subjects		
	Number	Percentage	Number	Percentage	Total num.
Diana	430	71,67%	170	28,33%	600
Martina	368	66,79%	183	33,21%	551
Raffaello	471	76,34%	146	23,66%	617
Rosa	594	77,14%	176	22,86%	770
Children	**1863**	**73,40%**	**675**	**26,60%**	**2538**
Adults	**688**	**73,50%**	**248**	**26,50%**	**936**

Besides the general data in Tab. 1, the distribution of overt/null subjects in Italian has often been claimed to be determined by the pragmatics. Serratrice (2005) found out that children, after the MLUW stage of 2.0, use null and overt subjects in a pragmatically appropriate way: she catalogued subjects on the basis of their informativeness. The subjects that are the most informative are realized overtly and conversely those that are the least informative are null. She investigated three parameters of informativeness: (1) the informativeness of the person morphology: 3rd person subjects are more likely to be realized overtly than first or second ones[2]; (2) the activation state of referents[3]; (3) disambiguation of the referent.[4]

---

[2] We will argue that the split between 1st / 2nd person vs. 3rd person is a grammatical and cognitive split and not only a pragmatic one (see section 3 for data and discussion).
[3] 1st and 2nd person referents are always active by definition, while 3rd person are inactive/ semi-active referents. (see Serratrice 2005, Serratrice and Sorace 2003).
[4] 3rd person active referents with more than one antecedent are more likely to be be realized overtly than 3rd person unanmbiguous active referents.

By the point of view of the acquisition of grammar, data like the ones in Tab. 1 can confirm that children early uses null *pro* element: the Italian rich verbal morphology permit their identification through the overt features of person and number. In other words, the Empty Projection Principle EPP (Chomsky 1981) is satisfied from the very first stage of the acquisition of Italian by the presence pf the null *pro* element. The discussion about the existence of *pro* has been a central topic in recent year (Barbosa 1995, Nicolis 2005, Holmberg, 2005 among others) especially within the minimalist framework of Chomsky (1995). Ruling out the presence of *pro* is under the scope of the present work, but in our respect the inflection of the finite verb has two roles: it identifies the phi –features of the referential subjects and satisfies the EPP principle in language in Italian.

In the terms of Manzini and Savoia (2007), the EPP property corresponds to a D(efiniteness) closure requirement: the subjects DP or the finite verb morphology have the denotational content D(efiniteness).[5] If we use the D(efinitiness) feature we can define the pro drop parameter as how different languages realize this feature (Manzini and Savoia, 2007). The D position of the sentential I domain can be lexicalized by a specialized head (such as subject clitics in northern Italian dialects), by a full noun phrase (English) or by either a specialized head or a full phrase (French). By contrast, in a language like Italian the D position of the sentential I domain is not lexicalized, while the D argument is lexicalized only at the morphological level by the inflection of the finite verb. In terms of the parametric condition on the lexicalization of the D properties, Manzini and Savoia (2007) propose a schematization like in (1). The divide between (a) and (b) in (1) corresponds to the classical divide between null subject languages and non-null subject ones.

(1) Lexicalization of the D properties of the sentential I domain:
    a. i   by clitic (e.g. northern Italian dialects)
       ii by clitic or noun phrase (e.g. Ladin dialects, French)
       iii by noun phrase (e.g. English)
    b. no lexicalization (e.g. Italian)

In our respect the pro drop parameter can be restated in the terms of Lexical Paremetrization: the parameter is given depending on how the D feature are lexicalized.

---

[5] Following Manzini and Savoia (2005, 2007, 2011) D is, in fact, the same category that we find in the highest position of nominals, where so called definite articles are inserted.

So, Italian children seem to acquire early on that the D feature are given. Nevertheless, the distribution of overt subjects in Italian is not homogeneous across syntactic frames (Serratrice 2005, Lorusso 2007, 2014), other lexical and morpho-syntactic features, which are in a Subset relation to the general pro drop (D) parameter, influence the distribution of the overt subjects: (1) the verb classes; (2) the scope discourse semantics implied by the pre or post verbal position of the overt subjects; (3) the person morphology; (4) the (in)definiteness of the subject DPs are the lexical(-syntactic) features. We will consider each of them in the next sections. We will start by showing in the next section that verb classes imply different use of overt subject both in adults and children's spontaneous speech.

3 Null subjects and verb classes

The general data about overt null subject in the spontaneous speech shows that children omit subjects at the same rate of the adults from the very earliest stage of the acquisition of Italian. However, the distribution of overt subjects is not uniform across all the sentences of the spontaneous speech. The first 'subset' that we analyze is the verbal class. We differentiate verb classes for the projection of an external argument in the *v*P. Unaccusative do not project external arguments (2), while unergatives (3) and transitives (4) do project an external argument in spec *v*P.

(2) Unaccusatives
 [$_{vP}$ ___ *v* [$_{VP}$ DP [$_{VP}$ V XP]]]

(3) Unergatives
 [$_{vP}$ DP *v* [$_{VP}$ DP [$_{VP}$ V XP]]]

(4) Transitives
 [$_{vP}$ DP *v* [$_{VP}$ DP [$_{VP}$ V XP]]]

External arguments are not true arguments (Pylkannen 2002, Kratzer 1996). In other words, Pylkkanen and Kratzer argue that the external argument is not introduced by the verb, but by a separate predicate, which Kratzer calls 'Voice'.[6] Voice is a functional head denoting a thematic relation that holds between the external argument and the event described by the verb; it combines with the VP by a

---

6 We represent Voice as a vP following Chomsky (1995).

rule called Event Identification. Event Identification allows one to add various conditions to the event that the verb describes; Voice, for example, adds the condition that the event has an agent (or an experiencer or whatever one consider possible thematic roles for external arguments). Verbs are supposed to be parameterized in the lexicon whether they project an external argument or not.

Children (and adults) show a systematic behaviors depending on whether the subject is an external argument or an internal argument. In Tab. 2 we report the data of Lorusso (2014) about the distribution of overt subjects across verb classes in children and adults.

Tab. 2: General data about the distribution of Overt subjects across verb classes in children and adults' productions (absolut numbers and percentage) (Lorusso 2014).

	Overt Subject across Verb Classes					
	Unergatives		Transitives		Unaccusatives	
	N.	%	N.	%	N.	%
Diana	12	23,53	113	26,40	45	37,19
Martina	24	26,97	115	32,67	44	40,00
Raffaello	22	25,00	70	18,23	54	37,24
Rosa	11	26,19	109	19,43	56	33,53
Children	69	**25,56**	407	23,59	199	36,65
Adults	35	**39,77**	129	20,00	84	41,38

The general results in Tab. 2 show a tendency in both adults and children in produce less overt subjects with transitives and unergatives than with unaccusative. Children significantly ($p < 0.05$) produce more overt subjects with unaccusative than with other verb classes ($\chi2= 36,21$ df=2 for P-Value = 0.00001).[7] Each verb is stored in the lexicon with the information on whether it projects an external argument or not. The lexical information about verb class influences the syntactic configuration of the VP shells and has an effect on the pattern of distribution of overt subjects for both children and adults. Children seem to be sensitive to the lexical parameterization of verbs. But why should the verb

---

[7] If we look at each child, we notice that the pattern of more overt subjects with Unaccusatives is confirmed: the data is statistically relevant for Diana ($\chi2= 6,04$; df=2 for P-Value = 0.048801), Raffaello ($\chi2= 21,16$; df=2 for P-Value = 0.000067) and Rosa ($\chi2= 14,8$; df=2 for P-Value = 0.000611), while for Martina there is a strong tendency although not statistically relevant, since it is relevant at P <0.10 ($\chi2= 3,9$; df=2 for P-Value =0,142274).

class influence the pattern of distribution of overt subjects? Our hypothesis is that the lexical parametrization of verbs has an effect on the syntactic derivation and interacts on the one side with the position of the overt subjects and on the other with the morpho-syntactic features of the overt subject DPs. In order to confirm this general hypothesis, we will check the position (preverbal or postverbal) of overt subjects in the spontaneous speech, since each lexical-syntactic verb class involves different syntactic derivation for pre or post verbal overt subjects.

4 Overt subject position

Following the formulation of the pro-drop parameter of Rizzi (1982, 1986), a pro-drop language, like Italian, also allows: (1) the possibility of free inversion of the subject and (2) the possibility of extracting a subject across a *that*-type complementizer. For the purpose of the present analysis we will focus mainly on the fata about free inversion in Italian. For what concerns the relation between the null subject parameter and the free inversion, different authors (Gilligan 1987, Holmberg, 2005, Newmeyer 2005, Nicolis 2005, Manzini and Savoia 2007, D'Alessandro 2015 among others) have shown that the null subject parameter and the free inversion of the overt subjects are independent or at least they stand in a subset relation (Manzini and Savoia 1997, 2007).

Children have already acquired that Italian is a null subject language (Tab. 1), since the D feature are lexicalized at the morphological level by the inflection of the finite verb. Internal arguments, as the subject of unaccusatives, are more likely to be produced overtly (Tab. 2). But are they produced in a preverbal or postverbal position? On the one side, the postverbal subject may be read (Cinque 1993; Zubizarreta 1998) in the scope of the Nuclear Stress Rule of Focus and in a language like Italian any inverted D element closes off the focus domain. On the other side, the lexicalization of the preverbal subject, which in Italian, by the hypothesis of Manzini and Savoia (2007) in (1), does not satisfy a syntactic requirement on the D position of the inflectional domain, corresponds to its interpretation as a topic. So, while the postverbal subject receives a focused reading, the preverbal subject is included within the topic material of the sentence. When children use preverbal and postverbal subjects are lexicalizing the scope discourse semantic properties of topicalization and focalization respectively. Lorusso (2014) checked whether children acquire early on the free inversion and if it is linked to the verb classes and their VP shells. In Tab. 3 we report the overall data (Lorusso 2014) about the percentage of

Tab. 3: General data about the distribution of postverbal and preverbal subjects across verb class in both Italian children and adults' spontaneous production (Lorusso 2014).

	Overt Subject Position across Verb Classes					
	Unergatives		Transitives		Unaccusatives	
	SV	VS	SV	VS	SV	VS
Diana	7 (58,3%)	5 (41,7%)	113 (57,4%)	84 (42,6%)	12 (26,7%)	33 (73,3%)
Martina	19(79,2%)	5 (20,8%)	84 (73 %)	31 (27%)	16 (36,4%)	28 (63,6%)
Raffaello	21 (95,5%)	1(4,5%)	45 (64,3%)	25 (35,7%)	20 (37%)	34 (63%)
Rosa	8 (72,7%)	3 (27,3%)	77 (70,6%)	32 (29,4%)	21 (37,5%)	35 (62,5%)
Children	55 (79,7%)	14 (20,3%)	319 (65%)	117 (35%)	69 (34,7%)	130 (65,3%)
Adults	29 (76,7%)	6 (20,3%)	81 (71,3%)	48 (28,7%)	36 (34,7%)	48 (65,3%)

preverbal and postverbal subjects across verb classes. We can see that the general tendency is producing preverbal subjects SV with unergatives and transitives and postverbal subjects with unaccusatives.

The general data is quite clear: all children and adults show a pattern of preferential SV order with unergatives and VS for unaccusatives. Furthermore, the percentages are very similar: both children and adults use in around the 70% of cases preverbal subjects when it is projected in the external argument position, while in the 65% of cases, postverbal subjects when it is projected in a direct object position. This distribution is statistically relevant for Children for p<0,05 ($\chi2$= 41,80107122 df=1 for P-Value = 0.00001)[8] and Adults ($\chi2$= 15,948 df=1 for P-Value = 0.00001).

Preverbal topicalized overt subjects are found with all verb classes. Unaccusatives are also produced with preverbal subjects, albeit fewer, showing that the Unique Check Constraint (UCC) Wexler (1998) does not apply: children are able to move outside the vP domain the internal subject DP.[9]

---

[8] Each child show a statistically relevant preference (p< 0,05) for preverbals with unergatives and postverbals with unaccusatives: Diana ($\chi2$= 4,275 df=1 for P-Value = 0.038677), Martina ($\chi2$= 11,39 df=1 for P-Value =0.000738), Raffaello ($\chi2$= 9,446538893 df=1 for P-Value = 0.002116) and Rosa ($\chi2$= 4.6476 df=1 for P-Value =0.038677).

[9] Following Borer and Wexler. (1987) and more recently Wexler (1998), HIrsch and Wexler (2007) children's problems with passive or raising predictes are due to a deficit in teh creation of an A chain or in more minimalist term children may interpret vP as a phase so that at spell out they are not able to raise Subject DPs for passives and unaccusatives. For a a discussion on the problems with th Chain A deficit hypothesis and the UCC with unaccusatives see Becker (2014) and Lorusso (2014).

Postverbal focused overt subjects, once more are found with all verb classes, but the higher number with unaccusatives suggest that these postverbal subjects may be left *in situ*. Following the original analysis of Belletti (1988), the position of licensing of the Object (an AgrOP position) is available. The case assigned in this position is not a proper nominative, but in terms of Belletti (1988) it is a partitive: the verb selects an indefinite meaning for the argument in internal argument position. In more recent analysis (Belletti 1988, 2001, 2004, Bianchi & Belletti 2014) Belletti proposes that the postverbal subjects with unaccusatives are licensed in situ through a Functional projection F that carries [gender] and [number] probe, independent of the I layer. This functional projection FP is a probe for the object F agrees (probe) in gender and number with the internal object and then is probed by the number agreement of the finite verb I.

(5)

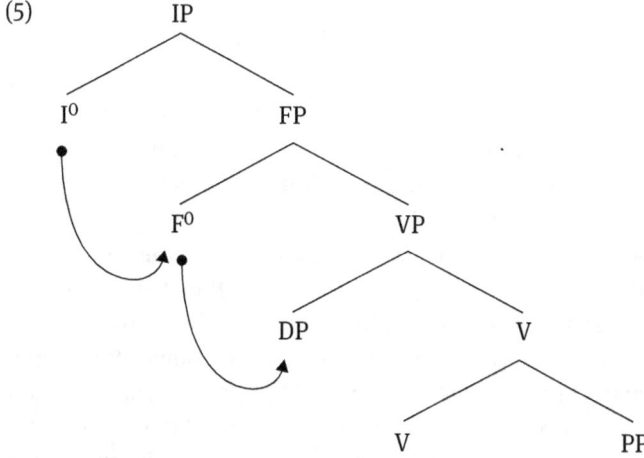

Due to characteristics of the agree mechanism of this postverbal position, nominative case is not assigned since the VP barrier blocks it. The features assigned by the FP in the VP periphery assign only an indefinite reading (6) since these postverbal subjects represented a property of the event denoted by the Unaccusative verb and not a mere participant.

(6) All'improvviso è entrato un uomo /*l'uomo/*ogni uomo dalla finestra.
     Suddenly is entered a man/ *the man/ *every man from the window
                                                (Bianchi & Belletti, 2014)

Manzini and Savoia (2007, 2011) analogously proposes that postverbal subject may undergo some (in)definiteness restrictions and different patterns of agreement found across languages depends on the split of definiteness (as in Sardinian, Manzini and Savoia 2005, 2007, will be back on their analysis in section 5). In order to understand the subset relation instantiated by the different lexical parameters that have a role in the distribution of overt subjects we now introduce the concept of informativeness that is encoded in the subject DPs which interacts with the discourse semantic interface of focus and topic: that is, the person morphology. Person morphology has a preferential pattern of distribution depending on the position of the overt subjects and consequently, as seen above, on the verb class. The informative status of 1st and 2nd person vs. 3rd person interacts with the lexical parametrization of verb classes.

4.1 Person morphology and overt subject

Different authors have showed that person marking across languages undergoes some morpho-syntactic pattern linked to the referential status of the person (Benveniste, 1966, Harley & Ritter, 2002 Bobaljik, 2008, Manzini and Savoia 2005,2007, 2011, Legendre, 2010, among others). In our respect, it is worth to remark that languages are sensitive to the person split between 1st and 2nd singular person and 3rd person.[10]

According to Manzini and Savoia (2005, 2007, 2010, 2011), the person split, in its various manifestations, depends on the fact that the speaker and the hearer (1st and 2nd persons) are anchored directly in the universe of discourse, independently of their role within the event; on the other hand, non-participants in the discourse (3rd persons) depend directly for their characterization on the position assigned to them within the structure of the event.

So 1st and 2nd persons are discourse anchored variables. In our respect they are easily recoverable from the universe of discourse. 3rd persons are event anchored variables. They are event participants but they are non-participants in the discourse, so they are mainly recoverable by the linguistic sentence context. In the distribution of overt subjects in Italian we expect that 1st and 2nd person subjects are omitted more than 3rd person subjects, since discourse anchored participants are more recoverable by the discourse than 3rd person subjects.

---

[10] Manzini and Savoia 2007 showed that the person split is relevant, for example, in the morphological make-up (gender and Case distinctions) or in the agreement properties of the object clitics in Italian and the subject clitic in Northern Italian dialects or in the or in the lexical selection involved by the auxiliary selection in many Italian dialects.

Serratrice (2005) (as Allen 2000, Serratrice and Sorace, 2003 among others) defines 1st and 2nd overt subjects as uninformative since they can be recovered by the discourse. 3rd person subjects are defined informative since there is no discourse cue to identify them. She finds very clear results: after the MLUW stage of 2.0, 3rd person (informative) overt subjects were produced two times more than of 1st or 2nd (uninformative) person subjects. We checked in the same corpus and we analyzed the spontaneous speech of the parents and the caregivers (Calambrone corpus (Cipriani et al 1989): CHILDES database. MacWhinney and Snow 1985). In the chart in Fig. 1 we resume the results about the production of overt subject depending on the person in the adults 'spontaneous speech. Infomative 3rd person subjects are produced overtly in the 33% of the sentences, while uninformative ones (1st and 2nd person are produced overtly only in the 17% of the sentences.

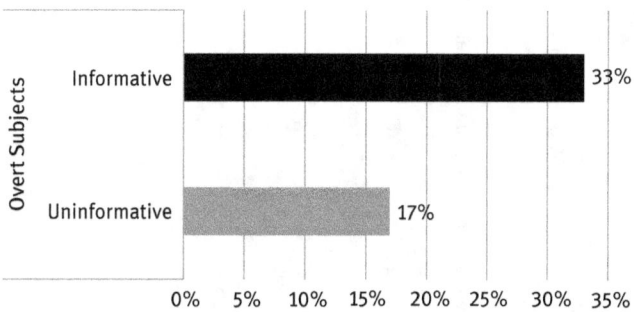

Fig. 1: General data about the distribution of overt informative (3rd person) and uninformative (1st and 2nd person) subjects in the spontaneous production of Italian adults.

Then we checked we if there was any difference for the person of the overt subjects depending on the verb class. Children seem to use more informative subjects with unaccusatives. In Fig. 2 we report the data about the distribution of the person of the overt subjects across the verb classes.

While adults use more informative subjects with both unergatives and unaccusatives, children show a strong preference in using 3rd person informative subject just in the case of internal argument. The verb class seems to influence the co-occurrence with 3rd person overt subjects. The lexical parametrization of verbs (whether they project an external or an internal argument) seems to influence the general distribution of overt/null subjects (as in Tab. 2) on both children and adults. However, children, not adults, use more 3rd person overt subjects just with the internal arguments of the unaccusatives. But why should

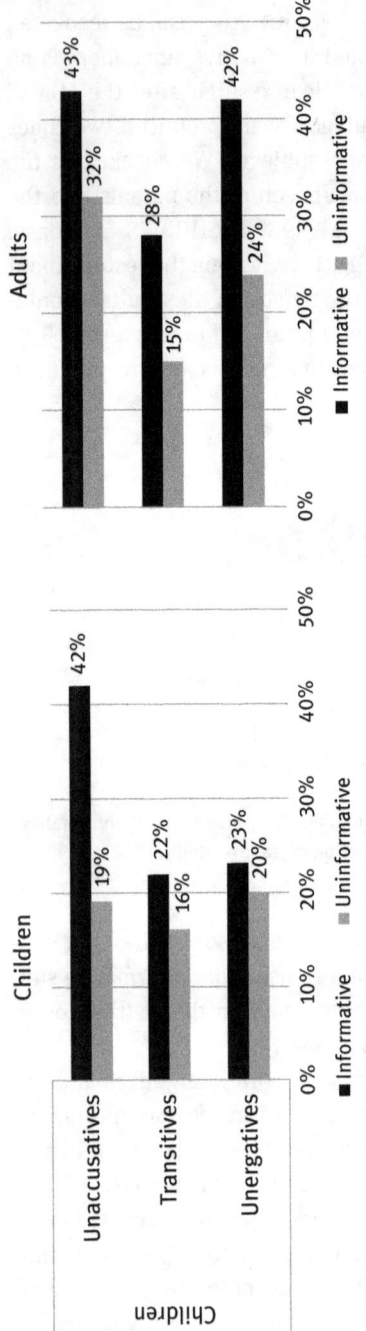

Fig. 2: General data about the distribution of overt informative (3rd person) and uninformative (1st and 2nd person) across verb classes subjects in the spontaneous production of Italian children and adults.

the argument structure of unaccusatives influence the appearance of more informative overt subjects? The answer is linked to the preferred postverbal position found for overt subjects with unaccusatives (see Tab. 3). We have been arguing that postverbal subjects are focalized and represent new information in a scope discourse semantic perspective. We checked the person morphology of the postverbal subjects in the spontaneous speech and we found that both children and adults use almost 3rd person for postverbal subjects with unaccusatives, but not with other verb classes. In Fig. 3 we report the data about the distribution of 3rd person postverbal subjects across verb classes in the spontaneous speech of adults and children.

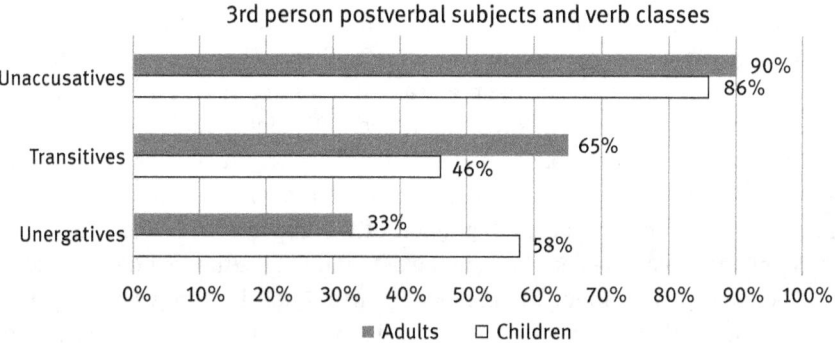

Fig. 3: General data about the distribution of overt informative (3rd person) postverbal subjects across verb classes in the spontaneous production of Italian children and adults.

So, the preferential position of overt subjects found with the different verb classes shows that the scope discourse semantics overlap the aktionsart of verbs. External (agentive) argument are more likely to be old information and they are expressed preverbally or omitted, they are more likely to be recovered by the context: for the very same reason in children's speech informative and uninformative person are found at the same rage for the subjects of unergatives and transitives (Fig. 2). Internal arguments are more likely to be expressed overtly and in postverbal position, they are part of the eventive structure of the verb and they are strictly linked to the linguistic context, they can not be inferred by the discourse. Both children and adults, in fact, use mainly 3rd person DPs for postverbal subjects with unaccusatives (Fig. 3).

Nevertheless, the 3rd person postverbal subjects are not linked only to the scope disourse semantic but other grammatical features seem to be involved. While 1st and 2nd person are definite DPs 3rd person DPs can be indefinite. The split of definiteness can have a role in explaining the pattern of early overt subjects in the Italian children's spontaneous speech (which is different from adults' productions): unaccusatives are found with more 3rd person subjects than other verb classes. Next section is devoted to some data and considerations on the indefinite postverbal subjects in children's speech and to the parametric variation that implies the split of definiteness which in a subset relation to the pro drop parameter.

5 (In)definiteness of the postverbal subjects

The data of the preferential use of 3rd person overt subjects with unaccusatives is linked to the argument structure of unaccusatives. The internal argument is part of the event expressed by the predicate: it measures out the event and it determines an eventive closure (Ritter and Rosen 1998, Mateu 2002, among others). In other words, the theme or the patient arguments are 'stucked' in the eventive relation predicated by the verbal head. Postverbal subjects with unaccusatives are a crucial element in the configuration of the unaccusative verb class: their (in)definiteness plays a central role in the definition of the the eventive structure.

Chomsky (1995), about the expletive construction in a non *pro* drop language like English points out that a definite associate is connected to a different interpretation than an indefinite one. Thus, an indefinite associate gives rise to the typical existential reading in (7a), while a definite associate gives rise to the list interpretation, as in (7b). Furthermore, in English the expletive constructions are restricted to unaccusatives.

(7) a. There is somebody outside
     b. There is John for a start

For what concerns Italian, postverbal indefinite subjects are possible with all verb classes, but just with unaccusatives they may represent a closure of the event denoted by the predicates. Lorusso (2014, 2017) found out that children in the corpus of spontaneous speech of the earliest stage of acquisition of Italian (18–36 months), use indefinite postverbal subjects just with unaccusatives. They never use a postverbal indefinite DP with unergatives and transitives as in Tab. 4. While adults do use indefinite postverbal subjects (in few cases) also with other verb classes.

Similar results are found also in a sentence repetition task (Vernice & Guasti, 2014) with older children (4;2 to 5;11 years of age): when children were

Tab. 4: Absolute numbers and percentage of indefinite postverbal subjects across verb classes (Lorusso 2014).

Distribution of Definite Subjects in SV or VS order accross Verb Classes

	Preverbal Subjects		Postverbal Subjects	
	Indefinite	Definite	Indefinite	Definite
Unergative	2 (4%)	55 (96%)	0 (0%)	14 (100%)
Unaccusatives	3 (4%)	70 (96%)	23 (18%)	130 (82%)
Transitives	3 (1%)	290 (99%)	0 (0%)	117 (100 %)

presented with an unaccusative verb and indefinite subject, they showed a preference in repeating it in a VS order. The same pattern was not found with definite subject and with other verb classes.

The learning component of the Subset Principle, "which orders parameter values according to the subset relations of the languages that the values generate ... (Manzini & Wexler, 1987: 414)" states that children must pick up the smaller subset of the language. Italian infants assume that the verb inflection introduces the D argument and satisfies the EPP principle. Then, with postverbal subjects with unaccusatives they pick up the smaller subset of the language, "..the variable introduced by the verb inflection is existentially closed [...] the identification of the variable by the argument in focus requires the argument itself to be compatible with existential quantification. An indefinite noun is straightforwardly predicted to satisfy this requirement, as it is itself in the scope of existential closure" (Manzini and Savoia 2007:75). So, children set the agree mechanism with postverbal indefinite subjects just for unaccusatives that project internal arguments. Recall that following also Belletti (2004) and Bianchi and Belletti (2014) these postverbal subjects represented a property of the event denoted by the unaccusative verb and not only a participant. The subset principle at work is that indefinites are allowed in postverbal position just when they denote a property of the event or are under the scope of the existential closure represented by the D properties of the verbal morphology (Manzini and Savoia 2007): that is, when they are internal argument of the verb and they represent a predication rather than a chain identification relation.

This kind of data follows by a real parametric option found across Romance languages. There is, in fact, a parametric variation involving null subject languages: the presence or absence of agreement of the I with postverbal subjects depending on the (in)definiteness of the postverbal DP.

Manzini and Savoia (2007,2011) reports that data coming form many dialects which display (some degree of) interaction between the agreement pattern and the (in)definiteness of the postverbal subject. In (8) we report about the dialect of Monreale where a definite postverbal plural subjects agree with the I (8a) while an indefinite postverbal subjects do not (8b). Auxiliary selection may also vary depending on the instantiation for the predicative relation instantiate by the indefinite subject: in the Sardinian variety of Orroli the agreeing postverbal definite subject is introduced by the *be* auxiliary (9a) while the non-agreeing post verbal indefinite subject is introduced by the *have* auxiliary (9b).

(8) Montereale (Friuli)
    a. i' veN i no fi'oi
       ClS come the our children
       'Our children come'
    b. a 'veN ka'nais
       ClS comes children
       'Children come'   (Manzini and Savoia 2007:72)

(9) Orroli
    a. **funti** e'niuzu is pittSCk'kEdduzu
       are come the children
       'The children came'
    b. dui **a** Be'niu pittSCk'kEdduzu
       here has come children
       'Children came here'   (Manzini and Savoia 2007:73)

Indefinite postverbal subjects agree[11] with the D properties of the verb although there is no lexicalization of the D properties within the postverbal indefinite DP (no chains identification): the postverbal indefinite can be the existential closure of the inflectional D morphology. The predicative relation between the unaccusative verbs and their internal argument is taken by children as the only syntactic environment where indefinite postverbal subject can be inserted. With unergatives and transitives there is no such a predicational relation within the subject and the event denoted by the verb.

---

[11] Or not, in languages like the ones in (8) and (9) where the absence of D properties within the postverbal DP may determin parametric variation on the agreement mechanism, for a detailed discussion on it see Manzini and Savoia 2007, 2011.

Children have set the pro-drop parameter: D properties (1) of the sentential I domain have no lexicalization in Italian other than the inflectional morphology of the verbs. Then, the argument structure of verbs influences the distribution of the overt subjects: the predicative relation between unaccusative verbs and their internal argument is the only syntactic environment where children allows overt indefinite postverbal subject since the event expressed by the unaccusative requires an existential quantification. The argument structure of unaccusatives and the indefiniteness of DPs defines a restrictive subset for the distribution of overt postverbal subjects in child Italian.

6 Conclusion

In this paper we accounted for the distribution of early and adult null subjects following the statement of the Lecial Parametrization Hypothesis (Manzini and Wexler, 1987) The lexical parameterization hypothesis states that: "values of a parameter are associated not with a particular grammar but with particular lexical items" (Manzini and Wexler 1987: 424) by children. By the data we have reported in the present work we found out that children set early on the prod-drop parameter, formulated as in (1) that we repeat here in (10), in the sense that they do not assign the D properties of the sentential to any lexical item other than the same inflectional morphology of the verb.

(10) Lexicalization of the D properties of the sentential I domain:
    a. i   by clitic (e.g. northern Italian dialects)
         ii   by clitic or noun phrase (e.g. Ladin dialects, French)
         iii by noun phrase (e.g. English)
    b. no lexicalization (e.g. Italian)

Although children acquire early on the pro-drop parameter, it does not mean that the distribution of overt subject DPs is random. The lexical parameter associated with different lexical items intervenes in the creation of subset condition which allows to account for the distribution of overt subject in Italian. We have collected old and new data to account for the distribution of overt subjects as a reflex of different lexical parameters that interacts.

The first lexical parameter at work is linked to the verb classes. When the verb projects external argument the omission of the subject DP is favoured in the spontaneous spoeech, conversely when the verb projects an internal argument, subject DPs are more likely to be produced overtly (Tab. 2). The preverbal and postverbal position of overt subjects seems to be inherently linked also to their loci of generation within the VP shells: overt external argument are found preferentially in a SV order, while overt internal arguments are found preferentially in a VS order in the spontaneous speech of both Italian children and adults.

This pattern matches the scope discourse semantic interface requirements: preverbal subjects are topic-like information while postverbal subjects are focus-like information. Agentive subjects found with unergatives and transitives are more likely to be omitted and recovered by the discourse than theme and patient subjects found with unaccusatives which measures out the event and are recoverable. The data about the informativeness of the person of the subject DPs (Serratrice 2005) also confirms that theta roles assigned to the subject by each verb influence the pattern of omission. While external argument in children's spontaneous speech are found with both uninformative (1st and 2nd singular) and informative (3rd singular) person, internal subjects of the unaccusatives are preferentially 3rd person DPs which are event related and not recoverable by the discourse. So informative persons are found with DPs that are focus-like: postverbal subject funs with unaccusatives, insfact, are mainly 3rd person DPs (around 90%).

The last lexical parameter is linked to the definiteness of the DP. Children produce indefinite postverbal subjects just with unaccusatives. In child Italian indefinite are allowed only when they are in the scope of the D properties and they are part of the eventive structure of the verb, that is, when they are not derived through event identification (Pylkannen 2002, Kratzer 1996) like the external arguments: they measure out (Ritter and Rosen, 1998) the event denoted by the verb and they allow a mechanism of agreement which does not involve the replication D properties on the indefinite DP, language may vary on the agreement mechanism with the postverbal indefinite DPs.

Lexical parametrization seems to be a predictive and powerful mechanism to account for the acquisition of a language for two main reasons. First because the parameters seem to be associated not with a particular grammar but with particular lexical items. In our respect for the distribution of overt subjects different paremeter are set on lexical items: D properties on the verb morphology allow the omission of the subjects, the loci of projection of the arguments and the definiteness of the DP influence the pattern of distribution of the overt subjects depending on the informativeness as it results by the morpho-syntactic properties of each overt nominal element.

Least but not last, the parameters associated with each lexical items defines some syntactic domains in a given language where lexical items are allowed (or not). They allow to have a subset of the sentences of the languages in which a given lexical item is allowed or banned. In our respect the interaction between verb classes and the (in)definitiness determines a subset within the Italian sentences. Children selects the value of a parameter that generates the smallest language that is compatible with the data (as for the Subset principle) so that indefinite postverbal subjects are found only with unaccusative.

References

Allen, Shanley. 2000. "A discourse-pragmatic explanation for argument representation in child inuktitut." *Linguistics* 38(3): 483–521.
Barbosa, Pilar. 1995. *Null subjects*. PhD dissertation: MIT.
Becker, Misha 2014. *The Acquisition of Syntactic Structure: Animacy and Thematic Alignment.* Cambridge, Cambridge University Press.
Belletti, Adriana. 1988. "The case of unaccusatives," *Linguistic Inquiry*, 19:1–34.
Belletti, Adriana. 2001. "Inversion as focalization," in Aafke Hulk and Jean-Yves Pollock (eds.), *Inversion in Romance and the theory of Universal Grammar*, New York: Oxford University Press (OUP), 60–90.
Belletti, Adriana. 2004. "Aspects of the low ip area," in Luigi Rizzi (ed.) *The structure of CP and IP. The Cartography of Syntactic Structures*, New York: Oxford University Press Volume 2, 16–51.
Benveniste, Emile. 1966. *Problèmes de linguistique générale*, Gallimard, Paris.
Bianchi, Valentina & Adriana Belletti. 2014. "Indefinite subjects of unaccusatives." talk at the workshop "Specificity in the grammar. Form and Interpretation", held in Trento University of Trento, 12 February 2014.
Bobaljik, Jonathan. 2008. "Missing persons: a case study in morphological universals," *The Linguistic Review, special issue Examples of Linguistic Universals* 25: 203–30.
Borer, Hagit. 1984. *Parametric Syntax*, Dordrecht: Foris.
Borer, Hagit, and Ken Wexler. 1987. "The maturation of syntax," in Thomas Roeper and Edwin Williams (eds.), *Parameter setting*. Dordrecht: Reidel, 123–172.
Bloom, Paul. 1991. Subjectless sentences in child language. *Linguistic Inquiry* 21: 491–504.
Chomsky, Noam. 1981. *Lectures on Government and Binding*. Dordrecht: Foris.
Chomsky, Noam. 1995. *The Minimalist Program*. Cambridge Mass.:MIT Press.
Chomsky, Noam. 2001. 'Derivation by phase', in Michael Kenstowicz (ed.), *Ken Hale: A Life in Language*. Cambridge, Mass, MIT Press 1–52.
Cipriani, Paola, Lucia Pfanner, Anna Maria Chilosi, Lorena Cittadoni, Alessandro Ciuti, Anna Maccari, Natalia Pantano, Paola Poli, Stefania Sarno, Piero Bottari, Giuseppe Cappelli, Colombo, and Edy Veneziano. 1989. *Protocolli diagnostici e terapeutici nello sviluppo e nella patologia del linguaggio. Protocollo n. 1/84*. Ministero della Salute della Repubblica Italiana: Stella Maris Foundation.
D'Alessandro, Roberta. 2015. "Null Subject", in Antonio Fábregas, Jaume Mateu and Michael Putnam (eds), Contemporary Linguistic Parameters. London: Bloomsbury Press, 201–226.
Gilligan, Gary M. 1987. *A cross linguistic approach to the pro-drop parameter*. PhD dissertation: University of Southern California.

Harley, Heidi. and Elizabeth Ritter 2002. "Person and number in pronouns: a feature geometric analysis," ms., University of Arizona and University of Calgary.

Holmberg, Anders. 2005. "Is there a little pro? Evidence from Finnish," *Linguistic Inquiry* 36: 533–64.

Hyams, Nina. 1986. *Language acquisition and the theory of parameters*. Dordrecht: Reidel.

Hyams, Nina. 2007. "Aspectual effects on interpretation," *Language Acquisition*, 14(3): 231–268.

Hirsch, Christofer and Ken Wexler. 2007. "The late acquisition of raising: What children seem to think about seem," in Stanley Dubinsky and William Davies (eds.), *New horizons in the analysis of control and raising*, 35–70. New York: Springer.

Kratzer, Angelika. 1996. "Severing the external argument from the verb," in Jphan. Rooryck and Laurie Zaring (eds.), *Phrase Structure and the Lexicon*, 109–137. Dordrecht: Kluwer.

Legendre, Geraldine. 2010. "A formal typology of person-based auxiliary selection in Italo-Romance," in Roberta D'Alessandro, Adam Ledgeway and Ian Roberts (eds.), *Syntactic Variation: the Dialects of Italy*. Cambridge, Cambridge University Press, 86–101.

Lorusso, Paolo. 2007. "The acquisition of aspect in L1 italian," in Alyona Belikova, Luisa Meroni, & Mari Umeda (eds.), *Proceedings of the 2nd Conference of GALANA*, ed., pages 253–264. Somerville: Cascadilla Press.

Lorusso, Paolo. 2014. *Verbs in Child Grammar The Acquisition of the Primitive Elements of the VP at the Syntax-Semantics Interface*. Doctoral Dissertation, Universitat Autónoma de Barcelona. http://www.tdx.cat/bitstream/handle/10803/283726/pl1de1.pdf?sequence=1.

Lorusso, Paolo. 2017. "Lexical Parametrization and early subjects in L1 Italian," *International Journal of Linguistics*, 9, 146–163.

Lorusso, Paolo, Caprin Claudia and Maria Teresa Guasti. 2005. Overt subject distribution in early italian children," in *BUCLD 29 Proceedings Supplement*. BU Boston,MA.: Online Publishing http://www.bu.edu/linguistics/APPLIED/BUCLD/supp29.html.

MacWhinney, Brian & Catherine Snow. 1985. "The child language data exchange system," *Journal of Child Language* 12: 271–296.

Manzini, M. Rita and Leonardo M. Savoia. 1997. "Null subjects without pro," *UCL Working Papers in Linguistics*, 9: 301–313.

Manzini, M. Rita and Leonardo M. Savoia. 2005. *I dialetti italiani e romanci. Morfosintassi generativa*. Alessandria: Edizioni dell'Orso.

Manzini, M. Rita and Leonardo M. Savoia. 2007. *A Unification of Morphology and Syntax*. London: Routledge.

Manzini, M. Rita and Leonardo M. Savoia. 2011. *Grammatical Categories. Variation in Romance Languages*, Cambridge Studies in Linguistics:128. Cambridge: CUP.

Manzini, M. Rita and Ken Wexler. 1987. "Parameters, Binding Theory and learnability," *Linguistic Inquiry*, vol. 18, pp. 413–44.

Mateu, Jaume. 2002. *Argument Structure: Relational Construal at the Syntax Semantics Interface*, Doctoral dissertation, Universitat Autónoma de Barcelona.

Newmeyer, Frederick. J. 2005. *Possible and Probable Languages: A Generative Perspective on Linguistic Typology*. Oxford: Oxford University Press.

Nicolis, Marco. 2005. *On pro-drop*, Doctoral dissertation: Università degli Studi di Siena.

Orfitelli, Robyn. M. 2008. *Null subjects in child language: The competing roles of competence and performance*, Master's thesis, UCLA, Los Angeles, California.

Pylkkänen, Liina. 2002. *Introducing Arguments*. Ph.D. thesis, MIT.

Rizzi, Luigi. 1982. *Issues in Italian Syntax*. Dordrecht: Foris.

Rizzi, Luigi. 1986. "Null-objects in italian and the theory of pro," *Linguistic Inquiry* 17: 501–559.

Rizzi, Luigi. 1993/1994. "Some notes on linguistic theory and language development: The case of root infinitives," *Language Acquisition* 3: 371–393.

Ritter, Elizabeth and Sara T. Rosen. 1998. "Delimiting events in syntax," in Miriam Butt and Wilhelm Geuder (eds.), *The Projection of Arguments*, Stansford, CA: CSLI, 135–164.

Serratrice, Ludovica & Sorace, Antonella. 2003. "Overt and null subjects in monolingual and bilingual italian acquisition," in Barbara Beachley, Amanda Brown and Frances Conlin, *Proceedings of the 27th Annual BUCLD*, Somerville: Cascadilla Press, Volume 2, 739–750

Serratrice, Ludovica. 2005. "The role of discourse pragmatics in the acquisition of subjects in Italian," *Applied Psycholinguistics* (26): 437–462.

Taraldsen, Knut T. 1978. 'On the NIC, Vacuous Application, and the That-t Filter', ms., MIT

Valian, Virginia. 1991. "Syntactic subjects in the early speech of american and italian children.," *Cognition* (40): 21–81.

Vernice, Mirta and Maria Teresa Guasti. 2014. "The acquisition of SV order in unaccusatives: manipulating the definiteness of the NP argument," *Journal of child language* 42(1): 210–237.

Wexler, Ken. 1998. "Very Early Parameter Setting and the Unique Checking Constraint: A New Explanation of the Optional Infinitive Sstage," *Lingua* 106, 23–79.

Wexler, Ken and Rita Manzini. 1987. "Parameters and Learnability in Binding Theory', in Thomas. Roeper and Edwin Williams (eds.), *Parameter Setting*. Dordrecht: Reidel, 41–76.

Ana Madeira and Alexandra Fiéis
Inflected infinitives in Portuguese

1 Introduction

Inflected infinitives in European Portuguese (EP) differ from their uninflected counterparts in several respects: they exhibit overt person/number morphology,[1] may occur with nominative subjects and are restricted to a subset of the contexts in which infinitives are allowed (namely, subject, adjunct and certain complement clauses). In most of these contexts, the inflected infinitival subject may be null or overt, and it is referentially free (see example in [1]).

(1) Os teus pais chegaram cedo para (tu) **poderes**
 the your parents arrived-IND.PAST-3PL early for (you) be-able-INF-2SG
 sair [EP]
 leave-INF
 'Your parents arrived early so you could go out'

Most analyses of the EP inflected infinitive (Madeira 1994; Martins 2001; Sitaridou 2002; Cowper 2002; Pires 2006; Gonçalves, Santos, and Duarte 2014) build on Raposo's (1987) proposal, according to which the inflected infinitive is made possible by two conditions: a syntactic condition (i.e., a positive value for the Null Subject Parameter, which allows for the morphological realization of

---

[1] In Portuguese, the inflected infinitive exhibits the following inflectional paradigm:
    falar ('speak')
    (eu) falar   [1st sing]
    (tu) falares   [2nd sing]
    (ele/ela) falar   [3rd sing]
    (nós) falarmos   [1st pl]
    (vós) falardes   [2nd pl]
    (eles/elas) falarem   [3rd pl]

Note: This paper is based upon work supported by the Foundation for Science and Technology (FCT) within the project PEst-UID/LIN/03213/2013. We thank an anonymous reviewer for his/her insightful comments and suggestions.

Ana Madeira, Alexandra Fiéis, CLUNL/FCSH – Universidade NOVA de Lisboa

https://doi.org/10.1515/9781501505201-023

the φ-features of I) and a morphological condition, the I(nfl)-parameter, responsible for the association of a complete set of φ-features to a [-Tense] I. Furthermore, this [-Tense] I must itself be Case-marked in order to be able to license nominative subjects, thus deriving the fact that inflected infinitival clauses are restricted to Case positions, unlike their uninflected counterparts. However, this assumption makes the incorrect prediction that we should expect inflected infinitival clauses in all Case positions where infinitival clauses may appear, which is not the case (subject control, etc.) (e.g. Madeira 1994:185–186; Mensching 2000:79–80).

Similarly, Cowper (2002) proposes that, in null subject languages, I may be associated with an uninterpretable Case feature, regardless of finiteness. Hence, from a minimalist perspective, in the case of the inflected infinitive, the uninterpretable Case feature on the infinitival I establishes an AGREE relation with a probe in a higher clause and, after feature valuation and deletion, the infinitival I acquires the ability to value and delete the Case feature of its subject and to spell out φ-features. The fact that, in standard EP, the inflected infinitive is excluded from certain positions – e.g., it reportedly never occurs embedded under modal verbs or temporal and aspectual auxiliaries (2), or as a complement to desiderative and other obligatory subject control verbs (3) – is attributed by Raposo (1987) to selectional restrictions (in selected contexts, the inflected infinitive is allowed only if the verb selects either a tensed or a nominal complement).

(2) *Os meninos devem / começaram a **tocarem** guitarra [EP]
the boys must-IND.PRS.3PL / start-IND.PAST.3PL to play-INF.3PL guitar
'The boys should / started to play the guitar'

(3) *Os meninos querem **tocarmos** guitarra [EP]
the boys want-IND.PRS.3PL play-INF.1PL guitar
'The boys want us to play the guitar'

However, it has been observed that there is some variation regarding the acceptance of constructions with inflected forms of the infinitive among speakers, both in standard EP and in other varieties of the language. Some aspects of the distribution and properties of the inflected infinitive are not predicted by the analyses described above. In this squib, we consider data from corpora of standard and nonstandard EP, Brazilian Portuguese (BP) and African varieties of

Portuguese and show that the properties and distribution of the inflected infinitive may differ in these varieties. These facts raise interesting questions regarding the morphosyntactic conditions which make a marked option such as the inflected infinitive possible and lead us to propose that the various occurrences of inflected infinitives observed do not constitute a unitary phenomenon, as they may be associated with different degrees of finiteness: in addition to the inflected infinitive described by Raposo (1987), we also find, on the one hand, an inflected infinitive which presents characteristics that are typical of finite verb forms and, on the other hand, another one which behaves like an uninflected infinitive, the so-called "pseudo-inflected infinitive" (Gonçalves, Santos, and Duarte 2014).

Hence, in the next section, we examine the distribution and properties of inflected infinitives in different varieties of Portuguese. Our primary focus is on describing the phenomena and identifying some of the questions which are of major interest in this domain. We consider that the data described here have potentially interesting implications for an understanding of the concept of *finiteness*, an issue which we touch on briefly in the final section of the squib.

2 The inflected infinitive: a non-unitary phenomenon

2.1 Inflected infinitives in finite contexts

Inflected forms of the infinitive, i.e. verbal forms which bear infinitival morphology associated with agreement inflection and license overt nominative subjects, are found in certain root contexts in standard EP, namely, in interrogative and exclamative contexts (4), in which the inflected infinitive bears a modal interpretation and may be associated with an exclamative intonation (cf. Ambar 1992; Ambar & Jiménez (2017); among others). These so-called 'independent infinitives' have been argued by Ambar (1992) and Ambar and Jiménez (to appear), among others, to involve a null modal operator which licenses Tense in C (assuming the verb to be in C).

(4) a. ***Telefonarmos*** *à mãe hoje ou amanhã?* [EP]
 phone-INF.1PL to.the mother today or tomorrow
 'Should we phone mum today or tomorrow?' (Oliveira 2014:80)

b. ***Dizeres*-me   tu   uma coisa dessas!²** [EP]
   tell-INF.2SG-me you-NOM a   thing of.those
   '(Imagine) you telling me a thing like that!'

In other varieties of Portuguese we find inflected infinitives in finite embedded contexts, standing for a subjunctive. See the examples in (5) from Angolan Portuguese (AP), where the inflected infinitive replaces the future subjunctive and the present subjunctive, respectively. Hence, in these contexts, the inflected infinitive appears to be associated with a mood specification, contrary to what has been argued by e.g. Pires (2006).

(5) a. <u>se</u> ***fazermos***   um balanço global dos   [AP]
       if make-INF.1PL a   balance global of.the
       dois últimos anos, achamos   que [...]
       two last   years, think-IND.PRS.1PL that [...]
       'if we make a global balance of the last two years, we think that [...]'
                                    (*African Varieties of Portuguese Corpus*)
   b. <u>para que</u> [...] ***ficarmos***   sossegados, sem
       for   that [...] become-INF.1PL calm,   without
       vestígios do   passado [AP]
       traces of.the past
       'so that [...] we can rest, without traces of the past'   (*Jornal de Angola*)

Examples (4) and (5) show that, in contemporary Portuguese, the inflected infinitive can be found in contexts where we would expect a finite form of the verb. This is reminiscent of what we find diachronically, namely, in Old Portuguese, where it occurred mainly in independent domains with an imperative/optative interpretation, alternating with the subjunctive (Martins 2001).³ However, its distribution is not uniform across varieties of Portuguese and that is what we will show in 2.2.

---

2 Subject-verb inversion is optional in these contexts.
3 Regarding the AP examples, a reviewer suggests that the inflected infinitive may have changed its category and is actually a subjunctive in this variety, in which case these examples should simply be considered finite verb forms. We leave this question for future research.

2.2 The "standard" inflected infinitive

As described in the introduction, the inflected infinitive standardly occurs in certain dependent non-finite contexts, where it can license a freely referring nominative subject. However, the distribution of the inflected infinitive bearing these properties appears to differ across varieties of Portuguese. For example, this inflected infinitive may appear in the complement position of certain subject control verbs in BP (see (6), where the inflected infinitival subject is interpreted as referentially disjoint from the matrix subject), but not in standard EP, and it is found with propositional verbs in EP (see [7]), but not in BP (Modesto 2010a).

(6) Eu_i prefiro $eles_j$ **ficarem**   lá   mesmo [BP]
      I   prefer-IND.PRS.1SG they meet-INF.3PL there right
      'I prefer for them to stay right there'   (Modesto, 2014)

(7)   O   presidente afirmou   **reunirem**-se   os   ministros
      the chair   say-IND.PAST.3SG meet-INF.3PL SE the ministers
      sempre às   6 [EP]
      always at.the 6
      'The chair said that the ministers always meet at 6'

As shown by Pires (2006), the inflected infinitive in these constructions displays properties which differ from those of control infinitives and are identical to those of finite verbs. For example, unlike its uninflected counterpart in (8b), the inflected infinitival subject in (8a) does not require a local c-commanding antecedent:

(8) a. Os $rapazes_i$ disseram   que os $amigos_j$
        the $boys_i$ say-IND.PAST.3PL that the $friends_j$
        lamentam $[-]_{i/j/k}$ **terem**   mentido [EP]
        regret-IND.PST.3PL $[-]_{i/j/k}$ have-INF.3PL lied
        'The boys said that their friends regret that they lied'
    b. Os $rapazes_i$ disseram   que os $amigos_j$
        the $boys_i$ say-IND.PAST.3PL that the $friends_j$
        lamentam $[-]_j$ **ter**   mentido [EP]
        regret-IND.PST.3PL $[-]_j$ have-INF lied
        'The boys said that their friends regret that they lied'

Moreover, unlike obligatory control uninflected infinitives (see [9b]), which trigger a sloppy reading under ellipsis, inflected infinitives only allow a strict interpretation, as shown in (9a).

(9) a. *Eu lamento (eles) **terem** mentido e a*
  I regret-IND.PST.1SG (they) have-INF.3PL lied and the
  Joana também [EP]
  Joana too
  'I regret that they lied and Joana does too'
  (= Joana regrets that they lied)
 b. *Eu lamento [-] **ter** mentido e a*
  I regret-IND.PST.1SG [-] have-INF lied and the
  Joana também [EP]
  Joana too
  'I regret that I lied and Joana does too'
  (= Joana regrets that she lied)

2.3 The inflected infinitive in control structures

Contrary to what was claimed by Raposo (1987), inflected infinitives may be found embedded under subject control verbs in standard EP. However, their distribution in these contexts appears to be highly restricted and, when they occur, they seem to display control properties, not allowing a freely referring subject (in contrast to the BP example in (6) above), as shown in (10)[4]:

(10) a. *??Eu prefiro (eles) **irem** ao cinema* [EP]
  I prefer-IND.PRS.1SG (they) go-INF.3PL to.the cinema
  'I prefer that they go to the cinema'
 b. **Eu decidi (eles) **irem** ao cinema* [EP]
  I decide-IND.PAST.1SG (they) go-INF.3PL to.the cinema
  'I decided that they should go to the cinema'

---

[4] In these contexts, there seems to be some variability regarding the acceptability of inflected infinitives, which appears to be determined by the matrix verb, as illustrated in the examples in (10).

According to Sheehan (2014), in sentences like those in (11), if the two subjects are correferential, only the uninflected form is allowed (11a), although some speakers may accept the inflected infinitive if an argument intervenes between the two subjects (11b). Similarly, if a partial control reading obtains, i.e., if the reference of the matrix subject is included in the reference of the infinitival subject, the inflected infinitive is acceptable for some speakers (11c), particularly in the presence of an intervening argument (11d).

(11) a. *Preferias* **chegar(*es)** *a tempo* [EP]
prefer-IND.IMPF.2SG arrive(-*INF.2SG) on time
'You would prefer to arrive on time'
b. *Prometemos à professora* **chegar(%mos)** *a tempo* [EP]
promise-IND.PAST.1PL to.the teacher arrive(-%INF.1PL) on time
'We promised the teacher to arrive on time'
c. *O João preferia* **reunir(%em)-se** *mais tarde* [EP]
the John prefer-IND.IMPF.3SG meet(-%INF.3PL)-SE more late
'João would prefer to meet later'
d. *O Pedro prometeu à Ana* **reunir%(em)-se** *em Braga* [EP]
the Pedro promise-IND.PAST.3SG to.the Ana meet(-%INF.3PL)-SE in Braga
'Pedro promised Ana to meet in Braga' (Sheehan 2014)

According to Modesto (2010b), the inflected infinitival complements of propositional verbs also exhibit the properties of control structures. Hence, contrary to what happens in EP, where the subject may be lexically realized and interpreted as disjoint from the matrix subject, as shown in (7) above, the subject of these complements cannot be lexically realized[5] in BP and must have a partial control reading, as in (12)[6]:

(12) O   presidente$_i$ afirmou   [-]$_{i+}$ se **reunirem**
     the   chair$_i$ say-IND.PAST.3SG   SE meet-INF.3PL
     (sempre) às   6 [BP]
     (always) at.the   6
     'The chair said that they (always) meet at 6'   (Modesto 2010b)

Furthermore, it appears that some speakers of standard EP both accept and produce inflected infinitives with subject control verbs with a correferential reading in the presence of a local controller. In these cases, the subject is not realized lexically. For instance, Pires, Rothman and Santos (2011) found significant acceptance of inflected infinitives with volitional verbs (e.g., *querem irem* 'want-IND.PST.3PL go-INF.3PL'). Similarly, an analysis of the *CETEMPúblico* corpus[7] reveals a number of examples, as illustrated in (13) below.[8] Similar examples are found in other varieties of the language – see (14), from oral Mozambiquean Portuguese (MP).

(13) se não querem   **serem**   [...] apoiantes
     if not want-IND.PRS.3PL   be-INF.3PL   [...] supporters

---

5 There appears to be some variation regarding the possibility of lexically realized subjects in this context in BP. Hence, Mensching (2000) notes that not only are they possible for some speakers, but, unlike in EP, where subjects are obligatorily postverbal in this context, they may also be acceptable in preverbal position, as shown in (i):
(i) ?*O aluno compreendeu [isto ser inútil]*
     the pupil understood this be-INF-3PL useless
     'The pupil understood that this was useless.'
     Mensching (2000:29)
6 A disjoint reading is possible in certain cases, e.g., if the subject has undergone wh-movement (Modesto 2010):
(i) *Que estudantes o Pedro acredita [-] terem passado?*
     'Which students does Pedro believe to have[INF.3PL] passed?'
7 The *CETEMPúblico* is a 180-million-word European Portuguese *corpus*, made up of texts extracted from the daily newspaper *Público*.
8 Only one example with a referentially disjoint subject was found in our analysis of this corpus, which involved a wh-moved subject:
(i) (...) «*distorções, erros e injustiças*» (...) *que diz não desejar virem «a beliscar minimamente a vitória do PS»*
     (...) '"distortions, mistakes and injustice" (...) which he says that he does not wish (them) to come[Inf-3pl] "to affect PS's victory minimally"' (CETEMPúblico)

  de um [...] *governo*   *corrupto* [EP]
  of a   [...] government corrupt
  'if they do not want to be [...] the supporters of a [...] corrupt government'
                   (*CETEMPúblico*)

(14) *até alguns já tencionavam **fazerem***
   even some already intend-IND.IMPF.3PL make-INF.3PL
   atentados físicos aos professores [MP]
   attempts physical to.the teachers
   'even some were already intending to assault their teachers'
              (*Spoken Corpus Mozambique*)

There are other constructions in standard EP that allow infinitives which, despite being associated with agreement inflection, do not license nominative subjects. This is the case, for instance, of complements to object control verbs (15) and Exceptional Case Marking (ECM) complements to causative and perception verbs (16). In the case of object control, the subject has to be null and is obligatorily controlled by the matrix object. In the case of ECM structures, on the other hand, the subject may be realized but it surfaces with accusative Case (Martins 2018).

(15) *O Pedro convenceu   os filhos a (*eles)*
   the Pedro convince-IND.PAST.3SG the children to (*they)
   estudarem [EP]
   study-INF.3PL
   'Pedro convinced his children to study'

(16) *O Pedro viu-   os **estudarem*** [EP]
   the Pedro see-IND.PAST.3SG them-ACC study-INF.3PL
   'Pedro saw them study'

Unlike standard inflected infinitives, controlled inflected infinitives display the same properties as uninflected infinitives selected by control verbs (Modesto 2010b; Sheehan 2014), e.g. they require a local c-commanding antecedent (cf. [17] and [18]) and trigger a sloppy reading under ellipsis (cf. [19]):

(17) **O Pedro acha   que <u>eu</u> preferia*
   the Pedro believe-IND.PRS.3SG that I prefer-IND.IMPF.1SG
   reunirem*-se mais cedo* [EP]
   meet-INF.3PL-SE more early
   'Peter believes that I preferred that they meet earlier' (Sheehan 2014)

(18) a. %[A chefe do   João$_i$]$_j$ preferia   **reunirem**-se   sem
         the   boss of.the João   prefer-IND.IMPF.3SG meet-INF.3PL-SE without
         ele$_i$ [EP]
         him
         'João's (female) boss would prefer to meet without him'
    b. *[A chefe do   João$_i$]$_j$ preferia   **reunirem**-se   sem
         the boss of.the João   prefer-IND.IMPF.3SG meet-INF.3PL-SE without
         ela$_j$ [EP]
         her
         'João's (female) boss would prefer to meet without her'   (Sheehan 2014)

(19) a. Ele decidiu   **irem**   ao   cinema   e   eu
         he   decide-IND.PAST.3SG go-INF.3PL to.the cinema and I
         também [EP]
         too
         'He decided that they would go to the cinema and so did I'
         (= I decided that I/we would go to the cinema)
    b. Nós preferimos   irmos   ao   cinema   e   eles
         we   prefer-IND.PRS.1PL go-INF.1PL to.the cinema and they
         também [EP]
         too
         'We prefer to go to the cinema and so do they'
         (= they prefer to go to the cinema)

These facts confirm that, unlike the inflected infinitives described in the previous sections, which take overt or null (pro) nominative subjects, the infinitival constructions described in this section are control structures with PRO subjects ("pseudo-inflected infinitives", according to Gonçalves, Santos, and Duarte 2014). As argued by, for example, Gonçalves, Santos, and Duarte (2014), these structures are evidence for a dissociation between overt agreement inflection and nominative Case licensing.

2.4 The inflected infinitive in raising structures

Inflected infinitives may also be found with modal verbs (which, following Wurmbrand 2001, we assume to be raising predicates) in standard EP (20), dialectal EP (21), and AP (22), either in coordination with an uninflected infinitive or not. The example in (22b) apparently differs from the other examples, in that the subject of the second conjunct does not coincide with the subject of the first conjunct (although it includes it). However, it may be assumed that, in this example, the modal in the second conjunct has undergone ellipsis ("podem juntar-se-nos e (podemos) fazermos uma lista de consenso" = '(they) may join us and (we can) make a consensual list'), in which case this example does not actually differ from the other ones.

(20) A   necessidade de os   pais   deverem
     the   need   of the parents   have.to-INF.3PL
     verem   televisão com os filhos   [EP]
     watch-INF.3PL television with the children
     'the need for parents to watch television with their children'
     (CETEMPúblico)

(21) Então podem **levar**   um panito caseiro   do
     So   can-3PL take-INF a bun   homemade   from.the
     forno, e   levarem   coentros   [EP]
     oven   and   take-INF.3PL   coriander
     'So you can take a homemade bun from the oven and take coriander'
     (Cordial-SIN)

(22) a. para que possamos   **viver**   em paz   e
        for that can-SUBJ.PRS.1PL live-INF   in peace and
        fazermos   uma luta   política [AP]
        make-INF.1PL   a   fight   political
        'for us to be able to live in peace and undertake a political fight'
        (Jornal de Angola)
     b. podem **juntar**-se-nos e **fazermos**   uma lista de consenso   [AP]
        can-3PL join-INF-SE-us and make-INF.1PL a   list of consensus
        '(they) may join us and (we can) make a consensual list'
        (African Varieties of Portuguese Corpus)

Finally, inflected infinitives may also be found embedded under aspectual verbs – see the examples below for standard EP (23), oral MP (24) and BP (25). In all of these cases, there is agreement between the aspectual verb and the infinitive.

(23) os holandeses continuam   a **puxarem**   pela   sua
     the Dutch   continue-IND.PST.3PL   to pull-INF.3PL   for.the their
     equipa [EP]
     team
     'the Dutch keep rooting for their team'(World Cup TV commentary)

(24) estavam   lá   os escravos reunidos **fazerem**
    be-IND.IMPF.3PL there the slaves gathered do-INF.3PL
    lá   nas   suas reuniões [MP]
    there in.the their meetings
    'the slaves were gathered there having their meetings'
                                        (*Spoken Corpus Mozambique*)

(25) quando os filhos   de vocês   começarem   a **serem**
    when   the children of you-PL start-SUBJ.PRS.3PL to be-INF.3PL
    mal-tratados [BP]
    ill-treated
    'when your children start being abused'   (Modesto 2014)

Like the controlled inflected infinitive described in 2.3., the inflected infinitive which appears embedded under modal and aspectual auxiliaries does not license an overt nominative subject. Given that it has been shown that inflected infinitives do not allow A-movement of the embedded subject (Quicoli 1996) and are thus excluded from raising structures, we may conclude that the infinitive which appears in these contexts in Portuguese bearing morphological person/number inflection displays the characteristics of what Gonçalves, Santos, and Duarte (2014) term as a "pseudo-inflected infinitive", i.e., a verbal form which is morphologically an inflected infinitive, but does not exhibit the syntactic properties of 'real' inflected infinitives.

In a nutshell, it is clear that the inflected infinitive is allowed in Portuguese in a wider number of contexts than is generally recognised. On the one hand, it is also found in certain finite contexts (subjunctive clauses in AP and exclamative and interrogative clauses in standard EP). On the other hand, both in standard and nonstandard EP, as well as in the other varieties of Portuguese considered (BP, and the Angolan and oral Mozambiquean varieties), inflected infinitives may be found embedded under subject control, modal and aspectual verbs. At least in some of these contexts, the inflected infinitive appears to exhibit different properties from those which it typically displays, regarding the lexical realization of the subject and its interpretation.

3 Final remarks

The characterisation of the Portuguese inflected infinitives (i.e., infinitives associated with agreement morphology) provided in section 2 shows that they are found in a wider number of contexts than observed by Raposo (1987) and,

moreover, that they display different properties in each of the contexts in which they are found. We considered four contexts:
(1) independent clauses (restricted to contexts with a modal value): in these clauses, the inflected infinitive licenses an overt subject which bears nominative case;
(2) embedded clauses (complements to propositional and factive verbs, and subject and adjunct clauses) in which the inflected infinitive licenses an overt subject which bears nominative case and may be referentially disjoint from the matrix subject;
(3) obligatory control complements: in these contexts, the inflected infinitive does not license an overt nominative subject and the implicit infinitival subject is either interpreted as correferential with the matrix subject (or object) or its reference must include that of the matrix subject/object;
(4) raising complements: in this case, the inflected infinitive does not license an overt nominative subject and the implicit infinitival subject is interpreted as correferential with the matrix subject.

Controlled inflected infinitives are assumed by Gonçalves, Santos, and Duarte (2014) to behave as "pseudo-inflected infinitives" and the person-number inflection on the infinitive is argued to correspond to the spell-out of an AGREE operation between infinitival T and a higher functional head (see also Landau 2000). The properties of this "pseudo-inflected infinitive" clearly indicate that morphological person/number agreement does not necessarily correlate with a positive specification for φ-features associated with uninterpretable Case features responsible for licensing nominative subjects. This conclusion has a bearing on our understanding of the concept of finiteness, which has standardly been correlated, among others, with syntactic context – morphologically non-finite verb forms are assumed to be excluded from independent contexts –, the presence of tense/agreement morphology and the presence of lexical nominative subjects. These are properties, as we have seen, regarding which the four types of inflected infinitives that we have described differ. Whereas the forms which appear in the contexts standardly described by Raposo (1987), as well as the forms found in independent contexts, exhibit all the hallmarks of finiteness, those found in control and raising structures do not – although they have morphological agreement inflection, they do not show the syntactic properties of finite verb forms, in particular, they do not license overt nominative subjects. Hence, as Ledgeway (2007:352) states, "finiteness may surface in apparently conflicting ways across different areas of the grammar". Hence, the picture which emerges from the description of the variation observed in the distribution and properties of the inflected infinitive could be argued to follow straightforwardly from a view of finiteness as a scalar, rather than a dichotomic, notion (Ledgeway 1998, 2007; Vincent 1998; Landau 2004). Thus, the facts described in this paper raise interesting questions for the definition of finiteness, in particular, regarding the relationship between the presence/absence of inflectional morphology and the morphosyntactic and semantic properties of (non-)finite verbs. These are questions which will be addressed in future work.

References

Ambar, Manuela. 1992. *Para uma Sintaxe da Inversão Sujeito Verbo em Português* [Towards a syntax of subject verb inversion in Portuguese]. Lisboa: Colibri.

Ambar, Manuela & Ángel Luis Jiménez. 2017. Inflected infinitives in Romance. In Everaert, Martin & Henk van Riemsdijk (eds.), *The Blackwell Companion to Syntax*, 2nd edn. Wiley-Blackwell.

Cowper, Elizabeth. 2002. Finiteness. Toronto: University of Toronto, MS. Online: www.chass.utoronto.ca/-cowper/Cowper.finiteness.pdf

Gonçalves, Anabela, Ana Lúcia Santos & Inês Duarte. 2014. (Pseudo-) inflected infinitives and control as Agree. In Lahousse, Karen & Stefania Marzo (eds.), *Selected Papers from 'Going Romance' Leuven 2012*, 161–180. Amsterdam: John Benjamin.

Landau, Idan. 2004. The scale of finiteness and the calculus of control. *Natural Language & Linguistic Theory* 22. 811–877.

Landau, Idan. 2000. *Elements of Control. Structure and Meaning in Infinitival Constructions*. Dordrecht: Kluwer.

Ledgeway, Adam. 2007. Diachrony and Finiteness: Subordination in the Dialects of Southern Italy. In Nikolaeva, Irina (ed.), *Finiteness: Theoretical and Empirical Foundations*, 335–365. Oxford: Oxford University Press.

Ledgeway, Adam. 1998. Variation in the Romance infinitive: The case of the Southern Calabrian inflected infinitive. *Transactions of the Philological Society Volume* 96,1. 1–61.

Madeira, Ana. 1994. On the Portuguese inflected infinitive. *UCL Working Papers in Linguistics* 6. 179–203.

Martins, Ana Maria. 2018. Infinitival complements of causative/perception verbs in a diachronic perspective. In Gonçalves, Anabela & Ana Lúcia Santos (eds.), *Complement Clauses in Portuguese: Syntax and Acquisition*, 101–128. Amsterdam/Philadelphia: John Benjamins.

Martins, Ana Maria. 2001. On the origin of the Portuguese inflected infinitive: A new perspective on an enduring debate. In Brinton, Laurel (ed.), *Historical Linguistics 1999: Selected Papers from the 14th International Conference on Historical Linguistics*, 207–222. Amsterdam & Philadelphia: John Benjamins.

Mensching, Guido. 2000. *Infinitive Constructions with Specified Subjects: A Syntactic Analysis of the Romance languages*. Oxford: Oxford University Press.

Modesto, Marcello. 2014. Epicene agreement, null finite subjects and inflected infinitives in BP. Unpublished manuscript. University of São Paulo.

Modesto, Marcello. 2010a. What Brazilian Portuguese Says about Control: Remarks on Boeckx & Hornstein. *Syntax* 13,1. 78–96.
Modesto, Marcello. 2010b. Inflected infinitives in BP and the structure of nonfinite complements. Unpublished manuscript. University of São Paulo.
Oliveira, Inês. 2014. *Usos Verbais e Nominais do Infinitivo em Português Europeu* [Verbal and nominal uses of the infinitive in European Portuguese]. University of Porto. PhD dissertation.
Pires, Acrisio. 2006. *The Minimalist Syntax of Defective Domains: Gerunds and Infinitives*. Philadelphia: John Benjamins.
Pires, Acrisio, Jason Rothman & Ana Lúcia Santos. 2011. L1 acquisition across Portuguese dialects: Modular and interdisciplinary interfaces as sources of explanation. *Lingua* 121. 605–622.
Quicoli, A. Carlos. 1996. Inflection and parametric variation: Portuguese vs. Spanish. In Freidin, Robert (ed.), *Current Issues in Comparative Grammar*, 46–80. Dordrecht: Kluwer.
Raposo, Eduardo. 1987. Case theory and Infl-to-Comp: The inflected infinitive in European Portuguese. *Linguistic Inquiry* 18. 85–109.
Sheehan, Michelle. 2014. Portuguese, Russian and the theory of control. In Huang, Hsin-Lun, Ethan Poole & Amanda Rysling (eds.), *Proceedings of the 43rd Annual Meeting of the North East Linguistic Society (NELS 43)*, vol. 2, 115–126. Amherst, Mass.: GLSA.
Sitaridou, Ioanna. 2002. *The Synchrony and Diachrony of Romance Infinitives with Nominative Subjects*. University of Manchester. PhD dissertation.
Vincent, Nigel. 1998. On the grammar of inflected non-finite forms (with special reference to Old Neapolitan). In Korzen, Iørn & Michael Herslund (eds.), *Clause Combining and Text Structure, Copenhagen Studies in Language* 22. 135–58.
Wurmbrand, Susanne. 2001. *Infinitives. Restructuring and Clause Structure*. Berlin: Mouton de Gruyter.

Corpora

CETEMPúblico: http://www.linguateca.pt/cetempublico/
Cordial-SIN – Corpus Dialetal para o Estudo da Sintaxe [Cordial-SIN – Dialectal Corpus for the Study of Syntax]:http://www.clul.ul.pt/en/resources/411-cordial-corpus
Spoken Corpus Mozambique 1986–87:
 http://metashare.metanet4u.eu/repository/browse/spoken-corpus-mozambique /f843c67a492311e2a2aa782bcb07413511cf382137004 b7f8961efc791d9586a/
Corpus de Variedades Africanas do Português [African Varieties of Portuguese Corpus]: http://www.clul.ul.pt/pt/recursos/219-online-queries-to-crpc-subcorpora-corpus-query-tool-concor-r2

Guido Mensching
Some notes on the Sardinian complementizer systems

1 Aims and background

The aim of this squib is to assess some of the Sardinian data provided by Rita Manzini and Leonardo Savoia (2003; 2005, vol. I, chap. 3; 2011), particularly their reconstruction of the complementizer systems in several varieties of this language. I will first comment on the value of Manzini and Savoia's work for Sardinian linguistics, then summarize their reconstruction of the Sardinian complementizer system and their theories on complementizers in general, also contextualizing it within the study of Sardinian (Sections 2 and 3). Next, I will discuss the data and theories that the authors advance, building on Sardinian and Italian dialect data, in particular in Manzini and Savoia (2005, 2011). More precisely, I will focus on the alignment of the Sardinian complementizers *ca* and *chi* with mood (Section 4) and the complementizer structures used in causal clauses (Section 5). I will finish with some remarks on Sardinian *wh*-items and their relationship to complementizers (Section 6).

In contrast to Sardinian morphology, which has been the subject of scholarly work since Wagner (1938/1939), the first serious studies on Sardinian syntax did not appear until the end of the 1980s with some articles by Michael Allan Jones (1988, 1992) and his seminal *Sardinian Syntax* (Jones 1993). This book, which has ever since been the basis of further studies in this field, describes just one Sardinian variety, namely the central Sardinian (Nuorese) dialect of Lula (Sard. Lùvula). Jones briefly addresses the question of whether the study of one local variety can be representative for Sardinian syntax as a whole. Concerning this issue, he offers the following remarks:

> From a syntactic point of view Sardinian appears to be much more homogeneous [than phonology, morphology, and lexis], though this perception may be due in part to the fact that the syntax of Sardinian has not been investigated as extensively as other aspects of the language and to the more general fact that syntactic differences are less amenable to direct observation.
> (Jones 1993: 6)

In subsequent years, other authors contributed to our knowledge of Sardinian syntax (e.g., La Fauci and Loporcaro 1997; Loporcaro 1998; Bentley 2004, 2011;

Guido Mensching, Georg-August-Universität Göttingen

https://doi.org/10.1515/9781501505201-024

Floricic 2003, 2009; Remberger 2006, 2009, 2010; Padovan and Penello 2006 [within the ASIt initiative]; Mensching and Remberger 2010a, 2010b, 2016; Mensching 2005, 2012, 2016, 2017). In some of these works, diatopic syntactic variation plays a certain role, but this issue has never been the focus in the study of Sardinian syntax. As far as I can see, Manzini and Savoia (2005) is the only work that provides data and classifications of a greater number of phenomena of syntactic variation in Sardinian, which show that Sardinian syntax is much less uniform than it previously appeared.

Hence, the Sardinian complementizer systems – the subject of the following pages – remained largely unknown before Manzini and Savoia (2003) presented a substantial amount of data and a first classification, which was then completed in Manzini and Savoia (2005, 2011). Apart from some rather obscure remarks by Wagner ([1951] 1997: 326–327) and DES I: 251, s.v. *ca*), the phenomenon was mentioned in greater detail by Blasco Ferrer (1986: 195–196), according to whom (i) the Logudorese varieties (including Central Sardinian) use the complementizer *chi*, whereas a distinction between two complementizers (*ca* and *chi*, from Lat. QUID and QUIA, respectively) is mostly restricted to Campidanese; and (ii) in the varieties that have the double complementizer system, *ca* appears after verba dicendi, sentiendi, and putandi and *chi* after verba timendi and volitional verbs, usually triggering the indicative and the subjunctive, respectively.

2 Sardinian complementizer systems: Typology and geographic distribution

The great accomplishment of Rita Manzini and Leonardo Savoia is not only to have provided, for the first time, a large amount of data concerning the geolinguistic and syntactic distribution of the Sardinian complementizers *ca* and *chi*, but also to have included other elements and phenomena commonly attributed to the complementizer phrase (CP), namely *wh*-items, relative clauses, and the complementizers meaning 'if'. They thus arrive at a much more differentiated view leading to four different systems, which can be schematized as shown in Figure 1.

It is a general property of all Sardinian varieties that the complementizers meaning 'that' (*chi*/*ca*)[1] are not identical and not even similar to the *wh*-

---

[1] For the representation of Sardinian varieties, I use the orthographic system of the Limba Sarda Comuna (LSC) proposed by RAS (2006). The item *ca* is pronounced [ka], with the

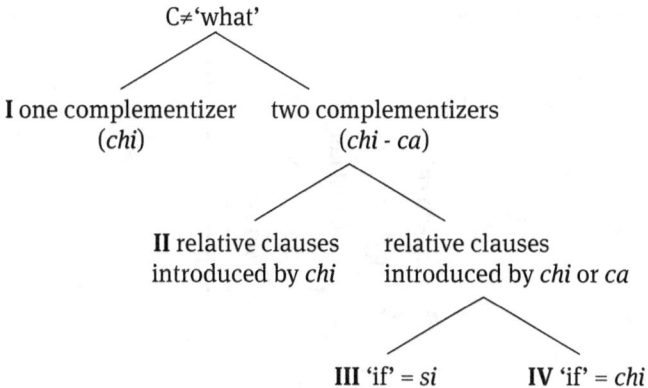

Figure 1: Sardinian complementizer systems.

element meaning 'what', which is *ite* (var. *iti* and *ita*, unlike most other Romance languages, cf. It. *che*, Fr. *que*, Sp. *que/qué*). A first basic subdivision is the distinction already introduced in Section 1 (one vs. two complementizers). System I, which only has *chi*, corresponds to the Logudorese and most of the Central Sardinian/Nuorese areas. On the basis of the data in Manzini and Savoia (2005) and some other data (see Mensching 2012), we conducted further fieldwork and reconstructed the isogloss shown in Figure 2 (cf. Bacciu and Mensching 2018: 355, map 12.5; for a previous version, see Mensching and Remberger 2016: 280, map 17.3) Extending from above Dorgali in a southwest direction, the isogloss traverses the Barbagia di Ollolai and then enters the so-called Arborense area, both zones in which a broad bundle of other, mostly historico-phonetic isoglosses separate Logudorese and Nuorese on the one hand from Campidanese on the other (cf. Virdis 1988: 908; Bacciu and Mensching 2018). The varieties above the isogloss shown in Figure 2 have system I of Figure 1. Places immediately below the isogloss, such as Dorgali, Fonni, Ardauli, and Paulilatino, seem to have system II. More southern localities tend to have system III or IV, with the latter extending to the extreme south of the island. Following Manzini and Savoia (2005: 414–417, 452–455, 464–469, 496–503), the varieties that correspond to systems III and IV employ *chi* in

---

exception of the Barbagia dialects of the so-called Fonni group, where /k/ is usually articulated as a glottal stop (cf. Wolf 1985), and of Dorgali, where *ca* appears as [xa]. In some Campidanese varieties, *chi* has become *ci* ([tʃi]).

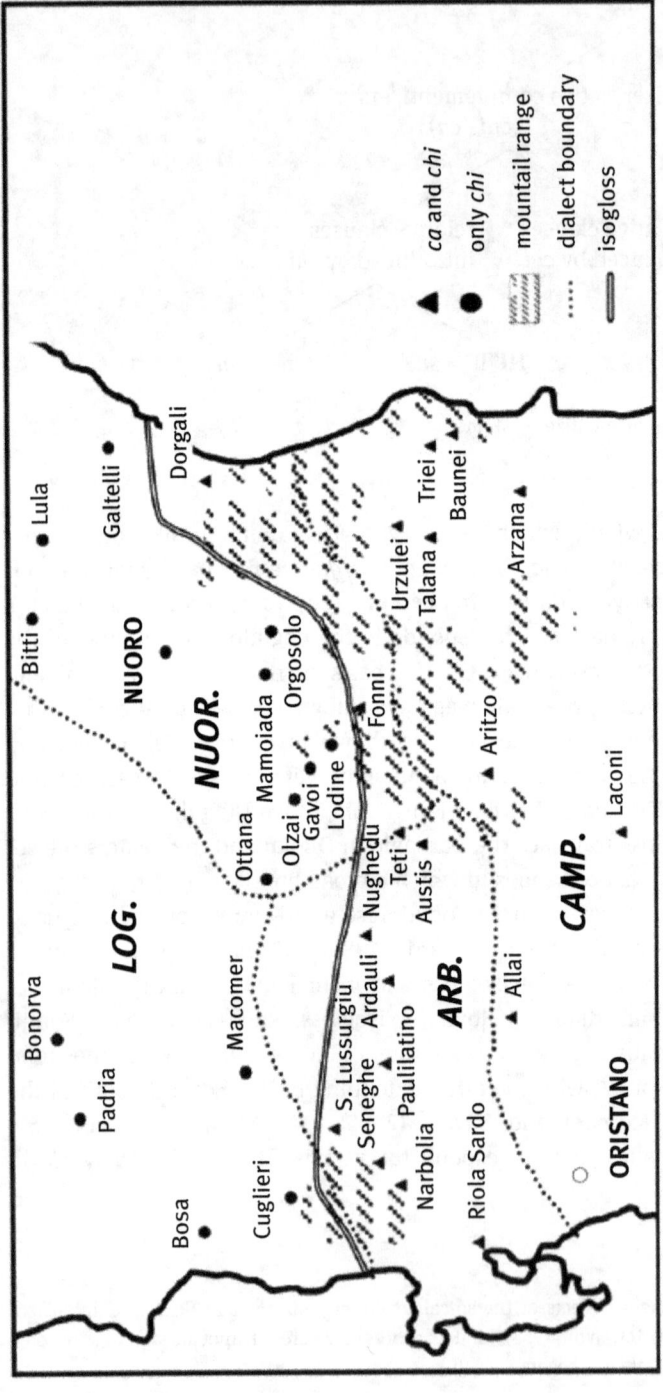

Figure 2: Isogloss of the *ca–chi* distinction (Bacciu and Mensching 2018: 355, map 12.5).

restrictive and *ca* in appositive relative clauses (systems I and II show *chi* for all relative clauses). In addition, system IV also uses *chi* in the sense of 'if'.

3 Sardinian complementizers within Manzini and Savoia's (2003, 2005, 2011) theory

The interesting theory within which Manzini and Savoia interpret the data, in particular as presented in Manzini and Savoia (2011), cannot be discussed in detail here. In a nutshell, the authors assume that complementizers are nominal in nature, i.e., they are considered as nominal heads merged above C°, which is verbal (and can thus host verbs, e.g., in V2 structures). Complementizers correspond to – or rather project – propositions, whereas regular nouns represent individuals (Manzini and Savoia 2011: 30). As *wh*-items, which are often identical or at least very similar to complementizers (such as It. *che*, Fr. *que*, Sp. *que/qué*), are also nominal, they in principle have the same position as complementizers. Both types of elements are operators introducing a variable, with "the main difference between them being the nature of the variable. This ranges over individuals for the *wh*-phrase *che* [...], while for complementizer *che* it ranges over situations/possible worlds" (Manzini and Savoia 2011: 16). The content of the propositional variable introduced by "the finite *k*-type complementizer in Romance languages" is restricted by the subclause (Manzini and Savoia 2011: 54–55).

Now, for the Sardinian complementizer systems II–IV and similar Italian systems, the authors assume that *ca* is definite and *chi* is indefinite. The former introduces a definite description, whereas the latter "introduces a propositional variable subject to existential closure" (Manzini and Savoia 2011: 55). Among other arguments, they derive the distribution of the indicative (with *ca*) and the subjunctive (with *chi*) from the idea that *ca* introduces a description outside the scope of polarity operators, which amounts to a "propositional definite description," whereas *chi* is within the scope of polarity operators, thus introducing an indefinite propositional variable (Manzini and Savoia 2011: 57). As definiteness is not compatible with *wh*-elements and *wh*-elements also introduce variables subject to existential closure, this theory predicts that in double complementizer systems, "it is always the indefinite complementizer that overlaps with a *wh*-quantifier" (Manzini and Savoia 2011: 55). The Sardinian system diverges from the latter generalization, a point to which I will return.

As mentioned in Section 2, systems III and IV use *chi* for restrictive relative clauses and *ca* for non-restrictive (appositive) ones (Manzini and Savoia 2005: I, 464–466). The basic idea is that the variable in appositive relatives is an individual variable, whereas it is an indefinite variable in restrictive relative clauses (Manzini and Savoia 2003: 104–105; 2011: 64). Although this would have required further explanation, it is an interesting attempt to explain the distribution of *ca* and *chi* in relative clauses of these Sardinian varieties. In particular, the authors argue that an appositive relative clause "is introduced by the definite sentential operator, i.e. *ka*" (Manzini and Savoia 2003: 105). Finally, an additional property of most Campidanese varieties (i.e., those of type IV) is that they employ *chi* for both conditional and interrogative 'if'. According to the authors, this is because, like interrogatives, conditional subclauses restrict a propositional variable. The difference is that in interrogatives, the variable is licensed in the scope of a question operator (Manzini and Savoia 2011: 68–69). Thus, 'if' has "indefinite quantification properties" (Manzini and Savoia 2003: 106), which predicts the choice of *chi* and not of *ca*. Finally, it is important to note that the overlap of the items meaning 'if' and 'that' seems to be typical for Sardinian (namely the type-IV varieties) and is not found elsewhere in Italo-Romance (Manzini and Savoia 2011: 66).

Manzini and Savoia's discovery of the basic typology of the Sardinian complementizer systems and syntactic variation within Sardinian has tremendously stimulated the work of my research group in recent years (see Mensching 2012, 2015–2017; Bacciu and Mensching 2018; Kellert (2019)).[2] Caroline Bacciu has recently begun working on a PhD thesis that aims to identify further parameters of morpho-syntactic variation in Sardinia, including geolinguistic mapping, using both traditional and dialectometric methods of linguistic geography. Some of the issues concerning the Sardinian complementizer systems that have arisen in these studies and might help to further elaborate Manzini and Savoia's theories are sketched in Sections 4 to 6 below.

4 Alignment of the complementizers *ca* and *chi* with mood

Systems II–IV in Figure 1 can be further subdivided into systems in which *ca* and *chi*, when used for introducing complement clauses, show a stable

---

[2] In addition, I directed the BA thesis by Janina Vahl (2012) and the MA thesis by Gabriele Kampmann (2010). The former investigates the *ca–chi* system in the Alta Ogliastra area (also cf. Blasco Ferrer 1988), whereas the latter is an attempt to put the most important parameters of syntactic variation in Sardinian from Manzini and Savoia (2005) on geographic maps.

correlation with the subjunctive (*ca*) and the indicative (*chi*) and others in which they do not. An example for the latter is Làconi (system IV, Manzini and Savoia 2011: 54, 60), where the verb *crèiri* 'to believe' is shown to select either *chi* or *ca*, which can both appear with either mood:

(1) Làconi (cf. Manzini and Savoia 2011: 60)
    a. dɛɔ krɛɔ   ka/tʃi issu βuru / kraza   'eniði
       I   believe that he too   tomorrow comes-IND
      'I believe that he will come as well/tomorrow.'
    b. dɛɔ krɛɔ   ka/ tʃi issu βuru / kraza   'ɛɳdʒaða
       I   believe that he too / tomorrow comes-SUBJV
      'I believe that he will come as well/tomorrow.'

However, it is unclear whether this is triggered by the special structure in the examples, with a focused element following the complementizer, particularly because Manzini and Savoia's (2005: I, 467) examples (26a/a.') neatly distinguish between *ca*+indicative and *chi/ci*+subjunctive. A better example is the one from Baunei (also system IV), provided by Damonte (2006), where *ca* appears with the subjunctive:

(2) Baunei (from Damonte 2006: 77, adapted to the LSC orthographical system)
    Mi   paret ca   custas cadiras sient   meda comodas.
    me= seems that these chairs are-SUBJV very comfortable
    'It seems to me that these chairs are very comfortable.'

Such systems must not be confused with those that show a stable correspondence in complement clauses with *ca* selecting the indicative and *chi* the subjunctive.[3] This is exemplified by Paulilatino (system II) (see Manzini and Savoia 2005: I, 465; 2011: 53–54). In my own inquiry at Dorgali within the ASIt initiative, I was able to replicate the same stable system with much more data (cf. Bacciu and Mensching 2018). These data show that deontic, volitional, and directive predicates always select complement clauses with *chi* and the verb in the subjunctive, whereas strong assertive predicates and epistemic predicates

---

[3] Except for *apustis chi* 'after' and *primma chi* 'before', which systematically select the indicative.

expressing certainty trigger *ca* with the indicative mood. My data from Dorgali confirm that it is not the matrix predicate itself that triggers these properties (for mood, see Manzini 2000; Manzini and Savoia 2011: 57). Thus, doxastic predicates such as *pàrrer(e)* 'to seem' and *pessare* 'to think' can select either *ca* +indicative or *chi*+subjunctive, depending, as I believe, on the speaker's degree of certainty:

(3) Dorgali (from Bacciu and Mensching 2018: 336–337)
  a. Mi paret ca in custas cradeas s' istat bene.
     me= seems that in these chairs REFL= stays-IND good
     'It seems to me that these chairs are comfortable.'
  a.' Mi paret chi apat abboghinau calincunu.
      me= seems that has-SUBJV called someone
      'It seems to me that someone has called.'
  b. Totus an pessau ca proiat.
     all have thought that rained-IND
     'Everybody thought that it would rain.'
  b'. Pesso chi los apan aprovaos totu.
      think-1SG that them= have-3PL-SUBJV approved all
      'I think that everybody has passed (the exam).'

It is important to note that the alignment of mood with the complementizer remains stable. An interesting issue for future research is whether this stability is typical for system II (to which both Paulilatino and Dorgali belong) and the instability is typical for system IV, attested for Làconi and Baunei. The idea that system IV is particularly unstable with respect to the complementizer–mood alignment may be corroborated by the fact that the same kind of instability has also been documented for Arzana (about 25 kilometers southwest of Baunei, cf. Mensching 2012), also a type-IV system. This raises the additional question of whether this is really a property related to the parametric division that we have discussed or whether it is a geolinguistic phenomenon typical of that area.

5 *Ca* and *chi* and causal clauses

A fact that has not been considered in the theory sketched by Manzini and Savoia (2011) is that in all varieties of Sardinian (i.e., systems I–IV), *ca* is also the canonical causal conjunction meaning 'because'. An example is given in (6):

(4) Ittiri (from Manzini and Savoia 2005: 453)
sɔɛ 'essidu ka vu fat'tɛndɛ 'kaððu
am gone-out because was doing hot
'I went out because it was hot.'

This example figures in Manzini and Savoia (2005: 453) as a correspondence to It. *Sono uscito che era facendo caldo*, which gives the impression that *ca* here corresponds to the Italian complementizer *che*. This would be odd, as Ittiri belongs to system I, where the complementizer is always *chi*. Instead, it introduces a regular causal adjunct clause. As this type of clause is factive, examples such as (4) would still fit into Manzini and Savoia's theory in that *ca* is definite – we would just have to state more precisely that in varieties of type I, the definite complementizer is specialized to a causal meaning. Causal *ca* can optionally be preceded by other prepositions or adverbs, such as *pro* ('for') or *sicomente* (causal 'since') in (5)[4]:

(5) a. Non bi semus andaos pro ca pessavamus (Orgosolo, type I)
       not LOC= are-1SG gone for that thought-1PL
       chi aèret pròiu.
       that had-SUBJV rained
       'We didn't go there because we thought that it had rained.'
    b. Sicomente ca aiat acabbau su tùcaru, (Dorgali, type II)
       since that had-3SG finished the sugar
       nde l' apo imprestau.
       of.it= him/her= have-1SG lent
       'Since he had finished the sugar, I lent him some.'

The situation is more complex and needs further research: when *sicomente* (log. *sigomente*, camp. *sigomenti*) is present, the complementizer is optional, and it seems that it is *chi* in varieties of type I and *ca* in the others, but note that Blasco Ferrer (1986: 201) quotes a Campidanese example with *chi*. As for (5a), unless the verb is in the infinitive, *ca* is obligatory with *pro* (camp. *po*) and the complementizer cannot be changed to *chi*, as *pro chi* introduces a final clause with the subjunctive and means 'so that', 'in order to'. Another option is *proite/poita* (lit. 'for what', similar to It. *perché*, Sp. *porque*), which can stand alone without a complementizer. If present, the complementizer behaves as with *pro*, i.e., it is *chi* for final and *ca* for causal subclauses (Blasco Ferrer 1986:

---

[4] The examples are taken from my own inquiry using the ASIt-sud questionnaire.

200; Jones 1993: 248–249). The exact diatopic distribution of these and other constellations is subject to future research. Here, I just observe that the elements preceding causal *ca* have a different status. For example, whereas *proite* is surely located in what is treated as the left periphery of the complementizer in Manzini and Savoia (2011: Section 1.2), *pro* is clearly a preposition that selects the CP (2011: 30–31). When the complementizer is *ca*, it can have a causal interpretation alone, but when it is *chi*, it cannot, regardless of the type of complementizer system.

6 Observations on Sardinian *wh*-items

All varieties of Sardinian are characterized by the fact that the *wh*-item meaning 'what' (*ite*) does not coincide with the complementizer(s) (*chi/ca*), although other interrogative elements clearly do belong to the *k*-series (*chie*, var. *chine* and *chini* 'who', *cale* 'which', cf. Manzini and Savoia 2005: 415; 2011: 33). However, it is interesting to note that, diachronically, the item *ite* originally did belong to the *k*-series. *Ite* and its variants *iti* and *ita* derive from *QUID DEU, lit. 'what/which God' (Meyer-Lübke 1902: 36; DES I: 349–350), and are documented in medieval texts as *kit(t)eu* or *git(t)eu*. The modern form *ite* is already documented in the Statuti Sassaresi (fourteenth century) as *itte*, along with the earlier form *itteu*. In this document, the element already appears in adjectival use, too, in the sense of 'what [kind of] N' (Manzini and Savoia 2003: 464–465).

Against this background and within a kind of nanosyntactic approach, one might ask whether the features [+definite] and [-definite] assumed by Manzini and Savoia are in reality encoded in the segments /a/ and /i/, respectively, and not in the full items *ca* and *chi*. This might also account for the difference between *ite* + N and *cale* + N, the former meaning 'what [kind of] N' and the latter 'which N'. The item *cale* is D-linked and might therefore be argued to be definite, whereas *ite* is clearly indefinite.

Apart from these rather speculative ideas, it is worth noting that *ite* has been further grammaticalized to become a marker for direct yes/no questions in some places, as witnessed in the following examples (see Mensching 2012, 2015, 2017):

(6) a. Ite as intopadu unu pitzinnu piliruju? (Ittiri, system I)
    Q have-2G met a boy red-headed
    'Have you met a red-headed boy?'

b.		Ite	azes	bisonzu	de	unu teracu?	(Nuoro, system I)
b.'	E	ite	tenies	bisongiu	de	unu seracu?	(Perdasdefogu, system IV)
	and Q		have-2PL	need	of a	worker	

'(And) do you need a worker?' (data from VIVALDI)

In Mensching (2016), I analyze this use of *ite* within a cartographic approach (cf. Rizzi 1997, 2001), showing that it must occupy the specifier of FocP. This is in conformity with the observation that yes/no questions in Sardinian usually show the activation of FocP via focus or predicate fronting (also cf. Jones 2013). Hence, the varieties that allow the structures in (6) seem to have developed an expletive that is inserted when no fronting occurs.[5] These data and my focus-related interpretation in Mensching (2016) are highly compatible with the framework of Manzini and Savoia, who hypothesize (for similar data with *che* in Fiorentino) "that the insertion of *ke* in yes–no questions corresponds to the presence of a focalization bearing on the main verb, paralleling the focalization on the *wh*-constituent in *wh*-questions, but consistent with the yes–no interpretation." (2011: 36).

This use of *ite* as a question marker must be kept distinct from the question marker *a* (< Lat. AUT, cf. DES I: 34; Jones 1993: 24–25; Remberger 2010), which Mensching (2015) has shown to exclusively encode non-standard yes/no questions (i.e., "special" questions in the sense of Obenauer 2004, 2006). Within the framework established by Rita Manzini and Leonardo Savoia and considering my speculations above, it might be worth-while asking whether the occurrence of /i/ (in *ite* encoding standard yes/no questions) versus /a/ (= *a* encoding special yes/no questions) might fit into the system. In any case, the fact that a *wh*-item is identical with a yes/no-question marker is predicted in Manzini and Savoia's system (2011: 15, 17, 36).

References

ASIt = *Atlante Sintattico d'Italia*, http://asit.maldura.unipd.it/ (last consulted November 25, 2018).
Bacciu, Caroline & Guido Mensching. 2018. The Complementizers *ca* and *chi* in Sardinian: Syntactic Properties and Geographic Distribution. In Roberta D'Alessandro & Diego Pescarini (eds.), *Advances in Italian Dialectology. Sketches of Italo-Romance Grammars*, 321-366. Leiden & Boston: Brill.

---

[5] According to Theresa Biberauer (personal communication), the fact that an expletive is available indicates that the position at issue (spec,FocP in my approach) is an essential position, in this case for marking yes/no questions.

Bentley, Delia. 2004. Definiteness Effects: Evidence from Sardinian. *Transactions of the Philological Society* 102. 57–101.

Bentley, Delia. 2011. Sui costrutti esistenziali sardi. Effetti di definitezza, deissi, evidenzialità. *Zeitschrift für romanische Philologie* 127. 111–140.

Blasco Ferrer, Eduardo. 1986. *La lingua sarda contemporanea. Grammatica del logudorese e del campidanese. Norma e varietà dell'uso. Sintesi storica*. Cagliari: Edizioni della Torre.

Blasco Ferrer, Eduardo. 1988. *Le parlate dell'Alta Ogliastra*. Cagliari: Edizioni della Torre.

Damonte, Federico. 2006. Complementatori e complementi congiuntivi in alcuni dialetti sardi. In Andrea Padovan & Nicoletta Penello (eds.), *Osservazioni sul sardo. Giornata conclusiva dei seminari ASIM (Atlante Sintattico dell'Italia Centro-Meridionale), Padova, 31 maggio 2005* (ASIt working papers 6). Padova: Università di Padova (http://asit.maldura.unipd.it/documenti/ql6/damonte6_2006.pdf, last consulted November 25, 2018).

DES = Wagner, Max Leopold (1960-1964), *Dizionario Etimologico Sardo*. 3 vols. Heidelberg: Winter.

Floricic, Franck. 2003. Notes sur l'"accusatif prépositionnel" en sarde. *Bulletin de la Societé de Linguistique de Paris* 98. 247–303.

Floricic, Franck. 2009. Negation and "focus clash" in Sardinian. In Lunella Mereu (ed.), *Information Structure and its Interfaces*, 129–152. Berlin & New York: de Gruyter.

Jones, Michael Allan. 1988. Auxiliary Verbs in Sardinian. *Transactions of the Philological Society* 86. 173–203.

Jones, Michael Allan. 1992. Infinitives with Specified Subjects in Sardinian. In Christiane Laeufer & Terrell A. Morgan (eds.), *Theoretical Analyses in Romance Linguistics. Selected Papers from the Nineteenth Linguistic Symposion on Romance Languages (LSRL XIX), The Ohio State University, 21-23 April 1989*, 295–309. Amsterdam & Philadelphia: John Benjamins.

Jones, Michael Allan. 1993. *Sardinian Syntax*. London & New York: Routledge.

Jones, Michel Allan. 2013. Focus, fronting and illocutionary force in Sardinian. *Lingua* 134. 75–101.

Kampmann, Gabriele M. 2010. *Kartographische Auswertung zu Studien der Dialektsyntax Italiens: Separierung sardischer Territorien durch Isoglossen und Beschreibung diverser sprachlicher Äußerungen*. Berlin: Freie Universität MA thesis.

Kellert, Olga. 2019. Complementizers in Sardinian wh-exclamatives and clefts. Italian Journal of Linguistics, 31. 125–148 (DOI: 10.26346/1120-2726-134, last consulted August 26, 2019).

La Fauci, Nunzio & Michele Loporcaro. 1997. Outline of a Theory of Existentials on Evidence from Romance. *Studi Italiani di Linguistica Teorica e Applicata* 26. 5–55.

Loporcaro, Michele. 1998. *Sintassi comparata dell'accordo participiale romanzo*. Torino: Rosenberg & Sellier.

Manzini, Maria Rita. 2000. Sentential complementation: the subjunctive. In Peter Coopmans, Martin Everaert & Jane Grimshaw (eds.), *Lexical Specification and Insertion*. 241–267. Amsterdam: John Benjamins.

Manzini, Maria Rita & Leonardo Savoia. 2003. The nature of complementizers. *Rivista di Grammatica Generativa* 28. 87–110.

Manzini, Maria Rita & Leonardo Savoia. 2005. *I dialetti italiani e romanici: Morfosintassi generativa*. 3 vols. Alessandria: Edizioni dell'Orso.

Manzini, Maria Rita & Leonardo Savoia. 2011. *Grammatical categories: Variation in Romance languages* (Cambridge studies in linguistics 128). Cambridge: Cambridge University Press.

Mensching, Guido. 2005. Remarks on Specificity and related Categories in Sardinian. In Klaus von Heusinger, Georg Kaiser & Elisabeth Stark (eds.), *Nereus II: Specificity and the evolution/emergence of nominal determination systems in Romance. Proceedings of the International Workshop at the Freie Universität Berlin, October 8th-9th 2004*, 81–106. Konstanz: University of Konstanz (https://kops.uni-konstanz.de/bitstream/handle/ 123456789/3798/AP_119.pdf, last consulted November 25, 2018).

Mensching, Guido. 2012. Anmerkungen zur sardischen Syntax anhand des Vivaio Acustico delle Lingue e dei Dialetti d'Italia (VIVALDI). In Carola Köhler & Fabio Tosques (eds.), *(Das) DISKRETE TATENBUCH. Digitale Festschrift für DIETER KATTENBUSCH zum 60. Geburtstag*. Berlin: Humboldt-Universität (http://www2.hu-berlin.de/festschrift-kattenbusch/mensching-sardisch-syntax.html, last consulted November 25, 2018).

Mensching, Guido. 2015. New insights on the question particle *a* in Sardinian. *Isogloss* 2. 1–33 (http://dx.doi.org/10.5565/rev/isogloss.22, last consulted November25, 2018).

Mensching, Guido. 2016. Yes/no interrogatives and focus in Sardinian. In Ernestina Carrilho, Alexandra Fiéis, Maria Lobo & Sandra Pereira (eds.), *Romance Languages and Linguistic Theory 10 – Selected Papers from 'Going Romance 28', Lisbon*. 139–169. Amsterdam & Philadelphia: John Benjamins.

Mensching, Guido. 2017. Morfosintassi: sincronia. In Eduardo Blasco Ferrer, Peter Koch & Daniela Marzo (eds.), *Manuale di linguistica sarda* (Manuals of Romance Linguistics 15), 376-396. Berlin & New York: de Gruyter.

Mensching, Guido & Eva-Maria Remberger. 2010a. Focus Fronting and the left periphery in Sardinian. In Roberta d'Alessandro, Ian Roberts & Adam Ledgeway (eds.), *Syntactic Variation. The dialects of Italy*, 261–276. Cambridge: Cambridge University Press.

Mensching, Guido & Eva-Maria Remberger. 2010b. La periferia sinistra romanza: topicalizzazione, focalizzazione e interrogazione in sardo. In Maria Iliescu, Heidi Siller-Runggaldier & Paul Danler (eds.), *Actes du XXVe Congrès International de Linguistique et de Philologie Romanes*. vol. 7, 189–197. Tübingen: Niemeyer.

Mensching, Guido & Eva-Maria Remberger. 2016. Sardinian. In Adam Ledgeway & and Martin Maiden (eds.), *Oxford Guide to the Romance Languages (OGRL)*, 270–291. Oxford: Oxford University Press.

Meyer-Lübke, Wilhelm.1902. *Zur Kenntnis des Altlogudoresischen*. Vienna: Gerold.

Obenauer, Hans-Georg. 2004. Nonstandard *wh*-questions and alternative checkers in Pagotto. In Horst Lohnstein & Susanne Trissler (eds.), *Syntax and Semantics of the Left Periphery. Interface Explorations 9*. 343-384. Berlin & New York: Mouton de Gruyter.

Obenauer, Hans-Georg. 2006. Special Interrogatives – Left Periphery, *Wh*-Doubling, and (Apparently) Optional Elements. In Jenny Doetjes & Paz Gonzalves (eds.), *Romance Languages and Linguistic Theory 2004 – Selected Papers from 'Going Romance 2004'*, 247-273. Amsterdam & Philadelphia: John Benjamins.

Padovan, Andrea & Nicoletta Penello (eds.). 2006. *Osservazioni sul sardo. Giornata conclusiva dei seminari ASIM (Atlante Sintattico dell'Italia Centro-Meridionale), Padova, 31 maggio 2005* (ASIt working papers 6). Padova: Università di Padova (http://asit.maldura.unipd. it/papers.html#6, last consulted November 25, 2018).

RAS 2006 = Regione Autonoma della Sardegna. 2006. *Limba Sarda Comuna. Norme linguistiche di riferimento a carattere sperimentale per la lingua scritta dell'Amministrazione regionale*, http://www.regione.sardegna.it/documenti/1_72_20060418160308.pdf (last consulted November 25, 2018).

Remberger, Eva-Maria. 2006. *Hilfsverben. Eine minimalistische Analyse am Beispiel des Italienischen und Sardischen* (Linguistische Arbeiten 504). Tübingen: Niemeyer.

Remberger, Eva-Maria. 2009. Null Subjects, Expletives and Locatives in Sardinian. In Georg Kaiser & Eva-Maria Remberger (eds.), *Null Subjects, Expletives and Locatives in Romance* (Konstanzer Arbeitspapiere des Fachbereichs Sprachwissenschaft 123), 231–261. Konstanz: Universität.

Remberger, Eva-Maria. 2010. Left peripheral interactions in Sardinian. *Lingua* 120. 555–581.

Rizzi, Luigi. 1997. The fine structure of the left periphery. In Liliane Haegeman (ed.), *Elements of Grammar: Handbook in Generative Syntax*, 281–337. Dordrecht: Kluwer.

Rizzi, Luigi. 2001. On the position "Int(errogative)" in the left periphery of the clause. In Guglielmo Cinque & Giampaolo Salvi (eds.), *Current Studies in Italian Linguistics Offered to Lorenzo Renzi*, 287–296. Dordrecht: Foris.

Vahl, Janina. 2012. *Ricerche sul sistema a due complementatori nella lingua sarda*. Berlin: Freie Universität BA thesis.

Virdis, Maurizio. 1988. Sardisch: Areallinguistik. In Günter Holtus, Michael Metzeltin & Christian Schmitt (eds.), *Lexikon der Romanistischen Linguistik*. Vol. IV: *Italienisch, Korsisch, Sardisch*, 897–913. Tübingen: Niemeyer.

VIVALDI = *Vivaio Acustico delle Lingue e dei Dialetti d'Italia*, ed. by Dieter Kattenbusch. Berlin: Humboldt-Universität, http://www2.hu-berlin.de/vivaldi/ (last consulted November 25, 2018).

Wagner, Max Leopold. 1938/1939. Flessione nominale e verbale del sardo antico e moderno. *Italia dialettale* 14. 93–70. 15. 207–247.

Wagner, Max Leopold. 1997 [1951]. *La lingua sarda: Storia, spirito e forma*. A cura di Giulio Paulis. Nuoro: Ilisso.

Wolf, Heinz Jürgen. 1985. Knacklaut in Orgosolo. Überlegungen zur sardischen Lautchronologie. *Zeitschrift für romanische Philologie* 101. 269–311.

Léa Nash
Structural source of person split

1 Introduction

Many ergative languages exhibit splits based on the nominal type of main arguments. The most typical manifestation of this type of split involves marking of 3rd person arguments (3P pronouns and full noun phrases, henceforth 3PA) according to the ergative case-schema (ergative case on transitive subjects and nominative/absolutive case on intransitive subjects), but not of 1st and 2nd person arguments (henceforth 1/2PA), which follow nominative case- alignment (nominative case on all subjects).

Dyirbal is a typical case of an ergative language with nominal split, where a transitive sentence containing 1/2P subject does not show evidence of ergative case-alignment. In (1a–b), the subject of the transitive and intransitive clauses is marked alike, *n^{y}urra*. Once the arguments are 3P, as in (2a–b), the language follows the ergative pattern and marks alike the transitive object and the intransitive subject *yabu*.

(1) a. *n^{y}urra*   nana-na   bura-n
    you-all.NOM we all-ACC see-NONFUT
    'You all saw us'
b. *n^{y}urra*   banaga-n^{y}u
    you-all.NOM return_NONFUT
    'You all returned'

(2) a. *yabu*   ŋuma-ŋgu bura-n
    mother.ABS father-ERG see-NONFUT
    'The father saw the mother'
b. *yabu*   banaga-n^{y}u
    mother.ABS return-NONFUT
    'The mother returned'   (Dixon 1994:14)

A number of questions arise with respect to the pattern in (1–2) in Dyirbal, as opposed to Basque (3), where all types of transitive subjects are marked with ergative.

Léa Nash, Université Paris 8 and CNRS

https://doi.org/10.1515/9781501505201-025

(3) a. zu-k   ni   ikusi n-au-zu
       you-ERG me.ABS see 1A-AUX-2E
       'You have seen me'
    b. gizona-k   Miren   ikusi du
       child-ERG Miren.ABS see 3A-AUX-3E
       'The child has seen Miren'

(i) Is the case-shift observed in (1–2) motivated by structural differences of clauses with 1/2PA and 3PA?
(ii) Is person split a more superficial phenomenon that has no structural source? Is the ergative morphological marking incompatible with certain feature specifications of 1/2PA?
(iii) Can person split receive a unitary explanation in languages where it is manifested?

1.1 Previous accounts of nominal splits

Person split has received considerable attention within functional and formal frameworks of theoretical linguistics. Silverstein (1976) proposes a functionalist explanation in terms of Nominal Hierarchy. According to this hierarchy in (4), arguments in the leftmost part are most likely to function as transitive subjects, and arguments in the rightmost part are most likely to be transitive objects. Ergative and accusative cases are morphologically marked cases, as opposed to nominative, they are hence most likely to signal the lowest and the most marked functions of nominal constituents. 1/2PA are not marked with ergative because they are typical Agents, *functionally*.

(4) 1st person 2nd person Demonstratives   Proper
    pronoun   pronoun   3rd person pronouns names
    Common nouns:
    Human Animate Inanimate
    <---
    Nominative   Ergative
                                                            Accusative
                                            (adapted from Dixon 1994:85)

Dixon (1994) proposes a cognitive explanation of person split: as the speaker sees himself as a prototypical "quintessential" agent, it is superfluous to further stress this basic fact by special morphological means. Diachronic explanations of person split have also been proposed, which account for the appearance of ergative only on inanimate nominals (the lowest nominal type on Silverstein's hierarchy) in some languages in terms of its diachronic reanalyses from an instrumental preposition (Garrett 1990).

Within the generativist tradition, person split has been extensively investigated. The analyses propose syntactic or morphological explanations of the phenomenon. Structural accounts focus on differences in functional categories present and activated in clauses with each type of nominal arguments, while morphological explanations focus on the parallel syntactic behaviour of 1/2PA and 3P/A and attribute the split to post-syntactic mechanisms which delete the ergative marking on 1/2PA.

Structural accounts base their argumentation on different discourse properties of 1/2PA and 3PA which motivate either (i) different argument licensing sites of each nominal type in the clause, or (ii) different feature makeup of predicates or functional categories that licence each nominal type.

Proponents of (i) hold that 1/2PA are inherently discourse presupposed as they denote participants in the speech act, as opposed to 3PA, and are hence licensed outside vP. (Jelinek 1993, Nash 1995, 1997, Manzini and Savoia 1998, a. o.). This idea that 1/2PA are special types of arguments, subject to special licensing conditions, is not restricted to ergative systems, and is promoted by Bianchi (2003) who claims that 1/2PA must be directly merged in a special ParticipantP in the left(er) field of the clause, between T and C. As ergative case is widely assumed to be assigned in vP, either as an inherent case (Woolford 2006, a.o.) or as a dependent case (Nash 2017, Baker 2014), the "high" discourse-related 1/2PA escape this marking. This type of reasoning tacitly admits that 1/2PA are not subject to the same thematic licensing requirements as 3PA arguments, which can be viewed as a weakening of Theta theory: discourse constraints should not interfere in establishing predicate argument relations. Coon and Preminger (2012) try to overcome the aforementioned weakness and argue that all arguments are projected within vP, yet a special Part(icipant)P, which serves as a locus for 1/2PA, is merged between v and V. PartP splits vP into two phases leading to a modification of case assignment modalities. Again, this analysis still allows discourse parameters to reshape the structure of vP, which is normally composed according to thematic and Aktionsart instructions.

Advocates of (ii) avoid the projection of special positions for speech-act participants, and propose that the features of v vary according to the person specification of its argument. In nominative languages, v case-licenses the object and T the subject, while in ergative systems the little v directly licenses the transitive subject, via ergative case marking. Yet, when the 1/2PA hold the agent role, they are licensed by Tense, due to their mutual feature compatibility. In such circumstances, *v*, free from its licensing responsibilities acquires a nominative behaviour, (cf. Müller 2004, Alexiadou and Anagnostopoulou 2006, D'Alessandro 2012).

In an attempt to combine the advantages of (i) and (ii), Merchant (2005) argues that all transitive subjects in ergative languages are licensed alike in vP, but in languages where person split is manifest, 1/2PA must also move to special PersonP above *v*P, resulting in double licensing or in double case. The upper case-marker provokes the morphological deletion of the lower ergative case affix.

All structural accounts of person split share the idea that 1/2PA entertain a closer relation with T than 3P arguments, because 1/2PA designate speech-act participants and T (or other functional head associated with it in the left field) plays an important role in anchoring events in speech situations. This link is captured by Béjar and Rezac's (2003) Person Licensing Condition (PLC), which states that "interpretable 1st/2nd person features must be licensed by entering into an Agree relation with an appropriate functional category", and more directly by Nash's (1997) Tense-Person Generalisation which attributes person split to the accessibility of 1/2PA to T in some ergative languages.

On the other side, Legate (2014) contests the validity of syntactic explanations of person split and presents robust cross-linguistic evidence for the parallel syntactic behaviour of distinctly case-marked 1/2PA and 3PA. She argues that if 1/2PA structurally lack ergative they are expected to trigger non-ergative case agreement. But if the absence of ergative marking is purely morphological then agreement mismatches between the ergativeless argument and its modifiers are expected. Cross-linguistic evidence confirms the latter prediction: while 1/2PA are not marked with ergative, any modifier in their local domain, or any constituent coindexed with them, such as floating quantifiers or appositive clauses, is marked ergative, (5).

Moreover, coordination constructions in the same languages reveal that 1/2PA can coordinate with 3PA regardless different case-markers, which would be excluded if different case- marking reflected different underlying structures, (6).

Marathi
(5) *case-concord*
   Mi   bicharii-ne sagla kaam ke-la
   I.NOM poor-ERG   all   work do-PERF.3SG
   'Poor little me did all the work'

(6) *coordination*
   Liki-ne   ani mi   keli   kha-ll-i
   Liki-ERG and I.NOM banana.NPL.NOM eat-PERF-NPL
   'Liki and I ate bananas'   (Legate, 2014: 194–195)

Legate concludes that person split cannot have a structural source and must therefore be accounted for in terms of superficial morphological factors, such as case syncretism. The motivation for case syncretism lies in markedness: the more specific is the feature makeup of a personal pronoun the more resistant it is to the special case-marking. The postsyntactic rule (7), (adapted from Legate's ex. 50:205) entails that arguments endowed with person features repel the ergative marking.

(7) postsyntactic rule: ERG—>ø [+participant; -/+singular]

Legate acknowledges in a footnote that her analysis does not in principle bar the existence of ergative languages where person split is structurally motivated, and predicts that in these languages the modifier of 1/2PA will bear nominative case in case agreement configurations, rather than ergative. Deal (2016) provides an analysis of exactly such a language, Nez Perce, where 1/2PA cannot be modified by ergative modifiers and cannot coordinate with 3PA, in which case the language has recourse to the commitative strategy.

1.2 Introducing person split in Georgian: Outline of the proposal

The phenomenon of person split is attested in Georgian: 1/2P pronouns have invariant forms while 3PA are distinctively marked with nominative, accusative or ergative cases. When the language manifests ergative alignment, only 3P transitive subjects are marked with ergative (8), which makes Georgian look akin to Dyirbal and distinct from Basque.

(8) a. ekim-ma   nax-a   pilm-i
        doctor-ERG   see-AOR.3SG   film-NOM
        'A/The doctor saw a/the film'
    b. čven(-*ma)   v-naxe-t   pilm-i
        we-ERG   1-see.AOR-pl   film-NOM
        'We saw a/the film'

However, the behaviour of 1/2PA reveals two contradictory patterns. On the one hand, 1/2P and 3P transitive subjects and 1/2P and 3P unaccusative subjects constitute distinct natural classes in Georgian with respect to case agreement. Example (9b) reveals that when a caseless 1P plural pronoun functions as a transitive subject it triggers the same agreement on the coindexed floating quantifier as the ergative nominal in (9a), similar to the situation reported in (5) in Marathi. But when the 1P plural pronoun is the subject of an unaccusative verb in (10b), it triggers nominative case-agreement with the quantifier.

(9) a. ekim-eb-ma$_i$ pilm-i q'vela-m$_i$/ *q'vela(-n-i)$_I$ naxe-s
   doctor-pl-ERG film-NOM all-ERG/ all-pl-NOM see-AOR.3PL
   'Doctors all saw the film'
b. čven$_i$ pilm-i q'vela-m$_i$/ *q'vela(n-i)$_i$ v-naxe-t
   we film-NOM all-ERG/ all-pl-NOM 1-see.AOR-PL
   'We all saw the film'

(10) a. ekim-eb-i$_i$ ik q'vela(n-i)$_I$ / *q'vela-m$_i$
    doctor-pl-NOM there all-pl-NOM/ all-ERG
    da=i-Karg-nen
    prev=nonact-lose-AOR.3PL
    'Doctors all got lost there'
b. čven$_i$ ik q'vela(n-i)$_i$/ *q'vela-m$_i$ da=v-i-Karge-t
   we there all-pl-NOM/ all-ERG prev=1-nonact-lose.AOR-pl
   'We all got lost there'

On the other hand, 1/2P transitive subjects and 1/2P unaccusative subjects constitute a natural class in triggering the identical person agreement on the verb, manifesting thus a typical behaviour of nominative languages.

(11) a. čven da=**v**-saje-**t** levan-i
    we prev=1-punish.AOR-PL Levan-NOM
    'We punished Levan'
b. čven da=**v**-i-Karge-**t**
    we prev=1-nonact-lose.AOR-PL
    'We got lost'

With respect to the two syntactic phenomena – case agreement and person agreement – Georgian 1/2PA simultaneously display ergative syntax and nominative syntax, which constitutes a serious challenge to structural and morphological accounts alike.

The aim of this paper is to contribute to the investigation of person split by putting forth an analysis for the mixed behaviour of 1/2PA in Georgian which manifest both ergative and nominative properties when they function as transitive subjects in ergative environments. A close investigation of three types of 1/2PA – (i) 1/2P pronouns, (ii) constructions with 1/2P pronominal determiners of type *we linguists* (Postal 1969) dubbed 1/2Pron-N, and (iii) superficially standard nominals triggering person agreement on the verb, 1/2P-N – leads to the conclusion that person split is best accounted in structural terms. It is conditioned by structural differences of nominal constituents rather than by structural asymmetries of clauses containing them. 1/2PA and 3PA are not structured alike: only 1/2PA are endowed with person features bundled in the category Person and projected in the specifier positions of their maximal projections. The two key properties – absence of case-marking and uniform person-agreement on the verb – are directly correlated with the presence of Person. Externally, it Agrees with the similar person specification on T yielding person agreement on the verb.

Internally, when Person occupies Spec,DP, it supplies in D-domain the necessary deictic specification for Person+D to function as a pronominal demonstrative determiner, as well as the necessary phi-features for the same Person+D to function as a strong indexical pronoun, hence making it *possible*, albeit not mandatory, for D to be intransitive. Georgian 1/2PA with intransitive D are spelled out as 1/2P pronouns, whereas 1/2PA with transitive D are spelled out as (pronoun-)noun constructions, 1/2Pron-N. As case-marking in Georgian only appears on the final nominal head, its absence is expected on constituents with intransitive D (1/2P pronouns), but not on constituents with nominal structure (1/2Pron-N). Person can be merged as the specifier of nominals with smaller, NumP structures, yielding 1/2P-N. While it does not affect the form of the nominal internally, Person in NumP induces interpretative effects: plural sets must include a speech-act participant as one of their variables.

Unlike 1/2P pronouns, 3P pronouns must be case-marked. Like 1/2P pronouns, they are strong indexical elements in Georgian. Their indexical property is not surprising as they are derived from demonstrative determiners. I argue that demonstrative DPs are formed by movement of the deictic spatial adjective from *n*P to DP (cf. Giusti 1997 a.o.). As the deictic adjective does not carry any phi-features – Georgian adjectives do not agree in number with the modified noun – the ellipsis of nominal structure NumP-*n*P-NP is disallowed in cases of pronominalisation: in spite of the deictic specification, the material in DP is not strong enough, in the sense of Lobeck (1995), to identify its discourse referent. Therefore, Georgian 3P pronouns, unlike 1/2P pronouns, must be headed by a transitive D, and include the nominal structure in their representation. This is transparently signalled by the addition of case and number morphemes to the demonstrative determiner in contexts of pronominalisation. The present analysis reveals that while all the grammatical information in 1/2P pronouns is available in the local domain of D, the required features of 3P are distributed in two domains, D-domain and nominal domain (cf. Manzini 2015). The systematic presence of the nominal layer in the structural representation of 3P pronouns and in a subclass of 1/2PA is the reason why ergative case marking (or any case marking) is present on these arguments.

The most important conclusion of the present analysis is that person split in Georgian is directly correlated with the presence of the nominal structure in the structural representation of arguments. When nominal structure is instantiated, case-marking is obligatory, when it is absent, the corresponding argument is not marked for case.

The paper is structured as follows. Section 2 is devoted to the description of main properties of 1/2PA. I first show that person split, unlike aspect split, does not affect case-alignment patterns of the language. Then person agreement is exposed which despite its clear nominative properties is triggered by 1/2P subjects that manifest ergative syntax and even ergative case-marking in Georgian. Section 3 details structural and interpretative differences of three types of 1/2PA: 1/2P Pron(ouns), 1/2Pron-N (pronominal determiner-noun constructions), and 1/2P-N (noun constituents that trigger person agreement). It is shown that person agreement, as well as the absence of case-marking on 1/2P pronouns, cannot be adduced to the overt or covert movement of a pronominal argument to T: 1/2P-N trigger person agreement but do not contain a pronoun or a pronominal determiner. Section 4 introduces the notion of Person and its role in person agreement and in shaping the form and the meaning of the three types of 1/2PA. Section 5 is devoted to the analysis of 3P pronouns, offering an account of their obligatory case-marking. Section 6 concludes.

2 External properties of 1/2PA

2.1 Aspect split vs. person split

Before tackling the issue of person split in Georgian, it is important to bear in mind that the language manifests another typical split of ergative systems, whereby the case-alignment shifts from ergative to nominative in certain tense-aspect systems. In the aorist and the subjunctive tenses, Georgian follows ergative case-alignment, whereas in imperfective tenses or in tenses derived from them, such as the conditional and the future, the language follows the nominative case-alignment. (cf. Nash 1995, 2017).[1] Following Nash (2017), I will refer to

---

[1] Nash (2017) provides an account of aspect split in terms of clausal functional complexity between *v*P and TP. Clauses in nominative tenses contain a functional category Event above

the former tense-aspect systems as ergative tenses and to the latter as nominative tenses. The direct object is morphologically distinct from the nominative subject in nominative tenses and bears the accusative case affix –s (12b).

(12) a. ekim-ma   xaT-a   saxl-i
       doctor-ERG draw-AOR.3SG house-NOM
       'A/the doctor drew a/the house'
   b. ekim-I   xaT-av-d-a   saxl-s
       doctor-NOM draw-imperf-PAST-3SG house-ACC
       'A/the doctor was drawing a/the house'

In ergative tenses, 1/2P pronouns and 3PA are not case-marked alike. While the former are invariable (13), all other arguments must carry the ergative case-suffix –ma (-m after vowel ending roots) when they function as transitive subjects, and the nominative marker –i when they are subjects of unaccusative verbs, (14). 3P pronouns behave like full referential expressions and have distinct forms depending on the valency of the predicate: e.g. *is/igi* is the third person singular nominative pronoun and *man/magan* is its ergative variant, (15) (cf. Section 5.1.).

(13) a. šen/*šen-ma es   saxli   da=ø-xaTe
       you/you-ERG this house-NOM prev=2-draw.AOR
       'You drew this house'
   b. šen/*sen-ma   da=ø-i-Karge
       you/you-ERG prev=2-nonact-lose.AOR
       'You got lost'

(14) a. ekim-ma/*ekim-i   es   saxl-I   da=xaT-a
       doctor-ERG/doctor-NOM this house-NOM prev=draw-AOR.3SG
       'A/the doctor drew this house'
   b. ekim-i/*ekim-ma   da=i-Karg-a
       doctor-NOM/doctor-ERG prev=nonact-lose-AOR.3SG
       'A/the doctor got lost'

---

vP which (i) thematically licenses the external argument and (ii) expresses the view-point aspect. As this category is absent in ergative tenses, the two arguments of transitive verbs are case-licensed inside vP. Tense is the only direct case-licenser for both arguments, and their case is determined by the dependent case algorithm: the higher of the two competing nominals is marked with the dependent ergative case. (Marantz 1991, Baker and Vinokurova 2010, Bobaljik 2008).

(15) a. man/   *is/   *ig-i   es saxl-i
        3SG.ERG/ 3SG.NOM/   3SG-NOM   this house-NOM
        da=xaT-a
        prev=draw-AOR.3SG
        '(S)he drew this house'
    b. is/   ig-i/   *man   da=i-Karg-a
        3SG.NOM/ 3SG-NOM/   3SG.ERG   prev=nonact-lose-AOR.3SG
        '(S)he got lost'

As already observed in (12b) and repeated in (16a), direct objects are marked with accusative in nominative tenses. When a 1/2P pronoun functions as a direct object in the same tenses, marking it with accusative is banned, (16b).

(16) a. levan-i   saxl-s   xaT-av-s
        Levan-NOM   house-ACC   draw-imperf-PRES.3SG
        'Levan is drawing a/the house'
    b. levan-i   šen/*šen-s g-xaT-av-s
        Levan-NOM   you/you-ACC 2O-draw-imperf-PRES.3SG
        'Levan is drawing you (your portrait)'

We conclude that 1/2P pronouns are not marked for accusative or ergative cases, neither for nominative, as nominals with consonant ending roots are followed by an overt nominative suffix –*i*, absent on 1/2P pronouns (cf. *šen* in 13b), but present on 3P pronouns (cf. *ig-i* in 15b). The forms of four invariable 1/2P pronouns are summarized in (17).

(17)   1   2
    SG me   šen
    PL čven   tkven

2.2 Case agreement

The absence of case-marking on 1/2P pronominal subjects does not affect the case-marking of 3P direct objects: in ergative tenses, 3P direct objects are always nominative/absolutive regardless the presence of the actual case affix on the agent.

(18) a. ekim-ma   da=xaT-a   saxl-i/*saxl-s
       doctor-ERG prev=draw-AOR.3SG house-NOM/house.ACC
       'A/the doctor drew a/the house'
   b. šen da=ø-xaTe   saxl-i/*saxl-s
      you prev=2-draw.AOR house-NOM/house-ACC
      'You drew a/the house'

Person split does not affect case-alignment in the same way as aspect split does, in Georgian. The absence of the ergative case on transitive subjects in imperfective tenses entails the presence of accusative on the corresponding direct objects, yet the absence of the ergative on 1/2P pronouns does not ensue in the presence of the accusative on the direct object in ergative tenses. As case-alignment directly depends on the properties of licensing heads, T or v, we conclude that their properties remain intact when one of the main arguments in the clause is 1/2P, contra Müller (2004).

The absence of ergative case-marking on 1/2P pronouns seems to be illusory in (18) from the point of view of case alignment mechanisms. Under the theory of dependent case which I adopt in this work following Nash (2017) (cf.fn.1), the two arguments of transitive verbs in ergative tenses have one case-licenser, Tense. The 3P direct object, which we saw to be uniformly marked with nominative, must "see" both 1/2P and 3P agents as its case- competitors. The phenomenon of case agreement confirms this hypothesis: 1/2P and 3P transitive subjects pattern alike in triggering ergative case agreement on secondary nominal predicate modifiers in (19), coindexed floating quantifiers in (21) and appositive NPs in (23). Likewise, in identical syntactic environments, 1/2P and 3P subjects of unaccusative verbs trigger nominative case agreement, (20, 22, 24).

Depictive secondary predicates
(19) a. ekim-ma   da=xaT-a   saxl-i   sruliad   mtvral-ma/
       doctor-ERG prev=draw-AOR.3SG house-NOM completely drunk-ERG/
       *mtvral-i
       drunk-NOM
       'The doctor drew a house completely drunk'
   b. me   da=v-xaTe   saxl-I   sruliad   mtvral-ma
      I   prev=1-draw.AOR house-NOM completely drunk-ERG/
      /*mtvral-i
      drunk-NOM
      'I drew a house completely drunk'

(20) a. ekim-i   da=i-Karg-a   sruliad   mtvral-i/
       doctor-NOM prev=nonact-lose-AOR.3SG completely drunk-NOM/
       *mtvral-ma
       drunk-ERG
       'The doctor got lost completely drunk'
   b. me   da=v-i-Karge   sruliad
       I   prev=1-nonact-lose.AOR completely
       mtvral-i/*mtvral-ma
       drunk-NOM/drunk-ERG
       'I got lost completely drunk'

Floating quantifiers

(21) a. kal-eb-ma$_i$ saxl-i   q'vela-m$_i$/ *q'vela$_i$ da=xaTe-s
       woman-pl-ERG house-NOM   all-ERG/   all.NOM   prev=drawAOR-3PL
       'The women all drew a house'
   b. čven$_i$ saxl-i   q'vela-m$_i$/ *q'vela$_i$ da=v-xaTe-t
       we   house-NOM all-ERG/   all.NOM   prev=1-drawAOR-PL
       'We all drew a house'

(22) a. kal-eb-i$_i$ kutais-ši   q'vela(n-i)$_i$/ *q'vela-m$_i$
       woman-pl-NOM   Kutaisi-in   all-pl-NOM/   all-ERG
       da=i-Karg-nen
       prev=nonact-lose-AOR.3PL
       'The women all got lost in Kutaisi'
   b. čven$_i$ kutais-ši   q'vela(n-i)$_i$/ *q'vela-m$_i$ da=v-i-Karge-t
       we   Kutaisi-in   all-pl-NOM/   all-ERG   prev=1-nonact-lose.AOR-PL
       'We all got lost in Kutaisi'

Appositive nominal expressions

(23) a. levan-ma, čveni sopl-is   ekim-ma/   *ekim-i,   saxl-i
       Levan-ERG our   village-GEN doctor-ERG/ doctor-NOM house-NOM
       da=xaT-a
       prev=draw-AOR.3SG
       'Levan, our village's doctor, drew a house'
   b. šen, čveni sopl-is   ekim-ma/   *ekim-i,   saxl-i
       you   our   village-GEN doctor-ERG/ doctor-NOM house-NOM
       da=ø-xaTe
       prev=2-draw.AOR
           'You, our village's doctor, drew a house'

(24) a. levan-i čveni sopl-is ekim-i/ *ekim-ma, kutais-ši
   Levan-NOM our village-GEN doctor-NOM/ doctor-ERG Kutaisi-in
   da=i-Karg-a
   prev=nonact-lose-AOR.3SG
   'Levan, our village's doctor, got lost in Kutaisi'
 b. šen, čveni sopl-is ekim-i/ *ekim-ma, kutais-ši
   you our village-GEN doctor-NOM/ doctor-ERG Kutaisi-in
   da=ø-i-Karge
   prev=2-nonact-lose.AOR
   'You, our village's doctor, got lost in Kutaisi'

The parallel behaviour of 1/2P pronouns and 3PA in case concord configurations prompts Legate (2014) to view person-split as a superficial phenomenon that masks the fact that all nominal types display the same underlying ergative syntax in their agent role, as opposed to unaccusative subjects (cf. Section 1.1).

But concluding that 1/2P transitive subjects do not behave as 1/2P unaccusative subjects seems compromised given that 1/2P subjects of transitive or unaccusative predicates trigger the identical person agreement on the verb, manifesting thus a typical behaviour of nominative systems where all subjects are marked with the same case and trigger the same person agreement. The next section is devoted to person agreement in Georgian, triggered by three types of 1/2PA: 1/2Pron(ouns), 1/2Pron-N (1st or 2nd pronominal determiner-noun constituents of type *we linguists*) (cf. Postal 1969), and 1/2P-N (1st or 2nd person-noun constituents) that represent NPs lacking all overt signs of 1/2P morphology but triggering person agreement on the verb.

2.3 Person agreement

Georgian is a pro-drop language with rich verb agreement. 1/2PA agree in person with the finite verb.[2] I limit the discussion to subject person agreement, putting aside contexts where is always a prefix and the number marker a suffix; (ii) allowing only one "slot" for the direct object is (also) 1/2P. Switching from

---

[2] The morphological mechanism of person agreement with 1/2PA objects is quite complex; it implies: (i) distributing the person exponent and the number exponent of each argument on different sides of the inflected verb (except for 1P plural object marker *gv-*), the person marker person exponent in contexts when both main arguments are 1/2P, and one "slot" for number exponent in contexts where both main arguments are plural. (cf. Bejar 2003, Bejar and Rezac 2009, Nash-Haran 1993, Halle and Marantz 1993, Wier 2011).

ergative to nominative tenses does not affect person agreement, *all* 1/2P subjects of eventive predicates in nominative and ergative tenses trigger the same person agreement on the verb, (25–28). When the subject is 1P, the affix *v-* is present on unaccusative and transitive verbs, in ergative and nominative tenses alike, and in case of 1P plural, the plural suffix *–t* is added, as summarized in (29).³

(25) a. me **v**-xaTe es saxl-i
 I 1-drawAOR this house-NOM
 'I drew this house-NOM'
 b. me **v**-xaT-av am saxl-s
 I 1-draw-imperf.PRES this house-ACC
 'I am drawing this house'

(26) a. me da=**v**-i-Karge
 I prev=1-nonact-lose.AOR
 'I got lost'
 b. me **v**-i-Karg-ebi
 I 1-nonact-lose-imperf.PRES
 'I am getting lost'

(27) a. čven **v**-xaTe-**t** es saxl-i
 we 1-draw.AOR-PL this house-NOM
 'We drew this house'

---

3 3PA do not agree in person. 3P subjects agree in number but the form of the plural- agreement marker on the verb depends on the valency of the predicate and on case-alignment system. In ergative tenses, ergative subjects trigger *–es* plural agreement, while nominative subjects of unaccusative verbs trigger *–(n)en* agreement:
(i) ekim-eb-ma Čam-es/ da=xaT-es
 doctor-pl-ERG eat-AOR.3PL/ prev=draw-AOR.3PL
 'Doctors ate/drew (something)'
(ii) ekim-eb-i da=i-Karg-nen/ mo=Kvd-nen
 doctor-pl-NOM prev=nonact-lose-AOR.3PL/ prev=die-AOR.3PL
 'Doctors got lost/died'
It is worth noting that in some Western dialects of Georgian, the plural agreement in the aorist is unified as *–en*, regardless the case of the subject and the (in)transitivity of the predicate.

b. čven **v**-xaT-av-**t** am saxl-s
   we 1-draw-imperf.PRES-PL this house-ACC
   'We are drawing this house'

(28) a. čven da=**v**-i-Karge-**t**
       we prev=1-nonact-lose.AOR-PL
       'We got lost'
    b. čven **v**-i-Karg-ebi-**t**
       we 1-nonact-lose-imperf.PRES-PL
       'We are getting lost'

(29)   1   2
     SG   v—   ø,x—
     PL   v—t   ø,x—t

Given the fact that 1/2P pronominal subjects trigger the same agreement in ergative and nominative contexts, it can be argued that they always occupy a special syntactic position where they do not need to be case-marked and where person agreement with the verb is triggered. As mentioned in Section 1.1., Merchant (2005) argues for the obligatory movement of person arguments into designated Person positions above vP where the original ergative case-marking is "erased" from the arguments and a second case, Nominative, is assigned.

However, this approach, or any other analysis that maintains that 1/2PA are licensed in higher functional layers of the clause, fails to account for the behaviour of case-marked noun phrases that contain a 1/2P pronoun acting as a determiner, of type *we linguists* (Postal 1969), which I will refer to as 1/2Pron-N, as well as of case-marked noun phrases that do not contain an overt 1/2P pronoun or determiner but still trigger person agreement, 1/2P-N. Their properties are exposed in the next section.

2.4 1/2Pron-N and 1/2P-N

Generally, 1/2Pron-N are plural, they are marked with ergative marker when they function as transitive subjects in ergative tenses and they trigger the same person agreement on the verb as 1/2P Pron(ouns), (30).

(30) a. čven <u>ekim-eb-ma</u> da=v-xaTe-t es saxl-i
       we doctor-pl-ERG prev=1-draw.AOR-PL this house-NOM
       'We doctors drew this house'

b. *tkven geograpi-is sTudenT-eb-ma* da=ø-male-t
you geography-GEN student-pl-ERG prev=2-hide.AOR-PL
ruk-eb-i
map-pl-NOM
'You geography students hid the maps'

The italicised sequences in (30) can be easily shown to function as one constituent and do not present a case of apposition of two nominals [_NP_we][_NP_doctors] akin to configurations in (23–24). In Georgian, left-adjacency to the verb is one of the main strategies for focussing a constituent. Additionally, focalised constituents can be modified by the adverb *marTo* 'only' or by the additive suffix *–c* 'too' (Nash 1995). Examples in (31–32) clearly demonstrate that 1/2Pron-N pattern with regular NPs with an adjectival modifier with respect to focalisation, while appositive constructions and a 1P singular pronoun followed by a modified noun fail the test and are composed of two juxtaposed constituents. This leads to conclusion that a plural 1/2 pronoun followed by a noun can function as a constituent whereas a singular 1/2 pronoun and its nominal complement cannot.

(31) a. marto *prang-ma ekim-ma* da=xaT-a saxl-i
only French-ERG doctor-ERG prev=draw-AOR.3SG house-NOM
'Only a French doctor drew a/the house'
b. marTo *čven prang-ma ekim-eb-ma* da=v-xaTe-t saxl-i
only we French-ERG doctor-pl-ERG prev=1-draw.AOR.PL house-NOM
'Only we French doctors drew a/the house'
c. *marto *Vano-m prang-ma ekim-ma* da=xaT-a
only Vano-ERG French-ERG doctor-ERG prev=draw.AOR.3SG
saxl-i
house-NOM
'Only Vano, the French doctor, drew a/the house'
d. *marto *me prang-ma ekim-ma* da=v-xaTe saxl-i
only I French-ERG doctor-ERG prev=1-drawAOR house-NOM
'Only I, the French doctor, drew a/the house'

(32) a. *prang-ma ekim-ma-c* da=xaT-a saxl-i
French-ERG doctor-ERG-too prev=draw-AOR.3SG house-NOM
'The French doctor too drew a/the house'
b. *čven prang-ma ekim-eb-ma-c* da=v-xaTe-t saxl-i
we French-ERG doctor-pl-ERG-too prev=1=draw.AOR.PL house-NOM
'We French doctors too drew a/the house'

c. *Vano-m   prang-ma   ekim-ma-c   da=xaT-a   saxl-i
   Vano-   French-   doctor-ERG-   prev=draw.AOR-   house-
   ERG   ERG   too   3SG   NOM
   'Vano, the French doctor, too drew a/the house'
d. *me prang-ma   ekim-ma-c   da=v-xaTe   saxl-i
   I   French-ERG   doctor-ERG-too   prev=1-draw.AOR   house-NOM
   'I, the French doctor, too drew a/the house'

The existence of 1/2Pron-N constituents marked with ergative makes it difficult to justify that arguments denoting speech-act participants move to designated projections where ergative case does not need to be assigned. They also illustrate that person agreement can be triggered by nominals bearing ergative case, which calls to reconsider the idea that person agreement follows the nominative pattern because it is triggered by arguments whose form does not shift according to case-alignment requirements of the clause and the valency of the predicate. And finally the existence of ergative 1/2Pron-N shows that person features on an argument do not ban the ergative case marking by a mechanism of morphological markedness, as proposed by Legate (2014) and illustrated in (7).

However, these conclusions can be countered by an analysis that treats pronouns and pronominal determiners in 1/2Pron-N as structurally identical (a version of which will be defended below) and argues for their covert movement to ParticipantP outside vP where person agreement on the verb is triggered. Such a conclusion may even constitute a welcome step in view of the behaviour of standardly looking noun constituents that trigger person agreement, which I refer to as 1/2P-N to distinguish them from 1/2Pron-N. In what follows, 1/2P-N will be translated in English with the pronoun in superscript. Examples (33a–b) contain 1/2P-N, while (33c–d) illustrate that the same constituents trigger the expected third- person agreement.

(33) a. _ekim-eb-ma_   da=v-xaTe-t   es   saxl-i
        doctor-pl-ERG   prev=1-draw.AOR-PL   this   house-NOM
        'We doctors drew this house'
    b. _geograpi-is_   _sTudenT-eb-ma_   da=ø-male-t   ruk-eb-i
        geography-GEN   student-pl-ERG   prev=2-hide.AOR-PL   map-pl-NOM
        'You geography students hid the maps'
    c. _ekim-eb-ma_   da= xaTe-s   es   saxl-i
        doctor-pl-ERG   prev=draw-AOR.3PL   this   house-NOM
        '(The) doctors drew this house'
    d. _geograpi-is_   _sTudenT-eb-ma_   da= male-s   ruk-eb-i
        geography-GEN   student-pl-ERG   prev=hide-AOR.3PL   map-pl-NOM
        '(The) geography students hid the maps'

Similar constructions exist in Spanish and Greek, among other languages. But unlike Spanish and Greek, Georgian 1/2P-N do not contain a determiner, as Georgian has no articles.

(34) Las organizadoras entrevist-amos a muchos candidatos.
      the organizers   interview-1.PL   many candidates
      'We organizers interview many candidates'
      (adapted from Torrego and Laka 2015)

The phenomenon, whereby a nominal expression triggers either a 3P agreement or a 1/2 person agreement on the verb, was named by Hurtado (1985) as unagreement. A number of researchers working on unagreement in Spanish and in Greek note that this phenomenon is only observed in null subject languages and propose that nominals in (33–34) and 1/2Pron-N, which are much largely attested crosslinguistically, represent the same structures yet differ in form as 1/2P-N contain the silent variant of the overt pronoun in 1/2Pron-N, (35). (Torrego and Laka 2015, Höhn 2016).

(35) (Nosostros) las organizadoras entrevist-amos a muchos candidatos.
      We   the organizers   interview-1.PL   many candidates
      'We organizers interview many candidates'

For Torrego and Laka, pronouns in 1/2Pron-N and their silent variants in 1/2P-N are full constituents with articulated internal structure that function independently of their NP complement. The overt variant *nosostros* 'we' is bimorphemic composed of the person part *nos* and the number part *ostros*.[4] Transposing this idea to Georgian 1/2Pron-N and 1/2P-N, one could maintain that the pronoun in the former covertly raises to a position above vP in and

---

4 Ackema and Neelman (2013) correctly point out that this type of approach presupposes that the pronoun somehow stands in apposition relation to the noun. This analysis is problematic for unagreement contexts as it is highly unusual for a pronoun to be null or even weak in apposition structures. French has weak and strong 1/2P pronouns but only the latter can be employed in apposition structures, (i). Furthermore, clitics, the weakest pronominal elements, cannot be used in appositive structures either, (ii).
(i)   a. *Je, une vraie social-démocrate, je n'accepterai jamais ça
      b. Moi, une vraie social-démocrate, je n'accepterai jamais ça
          'I, a true social-democrat, will never accept this.'
(ii) a. *Paul m'a vue, une vraie social-démocrate, pleurer comme une gamine
      b. Paul m'a vue moi, une vraie social-démocrate, pleurer comme une gamine
          'Paul saw me, a true social-democrat, crying as a little girl'.

so does its covert counterpart in (33a–b). This covert raising of overt and covert pronominal elements yields person agreement on the verb.

Importantly, any analysis that adduces the same structure to 1/2Pron-N and to 1/2P-N implies that they share the same meaning. In the next section I show that the two constructions have different referential properties and that 1/2P-N do not contain the silent homologue of the overt pronoun or overt determiner. In fact, 1/2P-N do not contain a definite determiner at all and cannot be analysed as DPs. On the basis of theses conclusions, I will claim that person agreement is not triggered by pronominal constituents.

3 Internal properties of 1/2P-N, 1/2Pron-N and 1/2Pron

We have seen in the previous sections that 1/2P person agreement on the verb can be triggered in Georgian by 1/2P pronouns not marked for ergative case, but also by 1/2Pron-N and 1/2P-N constructions marked for ergative. Examples in (36) further illustrate that the three types of 1/2PA trigger the same person agreement when they function as subjects of unaccusative verbs, irrespective of the presence of the nominative case marker on 1/2Pron-N and 1/2P-N and its absence on 1/2Pron.

(36) a. čven da=v-brundi-t [1/2Pron]
    we prev=1return.AOR-PL
    'We returned'
 b. čven kal-eb-i da=v-brundi-t [1/2Pron-N]
    we woman-pl-NOM prev=1-returnAOR-PL
    'We women returned'
 c. kal-eb-i da=v-brundi-t [1/2P-N]
    woman-pl-NOM prev=1-returnAOR-PL
    'We women returned'

Although it is tempting to attribute the uniformity of person agreement to caselessness of 1/2P pronouns by claiming that they make part of the three constructions at hand, my aim in this section is to show that 1/2P-N do not contain a pronoun nor are headed by the same functional category D as the other two types of 1/2PA.

3.1 Meaning asymmetries between 1/2P-N and 1/2Pron-N

1/2P-N exhibit the following properties: they can (i) contain quantifiers (37), (ii) cannot be preceded by a demonstrative article (38), (iii) cannot be a 3P pronoun (39), (iv) cannot contain coordinated singular proper names (40), but (v) can contain coordinated singular common nouns (41).

(37) sam(-ma)/ bevr(-ma)/ q'vela / arcert(-ma)/ qovel(-ma) kal-ma
three-ERG/ many-ERG/ all/ none-ERG/ each-ERG woman-ERG
v-tkvi-t
1-say.AOR-PL
'We three/many/all/no/each women said (something)'

(38) *am/mag kal-eb-ma v-tkv-i-t
this/that woman-pl-ERG 1-say.AOR-PL
'We these women said (something)'

(39) *mat/ mag-at-ma v-tkv-i-t
they.ERG/ that-pl-ERG 1-say.AOR-PL
'We they said (something)'

(40) *?lia-m da keto-m v-tkv-i-t
Lia-ERG and Keto-ERG 1-say.AOR-PL
'We Lia and Keto said this'[5]

(41) kal-ma da Kac-ma v-tkvi-t
woman-ERG and man-ERG 1-sayAOR-PL
'We woman and man said (something)'

---

5 A variant of (40) with two coordinated singular names can marginally trigger 2P plural person agreement (i), presumably due to the speech act context where the speaker addresses two individuals by isolating them from a larger salient group: (Out of you'll), *you Lia and Keto said this*. Such an utterance is infelicitous with the 1P plural agreement, as it is infelicitous to refer (by the speaker) to the speaker by name (cf. Ackema and Neelman 2013:17). This relates to an interesting pragmatic asymmetry whereby it as common to address an individual by her name as by the 2P pronoun, yet impossible to refer to oneself in a speech-act by the name instead of the 1P pronoun.
(i)   ?lia-m   da   keto-m   ø-tkvi-t es
Lia-ERG and keto-ERG 2-say-AOR-PL
'You Lia and Keto said this'.

1/2P-N can contain more than a quantifier and a noun and be heavily modified by adjectival and possessive constituents, (42).

(42) [ket-is   sam(-ma)   or-i   c'l-is   uK'an   vena-ši
     Keti-GEN three-ERG   two-NOM year-GEN   ago   Vienna-in
     gacnobil(-ma)   amxanag-ma]   v-tkv-i-t   es
     presented-ERG   friend-ERG   1-say.AOR-PL1 this.NOM
     'We Keti's three friends presented (to her) in Vienna two years ago said this'

In spite of their meaning similarities, witnessed by the English translations, 1/2Pron-N and 1/2P-N have partially overlapping properties. Both constructions are incompatible with demonstratives (43), with 3P pronouns (44) and with coordinated singular proper names (45). Both types can contain adjectival and genitive modifiers (46).

(43) (*čven) am/mag   (*čven) kal-eb-ma   v-tkv-i-t   es
     we   this/that   woman-pl-ERG   1-sayAOR-PL   thisNOM
     '*We these women said this'

(44) * čven   mat/   mag-at-ma   v-tkv-i-t   es
     we   theyERG/   that-pl-ERG   1-sayAOR-PL this.NOM
     '*We they said this'

(45) * čven lia-m   da   keto-m   v-tkv-i-t   es
     we   Lia-ERG and   Keto-ERG   1-sayAOR-PL thisNOM
     '*We Lia and Keto said this'

(46) [čven ket-is   sam(-ma)   or-i   c'l-is   uK'an   vena-ši
     we   Keti-GEN three-ERG   two-NOM year-GEN ago   Vienna-in
     gacnobil(-ma)   amxanag-ma]   v-tkv-i-t   es
     presented-ERG   friend-ERG   1-sayAOR-PL this.NOM
     'We Keti's three friends presented (to her) in Vienna two years ago said this'

However, 1/2Pron-N cannot contain coordinated singular common nouns in (47), unlike 1/2P-N in (41). The difference in meaning between the two sentences is salient: example (41) entails that a set contextually isolated from a larger set contains two individuals belonging to different classes (women and men) one of which is the speech act participant; the nouns here function as predicates and denote two different properties attributed to each of the individuals.

As opposed, in example (47), the coordinated group contains two definite expressions one of which is the speaker. Similarly to what is said in fn.5, it is infelicitous for the speaker to refer to herself by means of a definite description, unless we deal with an appositive construal 'I, the woman'.

(47) *čven kal-ma da Kac-ma v-tkvi-t es
we woman-ERG and man-ERG 1-sayAOR-PL this.NOM
'*We woman and man said this'

Furthermore, most quantifiers seen in (37) cannot be employed in 1/2Pron-N, (48).

(48) cven ok sam-(-ma)/ ok q'vela/ ?*zog(-ma)/ ??ramodenime/
we three-ERG/ all/ some-ERG/ several/
??bevr-ma/ ?*umravles(-ma)/
many-ERG /most-ERG/
??qovel(-ma) kal-ma v-tkvi-t es
each-ERG woman-ERG 1-sayAOR-PL this.NOM
'We three/all/some/several/many/most/each women said this'

Interestingly, sequences with 1/2P plural pronouns followed by a QP are judged as grammatical by some speakers, but in these cases they are interpreted as appositive constructions. When the same sequences are modified by the additive focus affix –c 'too' (cf. (32)) their acceptability is degraded even for these speakers, which proves that the italisized sequences in (49) do not function as single constituents.[6]

(49) a. ??čven zog(-ma) kal-ma-c v-tkvi-t es
we some-ERG woman-ERG-too 1-sayAOR-PL this.NOM
'We some women too said this'
b. ?*tkven bevr-(ma) ekim-ma-c ga=ø-sinje-t
you many-ERG doctor-ERG-too prev=2-examine.AOR-pl
avadmq'op-i
patient-NOM
'You many doctors too examined the patient'

---

[6] The similar incompatibility of quantifiers with pronominal determiners in unagreement contexts is reported for Greek and Spanish (Ackema and Neelman 2013, Höhn 2016). Ackema and Neelman point out that this asymmetry undermines analyses based on the assumption that 1/2P-N contain a pronominal element like 1/2Pron-N, in agreement to the view defended in this work.

Notice that the numeral quantifiers are equally licit in 1/2Pron-N and in 1/2P-N, due to their dual status of quantifiers and adjectival numeral modifiers. (cf. Höhn 2016:31). The same holds of *q'vela* 'all' which also functions as a group modifier.

(50) a. čven   q'vela sam-ma   kal-ma-c   ga=v-imeore-t
         we   all   three-ERG   woman-ERG-too   prev=1-repeat.AOR-PL
         es
         this.NOM
         'We all three women too repeated this'

The different behaviour of 1/2Pron-N and 1/2P-N in coordinated configurations and with respect to quantifiers suggests that the former denote *definite descriptions*, identified as groups containing speech-act participants, while the latter denote *quantificational constituents* where quantified or plural sets contain one variable identified as the speech-act participant.[7] This difference in meaning becomes clearer when we compare the two sentences in (51). In (51a), each conjunct contains a different set, [three women] and [four women] – the only property that they share is that each of these sets contains the same speech-act participant, namely the speaker, otherwise the two sets are formally distinct and can hence be contrastively coordinated. On the other hand, (51b) sounds as a contradiction as the set [we three women] is a definite group which contains a speech-act participant and other individuals and so is the set [we four women]. Each definite group must bear a distinct referential index, therefore in the same speech situation the determiner *we* cannot confer two different indices. The same meaning constraint can be observed in the following sentence *We arrived early and then we cooked*. The sentence entails that the group of "we"-early arrivers in the first conjunct and the group of "we"-cooks in the second is identical. The only plausible, but improbable, way to render the two groups of "we" formally distinct would be if the speaker gesturally designates the first group of early arrivers by including herself, and then gesturally designates a different group of cooks also including herself. Under a similar improbable scenario, the three women and the four women in (51b) can be formally different definite descriptions, and the outcome felicitous.

---

[7] Ackema and Neelman (2013) refer to these readings as referential and quantificational, respectively. They argue that in the first, speech act participants restrict the reference of the noun phrase, while in the second, speech participants act as a restriction on a variable, as in quantifier-bound variable relations (Heim and Kratzer 1998).

(51) a. sam(-ma)   kal-ma   v-tkvi-t   es   da   otx(-ma)
         three-ERG   woman-ERG   1-sayAOR-PL   this.NOM   and   four-ERG
         kal-ma   v-tkv-i-t   is
         1-sayAOR-PL that.NOM   woman-ERG
         'We three women said this and We four women said that'
    b.   #čven sam(-ma)   kal-ma   v-tkv-i-t   es   da   čven
         we   three-ERG   woman-ERG   1-say-AOR-PL   this.NOM   and   we
         otx(-ma)   kal-ma   v-tkv-i-t   is
         four-ERG   woman-ERG   1-say-AOR-PL   that.NOM
         '#We three women said this and we four women said that'

As expected, example (52) is well-formed because each definite group denoted by 1/2Pron-N is formally distinct as each conjunct contains a different speech participant, the speaker in the first group and the addressee in the second group.

(52) čven   sam(-ma)   kal-ma   v-tkvi-t   es   da   tkven
     we   three-ERG   woman-ERG   1-sayAOR-PL   this.NOM   and   you
     otx(-ma)   kal-ma   ø-tkvi-t   is
     four-ERG   woman-ERG   2-sayAOR-PL   that.NOM
     'We three women said this and you four women said that'

Consider now (53), where a 3P pronoun the second conjunct contrasts with 1/2P-N in the first conjunct in (53a), and with 1/2Pron-N in (53b). In (53a) the contrast is construed against a set: 1/2P-N in the first conjunct contains a numeral quantifier which ranges over a class of women picking up random three members including the speech-act participant and is contrasted with another set, which cannot be from the same class. However, in (53b) the pronoun contrasts with a definite expression. As 1/2Pron-N in the first conjunct refers to a definite group of three women including the speech-act participant, the referent of the pronoun in the second conjunct can refer to any other definite group, comprised of women or not.

(53) a. sam(-ma)   kal-ma   v-tkvi-t   es   da   magat-ma
         three-ERG   woman-ERG   1-sayAOR-PL   this.NOM   and   3pl-ERG
         tkv-es   is
         say-AOR.3PL   that.NOM
         'We three women said this and they said that'
         they: other individuals/*other women

b. čven sam(-ma) kal-ma v-tkv-i-t es da magat-ma
we three-ERG woman-ERG 1-sayAOR-PL this and 3pl-ERG
tkv-es is
say-AOR.3PL that.NOM
'We three women said this and they said that'
they: other individuals/other women

Examples in (54) further confirm that 1/2P-N are true QPs while 1/2Pron-N express definite descriptions: only the latter can be felicitously focused in contrast with another definite referent.[8]

(54) a. ??sam(-ma) kal-ma v-tkvi-t es, magat-ma Ki ara
three-ERG woman-ERG 1-sayAOR-PL this.NOM 3pl-ERG and not
'We three women said this, THEY did not.'
b. čven sam(-ma) kal-ma v-tkvi-t es, magat-ma
we three-ERG woman-ERG 1-sayAOR-PL this.NOM 3pl-ERG
Ki ara
and not
'We three women said this, THEY did not'
they: a definite group of other individuals/women

Evidence put forth above convincingly demonstrates that 1/2Pron-N and 1/2P-N do not have the same meaning, and consequently, their structure must be different too.

3.2 Structural asymmetries of 1/2PA

1/2Pron-N are best analysed as DPs that denote definite descriptions, or more specifically definite plural groups, while 1/2P-N have smaller structures. In line with much research on the functional structure associated with noun phrases, I contend that the nominal layer selected by D in (55) has an articulated structure whose functional spine above the lexical N is comprised of the classifier *n* (Borer 2005) and the quantifying category Number (Ritter 1991). For the ease of exposure I will continue to refer to the material embedded under D as the nominal (instead of Num-n-N) layer.

---

[8] The acceptability of (54a) improves if the noun *kalma* 'woman' is emphasized. In that case, the pronoun *they* in the second conjunct must refer to members of another class (e.g. men).

The lexical category N names a property. The categorizer *n* is endowed with the [class] feature that indicates whether the noun belongs to a class of common or mass nouns, and hence is individualisable/divisible. (cf. Borer 2005). Number specifies the quantity of individuals of the class that it ranges over, (cf. Borer's 2005 #P).[9] And finally, D provides a referential index to the quantified set of individuals defined by Number.

(55) [$_{DP}$ D [$_{NumP}$ Num [$_{nP}$ *n* [$_{NP}$ N]]]]

As 1/2P-N refer to indefinite plural or quantified sets, it is natural to view them as NumP: they denote individuated sets of entities where one of the variables is identified as the speech- act participant. Further confirmation for their asymmetric structures comes from variable binding capacity of 1/2P-N and 1/2Pron-N.

Déchaine and Wiltschko (2002, 2015) argue that pronominal elements that have a fixed denotation and fail to function as bound variables should be structurally represented as DPs since the locus of indexicality is in D. Referentially dependent elements that function as bound pronouns due to their indexical variability are to be analysed as smaller structures, φPs (the locus of all phi-features such as number, person, gender). In the present analysis,

1/2Pron-N are analysed as DPs and should function as strong indexicals, while 1/2P-N have a smaller structure and should allow a bound variable reading. Moreover, as 1/2P pronouns are identical in form with the pronominal

---

9 As plural marking on nouns in Georgian is generally mutually exclusive of quantifiers, I attribute the same structural origin to quantifiers and to the pluralizer *-eb*. Some quantifiers marginally tolerate plural nouns, but numerals and the quantity wh-word *ramdeni* 'how much/many' strictly require the singular noun as their complement:

(i) bevri kal-(?-eb)-i / zogi kal-(?*-eb)-i / sami kal(*-eb)-i
   many woman-pl-NOM / some woman-pl-NOM// three woman-pl-NOM
   what-quantity-NOM woman-pl-NOM
   ram-den-i   kal-(*-eb)-i
   'many women, some women, three women, how many women'

Notice that 3P plural agreement on the verb is only triggered by nominals formally marked as plural, (iia–b).

(ii) a. kal-eb-i   dadi-an/   *dadi-s
       woman-pl-NOM walk-PRES.3PL/ walk-PRES.3SG
       '(The) women walk'
    b. bevr-i   kal-i   dadi-s /   *dadi-an
       many-NOM woman-NOM walk-PRES.3SG/ walk-PRES.3pl
       'Many women walk'.

determiner in 1/2Pron-N they also should allow only fixed readings. The evidence presented below confirms this prediction.

Consider first English, where 1P and 2P pronouns do not always have a fixed denotation and can function as bound pronouns. Example (56) is felicitous under two scenarios: when nobody understood the question that they got (bound reading), and when nobody understood the question that I got (indexical reading).

(56) Only I got a question that I understood (nobody else did)
    i) (…nobody else got a question that I understood)
    ii) (…nobody else got a question that they understood)

In Georgian, 1/2P pronouns are not ambiguous as their English counterparts and always denote a fixed referent, (57a). On the other hand, in pro-drop contexts bound readings are available, (57b).

(57) a. marTo čven ga=gv-axsend-a rom čven is
      only we prev=1plO-recall-AOR.3SG that we that.NOM
      pilm-i uKve v-naxe-t
      film-NOM already 1-sawAOR-PL
      'Only we recalled that we saw that film'
      ≠ noone else recalled that he saw the film
      = no one else recalled that we saw the film
   b. marTo čven ga=gv-axsend-a rom is pilm-i
      only we prev=1Opl-recall-AOR.3SG that that.NOM film-NOM
      uKve v-naxe-t
      already 1- seeAOR-PL
      'Only we recalled that we already saw that film'
      = no one else recalled that they saw the film
      = no one else recalled that we saw the film

Examples in (58) illustrate that 1/2Pron-N have only indexical reading while 1/2P-N allow bound variable readings.

(58) a. marTo čven ga=gv-axsend-a rom čven kal-eb-ma
      only we prev=1Opl-recall-AOR.3SG that we woman-pl-ERG
      is pilm-i uKve v-naxe-t
      that.NOM film-NOM already 1-seeAOR-PL
      'Only we recalled that we women already saw this film'
      ≠ noone else recalled that they saw this film
      = no one else recalled that we women saw this film

b. marTo čven ga=gv-axsend-a rom kal-eb-ma
only we prev=1Opl-recall-AOR.3SG that woman-pl-ERG
is pilm-I uKve v- naxe-t
that.NOM film-NOM aleady 1-seeAOR-PL
'Only we recalled that we women already saw this film'
= no one else recalled that they saw this film
= no one else recalled that we women saw this movie

These binding facts serve as an important proof against the unified structural treatment of 1/2P pronouns, 1/2Pron-N and 1/2P-N. Only one type, 1/2P-N allows bound variable readings and should not be analysed as DP.

To conclude, in ergative tenses, subject person agreement is triggered by caseless 1/2P pronouns but also by case-marked constituents, 1/2Pron-N and 1/2P-N. In order to locate the structural source of person agreement and at the same to correlate this source with the absence of case on personal pronouns, it is tempting to propose that the three nominal types comprise an overt or covert pronoun that is licensed in a high position above vP, where case-marking requirements do not apply and where person agreement with the finite verb is triggered. Such a conclusion is not warranted: despite the fact that the form and the indexicality of 1/2Pron and 1/2Pron-N are similar, 1/2P-N do not share the meaning and the structure with either of them. 1/2P-N behave as quantified expressions and have a smaller structure, NumP, whereas 1/2Pron and 1/2Pron-N are indexically rigid DPs that refer to definite descriptions. In the next section, the common property that makes all 1/2PA person agreement triggerers is identified. It concerns the feature bundle (or the category) Person, merged in the specifier of nominals of different structural complexity. This feature is indirectly tied to the absence of case-marking on 1/2P pronouns as it allows their D head to be intransitive. As only arguments that contain nominal structure can be case-marked in Georgian, the absence of case on DPs with intransitive D ensues.

4 Person

In this section, I propose an analysis of person agreement in Georgian which is not based on the movement or base-generation of 1/2P pronouns in the functional domain of the clause. This reasoning is based on the outcome of the preceding section: pronominal arguments cannot be the source of 1/2P person agreement because 1/2P-N do not contain pronouns but agree in person with the verb.

I contend that the three types of constituents, 1/2P-N, 1/2Pron-N and 1/2Pron share one structural property regardless of their functional complexity: they all carry person features. Following Harley and Ritter (2002) and a long linguistic tradition summarized in that work, I identify the grammatical concept of Person to express speech-act participants, the speaker and the addressee, and larger groups of individuals that contain them. Importantly, the notion of 3rd person is not defined in terms of the grammatical concept of Person (cf. Benveniste 1966). 1st and 2nd singular person are only specified for the speech-act participant feature [speaker] or [addressee]. However, 1st and 2nd plural person are more complex notions and denote groups that encompass the speech act participant: the feature bundle of Person in this case is made up of the number feature and the speech-act participant feature but these are compositionally arranged rather than listed, the number including the participant (Harbour 2011).[10] Concretely, 1P plural is composed of number which expresses individuation of entities, yet these entities are not 'speakers' but rather individuals of some unspecified (though contextually familiar) class to which the speaker is added: [group (x+speaker)]. The representation of 2P plural parallels that of 1P plural, except for the value of speech-act participant, [group (x+addressee)]. The notion of number in persons and in nouns has different meanings: whereas in common nouns it makes sense to distinguish between singular and non-singular sets, the same reasoning cannot be extended to persons. A plural person does not represent an augmented number of participants but the *addition* to the speech act participant of the augmented or non-augmented sets of referents. In short, number in Persons entails coordination rather than standard quantification (cf. Vassilieva and Larson 2005). I henceforth propose that singular persons, albeit conceptually expressing one individual do not *grammatically* correspond to a singleton of some set, and hence are not specified for grammatical number; they are featurally minimal and just name the speech-act participant.

Adapting an idea from van Koppen (2012) (cf. also Choi 2014), I propose that the feature bundle Person is projected in the specifier of the highest functional category heading a noun expression. In 1/2P-N constructions, Person occupies Spec,NumP, while in 1/2Pron-N and 1/2Pron, it is merged in Spec,DP.[11] In (59), I identify possible values for Person: s stands for speaker, a for addressee, g for group (i.e. plural number) and x for added variable(s) in case of plural

---

10 In Harley and Ritter's (2002) representations, the two features of plural persons are listed [Speaker, Group/Indiv(iduation)].
11 It is important to bear in mind that under this approach Person corresponds to a feature bundle, and not to a maximal projection. This deficient syntactic category has no selectional properties and does not count itself as an argument but rather as a modifier of an argument.

persons. Notice that only Person specified for number can surface in structures that also contain the nominal structure, such as 1/2P-N and 1/2Pron-N.

(59) a. [NumP[PERSON g(x+s/a)] Num [nP n...]]   1/2P-N
b. [DP [PERSON g(x+s/a)] D [NumP Num [nP n...]]] 1/2Pron-N
c. [DP [PERSON g(x+s/a)] D]   1/2Pron PLURAL
d. [DP[PERSON s/a] Det]   1/2Pron SINGULAR

Person features percolate from the specifier position to the maximal projection of the noun phrase and define it as a personal argument. From the left-periphery of the nominal constituent, this bundle may rise to T as a clitic, yielding person agreement on the verb (cf. Nash-Haran 1993, Halle and Marantz 1993). Alternatively, following Georgi (2013), person agreement can be viewed as an outcome of the operation Agree by which an unvalued person feature on a functional head T is valued against Person's features of the argument, (60). The two mechanisms capture the basic idea shared by standard approaches to person split (cf. Section 1.1.): 1/2PA entertain a closer relation with T than 3P arguments, because Tense and Person are directly related to speech-acts: Person denotes speech-act participants and T serves as a mediator in anchoring the event time to the speech act situation.

(60) $T_{[Person]i}$......$[_{XP}[Person]_i$ X...]

4.1 Person in DPs vs. Person in NumP

Person affects the interpretation of NumP and DP in different ways: in the former, it applies to a plural set denoted by NumP and identifies one variable thereof as the speech-act participant, while in the latter it provides a deictic proximal specification to the definite description by identifying it either as the speech-act participant or as the contextually unique group containing the speech act participant. I will first elaborate on the role of Person in NumP and then turn to DPs.

In NumP, Person specifies that a plural/quantified set of individuals contains one variable which corresponds to the speaker or the addressee. The functional category Number which selects nPs is intrinsically specified for the individuation feature. I propose that the number values of plural Person and Number match and the final number value percolated to the maximal projection NumP includes the participant feature, by virtue of its inclusion in the number specification of Person, cf. (59a–c). Concretely, the denotations of *three women* and *we three women* differ only in the sense that the number value [3] in the latter must contain the speaker and be read as a coordination [₃speaker+2]. Van Koppen (2012) proposes that the features of 1/2 plural pronouns can split and be distributed on different syntactic sites. My proposal shares the spirit of her analysis, in the sense that the number specification of plural persons must strictly match, via Spec-head agreement, the similar value of Number. Notice that the feature matching mechanism fails if Number is modified by the singular Person as the latter is not endowed with grammatical number features.

I turn next to the role of Person in Spec,DP in 1/2Pron-N and 1/2Pron. The combination of D features and Person features is morphologically spelled out as a person pronoun, which in Georgian is clearly bi-morphemic. All 1/2P pronouns are composed of two morphemes, one for Person and the invariant – *n* spelling out the determiner. I reproduce below a modified version of (17). The modification concerns the 1st person singular pronoun: even if it does not carry the affix –*n* in Standard Georgian, the suffix is reported to be present on the pronoun in some Eastern dialects, and was also encountered in Old Georgian texts (Martirosov 1964).

(61)(=17)

	1	2
SG	me(-n)	še-n
PL	čve-n	tkve-n

A clear evidence for the determiner status of –*n* comes from the fact that the affix is omitted when the pronoun accompanies expressive epithets in vocative contexts.

(62) a. sad   mi=di-x-ar,   še(*-n) mTirala(v)!
       where prev=go-2-be.PRES you   crybaby.VOC
       'Where are you going, you crybaby?'
    b. mo-ø-di-t   ak,   tkve(*-n) sazizyr-eb-o!
       prev=2-go-PL   here   you   disgusting-pl-VOC
       'Come here, you despising ones!'

Following Longobardi (1994) and much subsequent work on vocatives (cf. D'Hulst et al 2007), I propose that the noun raises to D when marked for vocative, yielding a configuration where only Person part of the adnominal pronoun is spelled out.[12]

---

[12] If Person is analysed as a clitic fleshed out as person agreement on the verb, the actual strong pronouns in (61) are to be analysed as the pronunciations of D which acquires the

Semantically, the role of Person in 1/2Pron-N is to supply deictic information that links the definite description to the speech-act situation by specifying that the speech-act participant makes part of the referents of the definite description. In this sense, the pronominal determiner in 1/2Pron-N behaves as a demonstrative rather than a definite determiner, which are not instantiated in Georgian. A similar observation is made for parallel English constructions by Sommerstein (1972), (cf. Höhn 2016), concerning Postal's (1969) treatment of pronominal determiners. When reporting the example (63a), the expression *you troops* must be replaced by *those troops* rather than by a standard DP in (63b).

(63) a. YOU troops will embark but the other troops will remain.
 b. He said that (those/*the) troops would embark but the other troops would remain.

Furthermore, pronominal determiners are cross-linguistically compatible with the definite article but not with the demonstrative determiner, e.g. in Spanish and in . (Choi 2014, Höhn 2016)

(64) a. Standard Modern Greek
 (*aftoi) emeis (*aftoi) oi glossologoi (*aftoi)
 dem.pl we   the linguists
 'we linguists'
 b. Spanish
 (*esos) nosostros (*esos) los lingüistas (*esos)
 dem.pl we   the linguists
 'we linguists'

These facts lead to the conclusion that Person and D are distinct categories, D supplies a referential index to a description, and Person further restricts that index by deictic proximal specification. This conclusion resonates with Elbourne's (2005) analysis of determiners whereby the difference between D and demonstratives involves the presence on the latter of a proximal feature in addition to the index. This proximal feature in 1/2Pron-N is provided by Person, in the present analysis.

---

features of Person through feature sharing resulting from Spec-head agreement. An alternative view would consist in viewing the pronoun as the spell-out of Person to which D attaches as an enclitic. The evidence from (62) makes the second hypothesis more attractive.

The representation in (65) summarizes the structure of 1/2Pron-N, where the feature combination of Person and Determiner is spelled out as a person pronoun.

(65) [$_{DP}$ Person D [$_{NumP}$ Num [$_{nP}$ n [$_{NP}$ N]]]] 1/2Pron-N

Finally, I turn to full pronouns. Given that they are analysed as DPs on par with 1/2Pron-N, the question is to understand which property distinguishes person pronouns from pronominal demonstratives in 1/2Pron-N. As shown in (57), person pronouns in Georgian are strong emphatic elements, easily pro-dropped. They are felicitously employed in all contexts where only strong pronouns are expected cross-linguistically: deictically, accompanied by gestural pointing, in focus positions, as answers (66) and in coordination structures (67):

(66) Q: vin   ici-s   sad   aris zaza?
        who know-Pres.3SG where is   Zaza.NOM
        'who knows where is Zaza?'
     A: me!/ čven !
        'I! / we!'

(67) nino   da   šen   x-ar-t   mosKov-ši
     Nino.NOM and you   2-be-PL   Moscow-in
     'You and Nino are in Moscow'

I propose that DPs containing the demonstrative pronominal determiner and 1/2P pronoun only differ in the valency of D: in pronouns, D is intransitive (68), whereas in 1/2Pron-N, D is transitive and selects the nominal complement NumP, (65).

(68) [$_{DP}$ [Person] D] 1/2Pron

An optional instantiation of the nominal layer in the structures of 1/2PA is allowed because the feature inventory of the local D-domain modified by Person is rich enough in order to refer to an argument in the clause. In the case of the 1st person singular pronoun, Person only carries the feature [speaker] which is added to the denotational index of D: the speaker *is* the definite argument in the sentence. The similar mechanism holds for the 2nd person singular pronoun. As for 1/2P plural pronouns, Person, specified for the number feature, and D contribute the necessary and sufficient information in order to identify a discourse salient group (i.e. non-atomic entity) that includes the speech-act participant. If we return to the list of person pronouns in (61) we observe that 1st person plural and 2nd person plural pronouns share the phoneme –v-. This fact can be thought as irrelevant for the morphosyntax of pronominal forms, but interestingly the same pattern of behaviour, where the 1st and 2nd person pronouns are morphologically maximally identical, is observed in other South Caucasian languages: in Svan: 1pl *næj*, 2pl *sgæj* (Tuite 1998), in Megrelian 1pl *čki/čkə*, 2pl *tkva*. And finally, it is significant to note that the morpheme *v*- spells an indefinite animate individual in interrogative and indefinite pronouns *v-in* 'who', *v-inme, v-igac* 'someone'. I hypothesize that the morphological representation of 1/2P plural pronouns in Georgian transparently spells out the number feature too and should be rather considered tri-morphemic consisting of the participant morpheme, number morpheme, and the definite index: *č-v-en, tk- v-en*.[13]

When D selects NumP, a singleton or a group gets the definite index. If D selects a singleton set it cannot be specified by 1st singular person: an expression referring to some nominal class cannot simultaneously grammatically denote the speech-act participant. In such cases, the language has recourse to the apposition structure *I, the linguist*.[14] But when D marks plural sets with the index, the number specification of 1/2 plural persons, whose range is only partially specified or saturated, matches the number of the definite group. The unsaturated number value of Person, fleshed out by the morpheme –v- in the pronoun, is fully valued by the same feature of Number. In other words, in *we linguists*, the unspecified set of individuals [other(s)] that are added to the speaker in the denotation of the 1P plural [$_{we}$I+other(s)] is identified as the individuals which NumP ranges over: [other(s)]=[$_{Num}$Plinguists]. To put differently, [class] features are incompatible with [speaker/addressee] in Georgian, unless the latter are embedded under the number feature in Person.

To summarize, 1/2Pron-N and 1/2Pron are DPs specified by Person, and 1/2P-N is NumP specified by Person. The role of Person varies in DPs and NumPs. In DPs, Person is deictic, akin to the demonstrative determiner in definite descriptions. In NumPs, Person is partitive because it identifies one member of the set as

---

[13] Typologically, the same phenomenon is widely attested, e.g. *nos-ostros, vos-ostros*, in Spanish. (Vassilieva and Larson 2005, Torrego and Laka 2015).

[14] Interestingly, if the singular definite description is not formally a referring expression, as in the case of epithets, specifying it with Person yields a grammatical outcome:

i) me meTicara-m v-tkvi is
   I bragger-ERG 1-say.AOR that.NOM
   'I bragger said that'

Notice further that epithets are illicit in 1/2P-N, as they may not function as quantified expressions.

the speech act participant. The fact that the Person (in combination with D) is pronounced in DPs as a pronoun but not in NumPs can be ascribed to the blending of number features of plural Person and the head of NumP, which bans their double spellout.

4.2 Interim conclusion

In this section, I presented an analysis of 1/2Pron, 1/2Pron-N and 1/2P-N in Georgian, which share the property of triggering person agreement on the verb. I showed that this agreement results from Agree relation between T and Person present in the three types of nominals. The presence of Person does not affect or determine the structural size or identity of these nominals, it is merged in the specifier of DP in 1/2Pron and 1/2Pron-N and in the specifier of NumP in 1/2P-N. Out of the three nominal types, only 1/2Pron are not marked for case. The only other property that sets 1/2Pron aside from both 1/2Pron-N and 1/2P-N is the absence of the nominal structure. I correlate these two properties and argue that the absence of case on 1/2Pron is due to the absence of the nominal layer in their structure. The question that we must address now is why the nominal layer *can* be absent in some types of 1/2PA, namely in 1/2Pron, but must be present in 3P pronouns. In order to elucidate this issue, a closer investigation of the properties of 3P pronouns is in order. I show in Section 5 that 3P pronouns share strong indexicality with 1/2P pronouns and must be analysed as DPs. The deictic and phi-feature content of 1/2Pron is provided by Person in the D-domain, making it possible to dispense with the nominal complement of D. On the other hand, the spatial deictic information in 3P pronouns as well as their necessary phi-features are located in the nominal layer, making it impossible to sever the complement of D. Hence, obligatory case-marking of 3P pronouns is the direct consequence of their internal structure which must include the nominal layer below D.

5 Structure of 3P pronouns

In this section, I present an account of person-split which hinges on the presence of the nominal layer in the structural representations of pronominal arguments in Georgian. The conclusion reached in the last section is that 1/2P pronouns are not case-marked because they are headed by intransitive D. As 3P pronouns *are* case-marked, the question arises as to why they cannot be structured as 1/2P pronouns. If the absence of the nominal referent is the property that unites all the pronouns, 3P pronouns are also expected to be headed by intransitive D (cf. Abney 1987). In what follows, I show that the intransitivity of D cannot be the unifying feature of all pronouns in Georgian. 3P pronouns are derived from demonstrative determiners, which is a widely attested crosslinguistic strategy of pronoun formation, but in Georgian a morphologically reduced nominal structure is not elided after the demonstrative determiner in cases of pronominalisation. Its presence in 3P pronouns is obligatory as it provides to the demonstrative determiner the necessary phi-features, and most significantly the number and the class features, enabling the resulting pronominal constituent to function as a phi-complete argument.

5.1 3P pronouns and demonstrative determiners

Georgian 3P pronouns, just as 1/2P pronouns, are strong emphatic elements that can be easily dropped when their referent is familiar in discourse.[15] Unsurprisingly, they disallow, just like their 1/2P counterparts, boundvariable readings (cf. Section 3.4.).[16]

(69) marTo vano-s ga=axsend-a rom man nax-a
 only Vano-DAT prev=recall-AOR.3SG that 3SG.ERG see-AOR.3SG
 es pilm-i
 this film-NOM
 'Only Vano recalled that he saw this film'
 ≠ no one else recalled that they saw this film
 =no one else recalled that Vano saw the film

Georgian has a number of 3P pronouns, some of which belong to the written literary register and others used in colloquial and dialectal registers. The leftmost

---

15 Although 3P pronouns can be easily dropped in Georgian, they are obligatory in donkey anaphora contexts, in line with the analysis of these constructions by Elbourne (2005) that takes pronouns to stand for deictic definite descriptions.

(i) q'ovel-i Kac-i vis-ac vir-i h-qav-s
 every-NOM man-NOM who.DAT-rel donkey-NOM 3-have-PRES.3SG
 *(ma-s) xsirad (s)cem-s
 it-ACC often 3-beat-PRES.3SG
 'Every man who owns a donkey often beats it'.

16 The bound reading of 3P pronouns becomes easier to obtain if the pronoun is formally defocalised in the sense that it occurs with another focalised constituent.

pronoun given for each case in (70) corresponds to the most standard form. 3P pronouns are not specified for gender and only show number and case distinctions. As (70) shows, most singular pronouns are distinctly marked for case (-*i* for nominative, -*n* for ergative, and –*s* for dative/accusative), while plural pronouns *all* contain plural markers –*n*, -*t*, which are archaic markers not productive any more to pluralise nouns in modern Georgian. We also observe that in some plural forms the case- affix syncretises with the plural affix in ergative and accusative, *ma-t*. Importantly, 3P pronouns that have *mag* as their base systematically show distinct case and number morphemes for every form in the paradigm.

(70) THIRD PERSON PRONOUNS
	SG	PL
	3-(Case)	3-Num(-)/(,)Case
NOM	is, ig-i, mag-i	is-in-i, mag-en-i
ERG	(i)ma-n, mag-an	(i)ma-t, (i)ma-t-ma, mag-at-ma
ACC/DAT	(i)ma-s, mag-as	(i)ma-t, mag-at

3P pronouns are clearly derived from demonstrative determiners, as shown in (71):

(71) DEMONSTRATIVE DETERMINERS
NOM **es** ekim-i/ekim-eb-I
this(here) doctor-NOM/doctor-pl-NOM
eg/mag ekim-i/ekim-eb-i
this(there) doctor-NOM/doctor-pl-NOM
is/ig ekim-i/ekim-eb-i
that doctor-NOM/doctor-pl-NOM
ERG **am** ekim-ma/ekim-eb-ma this(here)
doctor-ERG/doctor-pl-ERG
mag ekim-ma/ekim-eb-ma
this(there) doctor-ERG/doctor-pl-ERG
im ekim-ma/ekim-eb-ma
that doctor-ERG/doctor-pl-ERG
ACC **am** ekim-s/ekim-eb-s
this(here) doctor-ACC /doctor-pl-ACC
mag ekim-s/ekim-eb-s
this(there) doctor- ACC /doctor-pl-ACC
im ekim-s/ekim-eb-s
that doctor-ACC/doctor-pl-ACC

Comparing the two tables, we observe that unlike pronouns, demonstrative determiners are never marked for number. As for case distinctions, they only distinguish between nominative and non-nominative forms. But even nominative demonstratives are not formally marked with the case affix -*i*: the demonstrative *mag* is invariable regardless of the case of the noun phrase, *ig* lacks the nominative –*i* when it functions as a demonstrative but not when it functions as a pronoun. To summarize, Georgian demonstrative determiners do not exhibit number agreement with the noun, nor strict case agreement.[17]

Although they are not decomposed in (71), demonstrative determiners are clearly bimorphemic: they comprise the deictic morpheme *a/e-*, *ma-*, *i-*, (proximal, medial, distal, respectively) and the suffix *-g* (*-s* in nominative contexts, *-m* in non-nominative contexts). I take *-g* and its allomorphs to spell the determiner base. Notice also that in certain Western dialects of Georgian, *-g*, or *-s*, can be dropped in demonstratives.

(72) a. ra   u-nd-od-a,   **ma** dedakal-s?
  what.NOM APPL-want-IMPERF.3SG that woman-DAT
  'What did that (here) woman want?'
 b. **i** Kac-i   rodis mova?
  that man-NOM when come.FUT.3SG
  'When will that (there) man come?'

5.2 Differences between pronominal and demonstrative determiners

The decomposition of demonstratives reveals that their internal makeup resembles that of pronominal demonstratives in 1/2Pron-N: both types contain a D-index and a deictic morpheme that anchors the referential expression in the speech-act situation. Deictic affixes in (71) spatially relate the discourse referent to the speaker or the addressee. Proximal deictic specification *a/e-* stands for 'near the speaker', medial *m(a)-* for 'near the addressee', and distal *i-* reflects 'not near the speech participants'. The same morphemes are used to form demonstrative adverbs: *a-k* 'here', *ma-k* 'there-proximal', *i-k* 'there-distal'.[18] This

---

[17] In Old Georgian, demonstrative determiners were postnominal and fully agreed with noun in case and in number.
[18] It is worth noting that nominative and ergative case-endings –*i* and –*ma* are homophonous with distal and medial deictic morphemes. This similarity could point to the spatial/deictic source of case distinctions in Georgian. It can be hypothesized that the nominative marks the

parallelism between pronominal determiners and demonstrative determiners begs the following question: why can 1/2P pronouns and pronominal demonstratives share the form while 3P pronouns and standard demonstratives, albeit morphologically related, have different forms? Notice that both 1/2P pronouns and pronominal demonstratives show number distinctions, in fact pronominal demonstratives are felicitous only when they are plural. As for 3P pronouns and demonstrative determiners, only the former is marked for number. I take this property, namely the absence of number distinction in standard demonstratives, to be the source of structural asymmetry between pronominal demonstratives and demonstrative determiners. The deictic component in 3P demonstratives denotes place, which conceptually is insensitive of number, while the deictic component in pronominal demonstratives, Person, is inherently specified for number in plural persons. As a consequence, when a demonstrative determiner is pronominalized, the absence of number specification at D-level requires the presence its complement NumP, whereas when a pronominal determiner is pronominalised, Person provides number features to D heading pronominal determiners, rendering superfluous the presence of D's complement.

There is a long tradition in linguistic theorizing that views demonstratives as adjectival elements (Bernstein 1997, Elbourne 2005, Giusti 1994, 1997, Bruge 1996). Giusti, among others, argues that demonstratives are generated low in the nominal structure as adjectival modifiers and move to the left periphery, above D. Leu (2007), endorsing the low generation analysis of demonstratives, considers their meaning to be built from the abstract (and silent) locative adjective *HERE*. I follow these analyses and take the deictic locative markers *a-/e-, ma-, i-* to flesh out the concept of *HERE* and to function structurally as adjectival predicates. They move from the nominal domain to the left periphery of D, and the result of their merger yields a demonstrative determiner that has both adjectival and determiner properties.

---

argument which is distal to the speech-situation and the ergative the closer one. Notice also that in Old Georgian, the ergative marker was *-man*, which in Modern Georgian is homophonous to the ergative 3P pronoun. So if case affixes are fundamentally spatial-deictic in Georgian, it is expected not to find them on 1/2P pronouns which are intrinsitically person-deictic. The present analysis formalizes this intuition by claiming that person deixis and spatial deixis have different mutually exclusive sources, the former is directly merged in the upper functional domain of the argument, while the latter has its source lower, in the nominal layer. Notice that the spatial/deictic part of the English determiner *th-* may be at heart of its incompatibility with the pronominal determiner, yielding ungrammatical **we the linguists*, in contrast with their Spanish or Greek homologues (cf. (64)).

(73) a. [_DP_ *HERE*+D [_NumP_ Num [_nP_ n [_ADJ_ ~~HERE~~][_NP_N]]
    b. ***HERE*+D—>ma-g, i-g, e-s**. ...

5.3 Adjectives in NP ellipsis and 3P pronouns

Indeed, demonstrative determiners and adjectives have many properties in common: both are prenominal, both disallow number agreement with the noun (74), and both show deficient
    case agreement. Examples in (75) show that case agreement is required in nominative, optional in spoken Georgian in ergative, and banned in accusative. Furthermore, all case- agreement is banned when the adjective ends in a vowel, (76).

(74) *tbil-eb-i   Pur-eb-i/   *tbil-eb-ma   Pur-eb-ma /
     warm-pl-NOM bread-NOM/ warm-pl-ERG bread-pl-ERG/
     *tbil-eb-s   Pur-eb-s
     warm-pl-ACC bread-pl-ACC
     'warm breads'

(75) NOM: tbil-*(i) Pur(-eb)-i
     ERG: tbil(-ma) Pur(-eb)-ma
     ACC: tbil-(*s) Pur(-eb)-s
     'warm bread(s)'

(76) axalgazrda(*-i/*-m/*-s) ekim(-eb)-i/-ma/-s
     young-NOM/ERG/ACC doctor-pl-NOM/ERG/ACC
     'young doctor(s)'

In NP ellipsis (NPE) environments, adjectives exhibit an entirely different behaviour, where they mandatorily carry number and case markers, (77–78).

(77) moxuc(-ma) ekim-ma   tkv-a   es,   *axalgazrd-eb-ma*
     old-ERG   doctor-ERG say-AOR.3SG this.NOM   young-pl-ERG
     Ki   ara
     yes   no
     'The old doctor said this, not the young ones'

(78) Q: am   kab-eb-idan   romel-i-a   nino-s-i?
       this dress-pl-from which-NOM-be.3SG Nino-GEN-NOM
       'From these dresses, which one is Nino's?'
   A: *tetr-i/*   *tetr-eb-i*
       white-NOM/ white-pl-NOM
       'The white one. / The white ones.'

On the basis of a cross-linguistic comparison of NPE configurations, Lobeck (1995) proposes that languages such as French can license a phonologically empty NP after fully inflected adjectives, while languages such as English, with uninflected adjectives, have recourse to the pronominalisation strategy and employ the pro-noun *one*. (cf. Postal 1969, Panagiotidis 2003a,b, Kayne 2003). What is interesting about Georgian is that it stands somewhere in between the two language-types with respect to NPE: adjectives do show rich case and number agreement, but this agreement *only* occurs on adjectives in NPE contexts. I propose that Georgian employs the English-style pronominalisation strategy in NPE, yet unlike English, the grammatical counterpart of *one* is a morphologically deficient enclitic The enclitic comprises of a null nominal categorizer *n* endowed with class feature and a number morpheme: *n* moves to Number and the resulting *n*-Num cliticizes to the adjective. (Cf. Corver and van Koppen 2011). In this respect, what is lacking in NPE contexts in Georgian is the nominal root that provides the name to the class identified by the categorizer *n*, (79).

(79) ([$_{DP}$D) [$_{NumP}$ [$_{ADJ}$tetr] *n*-Num [$_{nP}$ [$_{ADJ}$tetr] *n*-[$_{NP}$ √N$_{ø}$]]()
     tetr-ø-eb-ma [$_{NP}$√N$_{ø}$]

(80) white-*n*-pl-ERG
     '(the) white ones'

The feature makeup of adjectives in NPE contexts as in (80) is quasi identical to that of 3P pronouns in (70). In order to refer to plural antecedents, the number marking is obligatory in both types, as the italicised forms show in (81a–b).

(81) a. did bavšv-eb-ma   es   pilm-i   mosKov-si nax-es
        big child-pl-ERG this film-NOM Moscow-in see-AOR.3PL
        PaTar-eb-ma   Ki   Kiev-ši
        small-pl-ERG yes Kiev-in
        'The big children saw this film in Moscow but the *small ones* in Kiev'
    b. mag bavšv-eb-ma   es   pilm-i   mosKov-ši nax-es

that child-pl-ERG this film-NOM Moscow-in see-AOR.3PL
im-at-ma Ki Kiev-ši
DEM-pl-ERG yes Kiev-in
'These children saw this film in Moscow but *those ones/they* in Kiev'[19]

Georgian 3P pronouns are derived from demonstrative determiners in the similar manner as adjectives in NPE constructions, the only difference being that instead of the lexical adjective in (80) or (81a), the demonstrative determiner resulting from the merger of the deictic *HERE* and D hosts the pronominal enclitic comprised of the classifier *n* and Num (82–83).

(82) [$_{DP}$**HERE**+D [$_{NumP}$ **n+Num** [$_{NP}$ [$_{ADJ}$~~HERE~~] ~~n~~ [$_{NP}$~~√N$_{ø}$~~]]]

(83) ma-[g-ø-at]-ma [$_{NP}$~~√N$_{ø}$~~]
HERE-D-n-pl-ERG
'they'

Georgian 3P pronouns are 'one-word' renditions of English demonstratives in NPE contexts *this/that one*. The difference between English and Georgian lies in the locus of number features: in English, the demonstrative and the pro-noun agree in number: *these ones*; in Georgian, the number is uniformly carried by the pro-nominal part and does not spread to the demonstrative. In this respect, Georgian shows more parallelism between adjectives and demonstratives in NPE contexts than English, where plural agreement is allowed for demonstratives but not for adjectives.

5.4 Nominal structure of 3P pronouns

At this point, we are able to provide an answer to the question in the beginning of this section: why does the structural representation of 1/2P pronouns contain an intransitive D, which is the property responsible for the absence of their case-marking, while 3P pronouns must contain a transitive D and hence be case-marked? Recall that Person in 1/2P pronouns is generated in Spec,DP and supplies to D-domain a deictic speech act participant feature, and additional

---

19 In (81b), the italicized form *imatma* is ambiguous between a demonstrative in NPE and a pronoun; it can refer to another contextually salient group of children, or to any group, not necessarily made up of children.

number information, in case of plural pronouns. This constitutes, with the definite index on D, all the necessary and sufficient information to form a referentially dependent expression which can function as an argument in a clause, i.e. a pronoun. D therefore need not take a complement in such contexts as all the above-mentioned features are generated and retrieved *above* D.

In 3P pronouns, no structure is generated higher than D. Unlike Person in 1/2P pronouns, the deictic specification in 3P pronouns comes from the nominal layer, in the guise of the adjectival spatial *HERE*. This element is not endowed with any feature other than its categorial adjectival feature and spatial content. Importantly, unlike Person, it is not specified for the necessary phi-features to identify the referent previously mentioned in the discourse. While 3P pronouns do not carry person features, they show number distinctions (the concept of grammatical gender is not instantiated in Georgian). Grammatical number must by definition apply to a class of entities, as it is impossible to quantify vacuously. 3P pronouns refer to singular or plural classes of entities but omit their lexical content (*book* vs. *girl* vs. *computer*). Following insights of Bernstein (1993), Alexiadou and Gengel (2011) and Borer (2005), I propose that among phi-features that a 3P pronoun must be endowed with in a language which differentiates between plural and singular pronouns, the most crucial ones are number and class, as the former entails the latter. The loci for these features are n and Num, respectively, which renders the presence of the nominal layer, complement of D, mandatory in 3P pronouns.

Coming back to the main objective of this work – the analysis of person split – I conclude that the phenomenon under study can receive a structural explanation in Georgian and is conditioned by the presence of the nominal layer in the structural representation of pronominal arguments. When this layer is instantiated, in all referential expressions, in 3P pronouns, and in a subclass of 1/2PA (1/2Pron-N and 1/2P-N), the argument is marked with case. When the layer is not instantiated, in 1/2P pronouns, the argument appears without case-marking. Hence, even if the actual spelling of (ergative) case-marking is a matter of morphology, in line with Legate's (2014) conclusion, it remains strictly conditioned by the structural representation of (pro)nominal expressions. In this sense, the role of morphology is to interpret the structure, rather than to explain it.

6 Conclusion

At the outset of the present work, three questions were formulated concerning the phenomenon of person split:

(i) Is the case-shift motivated by structural differences of clauses with 1/2PA and 3PA?
(ii) Is person split a more superficial phenomenon that has no structural source? Is the ergative morphological marking incompatible with certain feature specifications of 1/2PA?
(iii) Can person split receive a unitary explanation in languages where it is manifested?

The conclusions of the present analysis of Georgian person split offer the affirmative answer to (i). Yes, caseless 1/2PA, namely 1/2P pronouns, are the only argument type that lack the nominal layer in their structural representation and are headed by intransitive D. As morphological case in Georgian only marks *nominal* arguments, the absence of all case marking is expected on 1/2P pronouns. This conclusion is very different from many previous attempts of person split that located the source of the split in the differences of *clause* architecture between sentences that contain speech-act participants and those that don't. The present analysis identifies the source of the division in the structural representation of the (pro)nominal arguments themselves. Another important conclusion has emerged from the present analysis: the division of argument types into expressions referring to speech act participants and expressions that refer to any other type of event participants is not warranted in order to account for person-split. We saw that some arguments, such as 1/2Pron-N and 1/2P-N, refer to speech-act participants, by virtue of inclusion of Person in their structural representation, but they are marked for case. What determines the presence of case on the argument is not its semantic-pragmatic type or its discourse role but rather its *structure*: if Person cohabitates in the same maximal projection with the nominal layer, the argument will be marked for case.

The answer to (ii) is more nuanced. Clearly, case-marking in Georgian is sensitive to the presence of the nominal structure in the argument. If one has to consider the issue from the point of view of feature (in)compatibility, it is true that case-marking is sensitive to the nominal feature [class]. When this feature is included in the overall representation of an argument, case-marking follows. Generally, the feature [class] is non-separable from [number], especially for common nouns that are divisible and countable. However, [number] can be intrinsically associated with [participant] in the same feature bundle, Person, in Georgian, as we have seen for plural persons. Therefore, the key factor that repels case- marking is the absence of [class] feature (provided by *n*) on an argument.

Finally, the answer to (iii) is yes and no. I have identified the source of case-marking to reside in the nominal domain of arguments, and more concretely in the categorizer *n*, which I take to be valid for every language.

However, careful investigation of (pro)nominal systems is necessary in order to account for person split. Cardinaletti and Starke (1999) and Déchaine and Wiltschko (2002) convincingly argue that pronouns are not structurally built in the same fashion cross-linguistically. Georgian pronouns are strong emphatic elements that disallow bound variable readings, which entails that they are DPs. But there are languages where all person pronouns are NPs, e.g. Japanese (cf. Déchaine and Wiltschko 2002). It is an open issue to understand how the same category Noun (or *n*) can host both [participant] and [class] feature which as we saw were distributed on different categories in Georgian. But the present analysis makes a prediction that an ergative language where pronouns are structured as NPs, as in Japanese, will not be sensitive to person split and will mark all (pro)nominal arguments in the same fashion.

On a more general note, recent attempts have been made to account for ergative splits and for the division of language systems into ergative and nominative types in terms of structural complexity (Laka 2006, Coon and Preminger 2012, Nash 2017). These authors have differently arrived at the conclusion that complex (in terms of the number of functional projections) functional architecture of the clause above the lexical domain guarantees its nominative status. Nash (2017) shows that the impoverishment of the functional spine between vP and TP shifts Georgian from the nominative type into the ergative type. The conclusions of the present analysis of person split in Georgian resonate with the logic of the structural complexity accounts of ergative splits. The more complex is the functional structure above D, as in 1/2PA in Georgian where Person is merged, the higher is the probability that the argument can dispense with the nominal lexical component *below* D and surface without ergative case. Yet when an argument is headed (i) by D that needs the nominal complement from which to draw the deictic material and the phi-features, or (ii) by any category lower than D, along the functional hierarchy D>Num>*n*>N, the ergative case will surface.

References

Abney, Steven. 1987. *The English noun phrase in its sentential aspect*. MIT dissertation.
    Ackema, Peter and Ad Neeleman. 2013. Subset Controllers in Agreement Relations. *Morphology* 23: 291–323.
Ackema, Peter, and Ad Neeleman. 2013. Subset controllers in agreement relations. Morphology 23.2: 291–323.
Alexiadou, Artemis and Elena Anagnostopoulou. 2006. From hierarchies to features. In: Boeckx, C. (Ed.), *Agreement Systems*. John Benjamins, Amsterdam, 41–62

Alexiadou, Artemis and Kirsten Gengel. 2011. Classifiers as morphosyntactic licensors of NP ellipsis: English vs. Romance. *Proceedings of NELS* 39, 15–28

Baker, Mark. 2014. On dependent ergative case (in Shipibo) and its derivation by phase. *Linguistic Inquiry* 45: 3.

Baker, Mark, and Vinokurova, Nadezhda. 2010. Two modalities of case assignment in Sakha. *Natural Language and Linguistic Theory* 28: 593–642.

Béjar, Susana. 2003. *Phi-syntax: a Theory of Agreement*. Ph.D dissertation. University of Toronto.

Béjar, Susana and Milan Rezac. 2009. Cyclic Agree. *Linguistic Inquiry* 40: 35–73.

Benveniste, Émile. 1966. *Problèmes de linguistique générale*. Paris: Gallimard.

Bernstein, Judith. 1993. *Topics in the syntax of nominal structure across Romance*. Ph.D. Dissertation, CUNY.

Bernstein, Judy. 1997. Demonstratives and reinforcers in Romance and Germanic languages. *Lingua* 102:87–113.

Bianchi, Valentina. 2003. On the Syntax of Personal Arguments. Paper presented at the XXIX Incontro di Grammatica Generativa, Urbino, 13–15 February 2003.

Bobaljik, Jonathan. 2008. Where's Phi? Agreement as a post-syntactic operation. In *Phi Theory: Phi Features Across Interfaces and Modules*, eds. David Adger, Daniel Harbour and Susanna Béjar, 295–328. Oxford: Oxford University Press.

Borer, Hagit. 2005. *In Name only*. Oxford: Oxford University Press.

Bruge, Laura. 1996. Demonstrative movement in Spanish: A comparative approach.*University of Venice Working Papers in Linguistics* 1–53.

Cardinaletti, Anna, and Michal Starke. 1999. The typology of structural deficiency: A case study of three classes of pronouns. In *Clitics in the languages of Europe*, ed. by Henk van Riemsdijk, 145–233. Berlin: Mouton.

Choi, Jaehoon. 2014. The locus of person feature and agreement. In Hsin-Lun Huang, Ethan Poola and Amanda Rysling (eds.), NELS 43: Proceedings of the 43rd meeting of the North East Linguistic Society, 65–76. Amherst (MA): GLSA.

Coon, Jessica, and Omer Preminger. 2012. Towards a unified account of person splits. In: *Proceedings of the 29th West Coast Conference on Formal Linguistics*, 310–318. http://www.lingref.com/cpp/wccfl/29/paper2716.pdf

Corver, Norbert and Marjo van Koppen. 2011. NP-ellipsis with adjectival remnants: a microcomparative perspective. *Natural Language and Linguistic Theory*, 29(2): 371–421.

D'Alessandro, Roberta. 2012. Merging Probes. A typology of person splits and person-driven differential object marking. Ms. LUCL Leiden. http://ling.auf.net/lingbuzz/001771

Deal, Amy Rose. 2016. Person-based split ergativity in Nez Perce is syntactic. *Journal of Linguistics*, 52(3), 533–564.

Déchaine, Rose-Marie and Martina Wiltschko. 2002. Decomposing pronouns. *Linguistic Inquiry* 33(3): 409–442.

Déchaine, Rose-Marie and Martina Wiltschko. 2015. When and why can 1st and 2nd person pronouns be bound variables? In Patrick Grosz, Pritty Patel-Grosz and Igor Yanovich (eds.), *The semantics of pronouns*. Proceedings of the special session of the 40th North East Linguistics Society, 1–50. GLSA.

D'hulst, Yves, Coene, Martine, and Liliane Tasmowski. 2007. The Romance vocativeand the DP hypothesis. In: A. Cunita, C. Lupu and L. Tasmowski (eds), *Studii de lingvistica si filologie romanica. Hommages offerts à Sanda Reinheimer Rîpeanu*, 200–211. Bucharest: Editura Universitatii din Bucuresti.

Dixon, R.M.W. 1994. *Ergativity*. Cambridge: Cambridge University Press.
Elbourne, Paul. 2005. *Situations and individuals*. Cambridge (MA): MIT Press. Emonds, Joseph. 1985. *A unified theory of syntactic categories*. Dordrecht: Foris. Harbour, Daniel. 2011. Valence and Atomic Number. *Linguistic Inquiry* 42, 561–594.
Harbour, Daniel. 2011. Valence and atomic number." Linguistic inquiry 42(4): 561–594.
Harley, Heidi, and Elizabeth Ritter. 2002. Person and number in pronouns: A feature-geometric analysis. *Language* 78 (3): 482–526.
Hurtado, Alfredo. 1985. The unagreement hypothesis. In *Selected papers from the thirteenth linguistic symposium on Romance languages*, eds. L. King and C. Maley, 187–211.Amsterdam: John Benjamins.
Garrett, Andrew. 1990). The origin of NP split ergativity, *Language* 66 :1990 :261–296
Georgi, Doreen. 2013. A Relativized Probing Approach to Person Encoding in LocalScenarios, *Linguistic Variation* 12(2): 153–210.
Giusti, Giuliana. 1994. Enclitic articles and double definiteness: A comparative analysis of nominal structure in Romance and Germanic. *Linguistic Review*, 11(3–4): 241–255.
Giusti, Giuliana. 1997. The categorial status of determiners. In *The New Comparative Grammar*, ed. L. Haegeman, 95–123. New York: Longman.
Halle, Morris, and Alec Marantz. 1993. Distributed Morphology and the pieces of inflection. In *The view from Building 20: Essays in linguistics in honor of Sylvain Bromberger*, ed. by Kenneth Hale and Samuel Jay Keyser, 111–176. Cambridge, MA: MIT Press.
Heim, Irene and Angelika Kratzer. 1998. *Semantics in generative grammar*. Oxford: Blackwell.
Höhn, Georg. 2016. Unagreement is an illusion. Natural Language & Linguistic Theory 34.2: 543–592.
Jelinek, Eloise. 1993. Ergative "splits" and argument type. In: Bobaljik, J.D., Phillips, C. (Eds.), Papers on Case and Agreement I. MITWPL, Cambridge, MA. MIT Working Papers in Linguistics 18., pp. 15–42. MIT Working Papers in Linguistics 18.
Kayne, Richard. 2003. Silent years, silent hours. In: *Grammar in Focus. Festschrift for Christer Platzack*, vol 2, eds. Lars-Olaf Delsing et al, 209–226. Lund: Wallin and Dalholm.
Koppen, Marjo van. 2012. The distribution of phi-features in pronouns. *Natural Language and Linguistic Theory*, 30(1),135–177.
Laka, Itziar. 2006. Deriving split ergativity in the progressive: the case of Basque. In *Ergativity: emerging issues*, eds. Alana Johns, Diane Massam and Juvenal Ndayiragije, 173–196. Dordrecht: Kluwer Academic Publishers.
Legate, Julie. 2014. Split ergativity based on nominal type. *Lingua* 148 (2014) 183–212.
Leu, Thomas. 2007. These HERE demonstratives. *University of Pennsylvania WorkingPapers in Linguistics*: Vol. 13: Iss. 1, Article 12.
Lobeck, Anne. 1995. *Ellipsis*. Oxford: Oxford University Press.
Longobardi, Giuseppe. 1994. Reference and proper names: a theory of N-movement in syntax and logical form. *Linguistic Inquiry* 25.4: 609–665.
Manzini, Maria Rita. 2015. On the substantive primitives of morphosyntax and their parametrization: Northern Italian subject clitics. In: Marc van Oosterdorp, Henk van Riemsdijk. *Representing structure in phonology and syntax*, 167–194 Mouton De Gruyter.
Manzini, Maria Rita, and Leonardo Savoia. 1998. I Clitics and auxiliary choice in Italian dialects: Their relevance for the Person ergativity split. Recherches linguistiques de Vincennes, (27), 115–138.

Manzini, Maria Rita, and Leonardo Savoia. 2005. *I dialetti italiani e romanci. Morfosintassi generativa*. Alessandria: Edizioni dell'Orso, 3 vols.

Marantz, Alec. 1991. Case and licensing. In *Proceedings of the 8th Eastern States Conference on Linguistics (ESCOL 1)*, eds. German Westphal, Benjamin Ao and Hee-Rahk Chae, Ithaca, NY: CLC Publications, 58–68.

Martirosov. A. 1964. nacvalsaxeli kartvelur enebsi [Pronouns in the Kartvelian Languages]. Publishing House of the Academy of Sciences of the Georgian Soviet Socialist Republic, Tbilisi. (in Georgian).

Merchant, Jason. 2006. Polyvalent case, geometric hierarchies, and split ergativity. In: *Proceedings of the 42nd Annual Meeting of the Chicago Linguistics Society*.

Müller, Gereon. 2004. Argument encoding and the order of elementary operations. Ms. IDS Mannheim. Presented at the 27th GLOW Colloquium in Thessaloniki, Greece.

Nash, Léa. 1995. *Portée argumentale et marquage casuel dans les langues SOV et dansles langue ergatives: l'exemple du géorgian*. Thèse de Doctorat, Université de Paris VIII.

Nash, Léa. 1997. La partition personnelle dans les langues ergatives. In Anne Zribi-Hertz (ed.), *Les pronoms: morphologie, syntaxe et typologie*. Saint-Denis: Presses Universitaires de Vincennes.

Nash, Léa. 2017. On the structural source of split ergativity and ergative case in Georgian. In *Oxford handbook of ergativity*, eds. Jessica Coon, Diane Massam and Lisa Travis, Oxford: Oxford University Press.

Nash-Haran, Léa. 1993. La catégorie AGR et l'accord en géorgien. *Recherches Linguistiques* 21: 65–79.

Panagiotidis, Phoevos. 2003a. One, Empty Nouns and Theta Assignment. *Linguistic Inquiry* 34: 281–292.

Panagiotidis Phoevo. 2003b. Empty Nouns. *Natural Language and Linguistic Theory* 21: 381–432.

Postal, Paul. 1969. On so-called pronouns in English. In: *Modern studies in English*, eds. David Reibel and Sanford Schane, 201–223, Prentice-Hall, Englewood Cliffs, N.J.

Ritter, Elizabeth. 1995. On the syntactic category of pronouns and agreement. *Natural Language and Linguistic Theory* 13: 405–443.

Silverstein, Michael. 1976. Hierarchies of features and ergativity. In: Dixon, R.M.W. (Ed.), *Grammatical Categories in Australian languages*. Humanities Press, New Jersey, pp. 112–171.

Sommerstein, Alan H. 1972. On the so-called definite article in English. *Linguistic Inquiry* 3: 197–209.

Torrego, Esther and Itziar Laka. 2015. The syntax of φ-features: Agreement with plural DPs in Basque and Spanish. In Fernández, B. and Salaburu, P. (Eds.). *Ibon Sarasola, Gorazarre. Homenatge, Homenaje*. Bilbao: UPV/EHU, 633–646.

Tuite, Kevin. 1998. *A short descriptive grammar of the Svan language*. Université de Montréal.

Vassilieva, Masha, and Richard Larson. 2005. The semantics of the plural pronoun construction. *Natural Language Semantics* 13(2): 101–24.

Wier, Thomas. 2011. *Georgian morphosyntax and feature hierarchies in natural language*, PhD Dissertation, University of Chicago.

Woolford, Ellen. 2006. Lexical case, inherent case, and argument structure. *Linguistic Inquiry* 37:111–130.

Ad Neeleman and Hans van de Koot
The non-existence of sub-lexical scope

1 Introduction

There is a body of literature that suggests that simplex causative verbs must be syntactically complex since they appear to allow modification of parts of their lexical semantics. In what follows we argue (i) that simplex causative verbs never allow modifiers to take scope over part of their lexical semantics, and (ii) that where scope appears to be sub-lexical, this is a consequence of the construction of a presupposition in which not all the material in the scope of a modifier is used.

There are two theories of causative verbs that we will consider. In the theory we advocate, the semantics of causation is contained in a single terminal (see, for example, Pinker (1989), Jackendoff (1990), and Rappaport Hovav and Levin (1998)). In the alternative theory, the semantics of causation is distributed across several syntactic heads (see, for example, Hale and Keyser (1993), Pylkkänen (2008), and Ramchand (2008)). Each of these theories comes in various flavours, depending on one's assumptions about the semantics of causation. It is most commonly assumed that causative events consist of a causing event, a process or become event, and a resultant state, which is the culmination of the become event. For concreteness sake, we adopt this standard assumption in what follows, although nothing hinges on this.[1] Thus, we will compare two proposals, one in which lexical verbs are simplex heads with

---

[1] We have elsewhere defended the view that causative verbs have very sparse semantics and lexically encode only a process and a culmination, enriched with an external argument (see Pietroski (2003, 2005) and Neeleman and Van de Koot (2012)).

Note: We are delighted to contribute to this volume in honour of our erstwhile colleague Rita Manzini. We remember Rita's time at UCL as highly stimulating, with conversations in which we agreed with her on all preliminary steps in an argument, but typically ended up with different conclusions. We suspect that the same would happen if we were to discuss lexical decomposition and therefore offer the material in this paper as a new area in which to test this generalization. We would like to thank an anonymous reviewer for useful comments that prompted a comprehensive revision of the first version of this paper. We would like to thank the editors for the invitation to contribute to this volume.

Ad Neeleman, Hans van de Koot, (UCL)

https://doi.org/10.1515/9781501505201-026

a semantics as in (1a) and one in which they are the amalgamation of three heads, as in (1b).[2]

(1) a. $[\![V_{cause}]\!] = \lambda y \, \lambda x \, \lambda e_m \, \exists e_1 \, \exists e_2 \, [e_m = \text{CAUSE}(e_1, e_2) \wedge \text{subject}(x, e_1)$
$\wedge \, e_2 = \text{BECOME}(\text{RESULT}(y))]$
b. $[_{\text{CAUSEP}} \, \text{DP CAUSE} \, [_{\text{BECOMEP}} \, \text{DP BECOME} \, [_{\text{RESULTP}} \, (\text{DP}) \, \text{RESULT}]]]$

On the standard assumption that adverbials modify the node to which they attach, the theories in (1a) and (1b) make very different predictions. The latter predicts that modification can in principle target three different constituents. An adjunct can be adjoined to CAUSEP, BECOMEP or RESULTP. By contrast, the theory in (1a) only allows modification of the causative verbs as a whole, which is equivalent to modification of CAUSEP under syntactic decomposition.

The problem we address in this paper is that neither of these theories seems correct. On the one hand, there is evidence from manner, locational and temporal adverbs suggesting that causative verbs should not be syntactically decomposed. On the other hand, there is evidence from presuppositional adverbs that does seem to require such decomposition. In particular, example (2) is ambiguous between a repeated action and a restitutive reading. (In the literature the former is sometimes referred to as the repetitive reading.) Of particular interest here is the restitutive reading, which seems to require that the adverbial modifies sub-lexical material.

(2) *John opened the window again.*
 i. Agent's action is repeated (repeated action reading)
  again (CAUSE (John, BECOME (OPEN (the window))))
 ii. Resultant state is restored (restitutive reading)
  CAUSE (John, BECOME (again (OPEN (the window)))))

In section 2 we review the evidence from non-presuppositional adverbs. We show that such adverbs are unable to modify sub-lexical material, as predicted by the

---

[2] To be sure, when we use the term 'simplex head' what we mean is a single base-generated X^0-category. This is not to deny that certain simplex causatives are derived from adjectives. We would analyze the verb *open*, for example, as a V^0-category that contains the A^0-category *open* and a silent suffix. This V^0-category is not derived by movement, but base-generated. Its argument structure is composed on the basis of the semantics of its parts, and in this composition the external argument variable of the adjective *open* becomes the internal argument variable of the verb. An analysis along these lines makes it possible to capture observed regularities in pairs like $open_A$-$open_V$ without the need for syntactic decomposition.

theory in (1a). Additional hypotheses that can capture these facts in a theory like (1b) also rule out a syntactic account of the restitutive reading of *again*.

In section 3 we reinterpret the data involving *again* in terms of a specific procedure by which a presupposition is constructed. On this reinterpretation, the theory in (1a) can capture the data. In fact, we will demonstrate that it provides more insight into the phenomenon of apparent sub-lexical scope than theories based on syntactic decomposition.

2 The scope of non-presuppositional modifiers

2.1 Manner modifiers

A well-known piece of evidence against the syntactic decomposition theory comes from manner modification (see Fodor (1970), Fodor and Lepore (1997), and Pylkkänen (2008)). In example (3a), John rather than Bill is associated with an action that takes place in a grumpy manner. This suggests that the syntactic structure of this example does not contain a constituent corresponding to an embedded become event "Bill become awake" that *grumpily* could take scope over. Yet, in (3b) and (3c), *grumpily* modifies the very event that cannot be targeted by manner modification in (3a) (see also Higginbotham (2000)).

(3) a. *John awoke Bill grumpily.*
    b. *Bill awoke grumpily.*
    c. *John caused Bill to awake grumpily.*

Similarly, in (4a) the GP rather than the patient is associated with an action that takes place in a dignified manner, while in (4b) and (4c) *in a dignified manner* modifies the become event that is apparently inaccessible in (4a).

(4) a. *The GP killed the patient in a dignified manner.*
    b. *The patient died in a dignified manner.*
    c. *The GP caused the patient to die in a dignified manner.*

None of the examples in (3) and (4) allows a reading involving modification of the state in which their event culminates. This is, however, less informative, since states seem to resist manner modification:

(5) a. **John was awake grumpily.*
    b. **The patient was dead in a dignified manner.*

2.2 Locational modifiers

We next turn to data involving locational modifiers. Consider the scenario in (6). What happened can be felicitously reported using (6a), but not using (6b). This suggests that (6b) does not contain a constituent corresponding to the become event "John died in UCLH" or a constituent corresponding to the state "John (is) dead in UCLH". Rather, the modifier scopes over a constituent that represents the entire causative semantics, but this does not fit the context. Yet, in (6c) and (6d), the locational modifier takes scope over the very event that it could not target in (6b). The examples in (6e, f) indicate that locational modification of the state "John (is) dead" is not altogether impossible. Their marginality is presumably due to *dead* being an individual-level predicate: if a person is dead in location X, then that person is dead anywhere. However, a reading of (6b) as "A roof tile caused John to undergo an event that culminated in his being dead in UCLH" must be unavailable, or the example would have a status comparable to (6f).

(6) [Context: John steps out of his house in Whetstone, north London, and gets hit on the head by a falling roof tile. An ambulance transports him to UCLH, a hospital in central London, where he dies.]
    a.   *A roof tile killed John in London.*
    b.   #*A roof tile killed John in UCLH.*
    c.   *John died in London.*
    d.   *John died in UCLH.*
    e.   ?*John was dead in London.*
    f.   ?*John was dead in UCLH.*

In the scenario we turn to next, we explore the use of a causative verb (namely *fill*) expressing a stage-level resultant state. This allows us to test the extent to which locational modification can reach into the lexical semantics of a causative verb. Suppose John uses a machine that fills buckets. It works as follows. One places an empty bucket on a circular moving track that runs from point A to points B, C and D and then back to collection point E (which is right next to point A). At points B, C, and D, a volume of water equal to 1/3 of the volume of the bucket is added. The full bucket then continues to point E for collection. A picture of the machine appears in (7). Now consider which of the examples (7a–d) can be used to talk about what happened when John has filled a bucket using this machine.

(7) LOCATION F

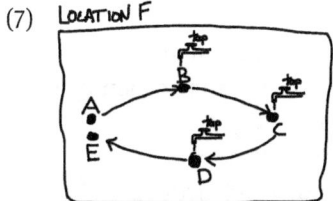

a. John filled the bucket in location F.
b. #John filled the bucket in location D.
c. The bucket filled in location D.
d. The bucket was full in location D.

The appropriateness of (7a) is unsurprising. The infelicity of (7b) is surprising on the decompositional approach, given that (7c) and (7d) are completely felicitous. It suggests that simplex causatives do not have an attachment site for locational modifiers at the level of the caused event or the resultant state, something which comes for free in non-decompositional theories.

2.3 Temporal modifiers

A considerably murkier picture presents itself when we turn to temporal modification of causatives and their unaccusative counterparts. Although we will not demonstrate this here, we believe that temporal adverbials cannot modify the process component of a simplex causative (much like what was demonstrated above for manner and locational modifiers). However, remarkably, temporal adverbials do seem to be able to modify the resultant state of such a verb. Thus, example (8a) has a reading on which the window was open for ten minutes as a result of John's actions, in addition to a less relevant reading on which John merely intended the window to be open for ten minutes (we ignore the repeated action reading, which is irrelevant to the present discussion). The unaccusative counterpart of (8a), given in (8b), lacks this 'intentionality' reading (which is unsurprising if the expression of intentionality requires the syntactic presence of a causer argument), but it apparently still allows modification of the resultant state: that is, on completion of the opening process, the window may stay open for ten minutes.

(8) a. *John opened the window for ten minutes.*
   (i) John caused the window to be open and the window stayed open for ten minutes.
   (ii) John opened the window with the intention for it to remain open for ten minutes.

b. *The window opened for ten minutes.*
   (i) The window opened and it stayed open for 10 minutes.
   (ii) *The window opened with the intention for it to remain open for ten minutes.

We put the 'intentionality' reading to one side for now and focus on the reading on which the window must actually be open for ten minutes for the sentence to be true.

As just mentioned, this reading appears to require modification of the end state of the verb *open*. However, the assumption that such modification is possible has unwanted consequences once it is combined with the widely-accepted view that the starting point of a become event is the negation of its culmination. Just like causative *open* describes a transition from "not open" to "open", *open for ten minutes* should describe a transition from "not open for ten minutes" to "open for ten minutes". But this reading is not available. What this modified verb describes is a transition from "not open" to "open for ten minutes". This is made clear by the infelicity of the examples in (9) in the contexts given.

(9) a. [Context: When we enter the room, we are informed that the window has been open for two minutes. Bill wants to close it, but John persuades him to leave it open. When a further eight minutes have passed, I say:]
   #*Look, John opened the window for ten minutes.*
   b. [Context: When we enter the room, we are informed that the window has been open for two minutes. When a further eight minutes have passed, I say:]
   #*It took only eight minutes for the window to open for ten minutes.*

This unwanted outcome is avoided if we maintain, as before, that the end state of a simplex causative verb is lexically encoded and therefore cannot be modified. Of course, this requires that we develop an alternative approach to temporal modification that can somehow operate on the lexically encoded end state in the absence of decomposition.

As a point of departure, consider the temporal interpretation of an unmodified verb of change. By definition, verbs of change (which include causative verbs and unaccusatives) describe a transition from $\neg p$ to p. Given that $\neg p$ and p are typically states, there is a great inherent flexibility in the temporal construal of verbs of change, as both $\neg p$ and p may persist over an interval of time. We propose that the interval covered by verbs of change is minimized by default, but can be stretched under specific circumstances. For example, if a puppy is born with a genetic defect that causes it to die after three months, it is fine to summarize what happened as *the puppy died in three months*. However, if a puppy is born healthy but contracts a disease after two months and dies a month later, it would be inappropriate to describe what happened in this way. Rather, one would have to say that the puppy died in a month (or after three months). Thus, the portion of ¬p (being alive) that can be covered by a verb of change like *die* is minimized to what is contextually relevant. (Much more can be said about this; see Neeleman and Van de Koot (2012).)

The example just given homes in on the portion of ¬p included in the event. We would expect that the same flexibility, constrained by minimization, characterizes the portion of p that can be included. In particular, we propose that temporal modifiers can stretch the portion of the resultant state covered by the verb of change by measuring backwards from the end of the event to the point preceding it in which p first holds. This will have the effect that the verb of change covers the portion of p measured by the modifier and no more. The proposal does not imply that the resultant state must terminate at the end of the event. Indeed, neither (8a) nor (8b) entail that the window closes after ten minutes.

A key fact about reading (i) of (8a) is that the duration for which the window is open is understood as being under the control of the causer arguments, as expected if the interval measured is construed as part of the interval covered by the causative verb. Thus, one would judge that John was being economical with the truth with the utterance in (10).

(10) [Context: John is part of a group of burglars who are targeting the local jeweller. The plan is that John will open the metal shutter and keep it open for ten minutes, while his mates loot the shop. On the day, John cuts the lock that secures the shutter and lifts it while the gang goes about their business. After nine minutes John can't hold the shutter anymore and his mate Bill takes over, keeping the shutter open for another crucial minute. On the way back, John boasts:]
#*I opened the shutter for ten minutes, didn't I?*

By contrast, on reading (ii) of (8a), the intentional reading, the interval measured by the for-phrase cannot be construed as part of the causation event: if some action is carried out with a particular intention, there is no guarantee that what is intended actually comes about. This implies that on the intentionality reading the modifier does not measure backwards into the causation event, but forwards from the culmination of that event. The fact that these modifiers measure in different directions can be illustrated in various ways. Consider first the contrast in (11), based on readings (i) and (ii) of (8a).

(11) a. reading (i):
John opened the window for ten minutes and then left for work.
⇒ John left for work ten minutes after opening the window.
b. reading (ii):
John opened the window for ten minutes and then left for work.
⇒ John left for work after opening the window.

On reading (i), where the window is in fact open for ten minutes, the ten minutes is included in the duration of the causation event, so that the implication of the example is that John left for work ten minutes after he opened the window. On the intentionality reading, however, this implication does not hold: John may well have left immediately after he opened the window (perhaps he asked someone else to close it after ten minutes).

The different ways in which measurement takes place on the two readings can also be made visible through interaction with a second modifier that measures the length of the causation event. If the length of the causation event is shorter that the duration measured by the for-modifier, only the intentionality reading survives:

(12) *In just a few seconds John opened the window for ten minutes.*
*reading (i); ✓reading (ii)

Finally, there are consequences for the 'reach' of the causer argument. On the intentionality reading, this argument bears responsibility for its intentions, which can be anchored in the culmination of the causation event. But since the interval linked with the causer argument's intentions falls outside the causation event, it is not interpreted as being under its control. Thus, there is a clear difference between (13) and the earlier example in (10): only in the former is John considered to have misrepresented the situation.

(13) [Context: John is part of a group of burglars who are targeting the local jeweller. The plan is that John will open the metal shutter and keep it open for ten minutes, while his mates loot the shop. On the day, John cuts the lock that secures the shutter, lifts it, and props it up with a piece of wood. The gang enter and go about their business. After five minutes the piece of wood collapses under the weight of the shutter and the gang only manage to escape after John lifts the shutter for a second time. On the way back, John says ruefully:]
As planned, I opened the shutter for ten minutes, but I misjudged the strength of the piece of wood I used to prop it up.

To summarize this section, although at first blush temporal modification seems to have access to the resultant state of a verb of change, on closer inspection this cannot be the case, as it makes incorrect predictions regarding the meaning of temporally modified verbs of change. *Open for ten minutes* does not describe a transition from "not open for ten minutes" to "open for ten minutes", but rather a transition from "not open" to "open for ten minutes". We have proposed an alternative account that does not suffer this defect and that is furthermore able to express the difference between the actual duration and the intended duration of a resultant state.

3 The scope of presuppositional modifiers

3.1 A two-way ambiguity with *again*

Having argued that sub-lexical modification is not attested with manner adverbials and the like, we now turn to the most famous case of apparent modification of this type, namely with the adverb *again*. This adverb is semantically compatible with states and events, as shown by the examples in (14).

(14) a. *John is asleep again.*
 b. *John works again.*

Again triggers a presupposition, based on its scope, that there was a previous eventuality of the same type. Given the standard claim that anything in the scope of *again* must be mapped to the presupposition, the theories in (1) make different predictions about the presuppositions that result from attaching *again* to a structure headed by a causative verb. The theory based on lexical semantic decomposition in (1a) predicts that all the information in the verb must reoccur in the presupposition. By contrast, the theory based on syntactic decomposition in (1b) predicts a three-way ambiguity, corresponding to modification of the entire causation event, the caused event, or the resultant state. Both theories face empirical hurdles, since the observation in the literature is that *again* creates a two-way ambiguity in the relevant structure, but not a three-way ambiguity. It can modify the matrix event or the result, but Von Stechow (1996) and Pylkkänen (2008), among others, claim that the intermediate reading, in which the modifier scopes exactly over the caused event (to the exclusion of the causing event), does not seem to exist.

(15) *John opened the window again.*
  i. Agent's action is repeated (repeated action reading)
     again (CAUSE (John, BECOME (OPEN (the window))))
  ii. *Caused event is repeated (intermediate reading)
     CAUSE (John, (again (BECOME (OPEN (the window))))))
  iii. Resultant state is restored (restitutive reading)
     CAUSE (John, BECOME (again (OPEN (the window))))))

We take reading (15i) to be easily accessible and we will not illustrate it further. However, the reading in (15iii) may require some contextualization. For example, if we enter a room with an open window, and Bill closes that window, then we may describe John's action of reopening it as in (15). In this context, the only reading that makes sense is one of restitution. The readings in (15i) and (15ii) are not felicitous in this context, as John did not open the window previously and neither did the window open previously.

The claim that the intermediate reading does not exist is not universally accepted (see for example Bale 2007 and Lechner et al. 2015).[3] However, its unavailability is manifest in the following scenario, suggested to us by an anonymous reviewer. Consider a situation in which a window has been nailed shut by Bill because it kept opening all by itself. Now imagine that John removes the nails, thereby allowing the window to spontaneously open again. While this action on John's part can be described by saying that John caused or allowed the window to open again, it cannot be described by uttering (15). (Some further examples illustrating the absence of the intermediate reading appear in (34) and (35) below.)

The two-way ambiguity just illustrated is also found with the unaccusative counterpart of causative verbs. Thus, *the window opened again* permits a reading in which the window opened before, as well as one in which it was open before. This is unremarkable in itself, but serves to make the point that the absence of the intermediate reading in (15ii) cannot be due to a ban on *again* modifying a become event.

---

3 To a large extent, this is a matter of what one considers to be the intermediate reading. The notion of intermediate reading relevant to our discussion is one in which *again* c-commands a causative verb and triggers a presupposition that includes the become event and its culmination but excludes the verb's causal layer (which contains the variable for the external argument). Lechner et al. (2015) consider cases where *again* scopes over anticausatives like *open* to be instances of the intermediate reading. These exist but do not involve sublexical scope and are therefore irrelevant to the issue discussed in this paper. Bale (2007) discusses what he calls "subjectless presuppositions" triggered by *again*. These exist, too, but we will argue that they do not exclude the semantics associated with the external argument but only the specific value of the argument variable.

There are two further peculiarities associated with the restitutive reading in (15iii). On the one hand, scope of *again* over the resultant state should give rise to a simple repeated state reading, rather than the more specific restitutive reading. A repeated state reading should not require restitution; that is, the undoing of the previous instantiation of the resultant state before its current instantiation is brought about. Yet in contexts that are incompatible with restitution, *again* cannot take low scope:

(16) [Context: When we entered the kitchen this morning, we found a broken glass on the floor.]
#*This afternoon John broke a glass again.*

What this seems to indicate is that a low construal of *again* requires the result to be contrastive.

On the other hand, while the repeated action reading does not trigger a marked stress pattern, the restitutive reading seems to require stress on the verb. Consider the following examples. The contexts in (17) and (18) have in common that they provide the example sentences with both an earlier mention of the resultant state *open* and a contrasting state, namely *closed*. This implies that the information-structural status of the resultant state in the two examples must be the same and can therefore not be responsible for the diverging stress patterns. Where the examples differ, though, is in their compatibility with a repeated action reading of *again*. In (17), which permits this reading, stress can fall on the adverbial, whereas in (18), which requires a restitutive reading, stress must fall on the verb.

(17) [Context: When we came into the room this morning, John opened the window. When we came in after lunch the window was closed.]
    a. *So, John opened it* AGAIN.
    b. *So, John* OPENED *it again.*

(18) [Context: When we came into the room this morning, the window was open. When we came in after lunch the window was closed.]
    a. #*So, John opened it* AGAIN.
    b. *So, John* OPENED *it again.*

The co-occurrence of these peculiarities suggests that contrastive focus on the result is necessary to license a low construal of *again*. After all, contrastive focus requires main stress and is associated at LF with a semantic representation that combines a proposition with the negation of an alternative proposition that differs exactly in the value of the focused constituent. This sort of representation is exactly right for situations of restitution.[4]

There is an alternative view of the effects of focus in sentences that contain *again*. Klein (2001) and Beck (2006) assume that stress on *again* triggers a repetitive reading. The intuition behind the proposal intended to explain this generalization is that stress on *again* in an example like *John opened the door* AGAIN implies destressing of the rest of the sentence, which in turn generates an anaphoric commitment that requires an occurrence of an identical event. In other words, John must have opened the door before and this information must be salient enough to trigger stress shift.

If we restrict the discussion to situations in which stress is placed either on the verb or on *again*, the generalization that the restitutive reading requires stress on the verb and the generalization that stress on *again* triggers the repetitive reading are empirically indistinguishable. What would distinguish them are situations in which neutral stress falls on the object. This stress pattern is available if the information that satisfies the presupposition triggered by *again* is satisfied by information present in the common ground but not in the linguistic context. We illustrate this in (19), where shared knowledge licenses the use of *again* on a repetitive reading, and the use of neutral stress on the object is available because the linguistic context does not provide an antecedent for stress shift to *again*.

(19) [Shared knowledge: For many years, John has opened the window whenever he came into the office. And for many years Mary has objected to this unsuccessfully. Recently a conflict mediator intervened and it was agreed that John would not open the window any longer.]
[Situation: Bill comes into the office and finds Mary in tears.]
[Linguistic context: Bill asks Lucy "What happened?"]
Lucy: *John opened the* WINDOW *again.*

---

[4] For presentational reasons, we will assume throughout that it is contrastive focus placed on the result that licenses the restitutive reading. It is likely, however, that what is required is contrastive focus placed on the verb. (For example, a restitutive reading of *weer nationaliseren* 'nationalize again' in Dutch requires stress on the stress-attracting suffix *–iseer* rather than the adjective *national*.) Contrastive focus on the verb and contrastive focus on the result yield the same semantics, as long as the presupposition triggered by a contrastive reading of the verb is chosen so that the antecedent verb is causative and has a result opposite to the verb bearing contrastive focus. Of course, nothing goes wrong if the presupposition is not chosen in this way, but the resulting interpretation will not be one of restitution.

The scenario should be compared with one in which the shared knowledge only licenses the use of *again* on a restitutive reading. The Klein/Beck generalization predicts that this should not affect the stress pattern in Lucy's answer, whereas the generalization proposed here implies that stress must shift to the verb. As shown in (20), the latter prediction is correct.

(20) [Shared knowledge: The window has been fixed open for many years. And for many years Mary has objected to this unsuccessfully, because John wanted the window permanently open and always got his way. As a result of a recent intervention by a conflict mediator, the window has finally been closed.]
[Situation: Bill comes into the office and finds Mary in tears.]
[Linguistic context: Bill asks Lucy "What happened?"]
a. #Lucy: *John opened the WINDOW again.*
b. Lucy: *John OPENED the window again.*

It would seem then that the correct generalization is that the restitutive reading requires stress on the verb, in line with our claim that this reading is dependent on contrastive focus on the resultant state. If so, any theory of *again* will have to answer the following three questions: (i) Why is there no intermediate reading?; (ii) What permits the low reading?; and (iii) Why does the low reading require contrastive focus on the resultant state?

A theory in which a causative verb corresponds to a complex syntactic structure rather than a single head provides a straightforward answer to question (ii). After all, if there is a complex structure, then part of that structure should be open to modification. However, decompositional theories fare less well with questions (i) and (iii). If syntactic structure is generally open to modification, decomposition should permit the intermediate reading, but as we have seen this reading is not available. Furthermore, the notion of decomposition in itself provides no insight into the relation between contrastive focus and the restitutive reading. In the following section we develop a non-decompositional account that provides an answer to all three questions.

3.2 Accounting for the ambiguity

Our analysis of *again* cannot rely on sub-lexical scope because we assume that lexical causatives are simplex verbs. The central idea is that the appearance of sub-lexical scope in restitutive readings is due to a process of presupposition impoverishment that takes place after an initial presupposition is constructed on the basis of scope relations in the syntactic representation. For ease of exposition, we develop our proposal in two steps, beginning with an illustration of the effects of scope on presupposition formation in repetitive readings. Once this is in place, we consider the effect of narrow contrastive focus on the verb for the process of presupposition construction, arguing that it can license impoverishment of the presupposition initially triggered by *again*.

Let us first formulate the two rules that govern the construction of the presupposition triggered by *again*[5,6]:

(21) *Rule 1*
Map all material c-commanded by *again* to the presupposition under type identity.
Rule 2
Map all internal arguments (of the eventuality) not c-commanded by *again* to the presupposition under token identity.

To get a flavour of the effects of these rules, consider the interpretation of *on Sunday* in the Dutch examples in (22). Rule 1 correctly predicts that this constituent must be mapped to the presupposition under type identity in (22a). In other words, (22a) presupposes that there was an earlier Sunday on which John opened a window. Given that rule 2 specifically mentions internal arguments, it follows that adverbials outside the scope of *again* will not be mapped to the presupposition at all. Thus, (22b) triggers the presupposition that John has opened a window before without specifying the day of the week on which this happened.

(22) a. Jan   heeft weer   op zondag een raam   geopend.
       John   has   again on Sunday a   window opened
       'John has opened a window on Sunday again.'

---

[5] See Fabricius-Hansen (2001) and Pedersen (2015) for alternative proposals that also do not rely on syntactic decomposition, but that assume that *again* is lexically ambiguous. The account developed here is non-decompositional but does not rely on an ambiguity of *again* in explaining the existence of repetitive and restitutive readings. For reasons of space we cannot offer a comparison.

[6] The notions of type identity and token identity are descriptive conveniences. It is likely that these interpretations correspond to an alternation in scope in the presupposition triggered by *again*, where an existential may or may not be interpreted in the scope of the temporal operator (informally represented as *before* throughout).

b. *Jan   heeft op zondag weer   een raam   geopend.*
   John has   on Sunday again a   window   opened
   'John has opened a window again on Sunday.'

Given the scopal positions of *again* with respect to external and internal arguments, there are three relevant structures when considering the interpretation of arguments under repetitive readings: (i) *again* may c-command only the verb, (ii) it may additionally c-command the internal argument, or (iii) it may additionally c-command both the external and internal arguments.

We first consider the behavior of indefinite internal arguments in the context of repetitive *again*. We initially use Dutch examples, as in this language c-command relations can be easily read off from the surface. Example (23a), where the indefinite *twee medewerkers* 'two employees' appears in the scope of *weer* 'again', is associated with the weak presupposition that previously two (different) employees were laid off. That is, the object is mapped to a type-identical object in the presupposition, as required by rule 1. By contrast, the example in (23b) triggers the stronger presupposition that previously the exact same two employees had been laid off. Thus, in this case, the object is mapped to a token-identical counterpart in the presupposition, as rule 2 dictates.[7] This explains the inappropriateness of the example in the context given.[8]

(23) [Context: Things are going downhill with John's company. On Monday, he had to lay off two employees. Unfortunately, that turned out not to be enough. And ...]
   a. *op dinsdag heeft Jan weer   twee medewerkers ontslagen.*
       on Tuesday has   John again two employees   fired
       'On Tuesday John fired two employees again.'
   b. *#op dinsdag heeft Jan   twee medewerkers weer   ontslagen.*
       on Tuesday has   John two employees   again   fired
       'On Tuesday John fired the same two employees again.'

---

7 It would be attractive if token identity reduced to specificity, which is in line with known interpretive effects of scrambling, but as we argue in section 3.3, this reductionist step is in fact unwarranted.
8 These examples and the ones below do not involve contexts in which windows are opened but ones in which employees are laid off. This is because the effects tested for rely on the identity of the object and this is often of little concern in contexts of the first type.

The context in (24) requires that the indefinite object in the examples are mapped under token identity (since the same two employees are laid off twice). This is possible in (24b) but not (24a), because objects in the scope of *again* are mapped under type identity rather than token identity.

(24) [Context: Things are going downhill with John's company. On Monday, he had to lay off ten employees. Unfortunately, he forgot to record who exactly he had fired. The next day, it became clear that another ten lay-offs were needed. Embarrassingly, John called up some people he had already fired. In other words, ...]
   a. #*Op dinsdag heeft Jan weer twee medewerkers ontslagen.*
       on Tuesday has John again two employees fired
      'On Tuesday John fired two employees again.'
   b. *Op dinsdag heeft Jan twee medewerkers weer ontslagen.*
       on Tuesday has John two employees again fired
      'On Tuesday John fired the same two employees again.'

We believe that the effects of our rules are also present with English repetitive *again*. The main argument supporting this view has to do with the observation that preverbal and postverbal *again* differ in the readings they permit: postverbal *again* allows the object to be mapped to the presupposition under either type or token identity, but preverbal *again* excludes the latter. This explains the pattern of judgments in (25) and (26).

(25) [Context: Things are going downhill with John's company. On Monday, he had to lay off two employees. Unfortunately, that turned out not to be enough. And ...]
   a. *on Tuesday John again laid off two employees.*
   b. *on Tuesday John laid off two employees again.*

(26) [Context: Things are going downhill with John's company. On Monday, he had to lay off ten employees. Unfortunately, he forgot to record who exactly he had fired. The next day, it became clear that another ten lay-offs were needed. Embarrassingly, John called up some people he had already fired. In other words, ...]
   a. #*On Tuesday John again laid off two employees.*
   b. *On Tuesday John laid off two employees again.*

The contrast between postverbal and preverbal *again* can be understood as follows. In the postverbal domain English allows both ascending and descending structures (see Janke and Neeleman (2012), and references cited there). We may therefore assume that the scope of *again* may either include the object (in the regular left-branching VP in (27)) or exclude it (in the shell structure in (28)). This implies that, on the rules in (21), the object will be mapped to the presupposition triggered by *again* under type identity in (27) and under token identity in (28).

(27)
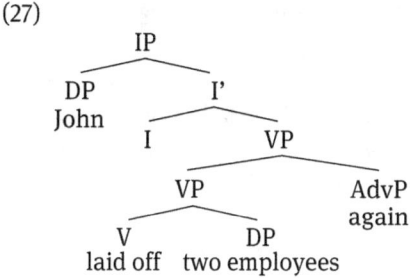

(28)
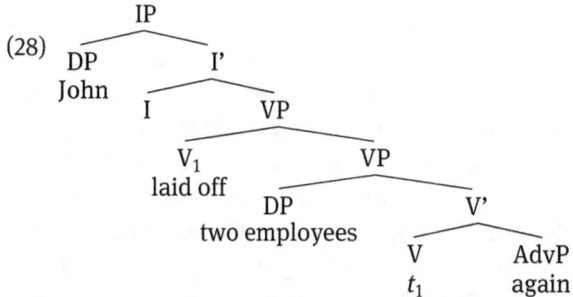

Preverbal adverbials uncontroversially c-command the object. Therefore, the examples in (25a) and (26a) only permit a reading in which the object is mapped under type identity. This fits the context in (25) but not that in (26).

Similar data and scenarios can be constructed to tease apart the type-identical and token-identical mapping of definite objects. For reasons of space, we restrict the discussion here to Dutch. Setting up appropriate scenarios is somewhat complicated, as one must control for interference of the uniqueness requirement associated with definites, and the fact that scrambled definites tend to be discourse-anaphoric. However, a nice minimal pair can be constructed using superlative modification: *the tallest boy* in the examples below could either be interpreted as a specific individual or as the tallest boy in whatever group John is meeting. The word order in (29a) requires the first reading, as 'the tallest boy' must be mapped to the presupposition under token identity. The word order in (29b) triggers the second reading, because it requires that 'the tallest boy' be mapped to the presupposition under type identity. Thus, John may have met one group in the morning and another group in the afternoon, and congratulated the tallest boy in each of these groups.

(29) [Context: This morning John congratulated the tallest boy.]
    a. En vanmiddag heeft Jan de langste jongen weer
       and this-afternoon has John the tallest boy again
       gefeliciteerd.
       congratulated
       'and this afternoon John has congratulated the tallest boy again.'
    b. En vanmiddag heeft Jan weer de langste jongen
       and this-afternoon has John again the tallest boy
       gefeliciteerd.
       congratulated
       'and this afternoon John has again congratulated the tallest boy.'

We now turn to interactions between *again* and the external argument. The rules in (21) state that internal and external arguments behave alike when they appear in the scope of *again* but differently when outside the scope of this modifier. That external arguments in the scope of *again* indeed map to the presupposition under type identity can be seen from examples like those in (30). Example (30a) triggers the strong presupposition that there was a previous act of opening the window performed by a boy. This is because rule 1 requires that material in the scope of *again* be mapped to the presupposition under type identity. By contrast, example (30b) merely presupposes that there was a previous act of the window being opened. This is because rule 2 is restricted to internal arguments, so that the indefinite subject of (30b) is not mapped to the presupposition under either type or token identity.

(30) a. *I believe that AGAIN a boy opened the window.*
    b. *I believe that a boy AGAIN opened the window.*

The same pattern is exhibited by the corresponding Dutch facts in (31), where only (31a) requires the previous opening of the window to have been carried out by a boy.

(31) a. Ik geloof dat er WEER een jongen het raam opende.
       I believe that there again a boy the window opened
       'I believe that again a boy opened the window.'

b. *Ik geloof dat er een jongen* WEER *het raam opende.*
   I believe that there a boy again the window opened
   'I believe that a boy again opened the window

These effects are also found with definite external arguments. At first sight, the data in (32) seem to pattern with what we observed for definite internal arguments in (29). 'The tallest boy', when c-commanded by *again*, is mapped to the presupposition under type identity, so that the two acts of glass breaking are performed by different boys (see (32b)). By contrast, the order in (32a) favours an interpretation in which the subject is mapped to the presupposition under token identity, so that the same boy is the agent of the two acts of glass breaking.

(32) [Context: This morning the tallest boy broke a glass.]
  a. *En vanmiddag heeft de langste jongen weer een*
     and this-afternoon has the tallest boy again a
     glas gebroken.
     glass broken
     'and this afternoon the tallest boy broke a glass again.'
  b. *En vanmiddag heeft weer de langste jongen een*
     and this-afternoon has again the tallest boy a
     glas gebroken.
     glass broken
     'and this afternoon again the tallest boy broke a glass.

This is only apparent, however, as demonstrated by the example in (33): if the subject c-commands *again* there is no requirement that the first glass was broken by a boy. Thus, the Dutch data with definite external arguments match the pattern established for indefinites.

(33) [Context: This morning the tallest girl broke a glass.]
  a. *En vanmiddag heeft de langste jongen weer een*
     and this-afternoon has the tallest boy again a
     glas gebroken.
     glass broken
     'and this afternoon the tallest boy broke a glass again.'
  b. **En vanmiddag heeft weer de langste jongen een*
     and this-afternoon has again the tallest boy a
     glas gebroken.
     glass broken

At this point, one might wonder whether a subject not c-commanded by *again* must be mapped to the presupposition at all. This is an important point: if the subject were not represented in the presupposition at all, this could be taken to be evidence for a reading where *again* selectively takes scope over the become event but not over the causation event (see also footnote 3).[9] However, as was already demonstrated in the discussion surrounding (15ii), intermediate readings are systematically unavailable. We support our conclusions in this regard with one further example that runs parallel to the ones given earlier in this section, but that lacks a representation of the causer argument in the context. This leads to considerable deterioration, indicating that when the event is mapped to the presupposition, it is mapped with its full argument structure. Hence, the causer argument must be present in the presupposition at the very least as an existentially bound variable.

(34) *This morning, a glass broke (all by itself).*
 #Later Bill AGAIN broke one.

We illustrate the same effect with the Dutch example in (35).

(35) *Vanmorgen   brak   er   (helemaal vanzelf)   een   glas.*
 this.morning broke there   (all by itself)   a   glass
 #Later brak   Jan   er   WEER   één.
 later   broke John there again one
 'This morning a glass broke (all by itself). Later John again broke one.'

We now turn to restitutive readings. Our task is twofold. On the one hand, we must explain why the low reading is permitted at all. After all, on the theory in (1a), which rejects syntactic decomposition, it is predicted that *again* cannot take scope exclusively over the resultant state. On the other hand, we must explain why the low reading invariably requires contrastive focus on the result (see the discussion in section 3.1). The thrust of our proposal is as follows. Contrastive focus on the result generates a presupposition which, under certain circumstances, is in conflict with the presupposition licensed by *again*. When

---

[9] A related observation is made by Bale (2007) under the heading of "subjectless presuppositions". The discussion below shows, however, that the presuppositions in question are not really subjectless, but merely involve underspecification of the subject: the subject variable is mapped to the presupposition, but the actual subject is not.

this is the case, a repair is needed that simplifies one of the two presuppositions, and it can be demonstrated that the only simplification that makes sense is one by which the presupposition triggered by *again* is reduced to a stative proposition.

Let us spell out the details of this proposal by going through a sample derivation. Consider the sentence in (36). As already explained, *again* triggers the presupposition in (i). Contrastive focus on the result does two things. First, focus generates a focus value, which consist of propositions that differ from the ordinary value of the sentence in exactly the focused element. Wagner (2005, 2012) has argued that the alternatives for the focused element must be mutually exclusive. In the case at hand, we are therefore dealing with the set of alternative results {open, closed}. Second, contrast negates a proposition in the focus value of the sentence and it may do so only, Wagner suggest, if this proposition is contextually salient. There are different ways in which salience can be achieved. The one we are interested in here is salience through previous occurrence of a similar event. In the case at hand, this results in the presupposition in (ii).

(36) *This morning, John OPENED the window again.*
 Presuppositions:
 (i) Again: Someone opened the window before.
 (ii) Contrast: Someone closed the window (before).

The presuppositions in (i) and (ii) are not contradictory if they pertain to different antecedent events. However, if (36) is construed with respect to a single antecedent event, a contradiction does ensue, as an event of opening a window cannot simultaneously be an event of closing that window. What determines whether the presuppositions are construed with respect to different antecedent events or just a single one? We assume that this decision is part of the procedure in which the presuppositional content of a sentence is determined, rather than something that is merely a matter of contextual felicity. Assuming that any contradiction between presuppositions is indeed detectable at the level of grammar, we may conjecture that repairs are possible before any presupposition failure is detected. There are two possible repairs: simplification of presupposition (i) or simplification of presupposition (ii). The first repair consists of a reduction of presupposition (i) to the stative proposition (i') below. These propositions are non-contradictory when associated with a single event, given that closing a window implies that at the start of the event that window was open.

(37) *This morning, John* OPENED *the window again.*
Presuppositions:
  (i') Again: The window was open before.
  (ii) Contrast: Someone closed the window (before).

The second potential repair would simplify the presupposition triggered by contrast. This would yield (38ii') alongside (38i). The problem with this repair is that the simplified presupposition associated with contrast is trivially true if John indeed opened the window. In other words, the mere use of the verb *open* already triggers the presupposition in (38iii).

(38) *This morning, John* OPENED *the window again.*
Presuppositions:
  (i)   Again: Someone opened the window before.
  (ii') Contrast: The window was closed (before).
  (iii) Open$_V$: The window was closed (before).

If we assume that contrast may not be used unless it has an interpretive effect, then the repair in (38) is blocked. Notice that this problem does not arise in (37), since the presupposition in (37ii) is stronger than that in (38iii).

At this point it is useful to compare our proposal with the one developed by Klein (2001) and Beck (2006). Unlike us, these authors assume syntactic decomposition of causative verbs, so that the high and low construals are the result of a syntactic ambiguity. But like us, they assume that focus is instrumental in determining whether *again* receives a high or low construal. In short, they argue that focus on *again* triggers the repetitive reading because it leads to anaphoric destressing of the remaining material in VP, which in turn requires an identical antecedent event. We have already show in section 3.1 that the correct generalization is not that stress on *again* triggers a repetitive reading, but rather than the restitutive reading requires stress on the verb. Apart from that, a problem with the theory developed by Klein and Beck is that it only acknowledges two potential readings of *again* and fails to take account of the fact that a third potential reading (which we have called the repeated state reading above) does not exist under any intonation (see the discussion surrounding (16)). Our proposal excludes this reading because contrastive focus on the result is necessary for a low construal of *again* and contrast is incompatible with the simple repetition of the resultant state. However, we do not see how the repeated state reading could be ruled out in the Klein/Beck approach.

We provide further motivation for our proposal by developing an argument first laid out by Jäger and Blutner (2000), who observe that restitutive readings are sometimes possible even if *again* c-commands the subject position. If this is true, and provided our theory can capture the relevant facts, an account of the scope ambiguity with *again* in terms of decomposition of causatives must be rejected, as on such an account a high attachment of *again* can never yield a low construal.

We begin, slightly off-center, by considering the effects of the rules in (21) for *again* on its restitutive reading. What we expect is that internal arguments c-commanded by *again* are mapped to the presupposition under type identity, while internal arguments outside *again*'s c-command domain are mapped to the presupposition under token identity. For external arguments, the prediction is that *again* cannot c-command them, as this would require that they be mapped to the presupposition, which would in turn stand in the way of the presupposition simplification required for a restitutive reading. These predictions are correct, as confirmed by the Dutch examples in (39), where c-command relations can be read off directly from linear order.

(39) a. *Gisteren heeft weer iemand twee ramen* GEOPEND.
yesterday has again someone two windows OPENED
*Restitutive reading
b. *Gisteren heeft iemand weer twee ramen* GEOPEND.
yesterday has someone again two windows OPENED
✓Restitution (of type-identical windows in open state)
c. *Gisteren heeft iemand twee ramen weer* GEOPEND.
yesterday has someone two windows again OPENED
✓Restitution (of token-identical windows in open state)
'Yesterday someone opened two windows again.'

A further prediction of the rules in (21) is that it should not be possible to include an adjunct in the c-command domain of *again* on a restitutive reading. The reason for this is that any material in the c-command domain of *again* must be mapped to the presupposition. However, adjuncts do not permit sub-lexical scope (see section 2.3), but must instead be construed as modifying the event denoted by the verb. On a restitutive reading, however, this event is removed from the presupposition leaving the adjunct without an interpretation. This prediction, too, is correct, as illustrated here for a temporal modifier (for related discussion, see Bale (2007)):

(40) a. *Toen heeft iemand weer op zondag twee ramen* GEOPEND.
then has someone again on Sunday two windows opened
*Restitutive reading

b. *Toen heeft iemand op zondag weer twee ramen* GEOPEND.
   then has someone on Sunday again two windows opened
   ✓Restitution (of type-identical windows in open state)
   'Then someone opened two windows again on Sunday.'

As we explained a little earlier, the external argument of a causative verb is typically not part of its resultant state and therefore it will typically be irrelevant to any restitutive reading. As pointed out by Jäger and Blutner (2000), there is an exception to this general rule, namely structures in which the external argument binds a reflexive internal argument. In such cases, the external argument *is* part of the result and must therefore appear in some form or other in the relevant presupposition. Jäger and Blutner present the examples in (41), which involve the inherently reflexive variant of the verb *settle*. Both examples permit a restitutive reading of *again*. That is, they are felicitous even though no Delaware settled in New Jersey before, and no Delaware lived there twice.

(41) [Context: The Delaware tribe was created in the area of New Jersey at the beginning of time. They never left the area until 200 years ago when they were forced into a reservation in Oklahoma. Recently, a member of the tribe moved to the home of his ancestors. Thus, ...]
   a. *a Delaware has settled in New Jersey again.*
   b. *again a Delaware has settled in New Jersey.*

Notice that in these examples the indefinite subject is mapped to the presupposition under type-identity, the typical effects of rule 1 of (21). Thus, this rule must be extended to external arguments of inherent reflexives. The same phenomenon can be observed in the Dutch variant of (41) below, which has an overt reflexive:

(42) ...*dat er zich weer een Delaware in New Jersey*
     that there self again a Delaware in New Jersey
     gevestigd heeft.
     settled has

If in examples of this type *een Delaware* 'a Delaware' finds itself outside the scope of *weer* 'again', it cannot be excluded from the presupposition and must be mapped under token identity, just like an internal argument. Thus, (43) implies that the very same Delaware lived in New Jersey before.

(43) ... dat er   zich een Delaware weer in New Jersey
         that there self a   Delaware again in New Jersey
         gevestigd heeft.
         settled   has

On a decompositional view, this constellation of data is not amenable to analysis. The observations in (39) and (40) demonstrate that high attachment of *again* is incompatible with a low construal. But the observations regarding (41) and (42) entail that a low construal of *again* must be allowed even when this adverbial is attached high. This paradoxical situation does not arise on the proposal advanced here, as a restitutive reading is compatible with a high attachment of *again*, provided the material in the c-command domain of this adverbial can find an interpretation in the stative presupposition it triggers.[10]

3.3 The scope of *re-*

In this section we explore the presuppositions triggered by the English prefix *re-*. These pattern in major respects with those we identified for *again*. *Re-* has both a repetitive and a restitutive reading, and at least in some verbs these display the same pattern of stress shift we observed with *again*. We give two sets of examples to illustrate how the repetitive and restitutive readings correlate with stress on the verbal base and the prefix, respectively:

(44) [Context: In this country the railways started as a collection of privately-owned enterprises. In the 1960s, prime minister Johansson nationalised them. Then, in the 1980s, prime minister Peterson privatised them. But fortunately ...]
   a. *his successor decided to REnationalise them.*
   b. #*his successor decided to reNATIONALISE them.*

---

10 Jäger and Blutner (2000) also propose a non-decompositional account of the ambiguity observed with *again*. *Again* can associate with the event variable of the verb, but they propose that in addition it can associate with the event variable of the resultant state (made available through the application of a result function). We have two main concerns about this analysis. First, we are unsure that it rules out sub-lexical modification by non-presuppositional modifiers. Second, we do not see how it explains why *again* – on a low construal – cannot give rise to a (non-restitutive) repeated state reading. For related discussion see Bale (2007).

(45) [Context: In this country the railways started as a publicly-owned enterprise. In the 1980s prime minister Peterson privatised them, but fortunately ...]
    a. #*his successor decided to REnationalise them.*
    b. *his successor decided to reNATIONALISE them.*

(46) [Context: The circus captured a strong and vicious bear, which they used for their show. After a few years it escaped, but I heard that ...]
    a. *they managed to REcapture it last week.*
    b. #*they managed to reCAPTURE it last week.*

(47) [Context: A bear was born in captivity. When it had grown into a strong and vicious specimen, it escaped, but I heard that ...]
    a. #*they managed to REcapture it last week.*
    b. *they managed to reCAPTURE it last week.*

In view of these data, an extension of the analysis for *again* to *re-* seems straightforward. However, *re-* allows us to develop three further arguments for aspects of our analysis.

To begin with, the distribution of *re-* militates against a decompositional analysis of lexical causatives. As pointed out by Wunderlich (2001) and Williams (2007), *re-* attaches to the verb and not to some higher node in the verbal extended projection. The main argument for this is that, as already noted by Keyser and Roeper (1992), *re-* cannot take scope over syntactically encoded results, although it can take scope over morphologically or lexically encoded results. This is shown by the contrast in (48). In (48a) *re-* fails to take scope over *red*, whereas *again* must do so in (48b), given the presuppositions triggered by these examples.

(48) a. *John repainted the door red.*
       Presupposition:
       someone painted the door before
   b. *John painted the door red again.*
       Presupposition:
       either: someone painted the door red before
       or: the door was red before

By contrast, *re-* must take scope over lexically or morphologically encoded results, and like *again* it permits a repetitive and a restitutive reading:

(49) a. *John reopened the door.*
Presupposition:
either: someone opened the door before
or: the door was open before
b. *The government renationalized the railways.*
Presupposition:
either: someone nationalized the railways before
or: the railways were national property before

Wunderlich and Williams both conclude that an account of these facts must refer to the notion of 'word': the prefix *re-* can only attach to a category if that category is a word. This is incompatible with a decompositional analysis of causative verbs, as on such an analysis there is no fundamental distinction between morphologically complex units (words) and syntactically complex units.

The second conclusion we can draw from verbs prefixed with *re-* is that they provide further evidence for the rule in (21). This rule states that objects not in the c-command domain of *again* must be mapped to the presupposition under token identity. As we noted, it is tempting to understand this rule as an effect of scrambling (or a comparable rule in English). On this view, the interpretation of an object outside the c-command domain of *again* is merely an instance of the general fact that scrambled objects tend to be discourse-given or specific. It turns out that this alternative view is incompatible with the interpretation of the object of verbs prefixed with *re-*. The crucial point is that *re-* is attached very low in the structure, so that the object must be generated outside its c-command domain. The rule in (21) therefore predicts that it will invariably be mapped to the presupposition under token identity. By contrast, an analysis of the type/token distinction in terms of scrambling predicts that the object of a verb prefixed by *re-* can either remain in its base position, and therefore be construed as new or non-specific, or scramble, and hence be interpreted as discourse anaphoric or specific. This implies that the mapping to the presupposition can take place under either type or token identity. The fact of the matter is that only mapping under token identity is permitted, as demonstrated by the contrast between (50) and (51).

(50) [Context: We came into a room with ten closed windows. John opened a window. A little while later he still felt hot and so ...]
   a. *he again opened a window.*
   b. #*he reopened a window.*

(51) [Context: When we came into the room, John opened all ten windows. A little while later Mary closed them, as she felt cold. John still felt hot, however, and so ...]
  a. *he again opened a window.*
  b. *he reopened a window.*

We may conclude, then, that the interpretation of objects of verbs prefixed with *re-* provides straightforward evidence for the rule in (21) (as opposed to a scrambling-based account).

The third way in which properties of verbs prefixed with *re-* support our proposal has to do with the selectional properties of this prefix, which attaches only to verbs:

(52) a. *The windows are open again.*
  b. **The windows are reopen.*

This implies that a verb like *renationalize* must have a structure in which *-ize* combines with *national* before *re-* combines with *nationalize*:

(53) [$_V$ re- [$_V$ national$_A$ -ize$_V$]]

Notice that *-ize* is the morpheme that introduces the become event that culminates in the result contributed by *national*. However, we have already seen that *renationalize* permits a restitutive reading (see (45)). Therefore, the conclusion seems inescapable that the presupposition triggered by *re-* need not contain all the semantic material contained in *nationalize* (its c-command domain). As this must be true, too, on the decompositional analysis, this analysis must permit simplification of the presupposition triggered by *re-* in much the same way as ours. It cannot be maintained, then, that the decompositional approach has a conceptual advantage in this domain.

4 Conclusion

The interpretation of manner, locational and temporal modifiers provides strong support for an analysis of causative verbs that does not permit sub-lexical modification. The only apparently convincing case of sub-lexical modification is based on the ambiguity found with presuppositional modifiers like *again*.

The detailed treatment of *again* (and *re-*) developed here favours non-decompositional theories over competitors that assign the semantic components of lexical causatives to independent syntactic positions. Such competitors fall short in a number of ways. They cannot account for the systematic absence of the "intermediate" scope reading and they cannot account for the systematic absence of repeated state reading (as opposed to restitutive reading). Moreover, the assumptions required to reconcile the interpretation of *again* with a non-decompositional analysis of lexical causatives (the rule in (21) and the option of presupposition simplification) are independently motivated in the sense that they cannot be avoided under decompositional accounts if these are extended to include the prefix *re-*.

Thus, on balance the evidence suggests that there is no such thing as sub-lexical scope.

References

Bale, Alan Clinton. 2007. Quantifiers and verb phrases: An exploration of propositional complexity. *Natural Language and Linguistic Theory* 25(3). 447–483.
Beck, Sigrid. 2006. Focus on 'again.' *Linguistics and Philosophy* 29(3). 277–314.
Fabricius-Hansen, Catherine. 2001. Wi(e)der and again(st). In Caroline Fery and Wolfgang Sternefeld (eds.), *Auditur vox sapientiae: A festschrift for Arnim von Stechow*, 101–130. Berlin: Akademie Verlag.
Fodor, Jerry. 1970. Three reasons for not deriving 'kill' from 'cause to die.' *Linguistic Inquiry* 1 (4). 429–438.
Fodor, Jerry, and Ernie Lepore. 1997. Morphemes matter; the continuing case against lexical decomposition. Ms. Center for Cognitive Science. Rutgers University.
Hale, Kenneth, and Samuel J. Keyser. 1993. On argument structure and the lexical expression of syntactic relations. In Kenneth Hale and Samuel J. Keyser (eds.), *The view from building 20*, 53–109. Cambridge: MIT Press.
Higginbotham, James. 2000. On events in linguistic semantics. In James Higginbotham, Fabio Pianesi, and Achille Varzi (eds.), *Speaking of events*, 49–79. Oxford: Oxford University Press.
Jackendoff, Ray. 1990. *Semantic structures*. Cambridge, MA.: MIT press.
Jäger, G, and Reinhard Blutner. 2000. Against lexical decomposition in syntax. *Proceedings of IATL*, 1–25.
Janke, Victoria, and Ad Neeleman. 2012. Ascending and descending VPs in English. *Linguistic Inquiry* 43(2). 151–190.
Keyser, Samuel Jay, and Thomas Roeper. 1992. Re: The abstract clitic hypothesis. *Linguistic Inquiry* 23(1). 89–126.
Klein, Wolfgang. 2001. Time and again. In Caroline Fery and Wolfgang Sternefeld (eds.), *Audiatur vox sapientiae. A festschriftfor Arnim von Stechow*, 267–86. Berlin: Akademie Verlag.
Lechner, Winfried, Giorgos Spathas, Artemis Alexiadou, and Elena Anagnasopoulou. 2015. On deriving the typology of repetition and restitution. Paper presented at GLOW 2015, Paris 8 & CNRS, April 15–17.

Neeleman, Ad, and Hans Van de Koot. 2012. The linguistic expression of causation. In Martin Everaert, Marijana Marelj, and Tal Siloni (eds.), *The theta system: Argument structure at the interface*, 20–51. Oxford: Oxford University Press.

Pedersen, Walter A. 2015. A scalar analysis of *again*-ambiguities. *Journal of Semantics* 32(3). 373–424.

Pietroski, Paul. 2003. Small verbs, complex events: Analyticity without synonymy. In Louise Antony and Norbert Hornstein (eds.), *Chomsky and his critics*, 179–214. Blackwell Publishers.

Pietroski, Paul. 2005. *Events and semantic architecture*. Oxford: Oxford University Press.

Pinker, Steven. 1989. *Learnability and cognition. The acquisition of argument structure*. Cambridge, Massachusetts: MIT Press.

Pylkkänen, L. 2008. *Introducing arguments*. Cambridge, Massachusetts: MIT Press.

Ramchand, Gillian. 2008. *Verb meaning and the lexicon: A first-phase syntax*. Cambridge: CUP.

Rappaport Hovav, Malka, and Beth Levin. 1998. Building verb meanings. In Miriam Butt and William Geuder (eds.), *The projection of arguments: Lexical and compositional factors*, 97–134. Stanford, CA: CSLI Publications.

Stechow, A. Von. 1996. The different readings of wieder 'again': A structural account. *Journal of Semantics* 13(2). 87–138.

Wagner, Michael. 2005. *Prosody and recursion*. PhD Dissertation. MIT.

Wagner, Michael. 2012. Focus and givenness: A unified approach. In Ivona Kucerova and Ad Neeleman (eds.), *Contrasts and positions in Information Structure*, 102–147. Cambridge: Cambridge University Press.

Williams, Edwin. 2007. Dumping lexicalism. In Gillian Ramchand and Charles Reiss (eds.), *The Oxford handbook of linguistic interfaces*. Oxford: Oxford University Press.

Wunderlich, Dieter. 2001. Prelexical syntax and the voice hypothesis. In Caroline Féry and Wolfgang Sternefeld (eds.), Audiatur vox sapientiae: A festschrift for Arnim Von Stechow. Berlin: Akademie Verlag.

Diego Pescarini
An emergentist view on functional classes

1 Introduction

Building on Manzini (2014), Manzini & Savoia (2014), this paper aims to challenge the hypothesis that function words fall into different *classes* (e.g. strong/weak/clitic), which are defined in syntactic terms. Strong elements are conceived as phrases with multiple layers, while *clitics* correspond – at least in the latter stage of their derivation – to a deprived structure, possibly to a single head exhibiting an affix-like behaviour. The correlation between the behaviour of function words and their syntactic make-up was first advanced by Kayne (1975), who argued that French clitics are heads inasmuch as they cannot be coordinated, focused, modified, used in isolation, etc. The hypothesis was further refined by Kayne (1983), who argued that certain clitics – noticeably, French subject clitics – are in fact *phonological clitics* as they show cues of phrasal behaviour. Phonological clitics resemble Germanic pronouns, e.g. German *es*, which cannot be coordinated, modified, etc., although they are not bound to a specific host or to a dedicated syntactic position (see Holmberg (1986), (1991) a.o.). The comparison between Germanic and Romance data led Cardinaletti (1991), (1994), (1998); Cardinaletti & Starke (1996), (1999) to a more articulated typology that includes a third class of pronouns, which Cardinaletti and Starke term *weak*. Inter- and intra- linguistic variation follows from the distribution of pronominal forms across the three classes, as exemplified in the following table, which illustrates the status of certain Italian and German pronouns (from Cardinaletti & Starke (1996: 27, 29)).

(1)

	Italian		German	
	3.sg.m.dat	3.pl.dat	3.sg.m.acc	3.sg.n.acc
Clitic	gli	–	–	–
Weak	–	loro	ihn	es
Strong	a lui	a loro	ihn	–

As previously mentioned, classes are modelled in terms of syntactic constituency. Functional elements are stored in the lexicon as triplets formed by *a syntactic subtree*, containing *a bundle of φ-features*, associated with *a phonological exponent* (see also Starke (2009)). Elements with the same

Diego Pescarini, CNRS, Université Côte d'Azur, BCL

https://doi.org/10.1515/9781501505201-027

syntactic subtree form a class, although they may differ from one another in terms of the features they express. In Cardinaletti & Starke's (1999) formulation, clitic and weak pronouns differ from strong pronouns in lacking the outer functional layer of the tree C_L (where L stands for any Lexical category), which allows pronouns to be coordinated, modified, contrasted, etc. Furthermore, clitics lack a further layer (namely, Σ_L), whose absence correlates with syntactic and morphophonological properties, e.g. doubling, prosodic deficiency, etc.:

(2) a. Strong b. Weak c. Clitic
    $[C_L [\Sigma_L [I_L LP]]]$ $[\Sigma_L [I_L LP]]$ $[I_L LP]$

Dèchaine & Wiltschko (2002) argued for a similar tripartition, see (3), but on the basis of a different set of phenomena (predicate/argument asymmetries, binding, obviation, switch reference, etc.). Dèchaine & Wiltschko's classification cuts across Cardinaletti & Starke's, meaning that the typology is, at best, far more complicated than previously thought.

(3) a. $[D [\Phi [N]]]$ b. $[\Phi [N]]$ c. $[N]$

Given (2) and (3), the crucial point is how to disentangle properties hinging on the internal structure of pronouns from phenomena attributable to external, clausal factors. For instance, some languages display a three-way system of possessive pronouns: Italian dialects, old Italian (Giusti (2010)), and old Gascon (Rohlfs (1970: 187)) exhibit strong postnominal possessives, as in (22a), weak prenominal possessives, as in (22b), and, with kinship nouns, clitic possessives,[1] which do not co-occur with the definite article, see (22c).

(4) a. el libro mio (Paduan)
       the book my
    b. el me libro
       the my book
       'My book'
    c. me= mama
       my= mum
       'Mum'

---

[1] The possessive clitic occurring with kinship nouns is enclitic in Romanian, old Italian (Giusti (2010)), and modern southern Italian dialects (Egerland (2013)), e.g. *fijə-mə* 'son=my', *mammə=mə* 'mum=my', *fretə-tə* 'brother=your', *tsiə-tə* 'uncle=your', etc. (Lanciano, Abr.).

However, the data in (4) are not conclusive evidence in favour of a three-way classification as the alternation between (4)b and (4)c is due to an external factor, i.e. the peculiar syntactic behaviour of (certain) kinship nouns (Benincà (1980), Longobardi (1994)). Hence, given the presence of an external, independent explanation, the hypothesis that the alternation in (4)b and (4)c follows from the internal structure of the pronoun *me* must be discarded in compliance with Occam's razor. Analogously, I show that several other phenomena point to clause-level explanations rather than class-based accounts.

The paper is organised as follows: section 2 summarises some of the phenomena that are normally taken as evidence for (pronominal) classes; section 3 focuses on the behaviour of clitic/weak pronouns in V2 environments; section 4 deals with doubling and resumption; section 5 addresses patterns in which the deficient pronoun is doubled by another deficient pronoun; section 6 is about climbing; section 7 examines the make-up of clitic combinations; section 8 discusses certain proclisis/enclisis asymmetries; section 9 deals with interpolation; section 10 focuses on the occurrence of clitics and weak pronouns in the complement position of prepositional phrases.

2 Deficient pronouns and non-canonical clitics

Many languages show a clear distinction between strong and deficient pronouns. The alternation between the two series is normally dependent on pragmatic factors (the latter usually denotes background information) and correlates with several syntactic, morphological, and phonological effects.

Several proposals have been advanced to distinguish different types of deficient pronouns, e.g. *phonological* vs *syntactic* clitics, *simple* vs *special* clitics, *weak* vs *clitics*. Definitions and criteria are not homogeneous and the taxonomies proposed so far are not easily comparable.

Furthermore, differences in the syntactic make-up of pronominal forms are usually assumed to be reflected in the morphophonological make-up of pronominal exponents: roughly speaking, strong pronouns behave prosodically and syntactically like words, while clitics are monosyllabic heads exhibiting an affix-like behaviour (I am not referring here to a specific formalization of the hypothesis, but to a rather naïve view, which is nonetheless tacitly assumed in part of the recent literature):

(5) strong > weak > clitic
 XP X' X^0
 PrW Ft σ

This idealised picture is often challenged by cases in which clitics are stressed, as in (6), have the same form of strong pronouns, as in (7b), do not climb in compound tenses, as in (8), may be separated from the verb by certain adverbs, as in (9), or are governed by a (lexical) preposition, as in (10).

(6) Finir-**lù** (Viozene, Rohlfs (1966: 442))
    To.end=it
    'to end it'

(7) a. Il **me** le donne (French)
       He to.me= it= gives
       'He gives it to me'
    b. Donne-le-**moi**!
       Give=it=to.me
       'Give it to me!'

(8) I an rangiò-**la**. (Cairo Montenotte, Parry (2005))
    They= have fixed=it.F
    'They fixed it.'

(9) I porti mi-**lla**. (Borgomanerese, Tortora (2015a))
    I= bring not=it
    'I'm not bringing it.'

(10) no sten ndar drio-**ghe** (Fossaltino, Vedovato & Berizzi (2011))
     not we.stay to.go behind=to.him/her
     'Let us not follow him/her'

Do the facts in (6)–(10) challenge or support the proposed distinction into pronominal classes? Laenzlinger (1993), (1994); Ordóñez and Repetti (2006), (2014); Repetti (2016); Cardinaletti (2015a), (2015b) argue that the clitics in (6)–(10) are in fact weak elements in the sense of Cardinaletti (1991), (1998); Cardinaletti & Starke (1999). Conversely, I argue that the phenomena in (6)–(10) end up challenging the class-based account in (1)–(2) as none of the properties distinguishing weak from clitic pronouns, listed in (11), hold systematically across languages.

(11) a. weak pronouns can occur in the first position of V2 clauses;
     b. clitics can double phrasal arguments;
     c. clitics climb to the auxiliary in compound tenses;
     d. clitics form tight clusters;

e. clitics are morphologically less complex than weak elements;
f. clitics, unlike weak elements, cannot occur as complement of Ps;
g. both weak and clitics can denote nonhuman referents.
h. weak are not subject to the Person Case Constraint
i. weak elements can bear lexical stress;
j. weak, unlike clitics, can be omitted under coordination;

The Romance languages, including dialects and historical vernaculars, exhibit a series of counterexamples and irregularities that lead us to reconsider the above tests and the overall claim that functional classes depends on the complexity of inner syntactic structures.

3 V2 syntax

Weak pronouns can occupy the first position of the clause in languages with a strict V2 syntax such as German and Dolomitic Ladin. If another constituent is fronted, as shown in (13)b, the weak element must be displaced after the inflected verb.

(12) Es ist zu teuer
 It is too expensive
 'It is too expensive'

(13) a. T vas gonoot a ciasa sua. (S. Leonardo, Poletto (2000: 89))
 You go.2.SG often at home his
 'You often visit him.'
 b. Gonoot vas-t a ciasa sua.
 Often go.2.SG=SCL at home his
 'You often visit him.'
 c. *Gonoot t vas a ciasa sua.
 Often you go.2.SG at home his

Clitics, by contrast, cannot fill the first position of V2 clauses. In medieval Romance, which exhibited a peculiar V2 syntax,[2] clitics pronouns never occur in the first position of the clause: in V1 environments or whenever the verb is preceded by left-dislocated elements (as in (14)a and (14)b), clitics occur

---

[2] Benincà (1983–4) a.o.; for a recent overview of the topic, see Wolfe (2016: 288).

enclitically, i.e. after the verb (the phenomenon is known as Tobler-Mussafia law). Clitics remain proclitic to the inflected verb when they are preceded by a focus-fronted element.

(14) a. Mando*lli* per li detti ambasciadori tre pietre (old Florentine)[3]
he.sent= to.him through the said ambassadors three stones

b. A voi le mie poche parole ch' avete intese ho *lle* dette con grande fede (old Florentine)[4]
to you the my few words that you.have heard I.have =them said with great faith
'The few words that you heard from me I pronounced with great faith.'

Given (14), one might argue that enclisis follows from the deficient structure of the clitic, which cannot act as the first maximal constituent of the clause. Since clitics cannot stand in the first position of the clause, the verb moves past the clitics *in order to* prevent the latter from occurring in the first position, yielding enclisis. This kind of explanation, adopted by Lema & Rivero (1991) and revised in Roberts & Roussou (2003), raises a look-ahead problem. In fact, it is likely that clitic placement is the *consequence*, not the trigger of verb movement, which means that in (14) the verb moves independently above the clitic (and irrespectively from the clitic's structure). In this respect, the distribution of proclisis and enclisis in early Romance seems orthogonal to the clitic/weak distinction and, in conclusion, the Tobler-Mussafia law does not provide any clue about the internal make-up of clitic (*vs* weak) pronominal forms.

4 Doubling (and resumption)

Some Romance languages allow clitic doubling:

(15) a. Le di un regalo a mi madre. (Spanish)
b. *Le diedi un regalo a mia madre. (Italian)
To.her= I.gave a gift to my mother
'I gave my mother a gift'

---

3 Anon., *Novellino*, II.
4 Schiaffini (1926: 282).

In standard Italian, doubling is not allowed – see (15)b – although in a lower/ colloquial register doubling is tolerated, in particular when the dative clitic is clustered with an accusative one as in (16)b (Benincà (1988); for a possible explanation, see Pescarini (2014: 174)):

(16) a. %gli ho dato un libro a Gianni (doubling)
to.them= I.have given a book to G.
'I gave him a book (to Gianni)'
b. ?glie-l' ho dato un libro a Gianni
to.them-it= I.have given a book to G.
'I gave it to him (to Gianni)'

Clitic resumption is always possible, although it is worth recalling that the resumption of elements other than direct objects may be optional.

(17) A Gianni, (gli) ho dato un libro (dislocation with resumption)
To G. to.him= I.have given a book
'I gave him a book (to Gianni)'

By contrast, the weak pronoun *loro* (Cardinaletti 1991) can neither double nor resume any dative complement:

(18) a. *Ai miei amici, diedi *loro*
To.the my friends I.gave to.them
un bacio. (dislocation with resumption)
a kiss
'I gave them a kiss (to my friends)'
b. *diedi *loro* un bacio ai miei amici (doubling)
I.gave to.them a kiss to.the my friends
'I gave them a kiss (to my friends)'

Given the data in (15)–(18), one might conclude that clitics can double or resume other elements, whereas weak pronouns cannot. The asymmetry is likely to result from the impoverished structure of clitics.

Things, however, are a bit more complicated. As for resumption, the ungrammaticality of (18)a does not probably depend on the internal structure of the pronoun as many languages allow nonclitic pronouns to resume left-dislocated elements, see (19).

(19) a. Your book, I read it yesterday.
   b. Peter, ich werde ihn morgen sehen
      P.   I   will   him tomorrow see
      'I will see Peter tomorrow'

Doubling, on the contrary, seems a rather robust property of clitic elements, although it is worth recalling that the correlation between clitichood and doubling is not biconditional as many languages with clitics do not allow doubling, cf. (15).

In the light of this provisional conclusion, let us focus on the syntax of subject clitics in central Romance. Rhaeto-Romance and French subject pronouns are regarded as weak elements by Cardinaletti & Starke as they cannot double a DP subject (at least in the formal register,[5] see Palasis (2015) for a recent overview), see (20)a vs (20)b. Northern Italian dialects, by contrast, have fully-fledged subject clitics that can co-occur with a non-dislocated phrasal subject (notice that French subject 'clitics' precede the preverbal negative marker, while northern Italian dialects display the order negation – clitic):

(20) a. *Jean il ne vient pas (French)
   b. Jean, il   ne vient pas
      J.   he= not comes NEG
      'He (Jean) comes'

(21) a. Giani no 'l vien mia (Veronese)
   b. Giani, no 'l   vien   mia
      G.   not he=   comes NEG

However, on a closer examination, the data shows that the distribution of subject clitics in several northern Italian dialects is more subtle and the divide between French and northern Italian is more nuanced. In several northern Italian dialects such as Paduan, subject clitics are ungrammatical whenever the subject is postverbal:

(22) *El riva   to   fradèo (Padovano, Benincà 1994)
     He= arrives your= brother
     'Your brother is coming'

---

[5] The pattern in (20b) is in fact widely attested in informal French, e.g. *Jean i-vient pas*, which is reminiscent of the situation found in northern Italian dialects.

With preverbal subjects, Benincà and Poletto (2004) notice that clitics seem optional, see (23)a. They argue that the (apparent) optionality in (23)a depends on whether the subject occupies its canonical position or not. In their analysis, the clitic occurs if and only if the subject is left-dislocated, which means that Paduan, like French, does not allow doubling, but only resumption. To support their analysis, Benincà and Poletto (2004) show that in contexts where the subject is clearly dislocated (for instance, when it precedes another left-dislocated element as in (23)b), the clitic cannot be omitted.

(23) a. Mario (l)   compra na casa   (Padovano)
        Mario (he=) buys   a   house
        'Mario is going to buy a house'
    b. Mario, na casa, no   *(l)   la   compra
        Mario, a house, not (he=)   it= will.buy
        'Mario is not going to buy a house'

The facts in (22) and (23) show that the distinction between French and northern Italian dialects is less clear than previously thought and, more generally, the data cast some doubts on the class-based account.

Furthermore, if Rhaeto-Romance, French, subject pronouns were weak pronouns, they would be expected to behave like fully-fledged weak pronouns such as Italian *egli* 'he'. The latter differs from its strong counterpart *lui* 'he' in displaying the canonical behaviour of weak elements, i.e. it cannot occur in isolation, cannot be focalised, coordinated,[6] etc.:

(24) a. Egli/lui è   stato visto.
        he   has been seen
        'He was seen'

---

[6] Nowadays weak *loro, egli* are confined to a rather formal/written register. I have searched for cases of weak dative *loro, egli* in a corpus of spoken Italian. For instance, out of 570 occurrences of the word *loro* (including possessive, subject, oblique, and dative instances of the pronoun), I have found only four occurrences of weak *loro*: one in an informal conversation (but *loro* follows a word ending in *-a*, so it could be a misunderstood strong dative *a loro*), another issue occurs in a homily ('and Jesus told them ...'), while the other two occurrences are from TV/radio news. The data above support the impression that Italian speakers have a kind of passive competence of the usage of *loro*. In this sense, the syntax of weak *loro* – as well as the syntax of other weak forms such as *egli* 'he', *cui* 'of which/whom', etc. – is nothing but a relic of the proto-Romance case system (Loporcaro 2002: 54; Manzini & Savoia 2014), which survives in old and, to a lesser extent, modern Italian as if it was part of a residual parallel grammar.

b. Chi è stato visto? *Egli/lui
   Who has been seen? He
   'Who was seen? He was'
c. è stato visto *egli/lui
   has been seen he
   'He was seen'
d. lui/*egli e Marco
   he and Marco
   'He and Marco'

However, *egli* can be separated from the verb, see (25), whereas subject clitics must always be adjacent to the inflected verb. If subject clitics of certain Romance languages and It. *egli* belonged to the same class, then the contrast in (25) would remain unaccounted for.

(25) a. il (*...) a mangé
   b. Egli sicuramente ha mangiato
      He certainly has eaten
      'He certainly ate'

In conclusion, the correlation between clitichood and doubling holds, although it is not biconditional and the boundary between doubling and resumption is less clear than usually thought. Doubling is a complicated diagnostic as many factors are at play besides the clitic/weak status of pronominal forms. In particular, it seems to me that an analysis of Rhaeto-Romance and French subject clitics as weak elements does not improve our account of the observed cross-linguistic asymmetries.

5 Being doubled

Although they cannot double another element, weak elements can be marginally doubled as shown in the following examples from modern Italian (Cardinaletti 1998: 138):

(26) a. ?Gli diede loro uno schiaffo
      to.him he.gave to.them a slap
   b. Glie-lo consegnò loro la settimana scorsa
      to.him-it= he.delivered to.them the last week

c. ?Ho   deciso   di   dir-glie-lo   loro   domani
   I.have decided to   say=to.him=it to.them tomorrow

Doubling of a clitic by another clitic, by contrast, is rather unexpected, e.g.

(27) *Gli   dovette   portar-gli   il   libro
     To.him= he.had.to bring=to.him the book
     'He had to bring him the book'

However, there are dialects in which doubling configurations such as (27) are in fact attested. In the 18th century, Piedmontese often showed two instances of the object clitic: one copy occurred proclitic to the auxiliary, while another copy of the same pronoun occurred after the lexical verb (Parry (1998: 107–110); Tortora (2014; 2015b)). In present-day dialects, this pattern is quite rare: it is attested in three AIS[7] datapoints (Jaberg & Jud 1928–1940), and in certain dialects of the Bormida valley such as Cairo Montenotte (Parry 2005: 179):

(28) a. A   l'   uma   visct-**le**   (Cairese)[8]
        We= him/it= have   seen=it/him
        'We saw him/it"
     b. A   'm   sun   fò-**me**   in fazing
        I= to.myself= am   made=to.myself a   cake
        'I baked me a cake'
     c. I   l'   an   catò-**le**
        they= it=   have   bought=it
        'They bought it"

Elsewhere, the proclitic copy does not occur anymore, giving rise to a pattern of generalised enclisis in compound tenses, as shown in (29). Nowadays, only the impersonal s- is allowed to occur twice, as shown in (30)b, or stand proclitic to the modal verb, cf. (30)b:

(29) a. a   l   peul di-lo   (18th century Piedm., Parry 1998: 108)
        (S)he= it= can   say=it

---

7 cf. AIS map. 1652: 122 Saint Marcel; 146 Montanaro; 147 Cavaglià.
8 In certain dialects of Piedmont auxiliaries exhibit a non-referential proclitic *l-* before auxiliary forms beginning with a vowel. Those in (28), however, are referential clitics as Cairese does not display clitics of auxiliary with these forms.

b. a   *(l) peul di-lo   (present day Piedm.)
      (S)he= it= can say=it
      '(S)he can say'

(30) a. a   s   peul di-**sse**
        EXPL= s= can say=s
     b. a   s   peul di
        EXPL= s= can say
     c. a   peul di-**sse**
        EXPL=   can say=s
      'One can say'

Similarly, in certain dialects of Piedmont (Parry 1997, Manzini & Savoia 2005), Friuli (Benincà 1986 e 1994:122–23) and Valle d'Aosta (Roberts 1993), interrogative clauses exhibit two subject clitics, one in proclisis and the other in enclisis (as usual, enclitic and proclitic forms are not identical, more on this in section 8):

(31) Còs   o   ra-**lo**   fat?   (Mondovì, CN, from Parry (1997: 93))
     What he=   has=he   done
     'What did he do?'

As in the case of object clitics, this peculiar pattern of doubling is found in dialects undergoing a change in clitic placement as, according to Parry 1997: 94–95 these dialects are progressively losing the structure with inversion, which is replaced by an alternative construction in which T-to-C movement (which yields enclisis) is blocked by inserting a complementiser after the *wh-* element:

(32) Còsa ch'   it   veule?
     What that you=   want
     'What do you want?'

The conclusion of the present section is twofold. First, if Piedmontese enclitics were analysed as weak elements, a logical paradox would result: it is fair to assume that weak pronouns evolve into clitics (Egerland 2005, 2010), but not *vice versa*. By contrast, if Piedmontese enclitics were analysed as weak, we would conclude that in these languages proclitic elements have been turned into weak forms.

Second, in the light of the above data one may conclude that doubling patterns of the type clitic/clitic are in fact attested, in particular in an area of

Italo-Romance subject to a radical and well documented change in clitic placement (more on this below). The above phenomena confirm that doubling is a multifaceted phenomenon that, in the end, is not very telling about the internal structure of pronominal elements.

6 Climbing

Climbing is a defining property of clitics. For instance, Cardinaletti 2015 claims that "sentences with auxiliaries (e.g., active sentences with compound tenses and passive sentences) are contexts of obligatory clitic climbing: clitic pronouns do not attach to the past participle but occur in the high clitic position attached to the auxiliary". Weak pronouns like It. *loro*, conversely, are not forced to climb with the verb. More precisely, one might argue that
a. clitics must climb, weak cannot;
b. clitic must climb, weak can climb;
c. clitics can climb, weak cannot;

Under (a) or (b), all cases of (apparent) enclisis to the participle in compound tenses would involve weak pronouns, as proposed by Cardinaletti 2015. However, in what follows I will show that none of the above generalisation holds: (c) is falsified by data from medieval Romance, see 6.1; while (a/b) are contradicted by data from several Romance varieties, see 6.2.

6.1 Preverbal weak pronouns in Romance

In modern Italian, weak *loro* never occurs before the finite verb, while clitics normally stand proclitic to the inflected verb. In compound tenses, *loro* normally occurs after the past participle, but it can marginally occur before the participle in (34) (although some speakers say that the latter order is restricted to a very bureaucratic register) and, in restructuring contexts like (35), *loro* can climb above the infinitive.

(33) (*loro)   diedi   (loro)   un   bacio
     to.them I.gave   to.them   a   kiss
     'I gave them a kiss'

(34) Ho   (?loro)   regalato (loro)   il   mio libro
     I.have to.them given   to.them the my   book
     'I gave them my book'

(35) a. Posso (loro)   dire   (loro)   che...
        I.can to.them say   to.them that
        'I can tell them that...'
     b. Farò   (loro)   pulire (loro)   la   macchina
        I.will.make   to.them clean   to.them the car

Old Italian, which exhibits a full paradigm of dative weak forms, allowed weak pronouns to occur between the auxiliary and the participle as in (36) and, unlike modern Italian, before the inflected verb in sentences without T-to-C movement as in (37) (Cardinaletti 2010: 418–424, 427–429):

(36) i quali denari avea loro   lasciati Baldovino[9]
     which money   had   to.them lent   B.
     'money that Baldovino had lent to them'

(37) a. Vertute [...] lui   obedisce e   lui   acquista onore[10]
        Virtue   to.him   obeys   and to.him   acquires honor
        'virtue obeys him, and so honors him,'
     b. quello che   lloro   piacie[11]
        that   that to.them pleases
        'what pleases them'

In conclusion, the above data show that, although weak elements climb less readily than clitic pronouns and, diachronically, tend to climb less and less, they are not necessarily bound to a postverbal position in the low IP area.

---

9 [1278], Libro d'amministrazione dell'eredità di Baldovino Iacopi Riccomanni p. 438, vv. 20–21 (La prosa italiana delle origini: I, Testi toscani di carattere pratico, a cura di Arrigo Castellani, Bologna, Pàtron, 1982).
10 Dante, Rime, 49 CVI.
11 Libricciolo di Bene Bencivenni I, p. 305, rr 20–21.

6.2 Generalised enclisis

Enclisis in compound tenses is attested in several Romance areas: Franco-Provençal (Chenal 1986), Piedmontese (Parry 2005 a.o.), Dolomitic Ladin (Rasom 2008), Abruzzese (Benincà & Pescarini 2015), Romanian (limited to the accusative feminine clitic *o*):

(38) L'   an   tot   portà-lèi   vià.   (Chenal 1986:340)
     They= have everything carried=to.him away
     'They have taken everything away from him.'

(39) a. I   an   rangiò-la.   (Cairo Montenotte, Parry 2005)
        They= have fixed=it.F
        'They fixed it.'

(40) a. 'ajə   ddʒa   məɲ'ɲetəmǝlu
        I.have already eaten=to.me=it
        (San Valentino in Abruzzo citeriore, Benincà & Pescarini 2015)
     b. 'ajə   ddʒa   mə   lu   məɲ'ɲetə
        I.have already to.me= it= eaten
        'I have already eaten it'

(41) a. Am   mâncat-o   (Romanian, Dragomirescu 2013: 193)
        I.have eaten-it.F
        'I ate it'
     b. aş   mâncat-o
        I.would eat- it.F
        'I would eat it'

By assuming that clitics always climb, than we must conclude that all the pronouns in (38)–(41) are not clitic. This, however, leads us to some paradoxes.

First, in Romanian and Italian dialects enclisis and doubling co-occur, see (42). Then, if doubling is a defining property of clitics (see above), then the pronouns in (42) cannot be weak (*tertium non datur*).

(42) Am   vazut-o   pe   ea.   (Romanian)
     I.have seen-her DOM her
     'I have seen her.'

Second, it seems to me that the lack of climbing can be better analysed in terms of external (namely, clausal) factors. In section 4 I have already argued – following previous works by Parry 1997, 1998, 2005 – that enclisis in northwestern Italian dialects results from a change affecting the climbing mechanism, rather than a change in the status of the pronoun. According to Tortora 2015a, climbing is blocked as compound tenses are reanalysed as a kind of biclausal structure. The hypothesis that compound tenses in certain varieties are 'less monoclausal' than in others may then account for data from early Italian (Poletto 2014), in which enclisis to the past participle is attested in compound tenses under ellipsis:

(43) a. m'ha con un bastone tutto rotto e detta**mi** la
me=has with a cudgel all broken and said=to.me the
maggior villania che mai si dicesse a niuna cattiva femina[12]
greatest rudeness that ever one said to any bad woman
b. trovò l' arme del re Meliadus, che lli avea
found the weapons of.the king M. that to.him =he.had
fatta sì bella deliberanza, e donato**gli**
done so nice disposal, and given=to.him[13]
c. avea una sola pecora, la quale avea comperata, nutricata,
he.had one only sheep, the which he.had bought, fed
e cresciuta e dato**le** a mangiare del suo pane[14]
and raised and given=to.her to eat of.the his bread

In modern Italian, sentences like those illustrated in (43) are ungrammatical as clitics always climb and ellipsis is allowed if and only if the same (kind of) argument is pronominalized in both conjoints:

(44) a. ***mi** ha sgridato e picchiato-**mi**.
me= has scolded and hit=me
b. **mi** ha sgridato e picchiato.
me= has scolded and hit
'He/she scolded and hit me'

---

12 Boccaccio, *Decam*.
13 Novellino, 63.
14 Ottimo, p. 304.

The contrast between old and modern Italian is arguably due to the syntactic structure of sentences featuring compound tenses in concert with the conditions ruling clitic climbing, i.e. external, clausal factors. Conversely, an analysis in terms of pronominal classes would not offer any promising account of the facts illustrated in (43)–(44) or improve our understanding of clitic placement in the languages exemplified in (38)–(41) (more on this in the next section).

7 Split clusters

In many Romance languages, clitics form tight clusters with a rigid order. However, clitics can sometimes co-occur without forming a cluster. For instance, in some Franco-Provençal dialects dative and accusative clitics are not adjacent as the dative clitic climbs, while the accusative remains enclitic to the past participle:

(45) a. T'   an- të   prèdzà-nen?
        to.you= have=they spoken=of.it?
        'Did they speak of it to you?'
    b. T'   an-të   deut-lo?
        to.you= have=they said=it?
        'Did they say it to you?'

Arguably, this state of affairs is a consequence of the climbing mechanism illustrated in the previous section. On the basis of data from different Italian dialects, Rasom (2008) and Tortora (2014a/b) show that changes in clitic placement do not affect all clitic forms at the same time. As a consequence, certain dialects may exhibit patterns of 'selective' climbing (the terminology is mine) as some clitics must/can climb, while others must attach to the past participle, thus resulting in a split configuration.

Similar phenomena occur in restructuring environments, where clitic sequences can be split even in languages in which clitics normally form tight clusters. Old Italian displays few examples, in (46), but a similar pattern is allowed in modern Italian as well, see (47), in particular with clusters featuring the impersonal clitic *si* (Pescarini 2014):

(46) a. Ma la cosa incredibile **mi** fece[15]
But the incredible thing me= made
indur-**lo** ad ovra ch'a me stesso pesa
induce=him to work that to my self weighs
'But your plight, being incredible, made me goad him to this deed that weighs on me'
b. se 'n tal maniera **mi** dovete dar-**lo**.[16]
if in such way to.me= you.have.to give=it
'if you have to give it to me in this way'

(47) a. **si** può portar-**lo** domani[17]
one= can take=it tomorrow
'we can take it tomorrow'
b. %**mi** ha dovuto portar-**ci** un'amica[18]
me= has had take=there a friend.F
'A friend of mine had to take me there'
c. %**c'** ha dovuto portar-**mi** un'amica
there= has had take=me a friend.F
'A friend of mine had to take me there'

The data above show that 'forming a tight cluster' is not *per se* a defining property of clitic combinations as, whenever they are not subject to mandatory placement conditions (as in restructuring contexts), they are free to occur separately.

In my opinion, the data in (46)–(47) and those in (45) point towards a finer theory of clitic climbing. Conversely, if we pursue an analysis in terms of pronominal classes (by claiming that all non-climbing pronouns are weak), we end up missing the link between (45) and (46)–(47) and reach the (disputable) conclusion that the pronouns in (46)–(47) are weak as well.

---

15 Dante, Inf. 13: 50–51.
16 Amico di Dante, Rime, Son. 44.
17 Notice that the impersonal *si* follows the accusative clitic, e.g. *lo si*, while the reflexive *si* exhibits the mirror order. Furthermore, it is worth noting that the impersonal clitic must climb in restructuring construction, this is why the counterpart of (26a) with the opposite order of clitics, e.g. **lo può portarsi domani*, is ungrammatical. Notice that this is orthogonal to the issue of separability.
18 Retrieved via Google on 30.10.12.

8 Proclisis/enclisis asymmetries

Laenzlinger (1993), (1994), Ordóñez and Repetti (2006), (2014); Cardinaletti (2015a), (2015b) argued that some puzzling morphophonological alternations between proclitics and enclitics could be accounted for if certain enclitic pronouns were analysed as weak elements.

In many languages, enclitic pronouns tend to be 'heavier' than proclitics even in absence of stress shift phenomena (see also Renzi and Vanelli 1983 on subject clitics). Several asymmetries can be accounted for under trivial phonological accounts, but not all alternations lend themselves to a phonological analysis (Ordóñez and Repetti 2006, 2014; Pescarini 2018). For instance, in modern French 1/2p enclitics are identical to strong forms:

(48) a. Il **me le** donne
    He to.me it gives
    'He gives it to me'
  b. Donne-**le**-**moi**!
    Give-it-to.me
    'Give it to me!'

Laenzlinger (1993) argues that the *me/moi* alternation is syntactic in nature and that *moi* is in fact a weak pronoun. He discards the hypothesis that the *me/moi* alternation may be due to the assignment of stress to the word-final syllable (Foulet 1924) because, although it might be a possible diachronic explanation, the phonological account cannot hold synchronically, as the same alternation is observed in non-standard varieties displaying the inverted order of clitics, e.g., subst. Fr. *donne=**moi**=**le***.

(49) a. Donne-**le**-**moi**!
  b. Donne-**moi**-**le**!
  c. Donne-**me**-**le**!
  d. *Donne-**le**-**me**!
    'give it to me'

However, by the same token, all third person dative clitics of French should be weak, as the original dative clitic *li* ('to him/her' > Lat. ILLI) was then replaced, in enclisis and in proclisis, by the oblique form *lui*:

(50) a. Et il **li**   dit: (Old French)
     And he to.him/her= says
     'and he says to him/her:'
   b. Et il **lui**   dit: (Modern French)
     And he to.him/her says
     'and he says to him/her:'

Following Laenzlinger's view, the change in (50) results from the substitution of a clitic with a weak element and, similarly, we can reconstruct the same change for the plural clitic *lor* (< ILLORUM), instead of the expected **lis* (< ILLIS). The point is that no empirical or theoretical gain results from this approach.

In general, such analyses rest on theories envisaging a direct mapping from syntax to morphology. In this view, weak pronouns are expected to exhibit a richer morphology insofar as they correspond to a larger chunk of structure (Manzini & Savoia 2004). However, clitics often have a rather complex morphology and sometimes they are 'bigger' than strong pronouns.

For instance, several Romance languages exhibit cases of 'compound' clitic forms, i.e. clitics expressed by a combination of two clitic formatives. In many Veneto dialects, for instance, the genitive/partitive clitic is formed by a combination of the locative clitic *ghe* [ge] and the partitive element *ne*, see (51)a. The composite structure of the partitive is synchronically evident, as in several Veneto varieties the former item (*ghe*) disappears when the partitive is combined with a dative or locative clitic (Benincà 1994), see (51)b:

(51) a. ghene=   magno do   (Pad.)
      of.it/them= I.eat   two
      'I eat two of them'
   b. te=   (*ghe)ne= porto   do   (Pad.)
      to.you of.it/them I.bring two
      'I bring you two of them'

Similarly, certain third person accusative pronouns result from the combination of different clitics and agreement markers. As shown in (52)a, the Gascon clitic *lousi* 'to them.M' can be decomposed into an accusative form *lous* 'them' plus the oblique marker *i* (identical to the so-called locative clitic corresponding to the Venetan *ghe* in (51)). In turn, the accusative clitic *lous* is formed by several formatives (*l*- -*ou*- -*s*). Analogously, the Catalan dialect spoken in Barcelona (Bonet 1991) exhibits a similar compound plural dative form due to the combination of the accusative clitic *elz* (*el* + plural -*z*) with *i*:

(52) a. Gascon (Rohlfs 1970):   b. Barceloní Catalan (Bonet 1991)
       lou   'it/him'   *(e)l*   'it/him'
       lous   'them'   *(e)lz*   'them'
       i   'there'   *hi*   /i/   'there'
       lousi 'to them'   *(e)lzi*   'to them'
                                          (sometimes written *elz'hi*)

This shows that certain clitic forms have a composite structure due to the combination of several clitic items and that such compound structures have not undergone reanalysis. In fact, the morphological boundary between the two is still active as they undergo partial dropping (as in the case of Venetan *ghene*) or allow the insertion of intervening clitic material as in the case of Barceloní (Bonet 1991).

In conclusion, the data above show that morphological complexity cannot be taken as evidence to distinguish clitic from weak pronouns and, more generally, to argue that functional elements fall into different classes on the basis of their inner structure.

9 Interpolation

Benincà & Cinque (1993) elaborate on a series of asymmetries between proclitics and enciltics and conclude that the latter are 'closer' to the verbal host than the former. Among the various diagnostics, the generalisation is supported by interpolation phenomena, i.e. the occurrence of adverbs or other constituents between the clitic and its host. With proclitics, interpolation is attested in a number of present-day languages such as western Ibero-Romance (Uriagereka 1995) and in several Italo-Romance dialects: Triestino (Benincà 1997: 129; Paoli 2007), Cosentino (Ledgeway and Lombardi 2005), the dialect spoken in Antrodoco (Scorretti 2012) and other (upper) southern Italian varieties (see references in Ledgeway and Lombardi 2005).

(53) a. Si   sempre lava   (Cosentino, Ledgeway & Lombardi 2005)
       Self= always   he.washes
       'he always washes himself'
   b. el   me   sempre dizi   (Triestino, Benincà 1997: 129)
       He= to.me= always says
       'He always speaks to me'

Interpolation between proclitics and the verb was marginally allowed in old Italian and old French, while in old Spanish and Portuguese (but not in Catalan), interpolation was more productive as several constituents of any kind could be interpolated.

With enclitics, conversely, Benincà and Cinque (1993) concluded that interpolation was not attested. The generalisation, however, was later challenged by data from some dialects spoken at the Piedmont/Lombardy border, in which enclitics can be separated from the verb by aspectual adverbs, see (54) from Tortora (2002, 2015). It is worth recalling that Piedmontese dialects exhibit enclisis is compound tenses and some of them, including Borgomanerese, have generalised enclisis in all finite clauses

(54) a. I   porti   mi-lla.
         I= bring   not=it
         'I'm not bringing it.'
     b. I   vangumma   già-nni   da dü agni.
         We=   see   already=us   of two years
         'We've already been seeing each other for two years.'
     c. I   vônghi   piö-llu.
         I= see   anymore=him
         'I don't see him anymore.'

Cardinaletti (2015) entertains the hypothesis that, when interpolation happens with enclitics, the pronouns must be weak. In fact, the pronouns in (54) occur in the same position of Italian *loro*, which can follow certain aspectual adverbs, while enclitics are always adjacent to the verb. However, if we take interpolation at face value, I cannot see why interpolation is a clue of weak pronouns in (54), but not in (53). As a matter of fact, Benincà and Cinque argued that the structural 'distance' between the host and enclitics is smaller than that occurring between the host and proclitics. Then, given (54), one is expected to conclude that Borgomanerese enclitics have the same status of proclitics in western Ibero-Romance, southern Italo-Romance, and Triestino. Then, if an analysis in terms of weak pronouns was advanced for the former, the same explanation should hold for the latter as well.

In conclusion, one can claim that either interpolation is a hallmark of weak pronouns (both in enclisis and in proclisis) or, more probably, interpolation is orthogonal to the weak/clitic divide.

10 Complement of P

Cardinaletti & Starke (1996: 24) notice that one of the properties distinguishing Romance clitics from Germanic weak pronouns is the possibility of occurring in the complement position of prepositional phrases:

(55) a. Je pars avec *le/lui
    I= leave with him
    'I leave with him'
 b. Ich kann ohne es nicht leben
    I can without it not live
    'I cannot live without it'

Clitics pronouns can in fact be the complement of prepositions, but then they must climb to the inflected verb. Again, the ungrammaticality of clitics under prepositions can be seen as a side effect of the climbing requirement and, in principle, I do not see any connection between the inner structure of pronouns and their need of climbing out of prepositional phrases.

(56) a. Va-lle dietro (*le)!
    Go=to.her beside
    'Follow her'
 b. Ci sei seduto sopra (*ci).
    There= you.are sit on
    'you are sitting on it'
 c. Mi era seduto accanto (*mi).
    To.me= he/she.was sit near
    'He/she was sitting near me'

Moreover, if weak were not allowed to climb out of prepositional phrases, one would expect that the Italian weak pronoun *loro* 'to them' should remain under P (like Germ. *es*). Contrary to our expectations, *loro* must occur in the usual postparticipial position. In this respect, *loro* does not pattern like Germ. *es*, but – *mutatis mutandis* – like a clitic.

(57) a. Si era seduto loro vicino
    Him/herself= he/she.was sit to.them near
    'He/she was sitting near them'

b. Si   era   seduto vicino *loro   / a loro
   Him/herself= he/she.was sit   near   to.them / to them
   'He/she was sitting near them'

Furthermore, certain Italian vernaculars show cases of fully-fledged clitics following the preposition. This is attested in some examples from old Italian in which the dative clitic *gli* 'to him' follows a lexical preposition, see (58). Cardinaletti (2015b: §7.1) proposes that *gli* in (58) is a weak element. However, it is worth recalling that old Italian weak pronouns are identical to strong pronouns (e.g. *lui* = weak 'to him', strong 'him', Cardinaletti 2010), while *gli* is a fully-fledged clitic.

(58) a. essa incontro-gli   da tre gradi   discese[19]
        She   towards=him   from three steps took.down
        'She took three steps down towards him'
     b. e   l' altro   dietro-gli[20]
        and the other   behind=him
        'and the other after him'
     c. e   'l maestro Dino allato-gli[21]
        and the master D.   along=him

Instances of enclitics to prepositions are found in present-day dialects such as the one spoken in Cairo Montenotte, see (59) (Parry 2005: 179).

(59) a. S' u   n'   ièra chila dedré-me, mi i   perdiva
        If she= not= was she   behind=me, I   them=   lose
        'If she had not been behind me, I would have lost them'
     b. u   iè ina sc-trò própi lì   dedré-te
        SCL= is a   street just there behind=you
        'there is a street just behind you'

It is worth recalling that Cairese is one of the aforementioned Piedmontese dialects in which clitic pronouns occur twice, in proclisis and in enclisis of compound tenses (I repeat below the relevant examples):

---

[19] Boccaccio, *Decameron*, II.5: p. 100.
[20] Sacchetti, Franco [1400], *Trecentonovelle (Il)* (a cura di Vincenzo Pernicone, Firenze, Sansoni, 1946.), p. 245, v. 29.
[21] Ibidem, p. 199, v. 6.

(60) a. A   l'   uma   visct-le   (Cairese)
         We= him/it= have   seen=it/him
         'We saw him/it"
    b. A   'm   sun   fò-me   in   fazing
         I= to.myself= am   made=to.myself a   cake
         'I baked me a cake'
    c. I   l'   an   catò-le
         they= it= have   bought=it
         'They bought it"

Enclisis to certain prepositions is attested in several other varieties that do not display enclisis in finite clauses (Salvioni 1903; Vedovato and Berizzi 2011; Cuzzolin 2015):

(61) no   sten   ndar   drio-ghe   (Fossalta di Piave)
      not we.stay   to.go   behind-to.him/her
      'Let us not follow him/her'

In conclusion, the data discussed so far corroborate the idea that being the complement of prepositions is not a solid diagnostic distinguishing between pronominal classes. In fact, alleged weak pronouns such as Italian *loro* are obligatorily raised from PPs, while enclisis to prepositions is allowed in a few Romance dialects.

11 Conclusions

In some Romance varieties, clitics have an unexpected, 'non-canonical' behaviour: they are stressed, they do not always climb to the inflected verb, they are separated from the verb by certain adverbs, they have a rich morphology, they can be governed by prepositions, they do not form tight clusters, etc.

Laenzlinger 1993, 1994; Ordóñez and Repetti 2006, 2014; Cardinaletti 2015 among others have argued that non-canonical clitics are in fact weak elements in the technical sense of Cardinaletti 1991, 1994, 1998; Cardinaletti & Starke 1996, 1999. However, many tests that are normally used for the definition of classes do not hold cross-linguistically, while other diagnostics are often contradictory.

From a theoretical point of view, this means that there is no clear evidence for a principled distinction between classes and, in particular, there is no conclusive evidence supporting the idea that the distribution, shape, and further characteristics of pronouns depend on their internal make up, i.e. their inner syntax. Although (2) provides an elegant and appealing analysis of several puzzles, the overall scenario shows that so called *classes* are to be defined as clusters of properties emerging at the clausal level.

References

Benincà, Paola. 1980. Nomi senza articolo. *Rivista di grammatica generativa* 5. 51–63.
Benincà, Paola. 1983. Il clitico *a* nel dialetto padovano. In Benincà et al., *Scritti linguistici in onore di G. B. Pellegrini*, 25–35. Pisa: Pacini.
Benincà, Paola. 1983–4. Un'ipotesi sulla sintassi delle lingue romanze medievali. *Quaderni Patavini di Linguistica* 4. 3–19.
Benincà, Paola. 1986. Punti di sintassi comparata dei dialetti italiani settentrionali. In G. Holtus and K. Ringger (eds.), *Raetia antiqua et moderna. W. Th. Elwert zum 80*, 457–79. Tübingen: Geburtstag.
Benincà, Paola. 1988. L'ordine degli elementi della frase e le costruzioni marcate. In L. Renzi, *Grande grammatica italiana di consultazione*, 115–192. Bologna: Il Mulino.
Benincà, Paola. 1994. *La variazione sintattica*. Bologna: Il Mulino.
Benincà, Paola. 1995. Complement clitics in Medieval Romance: the Tobler-Mussafia Law. In A. Battye and I. Roberts, *Clause Structure and Language Change*, 325–344. New York and Oxford: Oxford Universiry Press.
Benincà, Paola. 2006. A detailed map of the Left Periphery in Medieval Romance. In R. Zanuttini, H. Campos, E. Herburger, and P. Portner (eds.), *Negation, Tense, and Clausal Architecture: Crosslinguistic Investigations*, 53–86. Washington: Georgetown University Press.
Benincà, Paola, & Cinque, Guglielmo. 1993. Su alcune differenze tra enclisi e proclisis. In Michele A. Cortelazzo, Erasmo Leso, Pier Vincenzo Mengaldo, Gianfelice Peron, and Lorenzo Renzi, *Omaggio a Gianfranco Folena*, 2313–2326. Padova: Editoriale Programma.
Benincà, Paola & Diego Pescarini. 2015. Clitic placement in the dialect of S. Valentino in Abruzzo citeriore. *Archivio Glottologico Italiano* 101. 37–65.
Benincà, Paola & Cecilia Poletto. 2004. Topic, focus and V2: defining the CP sublayers. In Rizzi, L. (ed.), *The Structure of CP and IP: The Cartography of Syntactic Structures, Volume 2*, 52–75. New York: Oxford University Press.
Bonet, Eulalia. 1991. *Morphology after syntax: Pronominal clitics in Romance*. Cambridge (Mass.), Massachusetts Institute of Technology: Doctoral dissertation.
Cardinaletti, Anna. 1991. On pronoun dative movement. The Italian dative *loro*. *Probus* 3. 127–153.
Cardinaletti, Anna. 1994. On the internal structure of pronominal DPs. *The Linguistic Review* 11. 195–219.
Cardinaletti, Anna. 1998. On the deficient/strong opposition in possessive systems. In A. Alexiadou & Ch. Wilder (eds.), *Possessors, Predicates, and Movement in the Determiner Phrase*, 17–53. Amsterdam: Benjamins.

Cardinaletti, Anna. 2010. Il pronome personale obliquo. In Giampaolo Salvi and Lorenzo Renzi, *Grammatica dell'italiano antico*, vol. I, 414–450. Bologna: il Mulino.
Cardinaletti, Anna. 2015a. Cases of apparent enclisis on past participles in Romance varieties. *Isogloss* 1(2). 179–197.
Cardinaletti, Anna. 2015b. Syntactic Effects of Cliticization. In T. Kiss and A. Alexiadou, *Syntax. Theories and Analyses*, Vol. I, 595–653. Berlin: Mouton de Guyter.
Cardinaletti, Anna & Starke, Michel. 1996. Deficient pronouns: A view from Germanic. In Hoskuldur Thrainsson (Ed.), *Studies in Comparative Germanic Syntax II*, 21–65. Dordrecht: Kluwer.
Cardinaletti, Anna & Starke, Michel. 1999. The typology of structural deficiency: a case study of the three classes of pronouns. In Henk van Riemsdijk, *Clitics in the Languages of Europe*, 145–233. Berlin and New York: Mouton de Gruyter.
Chenal, Aimé. 1986. *Le franco-provençal valdôtain*. Aoste: Musumeci.
Cuzzolin, Pierluigi. 2015. *Vae drioghe, mi!* Sull'interpretazione del clitico *ghe* in alcune varietà di Veneto. In Mariagrazia Busà and Sara Gesuato, *Lingue e contesti. Studi in onore di Alberto M. Mioni*, 573–582. Padova: Cleup.
Dèchaine R.-M. & Wiltschko, M. (2002). Decomposing pronouns. *Linguistic Inquiry* 33. 409–422.
Dragomirescu, Adina. 2013. Complex predicates. In Gabriela Pană Dindelegan (ed.), *The grammar of Romanian*. Oxford: Oxford University Press.
Egerland, Verner 2005. Diachronic change and pronoun status: Italian dative 'loro'. *Linguistics* 43. 1105–1130.
Egerland, Verner. 2010. I pronomi 'lo' e 'ro' nel toscano dei primi secoli. *L'Italia Dialettale* 71. 111–145.
Egerland, Verner. 2013. On the grammar of kinship: Possessive enclisis in Italian dialects. In Jeppesen Kragh, K. & Lindschouw, J., *Deixis and Pronouns*, 69–83. Amsterdam: Benjamins.
Foulet, Lucien. 1919. *Petite syntaxe de l'ancien francais*. Paris: Champion.
Foulet, Lucien. 1924. L'accent tonique et l'ordre des mots: formes faibles du pronom personnel après le verbe. *Romania* 50. 54–93.
Foulet, Lucien. 1935. L'extension de la forme oblique du pronom personnel en ancien français. *Romania* 61. 257–315, 401–63.
Giusti, Giuliana. 2010. I possessive. In Salvi, Giampaolo and Lorenzo Renzi, *Grammatica dell'italiano antico*, 359–375. Bologna: Il Mulino.
Holmberg, Anders. 1986. *Word order and syntactic features in the Scandinavian languages and English*. Unpublished doctoral dissertation, Department of General Linguistics, University of Stockholm.
Holmberg, Anders. 1991. The distribution of Scandinavian weak pronouns. In Henk van Riemsdijk and Luigi Rizzi, *Clitics and their Hosts*, 155–174. Geneva and Tilburg: ESF-Eurotype.
Jaberg, Karl & Jakob Jud (1928–1940). *Sprach- und Sachatlas Italiens und der Südschweiz*, Vol. 1–8, Zofingen, Bern. Digital version by Graziano Tisato: http://www3.pd.istc.cnr.it/navigais-web/
Kayne, Richard. 1975. *French syntax: the transformational cycle*. Cambridge (Mass.): MIT Press.
Kayne, Richard. 1983. Chains, Categories External to S and French Complex Inversion. *Natural Language and Linguistic Theory* 1. 107–139.

Laenzlinger, Christopher. 1993. A syntactic view of Romance pronominal sequences. *Probus* 5. 242–270.
Laenzlinger, Christopher. 1994. Enclitic clustering: The case of French positive imperatives. *Rivista di Grammatica Generativa* 19. 71–104.
Ledgeway, Adam & Linda Lombardi. 2005. Verb Movement, Adverbs and Clitic Positions in Romance. *Probus* 17. 79–113.
Loporcaro, Michele. 2002. Il pronome loro nell'Italia centro-meridionale e la storia del sistema pronominale romanzo, *Vox Romanica* 61. 48–116.
Rivero, María Luisa. 1986. Parameters in the Typology of Clitics in Romance and Old Spanish. *Language*, 62(4). 774–807.
Rivero, María Luisa & José Lema. 1991. Types of Verbal Movement in Old Spanish: Modals, Futures and Perfects. *Probus* 3. 237–278.
Longobardi, Giuseppe. 1994. Reference and proper names: a theory of N-movement in syntax and logical form. *Linguistic Inquiry* 25. 609–665.
Manzini, Maria Rita. 2014. Grammatical categories: Strong and weak pronouns in Romance. *Lingua* 150. 171–201.
Manzini, Maria Rita, and Savoia, Leonardo. 2004. Clitics: Cooccurrence and mutual exclusion patterns In Luigi Rizzi (ed.), *The structure of CP and IP*, 211–50. Oxford: Oxford University Press.
Manzini, Maria Rita, and Savoia, Leonardo. 2005. *I dialetti italiani e romance. Morfosintassi generativa*. Alessandria: Edizioni Dell'Orso.
Manzini, Maria Rita, and Savoia, Leonardo Maria. 2009. Morphology dissolves into syntax: Infixation and Doubling in Romance languages. *Annali Online di Ferrara – Lettere* 1. 1–28.
Manzini, Maria Rita & Savoia, Leonardo Maria. 2014. From Latin to Romance: case loss and preservation in pronominal systems. *Probus* 26. 217–248.
Ordóñez, Francisco & Lori Repetti. 2006. Stressed Enclitics? In Jean-Pierre Montreuil, *New Analyses on Romance Linguistics: Volume II: Phonetics, Phonology and Dialectology (Selected Papers from the 35th LSRL 35)*, 167–181. Amsterdam: Benjamins.
Ordóñez, Francisco & Lori Repetti. 2014. On the morphological restriction of hosting clitics in Italian and Sardinian dialects. *Italia dialettale* 75. 173–199.
Palasis, Katerina. 2015. Subject clitics and preverbal negation in European French: Variation, acquisition, diatopy and diachrony. *Lingua* 161. 125–143.
Paoli, Sandra. 2007. Interpolation structures and clitics in Triestino. In Bentley, Delia and Ledgeway, Adam (eds.), *Sui dialetti italoromanzi: saggi in onore di Nigel B. Vincent, The Italianist* 27, Special Supplement 1. 184–199.
Parry, Mair. 1993. Subject clitics in Piedmontese: a Diachronic Perspective. *Vox Romanica* 52. 96–116.
Parry, Mair. 1997. Preverbal negation and clitic ordering, with particular reference to a group of North-West Italian dialects. *Zeitschrift für Romanische Philologie* 113(2). 243–70.
Parry, Mair. 2005. *Parluma 'd Coiri. Sociolinguistica e grammatical del dialetto di Cairo Montenotte*. Savona: Editrice Liguria.
Pescarini, Diego. 2014. Prosodic restructuring and morphological opacity. The evolution of Italo-Romance clitic clusters. In Ledgeway A, Benincà P, Vincent N. (eds.), *Diachrony and Dialects: Grammatical Change in the Dialects of Italy*. New York – Oxford: Oxford University Press.
Pescarini, Diego. 2018. Stressed enclitics are not weak pronouns: a plea for allomorphy. In F. Ordóñez, L. Repetti (eds.)*Romance Languages and Linguistic Theory 14: Selected*

papers from the 46th Linguistic Symposium on Romance Languages (LSRL), Stony Brook, NY. Amsterdam: Benjamins, 231–244.

Poletto, Cecilia. 2000. *The Higher Functional Field. Evidence from Northern Italian Dialects.* Oxford – New York: Oxford University Press.

Poletto, Cecilia. 2002. The left periphery of V2 Rhaetoromance dialects: a new view on V2 and V3. In *Syntactic Microvariation*, ed. by Sjef Barbiers, Leonie Cornips, and Susanne van der Kleij, 214–242. Amsterdam: Meertens Institut (https://www.meertens.knaw.nl/books/synmic/)

Poletto, Cecilia. 2014. Word Order in Old Italian. Oxford: Oxford University Press.

Rasom, Sabrina. 2008. *Lazy concord in the Central Ladin feminine plural DP: A case study on the interaction between morphosyntax and semantics.* Doctoral dissertation, University of Padua. Available at http://paduaresearch.cab.unipd.it/268/1/tesiSabrinaRasom.pdf.

Renzi, Lorenzo & Laura Vanelli. 1983. I pronomi soggetto in alcune varietà romanze, In Paola Benincà et al. (eds.), *Scritti in onore di G.B. Pellegrini*, 120–145. Pisa, Pacini.

Repetti, Lori. 2016. The phonology of postverbal pronouns in Romance languages. In Christina Tortora, Marcel den Dikken, Ignacio L. Montoya and Teresa O'Neill, *Romance Linguistics 2013: Selected papers from the 43rd Linguistic Symposium on Romance Languages (LSRL)*, New York, 17–19 April, 2013, 361–378. Amsterdam: Benjamins.

Rivero, Maria. Luisa. 1991. Clitic and NP Climbing in Old Spanish. In H. Campos and F. Martínez-Gil, *Current Studies in Spanish Linguistics*, 241–282. Washington, D. C.: Georgetown University Press.

Rivero, Maria. Luisa. 1997. On two locations for complement clitic pronouns: Serbo-Croatian, Bulgarian and Old Spanish. In A. van Kemenade and N. Vincent, *Parameters of Morphosyntactic Change*, 170–206. Cambridge: Cambridge University Press.

Roberts, Ian. 1993. The nature of subject clitics in Franco-Provençal Valdôtain. In A. Belletti (ed.), *Syntactic Theory and the Dialects of Italy*, 319–353. Turin: Rosenberg & Sellier.

Rohlfs, Gerhard. 1966. *Grammatica storica della lingua italiana e dei suoi dialetti*. Torino: Einaudi.

Rohlfs, Gerhard. 1970. *Le gascon*. Tübingen: Niemeyer.

Salvioni, Carlo. 1903. Del pronome enclitico oggetto suffisso ad altri elementi che non sieno la voce verbale. *Rendiconti del reale istituto lombardo di scienze e lettere* 36. 1012–1021.

Scorretti, Mauro. 2012. *Il dialetto di Antrodoco*. Pescara: Fondazione Ernesto Gianmarco.

Starke, Michal. 2009. Nanosyntax A short primer to a new approach to language. *Nordlyd* 36 (1). 1–6.

Tortora, Christina. 2002. Romance enclisis, prepositions, and aspect. *Natural Language and Linguistic Theory* 20. 725–758.

Tortora, Christina. 2014a. Patterns of variation and diachronic change in Piedmontese object clitic syntax. In P. Benincà, A. Ledgeway, & N. Vincent (eds.), *Diachrony and Dialects*, 218–240. Oxford: Oxford University Press.

Tortora, Christina. 2014b. On the relation between functional architecture and patterns of change in Romance clitic syntax. In M.-H. Côté & E. Mathieu (eds.), *Variation within and across Romance Languages*, 331–348. Amsterdam: Benjamins.

Tortora, Christina. 2015. *A Comparative Grammar of Borgomanerese*. New York: Oxford University Press.

Uriagereka, Juan. 1995. Aspects of the syntax of clitic placement in Western Romance. *Linguistic Inquiry* 26. 79–123.

Vanelli, Laura. 1989. *I dialetti italiani settentrionali nel panorama romanzo*. Roma: Bulzoni.

Vedovato, Diana. 2009. Weak pronouns in Italian: Instances of a broken cycle? In Elly van Gelderen, *Cyclical Change*, 133–156. Amsterdam: Benjamins.

Vedovato, Diana and Mariachiara Berizzi. 2011. Enclisi pronominale alle preposizioni *drio* e *sora* in alcune varietà venete. *Rivista Italiana di Dialettologia* 35. 37–50.

Wolfe, Sam. 2016. On the Left Periphery of V2 Languages. *Rivista di Grammatica Generativa* 38. 287–310.

Francesca Ramaglia and Mara Frascarelli
The (information) structure of existentials

1 Introduction

1.1 Aim of the study

This paper proposes an interface analysis of a specific type of existential sentence (illustrated in [1]) which – according to the present approach – constitutes a marked copular construction:

(1) There is [a man] [in the garden]

A sentence of this type is used to assert the existence of the referent denoted by the post-copular phrase (*a man* in our example) in the location connected with the (optional) final PP (*in the garden*), or else – if the latter is missing – in a location given in the universe of discourse.

The paper is organized as follows. The introductory section is dedicated to an overview of the literature concerned with copular constructions and information-structurally marked structures. Section 2 deals with existential sentences, presenting first some of the most influential works dedicated to this topic, so as to propose an interface analysis which takes into account the formal, semantic and discourse properties of the relevant constructions. Section 3 is concerned with a well-known phenomenon associated to existential sentences in many languages, namely the Definiteness Effect (henceforth, DE). Comparing data from languages showing DE (like English) with languages which apparently do not (like Italian), the present approach reveals that *there*-sentences with a definite post-copular phrase do not qualify as existential constructions

---

Note: This research was partially funded by MIUR (Ministero dell'Istruzione, dell'Università e della Ricerca) within the "SIR Programme 2014" (Principal Investigator: Francesca Ramaglia; research project title: "Comparing Nominal Predication at the Interfaces: a cross-linguistic study"; project code: RBSI140Q5F).

An earlier version of this paper was presented at the *42nd Incontro di Grammatica Generativa* (February, 18–20, 2016 – University of Salento). We wish to thank the audience, and in particular Maria Teresa Guasti, Olga Kellert and Roberto Zamparelli for their comments and suggestions.

Francesca Ramaglia and Mara Frascarelli, University of Roma Tre

proper, as they are characterized by different interpretive and formal properties. Results are summarized in section 4.

1.2 Background

1.2.1 Copular constructions

The term "copular construction" is generally used in the literature to indicate a structure in which two phrases of any category are linked by means of a copula:[1]

(2) XP – copula – YP

This structure is related to various types of copular constructions, which allow for different phrasal categories in the positions indicated in (2) as XP and YP (cf. Den Dikken 2006a). Limiting our attention to structures featuring two (major) nominal constituents, at least two types of copular constructions can be distinguished on the basis of their semantic and syntactic properties. In particular, many scholars have proposed a typology of these structures based on the referential quality of the post-copular phrase (i.e., YP in [2]).[2] In order to illustrate this two-fold classification, consider the following example (taken from Den Dikken 2006a):

(3) [$_{XP}$ *His supper*] *is* [$_{YP}$ *food for the dog*]

This sentence is ambiguous because the post-copular constituent can be interpreted as either referential or not.[3] In the latter case, it is interpreted as 'his supper serves as food for the dog', whereas in the former the sentence can be

---

[1] Notice that the same term is also used to indicate similar structures in which the copular element is not (necessarily) overtly realized and the three elements in (2) may appear in a different linear order.

[2] For an overview, cf. Den Dikken (2006a: § 1.2) and the references cited therein. As the author discusses in § 1.3, a more fine-grained typology of copular constructions can also be put forward, which is not limited to the referentiality of the post-copular constituent but include additional properties (e.g., discourse function, syntax and intonation) of both copular phrases; see, for instance, Higgins (1979) and Declerck (1988).

[3] It should be noticed that there is no general agreement as to whether this distinction depends on the referentiality of the post-copular constituent or to specific properties of the copula itself. As a matter of fact, it has been proposed that copulas have two different lexical

rephrased as 'he has food for the dog for supper'. Given that the post-copular YP *predicates something* about XP in the former reading, while its denotation *identifies* or *specifies the value for* the referent denoted by XP in the latter, the two relevant copular constructions are usually referred to as *predicative* and *identifying/ specificational*, respectively. As will become clearer in the remainder of this work, these two structures are correlated with different types of marked copular constructions (i.e., existential/locative sentences and (pseudo)clefts, respectively).

As far as their syntactic analysis is concerned, since Stowell's (1981) influential work copular constructions are usually treated as Small Clauses (SCs; cf., among many others, Cardinaletti and Guasti, eds. 1995; Moro 1997; Den Dikken 2006b):

(4)
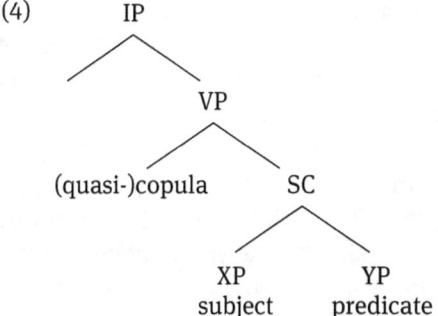

In this configuration (from Moro 1997), a subject and a predicate are linked by means of a Merge operation. Specifically, this predicative structure is selected by a copula (or, alternatively, by "quasi-copular" verbs such as *seem, become*, etc.) and, in languages like English, it is derived through the raising of either the subject or the predicate (depending on their specific properties) to Spec, IP, where Case and φ-features can be checked (cf. Moro 1997; Den Dikken 2006b).

1.2.2 Marked structures

Since Rizzi's (1997) seminal work, syntactic research in the generative framework has been paying special attention to information-structurally marked

---

entries – one with an identifying function and the other with a predicative nature (cf., for instance, Safir 1985). Nevertheless, in the generative literature there is a prevalent tendency to attribute the semantic and syntactic properties of the two constructions to the nature of the two major constituents.

constructions, in which the discourse interpretation of constituents is connected with formal features. In particular, discourse features are assumed to be encoded in the left periphery of the sentence (i.e., the C-domain), which is constituted by an array of rigidly ordered functional projections, each of which is dedicated to the interpretation of a specific information-structural feature. Following Frascarelli and Hinterhölzl (2007) (henceforth, F&H 2007) and Frascarelli (2007), we assume the following articulation:

(5) [$_{ForceP}$ [$_{ShiftP}$ [$_{GP}$ [$_{ContrP}$ [$_{FocP}$ [$_{FamP}$ [$_{FinP}$ [$_{IP}$ ....]]]]]]]]

The projections indicated as ShiftP, ContrP and FamP represent the functional projections in which Aboutness-Shift (A-)Topics, Contrastive (C-)Topics and Familiar/Given (G-)Topics are realized, respectively. Notice that this hierarchy refers to the array of Topics in root/root-like clauses, since not all types of Topics can be realized in any clausal type. As is argued in Bianchi and Frascarelli (2010), different types of Topics have different requirements with respect to conversational dynamics; specifically, A-Topics qualify as root phenomena (i.e., they require sentences with context update potential), C-Topics must be realized in (no less than) a proposition, while only G-Topics can be found in any clausal type (and can be recursive).[4] Finally, the Ground Phrase projection (GP) is drawn from Poletto and Pollock (2004) and assumed as the target of (remnant) IP movement in the case of right-hand Topics.

Assuming this structural array for copular sentences, Frascarelli and Ramaglia (2013) (henceforth, F&R 2013) argue for a SC analysis of clefts and pseudoclefts, in which the two copular constituents are connected to specific left-peripheral positions depending on their discourse properties. In particular, it is proposed that (pseudo)clefts – besides focalization of the post-copular DP – also implement a Topic-Comment structure. This is supported by the interface analysis of naturalistic data, showing that the free relative DP (*that/what I gave John* in the examples below) qualify as a Topic in both constructions:[5]

(6) a. *It is A BOOK [that I gave John]*$_{Topic}$ (cleft)
 b. *[What I gave John]*$_{Topic}$ *is a book* (pseudocleft)

---

[4] Also notice that, according to F&H's (2007) analysis, C-Topics and Contrastive Foci never co-occur in the same clause and are both characterized by a H* prosodic contour. This suggests that ContrP is endowed with a [+contrast] feature that can be associated to both types of constituents, realized in the same syntactic position (i.e., Spec,ContrP).
[5] Specifically, the right-hand Topic of clefts (cf. [6a]) is a G-Topic, while the (matrix) left-hand Topic of pseudoclefts (cf. [6b]) can instantiate any type of Topic, depending on the context.

The authors thus propose that in the basic SC structure of both constructions the (pseudo)clefted phrase constitutes the predicate (consistent with cross-linguistic analysis of Focus; cf. Frascarelli 2010), whereas the free relative DP is connected with the subject position. In particular, in pseudoclefts the free relative DP is merged in the subject position of the SC and is raised to the Specifier of a Topic projection (depending on discourse requirements). This is illustrated in (7) for English, assuming an A-Topic discourse function for the relative DP:

(7) Pseudoclefts:
 [$_{ShiftP}$ [$_{DP}$ *what I gave John*]$_i$ [$_{IP}$ t'$_i$ *is* [$_{SC}$ t$_i$ [$_{DP}$ *a book*]]]]

As far as clefts are concerned, F&R (2013) propose the derivation indicated in (8), which shows right-hand Topics to be derived through IP-inversion to Spec,GP (cf. also Cardinaletti 2002; Frascarelli 2004; Samek-Lodovici 2006; F&H 2007):

(8) Clefts:
 a. [$_{FamP}$ [$_{DP}$ *that I gave John*]$_i$ [$_{IP}$ [$_{DP}$ *it*]$_i$ *is* [$_{SC}$ t$_i$ [$_{DP}$ *a book*]]]] →
 b. [$_{FocP}$ [$_{DP}$ *A BOOK*]$_k$ [$_{FamP}$ [$_{DP}$ *that I gave John*]$_i$ [$_{IP}$ [$_{DP}$ *it*]$_i$ *is* [$_{SC}$ t$_i$ t$_k$]]]] →
 c. [$_{GP}$ [$_{IP}$ [$_{DP}$ *it*]$_i$ *is* [$_{SC}$ t$_i$ t$_k$]] [$_{FocP}$ [$_{DP}$ *A BOOK*]$_k$ [$_{FamP}$ [$_{DP}$ *that I gave John*]$_i$ t$_{IP}$]]]

As is widely discussed in F&R (2013), syntactic evidence for this analysis comes from extraction, Case marking and antiagreement effects, and is supported by intonational analysis. Finally notice that, as shown by indices in (8), the initial *it*-pronoun of clefts is *not* an expletive but is coreferent with the right-dislocated free relative DP.

2 Existential sentences

A major working hypothesis that the present study aims to explore is the possibility to extend F&R's (2013) analysis of (pseudo)clefts illustrated in § 1.2.2 to other types of marked copular constructions, that is to say, existential (9) and locative sentences (10):[6]

---

[6] This work is only concerned with existential constructions of the copular type (cf. [9] in the text), whereas other types of *there*-sentences showing an existential meaning (e.g., *There worked many men in the harbor, There arrived many men*) are beyond the limits of the present paper and may constitute the topic of future research. In particular, since the alternative types of *there*-sentences seem to share crucial properties with the copular ones (including the

(9) *There is a man in the garden*

(10) *A man is in the garden*

Our hypothesis is that existentials like (9) can be treated on a par with clefts, whereas locative sentences like (10) pattern with pseudoclefts. Before illustrating our proposal, a brief overview on previous analyses of existential and locative sentences is proposed in § 2.1.[7]

2.1 Former analyses: An overview

The early studies on existential constructions in the generative tradition date back to the '70s. In this period, some scholars (Milsark 1974; Stowell 1978) propose a structural analysis in which the post-copular DP (i.e., *a man* in [9]) is the subject and the locative PP (*in the garden*) is the predicate in a SC configuration (11a). Following this type of approach, it has been proposed that *there* is as an expletive pronoun associated with the post-copular DP (11b), which is subject to covert (LF) movement to substitute (or else adjoin) to it (11c) (Chomsky 1986, 1991):

(11) a. [$_{SC}$ [$_{DP}$ *a man*] [$_{PP}$ *in the garden*]] → insertion of the expletive *there*
b. *there*$_i$ ... *is*... [$_{SC}$ [$_{DP}$ *a man*]$_i$ [$_{PP}$ *in the garden*]] →
 LF-raising of the post-copular DP
c. [$_{DP}$ *a man*]$_i$ ... *is* ... [$_{SC}$ t$_i$ [$_{PP}$ *in the garden*]]

A different approach is proposed in Moro (1997), where existential sentences are derived from a basic SC structure which differs from (11) above in that the post-copular DP is the subject, *there* is the predicate (which is raised to Spec, IP), and the locative PP (when present) is a right-adjunct:

Definiteness Effect; cf. § 3), the possibility should be explored to extend the present analysis to non-copular existential constructions. In this case, a feasible hypothesis might be to analyze the relevant verb (*work, arrive* in the examples cited above) as a sort of light verb, so as to capture its structural parallel with the copula. We thank an anonymous reviewer for drawing our attention to these structures.

7 As is clear, this overview cannot do justice to the vast debate on existential and locative constructions. For the purposes of the present paper, we will just mention some of the most influential studies, so as to show the different approaches assumed for the relevant structures.

(12) a. be [SC [DP *a man*] [DP *there*]] ... [PP *in the garden*]
    b. [DP *there*]ᵢ *is* [SC [DP *a man*] tᵢ] ... [PP *in the garden*]

According to this analysis, existential constructions and the corresponding locative sentences (cf. [9–10] above) share the same "deep" structure (i.e., [12a]) and are differentiated by derivation; the copular constituent attracted to Spec, IP is *there* in existentials (cf. [12b]), while it is the DP merged as the subject of the SC (*a man*) in locative structures:

(13) a. be [SC [DP *a man*] [DP *there*]]
    b. [DP *a man*]ᵢ *is* [SC tᵢ [DP *there*]]

However, the interpretive asymmetries existing between existential and locative constructions led other scholars to propose alternative analyses. For instance, Zamparelli (2000) argues that the two structures under examination have opposite configurations. Specifically, a locative sentence like (10) is about [*a man*] (which is therefore analyzed as the subject) and asserts that it occupies a location referred to as *there* (the predicate); Moro's derivation in (13) can be thus maintained for locative constructions. On the other hand, the subject of an existential sentence is *there*, and the post-copular DP (*a man*) is the predicate:[8]

(14) a. be [SC [DP *there*] [DP *a man*]]
    b. [DP *there*]ᵢ *is* [SC tᵢ [DP *a man*]]

In this approach, a sentence like (14) is *about* a location in space and asserts "the property that that space "is" or [...] "contains" a man". Accordingly, the relevant sentence is true when "a man is in existence, or "instantiated", in the sense of McNally [(1997)]" (from Zamparelli 2000: § 5.2.4). As for the locative PP, Zamparelli (2000) follows Moro's (1997) suggestion (cf. [12]) and considers this element as right-adjoined.

---

[8] For the sake of simplicity, the two copular constituents in (14) are labelled as DPs, thus differing from Zamparelli's (2000) account in which nominal phrases are associated to different types of functional layers in the extended projection of the NP. As we will propose in § 2.2.1, the present analysis also takes predicative noun phrases to have a reduced functional structure (as opposed to nominal arguments); hence the "DP" label used so far to indicate both copular constituents must be considered as a temporary solution.

2.2 Existentials as marked copular constructions

The present study draws from Zamparelli's (2000) proposal and, as mentioned above, it is aimed at providing evidence that existential structures can be analyzed as clefts (cf. [15]), whereas locative sentences pattern with pseudoclefts (cf. [16]).

(15) a. *be* [$_{SC}$ [$_{DP}$ *it*]$_i$ [$_{DP}$ *a book*]] ... [$_{DP}$ *that I gave John*]$_i$ (cleft)
  b. *be* [$_{SC}$ [$_{DP}$ *there*]$_i$ [$_{DP}$ *a man*]] ... [$_{PP}$ *in the garden*]$_i$ (existential sentence)

(16) a. *be* [$_{SC}$ [$_{DP}$ *what I gave John*] [$_{DP}$ *a book*]] (pseudocleft)
  b. *be* [$_{SC}$ [$_{DP}$ *a man*] [$_{PP}$ *in the garden*]] (locative sentence)

While the analysis of locative sentences illustrated in (16b) can find strong support in the literature, the structural hypothesis on existential constructions (15b) might sound more controversial. The remainder of this section is dedicated to an illustration of semantic (§ 2.2.1), syntactic (§ 2.2.2) and prosodic arguments (§ 2.2.3) supporting this proposal.

2.2.1 Semantic analysis

In his multi-layered analysis of DPs, Zamparelli (2000) observes that the functional structure constituting the extended projection of a noun phrase is dependent on its semantic and syntactic role. More generally, it is commonly acknowledged that predicative (as opposed to argumental) noun phrases have a "reduced" functional structure and should not be analyzed as full DPs (cf., among others, Szabolcsi 1987, 1989, 1994; Stowell 1989; Longobardi 1994, 2001, 2005; Bernstein 2001; Ramaglia 2011). In particular, it has been argued that predicative noun phrases lack the functional projections dedicated to features such as referentiality, definiteness and specificity, which typically characterize arguments (rather than predicates). Furthermore, it has been proposed that the presence of the D° head is required for theta-role assignment; accordingly, D° contributes to making nominal elements able to serve as arguments; this means that noun phrases can appear as arguments if and only if they are dominated by the DP-layer. In this kind of syntax-semantics approach, argumental noun phrases are DPs, whereas nominal predicates are NPs.

However, since Abney's (1987) proposal that NPs are dominated by the DP functional layer, all noun phrases are generally assumed to have some kind of (more or less complex) extended projection (cf., among others, Szabolcsi 1987,

1989, 1994; Giorgi and Longobardi 1991; Grimshaw 1990; Ritter 1991; Valois 1991; Cinque 1994, ed. 2002, 2010; Zamparelli 2000; Bernstein 2001; Longobardi 2001; Scott 2002; Laenzlinger 2005; Giusti 2006; Alexiadou, Haegeman, and Stavrou 2007; Svenonius 2008; Ramaglia 2011, 2013); as a consequence, the hypothesis that predicative noun phrases lack the DP layer does not necessarily mean that they are to be analyzed as bare NPs. Following the analysis put forth in Ramaglia (2011: 178), we take nominal arguments to be full DPs (endowed with an array of functional projections constituting the left periphery of the DP), while predicative noun phrases are not limited to bare NPs and include functional projections for inflectional features, which will be indicated as NumP (on this phrasal category, see also Ritter 1991).

Assuming that existential sentences are copular constructions of the predicative type (cf. Zamparelli's 2000 proposal in § 2.1), it follows that the post-copular DP, which is merged as the predicate of the SC, should be analyzed as a NumP (rather than a full DP):

(17) *be* [$_{SC}$ [$_{DP}$ *there*]$_i$ [$_{NumP}$ *a man*]] ... [$_{PP}$ *in the garden*]$_i$

It is important to notice that this modification is not a mere descriptive issue concerning the label to be assigned to the nominal predicate; on the contrary, the assumption of a reduced functional structure for the predicate in (17) has crucial consequences on the types of constituents that can be merged in this position. As a matter of fact, referential/definite/specific elements (which are full DPs) are excluded from the post-copular position of existential sentences, and this can account for an important property of existential constructions in a number of languages, namely the DE (to be discussed in § 3.1).

2.2.2 Syntactic evidence

In the present section, syntactic diagnostics will be used to support the structural analysis put forth in this study for existential and locative sentences.

Based on Zamparelli's (2000) considerations, we have proposed that in existential constructions *there* is merged as the subject and the post-copular noun phrase as the predicate of a SC (cf. [17]). Syntactic evidence for this approach comes from extraction, as illustrated below by means of Italian examples:

(18) ci   sono   [tre   pagine [di esercizi]] [nel   libro [di inglese]]
     there be.3PL three pages of exercises in.the book of English
     'There are three pages of exercises in the English book.'

a. [Di cosa]_i pensi che ci siano [tre pagine t_i]
of what think.2SG that there be.SUBJ.3PL three pages
[nel libro [di inglese]]?
in.the book of English
'[Of what]_i do you think there are [three pages t_i] in the English book?'
b. *[Di quale lingua]_i pensi che ci siano [tre pagine
of which language think.2SG that there be.SUBJ.3PL three pages
[di esercizi]] [nel libro t_i]?
of exercises in.the book

As is commonly acknowledged in the literature, extraction is not allowed from subject DPs, while no restriction is imposed on the movement of predicate-internal material (cf. Moro 1997; Heycock and Kroch 1999; Den Dikken 2006b). The contrast in (18) thus provides syntactic evidence for the predicative nature of the post-copular element *tre pagine di esercizi* ('three pages of exercises'): as is illustrated in (18a), extraction from this constituent is fully accepted. On the other hand, the ungrammaticality of (18b) excludes the analysis illustrated in (11) above, which takes the locative PP *nel libro di inglese* ('in the English book') to be a predicate.[9]

If we now consider extraction effects in locative constructions, the present proposal predicts that extraction should be excluded from the subject DP *tre pagine di esercizi* ('three pages of exercises'), and allowed from the locative PP (as it is the predicate). The following data from Italian show that this prediction is (partially) borne out:

(19) [tre pagine [di esercizi]] sono [nel libro [di inglese]]
three pages of exercises be.3PL in.the book of English
'Three pages of exercises are in the English book.'
a. *[Di cosa]_i pensi che [tre pagine t_i] siano [nel libro
of what think.2SG that three pages be.SUBJ.3PL in.the book
[di inglese]]?
of English

---

[9] We acknowledge that the ungrammaticality of (18b) might be ascribed to a (general) restriction operating on the extraction out of a complex PP. However, the grammaticality of (18a) unambiguously proves the predicative function of the post-copular DP *tre pagine di esercizi* ('three pages of exercises'). This excludes a predicate merge for the locative PP *nel libro di inglese* ('in the English book').

b. *[Di quale lingua]$_i$ pensi che [tre pagine [di esercizi]]
   of which language think.2SG that three pages of exercises
   siano [nel libro t$_i$]?
   be.SUBJ.3PL in.the book

As can be observed, both sentences in (19a–b) are ungrammatical. The ungrammaticality of (19a) is consistent with our expectations, whereas the ungrammaticality of (19b) might be considered a counterexample. On the contrary, we argue that it is due to the fact that the predicate is a complex PP, from which extraction is banned for independent reasons (i.e., it is a "syntactic island").

The data presented in this section thus provide sound evidence in favor of the present structural account for both existential and locative constructions and also show that an analysis that derives both constructions from one and the same underlying structure cannot be maintained.

2.2.3 Discourse properties and prosodic realization

The parallelism between clefts and existentials, on the one hand, and between pseudoclefts and locative sentences on the other (cf. [15–16]) is not limited to a common underlying structure, but also concerns the discourse role of constituents. As already mentioned, our analysis of existential sentences, much like F&R's (2013) approach to clefts, takes the post-copular noun phrase to be a Narrow Focus, whereas the locative PP is a right-hand G-Topic. Extending the structure of clefts illustrated in (8) above to existential sentences, the latter thus have a derivation in which, after raising of the post-copular DP to Spec,FocP (20b), IP-inversion to Spec,GP takes place (20c):

(20) Existential sentences:
   a. [$_{FamP}$ [$_{PP}$ *in the garden*]$_i$ [$_{IP}$ [$_{DP}$ *there*]$_i$ *is* [$_{SC}$ t$_i$ [$_{NumP}$ *a man*]]]] →
   b. [$_{FocP}$ [$_{NumP}$ *A MAN*]$_k$ [$_{FamP}$ [$_{PP}$ *in the garden*]$_i$ [$_{IP}$ [$_{DP}$ *there*]$_i$ *is* [$_{SC}$ t$_i$ t$_k$]]]] →
   c. [$_{GP}$ [$_{IP}$ [$_{DP}$ *there*]$_i$ *is* [$_{SC}$ t$_i$ t$_k$]] [$_{FocP}$ [$_{NumP}$ *A MAN*]$_k$ [$_{FamP}$ [$_{PP}$ *in the garden*]$_i$ t$_{IP}$]]]

It is also important to notice that the locative PP is coindexed with *there* in (20): following F&R's (2013) analysis of the initial *it*-pronoun of clefts (cf. [8] and the relevant discussion), we propose that in existential sentences *there* is not an expletive but is coreferent with the dislocated PP (with which it shares a locative interpretation).¹⁰

In the remainder of this section, prosodic evidence will be provided to support both the predicative (and focal) nature of the post-copular noun phrase and the right-dislocation of the locative PP in the structure under examination. Consider the following data, drawn from an Italian corpus of naturalistic data (cf. Pietrandrea 2004):

(21) ci   sono   diversi   dialetti – credo –   nelle   cassette
      there be.3PL different dialects   believe.1SG in.the tapes
      'There are different dialects – I think – in the tapes.'

As is shown in Figure 1, the post-copular phrase *diversi dialetti* ('different dialects') presents the typical downgrading contour of Broad Focus sentences (cf. Pierrehumbert and Hirschberg 1990; Selkirk 1995; Frascarelli 2004), while the locative PP is totally destressed in the right periphery and separated from the post-copular noun phrase by a break. Also notice the presence of the parenthetical *credo* ('I think'), which further supports the dislocated nature of the subsequent material.

In the following sentence, on the other hand, the post-copular noun phrase shows the prosodic contour of a Contrastive Focus (i.e., a H* tone; cf. Figure 2), which is consistent with its discourse role (cf. the contrastive operator *addirittura* 'even'):

(22) (addirittura)   c'   erano   delle scenografie
      even   there be.PST.3PL some scenes
      'There were (even) some scenes.'

---

10 It is worth noting that *there* can only be coindexed with a locative element, which qualifies as a dislocated constituent in the present account. Other types of phrases predicating something about the post-copular element should be thus attributed a different analysis. This is for instance the case of the bracketed item in the following examples:
(i)   *After the seafood dinner there were several guests [sick] and had to be taken to the hospital*
(ii) *There are two rooms [available]*
In these cases *sick* and *available* are not to be taken as dislocated phrases coindexed with *there*; rather, they constitute a secondary predication about *several guests* and *two rooms*, respectively, and as such, they should be analyzed as predicates internal to the post-copular noun phrases. This means that the relevant sentences lack a locative PP, which is confirmed by the possibility for the latter to be overtly realized: cf. *There were several guests [sick] [at the party]*, *There are two rooms [available] [in this hotel]*.

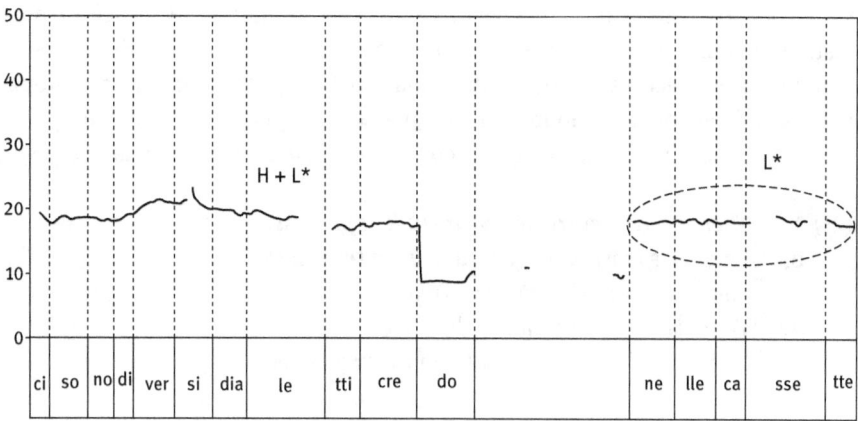

Figure 1: Non-contrastive existential sentence.

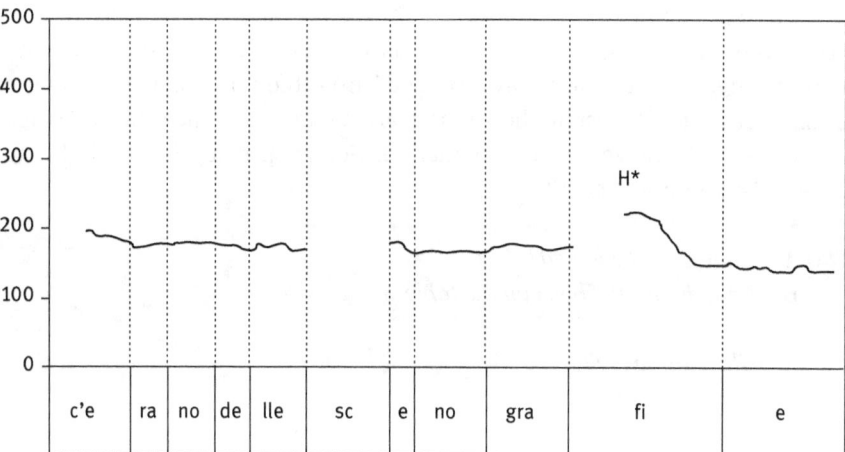

Figure 2: Contrastive existential sentence.

3 The Definiteness Effect (DE)

The DE is a phenomenon associated with a number of constructions in many languages, showing that the realization of definite DPs is excluded in certain syntactic positions.[11] In the case of existential sentences, "the definiteness restriction amounts to a restriction on the acceptability of definite, demonstrative, and necessarily quantificational noun phrases, including proper names and personal pronouns, in the [post-copular position]" (McNally 2011: 1832–1833), as is illustrated by the cited author in the following examples:

(23) a. ??*There is each/every first-year student present*
b. ??*There are most first-year students in that class*
c. ??*There is the neighbor's dog barking*
d. ??*There is that carpet under the table*
e. ??*There are them / Anna and Bob waiting outside*

Different analyses have been put forth in the literature to account for this phenomenon and, in the most influential works, DE has been attributed to either semantic and/or pragmatic properties of existential constructions (cf., among many others, Milsark 1974; Heim 1987; Abbott 1992; Ward and Birner 1995; Zucchi 1995; McNally 1997; Francez 2007; see McNally 2011: § 3 for an overview). These accounts, however, are rather controversial, as is the generalization that definite DPs are always excluded from the post-copular position of existentials. Indeed, despite the strong marginality of sentences like (23), definite DPs can be realized in post-copular position in specific cases, as in the so-called "list interpretation":[12]

(24) A. *What should we read?*
B. *Well, there's the book on the table*

(25) A. *Who can we invite?*
B. *Well, there's John*

In the next section evidence will be provided that the present analysis of existential constructions can easily account for DE, also suggesting an explanation for apparent counterexamples like the sentences in (24B) and (25B).

---

11 According to some scholars, the relevant restriction is not (only) connected to definiteness but (also) to specificity. Accordingly, the relevant effect is sometimes re-analyzed in terms of "specificity effect" (cf. Enç 1991). In this study, however, we use the DE term for simplicity, following the traditional terminology.

12 The examples in (24–25) are taken from Kayne (2016).

3.1 Explaining the Definiteness Effect

The impossibility for definite DPs to appear in post-copular position is predicted by the present analysis: since existential sentences are copular constructions of the predicative type (§ 2.2.1), the relevant noun phrase (merged as the predicate of a SC, cf. §§ 2.2.2–2.2.3) is not dominated by a DP-layer (it rather qualifies as a NumP, cf. [17]). Hence, definite noun phrases cannot appear in the post-copular position of existential constructions. The picture in (23) is thus expected.

Nevertheless, what appears to be problematic is (i) the possibility for definite DPs to be realized in the post-copular position of existentials in some contexts (e.g., [24–25]), and (ii) the existence of languages in which DE seems to be generally "relaxed" (as in Italian). As for the former, an explanation can be drawn from Kayne's (2016) analysis. Dealing with sentences like (24–25), the author proposes that the apparently definite noun phrases realized in post-copular position "are actually embedded within hidden indefinites" (Kayne 2016: § 9). Accordingly, a sentence like (25B) is to be understood as follows (caps are used to indicate silent – namely unpronounced – elements):

(26) *There's SOMEBODY WE CAN INVITE, (NAMELY) John*

Beside the cases of "list interpretation" like (24–25), Kayne's approach provides an explanation for other apparent counterexamples to DE in a language like English, assuming that the post-copular noun phrase should be analyzed as embedded in a more complex constituent including null elements. Some of the relevant examples (a), together with Kayne's analysis (b), are illustrated below; for further details, the reader is referred to Kayne (2016).

(27) a. *There is the most beautiful house for sale in the next block*
    b. *... [the most beautiful KIND] house ...*[13]

(28) a. *Where did there used to be the most syntacticians?*
    b. *... [the most NUMBER] syntacticians*

(29) a. *There is every reason to be suspicious*
    b. *... [every KIND] reason ...*

---

[13] Cf. *There is a house of the most beautiful kind for sale in the next block.*

The general absence of DE in languages like Italian will be approached from a different perspective in the following sections.

3.2 Exploring the absence of the Definiteness Effect in some languages

As mentioned in § 3.1, while we have strong evidence for DE in languages like English, definite noun phrases seem to be perfectly allowed in the post-copular position of *there*-sentences in other languages. Consider the following examples from Italian:

(30) a. C'   è   un uomo in giardino
        there be.3SG a   man   in garden
        'There is a man in the garden.'
    b. C'   è   Gianni   in giardino
        there be.3SG Gianni   in garden
        '*There is Gianni in the garden.'

As these examples show, existential constructions in Italian differ from the corresponding structures in English in that a definite description like *Gianni* is acceptable in post-copular position.

Assuming a cross-linguistic validity for the analysis proposed in this paper, the acceptability of sentences like (30b), against its ungrammaticality in languages like English, should receive a comprehensive explanation. As a matter of fact, if DE is predicted by the present analysis of existentials (cf. § 3.1), the grammaticality of (30b) seems to represent a challenge to it.

As a preliminary consideration, it should be noticed that the interpretation of *there*-sentences with definite and indefinite post-copular noun phrases (in languages that allow both constructions) is not exactly the same. As is discussed in Moro (1997), while a sentence like (30a) has an existential meaning, as it asserts the existence of an individual (*un uomo*, 'a man') in a certain location (*in giardino*, 'in the garden'), (30b) has a *locative* interpretation: rather than asserting the *existence* of an individual named *Gianni*, it asserts that it lies in a specific location. From a semantic perspective, the relevant sentence is therefore analogous to a locative sentence like *Gianni è in giardino* 'Gianni is in the garden'.

Based on similar considerations, a number of authors have proposed that the apparent counterexamples to DE represented by sentences like (30b) do not constitute existential sentences proper but should receive a different structural account (cf., for instance, Moro 1997; La Fauci and Loporcaro 1997; Cruschina 2012, 2015). In this paper, we follow this line of analysis and propose that DE is a *universal*, semantically-based, restriction on existential sentences and that apparent counterexamples like (30b) represent a different type of *there*-sentence, the analysis of which will be developed in the next section.

3.3 Appearances can be deceptive: Presentational constructions "in disguise"

Recent interface investigations focused on the use and interpretation of null subjects brought crucial evidence to light that what appears to be an existential clause (formally realized as a *there*-sentence) is in fact a *presentational construction*, introducing "what the sentence is about" (i.e., a Topic). To provide a comprehensive picture of such findings, some background reference is in order.[14]

3.3.1 A-Topics and Topic chains

In her interface investigations on the interpretation of null subjects, Frascarelli (2007, 2018) provides strong evidence that in (consistent and partial) null subject languages the interpretation of a referential *pro* depends on a matching relation (Agree) with a specific type of Topic. In a cartographic approach to discourse functions, this is identified with the A-Topic (cf. § 1.2.2) that is located in the high C-domain (cf. the hierarchy in [5]), is characterized by a L*+H tone (i.e., an intonational rise that is aligned with the tonic vowel in its full extension) and is endowed with a [+aboutness] edge feature (proposed as an "extended EPP" feature).

A Topic Criterion is thus proposed that correlates core grammar with discourse requirements and accounts for the syntactic identification of a referential *pro*. According to this Criterion, every predicational sentence contains

---

14 In this line of analysis, it is important to underline that a sentence like *Gianni è mio padre* ('Gianni is my father') does not pattern like (and cannot be analyzed on a par with) a sentence like (30b). Indeed, *Gianni è mio padre* is an *identificational* copular sentence and, as such, it does not implement a predicational, but an *identity statement* (Higgins, 1979: 263; cf. also Den Dikken 2006b). Consequently, a Topic-Comment discourse structure is excluded and a locative adverb like *ci* ('there') would have no role in that type of copular construction (**C'è Gianni mio padre*).

a position endowed with the [+aboutness] feature in the C-domain and, when it is kept continuous on the same referent across sentences, it can be silent and "maintained" by means of null (or low-toned) pronouns. From a discourse perspective, it is therefore assumed that predication can imply a *multiclausal domain*, in which *chains of clauses* are combined and refer to the same A-Topic. Crucially, A-Topics can only start a Topic chain (and interrupt the current chain to shift to a new one).

3.3.2 Introducing a Topic in post-copular position: Evidence from naturalistic data

The existence of Topic chains and their key role in the discourse has also been attested in recent acquisitional studies (Frascarelli 2015). Specifically, the interface analysis of short stories narrated by children shows that they correctly produce Topic chains at the age of four, linking null subjects to the DP produced with a L*+H tone.[15] Consider the Topic chain in the passage below:[16]

(31) <u>Lea e Bea c'hanno molti amici</u>,[17]
 Lea and Bea have.3PL many friends
 pro *fanno colazione con i biscotti e il latte, dopo* pro *vanno a scuola e leggono un libro, quando suona la campana* pro *escono dalla scuola –* <u>Lea si compra un gelato</u> *e* [...] pro *vanno a casa felici e contenti*
 'Lea and Bea have many friends, (they) have breakfast with biscuits and milk, then (they) go to school and read a book, when the school bell rings (they) go out the school – Lea buys an ice-cream and ... (they) go home happily ever after.'

---

15 The stimulus was provided by pictures showing the story of two rabbits ("Lea and Bea") on a powerpoint presentation originally created by Barbara Cerri (RCCS *Stella Maris Foundation*, Pisa, Italy) for different scientific purposes. This investigation is part of the Prin-2012 Project "Theory, Experimentation, Applications: Long distance dependencies in forms of linguistics diversity", funded by MIUR.
16 Notice that the Topic chain is not interrupted by *Lea* (in *Lea si compra un gelato* 'Lea buys an ice-cream'), because it is a C-Topic (the picture provided to children shows Lea with an ice-cream and Bea with a lolly-pop; since the child could not remember Bea's name, after a pause she decided to conclude the narration).
17 For space limitation, glosses are only provided for the (underlined) sentences to be illustrated in the subsequent Figures.

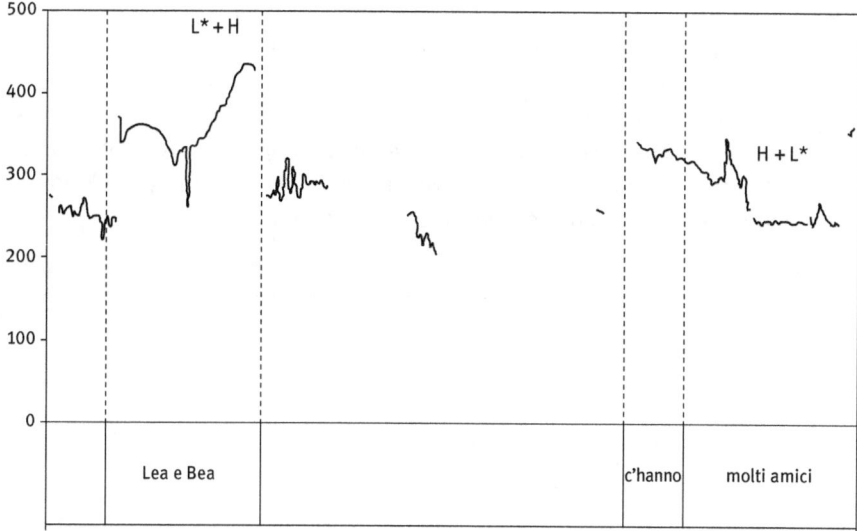

Figure 3: A-Topic starting a Topic chain.

As is shown, the DP *Lea e Bea* forms an independent prosodic domain, followed by a very long pause, as is expected for Topic constituents. Since Topics are located in the C-domain, a null subject must be assumed in the relevant sentence:

(31') [*Lea e Bea*]$_{\text{A-Top}}$ pro *c'hanno molti amici*

Given this competence in producing Topic chains, consistently attested across children, it is interesting to notice that when the fairy-tale incipit *c'era una volta* 'once upon a time' (lit. 'there was a time') is used to introduce the two protagonists, in most cases an A-Topic is produced in post-copular position. This means that the relevant DP is characterized by a L*+H tone, while the rest of the sentence shows the typical downgrading contour (H+L*) of Broad Focus sentences. A Topic-Comment structure is thus realized by means of a *there*-construction and a Topic chain is created. Consider (32) and the relevant Figure 4:[18]

---

[18] The presence of a *pro* in the *that*-clause following [*Lea e Bea*] in (32) will be clarified later in the paper (§ 3.3.3).

(32) <u>C'   era   una volta Lea e   Bea che</u> pro andavano
    there be.PST.3SG a   time Lea and Bea that   go.PST.3PL
    <u>a   casa</u>,
    to home
    poi pro prendevano i fiori e v enivano mamma e papà, pro c'avevano l'amici
    'Once upon a time, Lea and Bea were going home, then (they) took flowers
    and mummy and daddy arrived, (they) had friends.'[19]

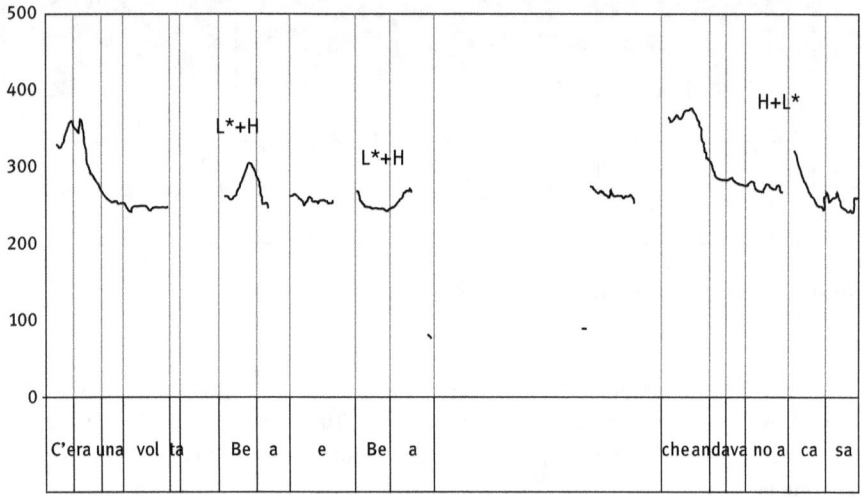

Figure 4: "*C'era una volta*" construction with a Topic-Comment structure.

On the other hand, when the post-copular DP is not realized with a L*+H contour, the Topic chain is not created and the use of null subjects is only started after the repetition of the DP *Lea e Bea* (or the realization of its pronominal counterpart) as an A-Topic.[20] Consider for instance the following passage, in

---

19 Incidentally notice that the postverbal subject *mamma e papà* 'mummy and daddy' does not interrupt the Topic chain, that is to say, it is not interpreted as the subject of the following sentence, though plural agreement makes this option theoretically available. This is predicted by the Topic Criterion: only A-Topics can interrupt a Topic chain and start a new one.
20 An anonymous reviewer observes that the existence of Topic chains and the discourse device of Topic maintenance are not necessarily connected with (hence, they are independent of) the presence of null subjects and s/he objects that analogous chains can be realized in a non-*pro*-drop language like English, by means of overt pronouns (e.g., *There were once (upon a time) Lea and Bea. They went home. They took flowers* ...). This observation is correct and beyond question: both pro-drop and non-pro-drop languages realize Topic chains in the

which a child uses a *there*-construction and provides a Focus interpretation for the post-copular DP *Lea e Bea* (marking the second conjunct with a H* tone, cf. Figure 5). As is shown in (33), the Topic chain only starts after the realization of the pronoun *loro* 'them', which qualifies as an A-Topic (cf. Figure 6). Also notice that this chain is not interrupted by the postverbal subject *la campanella* 'school bell', as expected (cf. fn. 19).[21]

(33) <u>C'</u>   <u>era</u>   <u>una volta</u> <u>Lea e</u>   <u>Bea</u> <u>con</u> <u>la</u> <u>mamma</u>
      there   be.PST.3SG a   time Lea and Bea with the mummy
      <u>e</u>   <u>con</u> <u>papà</u> <u>e</u>   <u>loro</u> <u>hanno</u>   <u>tanti</u> <u>amici</u>
      and with daddy and they have.3PL many friends
      pro *vanno a scuola,* pro *leggono un libretto, quando suona la campanella*
      pro *vanno via da scuola*
      'Once upon a time, Lea and Bea were with mummy and daddy, and they have many friends, (they) go to school, (they) read a little book, when the school bell rings, (they) go out from school.'

Based on these findings, we investigated the *ArCoDip* corpus (Pietrandrea 2004) in this respect, and found supporting evidence in adults' production as well. We can therefore conclude that the discourse strategy presented so far is not a "story-telling formula" used by children: *there*-constructions can function as presentational sentences, used to introduce either A-Topics (cf. [34]) or C-Topics (as is shown in [35] below and the relevant Figures):

---

discourse. The crucial point of the present argumentation is that the creation and licensing of such chains has been proved (Frascarelli 2007, 2017, 2018) to be dependent on their being *headed by an A-Topic* (i.e., by a DP that is *formally* characterized as such; cf. § 3.3.1 above). Assuming this theory, the observation that the DP following *c'era una volta* 'once upon a time' can function as the antecedent of null subjects pushed the hypothesis that this DP was not the predicate of a copular construction, but an A-Topic. This hypothesis has been confirmed by interface analysis, opening the way for the present innovative proposal. The expectation is therefore that in English as well the DP following *once (upon a time)* is realized with a raising tone and that coindexed overt pronouns are *low-toned*, consistent with Frascarelli's (2007) claim that low-toned pronouns share important discourse functions with null subjects (i.e., they can be part of a Topic chain as D-linked constituents). This expectation is the subject of current research.
21 We will resume the analysis of non-topical [+def] post-copular DPs in § 3.3.4.

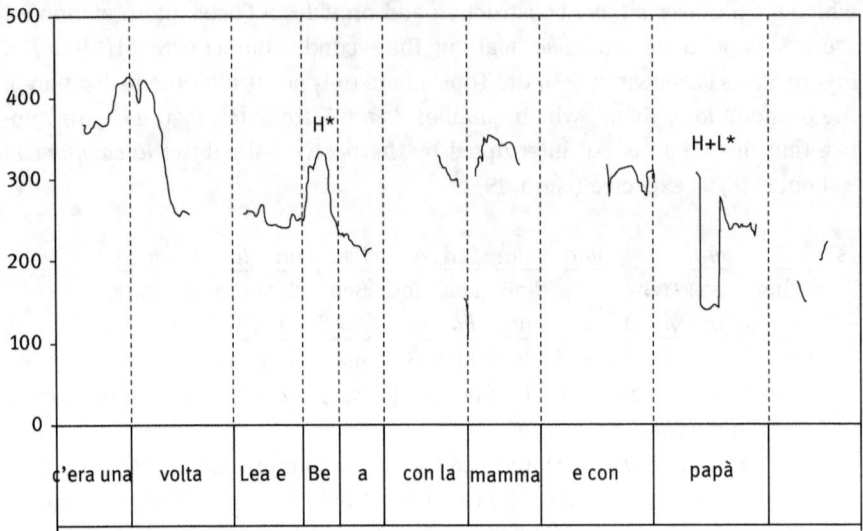

Figure 5: "*C'era una volta*" construction with a focused post-copular phrase.

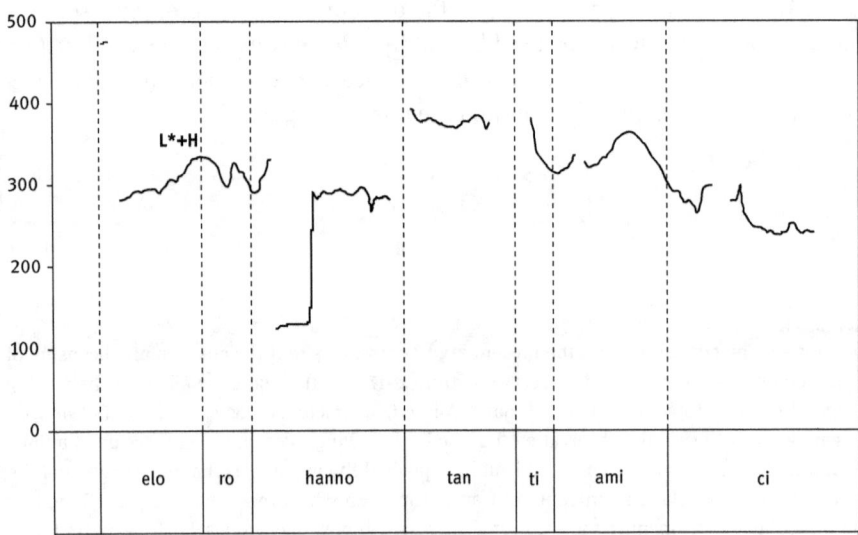

Figure 6: A-Topic starting a Topic chain.

(34) i   video   li   trovo   piuttosto noiosi <u>tanto più</u>   <u>che</u>
     the   videos   DO3PL.CL   find.1SG rather   boring all the more   that
     <u>ci</u>   <u>sono</u>   <u>quelle</u>   <u>schede</u>   <u>da</u>   <u>completare</u>   <u>che</u>   <u>sono</u>   <u>lunghissime</u>
     there be.3PL those   forms   to complete.INF that be.3PL long.SUP
     pro <u>non</u> <u>finiscono</u> <u>mai</u>
          NEG finish.3PL never
     'I find videos rather boring, all the more so because those forms to be filled are super-long, (they) are never-ending.'

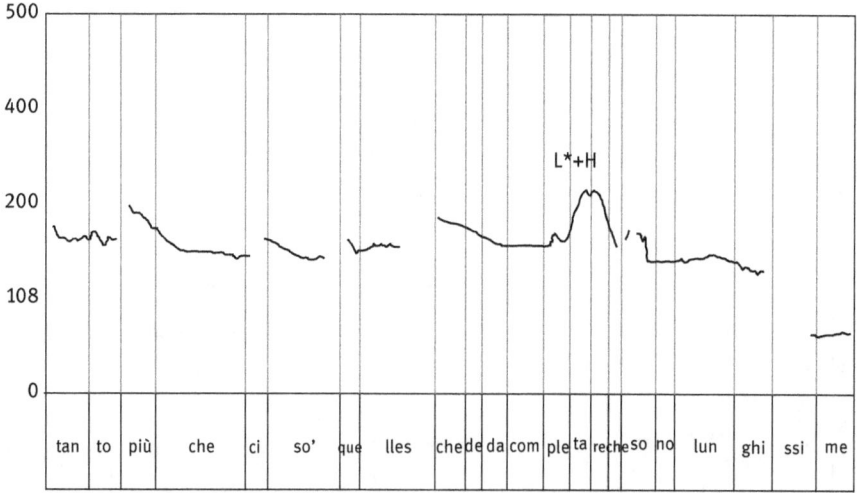

Figure 7: *There*-construction introducing an A-Topic.

(35) in   quello   dell'   investigatore   <u>c'</u>   <u>è</u>   <u>la</u>   <u>signora</u>   <u>elegante</u>
     in   that   of.the detective   there   be.3SG the woman   elegant
     <u>che</u>   pro <u>parla</u>   <u>in</u> <u>un</u> <u>determinato</u> <u>modo,</u>
     that   speak.3SG   in   a   certain   way
     <u>c'</u>   <u>è</u>   <u>la</u>   <u>cameriera</u>   <u>che</u>   pro <u>parla</u>   <u>proprio</u>
     there be.3SG the   waitress   that   speak.3SG   just
     <u>in</u> <u>tutt'</u> <u>altro</u>   <u>modo</u>
     in   quite   different way
     'In the detective's one [video] the elegant woman speaks in a certain way, while the waitress speaks in quite a different way.'

As is shown, the post-copular DP in (34) is marked with a L*+H tone, it implements a Topic shift with respect to the current Topic *i video* ('the videos',

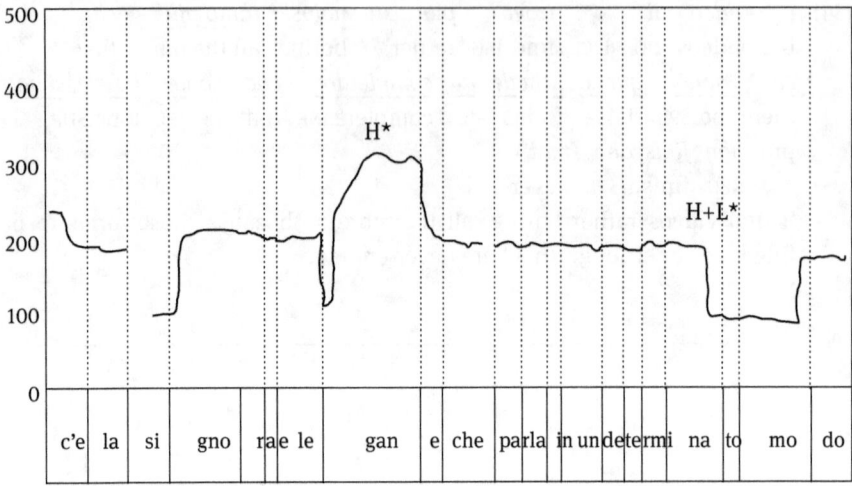

Figure 8a: *There*-construction introducing a C-Topic.

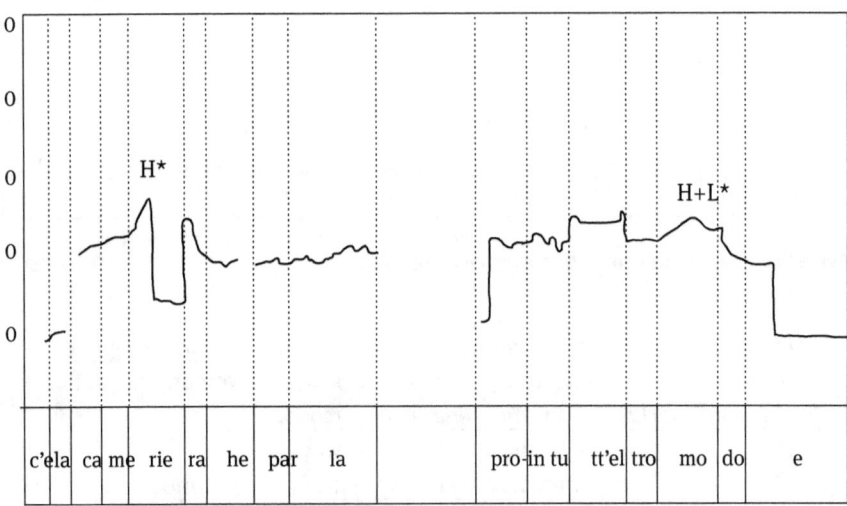

Figure 8b: *There*-construction introducing a C-Topic.

left-dislocated at the beginning of the extract) and is the antecedent of a following *pro* (the null subject of *non finiscono mai* '(they) are never-ending'). On the other hand, the two post-copular DPs in (35) are opposed with respect to different Comments. Hence, they qualify as C-Topics (cf. Bianchi and Frascarelli 2010) and, as such, they are marked with a H* tone (F&H 2007).

Notice that if a locative PP is realized in a *there*-construction, it can be either an element of the background (i.e., a G-Topic) or a *frame-setter*, that is to say, an element which has the function to *limit the truth-conditional validity* of the sentence it is associated with within some particular domain (Krifka 2007). Frame-setters in the left periphery are typically marked with a H* tone (Carella 2015; Frascarelli 2017), as is the case of the PP *in quello dell'investigatore* 'in the detective's one [video]' in (35) above (cf. Figure 9 below):

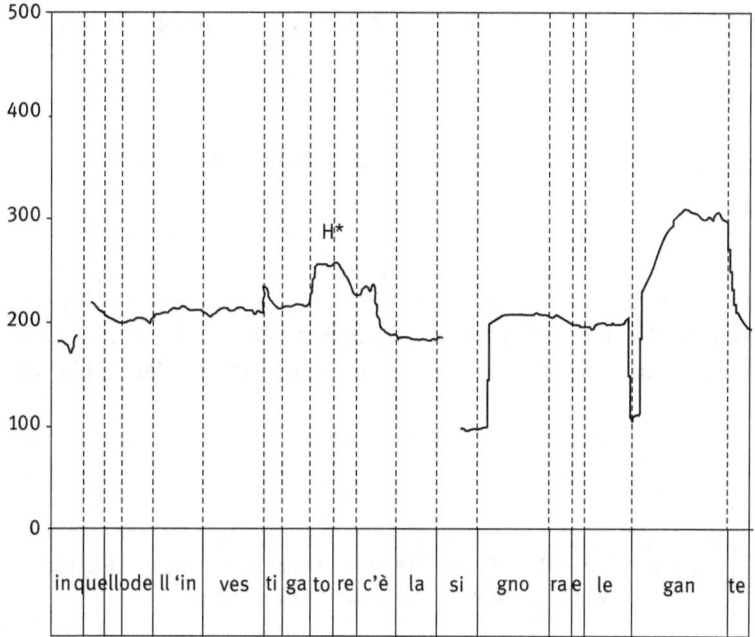

Figure 9: Frame-setter introducing a *there*-sentence.

To conclude, interface analysis shows the existence of different types of *ci*-sentences in Italian:
i) *existential sentences proper*: structures of the type illustrated in § 2 above, in which the post-copular noun phrase is the predicate (Focus) and the locative PP (when present) is a right-hand G-Topic;
ii) *presentational ci-sentences*: structures used to propose a Topic shift or a contrast between two (or more) propositions; in these constructions, the

post-copular DP is a left-hand Topic and the following material is the Comment (cf.§ 3.3.3);[22]

iii) *"c'era una volta"* ci-*sentences*: structures in which the story-telling formula *c'era una volta* ('once upon a time') is used. It will be argued (cf. § 3.3.4) that some of these constructions are presentational *ci*-sentences (cf. [ii] above), as they introduce a Topic-Comment (information) structure, while others must be provided a different analysis since the relevant formula is followed by a non-topical element (cf., for instance, [33] and the Figure 5).

In the following section syntactic evidence is discussed, providing further support to this proposal.

3.3.3 Presentational *ci*-sentences: Syntactic properties and derivation

When extraction operations are considered, presentational *ci*-sentences immediately show different properties with respect to existential sentences (cf. § 2.2.2). Specifically, the post-copular DP in a *ci*-sentence like (36) disallows extraction, exactly like the subject DP of a predicative sentence (37) and differently from the post-copular noun phrase in an existential clause like (18) above:

---

[22] It is important to notice that the existence of presentational *there*-sentences has been already attested in previous works, but from different perspectives and providing different explanations to the relevant construction. Specifically, Lambrecht (1994) clarifies that presentational sentences are different from other types of "sentence-focus" structures in that they do not introduce a new event, but a new referent in the discourse [...] often, but not always with the purpose of making it available for predication in subsequent discourse (Lambrecht 1994: 142–144). The author, however, does not provide an interface analysis for the relevant Topics and considers the "subsequent" proposition as a pseudo-relative clause (cf. also Lambrecht 2002) – a solution that suffers from different drawbacks, as is argued in § 3.3.3 below (cf. fn. 24). Lambrecht's analysis is then resumed in Cruschina's (2012, 2015) works. However, the author considers the referent introduced by *c'è/c'era* 'there is/was' to be a focal element and, consequently, argues for a sentence-focus analysis of the relevant structure. Specifically it is claimed that "the introduced referent is new in relation to the discourse, while the predicative constituent is new in relation to the newly introduced referent. Presentational sentences are therefore formed by two independent information units, that are both simultaneously focal" (Cruschina 2015: 94). We believe that this proposal cannot be maintained as well, given the discourse-prosody evidence provided in this paper (clearly supporting a Topic-Comment analysis) and the creation of Topic chains.

(36) *[di cosa]ᵢ c'   era   (una volta) [un pescatore tᵢ]
     of   what there be.PST.3SG a   time   a   fisherman
     che era   molto povero?
     that be.PST.3SG very poor
     Intended: '(Once upon a time), [a fisherman who fished for what] was very poor?'

(37) *[di cosa]ᵢ [un pescatore tᵢ] era   molto povero?
     of   what a   fisherman   be.PST.3SG very poor
     Intended: '[A fisherman who fished for what] was very poor?'

This parallel (as well as the contrast with existential sentences) strongly supports the existence of presentational sentences "disguised as existentials" and requires further insight on the structure and derivation of the relevant constructions.

As a matter of fact, assuming that the post-copular DP is a Topic implies that what follows is a proposition – not a DP-modifier (i.e., a relative clause) – despite the presence of the introducing element *che* ('that'). In this respect, immediate evidence against a relative clause analysis comes from the observation that the post-copular DP in a presentational *ci*-sentence can be coordinated with a [+def] DP disallowing a sloppy reading (cf. [38]). On the contrary, a sloppy interpretation is available for an existential sentence like (39), in which the *that*-clause can be either a restrictive or an appositive relative clause:

(38) Negli show degli anni '70 c'   era   sempre la Carrà
     in.the show of.the years 70 there be.PST.3SG always the Carrà
     che ballava.   E   anche Mina
     that dance.PST.3SG and also Mina
     'In the 70's shows Mrs. Carrà was always present, dancing. And Mina (was always present/*was dancing) as well.'   (STRICT / *SLOPPY)

(39) In quello show c'   era   una bimba   che ballava.
     in that   show there be.PST.3SG a   child.F that dance.PST.3SG
     E   anche una scimmietta
     and also a   monkey.DIMIN
     'In that show there was a young girl dancing. And a little monkey (was there/was dancing) as well.'   (STRICT / SLOPPY)

Furthermore, it should be noticed that the *that*-clause found in presentational *ci*-sentences does not qualify as a relative clause from an intonational viewpoint. As is known, a relative clause shows a pitch both on the relative head and on the rightmost element of the modifier clause (a scope-marking device, consistent with cross-linguistic analysis, cf. Frascarelli and Ramaglia 2014), while the clause under examination here shows the typical downgrading contour of a Broad Focus sentence (cf. Figures 4 and 8 above).

Based on this evidence, we argue that presentational *ci*-sentences qualify as *Topic-Comment constructions*. Accordingly, we propose that – differently from existential sentences – the [*ci* + copula] form in presentational *ci*-sentences is a complex *functional head* with a specific *discourse role*. In particular, we argue that it is an illocutionary marker and, as such, a grammaticalized form merged in a functional projection in the high C-domain (possibly, Force°) (see § 3.3.4 for further details concerning the relevant grammaticalization process).

As for the complementizer *che* ('that') preceding the Comment, we propose *a Focus marking function* for this element, specifically associated with propositional focalization. As a matter of fact, the "multi-functional" role of *che* is a well-attested phenomenon in Italian (Berruto 1998) and the present proposal is perfectly in line with the analysis provided in Manzini and Savoia (2011) for the complementizer *che* introducing matrix yes-no questions in some Romance varieties (as in Florentine and Roman; cf. [40] below):

(40) *Che esci stasera?*
    INT go.out.2SG tonight
    'Are you going out tonight?'

Specifically, the authors surmise that the insertion of *che* in yes-no questions "corresponds to the presence of a focalization expressed on the main verb" (Manzini and Savoia 2011: 36). This is exactly in the spirit of the present proposal.

Additionally consider that presentational *ci*-sentences can lack an initial Topic and serve exclusively as propositional Focus constructions. Indeed, given a question like *che c'è?* ('what's the matter (with you)?'), answers like (41a–b) are very common in Italian, in which a focal stress is intended on the main predicate and, importantly, the presence of the introducing *che* is compelling:

(41) a. *C' è *(che) sono stufo*
      there be.3SG that be.1SG fed up
      '(The point is that) I am fed up!'
   b. *C' è *(che) mi sono innamorato di te*
      there be.3SG that REFL be.1SG in.love of you
      '(The point is that) I am in love with you.'

We thus propose an analysis of the relevant *che* as a Focus marker and, consequently, its insertion in the head position of the Focus phrase projection in the C-domain. A sentence like *c'era la Carrà che ballava* 'Mrs. Carrà was present, dancing' (cf. [38] above) thus corresponds to the following (information) structural analysis:[23]

(42) [$_{ForceP}$ [$_{Force'}$ *c'era* [$_{ShiftP}$ [$_{DP}$ *la Carrà*]$_k$ [$_{FocP}$ [$_{Foc'}$ *che* [$_{FinP}$ [$_{IP}$ pro$_k$ *ballava*]]]]]]]

As is shown, the Comment is contained within an IP-structure having a *pro* in subject position that is matched with the A-Topic for referential interpretation (cf. Frascarelli 2007).[24]

---

23 It is important not to confuse presentational sentences like (42), in which the DP *la Carrà* is a Topic, with cleft constructions (e.g., *è la Carrà che balla* 'it's Mrs. Carrà who is dancing'), in which *la Carrà* is a Focus. This difference is immediately supported by evidence showing that a cleft can be used as an answer to a cleft wh-question (like [i] below), while this is not the case for a presentational sentence:
(i) Q: Chi è che balla?
 who be.3SG that dance.3SG
 'Who is it that is dancing?'
 A: È la Carrà che balla (cleft)
 be.3SG the Carrà that dance.3SG
 A': *C' è la Carrà che balla (presentational)
 there be.3SG the Carrà that dance.3SG
Furthermore, the post-copular DP in a cleft is typically associated to a corrective reading, while this interpretation is excluded for post-copular DPs in presentational sentences:
(ii) Q: In TV sta ballando Lorella Cuccarini
 In TV stay.3SG dance.GER Lorella Cuccarini
 'On TV you can see Lorella Cuccarini dancing.'
 A: No, è la Carrà che balla (cleft)
 A': *No, c'è la Carrà che balla (presentational)
Hence, in (42) *la Carrà* is not a Focus but a Topic, whereas the Focus is the following proposition (as in [41]).
24 The present proposal clearly excludes a pseudo-relative (PR) analysis for presentational *ci*-sentences (*contra* Cruschina 2015). As is known, PR is a type of finite construction found in many Romance languages that superficially looks like a relative clause but describes events giving rise to direct perception reports (cf., among others, Guasti 1988; Cinque 1992; Scarano 2002; Moulton and Grillo 2014). Though the presentational *che*-clause might "look like" a PR, Grillo and Moulton's (G&M) (2016) investigation on PRs immediately shows that this analysis is not tenable. Indeed, the authors convincingly show that PRs denote *event kinds* and that the DP heading a PR is part of the event itself. Consequently, a Topic-Comment structure cannot be associated to a PR since Topics typically denote individuals (*not* event kinds). Consider, for instance, spatial and temporal modifiers: G&M (2016) show that these are banned with Present

A final consideration concerning agreement is now in order for a comprehensive account of the relevant structure. Consider the presentational *ci*-sentence in (43), in which a plural Topic is realized, and the relevant structure in (44):

(43) Ci   sono   i   miei fratelli che   pro vivono   in America
     there be.3PL the my   brothers that   live.3PL in America
     'My brothers live in the States.'

(44) [$_{ForceP}$ [$_{Force'}$ *ci sono* [$_{ShiftP}$ [$_{DP}$ *i miei fratelli*]$_k$ [$_{FocP}$ [$_{Foc'}$ *che* [$_{FinP}$ [$_{IP}$ pro$_k$ *vivono in America*]]]]]]]

As can be noticed, plural agreement applies "downstairs" (i.e., within IP) and "upstairs" (i.e., with the "copula"). Since we argue that the relevant functional head is an illocutionary marker in Force°, the presence of agreement is not trivial an issue.

We propose to analyze this phenomenon as a case of "Agreement in COMP" (Rizzi 1990), revised from a Minimalist perspective. Assuming that grammatical agreement starts out at C ("φ-features and tense appear to be derivative [from C that is the phase head]", cf. Chomsky 2008: 143), we draw from Miyagawa (2012) the suggestion that in languages such as English and Italian, agreement lowers to T (i.e., I, in the traditional terminology used in this work) (via a mechanism of *feature-inheritance*), while it stays in C in others.

We therefore propose that in presentational *ci*-sentences, being Topic-Comment structures, the matrix *pro* is interpreted under long-distance Agree

---

PRs, as with other types of event kinds. This is not the case of presentational *ci*-sentences. Compare (i) and (ii) below:

(i)   *Ho   visto Maria che   balla   al   parco giovedì scorso
       have.1SG seen   Maria that dances.3SG at.the park Thursday last
       'I saw Maria dancing at the park last Thursday.'   (PR, from G&M 2016)

(ii)   C'   è   la   Carrà che   balla   in TV giovedì   prossimo / stasera
       there   be.3SG the Carrà that dances.3SG in TV Thursday next   tonight
       'Mrs. Carrà is dancing on television next Thursday/tonight.'

with the Shift° head through a "matching chain" between the subject *pro*, the Fin° head and the A-Topic (cf. Frascarelli 2007). Specifically it is proposed, in the respect of cyclicity, that after Merge of the subject *pro*, Agr is merged in Fin° and matches abstractly with *pro* (i.e., with a "variable matching"); subsequently the A-Topic is merged, matching (and valuating) Fin°. Agreement features are thus lowered to I and spelt out as the typical subject-verb agreement. Additionally, φ-features and tense features are transmitted to Force°, determining agreement between the "copula" and the Topic:[25]

(45)

[ForceP[Force'*ci sono*[ShiftP[DP *i miei fratelli*]k[FocP[Foc'*che* [FinPAgr [IPpro$_k$ *vivono*...]]]]]][26]

                        Agree   feature-
                                              inheritance

3.3.4 Explaining antiagreement effects and the lack of DE in (some) *there*-sentences

Given the present analysis, it is possible to provide a comprehensive explanation for the (apparent) antiagreement effects emerging on the "copula" in some presentational *ci*-sentences. As a matter of fact, browsing corpora and storytelling on internet blogs, it can be easily seen that the formula *c'era una volta*

---

25 This is consistent with Rizzi's (1997) suggestion that Force and Fin are "two sides of the same coin", as they constitute the two boundaries of the C-domain, dedicated to illocutionary force and finiteness, respectively. Even though Italian has no "Agr in C" phenomenon, the claim that Fin° is the career of Agr features can be maintained on empirical grounds insofar as Fin° is the projection related to finiteness in Italian as well. As a matter of fact, in Italian its overt realization (in the form of prepositional COMPs) is triggered by infinitive clauses. Hence, it might be argued that agreement morphology in C is parametrical (i.e., connected with either finite or infinitive Agreement).

26 Though we concentrated the analysis on presentational *ci*-sentences in which the postcopular DP is followed by a *that*-clause, it is important to underline that the relevant Topic can also be followed by a PP, usually having a locative function (e.g., *c'è tuo fratello alla porta* 'your brother is at the door', *c'è Gianni in giardino* 'Gianni is in the garden', cf. [30b]). We surmise that in this case an elliptical Comment is realized. In particular we propose that the relevant Topic is followed by the Comment (realized in IP), which only contains the predicative PP.

('once upon a time') is often followed by a coordinated DP, despite the 3SG person form of the "copula", as in:

(46) *C'era*$_{3SG}$ *una volta un re e una regina (che desideravano tanto...)*
 'Once upon a time a king and a queen (wanted so much...)'
(4950 Google occurrences)

It should be noticed, however, that such antiagreement effects do not appear either with plural (non-coordinated) DPs (47a-b) or when the first member of the coordination is plural (47c):

(47) a. **C'era*$_{3SG}$ *una volta [i sette nani]...*
 'Once upon a time the seven dwarfs...'
 b. **C'era*$_{3SG}$ *una volta [i cittadini poveri di un regno]*
 'Once upon a time the poor servants of a kingdom...'
 c. **C'era*$_{3SG}$ *una volta [due sorellastre e una regina molto cattiva]...*
 'Once upon a time two step-sisters and a very bad queen...'

We propose that the 3SG marking shown in (46) is not a case of antiagreement, and that it can be immediately explained through a bi-clausal structural analysis. Specifically, we argue that the formula *c'era una volta* constitutes an independent *existential* sentence, in which the post-copular NumP [*una volta*] has a predicate function, while the clitic pronoun *ci* is the subject (cf. § 2.2). The latter is coindexed with the Topic DP in the following (juxtaposed) presentational sentence (implementing a Topic-Comment structure). In other words, the presentational sentence represents the "logical complement" of the existential clause (like in a sort of direct speech narration):

(48) [$_{GP}$ [$_{IP}$ [$_{DP}$ *c'*]$_i$ *era* [$_{SC}$ t$_i$ t$_k$]] [$_{FocP}$ [$_{NumP}$ *una volta*]$_k$ t$_{IP}$]]
 [$_{ForceP}$ [$_{ShiftP}$ [$_{DP}$ *un re e una regina*]$_k$ [$_{FocP}$ [$_{Foc'}$ *che* [$_{FinP}$ [$_{IP}$ pro$_k$ *desideravano tanto*...]]]]]]

Hence, when "antiagreement effects" are found in presentational *ci*-sentences, we are dealing in fact with two separate sentences (as in [48]), in which copular agreement depends on the predicate NumP of the former; on the other hand, when the "copula" (i.e., the illocutionary marker) and the main verb both agree with the post-copular DP, a unique Topic-Comment structure must be assumed (as in [45]).

It is now important to observe that the bi-clausal construction in (48) can be taken as the source structure for the grammaticalization process deriving the

complex illocutionary head *c'è/c'era* ('there is/was'), which is merged in Force°
in presentational *ci*-sentences. Our hypothesis is that, starting from the structure in (48), the existential sentence *c'era una volta* has been re-analyzed as
a formula (typically used to introduce fairy-tales). Then, with the loss of the
temporal NumP [*una volta*], the relevant structure has reduced to *c'era*, which
has finally lost its structural articulation and completed its grammaticalization
process to become a functional head.

The bi-clausal structure proposed in (48) can also provide an explanation
for *there*-sentences like (33) above (repeated below as [49]), in which the formula *c'era una volta* is followed by a non-topical DP (cf. Figure 5 and the relevant discussion):

(49) *C'era una volta [Lea e Bea] con la mamma e con papà*
 'Once upon a time, Lea and Bea were with mummy and daddy.'

Given the present analysis of *ci*-sentences, the structure in (49) cannot be analyzed as an existential construction, which excludes definite DPs in postcopular position (cf. § 3.1). Nor can the relevant sentence be considered
a presentational *ci*-construction of the type illustrated in § 3.3.3, as the latter
introduces a Topic-Comment structure. Since [*Lea e Bea*] in (49) is a definite
non-topical DP, we propose a bi-clausal analysis for it (like [48]). Accordingly,
it is formed by an existential construction (i.e., *c'era una volta*) followed by
a second sentence including a SC, in which the PP is the predicate and the subject DP [*Lea e Bea*] is a fronted Focus:

(50) [$_{GP}$ [$_{IP}$ [$_{DP}$ *c'*]$_i$ *era* [$_{SC}$ t$_i$ t$_k$]] [$_{FocP}$ [$_{NumP}$ *una volta*]$_k$ t$_{IP}$]]
 [$_{ForceP}$ [$_{FocP}$ [$_{DP}$ *LEA E BEA*]$_k$ [$_{SC}$ t$_k$ [$_{PP}$ *con la mamma e con papà*]]]]

Finally, the syntactic analysis proposed for presentational *ci*-sentences also allows for an independent and comprehensive explanation for the absence of DE
effects observed in languages like Italian (in which [+def] DPs are not excluded
from the post-copular position; cf. § 3.2). It should be now clear that this possibility is connected to the existence of presentational *ci*-constructions (or else of
bi-clausal structures like [48]), in which the post-copular DP cannot show DE
effects because it is not a predicate with a reduced functional structure (§ 2.2.1)
but a Topic and, as such, specific (and referential) by definition (Frascarelli
2007).

If this analysis is on the right track, the prediction is that DE can only be
found in languages in which presentational or bi-clausal *there*-sentences are not
(or only marginally) available, due to independent core grammar restrictions

(concerning, for instance, the realization of dislocated constituents in the C-domain). This interesting issue will be addressed in future investigations.

4 Conclusions

In this paper different types of copular constructions have been analyzed, providing syntactic, semantic and interface (discourse-prosody) evidence for three major claims.

First of all, it is argued that existential sentences are marked copular constructions in which the post-copular NumP is a Narrow Focus, whereas the locative PP is a right-hand G-Topic. Existential sentences thus require the raising of the relevant NumP to Spec,FocP and IP-inversion to Spec,GP. This derivation can account for a number of specific syntactic and intonational properties.

Secondly, presentational *ci*-sentences have been approached and, differently from recent proposals, a Topic-Comment structure has been proposed to account for their derivation. In particular, it is argued that in this type of copular constructions the post-copular DP is a left-hand A- or C-Topic, while the following material is the Comment. Discourse and intonational evidence has been discussed, from children's and adults' naturalistic data, clearly showing a Topic contour for the relevant post-copular DP and the creation of a Topic chain after its production. In this picture, the *c'è/c'era* 'there is/was' form is no longer a copula but a complex functional head, that is to say an illocutionary marker, merged in Force°. Its origins have been indicated in the *c'era una volta* ('once upon a time') formula introducing fairy-tales: a predicative copular structure which has been grammaticalized after the loss of the predicative NumP *una volta*.

Finally, a bi-clausal analysis has been proposed for structures in which an existential construction seems to "overlap" with the Topic-Comment articulation that is typical of presentational *ci*-sentences. This explanation can also account for those *ci*-sentences in which a non-topical definite DP follows the *c'era (una volta)* form.

To conclude, the present analysis provides an interface-based, comprehensive explanation for a number of morpho-syntactic properties and prosodic phenomena connected with existential sentences (and for important asymmetries with respect to other copular constructions). Furthermore, it allows to maintain, with Moro (1997), that DE is a *universal property* of existential sentences: when it is apparently violated, we are in fact dealing with presentational *ci*-sentences, which are parametrically available in different languages, possibly depending on independent information-structural restrictions concerning the realization of Topics.

References

Abbott, Barbara. 1992. Definiteness, existentials, and the 'list' interpretation. In Chris Barker & David Dowty (eds.), *Proceedings of Semantics and Linguistic Theory (=SALT) II*, 1–16. Columbus: The Ohio State University.
Abney, Steven P. 1987. *The English noun phrase in its sentential aspect*. Cambridge, MA: MIT dissertation.
Alexiadou, Artemis, Liliane Haegeman & Melita Stavrou. 2007. *Noun Phrase in the Generative Perspective*. Berlin & New York: Mouton de Gruyter.
Bernstein, Judy B. 2001. The DP hypothesis: Identifying clausal properties in the nominal domain. In Mark R. Baltin & Chris Collins (eds.), *Handbook of Contemporary Syntactic Theory*, 536–561. Oxford: Blackwell Publishers.
Berruto, Gaetano. 1998. *Sociolinguistica dell'italiano contemporaneo*. Roma: Carocci.
Bianchi, Valentina & Mara Frascarelli. 2010. Is topic a root phenomenon? *Iberia* 2(1). 43–88.
Cardinaletti, Anna. 2002. Against optional and null clitics. Right dislocation vs. marginalization. *Studia Linguistica* 65(1). 29–57.
Cardinaletti, Anna & Maria Teresa Guasti (eds.). 1995. *Small Clauses* (Syntax and Semantics 28). San Diego, CA: Academic Press.
Carella, Giorgio. 2015. The Limiting Topic. *Annali di Ca' Foscari, Serie Occidentale* 49. 363–392.
Chomsky, Noam. 1986. *Knowledge of Language*. New York: Praeger.
Chomsky, Noam. 1991. Some notes on the economy of derivation and representation. In Robert Freidin (ed.), *Principles and Parameters in Comparative Grammar*, 417–454. Cambridge, MA: MIT Press.
Chomsky, Noam. 2008. On phases. In Robert Freidin, Carlos P. Otero & Maria Luisa Zubizarreta (eds.), *Foundational Issues in Linguistic Theory. Essays in Honor of Jean-Roger Vergnaud*, 133–166. Cambridge, MA: MIT Press.
Cinque, Guglielmo. 1992. The Pseudo-Relative and Acc-*ing* Constructions after Verbs of Perception. *University of Venice Working Papers in Linguistics* 92(I.2). 1–31.
Cinque, Guglielmo. 1994. On the evidence for partial N-movement in the Romance DP. In Guglielmo Cinque, Jan Koster, Jean-Yves Pollock, Luigi Rizzi & Raffaella Zanuttini (eds.), *Paths towards Universal Grammar. Studies in honor of Richard S. Kayne*, 85–110. Washington, DC: Georgetown University Press.
Cinque, Guglielmo. 2010. *The syntax of adjectives: A comparative study*. Cambridge, MA: MIT Press.
Cinque, Guglielmo (ed.). 2002. *Functional Structure in DP and IP (The Cartography of Syntactic Structures 1)*. Oxford: Oxford University Press.
Cruschina, Silvio. 2012. Focus in existential sentences. In Valentina Bianchi & Cristiano Chesi (eds.), *Enjoy linguistics! Papers Offered to Luigi Rizzi on the Occasion of his 60th Birthday*, 77–107. Siena: CISCL Press.
Cruschina, Silvio. 2015. Focus structure. In Delia Bentley, Francesco Maria Ciconte & Silvio Cruschina (eds.), *Existentials and Locatives in Romance Dialects of Italy*, 43–98. Oxford & New York: Oxford University Press.
Declerck, Renaat. 1988. *Studies on Copular Sentences, Clefts and Pseudo-Clefts*. Leuven: Leuven University Press.

Den Dikken, Marcel. 2006a. Specificational copular sentences and pseudoclefts. In Martin Everaert & Henk van Riemsdijk (eds.), *The Blackwell Companion to Syntax*, Vol. IV, 292–409. Oxford: Blackwell Publishers.

Den Dikken, Marcel. 2006b. *Relators and Linkers. The Syntax of Predication, Predicate Inversion, and Copulas*. Cambridge, MA: MIT Press.

Enç, Mürvet. 1991. The semantics of specificity. *Linguistic Inquiry* 22(1). 1–15.

Francez, Itamar. 2007. *Existential Propositions*. Stanford, CA: Stanford University dissertation.

Frascarelli, Mara. 2004. Dislocation, clitic resumption and minimality: A comparative analysis of left and right constructions in Italian. In Reineke Bok-Bennema, Bart Hollebrandse, Brigitte Kampers-Manhe & Petra Sleeman (eds.), *Romance Languages and Linguistic Theory 2002. Selected Papers from 'Going Romance' (Groningen, 28–30 November 2002)*, 98–118. Amsterdam & Philadelphia: John Benjamins.

Frascarelli, Mara. 2007. Subjects, topics and the interpretation of referential *pro*. An interface approach to the linking of (null) pronouns. *Natural Language and Linguistic Theory* 25(4). 691–734.

Frascarelli, Mara. 2010. Narrow Focus, Clefting and Predicate Inversion. *Lingua* 120(9). 2121–2147.

Frascarelli, Mara. 2015. «Lea e Bea»: Catene topicali in età prescolare. Un'analisi di interfaccia. Paper presented at the PRIN-2012 Workshop on Theory, Experimentation, Applications: Long distance dependencies in forms of linguistics diversity, "La Sapienza" University of Rome, 23–24 October.

Frascarelli, Mara. 2017. Dislocations and framings. In Elisabeth Stark & Andreas Dufter (eds.), *Manual of Romance Morphosyntax and Syntax* (Manuals of Romance Linguistics), 472–501. Berlin & New York: Mouton de Gruyter.

Frascarelli, Mara. 2018. The interpretation of pro in consistent and partial NS languages: A comparative interface analysis. In Federica Cognola & Jan Casalicchio (eds.), *Null-Subjects in Generative Grammar. A synchronic and diachronic perspective*, 211–239. Oxford & New York: Oxford University Press.

Frascarelli, Mara & Roland Hinterhölzl. 2007. Types of Topics in German and Italian. In Kerstin Schwabe & Susanne Winkler (eds.), *On Information Structure, Meaning and Form*, 87–116. Amsterdam & Philadelphia: John Benjamins.

Frascarelli, Mara & Francesca Ramaglia. 2013. (Pseudo)clefts at the syntax-prodosy-discourse interface. In Katharina Hartmann & Tinjes Veenstra (eds.), *Cleft Structures*, 97–137. Amsterdam & Philadelphia: John Benjamins.

Frascarelli, Mara & Francesca Ramaglia. 2014. The interpretation of clefting (a)symmetries between Italian and German. In Karen Lahousse & Stefania Marzo (eds.), *Romance Languages and Linguistic Theory 2012. Selected papers from 'Going Romance 2012'*, 65–89. Amsterdam & Philadelphia: John Benjamins.

Giorgi, Alessandra & Giuseppe Longobardi. 1991. *The Syntax of Noun Phrases*. Cambridge: Cambridge University Press.

Giusti, Giuliana. 2006. Parallels in clausal and nominal periphery. In Mara Frascarelli (ed.), *Phases of Interpretation*, 163–184. Berlin & New York: Mouton de Gruyter.

Grillo, Nino & Keir Moulton. 2016. Kind of Perfect. Paper presented at the 42nd Incontro di Grammatica Generativa, University of Salento, 18–20 February.

Grimshaw, Jane. 1990. *Argument Structure*. Cambridge, MA: MIT Press.

Guasti, Maria Teresa. 1988. La pseudorelative et les phénomenènes d'accord. *Rivista di Grammatica Generativa* 13. 35–57.

Heim, Irene. 1987. Where does the definiteness restriction apply? Evidence from the definiteness of variables. In Eric Reuland & Alice ter Meulen (eds.), *The Representation of (In)definiteness*, 21–42. Cambridge, MA: MIT Press.

Heycock, Caroline & Anthony Kroch. 1999. Pseudocleft connectedness: Implication for the LF interface level. *Linguistic Inquiry* 30(3). 365–397.

Higgins, Francis Roger. 1979. *The Pseudo-Cleft Construction in English*. New York & London: Garland Publishing.

Kayne, Richard S. 2016. The Unicity of *There* and the Definiteness Effect. Ms., New York University. https://ling.auf.net/lingbuzz/002858 (accessed 30 January 2016).

Krifka, Manfred. 2007. Basic notions of information structure. In Caroline Féry, Gisbert Fanselow & Manfred Krifka (eds.), *Interdisciplinary Studies on Information Structure*, Vol. 6 (ISIS, Working papers of the SFB 632). Potsdam: University of Potsdam.

La Fauci, Nunzio & Michele Loporcaro. 1997. Outline of a theory of existentials on evidence from Romance. *Studi Italiani di Linguistica Teorica e Applicata* 26(1). 5–55.

Laenzlinger, Christopher. 2005. French adjective ordering: perspectives on DP-internal movement types. *Lingua* 115(5). 645–689.

Lambrecht, Knud. 1994. *Information structure and sentence form. Topic, focus and the mental representations of discourse referents*. Cambridge: Cambridge University Press.

Lambrecht, Knud. 2002. Topic, focus and secondary predication. The French presentational relative construction. In Claire Beyssade, Reineke Bok-Bennema, Frank Drijkoningen & Paola Monachesi (eds.), *Romance Languages and Linguistic Theory 2000*, 171–212. Amsterdam & Philadelphia: John Benjamins.

Longobardi, Giuseppe. 1994. Reference and proper names: A theory of N-movement in Syntax and Logical Form. *Linguistic Inquiry* 25(4). 609–665.

Longobardi, Giuseppe. 2001. The structure of DPs: Some principles, parameters, and problems. In Mark R. Baltin & Chris Collins (eds.), *Handbook of Contemporary Syntactic Theory*, 562–603. Oxford: Blackwell Publishers.

Longobardi, Giuseppe. 2005. Toward a unified grammar of reference. *Zeitschrift für Sprachwissenschaft* 24. 5–44.

Manzini, Maria Rita & Leonardo Maria Savoia. 2011. *Grammatical Categories Variation in Romance Languages*. Cambridge: Cambridge University Press.

McNally, Louise. 1997. *A Semantics for the English Existential Construction*. New York: Garland.

McNally, Louise. 2011. Existential sentences. In Klaus von Heusinger, Claudia Maienborn & Paul Portner (eds.), *Semantics. An International Handbook of Natural Language Meaning*, 1829–1848. Berlin & New York: Mouton de Gruyter.

Milsark, Gary. 1974. *Existential Sentences in English*. Cambridge, MA: MIT dissertation.

Miyagawa, Shigeru. 2012. Agreements that occur mainly in the main clause. In Lobke Aelbrecht, Liliane Haegeman & Rachel Nye (eds.), *Main Clause Phenomena*, 79–112. Amsterdam & Philadelphia: John Benjamins.

Moro, Andrea. 1997. *The Raising of Predicates*. Cambridge: Cambridge University Press.

Moulton, Keir & Nino Grillo. 2014. Pseudo Relatives: Big but Transparent. Paper presented at the 45th North Eastern Linguistic Society, MIT, 31 October – 2 November.

Pierrehumbert, Janet & Julia Hirschberg. 1990. The meaning of intonational contours in the interpretation of discourse. In Philip R. Cohen, Jerry Morgan & Martha Pollack (eds.), *Intentions in Communication*, 271–311. Cambridge, MA: MIT Press.

Pietrandrea, Paola (ed.). 2004. *ArCoDip, Archivio dei Corpora del Dipartimento*. Roma: University of Roma Tre.

Poletto, Cecilia & Jean-Yves Pollock. 2004. On the left periphery of some Romance wh-questions. In Luigi Rizzi (ed.), *The Structure of CP and IP* (The Cartography of Syntactic Structures 2), 251–296. Oxford: Oxford University Press.
Ramaglia, Francesca. 2011. *Adjectives at the Syntax-Semantics Interface*. München: Lincom.
Ramaglia, Francesca. 2013. *La struttura dell'informazione nel sintagma nominale: DP = CP?*. München: Lincom.
Ritter, Elizabeth. 1991. Two functional categories in noun phrases: Evidence from Modern Hebrew. In Susan D. Rothstein (ed.), *Perspectives on Phrase Structure*, 37–62. San Diego, CA: Academic Press.
Rizzi, Luigi. 1990. *Relativized Minimality*. Cambridge, MA: MIT Press.
Rizzi, Luigi. 1997. The fine structure of the left periphery. In Liliane Haegeman (ed.), *Elements of Grammar*, 281–337. Dordrecht: Kluwer.
Safir, Kenneth J. 1985. *Syntactic Chains*. Cambridge: Cambridge University Press.
Samek-Lodovici, Vieri. 2006. When right dislocation meets the left-periphery. A unified analysis of Italian non-final focus. *Lingua* 116(6). 836–873.
Scarano, Antonietta. 2002. *Frasi relative e pseudo-relative in Italiano. Sintassi, semantica e articolazione dell'informazione*. Roma: Bulzoni.
Scott, Gary-John. 2002. *The syntax and semantics of adjectival modification*. London: SOAS dissertation.
Selkirk, Elisabeth. 1995. Sentence Prosody: Intonation, Stress, and Phrasing. In John A. Goldsmith (ed.), *The Handbook of Phonological Theory*, 550–569. London: Basil Blackwell.
Stowell, Tim A. 1978. What was there before *there* was there. *Proceedings of the Chicago Linguistic Society* 14. 458–471.
Stowell, Tim A. 1981. *Origins of Phrase Structure*. Cambridge, MA: MIT dissertation.
Stowell, Tim A. 1989. Subjects, specifiers, and X-bar theory. In Mark R. Baltin & Antony S. Kroch (eds.), *Alternative Conceptions of Phrase Structure*, 232–262. Chicago & London: The University of Chicago Press.
Svenonius, Peter. 2008. The position of adjectives and other phrasal modifiers in the decomposition of DP. In Louise McNally & Chris Kennedy (eds.), *Adverbs and Adjectives: Syntax, Semantics, and Discourse*, 16–42. Oxford & New York: Oxford University Press.
Szabolcsi, Anna. 1987. Functional categories in the noun phrase. In István Kenesei (ed.), *Approaches to Hungarian*, Vol. II, 167–189. Jate: Szeged.
Szabolcsi, Anna. 1989. Noun phrases and clauses: Is DP analogous to IP or CP? In John R. Payne, (ed.), *The Structure of Noun Phrases*. The Hague & Paris: Mouton.
Szabolcsi, Anna. 1994. The Noun Phrase. In Ferenc Kiefer & Katain É. Kiss (eds.), *The Syntactic Structure of Hungarian*, 179–274. San Diego, CA: Academic Press.
Valois, Daniel. 1991. *The internal syntax of DP*. Los Angeles, CA: UCLA dissertation.
Ward, Gregory & Betty Birner. 1995. Definiteness and the English existential. *Language* 71. 722–742.
Zamparelli, Roberto. 2000. *Layers in the Determiner Phrase*. New York: Garland.
Zucchi, Alessandro. 1995. The ingredients of definiteness and the definiteness effect. *Natural Language Semantics* 3. 33–78.

Luigi Rizzi
Che and weak islands

1 Introduction

The study of locality has triggered much work on subtle, but stable, contrasts of acceptability between minimally different structures, giving empirical substance to the theoretical literature (Rizzi 1990, 2004, Manzini 1992, 1997, 1999 and much related work).

A very minimal, and yet very clear contrast involves the different forms of the inanimate wh-element in Italian. The wh-element *che*, functioning in colloquial varieties as a reduced variant of *che cosa* (what), is not extractable from weak islands, in contrast with the complete form *che cosa*, and the other reduced form *cosa*. This is clearly illustrated by negative island contexts[1]:

(1) a. Che cosa hai detto?
       'What did you say?'
    b. Cosa hai detto?
       'What did you say?'
    c. Che hai detto?
       'What did you say?'

(2) a. Che cosa non hai detto?
       'What didn't you say?'
    b. Cosa non hai detto?
       'What didn't you say?'
    c. *Che non hai detto?
       'What didn't you say?'

The same contrast holds at the level of relative acceptability for more robust weak islands such as the wh-island: extraction of *che cosa* and *cosa* is degraded, but extraction of *che* sounds more severely deviant:

---

1 I believe that the contrast has been discovered by Rita Manzini, even though I was unable to identify the appropriate reference in her publications. In any event, the empirical observations and analytic ideas of this short note have been inspired by discussions that Rita and I had on asymmetries and the proper theoretical treatment of weak islands over the years.

Luigi Rizzi, University of Geneva – University of Siena

https://doi.org/10.1515/9781501505201-029

(3) a. ?(?) Che cosa non sai come dire __?
   'What don't you know how to say?'
   b. ?(?) Cosa non sai come dire __?
   'What don't you know how to say __?'
   c. *Che non sai come dire __?
   'What don't you know how to say?'

The notation "?(?)" is meant to express the variability of the judgment across speakers, depending on lexical choices and other factors; here I use *not know* as the verb taking the indirect question; this choice may seem non-optimal, as it involves a negation, hence a negative island on top of the wh island; nevertheless, extractions from indirect questions selected by *not know* sound more natural than extractions from complements of *wonder* or other verbs taking indirect questions, so I will systematically use this kind of structures.

The asymmetry illustrated by (2) and (3) is very sensitive to minimal modifications. For instance, both the full and the reduced forms can be modified by *altro* (else); in this case, the contrast between *che* and the other forms disappears. All the forms sound fully acceptable in cases of extraction from a negative island:

(4) a. Che cos'altro non hai detto?
   'What else didn't you say?'
   b. Cos'altro non hai detto?
   'What else didn't you say?'
   c. Che altro non hai detto?
   'What else didn't you say?'

And the three forms are equally marginal in cases of extraction from a wh island:

(5) a. ?(?) Che cos'altro non sai come dire __?
   'What else don't you know how to say?'
   b. ?(?) Cos'altro non sai come dire __?
   'What else don't you know how to say?'
   c. ?(?) Che altro non sai come dire __?
   'What else don't you know how to say?'

In this paper I would like to relate the surprising properties of *che*, compared to *che cosa* and *cosa* to an hypothesis on the internal structure of these elements. The analysis will be expressed in terms of a theory of intervention locality based on Relativized Minimality, relying in particular on a fundamental factor which modulates the relative acceptability of extractions from weak islands, according to recent versions of this approach: the presence or absence in the moved wh-phrase of a lexical restriction.

2 The role of the lexical restriction

The beneficial effect of the pied-piping of an overt lexical restriction in contexts of intervention is straightforwardly shown by the following facts in French. With wh-element *combien* (how much/how many) in object position, the lexical restriction connected to the wh-element by preposition *de* (of) can be pied-piped, or left in situ, with subextraction of *combien*:

(4) a. [Combien de problèmes] a-t-il résolus __?
       'How many of problems did he solve __?
   b. Combien a-t-il résolu [__ de problèmes] ?
       'How many did he solve of problems ?'

If these two options are tested in weak island environments, we get a clear contrast. Across an intervening negation pied-piping is fine and subextraction is deviant:

(5) a. Combien de problèmes n'a-t-il pas résolus __?
       'How many of problems did he not solve __?
   b. *Combien n'a-t-il pas résolu [__ de problèmes] ?
       'How many did he not solve of problems ?'

In the context of extraction from an indirect question, pied-piping is also degraded to some extent, but the contrast persists and is clearly detectable at the level of relative acceptability:

(6) a. ? Combien de problèmes ne sait-il pas comment résoudre __?
       'How many of problems doesn't he know how to solve __?
   b. *Combien ne sait-il pas comment résoudre [__ de problèmes] ?
       'How many doesn't he know how to solve of problems ?'

These minimal pairs clearly show that the lexical restriction plays a crucial role in facilitating extraction from a weak island environment.

Italian does not have the equivalent of the *combien de NP* structure: the wh-element equivalent to *combien*, *quanto/quanti*, directly takes an NP complement without the mediation of a preposition, and agrees with it in gender and number; nevertheless, the NP can be extracted via *ne* cliticization:

(7) a. Quanti problemi hai risolto __?
   'How many problems did you solve ?'
   b. Quanti ne hai risolti __?
   'How many of-them did you solve?'

In case of extraction from a wh-island, the equivalent of (7)a is slightly marginal, whereas the equivalent of (7)b is more severely degraded:

(8) a. ? Quanti problemi non sai come risolvere __?
   'How many problems don't you know how to solve?'
   b. * Quanti non sai come risolverne __?
   'How many don't you know how to solve?'

We see different and interacting factors at work here, but a general conclusion which seems justified is that, all other things being equal, extraction of a lexically restricted wh-element is more acceptable than extraction of a bare wh-element. The contrast in (8) suggests that the trace of a lexical restriction (after *ne* cliticization) does not count to determine an improvement.

3 Featural Relativized Minimality

In terms of the featural characterization of Relativized Minimality developed in Friedmann, Belletti & Rizzi (2009), based on Starke (2001) and Rizzi (2004) (in turn elaborating on Rizzi 1990; see also Belletti & Guasti 2015 for an overview of the results of this approach in the acquisition of A-bar dependencies), the two structures of (6) have representations like the following, in which +Q is the familiar morphosyntactic feature involved in the attraction of wh-elements in questions, and +N designates a wh-phrase in which a lexical restriction is present:

(6') a. ? Combien de problèmes ne sait-il pas comment résoudre __?
   'How many of problems doesn't he know how to solve __?
   +Q+N   +Q   __

b.* Combien   ne sait-il pas   comment résoudre [__ de problèmes] ?
'How many   doesn't he know   how   to solve __ of problems ?'
+Q   +Q   __

Let us consider the following definition of featural Relativized Minimality (fRM):

(9) In ... X ... Z ... Y ... a local relation between X and Y is disrupted when
  i. Z structurally intervenes between X and Y, and
  ii. Z shares relevant morphosyntactic features with X

"relevant morphosyntactic features" are those involved in the local relation under scrutiny. As we are looking at movement dependencies, "relevant morphosyntactic features" are those which trigger movement: in (6'), +Q and +N. The relevance of +Q is straightforward: it is the feature attracting wh-elements to the left-periphery. As for +N, Friedmann, Belletti & Rizzi (2009) argue that the latter participates in attracting movement in that in many languages lexically restricted wh-phrases have distinct landing sites with respect to bare wh-elements, typically in the higher part of the cartography of CP.

The most straightforward piece of evidence comes from the North Eastern Italian dialects (such as Bellunese) in which lexically restricted wh-elements are pronounced before the rest of the clause ("Of which boy have you spoken?"), whereas bare elements are pronounces clause-finally ("Have you spoken with whom?"). According to Munaro's (1999) analysis, both types of wh-elements are moved to the left periphery to two distinct positions, according to the following partial map:

(10) ... +Q, +N ...... X .... +Q .... IP

Wh movement is followed by remnant movement of the IP to the intermediate position X, so that the lower +Q position ends up being spelled out at the end of the clausal structure. Regardless of the formal details of the analysis, the basic distributional properties of the two types of wh-elements provide straightforward evidence for differentiating the landing site of lexically restricted and bare wh-elements. Such a differentiation is supported by numerous kinds of evidence in other languages (Villata, Rizzi & Franck 2016, text below ex. (3)).

So, +N contributes to finely modulating the target of wh-movement, and as such it is taken into account as a relevant feature in the computation of intervention relations.

One goal of this approach is that the featural definition of RM can also capture the gradation of judgments: when the featural overlap is full, i.e., the target and the intervener have the same featural specification, the disruption is maximal; when the featural overlap is partial, the disruption is less severe.

In both cases (6')a–b, the extracted element and the intervener have a relevant feature in common (+Q), and this causes the deviance of the structures; but in (6')a the target of movement is partially distinct from the intervener (we have an **inclusion** relation between X (+Q, +N) and Z (+Q)), and this captures the more acceptable status of the configuration compared to the totally non-distinct case (6')b, characterized by an **identity** of relevant features (+Q) on both X and Z.

As for the fact that the trace of the lexical restriction does not improve things in (8)b, we can observe that under the copy theory of traces a full copy of the clitic, corresponding to the lexical restriction, is present in the representation of (8)b. Nevertheless, we may assume that for a feature to be taken into account in the calculation of locality, the feature must be internal to the phrase whose properties we are computing. In the case of the clitic trace, the feature is not fully internal in the sense that one of occurrence of *ne* is inside and the other is outside the wh-phrase:

(8') b. [Quanti <ne>] non sai come risolverne __
     +Q   <+N>   +Q   +N

If only fully internal specifications count, the clitic trace does not help here to improve things.

It is also important to notice that the negative island and the wh-island exhibit different levels of strength, particularly in cases in which the moved element is lexically restricted, such as (5)a and (6)a: in the negative island, extraction of the lexically restricted element produces a structure which sounds fully acceptable, as in (5)a (even though in dealing with such examples, speakers need an extra moment of reflection, to imagine a context in which the structure would be naturally produced; this could be made visible in reading time experiments, which would be worth conducting with systematicity in weak island environments), whereas the extraction of the lexically restricted element from the wh island is marginal, as in (6)a. The difference between the two cases probably resides in the fact that target and intervener share the same exact feature in (6)a (+Q), while they are characterized by features which, while both belonging to the same class of operator features, are distinct in (5)a (the target is +Q and the intervener is +Neg). The system clearly is sensitive to the feature class (Rizzi 2004), in that intervention effects are caused by interveners characterized by features belonging to the same featural class as the features characterizing the target; nevertheless, a higher level of disruption may be determined when the feature is identical, with respect to the case in which two distinct features belonging to the same class are involved. The featural distinction between target and intervener, combined with the +N specification of the target, may cause violations of negative islands with lexically restricted wh-phrases like (5)a to sound virtually perfect; whereas in cases of identity of the operator feature, as in the violation of wh-islands, we always perceive some degree of marginality, as in (6)a. An additional element in support of the view that distinct operator features on the target and intervener may determine weaker violations than identical operator features is provided by the observation that extractions from wh-islands through relativization in Italian yield, or approximate, full acceptability, in contrast with the marginality of extraction via main question formation, as pointed out in Rizzi 1982, ch. 2, p. 51 (+R is the criterial feature triggering movement in relatives, the analogue of +Q for questions):

(11) a. Ecco un incarico che non so proprio a chi potrei affidare __
     Here is a task that I really dont know to whom I could entrust __
           +R, +N   +Q

    b. ? Che incarico non sai proprio a chi potresti affidare __
       'What task do you really not know to whom you could entrust __
       +Q,+N   +Q

It may be conceivable to assimilate cases involving distinct attracting features belonging to the same feature class to the case of **intersection,** a set theoretic relation between target and intervener that has been shown to be more easily accessible to language learners than the relation of inclusion (Belletti, Friedmann, Brunato, Rizzi 2012). I will not pursue this possible development here.

4 Che, cosa, and che cosa

Back to our initial empirical observation, the structure of *che cosa* presumably is something like the following (see Manzini 2014 for a unified analysis of *che-*like forms occurring in the left periphery in different Italian dialects; see also Manzini & Savoia 2005):

(12)   DP
       / \
     Che₊Q NP
            |
           cosa

So, the first idea that comes to mind in connection with the two reduced forms *cosa* and *che* is that they correspond to (12) except for the lack of an overt occurrence of one or the other element. If that were the case, the very different behavior illustrated by (2), (3) would remain mysterious. But it should be noticed that there is a fundamental difference between the two reduced cases: *che* is the bearer of the Q feature, hence its presence is necessary to qualify the expression as an interrogative element (as in *che libro, che idea*, etc.: what book, what idea, …). Therefore, the representation of the reduced form *cosa* must necessarily contain a null occurrence of *che*, otherwise the phrase would not qualify as an interrogative element at all. So we must have

(13)   DP
       / \
     C̶h̶e̶₊Q NP
            |
           cosa

(where the overstrike intends to express the silent nature of the element carrying the Q feature). On the other hand in the reduced form *che*, as the necessary Q feature is expressed on *che*, the lexical restriction expressed by the functional noun *cosa* in *che cosa* can presumably be dispensed with, and be radically absent. Therefore, simple considerations on the necessary specification of the Q feature lead to assuming significantly different representations for *cosa* and *che*. For *che*, we would thus have something like the following:

(14) DP
      |
     Che₊Q

Under this analysis, here we have a bare, non-lexically restricted wh element, which is expected to pattern with other bare wh-elements such as *combien* in extraction environments. We can therefore capture the strong sensitivity of *che* to weak island environments, as well as the fact that *cosa* (represented as in (13)) is about on a par with *che cosa*.[2]

This analysis is supported by the observation in (4). If the element *altro* (other) is added to the structure, an analysis of *che* as a bare D becomes unavailable: the DP projection must expand to include the modifier *altro*. But presumably the modifier cannot occur alone, it must select and co-occur with the NP it modifies. So, when *altro* is present, we have to restore here a null NP *cosa*; therefore, the three cases are all akin to the full form (12), and the parallel pattern in the case of extraction from the weak island is thus to be expected.

5 Conclusion

Intervention locality effects appear to be sensitive to the richness of the internal structure of the moved elements. In particular, lexically restricted wh-elements are easier to extract, when the lexical restriction is pied-piped, than bare wh-elements in weak island environments. In this short paper we have described and analyzed a minimal contrast between different forms of the inanimate wh-element in Italian: while the full form *che cosa* and the reduced form *cosa* give rise to mild

---

2 In (12) and (13) the wh-element is lexically restricted in the sense that it contains an NP specification (as opposed to (14)); nevertheless, this specification is functional, expressed by the functional noun *cosa* (thing) not drawn from the contentive lexicon as *libro, idea* in in *che libro, che idea*, etc. (what book, what idea, etc.). Villata, Rizzi & Franck (2016) show that, in controlled grammaticality judgments expressed on a 7-point Likert scale, extraction of elements like *what* is systematically more degraded than extraction of elements like *what book* in French. Notice that we are now introducing a further and finer distinction in Italian, between wh-elements with a contentive lexical restriction (*che libro*), wh-elements with a functional restriction (*che cosa, cosa*), and wh-elements in which the lexical restriction is totally absent (*che*). In fact, the presence of a contentive lexical restriction, the presence of a functional restriction, and the radical absence of a restriction seem to correspond to three detectable levels of deviance in weak island contexts:

(i) ? Che libro non sai come procurarti?
    'What book don't you know how to get?'
(ii) ?? Che cosa non sai come procurarti?
    'What don't you know how to get?'
(iii) * Che non sai come procurarti?
    What don't you know how to get?'

This gradation suggests that the feature calculus should be refined to also take into account the distinction between contentive and functional lexical restrictions. I will not discuss here how to better capture these facts.

violations of locality, the other reduced form *che* triggers a strong violation, comparable in force to adjunct extraction, or subextraction of *combien* in French. This surprising asymmetry can be naturally captured by an analysis of the different internal structures of the three wh-forms, in interaction with a general approach to intervention locality based on featural Relativized Minimality.

References

Belletti Adriana, Friedmann Naama, Brunato, Dominique, & Luigi Rizzi. 2012. Does gender make a difference? Comparing the effect of gender on children's comprehension of relative clauses in Hebrew and Italian. *Lingua* 122: 1053–1069.

Belletti, Adriana, & Maria-Teresa Guasti. 2015. *The acquisition of Italian. Morphosyntax and its interfaces in different modes of acquisition.* Amsterdam: John Benjamins.

Friedmann, Naama, Belletti, Adriana, & Luigi Rizzi. 2009. Relativized relatives: Types of intervention in the acquisition of A-bar dependencies. *Lingua* 119: 67–88.

Manzini, M. Rita. 1997. A minimalist theory of weak islands. In Peter Culicover and Louise McNally (eds.), *The limits of syntax. Syntax and semantics vol.29*, pp. 185–209, New York: Academic Press.

Manzini, M. Rita. 1999. Locality theory: Competing models of weak islands. *The Linguistic Review* 16: 63–79.

Manzini, M. Rita. 2014. The Romance k- complementizers. In Peter Svenonius (ed), *Functional Structure from Top to Toe The Cartography of Syntactic Structures, Volume 9*, pp. 148–187, New York: Oxford University Press.

Manzini, M. Rita. and Leonardo Savoia. 2005. *I dialetti italiani e romanci. Morfosintassi generativa*, 3 vols. Alessandria: Edizioni dell'Orso.

Munaro, Nicola. 1999. *Sintagmi interrogativi nei dialetti italiani settentrionali*. Padua, Italy: Unipress.

Rizzi, Luigi. 1982. *Issues in Italian Syntax*. Dordrecht: Foris Publications.

Rizzi, Luigi. 1990. *Relativized Minimality*. Cambridge, MA: The MIT Press.

Rizzi, Luigi. 2004. Locality and left periphery. In *Structures and beyond*, edited by Adriana Belletti, 223–251. New York: Oxford University Press.

Starke, Michal. 2001. *Move dissolves into Merge: A theory of locality*. Unpublished doctoral dissertation, University of Geneva, Geneva, Switzerland.

Villata, Sandra, Luigi Rizzi and Julie Franck. 2016. Intervention effects and Relativized Minimality: New experimental evidence from graded judgments. *Lingua* 179: 76–96.

Anna Roussou
Complement clauses: Case and argumenthood

1 Introduction: Nominals and visibility

In traditional terms, subordinate clauses are distinguished to nominal and adverbial ones. Nominal clauses can function as objects or subjects, while adverbials distribute like modifiers. In more formal terms, nominal clauses are associated with A-positions[1] and are introduced by complementizers, which, at least in the languages of the Indo-European family, typically derive from the (pro)nominal system (relatives, interrogatives, indefinites, etc.). This is the case of English *that*, Romance *che/que*, Greek *oti* or *pu*, Russian *čto*, etc. In essence, complement clauses are expected to have the distribution of NPs. Kayne (1982) attributes their nominal distribution to the complementizer, arguing that its role is to turn the clause to an argument.

Rosenbaum's (1967) analysis directly captured the nominal nature of complement clauses with the embedded sentence (S) being dominated by an NP node, as in (1a). For Rosenbaum, complementizers "are a function of predicate complementation and not the property of any particular sentence or set of sentences" (p. 25). It is with Bresnan (1972) that complementizers are introduced as part of the phrase structure rules (and not transformationally), as in (1b):

(1) a. NP → S
    b. S´ → C S

---

[1] Complement clauses as subjects may not necessarily occupy an A-position, but function as Topics (Koster 1978, Davies & Dubinsky 2009), thus in an A'-position. If this analysis is correct, then subject clauses are indirectly (via chain-formation) related to an A-position.

Note: This paper is dedicated to Rita on the occasion of her 60th birthday, as a small sample of gratitude and respect to an influential and intellectually stimulating teacher, colleague and friend. Complementizers were the topic of my PhD dissertation supervised by Rita back in 1994, so that's the link to the past. Complementizers are also an important aspect of Rita's more recent work, so this topic is also the link to the present. Rita's intellectual influence is evident throughout the paper, and I have no regrets for that!

Anna Roussou, University of Patras

https://doi.org/10.1515/9781501505201-030

According to (1b), C expands the sentence, and following the generalized X'-schema (Chomsky 1986a), C projects its own phrase (CP). Being part of the phrase structure, C becomes the head defining the left periphery of the clause, realized not only by complementizers, but also by V-movement, as in Subj-Aux inversion or V2 constructions. Under this conception, C takes the characteristics of a 'hybrid' category, realized either by a complementizer or a verbal (V-to-C) element. Treating C as an abstract category of this sort has been quite useful for the expansion of the left periphery. However, it has blurred the association of the syntactic category C with the complementizing morphemes.

Concentrating on complementizers, their systematic coincidence with (pro)nominal elements cannot be treated as accidental. It is actually this coincidence that gave rise to the analysis of complement clauses as some sort of relatives (Arsenijević 2009, Kayne 2010, Manzini 2010). In particular, Manzini (2010) argues that complement clauses are akin to free relatives, in the sense that they do not modify another head. According to her analysis, *che* in Italian (and its Romance co-generics) binds different variables (see also Manzini and Savoia 2003, and for a 'lighter' version Roberts and Roussou 2003). More precisely, *che* as an interrogative or relative pronoun binds an individual variable in (2a) and (2c), while *che* as a complementizer binds a proposition (or a situation) in (2a) (Manzini 2010: 169):

(2) a. *So che fai questo.*
      know-1SG that do-2SG this.
      "I know that you do this."
   b. *Il lavoro che fai è noto.*
      the work that do-2SG is known
      "The work that you do is known."
   c. *Che (lavoro) fai?*
      what work do-2SG
      "What are you doing?" / "What work are you doing?"

The assumption that *che* is one and the same element in both constructions eliminates discrepancies in the lexicon, reducing multiple instances of homophony. Taking it a step further, complementizer *che* embeds a proposition and heads the argument selected by the predicate (see also Franco 2012).

Strictly speaking then, the relation between the selecting predicate and the embedded clause is indirect, mediated by the complementizer, which merges as the argument of the selecting predicate. This has some important implications. First, it allows us to retain the 'traditional' C position in the left periphery of the clause as a scope position of the verb (in this context 'C' is a misnomer). Second, it does not exclude the possibility that some clause-introducers may be part of the left periphery of the clause, merging either in C-positions (thus predicate-related) or in nominal positions within the left periphery, as is the case with the 'subjunctive' particles of the Balkan languages (Roussou 2015 for Greek; Manzini and Savoia 2018 for Aromanian). A third implication, relevant to the present discussion, has to do with the conditions that relate to the 'distribution' of nominals: complement clauses, being nominal as a function of their complementizer, are expected to be subject to the conditions that regulate the distribution of NPs (to a greater or lesser extent).

It is this latter property that brings us to the issue of case/Case. In the Government and Binding model (Chomsky 1981, 1986b), abstract Case assignment regulated the distribution of NPs, dictating their surface position. In Chomsky (1986b), the link between Case and argumenthood was captured under the Visibility Condition, according to which arguments become *visible* for theta-marking, only if they receive Case, thus allowing for Case to be expressed as a property of chains. Abstract Case involved a structural configuration between a (lexical) head and an NP. Case as an addressing mechanism was also implemented in argument A'-chains, eliminating the need for head government (Manzini 1992).

Complement clauses present a problem for the Visibility Condition, assuming Stowell's (1981) Case Resistance Principle (CRP):

(3) Case may not be assigned to a category bearing a Case assigning feature.

Given the CRP, finite complements have a Case-assigning category (Tense) and as such the clause cannot be assigned Case. In relation to this, Stowell argues that only +N categories can be assigned Case. So the question is why complement clauses, despite being arguments, resist Case assignment (see also Bošković 1995, Lasnik 2008). One option is to relate them to a case-marked (null) element. Another option is to assume that they are caseless, a view put forward by Pesetsky and Torrego (2004); some of the evidence Pesetsky and Torrego offer is that complement clauses are not affected by passivization, as in (4), and do not require the presence of a preposition, as in (5) (in fact *that*-complements cannot be embedded under a preposition)[2]:

---

[2] Whether or not a (finite) complement clause can be embedded under a preposition is subject to parametric variation. As an anonymous reviewer points out, Italian may allow for a *che*-clause to be embedded under a P (a), as in: *era contrario a che tu partissi* ('he was opposed to that you left'). See also the discussion on Greek nominalized clauses that follows.

(4) a. [That the world is round] is believed by everyone.
 b. It is believed [that the world is round].
 c. [The world] is believed to be round.
 d. *It is believed [the world] to be round.

(5) a. Bill was afraid that the storm would be destructive.
 b. Bill was afraid *(of) the storm.

Being caseless, complement clauses are distinguished from NP arguments, thus restricting Visibility to NP-arguments only.

The picture changes a bit, once we consider the role of Case in minimalism (for an overview, see Bobaljik and Wurmbrand 2008, Lasnik 2008). Case reduces to a purely uninterpretable feature whose sole role is to activate the NP as a Goal; as such, it is important for the establishment of an Agree relation with *v* (accusative) or T (nominative) for example. The obvious question is why complement clauses cannot bear such an uninterpretable feature. In fact, nothing rules out the possibility that the complementizer as the head of the complement clause carries this feature. This alternative would maintain the similarities between nominals and complement clauses. Furthermore, if complementizers are nominal, and only +N categories can bear Case, as argued by Stowell (1981), the obvious conclusion to be drawn is that complement clauses are or can be case-marked.

Still, there is another deeper question, regarding the Case feature as such, which is taken to be purely uninterpretable (thus part of narrow syntax but with no effects at the interfaces; Chomsky 1995). At least languages with morphological case systems show that case does play a role at the interfaces. The alternative then is to assimilate case to a categorial feature, dispensing with an abstract Case feature, while maintaining morphological case (hence abandoning the "Case" notation). Pesetsky (2013) actually argues, on the basis of Russian data, that morphological cases translate to categorial features; a genitive suffix is of category N, a nominative one is of category D, an oblique is of category P, while accusative is of category V. Manzini and Savoia (2010, 2011) also take case to correspond to a categorial feature, but propose a different categorization: nominative is a D feature, while accusative (direct internal argument) is N; based on dative and genitive syncretisms they assign the category of 'inclusion' ⊆ to the oblique case, which in many instances is realized as a Preposition.

Pairing the above with the view that complementizers are nominal we derive a situation whereby complement clauses are not exempt from Visibility (see also Knyazev 2016 on Russian). As arguments and as projections of a nominal category they can in principle be associated with the range of categorial features that are involved in nominal projections. Respectively, they can occur in positions that involve a D feature (subject), an N feature (object) or ⊆ (oblique object). To put it in more abstract terms, they can enter into an Agree relation with designated heads that allow for the expression of D, N or ⊆ (P) properties.

In what follows, I will adopt Manzini and Savoia's categorial approach on case. I will also use the term 'oblique' as a cover term that excludes nominative and accusative (also known as 'direct' cases). In Blake's (2001) terminology, this distinction concerns 'core' (nominative, accusative) vs 'peripheral' cases. I will next show that Greek distinguishes between direct and oblique complement clauses. In particular, the former are introduced by *oti*, while the latter by *pu*. Oblique complement clauses are those introduced by *pu* and are selected by factive emotive predicates. Support for the oblique nature of *pu*-complements will be provided by the fact that these may alternate with *oti*-complements embedded under a preposition.

2 The empirical data

In this section I introduce the declarative complementizers in Greek and outline their basic distributional properties. Greek has three such complementizers, namely *oti*, *pos* and *pu*, which all translate as *that* in English, *che* in Italian, etc. While *oti* and *pos* are in free distribution, *pu* is more restricted. The broad division between *oti/pos*- vs *pu*-complements is that their distribution is determined by factivity (Christidis 1982, Roussou 1994, Varlokosta 1994). In short, *pu*-complements are treated as factive, while *oti/pos*-complements are treated as non-factive. However, as was already pointed out by Christidis (1982), this division is rather simplistic, since *oti*-complements may also be selected by factive predicates, such as *know* and *remember* in (6a):

(6) a. *Thimame/ksero   oti   milises   sti   Maria.*
       remember-1SG/know-1SG that talked-2SG to-the Mary
       "I remember/know that you talked to Mary"
   b. *Thimame   pu   milises   sti   Maria.*
       remember-1SG   that talked-2SG to-the Mary
       "I remember that you talked to Mary."
   c. *Nomizo   oti/*pu milises   sti   Maria.*
       think-1SG   that/that talked-2SG to-the Mary
       "I think that you talked to Mary."

Note that substituting *oti* for *pos* in (6a) has no semantic import in the construction. The same verb *thimame* may also select for a *pu*-complement, as in (6b). Finally, a non-factive verb like *nomizo* in (6) excludes *pu*.

According to Christidis (1982), selection of *pu* in (6b) gives rise to direct perception (immediate recollection of an event in this case). This is supported by that fact that while *thimame* can be modified when *oti* is selected, as in (7a), this does not hold when *pu* is selected, as in (7b):

(7) a. Thimame   me dhiskolia,   oti   milises   sti   Maria.
       remember-1SG with difficulty that talked-2SG to-the Mary
       "I remember, with difficulty, that you talked to Mary."
    b. #Thimame   me dhiskolia,   pu   milises   sti   Maria.
       remember-1SG with difficulty that talked-2SG to-the Mary
       "I remember, with difficulty, that you talked to Mary."

As Christidis argues, the modifier 'with difficulty' implies that there is some effort in remembering and therefore is not compatible with immediate recollection. As a result, selection of the *pu*-complement is infelicitous.

The class of factive predicates that split between *oti* and *pu*, correspond to Hooper & Thompson's (1973) Class E and Class D predicates respectively:

(8) Class D: resent, regret, bother, be sorry, be happy,...
    Class E: realize, learn, discover, know, recognize, ...

Class D predicates are emotives (psych-verbs), while Class E are broadly construed as 'perception' verbs (mental perception, knowing, etc.). Apparently, class E predicates are the ones that typically take an *oti*-complement, while Class D, namely factive emotives, mainly take a *pu*-complement, as shown below:

(9) a. Xerome   pu   efije.
       be.glad-1SG that left-3SG
       "I'm glad that he left."
    b. Me=enoxlise   pu   efije.
       me=bothered-3SG   that left-3SG
       "It bothered me that he had left."

In the above examples, selection of *oti* is not available (unless it is nominalised, as we will see in the next section). On the other hand, as we saw in relation to the examples in (6) and (7), Class E predicates may take a *pu*-complement. In many cases though the *pu*-complement is available provided the matrix verb is focused (on the relation of focus and factivity see Kalluli 2008). I will not get into more details in the present paper, since this is not relevant to the discussion that follows (but see Roussou 2010 for a preliminary overview).

The picture we get so far is that there is no one-to-one mapping between factivity and complement selection. At this point, it is useful to outline our set of assumptions regarding factivity. First, factivity is a property of the selecting predicate (de Cuba and Ürögdi 2010) and not of the complement clause. Emotives present a subclass of factive predicates, and are the ones that require *pu*. Some emotives, such as *worry* and *fear* (verbs of fearing), have a factive reading only with a *pu*-complement; when the complement clause is introduced by *oti* there is no factive reading. Second, selection by a factive predicate imposes certain restrictions on the interpretation of its complement. The traditional view of factivity takes it that factive complements involve presupposition, i.e. the content of the embedded clause is taken as granted (presupposed). In relation to this, Haegeman and Ürögdi (2010) argue that factive complements are 'referential', that is they have a fixed truth value. Syntactically, this means that they have characteristics of definite DPs. Kastner (2015) argues that complements of presuppositional predicates (factives being a subset of them) have a DP projection, while complements of non-presuppositional ones are (bare) CPs. Assuming that in either case, complement clauses of the sort discussed here are nominal, as a property of the complementizer, the DP vs CP distinction can be understood in slightly different terms in the present discussion:

(10) a. Presuppositional complements = [$_D$ [$_N$ Complementizer [CP/ IP]]]
     b. Non-presuppositional complements = [$_N$ Complementizer [CP/ IP]]

According to (10), presuppositional complements project a D layer, while non presuppositional ones do not and are the clausal equivalent of (bare) NPs. The above structure simply translates their semantic properties into syntax. As we will see in the following section, *oti*-complements have an overt D head (the definite article *to*) when they occur as subjects, an option which is altogether excluded for *pu*; the restrictions on *pu* will be attributed to the fact that it introduces an oblique argument.

In the context of the above assumptions, the picture that emerges is that *pu* introduces a proposition with a fixed truth value (true), while *oti* does so only when selected by a factive predicate. So in the example (6c) above *Nomizo oti milises sti Maria* "I think that you talked to Mary", the embedded proposition can be construed as true or false (so the proposition corresponds to a variable; see also Baunaz 2015). So both *oti* (/*pos*) and *pu* embed a proposition which may or may not be referential, depending on the selecting predicate primarily and/or the complementizer. Going back to the differences between *oti* and *pu* when selected by a factive (non-emotive) predicate, I will assume, along with Christidis (1982) that their differences relate to some notion of indirect (*oti*) vs direct (*pu*) proximity. This is a well-known property of deictic (demonstrative) pronouns, underlying the difference between *that* (distal) and *this* (proximal) in English for example (*that book* vs *this book*, proximity in relation to the speaker). This assumption suffices for the purposes of the present discussion.

Consider next the other occurrences of *oti*, *pos*, and *pu*. Let us first start with *pu*: apart from being a complementizer, *pu* is also a relativizer (for restrictive and non-restrictive relative clauses) alternating with the relative pronoun, as in (11a) and (11b) respectively. There is also an interrogative *pu* 'where', which unlike the complementizer/relativizer *pu*, is stressed, as in the examples in (12):

(11) a. *Sinandisa tin kopela [pu pire to vravio].*
　　　　met-1SG　the girl　that got-3SG the prize
　　　　"I met the girl that got the prize."
　　b. *Sinandisa tin kopela [i opia pire to vravio].*
　　　　met-1SG　the girl　the who got-3SG the prize
　　　　"I met the girl who got the prize."

(12) a. *Pú　　pas?*
　　　　where go-2SG
　　　　"Where are you going?"
　　b. *Pú　　to=katalaves?*
　　　　where it=understood-2SG
　　　　"How did you understand this?"
　　c. *Pú　　to=edhoses?*
　　　　where it=gave-2SG
　　　　"Who did you give it to?"

First, relativizer *pu* is in complementary distribution with the relative pronoun, thus the co-occurrence of *pu* with a relative pronoun is excluded. Second, interrogative *pu* primarily has a locative reading, as in (12a), but can be interpreted as a manner adverbial (from which x, did you understand it from x), or stand for an indirect object, as in (12c) (on the latter, see Michelioudakis 2012).

Consider next *pos*, which is a declarative complementizer in (13a), but also has an interrogative meaning 'how' in (13b). Interrogative *pos*, just like interrogative *pu*, is stressed:

(13) a. *Nomizo pos Milise sti Maria.*
 think-1SG that talked-3SG to-the Mary
 "I think that he talked to Mary."
 b. *Pós tis= milise?*
 how her talked-3SG
 "How did he talk to her?"

Finally, *oti* does not have an interrogative counterpart but can introduce free relatives with an inanimate referent as in (14):

(14) *O Janis perni o,ti tu= dhosis.*
 the John take-3SG whatever him=give-2SG
 "John takes whatever you give him"

Orthographically, relative *oti* is written as *o,ti* (literally 'the what') and is treated separately from the complementizer *oti* in traditional grammatical descriptions. The same distinct categorization holds for the complementizers *pu* and *pos* and their interrogative counterparts.

As already pointed out in section 1, this systematic coincidence between (interrogative or relative) pronouns and complementizers within the same grammar, as well as in other grammars, cannot be treated as accidental, that is as multiple instances of homophony. The alternative adopted in this paper is that there is a single element, binding different variables. Interrogative *pos* and *pu* bind an individual variable (corresponding to an entity); the same extends to free relative *oti* (subject to universal quantification) and relative *pu*. As complementizers they all introduce a proposition and the variable they bind is that of the proposition, restricted to an individual proposition or individual event in factive readings, or ranging over a set of propositions in non-factive (embedded interrogative) readings.

Before leaving this section, it's worth providing some comparative evidence from English. The morpheme *that* introduces (declarative) complement clauses as in (15a) and relatives as in (15b), but is also used as a deictic pronoun as in (15c):

(15) a. *I think [that John left].*
 b. *I met the man [that Peter saw].*
 c. *Peter saw [that man].*

As already pointed out, the question has been whether complementizer/relativizer *that* and demonstrative *that* are the same element. As above, I assume that it is the same element which binds different variables (see also Roberts and Roussou 2003). More precisely, as a complementizer *that* binds a propositional variable; as a relativizer it binds an individual variable, identified under predication with the head of the relative clause; finally, as a demonstrative it binds an individual variable in a deictic context. Deixis in the latter case requires emphasis on the demonstrative.

English also uses *how* as a declarative complementizer, although its distribution is more restricted:

(16) a. *They told me how the tooth fairy doesn't really exist.*
b. *Your dad once said how I had legs like Betty Brable.*

Example (16a) is from Legate (2010) and (16b) from van Gelderen (2015: 161). So although *how* is typically an interrogative element, it may also appear as a non-interrogative complementizer, exhibiting an extreme resemblance in this respect with its Greek counterpart *pos*. Legate (2010) argues that *how*-complements involve a D-layer; Nye (2013) argues that they are associated with a factive interpretation. If this is right, then English also shows a 'dual' declarative-complementizer system. It should be noted though, that according to the discussion in Nye (2013), *how*-complements are disallowed with Class E predicates, i.e. the predicates we called 'emotive factives' in the present paper. In any case, what is worth bearing in mind is that despite differences, Greek and English exhibit some similar properties.

The pattern that arises so far is quite systematic: one form, different functions, as illustrated in Table 1 below:

Table 1: The distribution of complementizer(-like) elements.

	Complementizer	Relativizer	Interrogative
oti	✓	✓ (free relatives)	*
pos	✓	*	✓ (pós)
pu	✓	✓	✓ (pú)
that	✓	✓	*
how	✓	*	✓

The assumption is that there is a core element that is compatible with different interpretations depending on the variables it binds; thus the systematic 'coincidence' within the same grammar and across grammars is accounted for. According to Franco (2012) this core element is a (light) nominal. Baunaz and Lander (2017) put forward a similar proposal, arguing that complementizers of this sort exhibit 'cross-categorial syncretism': there is a core element but the different functions are structurally disambiguated. To be more precise, the core element, being an indefinite, can have different projecting layers as part of its internal structure (nanosyntax). Adding layers has an effect on the function of the element along the "(Dem) – Comp – Rel – Wh" sequence ('Dem' applies to English *that*). Without going into any further details, it should be noted that both *pos* and *how* pose a problem for cell-adjacency, invoked in cases of syncretism. That is, syncretic cells are not adjacent (see * on the relativizer), thus giving rise to an illicit *ABA pattern. Leaving these remarks aside, we keep the idea that there is a core indefinite (nominal) part, allowing us to unify the various instances and functions of these elements.

Having outlined the basic distribution of declarative complementizers in Greek, I next turn to the properties of *pu* with factive emotives arguing that these complements have the properties of oblique (indirect) arguments.

3 *Pu*-complements as oblique arguments

In this section I will consider the properties of *pu*-complements with emotive predicates. I will first outline the very basic syntactic properties of emotive predicates in terms of their argument structure, including complement clauses, and I will next provide the properties of *pu*-clauses in terms of extraction and nominalization. Recall that the claim is that *pu*-complements of this sort have the properties of oblique arguments. As such they are expected to alternate with PP arguments, where that is relevant, and to create strong islands. A number of properties such as the unavailability of being embedded under a P head will also follow from their oblique status.

3.1 Emotive predicates and pu-complements

Emotive (psych) predicates have an experiencer argument which may be realized as a subject or object. In Greek, the picture is slightly more complex since voice (active vs middle-passive) may also play a role (for a recent analysis see Alexiadou and Iordăchioaia 2014). Consider the following examples (MP = middle-passive):

(17) a. I   idhisis   stenoxorun ton Jani.
       the news   upset-3PL   the John
       "The news upset John."
    b. O   Janis   stenoxorjete me   tis   idhisis.
       the John   Upset.MP-SG   with the   news
       "John is upset with the news."

In (17a), The DP *i idhisis* is the Causer and the DP *ton Jani* the Experiencer (object), while in (17b), the Experiencer is in the subject position (*o Janis*), and the second argument is realized as a PP and is interpreted as the Target of Emotion (TE), according to Pesetsky's (1995) analysis. If the preposition was *ja* (for, about), as in *ja tis idhisis*, the interpretation in (17b) would be that of the Subject of Emotion (SE), following Pesetsky's terminology.

Some predicates may alternate between a Subject and an Object Experiencer pattern without changes in voice (i.e. they occur in active voice only). This is the case of *anisixo* (worry) in the example below:

(18) a. O   Janis   anisixise   ton Petro.
       the John   worried-3SG the Peter
       "John worried Peter" (i.e. John made Peter worry).
    b. O   Petros anisixi   me   ton Jani /ja   ton Jani.
       the Peter   worry-3SG   with the John /for the John
       "John worries (is worried) with John/ about John".

In (18a) the DP *ton Petro* is the Experiencer in object position, while in (18b) it is in subject position. Note here that the verb remains in the active voice in both consturctions. The DP *o Janis* is the Agent/Causer in (18a), but the TM or SM of Emotion in (18b) depending on the preposition. As in the examples in (17), object experiencers are marked with accusative, while subject experiencers with nominative. The TM or SM arguments are expressed as PPs, and as such they are not 'core' (or 'direct') arguments but oblique ones.

The above brief introduction is quite relevant in order to understand how emotive predicates behave with respect to sentential complementation. In particular, we would expect to find a complement clause functioning as a subject, with the Object Experiencer pattern, and as an oblique argument with the Subject Experiencer pattern. Consider next the following examples, starting with the verb *stenoxorjeme* (be upset):

(19) a. O Janis stenoxorjete [pu efije o Petros].
    the John upset.MP-3SG that left-3SG the Peter
    "John is upset that Peter left."
   b. O Janis stenoxorjete [me /ja to oti efije o Petros].
    the John upset.MP-3SG with /for the that left-3SG the Peter
    "John is upset with/about the fact that Peter left."

The verb in (19) is in the middle-passive voice, as in (17b) and the Experiencer is in subject position (nominative *o Janis*). When the second argument is clausal it is introduced by *pu*, or prepositionally (*me* or *ja*). Interestingly in the latter case, the complementizer is *oti* embedded under the neuter definite article *to*. These clauses are referred to as 'nominalized clauses' (Roussou 1991). The relevant structure is given below:

(20) [$_P$ me/ja [$_D$ to [$_N$ oti [efije o Petros]]]

I have labelled the projection of *oti* as N, based on the assumption that it is a nominal.

The PP-construction alternates with *pu*, as the example in (19a) shows. Before we analyze this further, let us consider the example where the experiencer *John* occurs in object position. Given the pattern with the nominals, we expect that the complement clause will assume a subject (or subject-like) position:

(21) a. *[Pu efije o Petros] (ton)=stenoxori ton Jani.
     that left-3SG the Peter him=upset-3SG the John
   b. [To oti efije o Petros] (ton)=stenoxori ton Jani.
    The that left-3SG the Peter him=upset-3SG the John
    "That Peter left is upsetting John."

What the above contrast shows is that *pu* cannot occupy a subject position. On the other hand, the nominalized clause can. As expected, in this case there is no PP, but only a DP. As shown in Roussou (1991), nominalization is obligatory with subject clauses and with objects of prepositions (a fact that is interpreted in terms of Case-assignment). If the article *to* is absent, then the result is ungrammatical in (21b), i.e. *Oti tha fiji o Petros (ton) stenoxori ton Jani*.

On the basis of the above, we observe that *pu*-complements behave like oblique (indirect) arguments. This is supported by the fact that the clausal complements introduced by *oti* are embedded under a P, exactly like their nominal counterparts. Furthermore, while *oti*-clauses in their nominalized form can occur in subject position (as nominative arguments), this is not the case for *pu*-clauses, which seem to be restricted to object position. The lack of nominalization with *pu* follows from its function as an oblique argument.

Let us now consider the predicate *anisixo*, as in the examples below:

(22) a. O Janis anisixi [oti efije o Petros].
       the John worry-3SG that left-3SG the Peter
       "John worries that Peter left".
   b. O Janis anisixi [pu efije o Petros].
       the John worry-3SG that left-3SG the Peter
   c. O Janis anisixe [me /ja to oti efije o Petros].
       the John worry-3SG with /for the that left-3SG the Peter
       "John worries (for the fact) that Peter left".

According to the above pattern, *anisixo* can take an *oti*-complement, as in (22a). Interestingly in this case there is no factivity involved. On the other hand, when the complement clause is introduced by *pu*, as in (22b), or as PP, as in (22c), only a factive reading is available. This is tested by using negation (*dhen*) in the matrix clause:

(23) a. *O Janis dhen anisixi oti efije o Petros*: implies that Peter didn't leave.
   b. *O Janis dhen anisixi pu efije o Petros*: doesn't imply Peter didn't leave.

Thus while the complement clause has a fixed truth value (true) with *pu* in (22b), or its PP counterpart in (22c), this is not the case with *oti* in (22a). Verbs like *anisixo* present another sub-case of emotive predicates, known as 'verbs of fearing' (*verbi timendi*). In Greek they also allow a complement introduced by the complementizer *mipos* (see Makri 2013, Roussou 2017).

The pattern we get with *anisixo* (also with the verb *fovame* 'fear') is that it can have an object experiencer (accusative) or a subject experiencer (nominative). In the latter case, the Cause argument is realized as a PP, including the nominalized *oti*-complement, or as a *pu*-complement. I next turn to some other properties of *pu*-complements which further support the oblique argument analysis.

3.2 Extraction patterns

Extraction out of factive complements has been discussed extensively in the literature, offering a syntactic or semantic approach (for an updated overview, see Kastner 2015). With respect to Greek, non-factive *oti*-complements are not islands, while factive *oti*-complements are weak islands, as they allow for argument but not for adjunct extraction; on the other hand, *pu*-complements are strong islands (Roussou 1994, Varlokosta 1994). Consider the following examples with argument (object) extraction in (24) and adjunct extraction in (25):

(24) a. Pjon nomizis   [oti apelisan ~~pjon~~]?
        who think-2SG that fired-3PL who
        "Who do you think that they fired?"
    b. *Pjon ksafniastikes   [pu apelisan ~~pjon~~]?
        who surprised.MP-2SG that fired-3PL who
        "Who were you surprised that they fired?"
    c. ?Pjon anakalipses   [oti apelisan ~~pjon~~] ?
        who discovered-2SG that fired-3PL who
        "Who did you discover that they fired?"

(25) a. Pos nomizis   [oti anteghrapse tin askisi   ~~pos~~]?
        how think-2SG that copied-3SG   the exercise how
        "How do you think that he copied the exercise?"
    b. *Pos ksafniastikes   [pu anteghrapse tin askisi   ~~pos~~]?
        how surprised.MP-2SG that copied-3SG   the exercise how
        "*How were you surprised that he copied the exercise?"
    c. *?Pos anakalipses   [oti anteghrapse tin askisi   ~~pos~~]?
        how discovered-2SG that copied-3SG   the exercise how
        "*How did you discover that he copied the exercise?"

Starting with the examples in (25b-c), the output is ungrammatical when *how/pos* is construed with the embedded predicate (grammatical only with matrix scope); extraction out of the non-factive *oti* is grammatical (25a). Turning next to argument (object) extraction in (24), we observe that there is a contrast between factive *oti*- and *pu*-complements. In the latter case, argument extraction yields ungrammaticality. Extraction out of the factive *oti*-complement in (24c) is only slightly degraded compared to argument extraction out of the non-factive *oti*-complement in (24a).

There have been different proposals put forward in the literature regarding the above contrasts. Since this is not a paper on factivity, I will not elaborate further. For present purposes, I will assume, following Kastner (2015) that the weak island effect is due to a semantic effect (presuppositional verbs do not introduce new referents) accompanied by a syntactic structure that involves an abstract D head. But if *pu*-complements also have a D projection, then we would expect them to behave like factive *oti*-complements. On the other hand, as we saw above, *pu*-complements of emotive factives share the distribution of oblique arguments. On these grounds, I suggest that the strong island effect is due to this property. Keeping the parallelism with DP arguments, we would expect to find similarities in terms of extraction patterns.

Bearing the above discussion in mind, let us then consider the following examples:

(26) a. *Anisixisa*   [*ti fili*   *tis*   *Marias*].
        worried-1SG   the friend   the.GEN Mary.GEN
        "I worried Marias's friend."
    b. *Tinos*   *anisixises*   [*ti fili*   *tinos*] ?
        who.GEN   worried-2SG   the friend   who.GEN
        "Whose friend did you worry?"
    c. *Anisixisa*   [*ja ti fili*   *tis*   *Marias*].
        worried-1SG   for the friend the.GEN Mary.GEN
        "I worried about Mary's friend."
    b. **Tinos*   *anisixises*   [*ja ti fili*   *tinos*]?
        who.GEN   worried-2SG   for the friend   who.GEN
        "*Whose friend did you worry about?"

Extraction of the genitive out of the direct (accusative) argument *tin fili tis Marias* is grammatical. However, extraction out of the oblique (PP) argument *ja tin fili tis Marias* is ungrammatical (on locality conditions in Greek, see Kotzoglou 2005). We expect that a similar pattern would be attested in extraction out of *oti-* vs *pu-* (and *P+to oti-*) complements:

(27) a. *Anisixisa*   [*pu* /*oti*   *sinandise*   *tin*   *Maria*].
        worried-1SG   that /that   met-3SG   the   Mary
        "I worried that he had met Mary."
    b. **Pja   anisixises*   [*pu   sinandise   pja*]?
        who   worried-2SG   that   met-3SG   who
    c. **Pja   anisixises*   [*ja to   oti   sinandise   pja*]?
        who   worried-2SG   for the   that   met-3SG   who
    d. *Pja   anisixises*   [*oti   sinandise   pja*]?
        who   worried-2SG   that   met-3SG   who
        "Who did you worry that he had met?"

The *oti*-complement in (27d) does not block argument extraction, while *pu* and the nominalized clause create a strong island effect.

Without going into details, there seems to be a difference between extraction out of direct vs indirect or peripheral arguments (accusative vs oblique). If oblique is an instance of an inclusion relation, involving some notion of quantification (part of, etc.), then the fact that arguments of this sort carry a quantificational property that interacts with the formation an Operator-variable dependency is to be expected. Baunaz (2015) attributes the different extraction patterns to the 'size' of the complementizer, i.e. the functional layers it may involve, which interact with the 'size' of the extracted element. Despite the different approaches invoked, the thing to bear in mind is that islandhood in factive complements is a function of the properties of the selecting ('presuppositional') predicate and the properties of the complement clause. The latter becomes relevant in the case of Greek, due to the selection of *pu* vs *oti* in certain environments which matches oblique argument realization.

4 Case and complementation: Some comparative evidence

The analysis suggested so far is built on a couple of assumptions: first, that the complementizers under consideration are nominal and can be associated with the range of features relating to nominals. Second, that case reduces to a syntactic category. Morphologically, case is realized as an affix attaching to a nominal head. Syntactically, the nominal (with or without an affix) functions as the Goal in an Agree relation with a head that qualifies as a Probe. So in the simplest cases, Agree with T (I) counts as nominative (D), while Agree with v counts as accusative (N).

In the discussion so far, the claim has been that complement clauses can be construed as direct (core) or indirect (peripheral) internal arguments. This, to a large extent, depends on the lexical properties of the selecting predicate, and can be manifested by selection of a distinct complementizer or by having a Preposition mediating this relation. In these terms, complement clauses are compatible with case, given that nominal arguments enter an Agree relation with different heads. What about the Case Resistance Principle then that we saw in section 1? Manzini and Savoia (2018: 254) provide the following reformulation:

(28) *Agree Resistance Theorem (ART)*
CPs cannot enter into Agree relations with v or I probes because of their lack of φ-features.

Given the ART, Agree takes as a Goal the complementizer; so the Agree relation is mediated by the complementizer, which turns the clause into an argument (as in Kayne 1982). Other ways to derive the desired Agree relation include full nominalization of the CP, as is Turkish for example, or embedding of the clause under a preposition (in an oblique argument realization).³

The point of the discussion so far has been that the oblique strategy may also be encoded on the complementizer, thus distinguishing between direct and oblique complement clauses, introduced by *oti* and *pu*-respectively in Greek. At this point it is worth mentioning that the P-strategy has been invoked, in an abstract fashion, for Bulgarian *deto*-clauses. In particular, Bulgarian also distinguishes between two declarative complementizers, *če* and *deto*, corresponding to *oti* and *pu* respectively; *deto* is also the main relativizer and introduces complements of factive emotive predicates (Krapova 2010). The relevant examples are given below:

(29) a. *Ninak   ne   săžaljavam*
      not-at-all no   regret-1SG
      deto sreštata   im   se   e   provalila.
      that meeting-DET their REFL is failed.PRT
      "I do not regret at all that their meeting has not taken place."
   b. *Săžaljavam za/*na/*Ø provala   na sreštata*
      regret-1SG for/of/   failure-DET of meeting-DET
      "I'm sorry about the failure of the meeting."
   c. **Deto toj e xubav   ne   me=iznenada*
      that he is handsome not me surprsed-3SG
      "That he is handsome, did not surprise me."

The distribution of *deto* is very much like that of *pu* (although note that Bulgarian allows for the complementizer *če* as well in (29a)): it is attested in relatives, factive emotives, correlates with PP objects and is excluded from a subject position.

Krapova (2010) argues that *deto*-clauses are concealed PPs, on the basis of the alternation with a PP, as in (29b). The preposition selects for an abstract

---

3 An anonymous reviewer raises the question of how 'verbal' complementizers are accommodated. For the purposes of the present paper, I can only acknowledge the problem. An account of this pattern needs to take into consideration the general complementation pattern of the languages that have V-type complementizers, bearing in mind the (un)availability of serial verb constructions and/or the initial vs final position positioning in the structure.

tova which is in turn modified by the *deto*-clause (thus treating *deto*-complements as relative clauses). The relevant structure is given below:

(30) săžaljavam [PP za/ [DP tova/ [CP deto . . . .]]]

With *deto*, the preposition *za* and the demonstrative *tova* can be deleted. In some cases, the preposition remains, as in *zadeto* (za+deto), without the demonstrative.

Whether or not this analysis can extend to Greek is questionable. In the Greek case, *pu* and the preposition cannot co-occur.[4] In fact, as we saw in the previous section, when the complement clause is expressed as a PP, then its complement is a nominalized (*to-oti* = the that) clause. So the empirical evidence from Greek does not support the schematic representation in (30). Note that it's not a generalized property of *pu* that it cannot participate in nominalization. Consider the following example:

(31) [To [pu   tha pame]] dhen to=gnorizo.
     the where will go-1PL   not   it=know-1SG
     "I don't know where we'll go."

In (31) *pu* functions as an interrogative 'where'. The wh-clause it introduces is topicalized, and is nominalized (forming a chain with the object clitic *to*). What is interesting is that *pu* as a complementizer resists nominalization, a property which in our analysis was attributed to the fact that it occurs in oblique argument positions.

Another instance of PP-complementation is discussed by Knyazev (2016) with respect to Russian. The relevant cases involve predicates that can be construed with an agentive or non-agentive reading. For example, as agentive, the verb *govorit* (say) takes a *čto*-complement or a complex PP complement, as in

---

4 A point of clarification here: if *pu* is part of an NP, as in *to jeghonos pu* (the fact that), it can only be construed as a relativizer. However, this is not necessarily the case when the nominal is an emotive one:
(i)   Eksefrase   tin lipi=tu/   xara=tu   [pu tha fighume].
       expressed-3sg the sadness his   happiness his   that will leave-1pl
       "He expressed his sadness/happiness for our leaving."

In this respect, Greek seems to differ from Bulgarian, which in this context reverts to the complementizer *če*, and excludes *deto* (see Krapova & Cinque 2015: fn. 9).

(32) However, in its non-agentive reading (meaning 'indicate') it only takes a PP, as in (33) (pp. 2–3):

(32) a. Učenye   govorjat, čto
       scientists.NOM say   that
       na ètoj territorii   ran'še žili   ljudi.
       on this territory.LOC earlier lived people.NOM
       "Scientists say that earlier people used to live on this territory."
    b. Učenye   govorjat o   tom čto
       scientists.NOM say   about it   that
       na ètoj territorii   ran'še žili   ljudi.
       on this territory.LOC earlier lived people.NOM
       "Scientists are talking about the fact that earlier people used to live on this territory."

(33) a. Èti   naxodki   govorjat *čto
       these findings.NOM say   that
       na ètoj territorii   ran'še žili   ljudi.
       on this territory.LOC earlier lived people.NOM
    b. Èti   naxodki govorjat o   tom, čto
       these findings say   about it.LOC that
       na ètoj territorii   ran'še žili   ljudi.
       on this territory.LOC earlier lived people.NOM
       "These findings indicate that earlier people used to live on this territory."

The picture is more complex than the one presented here. What is relevant to the present discussion though is Knyazev's claim that *čto*-complement clauses require case. More precisely, *čto* appears in 'accusative' contexts (what we would call Agree between v and *čto*), when the verb is agentive, but it is embedded under a PP in oblique contexts when the verb is non-agentive. When the verb cannot assign accusative independently of complement selection (i.e. DP vs CP), the claim is that there is a null P. For our purposes it suffices to mention two points relevant to our discussion: first, that the notion of case extends to complement clauses, and second, that complement clauses behave like their NP-counterparts.

In short, in the present section I looked at some comparative evidence on how complement clauses behave in relation to case. The relevant data were viewed in the context of the Greek data and the *Agree Resistance Theorem*, proposed by Manzini and Savoia (2018).

5 Conclusion

In this paper I have discussed the Visibility Condition on arguments, on the basis of complement clauses. The key idea has been that complementizers are nominal elements and as such they can be associated with the range of features (projections) of the nominal system. In relation to case, I have assumed that it is a categorial feature and therefore interpretable. The dual declarative complementizer system of Greek has supported the view that complement clauses may occur as direct (accusative) or indirect (oblique) arguments. The distinction between *oti-* and *pu*-complements has been quite revealing in this respect. In particular, the claim has been that *pu*-complements of factive emotives are oblique arguments; this has been supported by the fact that they can be substituted by PPs (P+*to oti*-clause). This latter option is attested in Bulgarian and Russian as well (in similar or different complementation contexts), thus offering further empirical support to the present analysis.

References

Alexiadou, Artemis & Gianina Iordăchioaia. 2014. The psych causative alternation. *Lingua* 148. 53–79.
Arsenijević, Boban. 2009. Clausal complementation as relativization. *Lingua* 119. 39–50.
Baunaz, Lena. 2015. On the various sizes of complementizers. *Probus* 27. 193–236.
Baunaz, Lena & Eric Lander. 2017. Syncretisms with nominal complementizers. *Studia Linguistica* 72. 537–570.
Blake, Barry J. 2001. *Case*. Cambridge: Cambridge University Press.
Bobaljik, Jonathan & Susi Wurmbrand. 2008. Case in GB/Minimalism. In Andrej L. Malchukov & Andrew Spencer (eds.), *The Oxford handbook of case*, 44–58. Oxford: Oxford University Press.
Bošković, Želko. 1995. Case properties of clauses and the Greed principle. *Studia Linguistica* 49. 32–53.
Bresnan, Joan W. 1972. *Theory of complementation in English syntax*. Cambridge, MA: MIT dissertation.
Chomsky, Noam. 1981. *Lectures on government and binding*. Foris: Dordrecht.
Chomsky, Noam. 1986a. *Barriers*. Cambridge, MA: MIT Press.
Chomsky, Noam. 1986b. *Knowledge of language: Its nature, origin, and use*. New York: Praeger.
Chomsky, Noam. 1995a. Categories and transformations. In Noam Chomsky, *The minimalist program*, 219–394. Cambridge, MA: MIT Press.
Christidis, A.Ph. 1982. Ότι/πως-που: επιλογή δεικτών συμπληρωμάτων στα Νέα Ελληνικά [*Oti/ pos-pu*: complementizer selection in Modern Greek]. *Studies in Greek Linguistics* 2. 113–177.

de Cuba, Carlos & Barbara Ürögdi. 2010. Clearing up the 'facts' in complementation. *UPenn Working Papers in Linguistics* 16. 41–50.
Davies, William D. & Stanley Dubinsky. 2009. On the existence (and distribution) of sentential subjects. In Donna B. Gerdts, John C. Moore J. C. & Maria Polinksy (eds.), *Hypothesis A/ hypothesis B: Linguistic explorations in honor of David M. Perlmutter*, 111–128. Cambridge, MA; MIT Press.
Franco, Ludovico. 2012. Against the identity of complementizers and (demonstrative) pronouns. *Poznań Studies in Contemporary Linguistics* 48. 565–596.
Gelderen, Elly van. 2015. The particle *how*. In Josef Bayer, Roland Hinterhoelzl & Andreas Trotzke (eds.), *Discourse-oriented syntax*, 159–174. Amsterdam: John Benjamins.
Haegeman, Liliane & Barbara Ürögdi. 2010. Referential CPs and DPs: An operator movement account. *Theoretical Linguistics* 36 (2/3). 111–151.
Hooper, Joan B. & Sandra A. Thompson. 1973. On the applicability of root transformations. *Linguistic Inquiry* 4. 465–497.
Kalluli, Dalina. 2008. Clitic doubling, agreement and information structure. In Dalina Kalluli & Liliane Tasmowski (eds.), *Clitic doubling in the Balkan languages*, 227–256. Amsterdam: John Benjamins.
Kastner, Itamar. 2015. Factivity mirrors interpretation: The selectional requirements of presuppositional verbs. *Lingua* 164. 156–188.
Kayne, Richard. 1982. Predicates and arguments, verbs and nouns. *GLOW Newsletter* 8. 24.
Kayne, Richard. 1994. *The antisymmetry of syntax*. Cambridge, MA: MIT Press.
Kayne, Richard. 2010. Why isn't *this* a complementizer? In Richard Kayne, *Comparisons and contrasts*, 190–227. Oxford: Oxford University Press.
Koster, Jan. 1978. Why subject sentences don't exist. In Samuel J. Keyser (ed.), *Recent transformational studies in European languages*, 53–64. Cambridge, MA: MIT Press.
Knyazev, Mikhail. 2016. *Licensing clausal complements. The case of Russian što-clauses*. Utrecht: LOT Publications.
Kotzoglou, George. 2005. *Wh-extraction and locality in Greek*. Reading: University of Reading dissertation.
Krapova, Iliana. 2010. Bulgarian relative and factive clauses with an invariant complementizer. *Lingua* 120. 1240–1272.
Krapova, Iliana & Guglielmo Cinque. 2015. On noun clausal "complements" and their non-unitary nature. http://lear.unive.it/jspui/handle/11707/164.
Lasnik, Howard. 2008. On the development of Case theory: triumphs and challenges. In Robert Freidin, Carlos P. Otero & Maria Luisa Zubizarreta (eds.), *Foundational issues in linguistic theory: Essays in honor of Jean-Roger Vergnaud*, 17–42. Cambridge, MA: MIT Press.
Legate, Julie Anne. 2010. On how *how* is used instead of *that*. *Natural Language and Linguistic Theory* 28. 121–134.
Manzini, M. Rita. 1992. *Locality. A theory and some of its empirical consequences*. Cambridge, MA: MIT Press.
Manzini, M. Rita. 2010. The structure and interpretation of (Romance) complementizers. In Phoevos Panagiotidis (ed.), *The complementizer phase*, 167–199. Oxford: Oxford University Press.
Manzini, M. Rita & Leonardo M. Savoia. 2003. The nature of complementizers. *Rivista di Grammatica Generativa* 28. 87–110.

Manzini, M. Rita & Leonardo M. Savoia. 2010. Case as denotation: variation in Romance. *Studi Italiani di Linguistica Teorica e Applicata*, vol. XXXIX, 3. 409–438.

Manzini, M. Rita & Leonardo M. Savoia. 2011. Reducing 'case' to denotational primitives: Nominal inflections in Albanian. *Linguistic Variation* 11. 76–120.

Manzini, M. Rita & Leonardo M. Savoia. 2018. *The morphosyntax of Albanian and Aromanian varieties*. Berlin & New York: Mouton de Gruyter.

Makri, Maria Margariti. 2013. *Expletive negation beyond Romance: Clausal complementation and epistemic modality*. University of York MA dissertation.

Michelioudakis, Dimitris. 2012. *Dative arguments and abstract case in Greek*. University of Cambridge dissertation.

Nye, Rachel. 2013. Complementizer-like *how* clauses and the distribution of finite clausal complements in English. CONSOLE 2013 Potsdam.

Pesetsky, David. 1995. *Zero syntax. Experiencers and cascades*. Cambridge, MA: MIT Press.

Pesetsky, David. 2013. *Russian case morphology and the syntactic categories*. Cambridge, MA: MIT Press.

Pesetsky, David & Esther Torrego. 2004. Tense, Case, and the nature of syntactic categories. In Jacqueline Guéron & Jacqueline Lecarme (eds.), *The Syntax of Time*, 495–537. Cambridge, MA: MIT Press.

Roberts, Ian & Anna Roussou. 2003. *Syntactic change. A minimalist approach to grammaticalization*. Cambridge: Cambridge University Press.

Rosenbaum, Peter S. 1967. *The grammar of English predicate complement constructions*. Cambridge, MA: MIT Press.

Roussou, Anna. 1991. Nominalized clauses in the syntax of Modern Greek. *UCL Working Papers in Linguistics* 3. 77–100.

Roussou, Anna. 1994. *The Syntax of complementisers*. University College London dissertation.

Roussou, Anna. 2010. Selecting complementizers. *Lingua* 120. 582–603.

Roussou, Anna. 2015. Is particle a (unified) category? In Josef Bayer, Roland Hinterhoelzl, & Andreas Trotzke (eds.), *Discourse-oriented syntax*, 121–158. Amsterdam: John Benjamins.

Roussou, Anna. 2017. The duality of mipos. *Proceedings of the ICGL12*, Vol. 2. CeMoG, Freie Universität Berlin: Edition Romiosini.

Rudin, Catherine. 1986. *Aspects of Bulgarian syntax: Complementizers and wh-constructions*. Columbus, Ohio: Slavica Publishers.

Stowell, Timothy. 1981. *Origins of phrase structure*. Cambridge, MA: MIT dissertation.

van Gelderen, Elly (see Gelderen Elly, van).

Varlokosta, Spyridoula. 1994. *Issues on Modern Greek sentential omplementation*. University of Maryland, College Park dissertation.

Tarald Taraldsen
The internal structure of Nguni nominal class prefixes

1 Introduction: The V-CV analysis of class prefixes

This section introduces the properties of Nguni nominal class prefixes that are invoked to motivate the analyses in Taraldsen (2010) and Taraldsen et al. (2018). It provides some basic motivation for a decompositional analysis of the class prefixes and should be read as a prelude to the new proposals in section 2.

1.1 Two morphemes lexicalizing three heads

Nguni languages (Xhosa, Zulu, Swati, Ndebele) sort nouns into 13 different noun classes each associated with a distinct class prefix. The Xhosa paradigm is shown in (1):

(1) Class 1 *u-m-*   Class 2 *a-ba-*
          3 *u-m-*   4 *i-mi-*
          5 *i-(li)-*[1]   6 *a-ma-*
          7 *i-si-*   8 *i-zi-*
          9 *i-N-*   10 *i-zi-N- / ii-N-*
         11 *u-(lu-)*
         14 *u-(bu-)*
         15 *u-ku-*

The initial vowel of the forms listed in (1) is uncontroversially analyzed as a separate morpheme generally called the "augment". It has a morphosyntactic

---

[1] The parenthesized pieces never show up on polysyllabic stems in class 5 and show up on polysyllabic stems in classes 11 and 14 only in contexts where the augment (the initial vowel) is dropped. Likewise, *ii-N-* rather than *i-zi-N-* occurs with polysyllabic stems except when the augment is dropped. *N* is a homorganic nasal.

Tarald Taraldsen, CASTL, University of Tromsø

https://doi.org/10.1515/9781501505201-031

life of its own falling away in certain syntactically defined environments, e.g. in the scope of negation and when preceded by a demonstrative.

There is a pairing of singular and plural classes. In (1), the classes in the left column are singular classes while those in the right column are plural classes. A noun in a singular class from 1 up to 9 generally has a plural form in the class to its right in (1). For example, the class 1 noun *u-m-ntu* "person" finds its plural form *a-ba-ntu* "people" in class 2. In general, each member of a singular/plural pair might be taken to have the same gender, but different number, and the shape of the prefix would be conditioned by this, e.g. as in Carstens (1991), but I'll take issue with this view in section 2.

The Xhosa paradigm is representative of the Nguni system except for Swati, which is discussed in section 3. Another property of Xhosa is also typical of the Nguni languages except for another special feature of Swati also discussed in section 3. A verb agreeing with a subject will have an agreement marker in the same class as the subject. and as seen in (2), there is a regular correspondence between the subject agreement markers ("subject concords": SCs) and parts of the corresponding class prefixes on nouns:

(2)
class	the class prefix	the SC
1	*u-m-*	*u-*
2	*a-ba-*	*ba-*
3	*u-m-*	*u-*
4	*i-mi-*	*i-*
5	*i-li-*	*li-*
6	*a-ma-*	*a-*
7	*i-si-*	*si-*
8	*i-zi-*	*zi-*
9	*i-N-*	*i-*
10	*i-zi-N-*	*zi-*
11	*u-lu-*	*lu-*
14	*u-bu-*	*bu-*

In the classes where the initial segment of the basic prefix on nouns is a nasal (the "weak classes"), the SC is identical to the augment,[2] but in the other

---

[2] There is an ill-understood exception. SC1, the subject agreement marker in class 1, is *u* only when the verb is in the "principal mood", i.e. roughly in main clauses and in subject-relatives. Otherwise, it is *a* (like SC6). (When the verb is associated with a "latent *i* including all verbs in the "participial mood", this *a* is changed to *e* just like SC6 *a* and just like SC2 *ba* is changed to *be*; cf. the cases of phonological coalescence discussed in section 3.)

classes, it is identical to the part following the augment, i.e. the basic class prefix. To capture this correspondence, Taraldsen (2010) proposes that the structure of a class prefix (including the augment) is as in (3) and that a single morpheme (a vowel) "spans" the heads Aug and SC in the weak classes, while a single morpheme (C(V)-shaped) spans SC and AC, as illustrated in (4):

(3) [Aug [SC [AC [N]]]]

(4) a. [Aug$_1$[SC$_1$[AC$_1$[N]]]]

　　　　u　　m ntwana

b. [Aug$_2$[SC$_2$[AC$_2$[N]]]]

　　　　a　ba　ntwana

In the context of the general theoretical assumptions adhered to in Taraldsen (2010), this predicts that when the head SC occurs in isolation as a subject agreement marker on a verb, it will lexicalized by the same morpheme that lexicalizes it when it occurs inside the class prefix of noun. That is, by the same morpheme that lexicalizes the augment in the weak classes, but by the morpheme that spells out the basic prefix elsewhere.

1.2 The class prefix contains a noun

I have mentioned that the spell-out of a class prefix on a noun might be seen as conditioned by a number feature combining with a gender feature inherited from the noun. But there are reasons to think that this is not quite right.

The first reason is that the pairing of singular and plural forms does not always give the result expected on this view. For example, some class 1 nouns have plurals in class 6 rather than class 2, e.g. *u-m-Xhosa* "a Xhosa" (class 1)/ *a-ma-Xhosa* "Xhosas" (class 6). Likewise, some class 9 nouns have plurals in class 6 rather than class (10), e.g. *i-n-doda* "man" (class 6)/*a-ma-doda* "men" (class 6). A priori, this might be handled by postulating extra genders X for *Xhosa* and Y for *doda* and engineering syncretisms on the model of the Romanian neuter nouns that look like masculine nouns in the singular and like feminine nouns in the plural:

(5)   SG   PL
    M *prieten* *prieten-i* "friend"
    N *deget*   *deget-e*   "finger"
    F *cas-a*   *cas-e*   "house"

This analysis of Romanian nouns makes the correct prediction that a participle or adjective agreeing with a conjunction of two singular neuter nouns will have the same inflection as when it agrees with a single plural neuter noun, i.e. it will have the feminine plural inflection:

(6) a. *Un deget și   un braț au   fost amputat-e/*-i*
        a   finger and an arm have been amputated-F.PL/*M.PL
        'A finger and an arm have been amputated.'
    b. *Degetele/brațele   au   fost amputat-e/*-i*
        fingers-the/arms-the have been amputated-F.PL/*M.PL
        "The fingers/arms have been amputated."

Since the gender feature of neuter nouns in combination with the number feature [plural] (associated with a conjunction of singular nouns) should yield inflection identical to the feminine plural, what we see in (6) is exactly what the three-gender analysis of Romanian predicts.

But by the same token, treating the Xhosa "irregular" singular/plural pairs in an analogous fashion cannot be correct. If nouns like *Xhosa* and *Zulu* belonged to a distinct gender X and the combination the gender feature X with the number feature [plural] is simply spelled out by the same morpheme that spells out the gender feature of classes 5 and 6 in combination with [plural], the SC in (7a) ought to be the class 6 SC *a*, as in (7b), but it isn't:

(7) a. *U-m-Xhosa no-m-Zulu   **ba**/***a**-sebenza ndawonye*
        1-1-Xhosa and.1-1-Zulu   SC2/*SC6-work   together
        'A Xhosa and a Zulu are working together.'
    b. *A-ma-Xhosa/Zulu   a/*ba-sebenza ndawonye*
        6- 6- Xhosa/Zulu   SC6-work   together
        'The Xhosas/Zulus are working together.'

Rather, the SC in (7a) must be the class 2 SC *ba* suggesting that the singular forms *u-m-Xhosa* and *u-m-Zulu* actually must have the gender feature associated with classes 1 and 2. But then, how come their plurals are in class 6, if the gender feature determining the spell-out of the prefix is always inherited from the host noun?

The same question arises with the class 9 nouns that have plurals in class 6:

(8) a. I-n-doda ne-n-kwenke **zi/*a**-ya-cula
     9-9-man and.9-boy   SC10/*SC6-DJ-sing
     'A man and a boy are singing.'
   b. A-ma-doda/kwenkwe **a**-ya-cula
     6-6-man/boy   SC6-DJ-sing
     'The men/boys are singing.'

To account for the "irregular" singular/plural pairs, Taraldsen et al. (2018) abandon the idea that the gender feature determining the spell-out of the prefix is inherited from the host noun in the class 6 plurals. Instead, the gender associated with the class 6 prefix comes from a noun embedded inside the structure lexicalized by the basic class 6 prefix *ma* as in (9):

(9) $[[_{\#P} \#_{\{PL, 6\}} [\ N_6]]\ N_Y]$

ma

Then, Taraldsen et al. (2018) go on to propose that all the C(V)-shaped class prefixes contain a noun which acts as a classifier:

(10) $[[_{\#P} \#_{\{PL, X\}} [\ N_X]]\ N_Y]$

prefix

This analytical decision is supported by the second observation that leads one to abandon the view that the gender associated with a class prefix comes from the host noun. In Bantu languages, the regular class prefix of a noun (its "primary prefix") can be replaced by a "secondary prefix" that seems to shift the meaning of the noun in a way similar to derivational morphology. For example, the class 1 prefix of *u-m-ntu* "person" can be replaced with the class 14 prefix *bu* to yield *u-bu-ntu* "humanity". Other secondary prefixes are comparable to augmentatives and diminutives in other languages. Like Carstens (1991, 1997), Taraldsen et al. (2018) take the secondary prefixes to be connected to a silent noun whose semantics impacts on the meaning of the overt host noun, but implement this idea as in (10). This extends the analysis of the plural prefixes to the secondary singular prefixes.

However, a secondary prefix generally also occurs as the primary prefix of a set of nouns. For example, the class 14 prefix *bu* which is used as a secondary prefix in *u-bu-ntu* "humanity" also occurs as the primary prefix of basic class 14 nouns like *u-bu-sika* "winter". The internal logic of the nanosyntactic approach adopted by Taraldsen et al. (2018) forces the assumption that the structure underlying *bu* is as in (10) also when it is used as a primary prefix and likewise for the other class prefixes that are used both as primary and secondary prefixes, e.g. the class 5 prefix in Shona. Thus, Taraldsen et al. (2018) conclude that all class prefixes have the structure in (10) containing a noun acting as a kind of classifier. This conclusion plays a critical role in the new analysis of class prefixes that will be developed in the following sections.

2 The V-C-V analysis of class prefixes

In this section, I first present a generalization that is not captured in previous accounts of the nominal class prefixes in Nguni. Then, I sketch a new analysis which accounts for the generalization. The consequences of adopting this new analysis will be explored further in sections 3 and 4.

2.1 The augment is identical to the vowel in the CV-shaped prefix

The basic CV-shaped prefixes are generally seen as monomorphemic and are treated as such both in Taraldsen (2010) and in Taraldsen et al. (2018). But the formal relation between the augment and the V of the CV-shaped prefixes suggests otherwise. As seen in the Xhosa paradigm in (1), the augment is always the same vowel as the V of the basic prefix in each class whenever the basic prefix does in fact contain a V, i.e. in all classes except 1 and 3.[3] As pointed out in footnote 1, a CV-shaped basic prefix always occur on monosyllabic host nouns even in classes 5, 10, 11 and 14, and its disappearance on polysyllabic roots should be seen as a phonological effect.

Conceivably, the identity relation between the augment and the V of the CV-shaped basic prefix could be captured by assuming that the augment copies the phonological features of the V inside the prefix (and perhaps taking the *u* in

---

[3] In classes 1 and 3, the basic prefix is just *m* in Xhosa, but in Zulu and Swati, *–mu* occurs on monosyllabic stems.

classes 1 and 3 as a default spell-out). However, this presupposes that the phonological copying rule can apply before the basic prefix is elided in classes 5, 10, 11 and 14, where, as we have seen, the basic CV-shaped prefix never surfaces in the augmented forms of polysyllabic nouns.

In any event, there is a second generalization that phonological copying plainly cannot account for. In the weak classes, the SC is a vowel identical to the vowel of the corresponding basic CV-shaped class prefix on nouns (hence, also identical to the augment). But a SC is never followed by a CV-shaped prefix from which the features of the vowel could be copied.

Both generalizations are accounted for if the structure of the basic prefix is as in (11), where X, Y and Z are lexicalized by different morphemes, Z always by a vowel and Y by a consonant (in the strong classes) or Ø (in the weak classes)[4] and X by *m* in the weak classes, but by the same consonant as Y elsewhere, so that basic prefixes are no longer mono-morphemic (as in Taraldsen (2010)), but composed of "C-morphemes" and "V-morphemes" (with no theoretical significance attached to these terms):

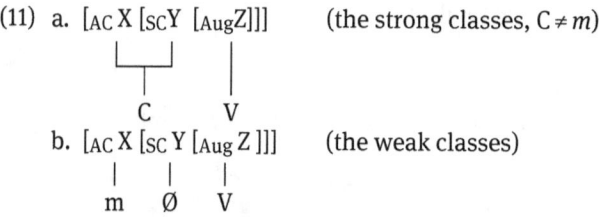

(11) a. [AC X [SC Y [Aug Z]]]   (the strong classes, C ≠ *m*)
         C   V

b. [AC X [SC Y [Aug Z]]]   (the weak classes)
    m   Ø   V

The fact that the SCs of the weak classes are identical to the vowel following *m* in the basic prefix, is now accounted for by saying that agreement copies the constituent labeled SC (= YZ) inside the basic prefix leaving out X, provided of course we adopt the analysis suggested in footnote 3 for the basic prefix in class 1 and 3. The identity between the augment and vowel inside the basic prefix is accounted for by saying that the augment is a second occurrence of the same morpheme that spells out Z inside the basic prefix, i.e. a second occurrence of the syntactic head Z agreeing in number and gender with the Z in the basic prefix.

However, this analysis meets an obvious challenge: Each C-morpheme only combines with a proper subset of the three V-morphemes *a, i* and *u*. So how do

---

4 In other Bantu languages, the C-morpheme is not Ø in the weak classes, but, for example, *k* in Lubukusu and *y/w* (depending on the following vowel) in the Tsonga languages Rhonga and Changana.

we ensure that we only allow the right CV combinations, e.g. *ba* (class 2) and *bu* (class 14), but not **bi*? At this point, the facts discussed in section 2 become relevant. There, I concluded that each class prefix contains a noun lexicalized together with Num by a single morpheme:

(10) [[#P #{PL, X} [NX]] NY]
         └─────────┬─────────┘
                 prefix

Implementing this idea in a different way, I now suggest that the structure of class prefixes is as in (12), which corresponds to (11) with Y = N, and that C-morphemes (including the Ø of the weak classes) lexicalize N:

(12) a. [AC X[SC N[Aug Z]]]   (the strong classes, C ≠ m)
            └─┬─┘ │
              C   V
     b. [AC X[SC N[Aug Z]]]   (the weak classes)
            │ │   │
            m Ø   V

We can then identify Z with # and assume as before that # also inherits the gender feature of N:

(13) a. [AC X[SC NG [Aug #{Sg/Pl,G}]]]   (the strong classes, C ≠ m)
            └─┬─┘   │
              C   V
     b. [AC X [SC NG [Aug #{Sg/Pl, G}]]]   (the weak classes)
            │   │   │
            m   Ø   V

Thus, the glue that holds C-morphemes and V-morphemes together is gender-agreement. From the point of view of the current analysis, the ingredients of a class prefix like class 2 [*a* [*b-a*]] relate to each other much like the ingredients of Portuguese *a cas-a* 'the house', for example.

2.2 Gender and number

The pairing of C-morphemes and V-morphemes emerges from the paradigm in (1) (repeated here for convenience):

(1) Class 1   u-m-   Class 2   a-ba-
          3   u-m-   4   i-mi-
          5   i-(li)-   6   a-ma-
          7   i-si-   8   i-zi-
          9   i-N-   10   i-zi-N- / ii-N-
         11   u-(lu-)
         14   u-(bu-)
         15   u-ku-

If the C-morphemes are Ns and V-morphemes are exponents of gender and number inheriting the gender of the N they follow, all C-morphemes that are paired with the same V-morpheme when number is held constant, should have the same gender. Assuming accidental syncretism (homophony) for the *l* of class 5 and the *l* of class 11,[5] we obtain the picture in (14) for the strong singular classes:

(14) Gender   N   # = singular
     A   l, s   i
     B   l, b, k   u

Minimizing gender-syncretism, we have (15) for the strong plural classes:

(15) Gender   N   # = plural
     A   z   i
     B   b   a

Putting together (14) and (15), we arrive at (16) as a characterization of the distribution of the V-morphemes in the strong classes:

(16) Gender   N   # = singular   # = plural
     A   l, s, z   i   i
     B   l, b, k   u   a

When the weak classes are taken into consideration, complications arise of two different sorts. The first arises from the fact that the C-morpheme Ø combines with three different vowels, i.e. *u* in classes 1 and 3, *i* in class 3 and *a* in class 6.

---

[5] In some languages, all class 11 nouns have been included in class 5.

Hence, it seems we must posit accidental homophony spanning at least two different Ns:

(17) | Gender | N | # = singular | # = plural |
| --- | --- | --- | --- |
| A | $\emptyset_4$ | | i |
| B | $\emptyset_{1,3,6}$ u | | a |

We return to this issue in section 4.

The second complication has to do with the pairing of singular and plural classes seen in (1). As mentioned earlier, an a priori plausible way of modeling this pairing would be to say that paired class prefixes have the same gender, i.e. they contain Ns with the same gender under the present account, possibly even the same N spelling out in different ways in the singular and the plural. But this cannot hold for classes 3 and 4 or classes 5 and 6, given the picture in (16): In class 3, the N must be of gender B, since the V-morpheme (when it occurs) is u, but in class 4 the N must be of gender A, since the V-morpheme is i. Similarly, the V-morpheme in class 5 is i, and the N inside the prefix must therefore be of gender A. But the V-morpheme in class 6 is a. Therefore, the N in class 6 must be assigned to gender B.

In section 2, however, we discovered that the class prefixes of a singular/plural pair do not always have the same gender. That is, they may contain different Ns in present terms. As it happens, the same agreement test used to show this for "irregular" singular/plural pairs in section 2 actually gives the same result for both 3/4 pairs and 5/6 pairs even though these should be "regular" in terms of (1). Agreement with a subject formed by conjunction of two singular class 3 nouns never gives the class 4 SC, and the class 6 SC never occurs with a conjunction of two singular class 5 nouns. Instead, the SC is in both cases the class 2 SC *ba* if one of the two nouns denote a human being, but the class 8/10 SC *zi* otherwise:

(18) a. *U-m-gewu   no-m-lwelwe   **ba**/*i-sebenza   ndawonye*
    3-3-criminal and.3-3-cripple SC2/*SC4-work together
    "A criminal and a cripple are working together."

  b. *I-mi-gewu   i-sebenza ndawonye*
    4-4-criminal SC4-work together
    'The criminals are working together.'

(19) a. *U-m-bhinqo no-m-nqathe   **zi**/*i-se-tafile-ni*
    3-3- skirt   and.3-3-carrot SC8/*SC4-LOC-table-LOC
    'A skirt and a carrot are on the table.'

b. *I-mi-bhinqo i-se-tafile-ni*
     4-4-skirt   SC4-LOC-table-LOC
     'The skirts are on the table.'

(20) a. *I-li-tya   ne-qanda   zi/*a-khataza   i-n-taka*
        5-5-stone and.5-egg   SC8/*SC6-annoy 9-9-bird
        'The stone and the egg annoy the bird.'
   b. *A-ma-tya   a-khataza   i-n-taka*
      6-6- stone SC6-annoy   9-9-bird
      'The stones annoy the bird.'

(21) a. *I-gqirha   ne-gosa   ba/*a-sebenza   ndawonye*
        5-healer   and.5-steward   SC2 work   together
        'The healer and the steward are working together.'

This suggests that 3/4 pairs and 5/6 pairs have the same status as irregular pairs like *u-m-Xhosa* "a Xhosa"/*a-ma-Xhosa* "Xhosas" (1/6) and *i-n-doda* "a man"/*a-ma-doda* "men" (9/6). That is, the singular prefix and the plural prefix don't have the same gender, just as our assignment of V-morphemes to genders requires.

2.3 A reevaluation of the agreement facts

However, the reasoning leading to the conclusion just drawn presupposes that subject/verb agreement is a simple matter of copying gender and number features, and this cannot actually be the case given the assumptions to be introduced in section 3. This is because the agreeing SC contains not only an exponent of gender and number, a V-morpheme, but also a C-morpheme (Ø in the weak classes) spelling out the same N as in the corresponding nominal class prefix. Thus, agreement as copying would have to include copying the noun inside the subject's class prefix as well, and the choice of V-morpheme within the SC would therefore be determined by the gender of this noun rather than by agreement with a subject.

Once it is recognized that both class prefixes on nouns and SCs contain classifier-like Ns, it becomes natural to regard subject/verb agreement in Bantu as a kind of semantic agreement rather than formal agreement of the sort discussed in section 2. Roughly, a specific classifier-like N is compatible with host nouns denoting things that are conventionally taken to possess certain defining characteristics, and likewise the N inside an SC restricts the applicability of the verbal predicate to entities conventionally associated with properties prescribed by that N. Agreement is then a matter of selecting the SC containing the N that comes closest to matching the properties associated with the entities denoted by the subject. But from this perspective, the agreement facts we have looked at, no longer tell us anything about gender-matching between singular and plural classes.[6]

The hypothesis that subject/verb agreement has nothing to do with gender-copying is consistent with the fact that the SCs of class 2 and 8/10 appear in (18)–(21) as well as in sentences where the subject is a conjunction of nouns belonging to different classes. The fact that the SCs of class 4 and 6 are impossible in (18)–(21) could plausibly be related to the fact that these also never appear with a subject formed by conjoining nouns of different classes. A possible explanation for both facts might turn on positing different types X and Y of plural denotations such that both the nominal class 4 and class 6 prefixes and the corresponding SCs denote pluralities of type X, the nominal prefixes and SCs of classes 2, 8 and 10 denote pluralities of type Y and the pluralities denoted by conjunctions of singular nouns also are of type Y.

This also means that what we see in (22)–(24) doesn't entail that the N inside the class 1 prefix (spelled out by Ø) and the N inside the class 2 prefix have the same gender, and likewise for the pairs 7/8 and 9/10:

(22) a. *U-m-ntwana no-m-fazi* **ba**-ya-dlala (Xhosa)
       1-1-child   and.1-1-woman SC2-DJ-play
       "The child and the woman are playing."
    b. *A-ba-ntwana / a-ba-fazi* **ba**-ya-dlala
       2-2-child   / 2-2-woman SC2-DJ-play
       'The children/women are playing.'

(23) a. *I-s-anuse ne-s-angoma* **zi**- sebenza ndawonye
       7-7-diviner and. 7-7-healer SC8-work together
       'The diviner and the healer work together.'
    b. *I-z-anuse / i-z-angoma* **zi**-sebenza ndawonye
       8-8-diviner / 8-8-healer SC8-work together
       'The diviners/healers work together.'

---

[6] In particular, examples (7)–(8) don't demonstrate that the N inside the prefix in the singular forms don't have the same gender as the N inside the plurals forms in pairs like *u-m-Xhosa* "a Xhosa"/*a-ma-Xhosa* "Xhosas" and *i-n-doda* "a man"/*a-ma-doda* "men". So the case for positing a classifier-like N inside class prefixes now rests entirely on the second observation mentioned in section 2.

(24) a. *I-n-tombi ne-m-bongi* **zi**-*ya-cula*
 9-9-girl and.9-9-poet SC10-DJ-sing
 'The girl and the poet are singing.'
 b. *Ii-n-tombi / ii-m-bongi* **zi**-*ya-cula*
 10-10-girl /10-10-poet SC10-DJ-sing
 'The girls/poets are singing.'

Nor is it inconsistent with seeing the V-morphemes *u/a* as a singular/plural pair of gender B as suggested by the fact that the C-morpheme *b* occurs with *u* in the singular (class 14) and with *a* in the plural (class 2), or with assigning *i* to gender A.

3 Swati

Turning back to an evaluation of the relative merits of the analysis mentioned in section 1 and the new analysis introduced in section 3, I will focus on a particular paradigm that at first seems to favor the old analysis, but which, I will argue, ultimately turns out to be better accounted for under the new analysis.

3.1 The distribution of initial vowels in Swati

In Swati, the augment (initial vowel) shows up only in the weak classes:

(25)
		pfx:	SC:			pfx:	SC:
Class	1	*umu-*	*u*	Class	2	*ba-*	*ba*
	3	*umu-*	*u*		4	*imi-*	*i*
	5	*li-*	*li*		6	*ema-*	*a*
	7	*si-*	*si*		8	*ti-*	*ti*
	9	*iN-*	*i*		10	*tiN-*	*ti*
	11	*lu-*	*lu*				
	14	*bu-*	*bu*				
	15	*ku-*	*ku*				

As can be gleaned from (25), another way of saying this is that there is an augment only in the classes where the SC is a just a vowel. This suggests an apparently straightforward account if the paradigm within the account proposed by Taraldsen (2010) where the Xhosa class prefixes are assigned the underlying structure in (3) (repeated below), and this structure is lexicalized as in (4)a in the weak classes, but as in (4)b in the strong classes:

(3) [Aug [SC [AC [N]]]]

(4) a. [Aug$_1$[SC$_1$[AC$_1$[N]]]]
            u   m ntwana

b. [Aug$_2$[SC$_2$[AC$_2$[N]]]]
            a   ba ntwana

If Swati is just like Xhosa except that the head Aug is not merged in prefixes on nouns so that the prefix on a noun has the smaller structure shown in (26), we expect that an initial vowel will show up only in the weak classes – not as a lexicalization of Aug, but as a lexicalization of SC:

(26) [SC [AC [N]]]

(27) a. [SC$_1$[AC$_1$[N]]]
           u   m   ntfwana
b. [SC$_2$[AC$_2$[N]]]
           ba   ntfwana

There is only one wrinkle (discussed briefly in Taraldsen 2010): The SC in class 6 is *a*, but the initial vowel of the class 6 prefix on nouns is *e*.

The new analysis proposed in section 3 posits a different structure for the augmented Xhosa prefixes and different lexicalization patterns:

(28) [$_{Aug}$ V$_i$ [$_{AC}$ X [$_{SC}$ N [$_{Aug}$ V$_i$]]]]

(29) a. $[_{Aug}V_1[_{AC}X[_{SC}N_1[_{Aug}V_1]]]]$
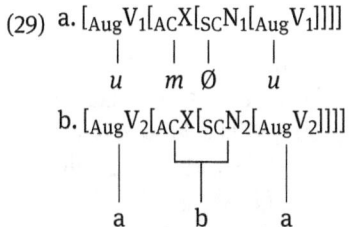
     u   m   Ø   u
 b. $[_{Aug}V_2[_{AC}X[_{SC}N_2[_{Aug}V_2]]]]$
     a   b   a

Clearly, the Swati paradigm doesn't emerge simply from peeling off the topmost Aug in these structures. Instead, the best way to relate Swati and Xhosa now seems to go through Lubukusu. In this language, the counterpart of the Xhosa augment is a full copy of the SC (where the C-morpheme is *k* in the weak classes except for classes 9/10):

(30)

class	class marker	SC (Lubukusu)
1	o-mu	a/o
2	ba-ba	ba
3	ku-mu	ku
4	ki-mi	ki
5	li-li	li
6	ka-ma	ka
7	si-si	si
8	bi-bi	bi
9	e-N	e
10	chi-N	chi
11	lu-lu	lu
12	kha-kha	kha
14	bu-bu	bu
15	khu-khu	khu
16	a-	a
17	khu	khu
18	mu-mu	mu
19	ku-ku	ku
23	e	e

Adopting a suggestion by P. Caha (p.c.), we can say that Swati is like Lubukusu except that the second occurrence of a repeated C-morpheme is deleted:

(31) Class: Class:
   1 [[$_{SC}$ ∅ [$_{Aug}$ u]] [$_{AC}$ m [$_{SC}$ ∅ [$_{Aug}$ u]]]]   2 [[$_{SC}$ b [$_{Aug}$ a]] [$_{AC}$ ɓ [$_{SC}$ ɓ [$_{Aug}$ a]]]]
   3 [[$_{SC}$ ∅ [$_{Aug}$ u]] [$_{AC}$ m [$_{SC}$ ∅ [$_{Aug}$ u]]]]   4 [[$_{SC}$ ∅ [$_{Aug}$ i]] [$_{AC}$ m [$_{SC}$ ∅ [$_{Aug}$ i]]]]
   5 [[$_{SC}$ l [$_{Aug}$ i]] [$_{AC}$ ɬ [$_{SC}$ ɬ [$_{Aug}$ i]]]]   6 [[$_{SC}$ ∅ [$_{Aug}$ a]] [$_{AC}$ m [$_{SC}$ ∅ [$_{Aug}$ a]]]]
   7 [[$_{SC}$ s [$_{Aug}$ i]] [$_{AC}$ s [$_{SC}$ s [$_{Aug}$ i]]]]   8 [[$_{SC}$ t [$_{Aug}$ i]] [$_{AC}$ ɬ [$_{SC}$ ɬ [$_{Aug}$ i]]]]
   9 [[$_{SC}$ ∅ [$_{Aug}$ i]] [$_{AC}$ [$_{SC}$ i [$_{Aug}$ i]]]]   10 [[$_{SC}$ t [$_{Aug}$ i]] [$_{AC}$ ɬ [$_{SC}$ ɬ [$_{Aug}$ i]]]]
  11 [[$_{SC}$ l [$_{Aug}$ u]] [$_{AC}$ ɬ [$_{SC}$ ɬ [$_{Aug}$ u]]]]
  14 [[$_{SC}$ b [$_{Aug}$ u]] [$_{AC}$ ɓ [$_{SC}$ ɓ [$_{Aug}$ u]]]]
  15 [[$_{SC}$ k [$_{Aug}$ u]] [$_{AC}$ k [$_{SC}$ k [$_{Aug}$ u]]]]

Provided adjacent identical vowels coalesce or one of them is elided, this too yields the paradigm in (25), but again with the wrinkle that the initial vowel should be *a* rather than *e* in class 6.

Comparing the two accounts of the Swati paradigm, one may prefer the first one, since the second one needs to posit a seemingly ad hoc deletion of repeated C-morphemes. However, it turns out that the second analysis fares better when it comes to eliminating the false prediction that the initial vowel in class 6 should be *a*.

3.2 The latent *i*

The account to be proposed for the initial *e* in class 6 in Swati is based on the fact that certain morphemes are associated with a so-called "latent *i*", e.g. verbal roots consisting only of a consonant both in Swati and Xhosa as illustrated in the following Swati examples from Ziervogel & Mabuza (1976:75, 95) (where FV – the final vowel – marks tense/mood):

(32) a. *Ba-nats-a*   vs. *Be-mb-a*
        SC2-drink-FV   SC2-dig-FV
        'They drink'   'They dig.'
     b. *A-nats-a*   vs. *E-mb-a*
        SC6-drink-FV   SC6-dig-FV
        'They drink.'   'They dig.'
     c. *U-nats-a*   *U-mb-a*
        SC1-drink-FV   SC1-dig-FV
        'He drinks.'   'He digs.'
     d. *I-nats-a*   *I-mb-a*
        SC9-drink-FV   SC1-dig-FV
        'He drinks.'   'He digs.'

The latent *i* connected with the root *mb* "dig" coalesces with a preceding *a* into an *e*, but leaves no trace elsewhere.

In Swati, but not in Xhosa, a latent *i* is also detectable with nouns. The preposition-like *na* "with, and" in (33) surfaces as *ne* when followed by a noun of any class as seen in (34):

(33) *na*   "with" plus pronoun: independent (strong) pronouns:
     class 1: *naye*   *yena*
            2: *nabo*   *bona*
            3: *nawo*   *wona*
            4: *nayo*   *yona*
            5: *nalo*   *lona*
            6: *nawo*   *ona*

(34) *na* "with" plus a noun: independent ("strong") noun:
     class 1:   *nemuntfu*   *umuntfu*   'man'
            2:   *nebantfu*   *bantfu*   'men'
            3:   *nemuti*   *umuti*   'village'
            4:   *nemiti*   *imiti*   'villages'
            5:   *nelibutfo*   *libutfo*   "regiment'
            6:   *nemabutfo*   *emabutfo*   'regiments'

In Xhosa and Zulu, the shape of *na* is determined by the initial vowel (augment) of the following noun:

(35) *na* "with" plus a noun: independent (strong) noun: (Zulu)
     class 1:   *nomuntu*   *umuntu*   'man'
            2:   *nabantu*   *abantu*   'men'
            3:   *nomuzi*   *umuzi*   'village'
            4:   *nemizi*   *imizi*   'villages'
            5:   *nefu*   *ifu*   'cloud'
            6:   *namafu*   *amafu*   'clouds'

(36) a.   *na* [*u* - → /no/
      b.   *na* [*a* - → /na/
      c.   *na* [*i* - → /ne/

This suggests that the *ne* in Swati is the result of coalescence with an initial vowel *I*, which is invariant across classes, i.e. (34) = (37):

(37) class 1: na [$_x$ *I* [$_{ac}$ mu [$_N$ ntfu]]] → /nemuntfu/
      2: na [$_x$ *I* [$_{ac}$ ba [$_N$ ntfu]]] → /nebantfu/
      3: na [$_x$ *I* [$_{ac}$ mu [$_N$ ti]]] → /nemuti/
      4: na [$_x$ *I* [$_{ac}$ mi [$_N$ ti]]] → /nemiti/
      5: na [$_x$ *I* [$_{ac}$ li [$_N$ butfo]]] → /nelibutfo/
      6: na [$_x$ *I* [$_{ac}$ ma [$_N$ butfo]]] → /nemabutfo/

In syntactic environments where the augment falls away, *na* surfaces unchanged both in Xhosa/Zulu and in Swati[7]:

(38) *na* "with" plus a noun under Neg: noun under Neg:

class		
1:	*namuntfu*	*muntfu* "man"
2:	*nabantfu*	*bantfu* "men"
3:	*namuti*	*muti* "village"
4:	*namiti*	*miti* "villages"
5:	*nalibutfo*	*libutfo* "regiment"
6:	*namabutfo*	*mabutfo* "regiments"

This is exactly as expected on the analysis of Xhosa/Zulu suggested by (35). For Swati, we need to assume that the latent *i* (represented as *I* in (37)) is part of the augment:

(39) class 1: na [$_{AC}$ mu [$_N$ ntfu]] → /namuntfu/
      2: na [$_{AC}$ ba [$_N$ ntfu]] → /nabantfu/
      3: na [$_{aAC}$ mu [$_N$ ti]] → /namuti/
      4: na [$_{AC}$ mi [$_N$ ti]] → /namiti/
      5: na [$_{AC}$ li [$_N$ butfo]] → /nabutfo/
      6: na [$_{AC}$ ma [$_N$ butfo]] → /namabutfo/

More precisely, I take the augment to have the structure in (40) in Swati except that, for reasons that remain to be understood, the constituent SC is not included when a noun is embedded under *na*:

(40) [[$_{SC}$ N$_i$ [$_{Aug}$ #$_i$]] *I*]

---

[7] Obviously, this speaks against the Taraldsen's (2010) proposal that the augment is never projected on top of nouns in Swati.

If so, it follows easily that the initial vowel is *e* rather than *a* in class 6 in Swati. In class 6, the #$_i$ in (40) is lexicalized by the V-morpheme *a* just like the # inside the basic prefix:

(41) [[$_{SC}$ Ø [$_{Aug}$ *a*]] *I*] [$_{AC}$ *m* [$_{SC}$ Ø [$_{Aug}$ *a*]]]

But coalescence converts the string *aI* to *e*.

When the vowel preceding *I* is *u* or *i*, the latent *i* has no detectable effect just as in (32). But one may wonder why the class 2 prefix is *ba* rather than *be*, since the vowel preceding *I* is *a* just as in class 6:

(42) [[$_{SC}$ *b* [$_{Aug}$ *a*]] *I*] [$_{AC}$ *b̶* [$_{SC}$ *b̶* [$_{Aug}$ *a*]]]

3.3 Vowel elision

Notice that coalescence and deletion of *b* inside the AC yields (43) where a CV-shaped constituent immediately precedes a vowel:

(43) [*be*] [*a*]

At this point, it becomes important to observe what happens when SCs are added to V-initial verbs, e.g. *enta* 'do' (Ziervogel & Mabuza (1976: 95):

(44) basic SC: on a V-initial verb:
cl		
1	u	w-enta
2	ba	b-enta
3	u	w-enta
4	i	y-enta
5	li	l-enta
6	a	Ø-enta
7	si	s-enta
8	ti	t-enta
9	i	y-enta
10	ti	t-enta
11	lu	lw-enta
14	bu	b-enta
15	ku	kw-enta

The vowel of the SC turns into a glide when it is *i* not preceded by a consonant or *u* not preceded by a labial consonant. Otherwise it is elided. We may then take it that the *e* preceding *a* is elided in (43) as well yielding *ba*. Thus, the difference between class 6 and class 2 follows from the fact that the *e* resulting from coalesced *aI* is immediately followed by a consonant, i.e. *m*, in (41), but not in (42).

The reason that *e* is not followed by a consonant in (42) is that the second *b* is erased in accordance with the analysis of the Swati paradigm in (25) forced by the approach proposed in section 3. But according to this analysis the C-morpheme inside the AC is erased only when it is identical to the C-morpheme in the augment as is always the case in the strong classes when nouns are not used as predicates. When nouns are used predicatively, however, there are exceptions from this pattern. So-called copulative forms of nouns may be formed by prefixing *ng* or *y* to the initial vowel in the weak classes:

(45) a. *ng-u-m- fati* (class 1)
COP-SC1-AC1-woman
'It is a woman.'
b. *ng-e-ma-khasi* (class 6)
COP-SC6- AC6-leaf
'It is leaves.'
c. *y-i-mi-fula* (class 4)
COP-SC4-AC4-river
'It is rivers.'

We may take *ng/y* to replace the C-morpheme Ø in the augment:

(46) [[$_{SC}$ *ng/y* [$_{Aug}$ V]] *I*] [$_{AC}$ *m* [$_{SC}$ Ø [$_{Aug}$ V]]]

Class 2 is the only strong class that can form copulatives the same way as the weak classes:

(47) *ng-e-ba-fati*
COP-IV-SC2-woman
'It is women.'

Notice that now an *e* appears even in class 2. This is exactly as our analysis predicts. Since the C-morpheme *b* doesn't also appear in the augment, the *b* in the AC is not erased, and the *e* resulting from coalescence therefore does not end up directly preceding a vowel:

(48) [[$_{SC}$ ng [$_{Aug}$ a]] I] [$_{AC}$ b [$_{SC}$ b [$_{Aug}$ a]]]

Thus, the occurrences of e that appeared problematic seem to receive a coherent account after all within the only account of the Swati paradigm consistent with the general account of class prefixes proposed in section 2.

By contrast, the wrinkle cannot be easily removed on the analysis based on Taraldsen (2010). Even though Taraldsen (2010) also suggests that the unexpected e may be the outcome of coalescence between a and a following latent i, this necessarily remains an ad hoc proposal in the context of the analysis of class prefixes pursued there. In particular, a latent i cannot be assumed for all the noun classes. In class 6, the latent i has to come between SC and AC in the general structural template assumed for Swati:

(49) [$_{SC}$ a [*I* [$_{AC}$ ma [N]]]

But then there would be an intervening *I* blocking lexicalization of the heads SC and AC by a single CV-shaped morpheme in the strong classes leading to the incorrect prediction that the class 2 prefix should be *beba with ba lexicalizing SC and AC separately:

(50) [SC [*I* [AC [N]]]]
　　　|　 　|
　　　ba　ba

If the CV-shaped morphemes were allowed to span all the three heads preceding the N. the CV-shaped morphemes would also lexicalize the *I* together with AC even when SC is absent, and so the analysis would fail to predict the uniform conversion of na to ne in (34) and the e in copulative class 2 forms.

4 The weak classes

I now return to an issue raised in section 2.2. Since the C-morpheme Ø combines with all three V-morphemes in the weak classes in Xhosa, it seems that we must posit an arbitrary syncretism between different Ns as in (17):

(17) | Gender | N | # = singular | # = plural |
| --- | --- | --- | --- |
| A | $Ø_4$ | | i |
| B | $Ø_{1,3,6}$ | u | a |

A similar conclusion suggests itself for the *k* occurring in all weak classes in Lubukusu and for the *y/w* in Rhonga and Changana (see footnote 4).

In this section, I suggest a way of getting around this conclusion. The proposal made in 4.1 is that the Xhosa Ø and its counterparts in Lubukusu and Tsonga languages isn't actually a classifier N, like the C-morphemes in the strong classes, but rather the lexicalization of a functional head. The proposal will rest on the assumption that the syntax of the weak class prefixes is different from the syntax of the strong class prefixes, and subsections 4.2 and 4.3 present some facts that seem to support this view.

4.1 A difference between weak and strong C-morphemes

We have seen three different C-morphemes occurring in all the weak classes: *m* at the AC-level (except in class 9), Ø inside SC and *ng/y* in the copulative forms. In addition, the weak forms used to express object-agreement (possibly object clitics) have distinct C-morphemes[8]:

(51) class 1 *m*   class 2 *ba*
           3 *wu*   4 *yi*
           5 *li*   6 *wa*
           7 *si*   8 *zi*
           9 *yi*   10 *zi*
           11 *lu*
           14 *bu*
           15 *ku*

By contrast, the strong classes have the same C-morpheme in all these cases.

The context-sensitivity exhibited by the C-morphemes in the weak classes suggests that they may be exponents of case-related properties. Adopting Caha's (2009) view of cases as syntactic structures composed of primitive case-heads, one would then say that the different C-morphemes occurring in the weak classes lexicalize different such structures in accordance with the nano-syntactic approach adopted by Caha (leaving out the copulative forms):

---

[8] The initial glides in (51) are not just hiatus breakers appearing in object-agreement markers, because these typically follow a vowel-final SC or TAM element: In imperatives, the object-marker is not preceded by any other element, and yet the it always has an initial glide in the weak classes.

(52) a. AC = m = [X [Y [Z]]]
   b. OC = y/w = [Y [Z]]
   c. SC = Ø = [Z]

Seen as exponents of case, the morphemes in (52) should also appear in the strong classes, but don't. A possibility is that each strong C-morpheme lexicalizes all three case-structures in (52) in addition to the classifier N they sit on top of[9]:

(53) C_i ⟷ [X [Y [Z [N_i]]]]

Each N_i in (53) would be a specific noun acting as a classifier in accordance with the conclusions reached in section 1.2.

Suppose now that there are no morphemes capable of lexicalizing a case-structure together with any of classifying Ns occurring in the weak classes as a matter of accidental lexical gaps. Then, the case-structures on top of N in (54) cannot be lexicalized in the weak classes unless the N moves away, if lexicalization only applies to constituents as assumed in Taraldsen et al. (2018)[10]:

(54) [X [Y [Z [N_i]]]]

The morphemes in (52) are the only morphemes capable of lexicalizing case-structures in isolation from the classifier N.[11] Therefore, m, y/w and Ø emerge in the weak classes as a result of N_i moving out of the three structures subsumed by (54).

At this point, we may hope to be able to connect with an idea in Kayne (2005): Syntactic constituents at a phase edge need not be spelled out. In other words, the hope is that weak Ns moving out of (54) move to a phase edge and therefore remain silent. If so, the syntax of the weak class prefixes must differ from the syntax of the strong class prefixes, since the strong C-morphemes b, l etc. must still be considered spell-outs of the classifying N (with case heads on top).

---

9 The Superset Principle (see Caha 2009, Starke 2009 among others) allows a morpheme associated in the lexicon with a tree T to lexicalize any piece of syntactic structure matching a constituent of T.
10 Following Starke (2009) and Pantcheva (2011), the lexicalization procedure disregards traces when determining constituency.
11 A morpheme C_i with the lexical entry in (53) will not be able to lexicalize [X [Y [Z]]], [Y [Z]] or Z if the lowest head in the structure lexically associated with C_i must be included in any syntactic structure lexicalized by C_i as proposed by Abels and Muriungi (2008).

4.2 The demonstratives

A particular fact about the shape of demonstratives in Xhosa may support the idea that the weak and the strong class prefixes involve different syntactic operations.

The basic demonstratives seem to be built on the pattern in (55) in Zulu and Swati:

(55) $l\ [_{of}\ a\ [_{Aug}\ V\ [_{SC}\ C\ [_{Aug}\ V\ ]]]]$

In this structure, the AC-layer is not included. This has the effect that although the C-morphemes that appear in SCs also occur inside the demonstratives, *m*, which only occurs at the AC-level is excluded from the demonstratives.[12]

The resulting Zulu forms are those in (56), where the first vowel is the outcome of coalescing *a* "of" with the following V:

(56) class 1 *lo*   class 2 *laba*
     3 *lo*   4 *le*
     5 *leli*   6 *la*
     7 *lesi*   8 *lezi*
     9 *le*   10 *lezi*
     11 *lolu*
     14 *lobu*
     15 *loku*

But Xhosa is slightly different in that the initial *l* only occurs in the weak classes, e.g. the demonstrative is *lo* in class 1, but *aba* in class 2, and this suggests an analysis different from (55):

(57) $[_{of}\ a\ [_{Aug}\ V\ [_{AC}\ X\ [_{SC}\ C\ [_{Aug}\ V\ ]]]]$
                            |
                           l/m

The idea is that *l* must originate at X preventing *m* from appearing there. As before, the Zulu paradigm in (56) is generated, since all C-morphemes other

---

[12] In Rhonga and Changana, the SC has the C-morphemes *y* and *w* in the weak classes rather than Ø (see footnote 4). Correspondingly, *y* and *w* also occur inside the weak demonstratives, e.g. class 4 *leyi* and class 6 *lawa*.

than *m* can occur inside the SC. For example, the class 2 demonstrative *laba* can have the derivation in (58):

(58) [$_{of}$ *a* [$_{Aug}$ *a* [$_{AC}$ *l* [$_{SC}$ *b* [$_{Aug}$ *a*]]]] → [*l* [$_{of}$ *a* [$_{Aug}$ *a* [$_{AC}$ *l̵* [$_{SC}$ *b* [$_{Aug}$ *a*]]]]]

For Xhosa, we might then say that the strong Ns (lexicalized by C) must also move to X blocking *l*:

(59) [$_{of}$ *a* [$_{Aug}$ *a* [$_{AC}$ X [$_{SC}$ *b* [$_{Aug}$ *a*]]]] → [$_{of}$ *a* [$_{Aug}$ *a* [$_{AC}$ *b* [$_{SC}$ *b̵* [$_{Aug}$ *a*]]]]

Of course, this suggestion needs to be elaborated in various ways and optimally in such a way that it connects with the idea that the classifier N raises to a phase edge in the weak classes, but not so in the strong classes. However, the basic claim that the contrast between the weak and the strong demonstratives in Xhosa is syntactic in nature, seems plausible.

4.3 SCs on *ka*

Another relevant fact has to do with possessive constructions. The general pattern in Xhosa is that the possessee occurs first, then the "associative" *a* "of" followed by the possessor. In addition, *a* is prefixed by a SC marking agreement with the possessee:

(60) a. *i-n-ja y-o-m-ntwana*
 9-9-dog SC9-of.Aug1-1-child
 "the child's dog"
 b. *i-n-ja y-a-ba-ntwana*
 9-9-dog SC9-of.Aug2-2-child
 "the children's dog"

However, when the possessor is in class 1a (proper names, kinship terms and inanimate class 1 nouns), *a* is replaced by *ka*, and then an SC appears only if the noun denoting the possessee belongs to one of the strong classes:

(61) a. *i-n-ja ka-Peter*
 9-9-dog of-Peter
 "Peter's dog"
 b. *i-zi-n-ja zi-ka-Peter*
 10-10-10-dog SC10-of-Peter
 "Peter's dogs"

This contrast between weak and strong SCs also seems to call for a syntactic explanation insofar as there is no morpho-phonological reason why the weak SCs should not appear preceding the possessive *ka*.

5 Conclusion

The main goal of this article has been to take a fresh look at the structures underlying the nominal class prefixes in Nguni languages. In particular, I have argued that the CV-shaped basic prefixes are bimorphemic with a C-morpheme lexicalizing a classifier-like N (in the strong classes) or case-related heads (in the weak classes) and a V-morpheme spelling out number and gender (under agreement with the classifier N). In the weak classes, the classifier N is moved to a phase edge and left unpronounced.

If this is approximately correct, we reach an unorthodox conclusion. Frequently, the noun classes in Bantu are identified with genders, e.g. in Carstens (1991). Taking paired singular and plural classes to have the same gender, a language like Xhosa would then have eight different genders, but would otherwise not be different from Romance or Germanic. Instead, I claim that Bantu languages are really classifier languages, and that each noun class is defined by the semantics of a distinct classifier N lexicalized by the prefix. Thus, noun classes are dissociated from gender.

On the other hand, each classifier N is associated with grammatical gender much like ordinary nouns in Romance or Germanic, but unlike ordinary nouns in Bantu. In fact, Nguni has a two-gender system (like Italian and Dutch) according to the proposal in section 2.2. As a corollary, it must be possible for a language to have both classifiers and grammatical gender, i.e. classifier systems and gender systems must be kept distinct.

Another somewhat unorthodox feature of the proposals I have made, is that the structures underlying the class prefixes are syntactic phrases to which syntactic operations may apply, as suggested in section 4. This is at odds with traditional accounts treating prefix+noun combinations as purely morphological entities, but is in agreement with much work aiming at obliterating the strict division line between syntax and morphology.

References

Abels, Klaus, and Peter Muriungi. 2008. The focus particle in Kîîtharaka: Syntax and semantics. *Lingua* 118. 687–731

Caha, Pavel. 2009. *The nanosyntax of case*. Tromsø: University of Tromsø dissertation

Carstens, Vicky. 1991. *The morphology and syntax of determiner phrases in Kiswahili*. Los Angeles: UCLA dissertation

Carstens, Vicky.1997. Null nouns in Bantu locatives. *The Linguistic Review* 14. 361–410

Kayne, Richard S. 2005. *Movement and Silence*. New York: Oxford University Press.

Pantcheva, Marina B. 2011. *Decomposing Path. The nanosyntax of directional expressions*. Tromsø: University of Tromsø dissertation

Starke, Michal. 2009. A short primer to a new approach to language. *Nordlyd* 36(1). 1–6

Taraldsen, Knut Tarald. 2010. The nanosyntax of Nguni noun class prefixes and concords. *Lingua* 120. 1522–1548.

Taraldsen, Knut Tarald, Lucie Taraldsen Medová and David Langa. 2018. Class prefixes as specifiers in Southern Bantu. *Natural Language and Linguistic Theory* 36 (4). 1339–1394

Jeroen van Craenenbroeck
Expletives, locatives, and subject doubling

1 Introduction

This paper focuses on *there*-expletives in a Brabant dialect of Dutch and shows how they display behavior that perfectly parallels that of regular subject pronouns in this dialect.[1] The paper is organized as follows. The next section provides some background on the pronominal system of the dialect under discussion here. I show that it makes a distinction between three types of pronouns (strong, weak, clitic), and that it features two types of pronominal doubling. Section 3 presents the new data and shows how expletive elements fit into the pronominal system outlined in the preceding section: they too make a distinction between deficient and strong forms, and they can undergo both types of pronominal doubling. In addition, I show that contrary to what is commonly assumed in the literature, the proximate locative adverb *here* can also display expletive(-like) behavior. Section 4 considers the implications of these data for existing analyses of *there*-expletives. I show that neither the standard Minimalist account nor predication-based theories are particularly suited to deal with these facts, and sketch the outlines of an alternative approach. Section 5 sums up and concludes.

2 Background: The pronominal system

2.1 Introduction

The central data in this paper come from one dialect of Dutch, namely that of the village of Wambeek (situated in the Belgian province of Brabant, close to

---

[1] Many thanks to Will Harwood, Sabine Iatridou, Dany Jaspers, Marjo van Koppen, Koen Roelandt, Jolijn Sonnaert, Cora Pots, Guido Vanden Wyngaerd, and the students of my Spring 2016 morphology class for discussion of the material presented in this paper. A special thanks also to Hilda Van Der Borght and Jef Van Craenenbroeck for invaluable help with the judgments. It gives me great pleasure to be able to dedicate this paper to Rita Manzini. It combines a number of topics which I know are dear to her heart – dialect syntax, subject doubling, expletives, and (apparent) homophony between functional categories – so I very much look forward to her insightful comments.

Jeroen van Craenenbroeck, KU Leuven/CRISSP

https://doi.org/10.1515/9781501505201-032

the border with East Flanders).² This section provides an introduction into the pronominal system of this dialect. It is against this backdrop that the expletive data in the next section will be presented and interpreted. I highlight two aspects of the Wambeek Dutch pronominal system: (1) the fact that Cardinaletti & Starke (1999)'s tripartition into strong, weak, and clitic pronouns is also applicable to this dialect (subsection 2.2), and (2) the fact that subject pronouns can undergo two types of pronominal doubling (subsection 2.3).

2.2 Three degrees of deficiency

As is well-known, Cardinaletti & Starke (1999) (henceforth C&S) provide an analysis of the internal structure and complexity of the pronominal system and in so doing arrive at a tripartition of increasingly structurally complex pronominal forms. Their system can be summarized as follows:

(1)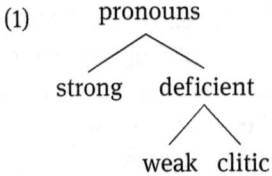

The first distinction is between strong and deficient pronouns, and the latter group can be further subdivided into weak pronouns on the one hand and clitics on the other. The three groups can be distinguished from one another on semantic, morphosyntactic, and phonological/prosodic grounds. C&S don't discuss Dutch pronouns (let alone non-standard varieties of this language), but Van Craenenbroeck & van Koppen (2000) show that the same tripartition can be applied to a variety of Dutch dialects (see also Haegeman 1990, 1992, 1993 for related discussion based on West Flemish). Consider for example the forms for the first person plural subject pronoun in the dialect of Wambeek in (2).

---

2 Informal consultation with informants from other dialects and regiolects as well as some preliminary corpus research suggests that the data patterns discussed in this paper are by no means restricted to this one dialect, but a systematic exploration of the variation in this area will have to await another occasion. For some discussion of expletive-related dialectal diversity in Dutch, see Haegeman 1986 and Van Craenenbroeck 2011.

(2) me / we / waaile
     we we we
     'we'

These three forms for the first person plural correspond nicely to the tripartition in (1). Let us use two tests from Van Craenenbroeck & van Koppen (2000) to illustrate this. First of all, as pointed out by C&S, strong pronouns differ from deficient ones in that they can be clefted. As shown in (3), this distinguishes the form *waaile* from the other two in (2).

(3) T   zen { * me / * we / waaile } da   da   muten duun.
     it are   we   we   we   that that must do
     'It's we who have to do that.'

On the other hand, pronominal clitics in (varieties of) Dutch are typically enclitic, which means that they differ from both weak and strong pronouns in being disallowed in sentence-initial position[3]:

(4) { * Me / We / Waaile } komme mergen.
         we   we   we   come   tomorrow
     'We're coming tomorrow.'

When taken together (and in combination with the other tests discussed in Van Craenenbroeck & van Koppen 2000), the examples in (3) and (4) provide a unique characterisation for each of the three forms in (2), thus lending credence to the hypothesis that the C&S-tripartition is operative in Wambeek Dutch as well. One thing that should be pointed out, though, is that it is relatively rare to find three morphologically distinct forms for the same pronoun. By far the more common pattern is one that only distinguishes between a strong and a deficient form. Given that this is also the pattern we will come across in the expletive paradigm in the next section, it is worth looking at it in a little more detail here. Consider in this respect the forms for the third person feminine singular subject pronoun in (5).

---

[3] Another way of interpreting the pattern in (4) is via C&S's claim that while weak and strong pronouns are XPs, clitics are syntactic heads. If this is on the right track, the clitic *me* would be unable to satisfy the V2-requirement of Wambeek Dutch.

(5) ze / zaai
    she she
    'she'

We can interpret such forms in (at least) three ways: (1) there is no subject clitic for the third person feminine singular in Wambeek Dutch, (2) there is no weak subject pronoun for the third person feminine singular in Wambeek Dutch, or (3) the subject clitic and weak subject pronoun for the third person feminine singular are homophonous in Wambeek Dutch. The following table schematically represents the three options:

(6)

clitic	weak	strong
	ze	zaai
ze		zaai
ze	ze	zaai

The next subsection will show that there are good reasons to think that the third option is correct: one type of subject doubling is limited to clitics, while another excludes clitics, and *ze* is able to participate in both.

2.3 Two types of doubling

Many of the Flemish dialects of Dutch exhibit subject doubling (see Haegeman 1991, 1992; Van Craenenbroeck & van Koppen 2002, 2008; De Vogelaer 2005; De Vogelaer & Devos 2008 for discussion and references). An important thing to note about this phenomenon is that it comes in two types. The first is illustrated in the following example.

(7) We   emme waaile   ie   niks   te zieken.
    we$_{weak}$ have we$_{strong}$ here nothing to seek
    'We have no business being here.'

In this example the subject is expressed twice: once in clause-initial position by the weak pronoun *we* 'we' and once in post-verbal position by the strong pronoun *waaile* 'we'. While the status of the second subject element is fixed – i.e. it is always a strong subject pronoun – the first is subject to variation. In particular, apart from weak pronouns, also strong pronouns, full DPs (9), and proper names (10) can be doubled in this way. Clitics, however, are excluded, as shown in (11).[4]

(8) Waaile emme waaile ie niks te zieken.
we$_{strong}$ have we$_{strong}$ here nothing to seek
'We have no business being here.'

(9) Dei vrau ei zaai ie niks te zieken.
that woman has she$_{strong}$ here nothing to seek
'That woman has no business being here.'

(10) Marie ei zaai ie niks te zieken.
Marie has she$_{strong}$ here nothing to seek
'Marie has no business being here.'

(11) *Me emme waaile ie niks te zieken.
we$_{clitic}$ have we$_{strong}$ here nothing to seek
INTENDED: 'We have no business being here.'

The generalization that weak pronouns can but clitics cannot be doubled in this way allows us to go back to an issue that was raised in the previous subsection, i.e. the status of the deficient third person feminine singular subject pronoun *ze*. As shown in (12), this element can occur in sentence-initial position in a doubling configuration, showing that it should at least be analyzed as a weak pronoun (while still leaving open the option that it is homophonous between a clitic and a weak pronoun).

(12) Ze ei zaai ie niks te zieken.
she$_{weak}$ has she$_{strong}$ here nothing to seek
'She has no business being here.'

The type of doubling illustrated in the preceding examples is commonly referred to as topic doubling (for reasons that will become clear below). It is

---

[4] The precise status of the sentence-initial pronominal element – clitic or weak pronoun? – is an issue that has garnered some discussion in the literature, see esp. the debate between Haegeman 1992, 2004 and Van Craenenbroeck & Van Koppen 2002, 2007b. However, given that most of the controversy is about (a dialect of) West Flemish, not about the dialect under consideration here, I gloss over it in what follows.

restricted to subject-initial main clauses, i.e. it does not occur in embedded clauses (13) or in inverted main clauses (14).

(13) *omda waaile waaile ie niks te zieken emmen.
because we$_{strong}$ we$_{strong}$ here nothing to seek have
INTENDED: 'because we have no business being here.'

(14) *Gisteren aume waaile waaile ie niks te zieken.
yesterday had we$_{strong}$ we$_{strong}$ hier nothing to seek
INTENDED: 'We had no business being here yesterday.'

As for the analysis of topic doubling, Van Craenenbroeck & van Koppen (2002) propose to treat it as a case of multiple spell-out: the subject moves from the canonical subject position (say, specTP) into the left periphery,[5] and rather than undergoing deletion, the lower copy of this movement chain is spelled out as a strong pronoun. The structure in (15) gives a schematic representation of this analysis for the example in (8).

(15)

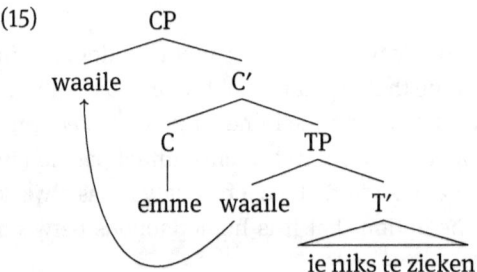

A major advantage of this type of approach is that it provides a straightforward explanation for the distribution of topic doubling. Given that the analysis crucially involves specCP as one of its ingredients, the account correctly predicts that topic doubling should be absent in embedded clauses (where specCP cannot be filled in Dutch, cf. Hoekstra & Zwart 1994) and inverted main clauses (where specCP is filled by some other element, cf. the adverb *gisteren* 'yesterday' in (14)).

---

[5] More specifically, to specTop, whence the name topic doubling. See Van Craenenbroeck & Van Koppen 2002 for certain interpretive effects in topic doubling with indefinite and interrogative subjects supporting this analysis.

The second type of subject doubling attested in Dutch dialects (including Wambeek Dutch) is clitic doubling. It is illustrated in (16).

(16) omdat   n   aai   ma guid elpen.
     because he$_{clitic}$ he$_{strong}$ me goes help
     'because he's going to help me.'

A clitic-doubled subject always consists of a clitic as the first subject element and a strong pronoun as the second element.[6] Note that clitic doubling can also involve the deficient pronoun *ze* 'she' as its first element, cf. (17). In combination with the topic doubling sentence in (12), this example thus shows that Wambeek Dutch has both a clitic and a weak pronoun for the third person feminine singular, but that they happen to be homophonous (i.e. the third option in the table in (6)).

(17) omda   ze   zaai   ma guid elpen.
     because she$_{clitic}$ she$_{strong}$ me goes help
     'because she's going to help me.'

Clitic doubling only occurs in embedded clauses (17) and inverted main clauses (18); it is disallowed in subject-initial main clauses (19).

(18) *Guit* n   aai   ma elpen?
     goes he$_{clitic}$ he$_{strong}$ me help
     'Is he going to help me?'

(19) **N   guid aai   ma elpen.*
     he$_{clitic}$ goes he$_{strong}$ me help
     INTENDED: 'He's going to help me.'

Rather than copy spell-out, Van Craenenbroeck & van Koppen (2008) propose that clitic doubling involves a so-called big DP (see also Belletti 2005; Uriagereka 1995; Laenzlinger 1998; Grohmann 2000; Poletto 2008; Kayne 2005), whereby a clitic doubled subject like *ze zaai* in (17) starts life as a single DP, and the occurrence of the clitic is due to subextraction of part of that DP. More specifically,

---

6 See Van Craenenbroeck & van Koppen 2008 for some exceptions involving coordinations of pronouns. As this complication is not relevant in the context of this paper, I don't discuss it here.

Van Craenenbroeck and Van Koppen use the tests from Déchaine & Wiltschko (2002) to show that while Wambeek Dutch strong subject pronouns are DPs, subject clitics are ϕPs:

(20) **stong subject prounoun**

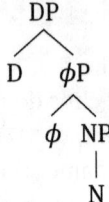

(21) **subject clitic**

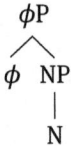

This means that subject clitics are quite literally subparts of strong subject pronouns. Clitic doubling now arises when a ϕP subextracts from DP (in this particular case because it is attracted by C, see the original paper for details): the moving ϕP is spelled out as the clitic and the remaining DP as the strong pronoun:

(22) **clitic doubled subject pronoun**

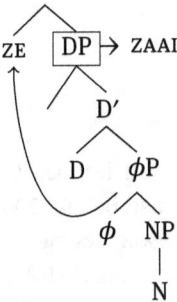

Note that nothing precludes topic doubling and clitic doubling from co-occurring in one and the same example: a sentence-initial subject element could be topic doubled by a strong subject pronoun, which is in turn clitic doubled by a subject clitic. Such cases of tripling do indeed occur:

(23) We   emme   me   waaile   ie   niks   te   zieken.
     we_weak have   we_clitic we_strong here nothing to   seek
     'We have no business being here.'

This concludes my overview of the subject doubling options in Wambeek Dutch. Before turning to expletives, however, there is one point that has remained implicit in the discussion so far but is worth emphasizing in the context of what follows: the only type of pronominal doubling attested in Dutch dialects is *subject* doubling. In other words, doubling of any other type of constituent is categorically ruled out. The following examples illustrate this for direct objects: both topic doubling (24) and clitic doubling (25) of direct objects is completely impossible.

(24) *Em   em   ik   em   gezien.
     him_strong have   I   him_strong seen
     INTENDED: 'I saw him yesterday.'

(25) *da   k   n   gisteren   em   wou   elpen.
     that I   him_clitic   yesterday him_strong wanted   help
     INTENDED: 'that I wanted to help him yesterday.'

This ban on non-subject doubling also applies to locative expressions. The following examples illustrate this for topic doubling. Note that the result is ill-formed regardless of whether the locative adverb is an argument (26) or an adjunct (27).[7]

(26) *Dui   em   ek   dui   gewoentj.
     there   have   I   there   lived
     INTENDED: 'I used to live there.'

(27) *Dui   ei   Jef Marie dui   gezien.
     there   has   Jef   Marie there   seen
     INTENDED: 'Jef saw Marie there.'

---

[7] These examples are grammatical under an irrelevant reading, whereby the two *there*'s refer to different (sizes or types of) locations, e.g. in (26) to indicate that in that city (there$_1$) I used to live in that house (there$_2$). I abstract away from such readings here and in the remainder of the paper. See Maienborn 2001 for relevant discussion.

As for the question of whether locative expressions can be clitic doubled, that requires first establishing that Wambeek Dutch has locative clitics to begin with. Interestingly, the structural configuration of subject clitic doubling provides a clear diagnostic for this. As pointed out by Van Craenenbroeck & van Koppen (2007a), the only elements that can intervene between the two parts of a clitic doubled subject are other clitics. This can be illustrated on the basis of pronouns that make a morphophonological distinction between weak and clitic pronouns (see above, subsection 2.2). Consider in this respect the following examples.

(28) da   ze   { n   /* em   } zaai   gezien eit.
     that she$_{clitic}$ him$_{DO.clitic}$ him$_{DO.weak}$ she$_{strong}$ seen   has
     'that she saw him.'

(29) da   ze   zaai   {* n   / em   } gezien eit.
     that she$_{clitic}$ she$_{strong}$ him$_{DO.clitic}$ him$_{DO.weak}$ seen   has
     'that she saw him.'

The third person masculine singular deficient object pronoun in Wambeek Dutch makes a morphophonological distinction between the clitic *n* and the weak pronoun *em*. As these examples show, when the object occurs in between the two parts of a clitic doubled subject, only the clitic form can be used, while to the right of the strong subject pronoun only the weak pronoun can appear. More generally, the possibility of occurring in between the two parts of a clitic doubled subject can be used as a diagnostic for clitichood in this dialect. Applying this test to the reduced form of the locative pronoun yields the following example.

(30) da   ze   er   zaai   gewoendj eit.
     that she$_{clitic}$ there she$_{strong}$ lived   has
     'that she has lived there.'

The fact that the reduced form of the locative pronoun can occur in between the two halves of a clitic doubled subject shows that it is – or at least can be – a clitic. This means that we can now legitimately ask whether a locative expression can be clitic doubled. As the following example shows, the answer is negative.

(31) *da   ze   er   zaai   dui   gewoendj eit.
     that she$_{clitic}$ there she$_{strong}$ there lived   has
     INTENDED: 'that she has lived there.'

Summing up, this subsection has shown that Wambeek Dutch has two types of subject doubling. The first, topic doubling, involves a variety of subject expressions in first position and a strong subject pronoun in second position, and it is only found in subject-initial main clauses. The second is clitic doubling. It consists of a clitic pronoun and a strong pronoun, and only shows up in embedded clauses and inverted main clauses. The two doubling processes can co-occur in one and the same example, resulting in subject tripling. Non-subjects can never be doubled, regardless of which doubling strategy is used. This also holds for locative expressions.

3 The new data: Expletives as part of the pronominal system

3.1 Introduction

This section focuses on the expletive system of Wambeek Dutch. Just like English – and Standard Dutch for that matter – this dialects uses expletive pronouns that are morphologically related to locative adverbs. What I will show is that these expletive forms fit perfectly into the pronominal system of the dialect as outlined in the previous section. In particular, they make a distinction between strong and deficient expletive forms, with the latter being homophonous between clitics and weak pronouns (subsection 3.2), and they can be both topic and clitic doubled (subsection 3.3). In addition, I show that even though it never loses its locative interpretation, the proximate locative adverb *here* can also display expletive-like behavior in this dialect (subsection 3.4).

3.2 Strong vs. deficient expletives

As is well-known (see for example Bennis 1986), Standard Dutch makes use of the form *er* 'there' as its expletive element in *there*-sentences. This *er* is the weak or reduced form of the distal locative adverb *daar* 'there', which is not used as an expletive. At first glance, Wambeek Dutch is no different in this respect: it uses the weak form *d'r* as its expletive pronoun. This is illustrated in (32)–(34).[8]

---

[8] Due to voice assimilation and /t/-deletion, the deficient expletive pronoun can surface as *d'r*, *t'r*, or *er*. Given that I have been unable to find any differences in syntactic behavior

(32) *D'r stui ne vantj inn of.*
    ER stands a man in.the garden
    'There's a man in the garden.'

(33) *Stuit t'r ne vantj inn of?*
    stands ER a man in.the garden
    'Is there a man in the garden?'

(34) *da t'r ne vantj inn of stuit.*
    that ER a man in.the garden stands
    'that there is a man in the garden.'

Unlike in Standard Dutch, however, the strong form of the distal locative adverb can also be used as an expletive pronoun in Wambeek Dutch. Consider in this respect the following example.

(35) *Dui stui ne vantj inn of.*
    there stands a man in.the garden
    'There's a man in the garden.'

As is clear from the English translation, the form *dui* 'there' adds no locative meaning to the sentence (or at least not necessarily, see fn. 10 below) and as such functions as a pure expletive here. This reading can be brought out more clearly by adding an additional, conflicting locative expression such as *ie* 'here' or *genner* 'over there' to the sentence.[9] This is illustrated in (36).

(36) *Dui stuid ie/genner ne vantj inn of.*
    there stands here/over.there a man in.the garden
    'There's a man here/over there in the garden.'

Moreover, the example in (35) becomes infelicitous in its intended meaning when the associate DP *ne vantj* 'a man' is replaced by a definite expression such as a proper name:

---

between these three forms, I treat them as different surface manifestations of the same underlying element, and I gloss all of them as ER.

[9] Wambeek Dutch has a tripartite distance-based locative system, which makes a distinction between proximate *ie* 'here', medial/distal *dui* 'there', and distal *genner* 'over there' (a cognate of the archaic English form *yonder*).

(37) # Dui stui Jef inn of.
 there stands Jef in.the garden

This example is not ungrammatical, but has a very specific interpretation. Imagine for instance that we are looking through a bunch of photos. I could point at one and utter the sentence in (37) to indicate that in that picture (i.e. there), Jef is standing in the garden.[10] The purely existential reading, however, in which *dui* 'there' adds no locative information, is lost in this example.

Another way to clearly bring out the non-locative, i.e. expletive, use of *dui* 'there' concerns sentences in which a locative dimension is completely absent, such as the existential sentence in (38). As the number of prime numbers smaller than ten is not tied to a particular location, a locative reading for *dui* would lead to a pragmatically odd or infelicitous sentence. Given that the example is perfectly well-formed, however, such a locative reading is missing, and *dui* is being used as a pure expletive pronoun.

(38) Dui zen mo vier priemgetalle klanjer as tien.
 there are only four prime.numbers smaller as ten
 'There are only four prime numbers smaller than ten.'

Note that the expletive use of *dui* is not restricted to sentence initial position. The declarative existential in (38) can be turned into an inverted main clause (39) or an embedded clause (40), without loss of the expletive reading.

(39) Zen dui mo vier priemgetalle klanjer as tien?
 are there only four prime.numbers smaller as ten
 'Are there only four prime numbers smaller than ten?'

(40) omda dui mo vier priemgetalle klanjer zen as tien.
 because there only four prime.numbers smaller are as ten
 'because here are only four prime numbers smaller than ten.'

Summing up, Wambeek Dutch has both a strong and a deficient expletive pronoun, and as such its expletive constructions mimic the structure of its pronominal system. Moreover, the two expletives are not completely interchangeable.

---

10 That same reading – *mutatis mutandis* – is also available in (35). Note that in both cases, the locative reading of *dui* requires heavy stress on this element. See below for more detailed illustration and ways of disambiguating such sentences.

For example, let's compare the two *dui*-examples in (39) and (40) with their *d'r*-counterparts in (41) and (42).

(41) Zen er mo   vier priemgetalle   klanjer as tien?
     are ER only four prime.numbers   smaller as ten
     'Are there only four prime numbers smaller than ten?'

(42) omda   t'r mo   vier priemgetalle   klanjer zen as tien.
     because ER   only four prime.numbers   smaller are as ten
     'because there are only four prime numbers smaller than ten.'

The examples in (41) and (42) are the most neutral way of expressing either the question or the (embedded) statement that there are only four prime numbers smaller than ten. The sentences in (39) and (40) express the same propositional content, but add emphasis or surprise, or they contradict a negative presupposition or a preceding statement. For example, one of my informants gives as a context for the question in (39) a math quiz, where someone has just listed the prime numbers smaller than ten and I want to grill him some more by asking something like 'Are there *really* only four prime numbers smaller than ten?' or 'Are you *sure* that there are only four prime numbers smaller than ten?'. This means that it is not only the case that Wambeek Dutch makes use of strong and deficient forms both in its pronominal and in its expletive system, the added emphasis that goes along with using a strong form is also present in both systems.

One question I have not tackled yet is what kind of deficient element *d'r* is exactly: a clitic or a weak pronoun? In order to answer that question it will be instructive to look at the doubling patterns expletive pronouns occur in. This is the topic of the next subsection.

3.3 Subject doubling of expletives

The strict subject requirement on pronominal doubling (see above, subsection 2.3) in combination with the fact that Wambeek Dutch has locative-based expletive pronouns allows us to test a central assumption that is shared by many existing accounts of *there*-expletives, namely the fact that *there* occupies the structural subject position (see Hartmann 2008:chapter 1 and section 4 below for an overview of different types of analyses, and see Bennis 1986 for an analysis of Standard Dutch *er* that does not share this assumption). Barring orthogonal intervening factors, expletive subjects should in principle be able to be doubled just like non-expletive ones (all the more so in light of the previous subsection, which has shown expletives to be like regular subject pronouns in having both strong and deficient forms). Let us first turn our attention to topic doubling. Consider the example in (43).

(43) Dui   eit   dui   niemand me   Jef geklapt.
     there has there no-one   with Jef talked
     'No-one spoke with Jef (there).'

This example contains two instances of the strong locative adverb *dui* 'there', with one of them clause-initial and the other in the immediately post-verbal position. As such, the example closely parallels the topic doubling one in (8). Note also that the example in (43) does not necessarily have a locative interpretation, suggesting that in (at least one version of) this example we are dealing with two instances of expletive *dui*, rather than, for example, a combination of expletive *dui* and locative *dui*. This can be brought out more clearly by adding a second, conflicting locative modifier, as in (44).

(44) Dui   leit dui   ie   e vliegsken op men and.
     there lies there here a fly.DIM   on my hand
     'There's a fly on my hand.'

The proximate locative adverb *ie* 'here' situates the state of affairs described in this sentence as being in the (extreme) vicinity of the speaker, thus showing that neither of the two *dui*'s adds any locative meaning.[11] Now, if (43) and (44) indeed represent cases of topic doubling of the expletive pronoun *dui*, we predict this pattern to be unavailable in embedded clauses and inverted main clauses (see above, examples (13) and (14)). At first glance, that prediction is not borne out, as the following two examples are perfectly well-formed:

(45) omda   dui   dui   niemand me   Jef geklapt eit.
     because there there no-one   with Jef talked has
     'because no-one spoke with Jef *(there).'

(46) Eit dui   dui   niemand me   Jef geklapt?
     has there there no-one   with Jef talked
     'Did no-one speak with Jef *(there)?'

---

11 Note that the example deliberately refers to a body part–and hence the extreme vicinity – of the speaker so as to make unlikely the kind of double locative reading described in fn. 7.

However, note that in both these examples there is an obligatory locative interpretation. This suggests that we are not dealing with pronominal doubling of the expletive element *dui*, but rather with a combination of expletive *dui* and locative *dui*. In other words, the type of doubling illustrated in (43) is restricted to subject-initial (or rather *dui*-initial) main clauses, exactly as would be expected from the description of topic doubling in subsection 2.3.[12] Summing up, the data just reviewed strongly suggests that, contrary to its homophonous locative counterpart (see above, the examples in (26) and (27)), the expletive use of the strong form *dui* 'there' can be topic doubled, just like regular subjects. This constitutes strong evidence in favor of analyzing *there*-expletives as occupying the structural subject position.

The existence of topic doubling in the expletive system also provides us with a first test to further determine the precise status of the deficient expletive form *d'r*. Recall from subsection 2.3 that weak pronouns can be topic doubled, but clitics cannot. If *d'r* can partake in expletive topic doubling, we know that it is (at least also) a weak pronoun. As the following example shows, this is indeed the case.

(47) *D'r leit dui ie e vliegsken op men and.*
ER lies there here a fly.DIM on my hand
'There's a fly on my hand.'

Turning next to the question of whether expletive subjects can also be clitic doubled, consider the following example.

(48) *dat er dui nen boek op tuifel leit.*
that ER there a book on tafel lies
'that there is a book (there) on the table.'

---

[12] For completeness' sake we can point out that the type of *dui*-doubling illustrated in (43) comes with a strong definiteness requirement on the thematic subject of the clause:

(i) * *Dui eit dui Marie me Jef geklapt.*
there has there Marie with Jef talked
INTENDED: 'Marie spoke with Jef (there).'

Note that this judgment is expected both under a topic doubling analysis of (43) and under an analysis of this example as containing a combination of expletive *dui* and locative *dui*. As such, it doesn't provide an additional argument in favor of the claim that expletives can be topic doubled in Wambeek Dutch.

The optionality of a locative interpretation in this example indicates that *dui* can once again be used as an expletive. Given that the sentence also contains an instance of the deficient expletive element *d'r*, this example features expletive doubling, albeit not topic doubling, but clitic doubling (see above, example (16)). This is further confirmed when we add another, conflicting locative modifier:

(49) dat er dui ie nen boek op tuifel leit.
 that ER there here a book on tafel lies
 'that there is a book here on the table.'

This sentence has a straightforward proximate interpretation, with *ie* serving as a locative modifier, *er* as the (expletive) subject clitic, and *dui* as the (equally expletive) strong doubling pronoun. What this suggests, then, is that expletive subjects can not only be topic doubled in Wambeek Dutch, but also clitic doubled. (Note also that this implies that the deficient expletive element *d'r* is homophonous between a clitic and a weak pronoun.) In fact, just like in the pronominal system (see above, example 2.3), expletive tripling is also attested:

(50) Dui eit er dui ie niemand me Jef geklapt.
 there has ER there here no-one with Jef talked
 'No-one spoke with Jef here.'

This example contains four locative expressions. The proximate locative adverb *ie* 'here' serves as an adjunct and assigns a locative interpretation to the sentence. The other three elements, *dui*, *d'r*, and *dui*, do not add any such meaning and serve as expletive pronouns. The sentence-initial *dui* is topic doubled by the post-verbal one, which is in turn clitic doubled by *d'r*. Note, crucially, that these extensive co-occurrence options between locative expressions do not imply that anything goes. In fact, if we force multiple locative expressions into a configuration where subject doubling is independently disallowed, the multiple expletive reading disappears and a locative one becomes obligatory. Consider in this respect the following example.

(51) Dui is niks gebeed.
 there is nothing happened
 'Nothing happened (there).'

As can be expected from the above discussion, this example is ambiguous between a locative and a non-locative (expletive) interpretation. If we add the deficient expletive pronoun to the right of the verb, however, the second reading disappears:

(52) Dui is t'r niks gebeed.
　　　there is ER nothing happened
　　　'Nothing happened *(there).'

In this example, *dui* is necessarily locative, i.e. the option of expletive doubling is unavailable. This perfectly mimics the fact that in this type of configuration – a strong form followed by the verb followed by a weak form – pronominal subject doubling is also categorically excluded:

(53) *Zaai ei ze ie niks te zieken.
　　　she_strong has she_deficient here nothing to seek
　　　INTENDED: 'She has no business being here.'

Summing up, the Wambeek Dutch expletive system shares with its pronominal counterpart not only the distinction between strong and deficient forms, but also the possibility of undergoing doubling. In particular, I have shown that expletive pronouns – unlike their homophonous locative counterparts – can undergo topic doubling, clitic doubling, and even tripling.

3.4 Expletive *here*

All the data I have examined so far featured the distal – or distal/medial, cf. fn. 9 – locative adverb *dui* 'there'. In this subsection I turn to its proximate counterpart *ie* 'here'. On the one hand, this element behaves exactly like a *bona fide* locative adverb in that it always retains its locative meaning. At the same time, however, it can be both topic and clitic doubled, and when it is, it imposes a definiteness restriction on the thematic subject, just like regular expletive pronouns.

Consider first the following example. It is identical to the one in (35), except that the distal locative *dui* 'there' has been replaced by the proximate *ie* 'here'.

(54) Ie stui ne vantj inn of.
　　　here stands a man in.the garden
　　　'There's a man in the garden *(here).'

Note that unlike the example in (35) the locative contribution of the clause-initial locative adverb is obligatory, suggesting that *ie*, unlike *dui*, cannot be used as an expletive pronoun. This intuition is further confirmed if we consider some more examples from the preceding sections but with *dui* replaced by *ie*:

(55) # Ie   zen   mo   vier   priemgetalle   klanjer   as   tien.
     here are   only four   prime.numbers smaller   as   ten
     'There are only four prime numbers smaller than ten here.'

(56) Ie   is   niks   gebeed.
     here is   nothing   happened
     'Nothing happened *(here).'

In both these examples *ie* makes an obligatory locative contribution (resulting in a pragmatically odd sentence in (55)). Neither of them allows for the location-neutral, expletive interpretation. Similarly, when *ie* is combined with other, conflicting locative expressions, the result is ill-formed[13]:

(57) *Ie   stuid   genner   ne   vantj   inn   of.
     here stands   over.there a   man   in.the   garden
     INTENDED: 'There's a man over there in the garden.'

In short, in accordance with what has been reported in the literature on expletives (see in particular Kayne 2008:195–196), the proximate locative adverb seems to lack the expletive uses of its distal counterpart. With that much as background, consider the following example.

(58) Ie   eid   ie   niemand   me   Jef   geklapt.
     here has   here   no-one   with   Jef   talked
     'No-one spoke with Jef *(here).'

This example contains two instances of *ie*, yet its interpretation reveals only a single proximate modification.[14] This means that at least one of the two *ie*'s is used as an expletive pronoun here (recall from examples (26) and (27) that locative modifiers cannot be doubled, so the two *ie*'s cannot be instances/copies of the same locative element). This is further confirmed by the fact that this construction imposes a strong definiteness requirement on the thematic subject of

---

13 More accurately: the only reading allowed in (57) is the double locative one described in fn. 7.
14 The double locative reading of fn. 7 is not impossible here, but very marked. It also requires heavy stress on both instances of *ie*, while the neutral pronunciation of (58) has the main stress falling on *niemand* 'no-one'.

the sentence, illustrated in (59). (Note that such a requirement is absent when the sentence contains only a single *ie* as in (60).)

(59) *Ie   eid   ie   Marie   me   Jef   geklapt.
    here has here Marie with Jef talked
    INTENDED: 'Marie spoke with Jef here.'

(60) Ie   eit   Marie   me   Jef   geklapt.
    here has Marie with Jef talked
    'Marie spoke with Jef here.'

The *ie*-doubling example in (58) resembles an instance of topic doubling with two strong subject pronouns (see above, example (8)), but at the same time it could also be analyzed as the combination of a locative and an expletive use of *ie*. As it turns out, however, it is also possible to have three instances of *ie*:

(61) Ie   eid   ie   ie   niemand   me   Jef   geklapt.
    here has here here no-one with Jef talked
    'No-one spoke with Jef *(here).'

The interpretation of this example is identical to the one in (58), i.e. there is only one (proximate) locative specification. This means that the other two *ie*'s are expletive pronouns. More specifically, not only can the proximate locative adverb be used as an expletive, in that capacity it can also undergo topic doubling. It is important to stress, though, that even in its topic doubled expletive use, *ie* still retains its locative interpretation. This can be shown by replacing the third *ie* in (61) by a conflicting locative expression such as *genner* 'over there'.

(62) *Ie   eid   ie   genner   niemand   me   Jef   geklapt.
    here has here over.there no-one with Jef talked
    INTENDED: 'No-one spoke with Jef over there.'

Given that (61) has shown that *ie* can be (topic doubled and) used as an expletive pronoun, it should in principle be possible to combine it with a conflicting locative expression such as *genner* 'over there' (see above, example (44)). The ill-formedness of (62) shows that this is not the case. This means that even in its use as an expletive pronoun, *ie* still retains its proximate locative interpretation.

Having established that *ie* can be topic doubled, this raises the question of whether it can be clitic doubled as well. The following example suggests that that is indeed the case.

(63) Eit   er   ie   ie   niemand   me   Jef geklapt?
     has ER here here no-one   with Jef talked
     'Did no-one speak with Jef here?'

There are three locative expressions in this example: the deficient expletive pronoun *d'r* and two instances of *ie*. Once again, the meaning of the sentence reveals only a single proximate dimension. This suggests that the other two elements are expletive in nature. In other words, it suggests that the expletive element *ie* is clitic doubled. Not surprisingly, then, the combination of topic doubling and clitic doubling, i.e. tripling, is also possible in the case of *ie*. This is shown in (64).

(64) Ie   eit   er   ie   ie   niemand   me   Jef geklapt.
     here has ER here here no-one   with Jef talked
     'No-one spoke with Jef here.'

Summing up, even though *ie* adds a proximate locative meaning to every sentence that contains it, it can undergo topic doubling and clitic doubling, two operations otherwise strictly preserved for XPs occupying the structural subject position. Moreover, whenever *ie* is doubled, it shows a defining characteristic of an expletive pronoun in that it imposes a definiteness requirement on the thematic subject. All of this suggests that in Wambeek Dutch the proximate locative adverb can be used as an expletive pronoun.

3.5 Summary

This section has examined the expletive system of Wambeek Dutch. I have shown that expletive pronouns fit into the pronominal system of this dialect in two ways: (1) they can be subdivided into strong and deficient forms (with the latter homophonous between clitics and weak pronouns), and (2) they can be pronominally doubled, both via topic doubling and via clitic doubling. In addition, the section has revealed that the proximate locative adverb also has an expletive use, in spite of it never occurring without its locative interpretation. The next section examines some of the implications of these findings for existing theories of *there*-expletives and sketches the outlines of an alternative approach.

4 Towards a new analysis of *there*-expletives

The generative literature on *there*-expletives is vast and it is not my intention to provide an exhaustive discussion of it in this paper (see Hartmann 2008: chapter 1 for an overview). What I do want to do in this section, though, is point out how the data presented in the previous section raise non-trivial questions for most if not all existing accounts of *there*-expletives, and sketch the outlines of an alternative approach that overcomes (at least some of) these problems.

Broadly speaking, we can identify two strands of analysis in the literature. The first is what one could call the canonical Minimalist approach (cf. Chomsky 2000). The central idea is that a *there*-expletive is a meaningless element that is inserted in the structural subject position (specTP) in order to satisfy some formal requirement that is imposed on that position (be it the EPP, an EPP-feature, an edge feature, or some other formal implementation of the same idea). This approach seems to be at odds with several of the findings described above. First of all, recall that Wambeek Dutch makes a distinction between strong and deficient expletive pronouns, and that the choice of a strong form over a deficient one has an impact on the interpretation of the sentence (see the discussion of the examples in (39)–(42)). This is quite unexpected from the point of view of *there* as a mere formal placeholder that makes no contribution to the meaning of the sentence. Secondly, recall that the proximate element *ie* can be used as an expletive even when it retains its locative interpretation. Consider in this respect the following example.

(65) *Ie woendj ie niemand nie.*
here lives here no-one not
'No-one lives here.'

In this example *ie* on the one hand clearly displays subject- and expletive-like properties: it is topic doubled and it imposes a definiteness requirement on the thematic subject. On the other hand, however, this element is not a meaningless placeholder: not only does it contribute a locative meaning to the sentence, it also serves as the (obligatory) internal argument of the locational verb *woenen* 'to live'. In other words, the standard Minimalist account of *there*-expletives seems to be a non-starter for the Wambeek Dutch data introduced in the previous section.

The other type of analysis of *there*-expletives starts from the idea that *there* is base-generated lower than specTP as a meaningful element of the structure (typically a predicate of some sort) and that it subsequently raises to specTP (possibly to satisfy the same formal requirement that drives *there*-insertion in the standard Minimalist account), see for example Moro (1997). At first glance, this type of account holds more promise for the Wambeek Dutch facts, as it takes into account the possibility that the expletive pronoun makes a semantic contribution to the clause. At the same time, however, the contexts in which *there* can be base-generated according to these accounts – which are mostly based on English *there*-sentences – constitute only a subset of the contexts in which Wambeek Dutch expletives can be found. In particular, *there* has been argued to be the predicate of a small clause (Moro 1997; Dikken 1992), the subject of such a small clause (Williams 1994; Hazout 2004), the spell-out of a spatio-temporal event variable (Kiss 1996; Ramchand 1996; Felser & Rupp 2001), and a presuppositional adjunct (Bennis 1986), and while these characterisations work well in the face of simple existential or locational sentences such as *There are many problems (in the world)* (Cresti & Tortora 1999:62), Wambeek Dutch expletives (exemplified here by *ie*-doubling) occur in a much wider variety of contexts: they can spell out the internal argument of a two-place predicate (66), an adjunct in an intransitive sentence (67), an adjunct in a transitive sentence (68) (a so-called transitive expletive construction, cf. Vikner 1995), or an adjunct in an impersonal passive (69). It is hard to see how all of these constructions could be reduced to the small set of *there*-configurations proposed in the literature.[15] Instead, the use of locative expressions as expletives seems to be parasitic on their use as locative adverbs: any structure that can host the adverb, be it as an adjunct or as an argument, can serve as the basis for the expletive use of this element. As far as I can tell, this is an intuition that none of the existing accounts of *there*-expletives incorporates.

(66) Ie   leid ie   ginnen boek.
     here lies here no   book
     'There's no book lying here.'

(67) Ie   eid ie   ne   noenkel va mou gewerkt.
     here has here an   uncle   of me worked
     'An uncle of mine used to work here.'

---

15 The same conclusion holds for Kayne's 2008 analysis, whereby *there* originates as a DP-internal modifier inside the associate DP and subsequently (remnant-)moves to specTP.

(68) Ie   eid ie   niemand nen boek gekocht.
     here has here no-one a   book bought
     'No-one bought a book here.'

(69) Ie   wedj   ie   gezeid dat Jef ziek is.
     here becomes here said   that Jef ill is
     'People are saying here that Jef is ill.'

Suppose we took this intuition as the starting point for an analysis of *there*-expletives in Wambeek Dutch: the expletive use of *dui* and *ie* (and possibly *d'r*)[16] is parasitic on their use as *bona fide* locative expressions. More specifically, whenever the structural subject position remains empty (because the subject is indefinite (Vangsnes 2002) or because there is no subject, like in impersonal passives, cf. (69)), a locative expression can be moved into this position.[17] While such a movement operation might seem unorthodox at first glance, it accords well with an observation that has been around in the literature on Dutch *there*-expletives since the early days (see for example Bennis 1986:214; Zwart 1992; Lightfoot 2002:95n4), i.e. the fact that the Dutch expletive pronoun *er* can be left out when it is followed by a locative expression. Interestingly, this idea is picked up and further worked out by Klockmann et al. (2015). On the basis of an online survey of 671 native speakers of Dutch, they observe that it is specifically the locative adverbs *daar* 'there' and *hier* 'here' that have this effect. Consider first two of their baseline examples, which show that Dutch is subject to an EPP-requirement, i.e. specTP can not remain empty willy-nilly.

(70) Werd   *(er   ) gedanst?
     became   there   danced
     'Was there dancing?'   (Standard Dutch)

---

16 I will mostly focus on the strong expletive pronouns *dui* and *ie* in what follows. While an account along the lines sketched below is also possible for the deficient form *d'r*, this element could also be given a standard Minimalist analysis in most of the contexts in which it occurs. See also fn. 18.

17 While I will leave the precise nature of this movement operation open, two options readily come to mind. One would be to assimilate it to Icelandic Stylistic Fronting (Holmberg 2000), another would be to endow T with a locative or distal feature along the lines of Ritter & Wiltschko 2009, which could then be checked by raising a locative expression to specTP, cf. Klockmann et al. 2015 (and see also Pots 2016 for related discussion).

(71) Gedanst werd   *(er   ).
     danced became   there
     'There was dancing.'   (Standard Dutch)

In the presence of the locative adverbs *daar* 'there' and *hier* 'here', however, the expletive pronoun is no longer obligatory:

(72) Werd   (er   ) hier/daar   gedanst?
     became   there   here/there danced
     'Was there dancing here/there?'   (Standard Dutch)

Interestingly, this effect is absent (a) when the locative element is not linearly adjacent to the expletive (73), or (b) when a non-locative adverb like *toen* 'then' is used instead (74). In fact, Klockmann et al. (2015) show that for many speakers even full locative PPs don't resort the same effect as *hier* 'here' and *daar* 'there' (75).

(73) Werd   *(er   ) wel gedanst daar?
     became   there   PRT danced   there
     'Was there really dancing there?'   (Standard Dutch)

(74) Werd   *(er   ) toen gedanst?
     became   there   then danced
     'Was there dancing at that time?'   (Standard Dutch)

(75) Werd   %(er   ) in het   park gedanst?
     became   there   in the   park danced
     'Was there dancing in the park?'   (Standard Dutch)

Like Klockmann et al. (2015) I take this to mean that in the absence of another filler of specTP, the locative adverbs *hier* 'here' and *daar* 'there' can move into this position. Moreover, given that the judgments in (70)–(75) carry over to Wambeek Dutch, I assume that the same analysis is applicable to this variety. What distinguishes Wambeek Dutch from Standard Dutch, is the fact that elements that occupy specTP in the dialect can be pronominally doubled. For instance, if *dui* 'there' moves on from specTP into the left periphery and the lower copy of this movement chain is spelled out, an expletive topic doubling configuration is derived. For the example in (76), this yields the (simplified) derivation in (77).

(76) Dui   woentj dui   niemand.
    there lives   there no-one
    'No-one lives there.'

(77)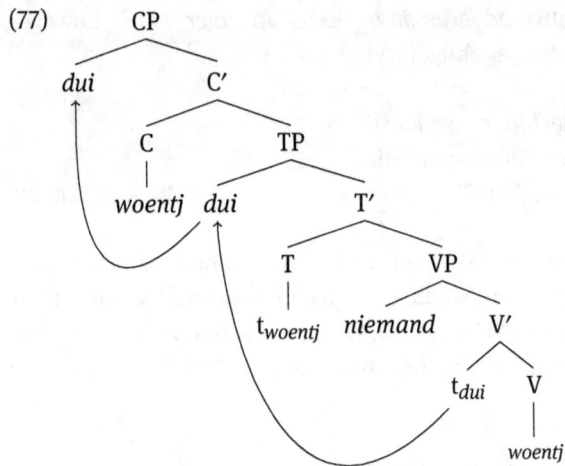

Similarly, the existence of expletive clitic doubling suggests that locative adverbs are morphologically complex, and that the deficient form *d'r* can be analyzed as a structural subset of the strong forms *dui* and *ie* (cf. also Rooryck 2003). Without going into any details regarding the categorial status of locative adverbs or the functional projections making up such elements, this means that the clitic doubled expletive pronoun in an example like (48) (repeated below as (78)) can be abstractly structurally represented as in (79).

(78) dat er   dui   nen boek op   tuifel leit.
    that ER   there a   book on   tafel lies
    'that there is a book (there) on the table.'

(79)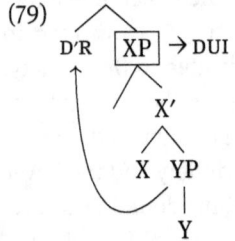

Summing up, the expletive facts from Wambeek Dutch reviewed in the previous section suggest that morphologically locative expletive pronouns can be parasitic on the regular locative use of these elements (be it as an argument or as an adjunct).[18] They move from their base position to specTP (see fn. 17 for possible implementations) and from there on are incorporated into the regular subject system of the language (which in the case of Wambeek Dutch includes the possibility of pronominal doubling). Neither the standard Minimalist analysis of *there*-expletives (Chomsky 2000) nor the predicate raising approach (Moro 1997) seems particularly suited to handle these facts.

5 Summary and conclusion

This paper has focused on *there*-expletives in a dialect of Dutch. I have shown that expletive elements show a remarkable similarity to the system of subject pronouns in this variety, in two ways: on the one hand, expletives show a distinction between strong and deficient elements, while on the other they can be pronominally doubled. In addition, an in-depth exploration of the data revealed that contrary to a commonly held opinion in the literature on *there*-expletives, the proximate locative adverb *here* can also be used as an expletive in Wambeek Dutch. These previously undiscussed facts raise significant challenges for existing accounts of *there*-expletives. Accordingly, I have sketched the outlines of an alternative approach, in which the expletive behavior of locative elements is made — or at least can be made — parasitic on their regular locative use.

---

18 Note that the account presented here leaves open the possibility of different types of expletives co-existing in a single language (see also Zwart 1992), see also fn. 16 on the reduced expletive pronoun *d'r*. Such an approach might also be suggested by examples such as (61), repeated below as (i).

(i) le   eid   ie   ie   niemand   me   Jef geklapt.
     here has   here here no-one   with Jef talked
     'No-one spoke with Jef *(here).'

Unless we want to say that the three *ie*'s represent three spelled-out copies in a single movement chain, the most plausible analysis of this example would be to assume that the third *ie* is a(n unmoved) regular locative adjunct, while the first two are copies of the same expletive element, which is base-generated in specTP, as per the standard Minimalist account. Similarly, the ambiguity of the basic example in (35) (cf. fn. 10) might be due to the possibility of base generating *dui* either in an adjunct position or directly in specTP. I leave the exploration of this 'double analysis' of *there*-expletives in varieties of Dutch as a topic for further research.

References

Belletti, Adriana. 2005. Extended doubling and the VP periphery. *Probus* 17(1). 1–35.
Bennis, Hans. 1986. *Gaps and dummies*. Dordrecht: Foris Publications.
Cardinaletti, Anna & Michal Starke. 1999. The typology of structural deficiency: a case study of three classes of pronouns. In Henk van Riemsdijk (ed.), *Clitics in the languages of Europe*, 145–233. Berlin: Mouton.
Chomsky, Noam. 2000. Minimalist inquiries: The framework. In Roger Martin, David Michaels & Juan Uriagereka (eds.), *Step by step: Essays on minimalist syntax in honor of Howard Lasnik*, 89–156. Cambridge, MA: MIT Press.
van Craenenbroeck, Jeroen. 2011. Germanic expletives revisited. In pursuit of Kayne's dream. Handout for an invited talk at the 26th Comparative Germanic Syntax Workshop.
van Craenenbroeck, Jeroen & Marjo van Koppen. 2000. On the pronominal system of Dutch dialects. Unpublished ms. University of Leiden.
van Craenenbroeck, Jeroen & Marjo van Koppen. 2002. Pronominal doubling and the structure of the left periphery in southern Dutch. In Sjef Barbiers, Leonie Cornips & Susanne van der Kleij (eds.), *Syntactic microvariation*, http://www.meertens.knaw.nl/books/synmic/.
van Craenenbroeck, Jeroen & Marjo van Koppen. 2007a. Feature inheritance and multiple phase boundaries. Handout of a talk at GLOW 30, CASTL, Tromsø, Norway.
van Craenenbroeck, Jeroen & Marjo van Koppen. 2007b. Theorie, empirie en subjectverdubbeling: een antwoord op Haegeman (2004). *Taal & Tongval* 59. 149–171.
van Craenenbroeck, Jeroen & Marjo van Koppen. 2008. Pronominal doubling in Dutch dialects: big DPs and coordinations. In Sjef Barbiers, Olaf Koeneman, Marika Lekakou & Margreet van der Ham (eds.), *Microvariation in syntactic doubling.*, vol. 36 Syntax and Semantics, 207–249. Bingley: Emerald.
Cresti, Diana & Christina Tortora. 1999. Aspects of locative doubling and resultative redication. In *Annual Meeting of the Berkeley Linguistics Society*, 62–73.
Déchaine, Rose-Marie & Martina Wiltschko. 2002. Decomposing pronouns. *Linguistic Inquiry* 33(3). 409–442.
Dikken, Marcel den. 1992. *Particles*. Dordrecht, The Netherlands: Holland Institute of Generative Linguistics.
Felser, Claudia & Laura Rupp. 2001. Expletives as arguments: Gemanic existential sentences revisited. *Linguistische Berichte* 187. 289–324.
Grohmann, Kleanthes K. 2000. *Prolific peripheries: a radical view from the left*. University of Maryland dissertation.
Haegeman, Liliane. 1986. *Er*-sentences in West-Flemish. Ms. Université de Genève.
Haegeman, Liliane. 1990. Subject pronouns and subject clitics in West Flemish. *The Linguistic Review* 7. 333–363.
Haegeman, Liliane. 1991. Subject clitics and clitic doubling in West Flemish. In Henk van Riemsdijk & Luigi Rizzi (eds.), *Clitics and heir host*, Tilburg: Gammatical Models.
Haegeman, Liliane. 1992. *Theory and description in generative syntax*. Cambridge: Cambridge University Press.
Haegeman, Liliane. 1993. The morphology and distribution of object clitics in West Flemish. *Studia Linguistica* 47(1). 57–94.
Haegeman, Liliane. 2004. Verdubbeling van subjectpronomina in de Zuid-Nederlandse dialecten: een reactie uit Lapscheure. *Taal & Tongval* 56. 119–159.

Hartmann, Jutta. 2008. *Expletives in existentials. English there and German da*. Tilburg University dissertation.
Hazout, Ilan. 2004. The syntax of existential constructions. *Linguistic Inquiry* 35(3). 393–430.
Hoekstra, Eric & Jan-Wouter Zwart. 1994. De structuur van CP. Functionele projecties voor topics en vraagwoorden in het Nederlands. *Spektator* 23(3). 191–212.
Holmberg, Anders. 2000. Scandinavian stylistic fronting: how any category can become an expletive. *Linguistic Inquiry* 31(3). 445–483.
Kayne, Richard. 2005. Pronouns and their antecedents. In *Movement and silence*, 105–135. Oxford: Oxford University Press.
Kayne, Richard. 2008. Expletives, datives, and the tension between morphology and syntax. In Theresa Biberauer (ed.), *The limits of syntactic variation*, 175–217. John Benjamins Publishing Company.
Kiss, Katalin É. 1996. Two subject positions in English. *The Linguistic Review* 13. 119–142.
Klockmann, Heidi, Coppe van Urk & Franca Wesseling. 2015. Agree is fallible, EPP is not: investigating EPP effects in Dutch. Handout of a talk at the Utrecht Syntax Interface Meetings.
Laenzlinger, Christopher. 1998. *Comparative studies in word order variations: pronouns, adverbs and German clause structure* (Linguistics Today 20). Amsterdam: John Benjamins.
Lightfoot, David. 2002. *Syntactic effects of morphological change*. Oxford: Oxford University Press.
Maienborn, Claudia. 2001. On the position and interpretation of locative modifiers. *Natural Language Semantics* 9(2). 191–240.
Moro, Andrea. 1997. *The raising of predicates: predicative noun phrases and the theory of clause structure*. Cambridge: Cambridge University Press.
Poletto, Cecilia. 2008. Doubling as a spare movement strategy. In Sjef Barbiers et al. (ed.), *Microvariation in syntactic doubling*, vol. 36 Syntax and Semantics, 36–68. Bingley: Emerald.
Pots, Cora. 2016. Object definiteness effects in Germanic wh-extraction. Handout of a talk at TABU 37.
Ramchand, Gillian Catriona. 1996. Two subject positions in Scottish Gaelic: The syntax-semantics interface. *Natural Language Semantics* 4(2). 165–191.
Ritter, Elizabeth & Martina Wiltschko. 2009. Varieties of INFL: Tense, Location, and Person. In Jeroen van Craenenbroeck (ed.), *Alternatives to cartography*, 153–202. Berlin: Walter de Gruyter.
Rooryck, Johan. 2003. The morphosyntactic structure of articles and pronouns in Dutch. In Jan Koster & Henk van Riemsdijk (eds.), *Germania at alia. A linguistic webschrift for Hans den Besten*, http://odur.let.rug.nl/koster/DenBesten/contents.htm.
Uriagereka, Juan. 1995. Aspects of the syntax of clitic placement in Western Romance. *Linguistic Inquiry* 26(1). 79–124.
Vangsnes, Øystein A. 2002. Icelandic expletive constructions and the distribution of expletives. In Peter Svenonius (ed.), *Subjects, expletives, and the EPP*, 43–70. New York: Oxford University Press.
Vikner, Sten. 1995. *Verb movement and expletive subjects in the Germanic languages*. New York: Oxford University Press.
de Vogelaer, Gunther. 2005. *Subjectsmarkering in de Nederlandse en Friese dialecten*: Ghent University dissertation.

de Vogelaer, Gunther & Magda Devos. 2008. On geographical adequacy, or: how many types of subject doubling in Dutch. In Sjef Barbiers, Olaf Koeneman, Marika Lekakou & Margreet van der Ham (eds.), *Microvariation in syntactic doubling*, vol. 36 Syntax and Semantics, 251–276. Bingley: Emerald.

Williams, Edwin. 1994. *Thematic structure in syntax*. Cambridge, Massachusetts: MIT Press.

Zwart, Jan-Wouter. 1992. Dutch expletives and small clause predicate raising. In K. Broderick (ed.), *Proceedings of North East Linguistic Society 22*, 477–491. Amherst, MA: GLSA.

Kenneth Wexler
Arbitrary control instead of obligatory control in temporal adjuncts in Child Grammar: An ATTRACT analysis

1 Introduction: The problem of temporal object control in child grammar

Among many other major achievements, Rita Manzini has contributed original and innovative solutions to the theory of control, solutions that have had much impact. Inspired by this work, in this paper I will attempt to work out an analysis of a long-standing problem in the theory of the acquisition of control using one of Manzini's important contributions, in particular the theory of ATTRACT in Manzini and Roussou (2000). The particular acquisition problem that will be the center of our attention is children's failure to provide the correct controller in a temporal adjunct.

A long-studied problem in the theory of grammatical development is that in sentences with control, although children at around ages 3 to 5 seem to behave perfectly on cases of obligatory control like (1a), they often make errors on cases of obligatory control into adjuncts like (1b and 1c).

(1) a. John tried [PRO to win the race]
   b. John pushed Bill before [leaving the room]
   c. John laughed [before PRO leaving the room]

For many years after the problem was first studied, it was thought that children go through a stage in which they took the controller of PRO to be the object of the matrix clause in (1b), with the most common idea being that the kids had incorrectly attached the embedded clause, *before leaving the room*, so that for them *Bill* c-commanded *leaving the room* and would therefore by the closest c-commander and therefore the controller of PRO (by the Minimum Distance Principle).

However, Wexler (1992) analyzed the data in the literature in detail and showed that the object stage didn't exist, or at best was extremely rare. Rather, children seemed to allow any discourse-appropriate DP to control PRO. The

Kenneth Wexler, Massachusetts Institute of Technology

https://doi.org/10.1515/9781501505201-033

reference for PRO in temporal adjuncts (like those in (1b, c)) was free for children,[1] subject to discourse conditions. He extended and made more precise an idea from Carlson that children might be treating the verbal gerund in (1b, c) as a DP. Kids were essentially treating "leaving the room" as "the leaving of the room." DP's like this can be interpreted as referring to an event that occurs at a certain time (just like *the wedding*), so that they can be interpreted as the object of a temporal preposition. But they do not specify their subject; they are not controlled at all. They come with a time of event occurrence, and the subject is free.

Broihier and Wexler (1995) further analyzed data from the literature. For example, they showed that in experiment in the literature in which the 2nd (non-subject) DP is embedded even deeper, so that there was no way it could be misattached to command PRO, this DP was often taken by children as the controller of PRO. There was no way that the misattachment analysis could work. Then they did 2 experiments, giving children the *choice* of an external DP (not even mentioned in the sentence) or an internal DP as the controller of PRO, the results being that the external DP (along with the grammatical subject DP and the object DP if there was one) could be quite often the controller of PRO.

It seems to me that by now, the "free reference" view of PRO in these temporal adjuncts has been amply supported, and accepted by all investigators.

The results were in particular further supported by Goodluck (2001), who, not only replicated these results, but showed, in creative experimentation, that children would accept a sentence like *John pushed Leo before/when dancing by Sam* to mean that John pushed Leo before/when Sam was dancing. Although this is grammatical (though dispreferred in the experiment by adults) with *before*, it is not grammatical with *when*; with *when* the sentence can only mean that John danced by Sam (*by* as a locative). Children took free reference to be very widely available. Goodluck took this as a test and confirmation of the DP theory of children's adjunct control errors. Since then, 2 dissertations have results confirming the free reference possibility of control in temporal adjuncts in children, while having many other things to say.

Why do children take the DP analysis of the gerunds? Wexler (1992) proposed that it was because children had difficulties with the empty temporal operators

---

[1] When I speak about "children" in this paper, I always mean children at the age at which the control errors are made, unless stated otherwise.

that existed in such sentences (see later sections for the evidence for this grammatical analysis in much more detail). The theory, although it's descriptively adequate, raises some questions. First, do children really not understand temporal operators? Second, and perhaps even more important, why should a difficulty with temporal operators lead to them adopting the DP analysis as a strategy? After all, it takes some effort and some ignoring of the morphological and syntactic conditions to take verbal gerunds in adjuncts like *John laughed before giving the answer* as a DP.

What would be more a welcome alternative to explaining free reference for temporal adjunct control is a theory that predicts that children take the relevant structures to be cases of arbitrary control. As is well known (and we'll discuss it further in the next section), arbitrary control is often interpreted specifically with relation to the discourse context. So if children believe that the structure of temporal adjuncts should lead to an analysis of arbitrary control, then we'd expect them to respond with discourse-related arbitrary control. There is no reason to think that the responses would be statistically equivalent to what happens when a pronoun is substituted for the empty subject (a pronoun might have its own discourse preferences), but nevertheless there should be the possibility of control by any discourse appropriate subject, whether sentence internal or external.

We need to look for a mechanism that causes the child's grammar to analyze temporal adjuncts like (1b, c) as cases of arbitrary control. We have to start from a theory that tells us what arbitrary control is. A promising theory in this regard is the theory of control governed by the ATTRACT relation outlined in Manzini and Roussou (2000). In section 1 I will very sketchily summarize a small (and most relevant) part of the theory of ATTRACT (from Manzini and Roussou), especially as it applies to adjuncts. Section 2 lays out Johnson's (1988) results on temporal prepositional adjuncts, that (following Larson 1990) makes the case not only for the existence of phonetically empty temporal operators in finite temporal adjuncts, but also shows that these operators are syntactically active, resulting in arguments for the existence of temporal operators in non-finite adjuncts (verbal gerunds) when they follow a temporal preposition like *before*. This means that we must assume that the verbal gerund in (1b, c) contains a temporal operator. Section 3 develops the theory of control in temporal adjuncts, integrating Manzini and Roussou's results with the results on temporal operators in Johnson's research. Section 4 develops the analysis that finds a small difference in children's grammar from that of the adult that was presented in section 3. This difference will result from a kind of intervention effect that happens in child grammar; the (non-finite) temporal adjunct will be controlled by the lower non-finite C that dominates it, a possibility in the theory of ATTRACT, but not one that applies in adult grammar in this case. The result will be that in temporal adjuncts, the child grammar will have arbitrary rather than obligatory control, predicting the empirical results that we very briefly reviewed in this section. We discuss a feature/operator based possibility for why children make this error. They follow the theory of ATTRACT and other relevant principles, but they misanalyse some featural properties of the temporal operator, resulting in their assuming an interrogative operator in the C dominating the adjunct, an operator that doesn't exist in adult grammar for temporal operators. The results of arbitrary control in children now follow ATTRACT theory exactly. Section 5 deduces a few more facts from the ATTRACT theory of children's errors and shows that they are empirically realized, making the case in more empirical detail for the existence of temporal operators in temporal adjuncts as being the cause of the problem in child grammar. Section 6 summarizes.

2 Attract and adjunct control

The larger goal of Manzini and Roussou (from now on MR) is to argue for a theory of grammar in which there is no A-movement (of DP's), but rather movement of predicates and requirements about lexicalization (as related to features).[2] A major application in the paper is to the theory of control, and this is the only application that we'll consider, ignoring the issue of the elimination of A-movement. We'll also not pay any attention to the arguments for the theory, but rather describe and use only those parts of the theory that we need to apply to the acquisition problem of adjunct control. A classical type of obligatory control is when PRO is in the subject position of an embedded infinitival, as in (2)[3]:

(2) John tried [PRO to win the race]

Chomsky (1981) assumed that the empty category PRO had particular features, +anaphoric, +pronominal. Since Principle A requires that PRO (as an anaphor) be bound in its governing category and Principle B requires that PRO (as a pronoun) be free in its governing category, he derived the result that PRO can

---

[2] Also, requirements about Connectedness, that we will not discuss.
[3] As will be obvious to those who know the paper, the following discussion follows closely Manzini and Roussou, both in idea and examples. I will not give credit to each of these separately.

only exist in ungoverned positions, where there is no governing category. This essentially derived in his framework that PRO could only occur in ungoverned positions, essentially in the subject position of non-finite clauses. This is called the *PRO Theorem*.[4]

Minimalist syntax (Chomsky 1995) discards much of the apparatus that earlier was used to derive the Pro Theorem. Empty categories are no longer defined in terms of features, binding theory itself is thought of in another way, and there is no need for the concept of governing categories. Thus the content of the PRO Theorem, that PRO can appear only in subject position of non-finite clauses, must be derived in another way. Chomsky and Lasnik (1995) propose that PRO is associated with "null case" and that null case can be checked only by a non-finite INFL. Thus PRO can only occur in subject position of non-finite clauses. For example, PRO cannot occur in object position or in the subject position of a finite clause (examples (3a, c) from MR):

(3) a. *John persuaded PRO
    b. *John(i) thought Bill likes PRO(i/j)
    c. *John believes that PRO will eat

MR critique the null case theory of control on several grounds, including the conceptual one that null case and PRO only occur together, so that reference to null case has no independent motivation.

A major issue in the theory of control is how to derive (rather than state) the *Minimal Distance Principle* (MDP) (Rosenbaum 1967), which says (in more modern terms) that PRO is controlled by the closest c-commanding antecedent. Thus in (4) (from MR), *John* must control PRO since it c-commands PRO and an alternative c-commander, *Mary*, is more distant from PRO.

(4) Mary [persuaded John [PRO to eat]]

---

4 Unless I am overlooking some paper, the issue of whether the kids know the PRO Theorem has never been directly discussed in the acquisition literature. Nevertheless, there is every reason to think that children *do* know the PRO Theorem. E.g. I know of no acquisition stage at which a child's grammar allows a direct object to be empty in a language that doesn't allow this (some languages allow the direct object to be empty for reasons independent of the PRO theory, e.g. discourse binding). Hyams and Wexler (1993) show that very young children (from before the age of 2) very rarely omit the direct object in English, despite being in a stage at which they often omit the subject ("null subject stage). Moreover, I know of no evidence that a child in English will omit a direct object in an embedded sentence because it is "controlled" by a higher DP in the matrix. For the purposes of this paper, we will follow earlier literature in assuming that children *do* know the PRO Theorem.

MR propose an account that they argue is conceptually and empirically superior to others. The account proposes that DP's don't undergo A-movement. Rather, DP's are merged in their surface position and ATTRACT a predicate that assigns a theta-role to the DO. For example, the derivation of *John left* is:

(5) [IP John I [VP left]]

The crucial aspect of this derivation is that the subject *John* is merged directly in [Spec,I]. This merger is required by a strong D-feature on I that requires a lexicalization (namely, lexical material in its Spec). How then does the DP *John* receive its theta-role, which is associated with the verb (predicate) *called*? As a result of the operation ATTRACT. ATTRACT is defined directly between D and V. In particular, D ATRRACTS V. Part of MR's argument for this approach is derived from Hale and Keyser's results, which argue that there is no particular list of theta-roles. Rather, the predicate has properties that assign a particular "theta" interpretation to the relevant DP. They presume the Configurational theory of theta-roles, which says that theta-roles "correspond to a relation directly defined between an argument and a predicate".

One of MR's major empirical arguments for the superiority of an approach to the phenomena of A-movement that doesn't involve movement is that in a Minimalist framework, the Copy Theory of Movement holds.[5] Since movement leaves behind a full DP copy, A-movement will have Reconstruction effects, just like A-bar movement. But, they argue, these reconstruction effects don't exist.[6] We won't go through any of the argumentation, but rather turn to MR's theory of control that follows from the ATTRACT theory.

---

5 What about the result of Chomsky that the Copy Theory of Movement follows directly from the theory of Merge, namely, as Internal Merge? If Internal Merge holds for A-bar movement, such as wh-movement, what is to rule it out for A-movement? Thus why does the Copy Theory of Movement not apply to A-movement? Possibly what MR would say is that the relevant configurations for Internal Merge in an "A" configuration never hold. For example, the subject DP John in (5) is merged directly into [Spec,I], via the assumption that I has a strong D-feature. Thus the relevant configurations for Internal Merge in an "A" configuration never hold. It's not that the Copy Theory of Movement is wrong; it's just that there is no A-movement, because of independent principles of grammar.

6 This is a point of controversy, of course. It is fairly standardly argued that in the ambiguous (i)

(i)   every cat isn't on the mat

the NEG>EVERY reading (which means that *it is not the case that every cat is on the mat*) is derived by reconstructing *every cat* (which has raised first to [Spec,I] then higher via QR), not just back into [Spec,I} but lower, into the original argument position below *not*. If *every cat is*

(6) [IP John I [VP tried [IP to [VP leave]]]

In (6), *John* merges directly into [Spec,I] to lexicalize the D-feature of I. MR assume that the I in non-finite structures do not have a strong D-feature, so there is nothing to license a DP in their subject position. Thus there is no subject at all in the lower IP. Thus no PRO (for MR, there is no PRO and none is needed, in fact no representation of a subject of the lower VP at all). Intuitively, the role of PRO in earlier theories is to insure that the "theta-role" of *leave* is assigned to *John*. This is done via some requirement for co-reference or binding between *John* and PRO. With no PRO, rather an operation of ATTRACT that can assign properties from a predicate to a DP when the DP ATTRACTS the predicate, it must be necessary for the "controller" *John* to ATTRACT the lower predicate *to leave*. Of course, *John* ATTRACTS the higher predicate *tried*, jut as in any finite subject-verb configuration, e.g. (5), as we have shown. This means that in (6) *John* must ATTRACT 2 predicates, *tried* and *leave*.

MR argue against the notion of a structurally defined "checking domain" in which 2 features interact. Rather, they argue that a potential attractor can attract down until it reaches the *next* potential attractor. This is defined as:

(7) *Scopal MINIMAL LINK CONDITION (Scopal MLC)*
Feature F ATTRACTs feature F_A only down to the next F' that also ATTRACTs F_A.

In (6), *John* can of course ATTRACT *tried*, but it can go further and *also* ATTRACT *leave* because there is no other potential attractor in between *John* and *leave*. Thus, *John* is correctly assigned properties from both predicates, *tried* and *leave*, without the use of PRO to effect this result. This is the crucial way in which control is analyzed within the ATTRACT theory, in which arguments are not merged directly into the most local positions of predicates. The same operation that assigns predicate properties ("theta roles") from *try* to *John* in (6) assigns predicate properties ("theta roles) from the predicate *leave* to *John*. We see a unification of "theta-role assignment) without positing PRO. Locality is observed, but, as MR put it, a locality via the attractor not the attractee. Intuitively, an attractor can ATTRACT relevant items up to the next potential attractor. A DP can ATTRACT a predicate up to the next DP.

---

generated in [Spec,I], so that no reconstruction under *not* is possible, how is the NEG>EVERY reading to be derived? Some theory of interpretation would be needed, possibly at complicating cost.

In fact, MR argue that a DP *must* ATTRACT a predicate if there is no other attractor closer to the predicate. This is formulated as:

(8) Scopal Last Resort + MLC
F ATTRACTs all and only the F_A's that are in its scope

We can now derive the PRO Theorem. (9) is an example showing that control can't occur into finite clauses.

(9) [IP John I [VP believes [CP that [IP will [VP eat]]]]

In terms of the current theory, why can't John attract both believes and *will* eat in (9)? Intuitively, finite clauses require lexicalized subjects. Suppose that *John* were merged into the matrix [Spec, I]. But finite *will* (that is, the embedded finite I) has a strong D-feature, which requires lexicalization, so that *John* merged into matrix I violates this requirement. So suppose that *John* is merged into the embedded [Spec, I]. MR assume that a given lexical items can lexicalize the same feature once and only once. Since *John* has lexicalized the D-feature of the embedded I, it cannot lexicalize the D-feature of the higher I. Thus there is a violation of the requirement to lexicalize the D-feature of the higher I. *John* is never merged into the specifier of matrix I, so there is no question of its ATTRACTing the lower DP.

Crucially, the ATTRACT theory also explains the Minimum Distance Principle (MDP).

(10) [IP Mary I [VP thinks that [IP John I [VP expected [IP to [VP eat]]]]]

In (10), unlike (9), there is no lexicalization of features violation. The D-feature of the Matrix I is lexicalized by *Mary* and the D-feature of the intermediate I is lexicalized by *John*. The most embedded IP is infinitival. Since infinitivals don't have D-features, there is no requirement to lexicalize.

Why is it that the most embedded *IP* is predicated of *John* and not *Mary*? This is the MDP question in (10). Via the Scopal MLC (8), *Mary* attracts only down to the scope of the next attractor, *John*. Therefore the only grammatical analysis is one in which *Mary* ATTRACTS *thinks* and *John* ATTRACTS both *expected* and *eat*. This is the correct result.[7]

---

[7] MR point out that in short passives, the ATTRACT theory doesn't allow an external argument to be syntactically present, since in that case the phonetically empty external argument (which lexicalizes a D-feature) would intercede between the surface subject and the verbal passive predicate,

We now turn to a property of the ATTRACT system that will be of suggestive importance for our analysis of child grammar, in particular since the analysis of temporal properties is involved. How is arbitrary control derived? Traditionally, in (11), the predicate *to work* has a PRO subject. Since there is no available controller for this PRO subject, PRO is assigned a free [arbitrary (ARB)] index, which accounts for the arbitrary interpretation of PRO. *To work* applies to any arbitrary DP; it is not controlled.

(11) [C [it is hard [to work]]

In (11), there is no DP argument that takes the predicate *work* in its scope.[8] So, how does the ATTRACT theory explain the arbitrary control status of *to work*? MR point out that the lack of a controller does not lead to a lack of interpretation in (11). Rather, it leads to an interpretation whereby *work* takes a "variable of a generic operator" as argument. This operator must be able to ATTRACT *work*. They call it an "abstract operator of quantification" and place it in C. C ATTRACTS *work*, yielding the generic interpretation.

MR argue for the proposal that C acts as the attractor in arbitrary control interpretations by the widely-accepted fact noticed by Bresnan (1982) and others that contexts of arbitrary control (no DP argument controller) can be interpreted as having "a specific, rather than a generic, argument given the appropriate context." Thus (12) associates a specific reading to the non-lexicalized argument, rather than the generic reading in (11).

(12) It was hard to work (on that beautiful sunny day).

---

thereby preventing (via the scopal MLC) the predicate from being ATTRACTed to the surface subject. They don't provide a picture, but one assumes that they mean that in (i)
(i) John was being pushed D(External Argument) the D-feature of the external argument is higher than *pushed*, so that the phonetically empty DP that lexicalizes the D-feature intercedes between *John* and *pushed* so that *pushed* cannot be ATTRACTed to *John*, a wrong derivation. This result does seem to be contra to the facts of disjointness for verbal passives such that in (ii), the phonetically empty external argument cannot be *John*, a fact usually explained as a binding theory result.
(ii) John is being dressed

I am not really sure how such considerations play into the theory of lexicalization.
8 We ignore complications arising from MR's discussion of the role of expletive *it* in the derivation.

(12) means that the generic operator is limited to working on that day. MR point out that the interpretation of the non-lexicalized argument in (11, 12) varies with the temporal context. They assume that the operator in C ATTRACTS a Tense just as it ATTRACTS a predicate. A generic operator in (11) determines a generic interpretation for both the non-lexicalized argument and for Tense while a specific operator determines a specific interpretation for the empty argument and Tense in (12). Thus the ambiguity of *it is hard to work* is determined by whether the operator in C is generic or specific (the specific operator licensed by context). Crucially, as MR point out, the correlation between the generic or specific nature of the argument and the temporal context does not occur when attraction of the predicate is done by an argument, that is in typical cases of obligatory control, e.g. (1). In such cases, the argument (rather than an operator) ATTRACTS the predicate, so there will be no cause for any such correlation. Thus in (13), the argument *us* ATTRACTS *work* (Scopal MLC) and C only ATTRACTS Tense. There will be no correlation of Tense and Specificity of argument.

(13) It is hard for us [to [work]]

Getting closer to the issue of temporal adjuncts, let's start by looking at adjuncts in general

(14) a. John left before eating
　　 b. John left without asking

For both the temporal adjunct (14a) and the non-temporal adjunct (14b), on the assumption (Larson 1988) that adverbials (e.g. the adjunct) are attached deeply, (say, as a sister of *left*), both the matrix predicate *left* and the embedded predicate *eating/asking* are in the scope of John. John ATTRACTS both the matrix predicate *left* and the embedded predicate *eating/asking*. This correctly implies that we get obligatory control of the adjunct by *John*. Only *John* is said to be doing the eating/asking in (14).

This attachment choice, however predicts that if we insert an object, as in (15), the embedded predicate *eating/asking* will be in the scope of the object, so that *John* only ATTRACTS the predicate *left* but the object ATTRACTS the embedded predicate *eating/asking*. This means that the object *us* will control the embedded predicate, incorrectly.

(15) a. John left us before eating
　　 b. John left us without asking

Thus we conclude that the attachment of the adjunct is higher, so that *us* does not command the adjunct, and, via the MDP and Scopal MLC, ATTRACT is only from *John*, not from *us*. *John* ATTRACTS both the matrix and embedded predicates in (15). For simplicity we can say that the adjunct PP adjoins to a VP that contains the verb and the object, forming a VP with VP PP as its 2 daughters, the lower VP containing the verb and object. The object does not command into the sister of its mother VP, as required.

A major point of relevance to child grammar is that in (15), only subject control is possible; there is no derivation in which arbitrary control is possible. We will consider later, however, the possibility that in (15a), there are temporal operators in the embedded sentence, and we have to ask whether these operators can prevent the subject from ATTRACTing the embedded predicate. As MR note in general, the possibility of the subject ATTRACTing an embedded predicate depends on there being no operators between that subject and the predicate that themselves ATTRACT the predicate.

That intervening operators can prevent a subject from ATTRACTing an embedded predicate is easy to see. Consider:

(16) a. What to do?
     b. I know what to eat

Starting with (16a), we notice first that the facts are that control is arbitrary; there is not even a DP that could be the controller. Nor is there a tensed C that takes the infinitival in its scope (there is no Tense at all), so that we need another mechanism to ATTRACT the predicate. MR argue that the ATTRACT theory of arbitrary interpretation requires that there be an "interrogative/exclamatives" modal operator (in C) that licenses this exceptional matrix use of the infinitive. This operator ATTRACTS the predicate *to do*, and, as in the cases of generic operators in finite C, assigns an arbitrary interpretation to the empty "subject" of *to eat* (16b).

(16b) is even more interesting because there is in fact a possible "controller", the subject *I*. However, MR argue that the same operator that is present in (16a) is also present in the embedded infinitival sentence in (16b). This operator ATTRACTS the embedded predicate *eat*, assigning it, as before, arbitrary interpretation. The subject *I* ATTRACTS *know*, but by the Scopal MLC cannot ATTRACT past the next attractor down (the empty operator), so that *I* cannot ATTRACT *to eat*. In fact, an arbitrary interpretation is correct in (16b), easily seen if we put a sentence like this in the proper context.

(17) SPEAKER A: I'm hungry, but I can't figure out what to eat.
     SPEAKER B: I know what to eat

Clearly Speaker B is using a sentence that allows an interpretation (in fact, the preferred interpretation in this context) in which what Speaker B knows is what Speaker A can/should eat, not what Speaker B can/should eat, despite the existence of a potential controller (ATTRACTOR) in the sentence. Speaker B is using a sentence that has arbitrary control properties because the operator in the embedded sentence blocks ATTRACT of *to eat* by *John*.

3 Temporal operators in nonfinite temporal adjuncts

Most of the acquisition research on control into adjuncts has focused on temporal adjuncts, like those introduced by *after, before*, etc., e.g. (15a). Wexler (1992) in fact, argued that the cause of errors in temporal adjuncts had to do with temporal operators that they contained. The major phenomenon of adjunct control, Wexler argued, was that instead of obligatory control into temporal adjuncts, children had a grammar with arbitrary control, the controller thereby being free in reference from a grammatical point of view, but of course, subject to pragmatic effects. For example, in (15a), the subject of the embedded predicate eating could be not only the adult-grammatical *I*, but also the ungrammatical *us* or even a referent not mentioned in the sentence. We'll review all of this in more detail in a later section.

Now, however, we want to ask about temporal adjuncts in the ATTRACT theory. First, following Wexler (1992) we should consider whether these adjuncts contain phonetically empty temporal operators. We'll review some evidence, trying to integrate some insights in especially Johnson (1988) about temporal operators in gerunds with insights from the theory of ATTRACT. In particular, we will sketch the reasoning that leads Johnson to conclude that in a clausal gerund that follows a temporal preposition (e.g. (14a)), there is an empty temporal operator in [Spec, C] of the gerund, between the preposition and the VP.

Johnson (1988) starts by reviewing Geis' (1970) observation that sentences like (18) are ambiguous with respect to the interpretation of the temporal subordinating conjunction (a preposition). Here are 5 examples with different temporal prepositions from his paper[9]:

---

[9] In this section I follow Johnson's paper closely, often using exactly his examples, without citing particular instances. I have not changed notation of S',S when he uses it, whereas current notation would use CP, IP. The idea is to adhere closely to his presentation, but updating such matters should be straightforward.

(18) a. Liz left before you said she had.
 b. Sam fell after you said he would.
 c. Betsy has used eye shadow (ever) since John said she has.
 d. Mikey denounced the Soviet Union (only) while[10] Joyce insisted that the party members should.
 e. Mittie drove until Daniel said she should stop.

(18a) means either that Liz left before that time at which you were talking and saying that she'd left. Or it can mean that Liz left before that time that you claimed she left. The former is the time of saying. The latter is the time that your saying asserted was true of her leaving.

Johnson accepts (and adds new evidence to support) Larson's (1990) argument that the ambiguity facts can be explained by assuming that the

---

10 Geis (1970) and Larson (1990) give some examples that they argue show that *while* does not show these scope ambiguities. While Johnson agrees with the examples that Larson gives, he argues that *while* in general does show the ambiguities as in (18d). Larson's examples are:
(i) I didn't see Mary in New York while she said she was there.
(ii) I will be in Boston while I promised I would be there.
I find (i) perfectly acceptable with the temporal operator modifying the lower VP, which is what is at issue. (ii) is perhaps slightly degraded. There are 2 considerations that might have something to do with varying judgments. First, the possibility of the temporal operator modifying the lower VP seems to be sometimes improved by mild focus/stress, suggesting that some pragmatic/information structure conditions are involved:
(iii) I will be in Boston while I PROMISED I would be there.
(iv) I will be in Boston while I said/SAID that I would be there.
(v) I WILL be in Boston while I said/promised that I will be there
For some reason *said* makes the ambiguity more transparent than *promise*. These sentences (especially (v)) appear perfectly fine to me. Second, there appears to be some subtle semantics to *while* concerning the temporal intervals to which it applies, and which might affect the judgment. The tenses are also involved: I find (v) and (vi) perfect. There might be some kind of interval matching requirement.
(vi) The witness was in Boston while he said he was (there)
(vii) The suspect was starting the fire while his wife said he was (at home) (taking care of the kids)
For some reason, using a subject of the most embedded clause that is disjoint from (not bound by) the subject of the matrix subject (e.g. *his wife* instead of *he*) in (vi) seems to my ear to often improve the sentence. Perhaps replacing *his wife* by *he* in (v) would tend to lead to a preference for the temporal operator modifying *said*, leading to a garden path effect (first trying the temporal operator as modifying *said*, that might lead to the feeling of slight deviance. For these reasons, I agree with Johnson's conclusion that *while does* show the temporal ambiguity. Thus *while*, like the other temporal prepositions, takes a sentential complement with a temporal operator in its CP.

CP complement of a temporal preposition contains a phonetically empty temporal operator, essentially an empty *when* that binds a temporal variable that marks the place from which the operator moves. This variable may occur in any embedded clause, moving to Spec, C of the temporal clause complement, leading to the interpretation corresponding to the position from which it moved. Johnson gives the following picture for this example:

(19) a. Liz left [$_{PP}$ before [$_{S'}$ Op$_i$ [$_S$ you said [$_S$ she had] t$_i$]]].
  b. Liz left [$_{PP}$ before [$_{S'}$ Op$_i$ [$_S$ you said [$_S$ she had t$_i$]]]].[11]

In both (19a) and (19b) there is a temporal operator *Op*. This operator binds a trace/variable. In (19a) the variable modifies *said*, the predicate of the higher embedded clause. The interpretation that that Liz' leaving was before you did the saying. In (19b), the variable modifies the elided VP *left*; the reference is to the time that she left according to your claim. Larson (1990) argues for this analysis and for movement of the operator *OP* from the one of the embedded positions to [Spec, CP] of the clause selected by the temporal preposition *before*.

We are most interested in Johnson's arguments concerning whether clausal gerunds also contain temporal operators when they follow a temporal preposition, because these will involve control and will be in fact the types of structures so subject to errors of child grammar (errors with respect to the adult grammar). At the same time, we will want to know whether there is an operator in the complement of a preposition that *isn't* temporal that contains a clausal gerund, because these analyses will cast light on whether any particular analysis of delay in child grammar applies to all clausal gerunds (at least to all that are complements of prepositions) or only to those that contain a temporal operator.

Johnson writes (p. 590): "Recall further that when temporal prepositions are followed by a finite clause, that clause must have a Comp containing Op. The simplest assumption would be that this requirement also holds when temporal prepositions are followed by clausal gerunds". Thus the structure of (20a) is "necessarily) (20b):

---

[11] I have inserted Johnson's analyses as in his paper. Of course, current theory/notation would replace S' by CP and S by IP, in these and later examples.

(20) a. Liz left after saying she wouldn't.
   b. Liz left [after [s· Opi [PRO saying [she wouldn't] ti]]].

In (20b), the embedded –ing clause (clausal gerund in Johnson's terms) contains a temporal operator in the specifier of the clause (which is assumes is S', so CP in current notation). This operator binds a temporal variable that modifies *saying*. Summarizing, he crucial assumption is:

(21) When a temporal preposition is followed by a clausal gerund, the specifier of the CP dominating the gerund contains a temporal operator *OP* (just as is the case for a finite clause instead of the clausal gerund).

Starting from this conceptual argument for the existence of temporal operators in clausal gerunds that are the complements of temporal prepositions, John builds a somewhat complex argument based on the assumption that a clausal gerund complement of a preposition contains an operator if and only if the preposition is temporal. This result will be central to the discussion of the kind of theory of development that I will want to discuss, so I will try to sketch the argument briefly here. The syntactic and acquisition evidence is crucial to the models. It would be easy to simply say clausal gerunds, they are non-finite and there is no reason to think that they contain operators. So operators shouldn't be involved in the explanation of the errors in child grammar, a conclusion that will leave us to date with no workable empirically adequate model of the acquisition facts. So Johnson's argument is crucial.

Johnson notes that nontemporal prepositions may take clausal gerunds. Alongside a structure with a temporal preposition in (22a) there is (22b).

(22) a. Liz left before telling a story
   b. Liz left without telling a story.

Other examples that Johnson gives of nontemporal prepositions that take clausal gerunds include *despite, by, about,* and *besides.* Like the temporal prepositions, these nontemporal ones *are* prepositions; they take DP complements.[12]

(23) a. Liz left before the story
   b. Liz left without the story

---

[12] Except for one or two of them, which Johnson attributes to the lack of ability to case-mark.

Johnson now discovers a major generalization. Some prepositions can take clausal gerunds with an over subject, some can't:

(24) a. *Liz left before him telling a story.
   b. *Gary fell after him telling a story.
   c. *Sam has left since him telling the story.
   d. Liz left without John telling a story.
   e. Sam left despite John saying that he wouldn't.
   f. Gary was bothered about him telling that story.
   g. Besides him stealing all that money, we also knew Bob had killed a guard.

(24) leads to the generalization in (25):

(25) A preposition may take an overt subject in its clausal gerund complement if and only if the preposition requires a temporal operator.[13]

Johnson now uses (21) to derive the generalization in (24). The structure of a clausal gerund with an over subject when the gerund follows a temporal preposition is as in (26):

(26) a. *Liz left after him saying that she wouldn't.
   b. Liz left [$_{PP}$ after [$_{S'}$ Op_i [$_S$ him saying [that she wouldn't] t_i]]].

On the plausible (and quite supported in current syntax) assumption that over subjects of gerunds (e.g. *him* in (26b)) can only be assigned case from outside the gerund, it is clear why (26a) is ungrammatical. *Him* in (26a) would have to receive case from *after*. But the operator in specific of S' (CP) interferes with the assignment of case.

For a preposition that doesn't have such a temporal operator, there is no such interference to case assignment. In (27b), *despite* assigns case to *John*; there is no interfering operator. This derives (25).

(27) a. Sam left despite John saying that he wouldn't.
   b. Sam left [despite [s John saying that he wouldn't]].

---

13 My account here simplifies Johnson's, for ease of exposition.

The argument crucially depended on (21), the necessary existence of a temporal operator in the complement of a temporal preposition (and the non-existence of an operator in nontemporal prepositions). So the data argue for the existence of a temporal operator in clausal gerunds following a temporal preposition, an assumption that will be crucial to the analysis of children's grammar of control into adjuncts.[14]

4 The analysis of control of temporal adjuncts with temporal operators in an ATTRACT theory

Johnson's results on the structure of adjuncts of temporal prepositions means that a sentence like (28a) would have the representation in (28b).

(28) a. Liz left before telling a story
 b. Liz left [$_{PP}$[$_P$ before [$_{CP}$[OP_i $_C$[telling a story t_i]]]]]

The temporal operator *OP* required by *before* is in Spec, C, having raised from its position in the verb phrase (the verbal gerund)).

Since (28a) yields obligatory control (*telling a story* can only be predicated of Liz), we know that *Liz* ATTRACTS *left* and *telling a story*, which implies that *OP* is not an intervener that prevents *Liz* from attracting *telling a story*. That is,

---

14 One important objection is that on the assumption (21) that clausal gerunds after temporal prepositions contain temporal operators is that we would expect the Geis ambiguities to hold when the complement to the preposition is a gerund. We would expect the analysis (i) to hold as well as the analysis in (20b).
(i) Liz left [$_{PP}$after [s, Op$_i$ [PRO saying [she wouldn't t_i]]]].
But the Geis ambiguities don't hold in this case. The meaning derived from (i) doesn't exist. The temporal operator in (i) *must* modify "saying" in the intermediate clause. (i) is not a possible representation. Johnson argues that this fact is due to independent considerations, namely the impossibility of extracting a temporal phrase out of the complement to a gerund:
(ii) a. *When do you remember [S2 saying [S1 that the Titanic sunk ti]]?
 b. When do you remember [s the Titanic sinking ti]?
The fact that (iib) is grammatical shows that the ungrammaticality of (iia) is due to the impossibility of extracting out of the mostly deeply embedded clause in (iia), the finite clause. Due to this impossibility, (i) and its corresponding interpretation can't be derived. The evidence for the existence of temporal operators depends on the generalization in (21) even though an independent factor prevents the Geis ambiguities from holding.

OP does not endow the infinitival C with the power to ATTRACT. This is perhaps surprising. As (15b) shows, *what* and other *wh* words do cause C to attract. In particular, *when* induces ATTRACT capacities to C.

(29) a. [$_C$ When to go]
 b. I know [$_C$ when to go]

When causes C in (29) to have the power to ATTRACT? That is, there is an interrogative/exclamative operator in Spec, C that is associated with *when*. Since *OP* is supposed to be a phonetically empty form of *when*, why doesn't *OP* ATTRACT?[15] It might be tempting to argue that phonetically empty operators don't have this power, but we know that *OP* is syntactically active, as in Johnson's use of *OP* to block case-assignment; see the explanation of (25) above. It would be quite unusual if a phonetically empty but syntactically active syntactic element (moreover one, that has clear semantic consequences) didn't have the same interpretive consequences as an audible one. (28a) and (29b) are repeated in (30), with relevant aspects of their syntax included so as to bring out their parallel structures.

(30) a. Liz left before [$_{CP}$ OP_i [$_C$ telling a story t_i]]
 b. I know [$_{CP}$ when$_{(i)}$ [$_C$ to go $t_{(i)}$]]

The question comes down to why C in (30b) ATTRACTS while what appears to be the quite similar C in (30a) (*OP* instead of when) doesn't ATTRACT. One possibility is that it is the *wh* feature of *when* that causes ATTRACT; perhaps *OP* doesn't have the *wh* feature, despite our intuitions that says it is a phonetically empty version of *when*.

As (31) shows, after a temporal preposition, *when* may not appear instead of *OP*. So it's not just that *when* can be not pronounced in these contexts.

(31) a. I read Piketty before *OP/*when* John did
 b. I read Piketty before *OP/*when* John said his brother did (on either of the 2 readings, high or low *OP*)
 c. I read Piketty before *OP/*when* deciding how to invest

---

15 To be clear, MR's discussion doesn't necessarily have this problem. They don't discuss the existence of the empty temporal operator in the complements of temporal prepositions, although they do gloss these as CP's, e.g. see their (57), which provides a phrase-marker for *John left before eating*.

The impossibility of *when* (or any other *wh* word) after *before* and in front of a tensed complement (31b) makes it quite possible that although *before* selects a CP with an empty temporal operator, it doesn't select a CP with a *wh* feature. Since Tense is associated with C (as well as T), it is possible that the Tense feature that the temporal preposition requires on C causes *OP* to move to C, via the usual syntactic assumptions. The semantic motivation for P requiring this Tense feature on C is obvious: a temporal preposition like *before* is interpreted as a relation between the time of the matrix event and the time of the subordinate event.

We won't take this inquiry further here,[16] but simply assume for concreteness that a temporal preposition places an uninterpretable Tense feature on the C that it selects. This feature attracts *OP* to [Spec, C], eliminating the uninterpretable Tense feature on C. Since *OP* is interpreted as the time of the relevant embedded event, the temporal preposition can be interpreted locally. In standard phase theory, this is fleshed out as the possibility that *OP* is interpreted locally, in the phase of the temporal preposition. If this phase is the phase of the matrix vP (as is usually assumed), the *OP* is still available for interpretation, since it is Spec, C for the embedded C and therefore on the edge of the embedded CP phase. It hasn't been shipped off for interpretation and is thus available

---

16 Sawada and Larson (2004), following Johnston (1994), gives a formal semantics for clauses introduced by *when* that, very briefly and informally, says that the sentence that follows *when* (e.g. *John did* in (31a) is an *open* event description (without an interpretation of the time of the event). "*When* is analyzed as taking an open event description and yielding an interval description", namely, "the interval that is the temporal "run-time" of the maximal event that it combines with ... ". For example, *Bill showed up* in (ia) is an open event description, and *when* yields the time interval description of the event.

(i)   a.   I left when Bill showed up.
       b.   I left before Bill showed up.

Sawada and Larson discuss how this discussion assures the Presuppositionality of the embedded clause headed by *when*. (ia) presupposes that Bill arrived. They also assume that the clauses headed by temporal presuppositions are presupposed. E.g. the standard assumption as they point is that *Bill arrived* would be presupposed in (ib). I'm not certain that this is true. It seems to me that I can use (ib) even if I don't know whether Bill showed up. This fact could be explained by *OP* not closing off the event in the same sense as *when* does. (An alternative would be to assume that there is some kind of covert modal in (ib).

when *before* is being interpreted as the relation between the matrix and embedded (the latter encoded in *OP*) times.[17]

The most difficult question that needs much more work is how indeed *OP* differs so that it doesn't have a *wh* feature (see footnote 16). If this can't be worked out, we will need some other way to explain why *when* and *OP* don't have the same distribution in CP. We can't just assume, of course, that a temporal preposition like *before* and *when* are simply different 'subordinating conjunctions". Their syntactic behavior is far too different, as a large literature (some of which we have discussed) shows.[18]

5 The mistaken *wh* feature/operator analysis of temporal adjuncts in child grammar

With this background in syntactic theory we are in a position to state a theory of why children come to have the property of arbitrary control for temporal adjuncts. Our assumption to explain the adult and child grammar facts is (32).

---

[17] The reader will note that I am using considerations from phase theory that are not part of MR's analysis. There is no room here to consider how these 2 set of ideas interact.

[18] We will also have to consider why some *wh* words (a) appear to be able to head clausal gerunds, yet (b) they don't block ATTRACT.

(i) a. John stumbled while/?*when leaving the room
     b. John got upset while/*when shopping at the supermarket
     c. John gets upset while/?when shopping at the supermarket

(ii) a. John stumbled while/when he was leaving the room
     b. John got upset while/when he was shopping at the supermarket
     c. John gets upset while/when he shops at the supermarket

As to (a), *when* seems to have difficulty heading with clausal gerunds. That this isn't due to the "progressive" property of the gerund is seen by the fact that the tensed sentences with progressive aspect in (ii) are fine. Interestingly *when* seems to accept a gerund more readily when it relates to a generic (ic). Perhaps this is because it doesn't select a particular time, "closing off" an open event. As to (b), it is clear that all of these sentences, whether completely grammatical or not, must be controlled by the matrix subject *John*. There is no possibility of an arbitrary interpretation. So while/when, to the extent that they are acceptable in heading a clausal gerund, do not endow their C with the power to ATTRACT. Presumably this is because they don't involve an interrogative operator in C in these cases. So we will have to assume that when *while/when* head a clausal gerund they either don't have a *wh* feature or they do, but in a (defective?) form, such that there is no required interrogative operator.

(32) The mistaken *wh* feature analysis of temporal adjunct errors:
   a. In adult grammar, *OP* does not have a *wh* feature and therefore cannot endow the C that attracts it with the power to ATTRACT (there is no interrogative operator).
   b. In immature child grammar, *OP has* a *wh* feature and therefore endows C with the power to ATTRACT (there *is* an interrogative operator).

Since *OP* doesn't have a *wh* feature for adults, the C that it moves to doesn't have an interrogative operator, which means that C doesn't block ATTRACT the embedded predicate by the matrix subject. This results to obligatory control by the matrix subject. For children, on the other hand, *OP does* have a *wh* feature; the C that it moves to *does* have an interrogative operator, which endows C with the power to ATTRACT the embedded predicate. This implies only arbitrary control is possible. Thus the empty subject of the embedded predicate can be interpreted in any way allowed by the discourse and subject to a specific operator in C. Given the considerations of footnote (18), *while* and *when* will also contain interrogative operators for children but not adults, so that children (and of course not adults) will also have arbitrary control in these clauses.

Suppose the clausal gerund is *not* temporal, that is, it doesn't contain *OP*, e.g. a clause headed by *without*. Then there is no reason for the child to assume that there is a *wh* feature in C or that an interrogative operator exists there. In such a case the prepositions (e.g. *without*) doesn't endow C with the power to ATTRACT. The matrix subject ATTRACTs the embedded predicate and obligatory control of the embedded predicate will result, for the child, just as for the adult.

(33) Prediction of the mistaken *wh* feature analysis of temporal adjuncts
   a. Children will show arbitrary control, that is free reference subject to discourse considerations, into temporal adjuncts, including those headed by *while* and *when*.
   b. Non-temporal prepositions heading clausal adjuncts (e.g. *without*) will not show errors by children.

In the next section we will discuss briefly the child data that is relevant to the predictions in (33).

6 A few additional facts about child grammar of control into adjuncts and their place in the theory: Is it really the temporal operators that are relevant?

This paper has not reviewed alternative proposals for the analysis of the child grammar of temporal adjuncts. I do want to mention a few facts and discuss whether they are expected. Let me first briefly discuss Adler (2006), which appeared after Wexler (1992), Broihier and Wexler (1995) and Goodluck (2001) established the case for free reference for the control of PRO in temporal adjuncts in child grammar.

Adler (2006)) reproduces the results on free reference in temporal adjuncts, using classic methods.[19] Let me just mention a few particular predictions of the ATTRACT theory of arbitrary control that can be tested.

Wexler (1992) argues that temporal adjuncts headed by *while* are delayed along with *before, after,* etc., a result confirmed by the studies in the literature. Adler points out correctly (p. 19) that adjuncts without a temporal operator are expected to show adult-like control in child grammar on the theory presented in Wexler (and, of course, the same result holds in our theory[20]). However, she assumes that *while* does not have a temporal operator, attributing this view to the "linguistic theory of Larson (1988) and Johnson (1988)." (p. 20). As we have seen, although Larson might endorse this view on the basis of the lack of Geis effects in some examples with *while,* Johnson came to exactly the opposite conclusion. He argued for the existence of temporal operators in *while* adjuncts (see Johnson's 4, (18d) of this paper (Johnson's example) and footnote10 of this paper for discussion.) So in fact, a theory that locates the problem of child adjuncts in the temporal operator applies to *while* adjuncts.

So, we have a rather explicit prediction, which follows also from the mistaken *wh* feature analysis of this paper (32):

(34) Children in the adjunct error stage should not make many errors on adjuncts headed by *without* but should make them on adjuncts headed by *while*.

---

[19] This dissertation has many arguments, results and alternative ideas. I am making no attempt to capture this content here, only to point out that the general results show that free reference for PRO in temporal adjuncts exists in child grammar and to discuss a few results that are discussed with respect to whether the theory that I have presented (in Wexler (1992) and here that takes temporal operators to be the cause of the problems in free relatives is correct.

[20] Assuming of course that there are no additional factors that cause issues in child grammar.

Adler's Experiment 1 studies children's performance on *without, while* and *after* adjuncts. Her results of correct adult-like responses (choice of controller) are in her Figure 1, p. 174. Her younger age group has mean age 3;6, the older age group has mean age 5.0. Children's responses didn't significantly differ for *after* and *while* adjuncts. However, performance on *without* adjuncts was significantly higher than for the 2 temporal adjuncts *after* and *while*. The younger group produced 59% and 52% correct responses on the 2 temporal adjuncts, but achieved 77% for *without*. The older group produced 79% and 82% correct responses on the 2 temporal adjuncts but achieved a perfect (100%) score on *without* adjuncts. These results are exactly as predicted by (33). It is the temporal adjuncts that cause difficulty.[21] Moreover, *while* patterns with the temporal operators, as predicted by (33) together with Johnson's positive results concerning the existence of a temporal operator in the complement of *while*. Children seem to know which "subordinating conjunctions" (among those tested so far) have temporal operators. Given that the evidence for their existence isn't all that transparent, this is an interesting result (We wouldn't intuitively expect that the Geis ambiguities would be available evidence for young children. Perhaps it's simply the temporal character of the adjuncts that is sufficient for the children to posit the temporal operator).

It might be worthwhile to think a bit more about Goodluck's results. Children heard sentences like (35), her (10).

(35) a. Snowy pushes Leo before dancing by Ellie.
 b. Snowy pushes Leo when dancing by Ellie.
 c. Snowy pushes Leo before some dancing by Ellie.

The idea of the experiment is that it is in principle possible to read *by Ellie* has either (a) a locative, so that some other character is dancing by (past) Ellie, or (b) the agent of a nominal (the agent reading produced as the object of *by*). In the latter case, Goodluck takes *dancing by Ellie* as a DP, the object of the preposition *before*. So with this "nominal" reading (35a) is good, and it has a meaning quite close to (35c). However, although *dancing by Ellie* in principle could

---

[21] One might ask, why only 77% correct on *without* adjuncts for the younger children? These children are a mean age of only 3.6. We can't be certain that they have learned the completely correct nature of *without* (which after all, has somewhat difficult semantics, incorporating a negative component, always difficult for children) and even if they have, children at this age might make mistakes even if they have the grammar. The important result is that the *without* adjuncts were much better than the temporal adjuncts, independently for each age group.

still get a nominal analysis in (35b), *when* doesn't take a DO object (*when* isn't a preposition, it doesn't assign case). So if children know that *when* doesn't assign case they should reject reading (b) of (35b). However children (unlike adults) accept this reading quite often of (35b) (they accept it in (35a) also, but it is in principle grammatical in that case).

The biggest question is why children accept (35b) in the nominal reading. If children have free reference in the control analysis of (35a) as (32) predicts, then *Snowy, Leo* or *Ellie* could in principle be the controller of PRO. More precisely, the prediction is that the embedded C contains an empty operator *OP* in (35a), so that the embedded C contains an interrogative operator for the child, so that this embedded C ATTRACTS *dancing*. By the ATTRACT theory, arbitrary control is the result. Any one of the 3 DP's is discourse relevant, so any of them can "control PRO", that is there is arbitrary reference for the "subject" of the predicate *dancing*. We have to assume that there is no reason that this subject can't be *Ellie*. This might be problematic. If there were a PRO subject of the adjunct in (35a), we would have a configuration where PRO c-commanded and was co-indexed (in traditional terms) with *Ellie*. Something like *Ellie's dancing by Ellie*, ruled out by at least Principle C of the binding theory. But in the ATTRACT theory there isn't a PRO; there is no "subject" of the embedded predicate since there is no lexicalization (D) feature that requires it. We might have a similar situation in (36).

(36) Ellie doesn't like herself even though it's hard to not like Ellie

The ATTRACT theory predicts arbitrary control (for adults) in (36). Can the discourse be set up so that we're considering that Ellie doesn't like Ellie. Yes. So it seems possible that (34a) can be construed as arbitrary control even though the *by Ellie* phrase spells it out as *Ellie*.

The harder question is why children often accept (35b) under a control analysis in the ATTRACT theory (32). First, *when* actually *is* a *wh* word, it has the *wh* feature, we expect an interrogative operator in the specifier of the *when* clause. Thus, arbitrary control is licensed. The "subject" of *dancing by Ellie* can be *Ellie*, presumably by the same kinds of considerations that we have just made for (35a).

Since there is no PRO occupying a structural position, we don't have Principle C ruling out PRO from being co-indexed with *Ellie* in the *by*-phrase for the child. If this is right, though, shouldn't (35b) be acceptable for *adults* with Ellie doing the dancing? Of course it isn't, as seen either by our intuitive judgments or by the results from Goodluck's experiment on adults. Perhaps in fact the children take the DP analysis in this particular case (not in the other cases that we've discussed); after all, with *before* the structure is grammatical (35a). Perhaps children use the DP analysis in (35a, b). The question is why this isn't ruled out for the child by the impossibility of *when* appearing before DP. A useful research project would be to test whether in fact children know that *when* can't take a DP object, the test being carried out either in natural production data or experimentally.

We leave these considerations here, as a problem for future research.

7 Conclusion

We have argued that children have arbitrary control in temporal adjuncts. The problem is related to the existence of temporal operators, which the child takes as implying an interrogative operator that licenses arbitrary control under the ATTRACT theory of control. Using Johnson's results on the existence of temporal operators in sentential gerunds and on the syntactically active aspect of these operators, we assumed that this would lead the child to create an interrogative operator in C so that arbitrary control is licensed. It remains an open question whether a traditional theory of control with PRO and the MDP, or any other theory of control can lead to the same results.

References

Adler, Allison. 2006. Syntax and discourse in the acquisition of adjunct control. Doctoral Dissertation, MIT.
Bresnan, Joan. 1982. Control and Complementation. *Linguistic Inquiry* 13, 343–434.
Broihier, Kevin, and Ken Wexler. 1995. Children's acquisition of control in temporal adjuncts. *MITWPPL* 26, 193–220.
Chomsky, Noam. 1981. *Lectures on Government and Binding*. Dordrecht: Foris.
Chomsky, Noam. 1995. *The Minimalist Program*. Cambridge, Mass.: MIT Press
Chomsky, Noam, and Howard Lasnik. 1995. The theory of Principles and Parameters. In N. Chomsky. *The Minimalist Program*. Cambridge, Mass.: MIT Press.
Geis, Michael. 1970. Adverbial Subordinate Clauses in English, Doctoral dissertation, MIT, Cambridge, Massachusetts.
Goodluck, Helen. 2001. The nominal analysis of children's interpretations of adjunct PRO clauses. *Language* 77: 494–509.
Hyams, Nina, and Ken Wexler. 1993. On the grammatical basis of null subjects in child Language. *Linguistic Inquiry* 24: 421–459.
Johnson, Kyle. 1988. Clausal gerunds, the ECP and government. *Linguistic Inquiry* 19: 583–609.

Johnston, Michael. 1994. The Syntax and Semantics of Adverbial Adjuncts. Doctoral Dissertation. UCSC.

Larson, Richard. 1988. On the double object construction. *Linguistic Inquiry* 19: 335–391.

Larson, Richard. 1990. Extraction and multiple selection in PP. *The Linguistic Review* 7: 169–182.

Manzini, M. Rita, and Anna Roussou. 2000. A Minimalist Theory of A-movement and Control. *Lingua* 110: 409–447.

Sawada, Miyuki, and Richard. K. Larson. 2004. Presupposition & root transforms in adjunct clauses. *Proceedings of NELS* 34, pp. 517–528. UMASS: GLSA.

Rosenbaum, Peter. 1967. *The grammar of English predicate complement constructions*. Cambridge, MA: MIT Press.

Wexler, Ken. 1992. Some issues in the growth of control. In R. Larson, S. Iatridou, U. Lahiri, & J. Higginbotham (Eds.), *Control and grammar*, 253–295. Berlin: Springer.

Language Index

Abruzzese 379, 388, 545
Albanian 2, 189
Amharic 286
Apulian 126–128, 131, 134, 139, 143, 144
Aromanian 2, 611

Balearic 362, 363
Balkan 126, 145, 611
Bantu 4, 197–215, 637, 639, 643, 658
Basque 453, 457
Bih 174
Breton 274
Bulgarian 176, 626, 627, 629
Burushaski 184

Calabrian 126, 128, 129, 134, 141, 144, 145, 363, 379, 385, 390, 394, 396, 397
Campanian 363, 379, 394, 396, 397
Catalan 189, 266, 359, 362, 363, 364, 368, 372, 550, 551, 552
Caucasian 486
Changana 639, 654, 656
Chichewa 199, 210, 371
Chinese 48, 264, 339
Chuj 183
Corsican 363, 364
Croatian 169, 175, 182, 183

Dutch 5, 65, 169, 217, 263, 336, 352, 433, 512, 514, 515, 517–520, 523, 524, 658, 661–664, 666–674, 676–678, 681–685, 687
Dyirbal 453, 457

Emilian 274
English 4, 10, 11, 15, 16, 49, 63, 141, 156, 166, 169, 171, 173–176, 178, 179, 188, 190, 202–204, 217, 221, 225, 231–246, 250, 255, 261, 263–265, 273, 284, 286, 290, 335–337, 339, 345, 346, 348–353, 357, 371, 385, 386, 392, 402, 404, 414, 417, 469, 473, 479, 484, 491, 493, 494, 516, 525, 527, 561, 563, 565, 569, 570, 575, 576, 580, 581, 590, 609, 613, 616–619, 671, 672, 683, 695

Finnish 261
Flemish 662, 664, 665
Florentine 2, 253, 254, 258, 275, 536, 588
Franco-Provençal 363, 545, 547
French 76, 79, 80, 82, 84, 159, 160, 161, 175, 183, 184, 185, 189, 209, 220, 274, 329, 330, 335, 336, 342, 346, 350, 352, 373, 374, 395, 404, 417, 468–470, 493, 531, 534, 538–540, 549, 550, 552, 601, 607, 608

Gascon 532, 550, 551
Gengbe 171
Georgian 457–460, 463, 465, 466, 468, 470, 471, 478, 479, 480, 483–497
German 47–49, 51, 53, 57, 60–62, 65, 66, 169, 178, 179, 187–189, 190, 336, 337, 340, 531, 535
Germanic 65, 531, 553, 658
Greek 107, 109, 110, 112, 114, 118, 141, 188, 289, 470, 474, 484, 491, 609, 611, 613, 618, 619, 622–629
Gungbe 171

Hebrew 286, 343
Hindi 225, 226

Ibero-Romance 372, 374, 551, 552
Icelandic 684
Indo-Aryan 175, 226, 227, 265
Inuktitut 264
Irish 7, 8, 11, 12, 14–17
Italian 1–3, 5, 6, 11, 12, 15–17, 40, 42, 43, 48, 65, 73–84, 87, 88, 90–93, 95, 98, 105, 106, 118, 119, 125–146, 149, 151, 152, 153, 154, 156, 158–161, 171, 174, 176, 177, 179, 185–190, 204, 206–210, 213, 214, 227, 249–267, 273–290, 336, 362, 364, 373, 374–377, 382, 384, 386, 387, 392, 395, 396, 397, 401–419, 439, 443, 447, 531, 532, 536–540, 543–547,

551–555, 561, 569, 570, 572, 575, 576, 585, 588, 590, 591, 593, 599, 602, 603, 605, 607, 610, 611, 613, 658
Italo-Romance 4, 87, 119, 120, 274, 275, 282, 284, 287, 444, 543, 551, 552

Japanese 48, 286, 497

Kannada 286
Kanuri 171
Konda 184

Ladin 404, 417, 535, 545
Lakhota 172, 175
Lango 171
Latin 87, 91, 92, 99–106, 108, 111, 113–120, 127, 203, 232, 238, 240–242, 245, 246, 274, 280, 286, 289, 358
Lezgian 286
Ligurian 363, 364
Lingala 203
Lubukusu 639, 647, 654
Lucanian 359, 362, 363, 364, 368

Makasae 171, 172
Malayalam 286
Marathi 456, 458
Megrelian 486
Melfi 120
Mina 172, 173, 587
Mongsen Ao 266
Mundurucu 353

Ndebele 633
Nguni 633–658

Obolo 171, 172
Occitan 362, 364

Paduan 179, 532, 538, 539
Pashto 266
Piedmontese 290, 541, 542, 545, 552, 554
Polish 175, 179, 181, 182, 188, 190
Portuguese 11, 132, 158, 423–436, 552, 640
Proto-Indo-European 4, 87
Punjabi 153

Rajasthani 226, 227
Rhaeto-Romance 538, 539, 540
Rhonga 639, 654, 656
Roman 588
Romance 1, 91, 131, 198, 209, 211, 213, 214, 342, 357, 361, 363, 365, 368, 415, 441, 443, 535, 536, 540, 547, 550, 589
Romanian 179, 346, 371, 532, 545, 635, 636
Romansh 238, 240–242, 244
Ronghong Qiang 172, 173
Russian 351–353, 609, 612, 627, 629

Salentino 119, 126, 128, 129, 138–141, 144
Sardinian 3, 6, 357–368, 410, 416, 439–449
Sesotho 286
Shona 638
Sicilian 126, 129–132, 134, 261, 280, 379
Sinhala 175
Spanish 156, 175, 189, 210, 217, 219–223, 225, 226, 364, 372, 470, 474, 484, 486, 491, 536, 552
Svan 486
Swahili 199, 203, 204, 205, 210, 213, 214
Swati 633, 634, 638, 645–653, 656

Tuscan 119, 133, 254, 274, 275, 280–289
Triestino 551, 552
Tshiluba 198–204, 207, 209–211, 213, 214
Tsonga 639, 654
Turkish 175, 286, 626

Umbrian 119
Uralic 264, 265
Uzbeki 264

Vedic 107, 108, 112

Wandala 266
Welsh 238, 274

Xhosa 633–636, 638, 643, 644, 646–650, 653, 654, 656–658

Yucatec Maya 175

Zina Kotoko 263
Zulu 286, 633, 636, 638, 649, 650, 656

Subject Index

addressee 44, 476, 481–482, 486, 490
adjective 112, 154, 197–198, 200, 201, 203–204, 211–215, 233–234, 241, 252, 343–344, 356, 459, 492–494, 502, 512, 596–597, 598, 636
adjunct 50 ffn4, 53, 79, 170 ffn4, 186–188, 362, 363, 435, 447, 502, 523, 566, 608, 623, 669, 677, 683, 687 ffn.18, 691–692, 694, 695, 697, 699, 700–703, 705, 707, 709–713, 715–716
adverb 47–49, 53–54, 66, 129 ffn.7–8, 187, 217, 259, 261 ffn.8, 274, 276–277, 284 ffn.8, 288, 330, 375, 385–386, 394–395, 447, 468, 490, 502, 505, 509, 511, 514, 517, 525, 534, 551–552, 555, 577 ffn.14, 616, 661, 666, 669, 671, 675, 677–681, 683–687, 700
– locative adverb 577, 618, 661, 669, 671, 675, 677–681, 683–687
Agree 9, 11, 14, 15, 50–53, 61, 63–66, 76–77, 107, 125, 127–129, 135–137, 140, 142–147, 159–160, 164–166, 200, 202–204, 206, 211, 213–214, 217, 223, 225–228, 231–232, 237–239, 241, 265 ffn.13, 287, 300, 317, 319, 321–322, 325, 339, 342, 344, 384, 402, 409–410, 415–416, 418, 424–425, 431–435, 456–460, 462–463, 465–467, 469–472, 480, 482–484, 487, 490, 492–494, 512, 550, 562, 565, 577, 580, 590–592, 602, 612–613, 625–626, 628, 634–636, 639–640, 642–644, 654, 657–658, 703 ffn.10
– long distance agreement 164, 590
– multiple agreement 125, 127, 135, 145
– number agreement 11, 107, 231, 238–239, 384 ffn.5, 402, 409, 434–435, 466 ffn.3, 470, 478, 482–483, 487, 490, 492–494, 634–635, 639–640, 643, 658
– object agreement 11, 76, 225–228, 321–322, 409, 463, 465, 654
– parasitic agreement 136–137
– person agreement 11, 107, 131, 133, 135–137, 227, 237–239, 402, 435, 456–460, 463, 465–467, 469–471, 480, 482–484, 487, 550, 634
– subject-verb agreement 11, 15, 76, 107, 129, 135, 202, 204, 237, 325, 384, 402, 409–410, 415–416, 418, 431–432, 434–436, 458, 463, 465–467, 471, 480, 580 ffn.19, 591–592, 634–635, 643–644
– Spec-Head agreement 11, 50, 61, 66, 164–165, 228, 483–484, ffn.12
anaphor 51 ffn.8, 82, 126, 135, 137, 139, 181–183, 318, 382, 488 ffn.15, 512, 517, 522, 527, 694
anti-agreement 239
anticausative 510
argument 11, 14, 16–17, 73, 75–79, 81–85, 126, 128 ffn.6, 138–140, 145, 149, 159, 161, 163–164, 170 ffn.4, 179 ffn. 28, 186–187, 206–213, 220, 232, 237, 241–242, 245, 263, 266, 279, 284 ffn. 7–8, 317–318, 321, 327, 347, 372, 376, 381, 386, 388, 390–391, 402, 404–409, 411, 413–418, 429, 453–457, 460–461, 463, 465, 469, 480–482, 485, 488, 495–497, 501 ffn.1, 502 ffn.2, 507–508, 510 ffn.3, 514–516, 518–520, 523–524, 526, 532, 534, 568–569, 609–612, 615, 619–626, 629, 669, 682–683, 687, 696, 698 ffn.7, 699–700
Aspect 82, 87, 91, 99, 106–109, 111–117, 121, 126–129, 133, 199, 279, 321, 422, 433–434, 460–461, 463, 710
– constructions 125–127, 424
– imperfective 99, 107, 460
– perfective 87, 99, 106–107, 463
– progressive 21, 137, 710
– stative 106–107, 111, 114, 525
Axial Part 249–251, 261–267

binding 166, 303–305, 317–318, 330, 382, 478, 480, 532, 611, 617, 695, 697, 699 ffn.7, 714
Binding Theory 166, 317, 695, 699 ffn.7, 714
by-phrase 78–84, 372, 381–382, 714

c-command 52, 154 ffn.2, 175, 190, 382, 427, 431, 510 ffn.3, 514–520, 523, 525, 527–528, 691, 695, 714
case 8, 11–16, 75–76, 81, 82, 103, 141, 154, 158–161, 169 ffn.1, 176, 184–186, 188–191, 205, 226, 231, 234, 240, 262 ffn.10, 264 ffn.12, 265, 318, 328, 409, 424, 431–432, 435, 453–471, 480, 487, 489–490, 491–497, 535, 563, 565, 611–613, 622, 625–628, 654–655, 658, 695–696, 706, 708
– absolutive case 453, 462
– abstract case 82, 93, 265 ffn.13, 611–613
– accusative case 14, 75–77, 154, 161, 190 ffn.48, 227, 240, 386, 431, 454, 457, 461–465, 466, 489, 612–613, 620, 622, 625, 628–629
– case assignment 11, 75–77, 158–159, 262 ffn.10, 455, 611, 621, 706, 708
– case attraction 16, 189
– case feature 11–14, 424, 480
– case hierarchy 189
– dative case 199 ffn.5, 221, 227, 233, 263–265, 267, 359, 375, 386, 489, 537, 539 ffn.6, 544, 547, 549, 550, 554, 612, 631
– default case 89, 95, 211
– dependent case 455, 463
– ergative case 453, 455, 456, 460–461, 463, 467, 469, 471, 490, 497
– genitive case 231, 236, 237, 240–241, 244–245, 263–265, 267, 351–352, 624
– inherent case 455
– instrumental case 259, 262
– locative case 138, 205
– morphological case 351, 496, 612
– nominative case 8, 14, 141, 158, 159, 161, 409, 424, 431–432, 435, 453–467, 469, 471, 489–490, 497, 612–613, 620–622, 625
– oblique case 264 ffn. 12, 265 ffn.13, 612
– structural case 10–12, 611
causative 74–75, 77–86, 101, 106, 108 ffn.17 112, 140, 144, 199, 371–379, 381–393, 396–397, 431, 501–502, 504–513, 522–524, 527–528

class, nominal 199–205, 207–209, 213–214, 477, 486, 488, 493, 495–497, 533, 633, 635–641, 643–645, 647, 649–651, 654–659
Classifier 171, 173ffn13, 191, 200, 335, 339–341, 344, 346 ffn.22, 354, 477, 494, 637–638, 643–644, 654–655, 657–658
cleft construction 280, 563–566, 568, 571, 589ffn23, 663
clitic 11, 73–75, 78, 82, 84, 138, 140–146, 159, 169 ffn.1, 183 ffn. 36, 189 ffn. 47, 208–211, 213–215, 221 ffn.1, 227, 258, 357, 358–370, 374–377, 383, 388–390, 392–397, 404, 410, 417, 470 ffn.4, 482–483, 494, 531–556, 592, 602, 604, 627, 654, 661–665, 668–671, 674, 676
– clitic doubling 537–538, 541, 630, 667, 668, 677–678, 681, 686
– clitic placement 137, 139, 142, 543–544
– clitic-climbing 126, 142, 144, 145, 372, 385, 548, 546–547, 548
– Clitic Left Dislocation (CLLD) 537
– enclitic 159 ffn.7, 357, 358–370, 380–382, 484, 493, 542, 545–547, 549–551, 551–552
– proclitic 337, 358–370, 380–382, 389, 536, 542, 549–552
complementizer 137, 145, 151–152, 154, 158, 179 ffn.27, 407, 439–449, 588, 609–612, 615–618, 621–622, 625, 626–627
compound noun 19, 22, 342
concord 456, 465
– negative 277, 279, 285, 287
control 214, 226, 317–330, 427–432, 434–435, 507–508, 691–705, 707, 710–715
– arbitrary control 693–695, 699, 701–703, 710, 711, 712, 714, 715
– ATTRACT theory of control 325, 691, 693–694, 696–699, 701–702, 707–708, 710–712, 714–715
– movement analysis of control 317–326, 328–329, 430 ffn.6, 434, 694, 696, 704

- object control 226, 318, 321–323, 328, 431, 435, 517, 691–692, 695, 700–701, 713–715
- obligatory control 317–319, 324, 326, 424, 428, 435, 691, 700, 702, 707, 711

coordination 127 ffn.4, 261 ffn.9, 286, 299, 345–346, 347 ffn.24, 348 ffn.26, 351, 353, 354, 432, 456, 481, 483, 485, 535, 592
- coordinate structure 127 ffn.4, 290, 335, 346–347, 348, 349, 354, 456, 457
- motor 299, 300

copular 73–74, 76–78, 233, 236, 561–572, 574–587, 589–594

Coreference 140, 169 ffn.1, 382, 565m 572

countability 232, 240, 242–246

cross-linguistic variation 149, 289 ffn.10, 531

default 89, 95 ffn.7, 113 ffn.21, 221 ffn.22, 226, 506, 639

demonstrative 202, 204, 213, 253, 341 ffn.15, 454, 459, 472, 473, 484–486, 488–492, 494, 498, 616, 618, 627, 634, 656–657

Dependency Phonology 19

determiner 151, 153–154, 159, 160, 175–177, 183 ffn. 37, 205–206, 209, 214, 237, 241, 244–245, 250–251, 306, 308, 337, 339, 344, 458–460, 465, 467, 469–471, 474–475, 479, 483–486, 488–492, 494

Differential Object Marking (DOM) 217–229, 545

ditransitive construction 221–222, 226, 263

doubling 47, 53, 55, 59, 61–67, 210–211, 273–274, 289, 532, 533, 536–540, 541–543, 545, 661–671, 674–681, 683, 685–690
- subject doubling 210–211, 538–540, 542–543, 661–664, 665–671, 673–681, 683, 685, 687–690

Element Theory 19, 21–23, 25–26

elision 136, 651

ellipsis 279, 288, 337 ffn.5, 428, 431, 433, 459, 492, 546

Event Identification 408, 418

Exceptional Case Marking (ECM) 10–11, 164, 166–167, 372, 374, 431

existential 16, 33, 176, 177 ffn. 21, 217–218, 225, 273, 281, 284, 287, 414–517, 443, 514 ffn.6, 520, 563, 565–569, 571–577, 585, 586–588, 592–594, 673, 683

experiencer 79, 226, 330, 406, 619–622

expletive 8, 11, 78–79, 217, 327–328, 336 ffn.1, 414, 449, 565–566, 572, 661–664, 671–678, 678–681, 682–687, 699 ffn.1
- there-expletives 336, 336 ffn.1, 414, 565 ffn.6, 566, 572, 661, 669, 671–678, 682–687

Extended Projection Principle (EPP) 7–8, 12–14, 16–17, 163–166, 206–208, 213, 241, 322, 324, 325, 328, 329, 404, 415, 577, 682, 684, 689

feature 8–16, 19–25, 33–34, 49–52, 61, 63 ffn.14, 90, 98–99, 106–107, 125–126, 131, 134–137, 144, 145, 151–153, 155, 156, 161, 163–166, 206, 231–232, 236–237, 240, 241–242, 244 ffn.23, 244, 245–246, 286–289, 305, 318, 387, 401–402, 407, 413, 424, 448, 454–459, 478, 493, 495–497, 602–605, 607 ffm.2, 611–613, 629, 634, 635–640, 677–678, 682, 687 ffn.17, 694–699, 708–712, 714
- feature bundle 90, 129, 145, 459, 480–482, 496, 531, 563, 568, 577–578
- interpretable feature 50, 273, 274, 629
- negative feature 273–274, 280, 286–289
- number feature 206, 231, 232, 240, 478, 481, 483–488, 491, 493, 494–496, 635–636
- person feature 131, 206, 231, 232, 236, 237, 404, 454–459, 480, 481, 482, 485–488, 491, 494, 495–497
- phonetic features 19–23, 294, 307
- phi-feature 8, 10–11, 13–16, 107, 163, 166, 225–227, 321–326, 328, 387, 399, 402, 404–405, 409, 424, 435, 454–459, 469, 478, 487–488, 495, 497, 531–532, 563, 625, 569, 590, 591, 625, 668
- prosodic feature 363–364, 564
- Prt feature 50–52, 61, 63

- quantificational feature 240, 241–242, 602–606
- uninterpretable feature 265 ffn.13
- unvalued feature 165 ffn.5, 482

Figure-Ground 249, 260 ffn. 6, 262–267
frequentative 106

gender 33, 342, 384 ffn.5, 409, 410 ffn.10, 478, 489, 495, 602, 634, 635, 636, 637, 639, 640, 641, 642, 643, 644, 645, 653, 658
gerund 131, 357, 692, 693, 702, 704, 705, 706, 707, 710 ffn.18, 711, 715
goal 51, 165, 166
goal dative 221, 226

hearer 19, 31, 410

imperative 107, 125 ffn.2, 127 ffn.5, 130, 131, 132, 199 ffn.3, 200, 205, 237 ffn.12, 357, 359, 360, 364, 375, 377, 383, 384, 385, 386, 387, 388, 391, 392, 393, 394, 395, 396, 654 ffn.8
impersonal 75 ffn.4, 221 ffn.1, 541, 547, 549 ffn.17, 683, 684
indefinite 172 ffn.10, 179 ffn.n 27, 202, 234, 245, 281, 335, 337–338, 340–341, 344, 346, 401–402, 409, 413–419, 443–444, 448, 478, 486, 515–516, 518–519, 524, 575, 576, 609, 619, 666 ffn.5, 684
infinitive 99, 126, 130 ffn.10, 131 ffn.11, 145, 212, 371–372, 374–377, 381, 385, 386, 387, 389, 390 ffn. 7, 391, 394, 396, 397, 447, 543, 591 ffn.25, 701
- inflected infinitive 423–429, 432–437, 543
interface 10, 11, 250, 301, 320, 322, 561, 564, 577, 581 ffn.20, 585, 586 ffn.22, 612
- conceptual-intentional (CI) 64, 307, 308, 309, 310
- discourse-prosody 586 ffn.22, 585, 586 ffn.22, 594
- phonology-syntax 310, 371
- scope-discourse semantics 410, 418, 561, 564, 577, 581, 586 ffn.22

- sensory-motor (SM) 24, 26, 300, 301, 304, 307
- syntax-lexicon 250
- syntax-morphology 90, 93, 100, 197, 205–206, 550, 556, 658
- syntax-semantics 319, 568
interpolation 394, 551–552
intervention effects 77, 154 ffn.2, 600, 601, 604, 607, 608, 694
intransitive 253, 254, 261 ffn.8, 372, 381, 453, 459, 480, 485, 487, 488, 494, 496, 683
island 571, 599–605, 607, 619
- strong island 170 ffn.4, 176, 624
- weak island 509, 603–605, 607–8, 623

labelling 9–10, 12, 14–16, 160, 307
Lexical parametrization 407, 410, 417
LF interface 9–10, 12, 14–16, 160, 307
legitimization 29–34, 40–43
linker 125fn3
locality 77, 87, 89, 98fn10, 99, 106, 109, 111, 118, 121, 154fn2, 155, 320, 326, 395, 599–600, 604, 607, 624, 697

Manipulation 37
Merge 9–1013–15, 20–21, 49–53, 61, 66, 90, 126, 128–129, 151, 154–155, 164–166, 169–170, 173–174, 187–188, 193, 203, 209, 212–214, 219, 221–222, 225, 236, 242, 287, 293, 300, 306, 308–311, 331–332, 348, 354, 367, 375, 443, 455, 459, 480–481, 487, 491, 494, 497, 563, 565, 567, 569–570, 575, 588, 591, 593–594, 610, 615, 646, 696–698
metaphor 38–39
modifier 169fn1, 173fn13, 174fn16, 178fn25, 198, 204, 222–223, 456–457, 463, 468, 473, 475, 481, 491, 501, 503–505, 507–509, 523, 525, 528, 587–589, 607, 609, 614, 675, 677, 679, 683
- locational 263fn11, 502, 504–505, 528, 682–683
- manner 21, 172fn9, 174, 259, 502–503, 505, 509, 528, 616

– temporal 62, 259–260, 502, 505–506, 509, 514, 523, 528, 589fn24, 593, 691–694, 699, 700–713, 715

negation 49, 53, 64–65, 271, 273–290, 321, 395, 506, 511, 538, 558, 600–601, 622, 634
nominal class (see class, nominal)
number 11, 21–22, 24, 26, 65, 98, 107, 118, 202, 206, 227, 231–236, 238–240, 340–341, 347–351, 353, 384fn5, 402, 409, 423, 434–435, 465–466, 477–478, 481–483, 485–497, 602, 634–636, 639–641, 643, 658
numeral 178, 335, 337, 340fn10, 342–345, 347–354, 475–476, 478

optionality 144, 195, 277, 285, 302, 539, 677
oscillatory rhythms 293, 295, 297, 302–303, 305–309, 311
overgeneration 21–22

participant 41, 43, 93, 95, 102, 409–410, 415, 455–457, 459, 469, 473, 475–476, 478, 481–482, 484–487, 490, 494, 496–497
participle 11, 76, 87–89, 131, 145–146, 149, 154, 156–157, 159, 161, 185, 199, 201, 226–227, 241, 388–389, 543–544, 546, 547, 557, 636
passive 73–84, 100, 106, 149, 153–154, 157, 199, 217, 221–222, 323, 372–373, 381, 384, 388–391, 397, 408, 539, 543, 619, 621, 683–684, 698
– smuggling analysis of passive 76–84
– se-passive 73
Person Case Constraint (PCC) 11, 535
Person Licensing Condition (PLC) 456
person split 132–133, 251, 403fn2, 410, 453–461, 463, 482–483, 487, 495–497
phase 9–13, 17, 163–164, 166, 298–302, 304–309, 320, 323, 387–389, 393, 408fn9, 455, 709–710
– phase edge 655, 657–658
– phase head 9, 11, 13–15, 163, 166, 590
– Phase Impenetrability Condition 390, 395

possessive 181–183, 202, 204, 223–224, 233–236, 238–239, 243–244, 246–247, 264, 382, 473, 532, 539, 657–658
post-syntactic 12, 455
preposition 15, 17, 78–79, 160–161, 170fn2, 174, 197–198, 202–203, 205, 212–215, 217, 219, 221, 225, 233–234, 249, 251–255, 257–261, 263–265, 267, 306, 308, 346fn22, 373, 447–448, 455, 533–534, 553–555, 591fn25, 601–602, 611–613, 620–621, 626–627, 649, 692–693, 702–711, 714
presupposition 276, 282, 501–503, 509–510, 512–529, 615, 623, 625, 630, 683, 709
Principle C 714
pro-drop 11, 15–16, 401–405, 407, 465, 479, 485, 580
probe-goal 51, 165–166, 625
Prolific Domain 317, 320–323, 330

quantifier 129, 178, 217, 241, 273, 276, 281, 284–285, 289–290, 329, 331, 333, 443, 456, 459, 464, 472–476, 478fn9
– indefinite quantifier 202

raising 12–13, 17, 50, 53, 90, 151, 153, 163–166, 169, 173–175, 181, 183–184, 186, 188fn44, 189, 237, 287, 317, 319–330, 390fn7, 408fn9, 432–435, 471, 563, 566, 571, 581, 594, 684fn17, 687
reflexive 11, 73–79, 81–84, 358, 524, 548fn17
relative 129fn7, 149–161, 169, 171, 173–175, 177–185, 187, 189, 191–196, 220, 303, 440–441, 443–444, 564–565, 587, 605, 608–610, 616–618, 626–627
Relativized Minimality 63, 77, 154fn2, 601–603, 608
relator 219–221, 223–224, 262, 264, 266fn15, 267

speaker 410, 454, 474–476, 481–483, 485–486, 490
subjunctive 93, 100, 107, 109, 126, 131–133, 135, 137, 141, 145, 220–221

stress 361, 512
- stress shift 357–359, 361–365, 367–370, 525, 549
Subset principle 415
syncretism 190, 227, 231, 245, 457, 612, 619, 635, 641, 653

Tense 87, 89, 91, 93–96, 99, 107, 110, 121, 125–126, 130–132, 134–137, 143–145, 152, 184, 186, 198, 211–212, 237–239, 279, 424–425, 435, 455–456, 460–461, 482, 590–591, 611, 648, 700–701, 703, 709
theta-role 154, 155, 237, 318, 322, 324–327, 418, 455, 568, 611, 696–697
transitive 11, 73, 76, 83, 154, 155, 161, 206–208, 271, 215, 372, 405–406, 408, 412–416, 453–459, 461, 463, 465–467, 485, 494, 683

unaccusative 7, 8, 11–17, 81, 149, 153–154, 156–158, 161, 164, 222, 384, 390–391, 401, 405–409, 411–419, 457–458, 461, 463, 465–466, 471, 505–506, 510
unergative 149, 155, 157, 159, 222, 381, 405, 406, 408, 411–416, 418
Unique Check Constraint 408
uninflected 137, 205, 423

vagueness 31
V2 65, 125–131, 134–137, 139–147, 187, 290, 443, 533–535, 556, 559–560, 610, 647, 663
Visibility Condition 611, 629
Voice 77, 100, 107, 219–222, 263, 388, 396, 405–406, 619–621, 671

weak island (see island)

www.ingramcontent.com/pod-product-compliance
Lightning Source LLC
Chambersburg PA
CBHW070753300426
44111CB00014B/2387